Uncertainty and Intelligent Information Systems

Uncertainty and Intelligent Information Systems

editors

Bernadette Bouchon-Meunier

Christophe Marsala

Maria Rifqi

Université Pierre et Marie Curie-Paris 6, France

Ronald R Yager

Iona College, USA

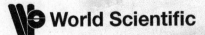 **World Scientific**

NEW JERSEY · LONDON · SINGAPORE · BEIJING · SHANGHAI · HONG KONG · TAIPEI · CHENNAI

Published by

World Scientific Publishing Co. Pte. Ltd.
5 Toh Tuck Link, Singapore 596224
USA office: 27 Warren Street, Suite 401-402, Hackensack, NJ 07601
UK office: 57 Shelton Street, Covent Garden, London WC2H 9HE

British Library Cataloguing-in-Publication Data
A catalogue record for this book is available from the British Library.

UNCERTAINTY AND INTELLIGENT INFORMATION SYSTEMS

ISBN-13 978-981-279-234-1
ISBN-10 981-279-234-1

Editor: Tjan Kwang Wei

Typeset by Stallion Press
Email: enquiries@stallionpress.com

Printed in Singapore.

Foreword

Uncertainty is an attribute of information. Decisions are based on information. More often than not, decision-relevant information is uncertain and/or imprecise. As we move further into the age of machine intelligence and automated decision-making the issue of how to deal with uncertainty and imprecision becomes a matter of pressing importance.

Uncertainty and Intelligent Information Systems is an important contribution to a better understanding of how to deal with information processing and decision-making in an environment of uncertainty, imprecision and partiality of truth. *Uncertainty and Intelligent Information Systems* draws on papers presented at the 2006 Conference on Information Processing and Management of Uncertainty (IPMU) which was held in Paris in 2006. IPMU was born in 1986, the brainchild of Bernadette Bouchon-Meunier and Ronald Yager. Over the years, IPMU evolved into a leading conference in its field, embracing a wide-variety of methodologies for dealing with uncertainty and imprecision. Unlike many other conferences, IPMU has not been committed to a particular methodology. It rolls out a welcome mat for all schools of thought. Representative of the breadth of scope of IPMU are the papers: "The Game-Theoretic Framework for Probability," by G. Shafer; "Generalized Naïve Bayesian Modeling," by Ronald Yager; "An Increment Hierarchical Fuzzy Clustering for Category-based News Filtering," by Gloria Bordogna, Marco Pagani, Gabriella Pasi; "A Possible Worlds Interpretation of Label Semantics," by Jonathan Lawry and Van Nam Huynh; "A Study on the Analytic Hierarchy Process," by Shin-ichi Ohnishi, Didier Dubois, Henri Prade and Takahiro Yamanoi; "Comparison of Spatiotemporal Difference of Brain Activity Between Correct and Approximation Answer Choices on Addition," by Takahiro Yamanoi, Yuta Fujiwara, Hisashi Toyoshima, Michio Sugeno and Elie Sanchez;

"Comparing Dynamical Systems by Using Temporal Fuzzy Models," by Juan Moreno-Garcia, Jose Jesus Castro-Schez and Luis Jimenez; "Improvement of Approximation Properties of a First-order Takagi Sugeno Fuzzy System," by Felipe Fernandez, Julio Gutierrez, Gracian Trivino and Juan Carlos Crespo; "Using the Fuzzy Spatial Relation 'Between' to Segment the Heart in Computerized Tomography Images," by A. Moreno, C.M. Takemura, O. Colliot, O. Camara and I. Bloch; "Neurofuzzy Network with On-Line Learning in Fault Detection of Dynamic Systems," by Walmir Caminhas and Fernando Gomide; "Imperfect Information Representation through Extended Logic Programs in Bilattices," by Daniel Stamate; "Geometric Representation of Weak Orders," by Sergei Ovchinnikov; "Efficient Tracking of the Dominant Eigenspace of a Normalized Kernel Matrix," by Geert Gins, Ilse Smets and Jan Van Impe.

In science, there is a deep-seated tradition of dealing with uncertainty and imprecision through the use of concepts and techniques drawn from probability theory. Until the advent of fuzzy logic, there was no questioning of this tradition. Today, this is no longer the case. More specifically, there has been and continues to be an ongoing debate between two schools of thought. First, there are those who believe that standard probability theory, PT, is sufficient for dealing with all kinds of uncertainty. An eloquent exponent of this school of thought — call it "PT is sufficient" school of thought — is the eminent Bayesian, Professor Dennis Lindley. In his view:

> *"The only satisfactory description of uncertainty is probability. By this I mean that every uncertainty statement must be in the form of a probability; that several uncertainties must be combined using the rules of probability; and that the calculus of probabilities is adequate to handle all situations involving uncertainty ... probability is the only sensible description of uncertainty and is adequate for all problems involving uncertainty. All other methods are inadequate ... anything that can be done with fuzzy logic, belief functions, upper and lower probabilities, or any other alternative to probability can better be done with probability."*

On the other side of the debate is the "PT is insufficient," school of thought. This school holds the view that even though PT is powerful and important, it is not sufficient for dealing with many types of real-world problems. More specifically, PT has fundamental limitations which are rooted in the fact that PT is based on bivalent logic — a logic which is intolerant of imprecision and partial truth. In PT, a concept is either true or false with no shades of truth allowed. Thus, an event either occurs or does not occur; a process is either stationary or nonstationary; events are either independent or not independent, and so on. Clearly, this is not a good model of reality. More importantly, PT does not provide effective tools for computation with imprecise probabilities and imprecise probability distributions — as most real-world probabilities and probability distributions are. There is a literature on imprecise probabilities and growing interest in computation with imprecise probabilities within PT, but what can be done through the use of bivalent-logic-based methods is rather limited. It is of interest to note that the debate between the Sufficients and the Insufficients has many historical parallels. Familiar examples are: Newtonian mechanics versus quantum mechanics; deterministic mechanics versus statistical mechanics; Euclidian geometry versus non-Euclidian geometry; and deterministic versus stochastic models in economics. In almost all cases, it is the Insufficients whose views eventually prevail.

Within the "PT is insufficient" school of thought there are those, as I am, who feel that probability theory has much to gain from addition of concepts and techniques drawn from fuzzy logic. Among such concepts are those of fuzzy event, fuzzy probability, fuzzy probability distribution, fuzzy relation, the concept of a protoform, the concept of a linguistic variable, the concept of fuzzy rule set and the concept of a generalized constraint. In fuzzy logic, computation with fuzzy probability distributions involves propagation of generalized constraints. Importantly, in fuzzy logic everything is or is allowed to be graduated, that is, be a matter of degree or, equivalently, fuzzy. Furthermore, in fuzzy logic everything is or is allowed to be granulated, with a granule being a clump of elements drawn together by indistinguishability, equivalence, similarity, proximity or functionality. Graduation and granulation play key roles in human cognition.

The most significant limitation of PT is that PT does not have NL-capability, that is, the capability to operate on information described in natural language. The importance of NL-capability derives from the fact that much of human knowledge is described in natural language. This applies, in particular, to perception-based knowledge. An example is the following problem. Assume that X is a real-valued random variable. I do not know the probability distribution of X but my perceptions are: (a) usually X is much larger than approximately a; and (b) usually X is much smaller than approximately b, with a < b. What is the expected value of X? Another example: I ask a cab driver to take me to address A the shortest way. This problem has a provably valid solution. But if I ask the driver to take me to address A the fastest way, the problem does not have a provably valid solution.

Generalization of PT through the addition of concepts and techniques drawn from fuzzy logic leads to what may be called the Generalized Theory of Uncertainty (GTU). The fundamental thesis of GTU is that information is representable as a generalized constraint. The traditional view that information is statistical in nature is a special case. Unlike PT, GTU is based on fuzzy logic. By construction, GTU is not a replacement for PT, but its conceptual framework is much broader than the conceptual framework of PT. In particular, as in fuzzy logic, graduation and granulation play pivotal roles in GTU.

In sum, "Uncertainty and Intelligent Information Systems," contains much that is forward-looking, informative and authoritative. Bernadette Bouchon-Meunier, Ronald Yager, Christophe Marsala, Maria Rifqi, the contributors and the publisher deserve our thanks, congratulations and loud applause.

Lotfi A. Zadeh
Berkeley, California
June 15, 2007

Contents

Chapter 31. On n-Contractive Fuzzy Logics: First Results   433

Chapter 32. Geometric Representations of Weak Orders   447

Chapter 33. Lexicographic Composition of Similarity-Based Fuzzy Orderings   457

Chapter 34. Efficiently Updating and Tracking the Dominant Normalized Kernel Principal Components   471

UNCERTAINTY MODELING

The Game-Theoretic Framework for Probability

Glenn Shafer

Rutgers Business School — Newark and New Brunswick,
180 University Avenue, Newark, New Jersey 07102 USA
Department of Computer Science, Royal Holloway,
University of London, Egham, Surrey TW20 0EX UK
gshafer@rutgers.edu

Abstract

The game-theoretic framework for probability was introduced by Vladimir Vovk and myself in *Probability and Finance*, published in 2001. But it has roots in the work of Jean Ville, who showed how Cournot's principle, the principle that an event of very small probability will not happen, can be given a game-theoretic interpretation. The framework allows us to generalize the classical limit theorems of probability and opens up new ways of making probability predictions.

1. Introduction

Cournot's principle says that an event of small or zero probability singled out in advance will not happen. From the turn of the twentieth century through the 1950s, many mathematicians, including Aleksandr Chuprov, Émile Borel, Maurice Fréchet, Paul Lévy, and Andrei Kolmogorov, saw this principle as fundamental to the application and meaning of probability. In their view, a probability model gains empirical content only when it rules out an event by assigning it small or zero probability.

In his doctoral dissertation, published in 1939, Jean Ville showed that Cournot's principle can be given a game-theoretic interpretation. The game-theoretic framework for probability published by Vladimir Vovk and myself in 2001 (in *Probability and Finance; It's Only a Game!*[20]) extends Ville's game-theoretic approach to cases where successive forecasts fall short of a full probability distribution for the quantities forecast.

2.   The Origins of Cournot's Principle

An event with very small probability is *morally impossible*; it will not happen. Equivalently, an event with very high probability is *morally certain*; it will happen. This principle was first formulated within mathematical probability by Jacob Bernoulli. In his *Ars Conjectandi*, published posthumously in 1713, Bernoulli proved that in a sufficiently long sequence of independent trials of an event, there is a very high probability that the frequency with which the event happens will be close to its probability. Bernoulli explained that we can treat the very high probability as moral certainty and so use the frequency of the event as an estimate of its probability.

Augustin Cournot, a mathematician now remembered as an economist and a philosopher of science,[15,16] gave the discussion a nineteenth-century cast in his 1843 treatise on probability.[9] Because he was familiar with geometric probability, Cournot could talk about probabilities that are vanishingly small. He brought physics to the foreground. It may be mathematically possible, he argued, for a heavy cone to stand in equilibrium on its vertex, but it is physically impossible. The event's probability is vanishingly small. Similarly, it is physically impossible for the frequency of an event in a long sequence of trials to differ substantially from the event's probability [9, pp. 57 and 106].

At the turn of the twentieth century, it was a commonplace among statisticians that one must decide what level of probability will count as practical certainty in order to apply probability theory. We find this stated explicitly in 1901, for example, in the articles by Georg Bohlmann and Ladislaus von Bortkiewicz in the section on probability in the *Encyklopädie der mathematischen Wissenschaften* [25, p. 825] [4, p. 861]. Aleksandr Chuprov, professor of statistics in Petersburg, was the champion of Cournot's principle in Russia.

He called it Cournot's lemma [18, p. 167] and declared it a basic principle of the logic of the probable [22, pp. 95–96].

Saying that an event of very small or vanishingly small probability will not happen is one thing. Saying that probability theory gains empirical meaning only by ruling out the happening of such events is another. Cournot may have been the first to make this second assertion:

> ... *The physically impossible event is therefore the one that has infinitely small probability*, and only this remark gives substance — objective and phenomenal value — to the theory of mathematical probability [9, p. 78].

Paul Lévy, a French mathematician who began writing on probability in the 1920s, stands out for the clarity of his articulation of the thesis that Cournot's principle is the only way of connecting a probabilistic theory with the world outside mathematics.[14] Lévy's views were widely shared in France. In the 1940s, Émile Borel called Cournot's principle first "the only law of chance" (la loi unique du hasard).[5,6] Neither Lévy nor Borel used the name "Cournot's principle," which was coined by Maurice Fréchet in 1949. Fréchet's inspiration was Oskar Anderson, who had talked about the Cournotsche Lemma (Cournot's lemma) and the Cournotsche Brücke (Cournot's bridge).[1,2] Anderson was following his teacher Chuprov in the use of "lemma." Fréchet felt that "lemma," like "theorem," should be reserved for purely mathematical results and so suggested "principe de Cournot." Fréchet's coinage was used in the 1950s in French, German, and English.[12,18,19,26]

3. Ville's Theorem

Vovk and I[20] use Cournot's principle in a game-theoretic form: a strategy for placing bets without risking bankruptcy will not multiply the bettor's capital by a large or infinite factor. In the case where the bettor can buy or sell any random variable for its expected value, this is equivalent to the classical form of the principle; Jean Ville demonstrated the equivalence in 1939.[24]

Consider a sequence $Y_1, Y_2, \ldots$ of binary random variables with a joint probability distribution P. Suppose, for simplicity, that P assigns every finite sequence $y_1, \ldots, y_n$ of 0s and 1s positive probability, so that its conditional probabilities for Y_n given values of the preceding variables are always unambiguously defined. Following Jean Ville,[24] consider a gambler who begins with \$1 and is allowed to bet as he pleases on each round, provided that he does not risk bankruptcy. We can formalize this with the following protocol, where betting on Y_n is represented as buying some number s_n (possibly zero or negative) of tickets that cost \$$P\{Y_n = 1 | Y_1 = y_1, \ldots, Y_{n-1} = y_{n-1}\}$ and pay \$$Y_n$.

BINARY PROBABILITY PROTOCOL
Players: Reality, Skeptic
Protocol:
> $\mathcal{K}_0 := 1$.
> FOR $n = 1, 2, \ldots$:
>> Skeptic announces $s_n \in \mathbb{R}$.
>> Reality announces $y_n \in \{0, 1\}$.
>> $\mathcal{K}_n := \mathcal{K}_{n-1} + s_n(y_n - P\{Y_n = 1 | Y_1 = y_1, \ldots, Y_{n-1} = y_{n-1}\})$.

Restriction on Skeptic: Skeptic must choose the s_n so that his capital is always non-negative ($\mathcal{K}_n \geq 0$ for all n) no matter how Reality moves.

This is a perfect-information sequential protocol; moves are made in the order listed, and each player sees the other player's moves as they are made. The sequence $\mathcal{K}_0, \mathcal{K}_1, \ldots$ is Skeptic's capital process.

Ville showed that Skeptic's getting rich in this protocol is equivalent to an event of small probability happening, in the following sense:

(1) When Skeptic follows a measurable strategy (a rule that gives s_n as a function of $y_1, \ldots, y_{n-1}$),

$$P\left\{ \sup_n \mathcal{K}_n \geq \frac{1}{\epsilon} \right\} \leq \epsilon \tag{1}$$

for every $\epsilon > 0$. (This is because the capital process $\mathcal{K}_0, \mathcal{K}_1, \ldots$ is a non-negative martingale; Equation (1) is sometimes called *Doob's inequality*.)

(2) If A is a measurable subset of $\{0, 1\}^\infty$ with $\mathrm{P}(A) \leq \epsilon$, then Skeptic has a measurable strategy that guarantees

$$\liminf_{n \to \infty} \mathcal{K}_n \geq \frac{1}{\epsilon}$$

whenever $(y_1, y_2, \dots) \in A$.

We can summarize these results by saying that Skeptic's being able to multiply his capital by a factor of $1/\epsilon$ or more is equivalent to the happening of an event with probability ϵ or less.

Ville's work was motivated by von Mises's notion of a collective.[27-29] Von Mises had argued that a sequence $y_1, y_2, \dots$ of 0s and 1s should be considered random if no subsequence with a different frequency of 1s can be picked out by a gambler to whom the ys are presented sequentially; this condition, von Mises felt, would keep the gambler from getting rich by deciding when to bet. Ville showed that von Mises's condition is insufficient, in as much as it does not rule out the gambler's getting rich by varying the direction and amount to bet.

4. The Game-Theoretic Framework

Although the preceding explanation of Ville's ideas was limited to the binary case, Ville made it clear that these ideas apply whenever conditional probabilities from a joint probability distribution for a sequence of random variables are used to make successive probability predictions. The framework of[20] generalizes the ideas further. The generalization has three aspects:

- Instead of beginning with a probability measure and using its conditional probabilities or expected values as prices on each round, we allow another player, Forecaster, to set the prices as play proceeds. This makes the framework "prequential";[11] there is no need to specify what the price on the nth round would be had Reality moved differently on earlier rounds.
- When convenient, we make explicit additional information, say x_n, that Reality provides to Forecaster and Skeptic before they make their nth moves.
- We allow the story to be multi-dimensional, with Reality making several moves and Forecaster pricing them all.

A convenient level of generality for the present discussion is provided by the following protocol, where $\mathbb{R}^k$ is k-dimensional Euclidean space, $\mathbf{Y}$ is a subset of $\mathbb{R}^k$, and $\mathbf{X}$ is an arbitrary set.

LINEAR FORECASTING PROTOCOL
Players: Reality, Forecaster, Skeptic
Protocol:
  $\mathcal{K}_0 := 1$.
  FOR $n = 1, 2, \ldots, N$:
      Reality announces $x_n \in \mathbf{X}$.
      Forecaster announces $f_n \in \mathbb{R}^k$.
      Skeptic announces $s_n \in \mathbb{R}^k$.
      Reality announces $y_n \in \mathbf{Y}$.
      $\mathcal{K}_n := \mathcal{K}_{n-1} + s_n \cdot (y_n - f_n)$.

Restriction on Skeptic: Skeptic must choose the s_n so that his capital is always non-negative ($\mathcal{K}_n \geq 0$ for all n) no matter how the other players move.

Here $s_n \cdot (y_n - f_n)$ is the dot product of the k-dimensional vectors s_n and $y_n - f_n$. Notice also that play stops on the Nth round rather than continuing indefinitely. This is a convenient assumption in this section, where we emphasize the finitary picture; we will return to the infinitary picture later.

The linear forecasting protocol covers many prediction problems considered in statistics (where x and y are often called *independent* and *dependent* variables, respectively) and machine learning (where x is called the *object* and y the *label*).[13,23,31] Market games can be included by taking f_n to be a vector of opening prices and y_n the corresponding vector of closing prices for the nth trading period.

A strategy for Skeptic in the linear forecasting protocol is a rule that gives each of his moves s_n as a function of the preceding moves by Reality and Forecaster, $(x_1, f_1, y_1), \ldots, (x_{n-1}, f_{n-1}, y_{n-1}), x_n, f_n$. A strategy for Forecaster is a rule that gives each of his moves f_n as a function of the preceding moves by Reality and Skeptic, $(x_1, s_1, y_1), \ldots, (x_{n-1}, s_{n-1}, y_{n-1}), x_n$. One way of prescribing a strategy for Forecaster is to choose a probability distribution for $(x_1, y_1), (x_2, y_2), \ldots$ and set f_n equal to the conditional expected value of y_n given $(x_1, y_1), \ldots, (x_{n-1}, y_{n-1}), x_n$. We will look at other interesting strategies for Forecaster in Sec. 7.

How can one express confidence in Forecaster? The natural way is to assert Cournot's principle: say that a legal strategy for Skeptic (one that avoids $\mathcal{K}_n < 0$ no matter how the other players move) will not multiply Skeptic's initial capital by a large factor.

Once we adopt Cournot's principle in this form, it is natural to scale the implications of our confidence in Forecaster the same way we do in classical probability. This means treating an event that happens only when a specified legal strategy multiplies the capital by $1/\epsilon$ as no more likely than an event with probability ϵ.

As in classical probability, we can combine Cournot's principle with a form of Bernoulli's theorem to obtain a statement about relative frequency in a long sequence of events. In a sufficiently long sequence of events with upper probability 0.1 or less, for example, it is morally certain that no more than about 10% of the events will happen [21, Sec. 5.3]. This is a martingale-type result; rather than insist that the events be independent in some sense, we assume that the upper probability for each event is calculated at the point in the game where the previous event is settled.

5. Extending the Classical Limit Theorems

One of the main contributions of Shafer and Vovk[20] was to show that game theory can replace measure theory as a foundation for classical probability.

We showed in particular that classical limit theorems, especially the strong law of large numbers and the law of the iterated logarithm, can be proven constructively within a purely game-theoretic framework. From Ville's work, we know that for any event with probability zero, there is a strategy for Skeptic that avoids bankruptcy for sure and makes him infinitely rich if the event fails. But constructing the strategy is another matter. In the case of the events of probability zero associated with the classical theorems, we did construct the requisite strategies; they are computable and continuous.

We provided similar constructions for classical results that do not require an infinite number of rounds of play to be meaningful: the weak law of large numbers, finitary versions of the law of the iterated logarithm, and the central limit theorem.

6. The Idea of a Quasi-Universal Test

If two events have very small probability, their union also has reasonably small probability. The analogous idea in game-theoretic probability is that of averaging strategies: if one strategy for Skeptic makes him very rich without risking bankruptcy if one event happens, and another makes him very rich without risking bankruptcy if a second event happens, then the average of the two strategies will make reasonably rich without risking bankruptcy if either of the events happens. This leads us to the notion of a quasi-universal strategy: we list the most important extreme events that we want to rule out, and by averaging the strategies that rule each out, we obtain a strategy that rules them all out.

Leaving aside how this idea has been developed in the past within measure-theoretic probability, let us consider how it can be developed measure-theoretically in this protocol of binary forecasting:

BINARY PROBABILITY PROTOCOL WITH FORECASTER AND OBJECTS
Players: Reality, Forecaster, Skeptic
Protocol:
$\quad \mathcal{K}_0 := 1.$
$\quad$ FOR $n = 1, 2, \ldots$:
$\quad\quad$ Reality announces $x_n \in \mathbf{X}$.
$\quad\quad$ Forecaster announces $p_n \in [0, 1]$.
$\quad\quad$ Skeptic announces $s_n \in \mathbb{R}$.
$\quad\quad$ Reality announces $y_n \in \{0, 1\}$.
$\quad\quad \mathcal{K}_n := \mathcal{K}_{n-1} + s_n(y_n - p_n).$

Restriction on Skeptic: Skeptic must choose the s_n so that his capital is always non-negative ($\mathcal{K}_n \geq 0$ for all n) no matter how the other players move.

In this protocol, where Forecaster gives a probability p_n on each round, taking into account the previous outcomes $y_1, \ldots, y_{n-1}$ and auxiliary information $x_1, \ldots, x_n$, we are mainly interested in two aspects of the agreement between the probabilities p_n and the outcomes y_n:

Calibration. Whenever there are a large number of rounds on which p_n is close to some fixed probability p^*, we want the frequency with which $y_n = 1$ on those rounds to be approximately equal to p^*.

Resolution. We want this approximate equality between frequency and p^* to remain true when we consider only rounds where p_n is close to p^* and also x_n is close to some fixed value x^* in the object space **X**.

As it turns out,[34] we can often average strategies that reject Forecaster's performance over a grid of values of (x^*, p^*) that are sufficiently dense to capture all deviations of practical interest. This average strategy, which is testing for calibration and resolution, will not necessarily test for more subtle deviations by $y_1, y_2, \dots$ from the forecasts $p_1, p_2, \dots$, such as those associated with the law of the iterated logarithm or Ville's refutation of von Mises's theory, but these more subtle deviations may hold little interest. So the average strategy can be regarded, for practical purposes, as a universal test. To avoid confusion, I call it a *quasi-universal strategy*.

7. Defensive Forecasting

In cases where we have a quasi-universal strategy, a new opportunity opens up for Forecaster. Forecaster will do well enough if he can avoid rejection by that strategy. Formally, he needs a winning strategy in a version of the game where Skeptic is required to follow the quasi-universal strategy but Reality is free to move as she pleases. Does Forecaster have such a winning strategy? The surprising answer is yes.

This is easiest to see in the case where the quasi-universal strategy gives a move for the nth round that is continuous in the forecast p_n. As it happens, this is not an unreasonable requirement. We can construct quasi-universal strategies for calibration and resolution that are continuous in this respect, and there is even a philosophical argument for ruling out any discontinuous strategy for Skeptic: discontinuous functions are not really computable.[7,17]

As it turns out, it is easy to show that for any forecast-continuous strategy for Skeptic there exists a strategy for Forecaster that does not allow Skeptic's capital to grow, regardless of what Reality does. Let me repeat the simple proof given in Refs. 32 and 34. It begins by simplifying so that Forecaster's job seems to be even a little harder.

Instead of requiring that the entire forecast-continuous strategy for
Skeptic be announced at the beginning of the game, we ask only
that Skeptic announce his strategy for each round before Forecaster's
move on that round. And we drop the restriction that Skeptic avoid
risk of bankruptcy. This produces the following protocol:

BINARY FORECASTING AGAINST CONTINUOUS TESTS
Players: Reality, Forecaster, Skeptic
Protocol:
    $\mathcal{K}_0 := 1$.
    FOR $n = 1, 2, \ldots$:
        Reality announces $x_n \in \mathbf{X}$.
        Skeptic announces continuous $S_n : [0,1] \to \mathbb{R}$.
        Forecaster announces $p_n \in [0,1]$.
        Reality announces $y_n \in \{0,1\}$.
        $\mathcal{K}_n := \mathcal{K}_{n-1} + S_n(p_n)(y_n - p_n)$.

Here S_n is Skeptic's strategy for the nth round; it gives his move
as a function of Forecaster's not-yet-announced move p_n.

Theorem 1. *Forecaster has a strategy that ensures* $\mathcal{K}_0 \geq \mathcal{K}_1 \geq \mathcal{K}_2 \geq \cdots$.

Proof Because S_n is continuous, Forecaster can use the following
strategy:

- if the function $S_n(p)$ takes the value 0, choose p_n so that $S_n(p_n) = 0$;
- if S_n is always positive, take $p_n := 1$;
- if S_n is always negative, take $p_n := 0$.

This guarantees that $S_n(p_n)(y_n - p_n) \leq 0$, so that $\mathcal{K}_n \leq \mathcal{K}_{n-1}$. $\square$

Some readers may question the philosophical rationale for requiring that S_n be continuous. As it turns out, dropping this requirement
does not cost us much; Forecaster can still win if we allow him to
randomize.[33] This means that instead of telling Reality his probability p_n, Forecaster may give Reality only a probability distribution P_n
for p_n, with the value p_n to be drawn from P_n out of sight of Reality
or perhaps after Reality has selected y_n.

A strategy for Forecaster is what one usually calls a probability model; given the previous outcomes $y_1, \ldots, y_{n-1}$ and auxiliary

information $x_1, \ldots, x_n$, it gives a probability p_n for $y_n = 1$. Such probabilities can be used in any repetitive decision problem.[30] So Theorem 1's guarantee that they are valid, in the sense that they pass any reasonable test of calibration and resolution, has immense practical significance.

References

1. O. N. Anderson, *Einführung in die mathematische Statistik*. Springer, Vienna (1935).
2. O. N. Anderson, Die Begründung des Gesetzes der grossen Zahlen und die Umkehrung des Theorems von Bernoulli. *Dialectica*, **3**(9/10), 65–77 (1949).
3. J. Bernoulli, *Ars Conjectandi*. Thurnisius, Basel, 1713. Edith Sylla's English translation, *The Art of Conjecturing, Together with Letter to a Friend on Sets in Court Tennis*, was published by Johns Hopkins University Press in 2005. Oscar Sheynin's English translation of Part IV, dated 2005, is at www.sheynin.de.
4. G. Bohlmann, Lebensversicherungs-Mathematik. In *Encyklopädie der mathematischen Wissenschaften, Bd. I, Teil 2*, pages 852–917. Teubner, Leipzig (1901).
5. É. Borel, *Les probabilités et la vie*. Presses Universitaires de France, Paris, 1943. Later editions in 1946, 1950, 1958, and 1967. The 1958 edition was translated into English by Maurice Baudin and published as *Probabilities and Life* by Dover, New York (1962).
6. É. Borel, *Probabilité et certitude*. Presses Universitaires de France, Paris, 1950. An English translation, *Probability and Certainty*, was published in 1963 by Walker, New York.
7. L. E. J. Brouwer, Begründung der Mengenlehre unabhängig vom logischen Satz vom ausgeschlossenen Dritte. Erster Teil. Allgemeine Mengelehre. *Koninklijke Nederlandse Akademie van Wetenschschappen Verhandelingen*, **5**, 1–43 (1918).
8. A. A. Chuprov, Очерки по теории статистики *(Essays on the theory of statistics)*. Sabashnikov, Saint Petersburg, second edition, 1910. The first edition appeared in 1909. The second edition was reprinted by the State Publishing House, Moscow (1959).
9. A.-A. Cournot, *Exposition de la théorie des chances et des probabilités*. Hachette, Paris, 1843. Reprinted in 1984 as Vol. I (B. Bru, ed.) of Ref. 1,
10. A.-A. Cournot, *Euvres complètes*. Vrin, Paris, 1973–1984. Vols. 10, with an eleventh to appear.
11. A. P. Dawid, Statistical theory: The prequential approach (with discussion). *Journal of the Royal Statistical Society. Series A*, **147**, 278–292 (1984).
12. B. de Finetti, Recent suggestions for the reconciliation of theories of probability. In Jerzy Neyman, editor, *Proceedings of the Second Berkeley Symposium on Mathematical Statistics and Probability*, pages 217–225. University of California Press, Berkeley and Los Angeles (1951).

13. T. Hastie, R. Tibshirani and J. Friedman, *The Elements of Statistical Learning Theory: Data Mining, Inference, and Prediction.* Springer, New York (2001).

14. P. Lévy, *Calcul des probabilités.* Gauthier-Villars, Paris (1925).

15. T. Martin, *Probabilités et critique philosophique selon Cournot.* Vrin, Paris (1996).

16. T. Martin, *Bibliographie cournotienne.* Annales littéraires de l'Université Franche-Comté, Besançon (1998).

17. P. Martin-Löf, *Notes on Constructive Mathematics.* Almqvist & Wiksell, Stockholm (1970).

18. H. Richter, Zur Begründung der Wahrscheinlichkeitsrechnung. *Dialectica*, **8**, 48–77 (1954).

19. H. Richter, *Wahrscheinlichkeitstheorie.* Springer, Berlin (1956).

20. G. Shafer and V. Vovk, *Probability and Finance: It's Only a Game.* Wiley, New York (2001).

21. G. Shafer and V. Vovk, On a review by V. N. Tutubalin. http://www.probabilityandfinance.com/reviews/tut_response1.pdf (2002).

22. O. Sheynin, *Aleksandr A. Chuprov: Life, Work, Correspondence. The making of mathematical statistics.* Vandenhoeck & Ruprecht, Göttingen (1996).

23. V. Vapnik, *The Nature of Statistical Learning Theory.* Springer, New York (1996).

24. J.-A. Ville, *Étude critique de la notion de collectif.* Gauthier-Villars, Paris, 1939. This differs from Ville's dissertation, which was defended in March 1939, only in that a 17-page introductory chapter replaces the dissertation's one-page introduction.

25. L. von Bortkiewicz, Anwendungen der Wahrscheinlichkeitsrechnung auf Statistik. In *Encyklopädie der mathematischen Wissenschaften, Bd. I, Teil 2*, pages 821–851. Teubner, Leipzig (1901).

26. G. von Hirsch, Sur un aspect paradoxal de la théorie des probabilités. *Dialetica*, **8**, 125–144 (1954).

27. R. von Mises, Grundlagen der Wahrscheinlichkeitsrechnung. *Mathematische Zeitschrift*, **5**, 52–99 (1919).

28. R. von Mises, *Wahrscheinlichkeitsrechnung, Statistik und Wahrheit.* Springer, Vienna, 1928. Second edition 1936, third 1951. A posthumous fourth edition, edited by his widow Hilda Geiringer, appeared in 1972. English editions, under the title *Probability, Statistics and Truth*, appeared in 1939 and 1957.

29. R. von Mises, *Wahrscheinlichkeitsrechnung und ihre Anwendung in der Statistik und theoretischen Physik.* Deuticke, Leipzig and Vienna (1931).

30. V. Vovk, Competitive on-line learning with a convex loss function. Working Paper No. 14, http://www.probabilityandfinance.com (2005).

31. V. Vovk, A. Gammerman and G. Shafer, *Algorithmic Learning in a Random World.* Springer, New York (2005).

32. V. Vovk, I. Nouretdinov, A. Takemura and G. Shafer, Defensive forecasting for linear protocols. In *AISTATS 2005: Proceedings of the 10th International Workshop on Artificial Intelligence and Statistics, Barbados, January 6–8*,

2005, pages 365–372, (2005). http://www.gatsby.ucl.ac.uk/aistats/proceedings.htm. Extended version: Working Paper No. 10, http://www.probabilityandfinance.com.

33. V. Vovk and G. Shafer, Good randomized sequential probability forecasting is always possible. *Journal of the Royal Statistical Society, Series B*, **67**, 747–764 (2005). Extended version: Working Paper No. 7 at http://www.probabilityandfinance.com.

34. V. Vovk, Akimichi Takemura, and Glenn Shafer. Defensive forecasting. In *Algorithmic Learning Theory: Proceedings of the 16th International Conference, ALT 2005, Singapore, October 8–11, 2005*, page 459. Springer-Verlag, 2005. Lecture Notes in Computer Science, Vol. 3734. Extended version: Working Paper No. 8, http://www.probabilityandfinance.com.

Aggregated Likelihoods: a Comparative Approach

G. Busanello[*,†], G. Coletti[*,‡], R. Scozzafava[**,§] and B. Vantaggi[**,¶]

*Dip. Matematica e Informatica,
Univ. of Perugia, Italy
†busanello@dipmat.unipg.it
‡coletti@dipmat.unipg.it
**Dip. Metodi e Modelli Matematici,
Univ. "La Sapienza" Rome, Italy
§romscozz@dmmm-uniroma1.it
¶vantaggi@dmmm.uniroma1.it

Abstract

Given a set of conditional events $E|H_i$, we characterize binary relations on the conditioning events H_i representable by aggregated likelihoods. This procedure can drive us to the "right" choice for extending a likelihood (defined on points) to an aggregated one.

1. Introduction

During the knowledge acquisition process (as in decision theory), a fundamental role is played by the problem of enlarging the domain of events of interest and the ensuing relevant values of the reference measure (such as uncertainty or information measure). This process is usually referred to as "inferential process". A well-known procedure of this kind is that related to the enlargement of a probability assessment, given on a class of (conditional) events $\{H_i, E|H_i\}$ (with incompatible and exhaustive $H_i = H_i|\Omega$, where Ω is the sure event), to the events $\{H_i|E\}$ through Bayes' theorem. The attractiveness

17

and the relevant success of this specific case is due mainly to its simplicity and to the uniqueness of the answer. Nevertheless, thanks to the particular logical structure of events $\{H_i\}$, it hides some of the steps necessary for the general process (see Ref. 3): besides the trivial checking of coherence for the assessment $\{P(H_i), P(E|H_i)\}$, we need to find all possible values of $\{P(H_i|E)\}$ for which the "global" assessment $\{P(H_i), P(E|H_i), P(H_i|E)\}$ is coherent. There is not a unique value (as in the case of Bayes' theorem): in fact, the coherent values usually belong to a real interval. A typical situation is related to the enlargement of a (coherent) assessment $\{P(E|H_i)\}$, with the H_i's incompatible (that is, a likelihood) to events $H \in \mathcal{H}$, where $\mathcal{H}$ is the algebra spanned by them. Also in this case the enlargement is not unique and the possible coherent enlargements are completely characterized in Ref. 7 (the case of a finite number of H_i's is essentially dealt with in Ref. 1). We summarize the following results established in Refs. 1, 5 and 6:

- extensions obtained by additivity, i.e. $P(E|H \vee K) = P(E|H) + P(E|K)$, in general are not coherent;
- if we require that $\varphi(\cdot) = \{P(E|\cdot)\}$ is an uncertainty measure on $\mathcal{H}$ (and so its monotonicity with respect to $\subseteq$), then the only coherent enlargement is that obtained by putting, for every $H, K \in \mathcal{H}$

$$P(E|H \vee K) = \max\{P(E|H), P(E|K)\} .$$

A similar situation occurs if $\varphi(\cdot)$ is a measure of information (and so antimonotone with respect to $\subseteq$), for which the only coherent extension is obtained by using "min" in place of "max";

- in the general (finite) case, any coherent enlargement is such that the value of the $\varphi(H)$ is a weighed mean (or convex combination, possibly also degenerated) of the values $\{P(E|H_i)\}$, $H_i \in H$.

It is interesting to stress that, in the approach to fuzzy set theory introduced in Ref. 5, also a membership function $\mu(x)$ can be seen as a likelihood. For example, if X is a numerical quantity and φ_X is the property "small", the membership function $\mu(x)$ may be put equal to 1 for values x of X less than a given x_1, while it is put equal to 0 for values greater than x_2; so the real problem is that we are doubtful (and so uncertain) on having or not the property φ_X those elements of C_X between x_1 and x_2. Then the interest is in fact directed toward *conditional events* such as $E|A_x$, where x ranges over the interval from x_1 to x_2, with

$$E = \text{We claim the property } \varphi_X, \quad A_x = \text{the value of } X \text{ is } x.$$

It follows that we are willing to assign a subjective probability $P(E|A_x)$ and identify it with the values of the membership function $\mu(x)$. Then some of the usual arguments appear counterintuitive: in fact, the "aggregated" membership should possibly decrease when the information is not concentrated on a given x but is "spread" over a larger set. So you may be willing, if you know that $x = 39$, to put $\mu(x) = 0.2$, while if you know that $x = 2$, you may be willing to put $\mu(x) = 0.9$; on the other hand, knowing that x is between 2 and 39, the corresponding value of the possibility measure is still 0.9. This would suggest to take as such aggregated measure a function which is **not** a capacity. Now the question is: which is the "best enlargement" of a likelihood, in a specific class of problems? Or, in other words: which is the best model to manage information during a knowledge acquisition process or during a decision process? To give an answer to these questions we try to study the problem in a comparative context, by using the classic methodology of the theory of measurements and of decision theory: in fact, we remove the constraints of the numerical structure, and so it is simpler to see the actual conditions on which a model is based. To pursue this goal we consider a binary relation $\preceq$ between events $E_i|H_i$ ($H_i \in \mathcal{H}$) expressing the idea of "no more likely than" and study necessary and sufficient conditions for the representability of $\preceq$ by a coherent aggregated likelihood, singling out various specific kinds of enlargements.

2. Coherent Conditional Probabilities

Definition 1. Given a Boolean algebra $\mathcal{B}$ and an additive set $\mathcal{A}$ (closed under finite unions) such that $\mathcal{A} \subset \mathcal{B}$ and $\emptyset \notin \mathcal{A}$, a *conditional probability* on $\mathcal{B} \times \mathcal{A}$ is a function $P(\cdot|\cdot)$ into $[0, 1]$, which satisfies the following conditions:

(i) $P(H|H) = 1$ for every $H \in \mathcal{A}$,
(ii) $P(\cdot|H)$ is a finitely additive probability on $\mathcal{B}$ for any $H \in \mathcal{A}$,
(iii) $P(E \wedge A|H) = P(E|H)P(A|E \wedge H)$, with $E, A \in \mathcal{B}$ and H, $E \wedge H \in \mathcal{A}$.

The notion of coherence is needed in order to manage partial probability assessments: in fact, coherence of a partial assessment p assures that p is the restriction of a *conditional probability P*.

Definition 2. Given an arbitrary set of conditional events $\mathcal{F}$, a real function P on $\mathcal{F}$ is a *coherent* conditional probability if there exists a conditional probability $P'(\cdot|\cdot)$ on $\mathcal{E}$ extending P, with $\mathcal{E} \supseteq \mathcal{F}$ and $\mathcal{E} = \mathcal{B} \times \mathcal{A}$ (where $\mathcal{B}$ is an algebra, and $\mathcal{A}$ is an additive set with $\mathcal{A} \subset \mathcal{B}$).

We recall, among the several characterizations of coherence, the following[4]:

Theorem 1. *Let $\mathcal{F}$ be an arbitrary family of conditional events. For any finite family $\mathcal{G} = \{E_1|H_1, \ldots, E_n|H_n\} \subseteq \mathcal{F}$ denote by $\mathcal{B}(\mathcal{G})$ the algebra generated by $\{E_1, H_1, \ldots, E_n, H_n\}$. For a real function P on $\mathcal{F}$ the following statements are equivalent:*

(i) P is a coherent conditional probability;

(ii) for every finite family $\mathcal{G} \subseteq \mathcal{F}$ there exists a family of probabilities $\mathcal{P} = \{P_0, \ldots, P_k\}$, each probability being defined on a suitable subset $\mathcal{A}_\alpha \subseteq \mathcal{B}(\mathcal{G})$ (with $\mathcal{A}_0 = \mathcal{B}(\mathcal{G})$ and, for $\alpha = 1, \ldots, k$, $\mathcal{A}_\alpha = \{A \in \mathcal{A}_{\alpha-1} : P_{\alpha-1}(A) = 0\}$), such that for any $E_i|H_i \in \mathcal{G}$ there exists a unique P_α, with $P_\alpha(H_i) > 0$ and

$$P(E_i|H_i) = \frac{P_\alpha(E_i \wedge H_i)}{P_\alpha(H_i)}.$$

Condition *(ii)* gives a characterization of P restricted to $\mathcal{G}$ in terms of an "agreeing" class of unconditional probabilities $\{P_0, \ldots, P_k\}$ and it allows a "local" representation of P. The unique index α such that $P_\alpha(H) > 0$ represents the *zero-layer* of the conditioning event H (see Ref. 4).

A particular, but interesting case of the previous result is the following:

Theorem 2. *Let $\mathcal{F}$ be a family of conditional events $\{E_i|H_i\}_{i\in I}$, where card(I) is arbitrary and the events H_i's are a partition of Ω. Then, any function $f : \mathcal{F} \to [0,1]$ such that*

$$f(E_i|H_i) = 0 \quad \text{if } E_i \wedge H_i = \emptyset$$
$$f(E_i|H_i) = 1 \quad \text{if } H_i \subseteq E_i$$

is a coherent conditional probability.

An important feature of coherence is the possibility to enlarge a coherent conditional probability assessment to new (conditional) events or, in other words, to make inference on any event.[4]

Theorem 3. *If P is an assessment on a family of conditional events $\mathcal{F}$, then there exists a (possibly not unique) coherent extension of P to an arbitrary family $\mathcal{K} \supset \mathcal{F}$, if and only if P is coherent on $\mathcal{F}$.*

3. Comparative Relations

Let $\preceq$ be a binary relation, expressing the intuitive idea of being "no more believable than", on a set of conditional events $\mathcal{F} = \{E_i|H_i, F_i|K_i\}_{i \in I}$. The symbols $\sim$ and $\prec$ represent, respectively, the symmetric and asymmetric parts of $\preceq$: $E|H \sim F|K$ means (roughly speaking) that $E|H$ is judged "equally believable" as $F|K$, while $E|H \prec F|K$ means that $F|K$ is "more believable" than $E|H$. The relation $\preceq$ expresses a qualitative judgement, and we need to set up a system of rules assuring the consistency of the relation with some numerical model. More precisely, given a numerical framework of reference (singled-out by a numerical conditional measure of uncertainty), we seek for the conditions which are necessary and sufficient for the existence of a numerical assessment on the events representing a given ordinal relation. We recall that a function f from $\mathcal{F}$ to $\mathbb{R}^+$ *represents* the relation $\preceq$ iff

$$E|H \preceq F|K \implies f(E|H) \leq f(F|K),$$
$$E|H \prec F|K \implies f(E|H) < f(F|K).$$

In Ref. 8 a comparative conditional probability is defined as any binary relation $\preceq$ satisfying the following condition (interpretable in terms of betting scheme):

(ccp) for every $E_i|H_i, F_i|K_i \in \mathcal{F}$ there exist $\alpha_i, \beta_i \in [0,1]$ with $\alpha_i \leq \beta_i$ if $E_i|H_i \preceq F_i|K_i$ and $\alpha_i < \beta_i$ if $E_i|H_i \prec F_i|K_i$, such that, for every $n \in \mathbb{N}$ and for every $E_i|H_i \preceq F_i|K_i$, $\lambda_i, \lambda_i' \geq 0$, $\lambda_i + \lambda_i' > 0$ $(i = 1, \ldots, n)$, the supremum over

$$H^0 = \left(\bigvee_{H_i : \lambda_i > 0} H_i \right) \vee \left(\bigvee_{K_i : \lambda_i' > 0} K_i \right),$$

of the following random quantity,

$$\sum_i \left[\lambda'_i (I_{F_i \wedge K_i} - \beta_i I_{K_i}) + \lambda_i (\alpha_i I_{H_i} - I_{E_i \wedge H_i}) \right]$$

where I_A is the indicator of event A, is greater than or equal to 0.

We recall that condition (ccp) is necessary and sufficient for the representability of $\preceq$ by a coherent conditional probability on an arbitrary family $\mathcal{F}$ of conditional events. Now, we focus on relations defined in a more specific setting (that of interest for a likelihood and its aggregations), so we consider the events $E|A_r$, with $\mathcal{C} = \{A_1, \ldots, A_n\}$ partition of Ω.

First of all we consider the family $\mathcal{G} = \{E|A_r, \emptyset|\Omega, \Omega|\Omega \ : \ A_r \in \mathcal{C}\}$.

Proposition 1. *Let $\preceq$ be a binary relation on $\mathcal{G}$ such that $\emptyset|\Omega \preceq E|A_r \preceq \Omega|\Omega$, and moreover $E|A_r \sim \emptyset|\Omega$, for every $A_r \wedge E = \emptyset$ and $E|A_r \sim \Omega|\Omega$ for $E \supseteq A_r$. If $\preceq$ is reflexive and transitive and if there is a countable subset $\mathcal{B}$ of $\mathcal{G}$ dense with respect to $\preceq$, then there exists a coherent conditional probability P on $\mathcal{G}$ representing $\preceq$.*

Proof. The requirement that $\preceq$ is a preorder and admits a countable dense subset assures that there exists a real function on $\mathcal{G}$ representing $\preceq$. So also any transformation of it giving 0 to $\emptyset|\Omega$ and 1 to $\Omega|\Omega$ represents $\preceq$. By Theorem 2, this function is a coherent conditional probability. $\qquad\qquad\square$

Let us consider now the additive class $\mathcal{H}$ spanned by $\mathcal{C}$ and the set $\mathcal{E} = \{E|H, \emptyset|\Omega, \Omega|\Omega \ : \ H \in \mathcal{H}\}$. The following proposition gives necessary conditions for the representability of $\preceq$ by a coherent conditional probability on $\mathcal{E}$ (which is called *aggregated likelihood*).

Proposition 2. *If there exists a coherent conditional probability on $\mathcal{E}$ representing $\preceq$, then the following conditions hold:*

(a) *$\preceq$ is a weak order such that $\emptyset|\Omega \prec \Omega|\Omega$;*
(b) *for any $E|H \in \mathcal{E}$, $\emptyset|\Omega \preceq E|H \preceq \Omega|\Omega$;*
(c) *for any $H \in \mathcal{H}$, $E \wedge H = \emptyset \Rightarrow E|H \sim \emptyset|\Omega$, and $E \supseteq H \Rightarrow E|H \sim \Omega|\Omega$;*
(d) *$H, K \in \mathcal{H}$, with $H \wedge K = \emptyset$,*

$$[E|K \preceq E|H] \Rightarrow [E|K \preceq E|(H \vee K) \preceq E|H];$$

(e) $H, K, K', G \in \mathcal{H}$ with $H \wedge K = \emptyset$ and $K' \subseteq K$, if either $E|(G^c \wedge H) \not\prec E|H$ or $E|H \not\prec E|(G \vee H)$ holds, then $[E|H \sim E|(H \vee K)$ and $E|K \not\prec E|H] \Rightarrow [E|G \sim E|(G \vee K')]$;

(f) $H_1, H_2, K \in \mathcal{H}$ and $(H_1 \vee H_2) \subseteq K$,
$[E|(H_1^c \wedge K) \not\prec E|K \not\prec E|(H_2^c \wedge K)] \Rightarrow [E|(H_1 \wedge H_2) \sim E|K]$.

The proof is based on the characterization Theorem 1, moreover these conditions can be deduced from (ccp). However the above conditions are not sufficient to assure the representability of $\preceq$ by means of a coherent conditional probability:

Example 1. Take the partition $\{A_1, \ldots, A_4\}$ and consider the following ordinal relation

$$\emptyset|\Omega \prec E|A_1 \prec E|(A_1 \vee A_2) \prec E|A_2 \sim E|(A_1 \vee A_3)$$
$$\sim E|(A_1 \vee A_2 \vee A_3) \sim E|(A_1 \vee A_4) \sim E|(A_1 \vee A_2 \vee A_4)$$
$$\prec E|(A_2 \vee A_3) \prec E|(A_2 \vee A_4) \prec E|A_3 \sim E|A_4 \sim E|(A_3 \vee A_4)$$
$$\prec \ldots$$

It is easy to check that $\preceq$ satisfies the conditions *(a)–(f)*, but there is no coherent conditional probability representing it. Consider in fact a coherent conditional probability $P(\cdot|\cdot)$ on $E \times \mathcal{H}$, and extend it on $\mathcal{B} \times \mathcal{H}$, with $\mathcal{B}$ the algebra spanned by $E, A_1, \ldots, A_4$. Putting $P(A_i) = p_i$, since $E|A_2 \sim E|(A_1 \vee A_3)$ we have that

$$P(E|A_2) = P(E|(A_1 \vee A_3)) = \frac{P(E|A_1)p_1 + P(E|A_3)p_3}{p_1 + p_3}$$

and so

$$(P(E|A_2) - P(E|A_1))p_1 = (P(E|A_3) - P(E|A_2))p_3.$$

Analogously, from $E|A_2 \sim E|(A_1 \vee A_4)$ it follows

$$(P(E|A_2) - P(E|A_1))p_1 = (P(E|A_4) - P(E|A_2))p_4.$$

Since $E|A_3 \sim E|A_4$, from the previous equalities we get $p_3 = p_4$. Moreover, $p_3, p_4 > 0$, since $p_1 > 0$ (and also $p_2 > 0$) by $E|A_1 \prec E|(A_1 \vee A_2) \prec E|A_2$. Now, taking into account conditions

$E|A_3 \sim E|A_4$ and $p_3 = p_4$ we obtain

$$P(E|(A_2 \vee A_3)) = \frac{P(E|A_2)p_2 + P(E|A_3)p_3}{p_2 + p_3}$$
$$= \frac{P(E|A_2)p_2 + P(E|A_4)p_4}{p_2 + p_4} = P(E|A_2 \vee A_4)$$

which violates the initial condition $E|(A_2 \vee A_3) \prec E|(A_2 \vee A_4)$.

Then, the above example shows that also in this simple situation (particular set of events) we cannot avoid a condition based on a betting scheme criterion.

Definition 3. A relation $\preceq$ on $\mathcal{E} = \{E|H, \emptyset|\Omega, \Omega|\Omega : H \in \mathcal{H}\}$ is an "evenly" aggregated comparative likelihood if it satisfies conditions (a), (b), (c) and the following one:

(al) for any $n \in N$, any $\{E|H_1, \ldots, E|H_n\} \subseteq \mathcal{E}$, and for any choice of positive real numbers μ_i, if $E|H_i \preceq E|K_i$ and

$$\sup_{H^0} \sum_I \mu_i[h_i I_{K_i} - k_i I_{H_i})] \leq 0, \tag{1}$$

then $E|H_i \sim E|K_i$ (where k_i is the number of atoms contained in K_i — analogously for h_i).

For evenly aggregated comparative likelihood we have the following result:

Theorem 4. *If $\mathcal{H}$ is an additive set generated by the partition $\mathcal{C} = \{A_1, \ldots, A_n\}$, for a binary relation $\preceq$ on $\mathcal{E} = \{E|H, \emptyset|\Omega, \Omega|\Omega : H \in \mathcal{H}\}$ the following two statements are equivalent:*

(i) *$\preceq$ is an evenly aggregated comparative likelihood;*
(ii) *there exists a coherent conditional probability on $\mathcal{E}$ representing $\preceq$. Moreover, this conditional probability is such that, for every $H \in \mathcal{H}$, $P(E|H)$ coincides with the average (with the same weights) of the values $P(E|A_r)$ for all $A_r \subseteq H$.*

Proof. If there exists a coherent conditional probability P as in condition (ii), then for any $E|H_i \in \mathcal{E}$

$$P(E|H_i) = \sum_{A_r \subseteq H_i} P(E|A_r)P(A_r|H_i) = \frac{1}{h_i} \sum_{A_r \subseteq H_i} P(E|A_r)$$

and so for $E|H_i \preceq E|K_i$ it follows

$$k_i \sum_{A_r \subseteq H_i} P(E|A_r) \le h_i \sum_{A_r \subseteq K_i} P(E|A_r).$$

Analogously, for $E|H_j \prec E|K_j$

$$k_j \sum_{A_r \subseteq H_j} P(E|A_r) < h_j \sum_{A_r \subseteq K_j} P(E|A_r).$$

For $E \wedge H_k = \emptyset$ one has $\sum_{A_r \subseteq H_k} P(E|A_r) = 0$, so $E|H_k \sim \emptyset|\Omega$. Moreover, for $H_r \subseteq E$ it follows $\sum_{A_r \subseteq H_r} P(E|A_r) = h_r$, so $E|H_r \sim \Omega|\Omega$. Then, conditions (a), (b) and (c) hold. Moreover, denoting by V_K the n-vector with rth component equal to 1 if $A_r \subseteq K$ and 0 otherwise, it follows from Theorem 1 that such $P(\cdot|\cdot)$ representing $\preceq$ exists iff for every $n \in N$ and for any $\{E|H_1, \ldots, E|H_n\} \subseteq \mathcal{E}$, the following system $\mathcal{S}$ admits a semi-positive solution (i.e. $w_r \ge 0$ and $\sum_r w_r > 0$)

$$\begin{cases} (h_i V_{K_i} - k_i V_{H_i}) \times W \ge 0, & E|H_i \preceq E|K_i \\ (h_j V_{K_j} - k_j V_{H_j}) \times W > 0, & E|H_j \prec E|K_j. \end{cases}$$

From a classic alternative theorem (see, e.g., Ref. 11) the system $\mathcal{S}$ has a semi-positive solution if and only if the inequality

$$\sum_I \lambda_i [h_i V_{K_i} - k_i V_{H_i})] + \sum_J \mu_j [h_j V_{K_j} - k_j V_{H_j})] \le 0$$

does not admit solution for non-negative λ_i, μ_j such that $\sum_J \mu_j > 0$. It is easy to see that the above condition has a solution iff $\preceq$ does not satisfy condition (al). $\quad\square$

Remark 1. Note that any P satisfying condition (ii) is such that its extension to events A_r is $P(A_r|\Omega) = \frac{1}{n}$.

In the case that the relation $\preceq$ is agreeing with a coherent conditional probability $P(E|\cdot)$ such that its extension on $A_r|\Omega$ is strictly positive, but not necessarily equal to $\frac{1}{n}$, we have the following result:

Theorem 5. *Let $\mathcal{H}$ be a finite additive set spanned by the partition $\mathcal{C} = \{A_1, \ldots, A_n\}$. For a binary relation $\precsim$ on $\mathcal{E} = \{E|H, \emptyset|\Omega, \Omega|\Omega : H \in \mathcal{H}\}$ the following two statements are equivalent:*

(i) for any $E|H_i \precsim E|K_i$ there exist $\alpha_i \leq \beta_i$ and $\alpha_i < \beta_i$ if $E|H_i \prec E|K_i$ such that the following system

$$\begin{cases} (V_{E \wedge K_j} - \beta_j V_{K_j}) \times W \geq 0, & E|K_j \in \mathcal{E} \\ (-V_{E \wedge H_i} + \alpha_i V_{H_i}) \times W \geq 0, & E|H_i \in \mathcal{E} \end{cases}$$

has a semi-positive solution;

(ii) there exists a coherent conditional probability on $\mathcal{E}$ representing $\precsim$. Moreover, this conditional probability is such that, for every $H \in \mathcal{H}$, $P(E|H)$ coincides with the average with positive weights of the values $P(E|A_r)$ for all $A_r \subseteq H$.

The result follows essentially from Theorem 1. For a detailed proof see Theorem 6 in Ref. 8. Since evenly aggregated comparative likelihoods are particular cases of the relation characterized by, means of Theorem 5, we show, through the following example, that this class of relations does not collapse in the class of evenly aggregated comparative likelihoods:

Example 2. Let $\{A_1, A_2, A_3\}$ be a partition of Ω and consider a relation on $E \times \mathcal{H}$ (with $\mathcal{H}$ the additive set generated by A_1, A_2, A_3)

$$E|A_1 \prec E|(A_1 \vee A_2 \vee A_3) \prec E|(A_1 \vee A_3) \prec E|(A_1 \vee A_2)$$
$$\prec E|A_2 \prec E|(A_2 \vee A_3) \prec E|A_3.$$

This relation is representable by the following coherent conditional probability

$$P(E|A_1) = \frac{1}{10}, \quad P(E|A_2) = \frac{7}{20},$$

$$P(E|A_3) = \frac{153}{380}, \quad P(E|(A_1 \vee A_3)) = \frac{2423}{41420},$$

$$P(E|(A_1 \vee A_2)) = \frac{73}{109}, \quad P(E|(A_2 \vee A_3)) = \frac{1483}{4180},$$

$$P(E|(A_1 \vee A_2 \vee A_3)) = \frac{6507}{75620}.$$

It is easy to check the coherence of the above assessment by Theorem 1. On the other hand, $\preceq$ is not an evenly aggregated comparative likelihoods: in fact considering the subset

$$\{E|A_2, E|A_3, E|(A_1 \vee A_2), E|(A_1 \vee A_3)\}$$

and taking e.g. $\mu_1 = 1$ and $\mu_2 = \frac{1}{2}$, from the statements $E|A_2 \prec E|A_3$ and $E|(A_1 \vee A_3) \prec E|(A_1 \vee A_2)$ one has that inequality (1) holds, while the relation is strict.

This implies that a relation representable by a coherent conditional probability, whose extension is such that $P(A_r|\Omega) > 0$ for any atom, it is not necessarily agreeing with a coherent conditional probability whose extension is such that $P(A_i|\Omega) = P(A_j|\Omega)$ for any pair of atoms. In other words, $P(E|H)$ is a mean with different positive weights.

Conditions (d), (e) and (f) are useful to split the problem into subproblems, by detecting the conditioning events belonging to different zero-layers,[4] as the following result shows:

Theorem 6. *Let $\preceq$ be an ordinal relation on $\mathcal{E}$ (with $\mathcal{H}$ a finite additive set) satisfying the conditions (a)–(f). Let H^0 be the union of the events in $\mathcal{H}$ and define H^i (for $i > 0$) as the union of $K \in \mathcal{H}$ such that $K \subseteq H^{i-1}$ and $E|K \not\sim E|(K^c \wedge H^{i-1}) \sim E|H^{i-1}$. If the restriction of $\preceq$ to the set $\mathcal{E}_j = \{E|H \, : \, H \in \mathcal{H}; H \subseteq H^j, H \not\subseteq H^{j+1}\}$ for any $j = 0, \dots, k$, is representable by a coherent conditional probability, then also $\preceq$ is representable by a coherent conditional probability.*

Proof. The proof is based essentially on the characterization result for coherent conditional probability (Theorem 1). Denoting by P^j a coherent conditional probability on $\mathcal{E}_j$ representing the restriction of $\preceq$ to $\mathcal{E}_j$, we consider the function f from $\mathcal{E}$ into $[0,1]$ such that, for any $E|H \in \mathcal{E}_j$, $f(E|H) = P^j(E|H)$, which is a coherent conditional probability. In fact, an agreeing class for it can be obtained by the "concatenation" of the agreeing classes of P^j. □

It comes out that a relation satisfying conditions (a)–(f) and decomposable into aggregated comparative likelihoods on $\mathcal{E}_j$ (with $j = 0, \dots, n$), is representable by a coherent conditional probability on $\mathcal{E}$.

Now we show how to get as particular case (when $H^i \wedge H^{i+1}$ contains only one suitable atom for $i = 0, \dots, k$) some specific relations.

To reach this aim we introduce the following axioms:

(A1) for every $H, K \in \mathcal{H}$ with $H \wedge K = \emptyset$ one has that either $E|(H \vee K) \sim E|H$ or $E|(H \vee K) \sim E|K$;

(A2) for every $H, K, C, D \in \mathcal{H}$ with H, K, C mutually incompatible and $D \subseteq (H \vee K)$, one has $[E|(H \vee K) \sim E|K$ and $E|(K \vee C) \sim E|C]$ implies $E|(D \vee C) \sim E|C$.

Actually these two axioms are a reinforcement of (d), (e), (f).

Proposition 3. *Let $\preceq$ be a relation on $\mathcal{E} = \{E|H, \emptyset|\Omega, \Omega|\Omega :$ $H \in \mathcal{H}\}$ satisfying conditions (a), (b), (c) and $(A1)$. Then, for every $H \in \mathcal{H}$, there exists a (unique, apart from equivalence) atom $A_r \subseteq H$ such that $E|A_r \sim E|H$.*

Proof. If for every atom $A_r \subseteq H$ we had $E|A_r \prec E|H$, by condition (A1) we would obtain $E|(A_i \vee A_j) \prec E|H$ for every pair of atoms A_i and A_j included in H, then, by induction, it would follow $E|H \prec E|H$. $\qquad\square$

The following result gives a characterization of relations satisfying, besides (a), (b), (c), axioms (A1) and (A2).

Theorem 7. *Let $\mathcal{H}$ be a finite additive set generated by the partition $\{A_1, \ldots, A_n\}$. For a binary relation $\preceq$ on $\mathcal{E} = \{E|H, \emptyset|\Omega, \Omega|\Omega :$ $H \in \mathcal{H}\}$ the following two statements are equivalent:*

(i) $\preceq$ satisfies (a), (b), (c), $(A1)$ and $(A2)$;

(ii) there exists a coherent conditional probability on $\mathcal{E}$ representing $\preceq$. Moreover, this conditional probability is such that, for every $H, K \in \mathcal{H}$ with $H \wedge K = \emptyset$, $P(E|H \vee K)$ is equal to either $P(E|H)$ or $P(E|K)$.

Proof. First we prove that (ii) implies (i). Any coherent conditional probability on $\mathcal{E}$ induces a relation $\preceq$ on $\mathcal{E}$ satisfying (a), (b), (c). Thus, we need to prove that $\preceq$ induced by a coherent conditional probability $P(E|\cdot)$, as in condition (ii), satisfies also (A1) and (A2). Since for every $H, K \in \mathcal{H}$ with $H \wedge K = \emptyset$ one has

$$P(E|H \vee K) = P(E|H)P(H|H \vee K) + P(E|K)P(K|H \vee K)$$

by the above hypothesis one has either $P(H|H \vee K) = 1$ or $P(K|H \vee K) = 1$. Then, either $P(E|H \vee K) = P(E|H)$ or $P(E|H \vee K) = P(E|K)$. This implies that $\preceq$ satisfies (A1). Moreover, if for every H, K, C mutually incompatible $P(E|H \vee K) = P(E|K)$ and $P(E|K \vee C) = P(E|C)$, then $P(H|H \vee K) = P(K|K \vee C) = 0$, which implies (through disintegration) that $P(E|H \vee K \vee C) = P(E|C)$ and so axiom (A2) holds.

Now we prove that (i) implies (ii). Since $\preceq$ is defined on $\mathcal{E}$, consider a partition $\mathcal{E}_0, \ldots, \mathcal{E}_l$ of $\mathcal{E}$ such that for all $E|H_i \in \mathcal{E}_s$ and $E|H_j \in \mathcal{E}_k$ we have $E|H_i \prec E|H_j$, if $s < k$. By condition (a) it follows that $l \geq 1$, and by (c) any $E|H_i \in \mathcal{E}_0$ is such that $E|H_i \sim \emptyset|\Omega$, and for any $E|H_j \in \mathcal{E}_l$ one has $E_j|H_j \sim \Omega|\Omega$. Now, consider a function $f : \mathcal{E} \to [0, 1]$ defined by putting

$$f(E|H) = \frac{s}{l} \text{ if } E|H \in \mathcal{E}_s \text{ (with } s = 0, \ldots, l),$$

which obviously represents $\preceq$. We need to prove that $f(\cdot|\cdot)$ is a coherent conditional probability on $\mathcal{E}$ satisfying the condition of statement (ii). From Proposition 3 there exists an atom A_r such that $E|A_r \sim E|\Omega$, let $I^0 = \{A_r : E|A_r \sim E|\Omega\}$. From transitivity one has that $E|A_r \sim E|\Omega \sim E|A_k$ for any $A_r, A_k \in I^0$. Thus, from (A1) one gets $E| \bigvee_{A_r \in I^0} A_r \sim E|\Omega$.

Analogously from Proposition 3 for the event $\bigwedge_{H \in I^0} H^c = \bigvee_{H \notin I^0} H$, which belongs to $\mathcal{H}$, there exists an atom $A_j \notin I^0$ such that $E|A_j \sim E|(\bigvee_{A_r \notin I^0} A_r)$. Moreover, from (A2) we get,

$$E \left| \left[\left(\bigvee_{A_r \notin I^0} A_r \right) \vee \left(\bigvee_{A_r \in I^0} A_r \right) \right] \sim E \left| \left(\bigvee_{A_r \in I^0} \right) A_r \sim E|A_i \right.\right.$$

for $A_i \in I^0$. Inside the set I^0 we can choose an arbitrary order among the atoms and we can take for $\beta = 0, \ldots, |I^0| - 1$

$$P_\beta(E \wedge A_{r_i}) = \begin{cases} \dfrac{s}{l} & i = \beta - 1, \ E|A_{r_i} \in \mathcal{E}_s \\ 0 & i \geq \beta \end{cases}.$$

Actually, $\{P_\beta\}$ is a class of coherent probabilities agreeing with the restriction of $f(E|\cdot)$ to the set of events $H \in \mathcal{H}$ such that there is an atom $A_r \in I^0$ with $A_r \subseteq H$. If $I^0 = \{A_1, \ldots, A_n\}$, then $f(E|\cdot)$ is a coherent conditional probability by Theorem 1. Otherwise, let us consider the atoms A_r such that $E|A_r \sim E|(\bigvee_{j \notin I^0} A_j)$ and consider this set I^1 which has been reordered as $A_{r_{|I^0|+1}}, \ldots, A_{r_{|I^0|+|I^1|}}$. Now define for $\beta \in \{|I^0|, \ldots, |I^0 \cup I^1| - 1\}$

$$P_\beta(E \wedge A_{r_j}) = \begin{cases} \dfrac{s}{l} & j = \beta - 1, \ E|A_{r_j} \in \mathcal{E}_s \\ 0 & i \geq \beta \end{cases}.$$

If $(I^0 \cup I^1) \subset \{A_1, \ldots, A_n\}$, we find $I^2 = \{A_r : E|A_r \sim E|(\bigvee_{j \notin I^0 \cup I^1} A_j)\}$ and so on, till $\{A_1, \ldots, A_n\}$ is covered and we build P_β (for $\beta = |I^0 \cup I^1|, \ldots, |I^0 \cup I^1 \cup I^2| - 1$) as before, an agreeing class for $f(E|\cdot)$. It follows that f is a coherent conditional probability. $\square$

Notice that the coherent conditional probability in condition (ii) of Theorem 7 admits an extension $\tilde{P}$ to $\mathcal{B} \times \mathcal{H}$ (with $\mathcal{B}$ the algebra generated by E and $\mathcal{H}$) such that $\tilde{P}(A_r|H)$ takes value either 0 or 1, for every $H \in \mathcal{H}$. From the above proof it comes out that if there is no pair of atoms A_r, A_k such that $E|A_r \sim E|A_k$, then the only coherent conditional probabilities P representing $\preceq$ are such that any atom belongs to a different zero-layer and any extension $\tilde{P}$ of P to $\mathcal{B} \times \mathcal{H}$ satisfies the above property. When there is a pair of atoms A_r, A_k such that $E|A_r \sim E|A_k$, then there are also extensions of $\tilde{P}$ such that the atoms A_r and A_k belong to the same zero-layer and so $\tilde{P}(A_r|H)$ can take values in $(0, 1)$. As particular case we can have a relation $\preceq$ satisfying also the following axiom (which is stronger than (A1) and (A2)): for any $H, K \in \mathcal{H}$:

$$E|H \preceq E|K \Rightarrow E|(H \vee K) \sim E|K.$$

By regarding $\preceq$ as relation on the *conditioning events*, it becomes a comparative possibility.[10] Thus, by regarding the coherent conditional probability $P(E|\cdot)$, representing $\preceq$, as a function of the conditioning events we obtain a possibility (see also Ref. 6). We recall that this aggregation function is largely used in fuzzy set theory for aggregating membership functions. On the other hand if $\preceq$ satisfies (besides (a), (b) and (c)) also the following condition: for any $H, K \in \mathcal{H}$

$$E|H \preceq E|K \Rightarrow E|(H \vee K) \sim E|H,$$

we get that the coherent conditional probability $P(E|\cdot)$ representing $\preceq$ is such that $P(E|H \vee K)$ is equal to the minimum of the two likelihoods $P(E|H), P(E|K)$. Hence, this class of relations covers a large choice for aggregating qualitative likelihoods or membership functions.

References

1. S. Ceccacci, C. Morici and T. Paneni, Conditional probability as a function of the conditioning event: characterization of coherent enlargements. *Proc. of 6th WUPES*, pp. 35–45 (2003).
2. G. Coletti and R. Scozzafava, Conditioning and inference in intelligent systems. *Soft Computing*, **3**(3), 118–130 (1999).
3. G. Coletti and R. Scozzafava, The role of coherence in eliciting and handling imprecise probabilities and its application to medical diagnosis. *Information Science*, **130**(1–4), 41–65 (2000).
4. G. Coletti and R. Scozzafava, *Probabilistic Logic in a Coherent Setting. Trends in logic n.15*, Kluwer, Dordrecht (2002).
5. G. Coletti and R. Scozzafava, Conditional probability, fuzzy sets, and possibility: a unifying view. *Fuzzy Sets and Systems*, **144**(1), 227–249 (2004).
6. G. Coletti and R. Scozzafava, Conditioning in a coherent setting: Theory and applications. *Fuzzy Sets and Systems*, **155**(1), 26–49 (2005).
7. G. Coletti, R. Scozzafava and B. Vantaggi, *Coherent Extensions of a Likelihood*. Submitted for publication (2006).
8. G. Coletti and B. Vantaggi, Representability of ordinal relations on a set of conditional events. *Theory and Decision*, **60**(2–3), 137–174 (2006).
9. B. de Finetti, La logique de la probabilité. *Actes du Congrès International de Philosophie Scientifique*, Hermann, Paris, **IV**, 1–9 (1935).
10. D. Dubois, Belief structure, possibility theory and decomposable confidence measures on finite sets. *Comput. Artificial Intelligence* **5**, 403–416 (1986).
11. W. Fenchel, Convex Cones, Sets and Functions. *Lectures at Princeton University* (1951).

The Moment Problem for Finitely Additive Probabilities

Enrique Miranda*, Gert de Cooman† and Erik Quaeghebeur‡

*Rey Juan Carlos University, Madrid, Spain
enrique.miranda@urjc.es
†,‡SYSTeMS Research Group, Ghent University, Ghent, Belgium
†Gert.deCooman@UGent.be
‡Erik.Quaeghebeur@UGent.be

Abstract

We study the moment problem for finitely additive probabilities and show that the information provided by the moments is equivalent to the one given by the associated lower and upper distribution functions.

1. Introduction

The moment problem in probability theory refers to the existence and uniqueness of a σ-additive probability measure with a particular sequence of moments m, or equivalently m_k, $k \geq 0$, i.e. of a measure μ such that $\int x^k \, d\mu = m_k$ for all $k \geq 0$. There are three classical moment problems: the Hamburger moment problem, where the support of μ is the real line; the Stieltjes moment problem, where it is $[0, +\infty)$; and the Hausdorff moment problem, where it is the closed interval $[0, 1]$. This last problem is the one we shall consider in this paper.

Extended versions of parts this paper, with proofs, are available.[6,7]

Hausdorff[4,5] has proved that there is a solution to the moment problem for a moment sequence m if and only if this sequence is completely monotone, meaning that $(-1)^n \Delta^n m_k \geq 0$ for all $n, k \geq 0$, with $\Delta^n m_k = \Delta^{n-1} m_{k+1} - \Delta^{n-1} m_k$ for $n \geq 1$ and $\Delta^0 m_k = m_k$. In this case, the existence of a probability measure μ with a sequence of moments implies its uniqueness, by virtue of the Riesz Representation Theorem.

In this paper, we study the Hausdorff moment problem for finitely additive probabilities. We consider a sequence m of real numbers and study whether there is a unique finitely additive probability (or *probability charge*) with this sequence of moments. We shall see that in this case the question of the existence of such a probability charge is a fairly trivial one, but the study of its unicity becomes much more involved as soon as we let go of the countable additivity (or continuity) axiom. Hence, it will be important to study for which functions (and in particular on which events) the expectation with respect to such probability charges μ is uniquely determined by the moments. It turns out that studying and solving this problem can be done quite efficiently using the language of Walley's behavioral theory of coherent lower previsions.[8]

2.   A Short Introduction to Lower Previsions

Let us give a short introduction to those concepts from the theory of coherent lower previsions that we shall use in this paper. We refer to Ref. 8 for their behavioral interpretation, and for a much more complete introduction and treatment. Consider a non-empty set Ω. Then a *gamble* on Ω is a bounded real-valued function on Ω. We denote the set of all gambles on Ω by $\mathcal{L}(\Omega)$.

A *lower prevision* $\underline{P}$ is a real-valued map defined on some subset $\mathcal{K}$ of $\mathcal{L}(\Omega)$. If the domain $\mathcal{K}$ of $\underline{P}$ only contains (indicators of) events A, then $\underline{P}$ is also called a *lower probability*. We also write $\underline{P}(I_A)$ as $\underline{P}(A)$, the lower probability of the event A. The *conjugate upper prevision* $\overline{P}$ of $\underline{P}$ is defined on $-\mathcal{K}$ by $\overline{P}(f) := -\underline{P}(-f)$ for every $-f$ in the domain of $\underline{P}$. If the domain of $\overline{P}$ contains indicators only, then $\overline{P}$ is also called an *upper probability*.

A lower prevision $\underline{P}$ defined on $\mathcal{L}(\Omega)$ is called *coherent* if it is super-additive: $\underline{P}(f + g) \geq \underline{P}(f) + \underline{P}(g)$, positively homogeneous: $\underline{P}(\lambda h) = \lambda \underline{P}(h)$ for $\lambda \geq 0$, and positive: $\underline{P}(h) \geq \inf h$. A lower prevision $\underline{P}$ on a general domain is then called *coherent* if it can be extended to some coherent lower prevision on all gambles. This is the case if and only if $\sup[\sum_{i=1}^{n} f_i - mf_0] \geq \sum_{i=1}^{n} \underline{P}(f_i) - m\underline{P}(f_0)$ for any $n, m \geq 0$, and $f_0, f_1, \ldots, f_n$ in the domain of $\underline{P}$.

A *linear prevision* P on $\mathcal{L}(\Omega)$ is a coherent lower prevision that is self-conjugate: $P(-f) = -P(f)$, or in other words, a linear functional that is positive and normalized: $P(1) = 1$ (1 also used as a constant function). A functional defined on an arbitrary subset $\mathcal{K}$ of $\mathcal{L}(\Omega)$ is called a *linear prevision* if it can be extended to a linear prevision on $\mathcal{L}(\Omega)$. This is the case if and only if $\sup[\sum_{i=1}^{n} f_i - \sum_{j=1}^{m} g_j] \geq \sum_{i=1}^{n} P(f_i) - \sum_{j=1}^{m} P(g_j)$ for any $n, m \geq 0$, and $f_1, \ldots, f_n, g_1, \ldots, g_m$ in the domain of P. The restriction Q of a linear prevision P on $\mathcal{L}(\Omega)$ to the set $\wp(\Omega)$ of all events is a finitely additive probability measure (*probability charge*). Moreover, it holds that $P(h) = (D) \int h \, dQ$ for any gamble h (Dunford integral). Hence, linear previsions are completely determined by the values they assume on events, and are simply expectations with respect to finitely additive probabilities.

The *natural extension* $\underline{E}_P$ to $\mathcal{L}(\Omega)$ of a coherent lower prevision $\underline{P}$ defined on $\mathcal{K}$, is the point-wise smallest coherent lower prevision that extends $\underline{P}$ to all gambles. It is equal to the lower envelope of the set $\mathcal{M}(\underline{P})$ of all linear previsions that point-wise dominate $\underline{P}$ on its domain $\mathcal{K}$: $\underline{E}_P(f) = \min_{Q \in \mathcal{M}(\underline{P})} Q(f)$ for any gamble f in $\mathcal{L}(\Omega)$. Moreover, $\mathcal{M}(\underline{E}_P) = \mathcal{M}(\underline{P})$.

A coherent lower prevision defined on a *lattice* of gambles $\mathcal{K}$ (a set of gambles closed under pointwise minima and maxima) is called *n-monotone* if $\sum_{I \subseteq \{1, \ldots, p\}} (-1)^{|I|} \underline{P}(f \wedge \bigwedge_{i \in I} f_i) \geq 0$ for all $1 \leq p \leq n$, and all $f, f_1, \ldots, f_p$ in $\mathcal{K}$. A coherent lower prevision is *completely monotone* when it is n-monotone for any $n \geq 1$. A thorough study of n-monotone coherent lower previsions, and their properties, can be found in Refs. 1 and 2.

3. Formulation and Initial Solution of the Problem

We are now ready to formulate the moment problem using the language established in the previous section. Consider a moment sequence m and the subset $\mathcal{V}_p([0,1])$ of the set of all polynomials on the unit interval given by $\mathcal{V}_p([0,1]) := \{p^k : k \geq 0\}$, where $p^k(x) = x^k$. We define a functional P_m on this set by letting $P_m(p^k) := m_k$. This functional can be *uniquely* extended to a linear functional $\hat{P}_m$ on the set of all polynomials as follows: $\hat{P}_m(\sum_{k=0}^{n} a_k p^k) = \sum_{k=0}^{n} a_k m_k$.

The following theorem summarises a number of results from the literature. It tells us under what conditions there exists a *linear prevision* on the set $\mathcal{L}([0,1])$ of all gambles on $[0,1]$, or equivalently a *finitely additive probability* on the set $\wp([0,1])$ of all subsets of $[0,1]$, for which the moments are given by m.

Theorem 1. *The following are equivalent.*

(1) *The functional P_m can be extended uniquely to a linear prevision on the set $\mathcal{C}([0,1])$ of all continuous gambles on $[0,1]$. We shall denote this extension by $\hat{P}_m$.*

(2) *For all polynomials $q = \sum_{k=0}^{n} a_k p^k$, $\min q \leq \hat{P}_m(q) \leq \max q$.*

(3) *The moment sequence m satisfies the Hausdorff moment condition:*[4,5] *$m_0 = 1$ and m is* completely monotone, *meaning that $(-1)^n \Delta^n m_k \geq 0$ for all $k \geq 0$ and $n \geq 0$.*

So we see that the Hausdorff moment problem has a solution (as a linear prevision) if and only if the Hausdorff moment condition is satisfied, and in that case the solution is uniquely determined on the set $\mathcal{C}([0,1])$ of continuous functions.

If we invoke the Riesz Representation Theorem (see for instance, [3, Sec. V.1]) we see that there is a *unique* σ-additive probability measure P_m^σ on the Borel sets of $[0,1]$, and a *unique* (right-continuous) distribution function F_m^σ on $[0,1]$ such that for all continuous gambles h, the expectation $E_m^\sigma(h)$ is equal to $(L) \int h \, dP_m^\sigma = (LS) \int h \, dF_m^\sigma = \hat{P}_m(h)$, where the first integral is the Lebesgue integral associated with the probability measure P_m^σ, and the second integral the Lebesgue–Stieltjes integral associated with the distribution function F_m^σ. Also, $F_m^\sigma(x) = P_m^\sigma([0,x])$. Note that, actually, the expectation operator E_m^σ, as well as both integrals are defined for all Borel-measurable functions on $[0,1]$.

In this sense, the moments determine a unique σ-additive probability measure on the Borel sets. But the solution is not as clear-cut if we look for the finitely additive probabilities on all events (or equivalently the linear previsions on all gambles) that correspond to the given moments. These are given by the set $\mathcal{M}(\hat{P}_m)$ of all linear previsions Q that dominate, or, equivalently, coincide with, $\hat{P}_m$ on continuous gambles.

For any gamble h on $[0,1]$, it follows that the linear previsions that solve the moment problem can assume a value in the real interval $[\underline{E}_m(h), \overline{E}_m(h)]$, where $\underline{E}_m(h) = \inf\{Q(h) \colon Q \in \mathcal{M}(\hat{P}_m)\}$ and

$\overline{E}_m(h) = \sup\{Q(h): Q \in \mathcal{M}(\hat{P}_m)\}$. In fact, given any real number a in this interval, there will be a solution Q to the moment problem such that $Q(h) = a$. The functional $\underline{E}_m$ on $\mathcal{L}([0,1])$ is the natural extension of $\hat{P}_m$, and it is the point-wise smallest coherent lower prevision that coincides with $\hat{P}_m$ on $\mathcal{C}([0,1])$. The functional $\overline{E}_m$ is its conjugate upper prevision and satisfies $\overline{E}_m(h) = -\underline{E}_m(-h)$ for all gambles h on $[0,1]$.

$\underline{E}_m$ is the smallest coherent lower prevision that satisfies $\underline{E}_m(p^k) = \overline{E}_m(p^k) = m_k$, $k \geq 0$. It is easy to see (use [8, Theorem 3.4.1]) that $\mathcal{M}(\underline{E}_m) = \mathcal{M}(\hat{P}_m) = \mathcal{M}(P_m)$. So we see that the lower prevision $\underline{E}_m$ *completely determines* the solution to the Hausdorff moment problem for linear previsions. In particular, the gambles h on $[0,1]$ where the lower and upper natural extensions coincide, i.e. $\underline{E}_m(h) = \overline{E}_m(h)$, are precisely those gambles to which P_m has a unique extension. We shall call such gambles *m-integrable*. One of the goals in this paper is precisely to study these m-integrable gambles. Another, closely related goal, is to study the functional $\underline{E}_m$.

With $\underline{E}_m$ and its conjugate $\overline{E}_m$ we can associate a *lower distribution function* $\underline{F}_m$ and an *upper distribution function* $\overline{F}_m$ on $[0,1]$,

$$\underline{F}_m(x) = \underline{E}_m([0,x]), \quad \overline{F}_m(x) = \overline{E}_m([0,x]),$$

for $x \in [0,1]$. We then ask: what are the properties of these distribution functions, what is their relationship to F_m^σ, and to what extent do they determine the functional $\underline{E}_m$, and therefore the solution to the Hausdorff moment problem?

4. The Natural Extension $\underline{E}_m$ and m-Integrable Gambles

Since $\mathcal{C}([0,1])$ is a linear subspace of $\mathcal{L}([0,1])$ that contains all constant gambles, we may apply another known result [8, Corollary 3.1.8] from the theory of coherent lower previsions to obtain the following expressions: for any gamble h on $[0,1]$, $\underline{E}_m(h) = \sup\{\hat{P}_m(g): g \in \mathcal{C}([0,1]), g \leq h\}$ and $\overline{E}_m(h) = \inf\{\hat{P}_m(g): g \in \mathcal{C}([0,1]), h \leq g\}$. We use these expressions to prove a number of interesting properties of $\underline{E}_m$ and the lower and upper distribution functions $\underline{F}_m$ and $\overline{F}_m$.

Proposition 1. *Consider a moment sequence m satisfying the Hausdorff moment condition.*

(1) $0 \leq \underline{F}_m \leq F_m^\sigma \leq \overline{F}_m \leq 1$.

(2) $\underline{F}_m$ and $\overline{F}_m$ are non-decreasing functions.

(3) $\underline{F}_m(0) = 0$ and $\underline{F}_m(1) = \overline{F}_m(1) = 1$.

It follows from Proposition 1 that the left and right limits of $\underline{F}_m$ and $\overline{F}_m$ exist everywhere. Let us denote by $\mathcal{D}_{\underline{F}_m} := \{x \in [0,1] : \underline{F}_m(x+) \neq \underline{F}_m(x-)\}$ the set of all points of discontinuity of $\underline{F}_m$, and similarly by $\mathcal{D}_{\overline{F}_m} = \{x \in [0,1] : \overline{F}_m(x-) \neq \overline{F}_m(x+)\}$ the set of points where $\overline{F}_m$ is not continuous. Let $\mathcal{D}_m := \mathcal{D}_{\underline{F}_m} \cup \mathcal{D}_{\overline{F}_m}$ denote their union. It follows from the non-decreasing character of $\underline{F}_m$ and $\overline{F}_m$ that $\mathcal{D}_{\underline{F}_m}$, $\mathcal{D}_{\overline{F}_m}$ and $\mathcal{D}_m$ are countable subsets of $[0,1]$.

Proposition 2. *Consider a moment sequence m satisfying the Hausdorff moment condition.*

(1) *For any $x \in [0,1]$, $\underline{F}_m(x+) = \overline{F}_m(x) = \overline{F}^{\sigma}_m(x) = \overline{F}_m(x+)$.*

(2) $\underline{F}_m(x-) = \underline{F}_m(x) = \overline{F}_m(x-) \; \forall x \in (0,1)$.

(3) $\underline{F}_m(0-) := \underline{F}_m(0) \leq \overline{F}_m(0-) := \overline{F}_m(0)$.

(4) $\underline{F}_m(1-) = \overline{F}_m(1-) \leq \underline{F}_m(1) = \overline{F}_m(1)$.

(5) $\mathcal{D}_{\underline{F}_m} \cap (0,1] = \mathcal{D}_{\overline{F}_m} \cap (0,1]$.

(6) *The following statements are equivalent for all $x \in (0,1)$: (i) $x \notin \mathcal{D}_m$; (ii) $\underline{F}_m(x) = \overline{F}_m(x)$; and (iii) F^{σ}_m is continuous in x.*

Hence, if m is a sequence satisfying the Hausdorff moment condition, the distribution function F^{σ}_m of the unique σ-additive probability with these moments is equal to the upper distribution function $\overline{F}_m$.

Example 1. Consider the moment sequence m given by $m_0 = 1$, $m_k = 0$, $k > 0$. It is completely monotone, because the probability measure all of whose mass is concentrated in 0 has these moments. If we consider the $\underline{F}_m$ and $\overline{F}_m$ produced by this sequence, it is easy to check that the fifth and sixth statements of Proposition 2 do not hold for $x = 0$, and that the inequality in the third statement may be strict.

Let us now define, for any gamble h on $[0,1]$, the gambles $h^{\downarrow}$ and $h^{\uparrow}$ on $[0,1]$ by $h^{\uparrow}(x) = \sup\{g(x) : g \in \mathcal{C}([0,1]), g \leq h\}$ and $h^{\downarrow}(x) = \inf\{g(x) : g \in \mathcal{C}([0,1]), h \leq g\}$ for all x in $[0,1]$. Then $h^{\uparrow}$ is the pointwise greatest lower semi-continuous gamble that is dominated by h, and $h^{\downarrow}$ is the pointwise smallest upper semi-continuous gamble that dominates h. Observe also that for any $A \subseteq [0,1]$, $(I_A)^{\uparrow} = I_{int(A)}$

and $(I_A)^{\downarrow} = I_{cl(A)}$, where $int(A)$ is the topological interior of A, and $cl(A)$ its topological closure.

Proposition 3. *Consider a moment sequence m satisfying the Hausdorff moment condition. Then for any gamble h on $[0,1]$ we have that $\underline{E}_m(h) = \underline{E}_m(h^{\uparrow})$ and $\overline{E}_m(h) = \overline{E}_m(h^{\downarrow})$. In particular, for any $A \subseteq [0,1]$, $\underline{E}_m(int(A)) = \underline{E}_m(A)$ and $\overline{E}_m(cl(A)) = \overline{E}_m(A)$.*

Now consider, for any set A its interior $int(A)$. It is easy to check that $int(A)$ is a countable union of disjoint open intervals. The following important result now tells us that it even suffices to know the values of $\underline{E}_m$ on open intervals.

Proposition 4. *Consider a moment sequence m satisfying the Hausdorff moment condition. Let B be a countable union of disjoint open intervals B_n, $n \geq 0$. Then $\underline{E}_m(B) = \sup_{n \geq 0} \sum_{k=0}^{n} \underline{E}_m(B_k)$.*

Summarising, $\underline{E}_m$ is completely determined on events if we know its values on all open intervals. The following proposition establishes that these values are determined by the lower and upper distribution functions $\underline{F}_m$ and $\overline{F}_m$.

Proposition 5. *Consider a moment sequence m satisfying the Hausdorff moment condition.*

(1) *$\underline{E}_m([0,x)) = \underline{F}_m(x-)$ for all $x \in [0,1]$.*
(2) *$\underline{E}_m((x,1]) = 1 - \overline{F}_m(x)$ for all $x \in [0,1]$.*
(3) *$\underline{E}_m((x,y)) = \underline{F}_m(y-) - \overline{F}_m(x)$ for all $0 \leq x < y \leq 1$.*
(4) *For all $0 \leq x < y \leq 1$, the interval (x,y) is m-integrable if and only if x and y do not belong to $\mathcal{D}_m$. For $x \in [0,1]$, $[0,x)$ and $(x,1]$ are m-integrable if and only if x does not belong to $\mathcal{D}_m$.*

We can also deduce from these results that there is *never* a unique linear prevision that solves the Hausdorff moment problem.

Remark 1. Consider the set $\mathbb{Q} \cap [0,1]$ of all rational numbers between zero and one, then $int(\mathbb{Q} \cap [0,1]) = \emptyset$ and $cl(\mathbb{Q} \cap [0,1]) = [0,1]$, so we infer from Proposition 3 that $\underline{E}_m(\mathbb{Q} \cap [0,1]) = \underline{E}_m(\emptyset) = 0$ and $\overline{E}_m(\mathbb{Q} \cap [0,1]) = \overline{E}_m([0,1]) = 1$. This shows that there is always either none (when m is not completely monotone) or an uncountable infinity of linear previsions that produce a given sequence of moments m_k, $k \geq 0$.

There are two further questions we would still like to look at in this section. First of all, are the values of $\underline{E}_m$ on events also completely determined by $\underline{F}_m$ and $\overline{F}_m$ in their points of continuity, or in other words, by F_m^σ in its points of continuity? By virtue of Proposition 5, this comes down to $\underline{E}_m$ being determined by its values on *m-integrable open intervals*. And secondly, can we say something similar about the values that $\underline{E}_m$ assumes on gambles, and not just events? We shall answer both questions in the positive in Theorem 3 further on.

But before we can address these issues, we need to prepare ourselves a bit better. In order to answer the first question, it will help us to consider the set of all m-integrable open intervals. By Proposition 5 this is the set $\{[0,1], [0,x), (x,y), (y,1] : x, y \notin \mathcal{D}_m\}$. This set is closed under intersections, so the lattice of events $\mathcal{O}_m$ generated by all m-integrable open intervals is the set made up of all finite unions of m-integrable disjoint open intervals. For the second question, let $\mathcal{L}_m$ denote the class of m-integrable gambles, $\mathcal{L}_m := \{h \in \mathcal{L}([0,1]) : \underline{E}_m(h) = \overline{E}_m(h)\}$, and let $\mathcal{F}_m$ denote the class of m-integrable events, i.e. those events with m-integrable indicators. Then we have the following:[1,2]

Theorem 2. *Consider a moment sequence* m *satisfying the Hausdorff moment condition.*

(1) $\underline{E}_m$ *is the natural extension of its restriction to events, which is a completely monotone coherent lower probability.*

(2) $\underline{E}_m$ *is completely monotone on* $\mathcal{L}([0,1])$, *and* $\underline{E}_m(h) = (C) \int h \, d\underline{E}_m$ *for any* $h \in \mathcal{L}([0,1])$, *where the integral is the Choquet integral of* h *with respect to* $\underline{E}_m$, *equal to (using the Riemann integral)* $\inf h + (R) \int_{\inf h}^{\sup h} \underline{E}_m(\{h > t\}) \, dt$.

(3) $\mathcal{L}_m$ *is a uniformly closed linear lattice that contains all constant gambles.*

(4) $\mathcal{F}_m$ *is a field of subsets of* $[0,1]$ *that includes* $\mathcal{O}_m$.

(5) *A gamble* h *is* m-integrable if and only if its cut sets $\{h \geq t\} := \{x \in [0,1] : h(x) \geq t\}$ *are* m-integrable for all but a countable number of t in $[0,1]$.

Let us denote by $\tilde{P}_m$ the restriction of $\underline{E}_m$ to $\mathcal{O}_m$. Then we know by Proposition 4 that $\tilde{P}_m$ is additive on this lattice of events. We show next that $\underline{E}_m$ is completely determined by $\tilde{P}_m$.

Theorem 3. *Consider a moment sequence m satisfying the Hausdorff moment condition.*

(1) *The natural extension of $\tilde{P}_m$ to all events is the inner set function $\tilde{P}_{m,*}$ of $\tilde{P}_m$, where, for any $A \subseteq [0,1]$, $\tilde{P}_{m,*}(A) = \sup_{B \in \mathcal{O}_m, B \subseteq A} P_m(B)$.*

(2) *For any $A \subseteq [0,1]$, $\underline{E}_m(A) = \tilde{P}_{m,*}(A)$.*

(3) *$\underline{E}_m(h) = (C) \int h \, d\tilde{P}_{m,*} \ \forall h \in \mathcal{L}([0,1])$.*

5. The Natural Extension of Lower and Upper Distribution Functions

In the rest of this paper, we intend to show that $\underline{E}_m$ is the natural extension of the lower and upper distribution functions $\underline{F}_m$ and $\overline{F}_m$. But before we can do that, we must make a small digression, in order to explain exactly what we mean by the phrase "natural extension of lower and upper distribution functions" in a general context. This is the subject of the present section. In the next section, we take up the thread of the moment problem again.

5.1. *A precise distribution function*

Let us begin with the simplest problem. We call any non-decreasing function $F \colon [0,1] \to [0,1]$ that satisfies the normalization condition $F(1) = 1$ a *distribution function* on $[0,1]$. The interpretation of such a distribution function is as follows: for any $x \in [0,1]$, the (lower and upper) probability $P_F([0,x])$ of $[0,x]$ is equal to $F(x)$. Consequently, the probability $P_F((x,1])$ of $(x,1]$ is equal to $1 - F(x)$. In other words, specifying a distribution function F is tantamount to specifying a set function P_F on the set of events $\mathcal{H} := \{[0,x] \colon x \in [0,1]\} \cup \{(x,1] \colon x \in [0,1]\}$, and it is easy to check that this P_F is a linear prevision. It can be uniquely extended to a linear prevision on the lattice $\mathcal{Q}$ generated by $\mathcal{H}$, where all elements have the form

$$[0,x_1] \cup (x_2, x_3] \cup \cdots \cup (x_{2n}, 1] \quad \text{or} \quad (x_2, x_3] \cup \cdots \cup (x_{2n}, 1]$$

where $0 \le x_1 \le x_2 \le x_3 \le \cdots \le x_{2n} \le 1$.

The natural extension $\underline{E}_F$ of P_F is the lower envelope of the set $\mathcal{M}(P_F)$ of all linear previsions Q for which $Q([0,x]) = F(x)$, $x \in [0,1]$. For any gamble h on $[0,1]$, $[\underline{E}_F(h), \overline{E}_F(h)]$ is the range of the value $Q(h)$ for all such linear previsions Q.

Using the results in Refs. 1 and 2, we see that $\underline{E}_F$ is a completely monotone coherent lower prevision, that the restriction of $\underline{E}_F$ to events is the inner set function $P_{F,*}$ of P_F, and that for all gambles h on $[0,1]$, $\underline{E}_F(h) = (C)\int h\,d\underline{E}_F$. If $\mathcal{L}_F := \{h \in \mathcal{L}([0,1]): \underline{E}_F(h) = \overline{E}_F(h)\}$ is the set of all F-integrable gambles, then we also know that $\mathcal{L}_F$ is a uniformly closed linear lattice containing all constant gambles, and that a gamble h is F-integrable if and only if its cut sets $\{h \geq t\}$ are F-integrable for all but a countable number of t.

Interestingly, it can be checked that *any distribution function F produces precise moments*, i.e. the polynomials p^k are F-integrable for any distribution function F.

5.2.   *Lower and upper distribution functions*

Suppose now that we have two maps $\underline{F}, \overline{F} \colon [0,1] \to [0,1]$, which we interpret as a lower and an upper distribution function, respectively. This means that $\underline{F}$ and $\overline{F}$ determine a lower probability $\underline{P}_{\underline{F},\overline{F}}$ on the set $\mathcal{H}$ by $\underline{P}_{\underline{F},\overline{F}}([0,x]) = \underline{F}(x)$ and $\underline{P}_{\underline{F},\overline{F}}((x,1]) = 1 - \overline{F}(x)$ for all $x \in [0,1]$. Walley [8, Sec. 4.6.6] has shown that $\underline{P}_{\underline{F},\overline{F}}$ is a coherent lower prevision if and only if $\underline{F} \leq \overline{F}$ and both $\underline{F}$ and $\overline{F}$ are distribution functions, i.e. non-decreasing and normalized. We shall assume in what follows that these conditions are satisfied.

The natural extension $\underline{E}_{\underline{F},\overline{F}}$ of the coherent lower probability $\underline{P}_{\underline{F},\overline{F}}$ to all gambles is the smallest coherent lower probability that coincides with $\underline{P}_{\underline{F},\overline{F}}$ on $\mathcal{H}$, or in other words, that has lower and upper distribution functions $\underline{F}$ and $\overline{F}$. Denote by $\mathcal{M}(\underline{F},\overline{F})$ the set of all distribution functions (non-decreasing and normalized) on $[0,1]$ that lie between $\underline{F}$ and $\overline{F}$.

Theorem 4. $\underline{E}_{\underline{F},\overline{F}}(h) = \inf\{\underline{E}_F(h)\colon F \in \mathcal{M}(\underline{F},\overline{F})\}$ *for all* $h \in \mathcal{L}([0,1])$.

6.   The Information Given by the Lower and the Upper Distribution Functions

Let us now go back to the Hausdorff moment problem. As we have seen, if we consider a sequence m of moments m_k, $k \geq 0$ that satisfies Hausdorff's moment condition, we can consider the lower and upper envelopes $\underline{E}_m$ and $\overline{E}_m$ of all linear previsions with those moments.

These lower and upper envelopes induce the lower and upper distribution functions $\underline{F}_m$ and $\overline{F}_m$. We now proceed to show that these two functions already capture all the information that is present in the moments.

Theorem 5. *Consider a moment sequence m satisfying the Hausdorff moment condition.*

(1) *For all F in $\mathcal{M}(\underline{F}_m, \overline{F}_m)$, the restriction of $\underline{E}_F$ to $\mathcal{O}_m$ is equal to $\tilde{P}_m$. Hence, $\underline{E}_F \geq \underline{E}_m$ and $\mathcal{L}_m \subseteq \mathcal{L}_F$.*
(2) $\underline{E}_m = \underline{E}_{\underline{F}_m, \overline{F}_m}$.

Corollary 1. *The following statements are equivalent.*

(1) $\underline{F}_m = \overline{F}_m$;
(2) $\underline{F}_m$, $\overline{F}_m$ *and F_m^σ are continuous on $[0, 1)$;*
(3) $\underline{E}_m = \underline{E}_F$ *for some $F \in \mathcal{M}(\underline{F}_m, \overline{F}_m)$;*
(4) $\underline{E}_m = \underline{E}_F$ *for all $F \in \mathcal{M}(\underline{F}_m, \overline{F}_m)$;*
(5) $\underline{E}_m = (RS)\int \cdot \, \mathrm{d}F$ *for all $F \in \mathcal{M}(\underline{F}_m, \overline{F}_m)$, where the integral is a lower Riemann–Stieltjes integral.*

We can also prove the following:

Theorem 6. *Consider a moment sequence m satisfying the Hausdorff moment condition. Then for any $F \in \mathcal{M}(\underline{F}_m, \overline{F}_m)$ such that $F(0) = 0$ and any gamble h on $[0, 1]$, $\underline{E}_m(h) \leq (RS)\underline{\int} h \, \mathrm{d}F \leq (RS)\overline{\int} h \, \mathrm{d}F \leq \overline{E}_m(h)$.*

Hence, if a gamble h is m-integrable, then the Riemann–Stieltjes integral of h with respect to F exists for any $F \in \mathcal{M}(\underline{F}_m, \overline{F}_m)$, and they all agree with $\underline{E}_m(h) = \overline{E}_m(h)$. It may happen nonetheless that a gamble h is Riemann-Stieltjes integrable with respect to some $F \in \mathcal{M}(\underline{F}_m, \overline{F}_m)$ but not with respect to all of them.

There is a final result that summarizes much of what has been said before in a concise manner. For this, note that any distribution function F in $\mathcal{M}(\underline{F}_m, \overline{F}_m)$ can be written as a convex mixture $F = \mu_m F_b + (1 - \mu_m) F_c$ of a continuous distribution function F_c and a 'pure break function' F_b, which is a uniformly and absolutely convergent sum (convex mixture) of simple break functions. Explicitly, we have for all $x \in [0, 1]$

$$\mu_m F_b(x) := F(x) - \underline{F}_m(x-) + \sum_{d \in \mathcal{D}_m, d < x} [\overline{F}_m(d) - \underline{F}_m(d-)]$$

and

$$(1 - \mu_m)F_c(x) := F(x) - \mu_m F_b(x) = \underline{F}_m(x) - \sum_{d \in \mathcal{D}_m, d < x} [\overline{F}_m(d) - \underline{F}_m(d-)],$$

where $0 \leq \mu_m = \sum_{d \in \mathcal{D}_m} [\overline{F}_m(d) - \underline{F}_m(d-)] \leq 1$, so the continuous part F_c is the same for all distributions F in $\mathcal{M}(\underline{F}_m, \overline{F}_m)$, and the pure break parts are identical in all the continuity points of $\underline{F}_m$ and $\overline{F}_m$, and differ only by the values $F(d)$ they assume in the countably many discontinuity points $d \in \mathcal{D}_m$. Define, for $d \in [0, 1]$, the functional $\underline{osc}_d$ by $\underline{osc}_d(h) := \sup_{d \in B \text{open}} \inf_{z \in B} h(z)$ for all gambles h on $[0, 1]$.

Theorem 7. *Consider a moment sequence m satisfying the Hausdorff moment condition, and $h \in \mathcal{L}([0, 1])$. Then $\underline{E}_m(h) = (1 - \mu_m)\underline{E}_{F_c}(h) + \sum_{d \in \mathcal{D}_m}[\overline{F}_m(d) - \underline{F}_m(d-)]\underline{osc}_d(h)$, and the following are equivalent:*

(1) *h is m-integrable.*
(2) *h is continuous in all the discontinuity points $d \in \mathcal{D}_m$, and Riemann–Stieltjes-integrable with respect to F_c if $\mu_m < 1$.*

7. Conclusions

We have proven that the existence of a (finitely additive) probability charge with a given sequence of moments is equivalent to the existence of a (σ-additive) probability measure with these moments. Perhaps more surprisingly, and contrary to what happens in the case of σ-additive probabilities, a sequence of moments does not determine a unique probability charge.

If we consider the set of all probability charges with the given moment sequence, we can also induce lower and an upper distribution functions. We have proven that these two functions (actually any of the two) capture all the information given by the moments, i.e. we can deduce the lower and upper natural extensions from them. Moreover, we can gain more insight in the problem by considering these functions. First, the (unique) σ-additive probability measure with these moments induces the greatest distribution function of all the compatible probability charges; secondly, if there exists a continuous distribution function with these moments, then the results in Sec. 6 imply that *all* the distribution functions with those moments coincide and are, therefore, continuous. In particular, we deduce that the moments of a continuous distribution function can never be induced by a different, and discrete, distribution function on $[0, 1]$. Note however that even this does not imply the unicity of probability charges producing them! This is a consequence of Remark 1.

Acknowledgments

Research supported by the project TSI2007-66706-C04-01 and by the research grant G.0139.01 of the Flemish Fund for Scientific Research (FWO). Erik Quaeghebeur's research was financed by a PhD grant of the Institute for the Promotion of Innovation through Science and Technology in Flanders (IWT Vlaanderen).

References

1. G. de Cooman, M. C. M. Troffaes and E. Miranda, *n-Monotone Exact Functionals.* Submitted (2006).
2. G. de Cooman, M. C. M. Troffaes and E. Miranda, *n*-Monotone lower previsions and lower integrals. F. Cozman, R. Nau and T. Seidenfeld (eds.), *Proceedings of ISIPTA'2005*, pp. 145–154, (2005).
3. W. Feller, *An Introduction to Probability Theory and Its Applications*, volume II. John Wiley and Sons, New York (1971).
4. F. Hausdorff, Summationmethoden und Momentfolgen I. *Mathematische Zeitschrift*, **9**, 74–109 (1921).
5. F. Hausdorff, Summationmethoden und Momentfolgen II. *Mathematische Zeitschrift*, **9**, 280–299 (1921).
6. E. Miranda, G. de Cooman and E. Quaeghebeur, The Hausdorff moment problem under finite additivity. *Journal of Theoretical Probability*, **20**(3), 663–693 (2007).
7. E. Miranda, G. de Cooman and E. Quaeghebeur, Finitely additive extensions of distribution functions and moment sequences: the coherent lower prevision approach. *International Journal of Approximate Reasoning*, in press.
8. P. Walley, *Statistical Reasoning with Imprecise Probabilities*. Chapman and Hall, London (1991).

Towards a General Theory of Conditional Decomposable Information Measures

B. Bouchon-Meunier[*,†], G. Coletti[§] and C. Marsala[*,‡]

*Université Pierre et Marie Curie-Paris6, CNRS UMR 7606
LIP6, 104 Avenue Kennedy, Paris, F-75016, France
†Bernadette.Bouchon-Meunier@lip6.fr
‡Christophe.Marsala@lip6.fr
§Dept. Matematica e Informatica
Università di Perugia, Italy
coletti@dipmat.unipg.it

Abstract

We start from a general concept of conditional event in which the "third" value is not the same for *all* conditional events, but depends on $E|H$. Following the same line adopted in previous papers to point out conditional uncertainty measures,[3,4,8,9] we obtain in a natural way the axioms defining a generalized $(\odot, \oplus)$-decomposable conditional information measure, which, for any fixed conditioning event H is a $\odot$-decomposable information measure in the sense of Kampé de Fériet and Forte.[15,17]

1. Introduction

What is usually emphasized in the literature, when any conditional measure $f(E|H)$ is taken into account, is only the fact that $f(\cdot|H)$ is, for every given H, a measure with the same properties of $f(\cdot)$. But this is a very restrictive view of conditional measure, corresponding trivially to just a modification of the "world". On the contrary the real richness of conditional measure is based on the possibility to regard the conditioning event H, which plays the role of hypothesis, as a "variable", with the same state of E. It must be regarded not just as a given fact, but as an (uncertain) event, for which the knowledge of its truth value is not required.

Usually conditional measures are obtained starting from an unconditional measure as a derived concept. This fact is particularly evident in information theory, in which usually the concept of independence precedes that of conditioning.

One starts from an (unconditional) information measure $I : \mathcal{A} \to [0, +\infty]$, ($\mathcal{A}$ Boolean algebra) and (pretend to) define, for every E and $H \in \mathcal{A}$ the "conditional measure" $I(E|H)$ through the values of $I(E \wedge H)$ and $I(H)$ by using some operation $\oplus$. More precisely $I(E|H)$ is defined as the unique solution of the equation

$$I(E \wedge H) = x \oplus I(H).$$

Nevertheless, for every choice of $\oplus$ there are some events H for which the equation admits a non-unique solution. Then usually one tries, through some *adhocheries*, to extend the conditioning to all pairs of events without taking into account the inconsistencies that come out from this procedure.

Where is the problem? In fact one cannot pretend to capture the complexity of the concept of conditional measure (obviously interesting when we consider different conditioning events) by means of the essentially "poor" concept of unconditional measure.

We propose to invert the process: defining conditional information measures $I(\cdot|\cdot)$ as a primitive concept, by means of some properties (axioms) and, so, studying the connections with the relevant unconditional information measures $I(\cdot) = I(\cdot|\Omega)$.

The problem now becomes: which axioms are required to define a conditional information measure?

Our aim is to find "reasonable" axioms for generalized conditional information measures. The starting point is a "logical" one, in the sense that we consider a family $\mathcal{T}$ of *conditional events* $E|H$, each one being represented by a suitable *three-valued random variable* whose values are 1, 0, or $t(E|H)$. By using a monotone transformation λ of those random variables and introducing two commutative, associative, and increasing operations $\odot$ and $\oplus$, we get "automatically" (so to say) conditions on $\lambda(t(E|H))$ that can be taken as the "natural" axioms for a conditional information measure.

We show also that, as proved for conditional decomposable uncertainty measures, conditional information measures can be characterized in terms of a class of unconditional information measures.

Finally we introduce the concept of coherence for information measures only partially assessed and prove that the above characterization is an efficient tool to provide algorithms to check coherence.

2. Kampé de Fériet Information Measures

We recall the definition of (generalized) information measure given by Kampé de Fériet and Forte.

Definition 1. A function I from an algebra $\mathcal{E}$, and with values on $R^* = [0, +\infty]$, is an *information measure* if it is *antimonotone*, i.e. the following condition holds: for every $A, B \in \mathcal{E}$

$$A \subseteq B \Longrightarrow I(B) \leq I(A). \tag{1}$$

So, if both $\emptyset$ and Ω belong to $\mathcal{E}$, it follows that

$$0 \leq I(\Omega) = \inf_{A \in \mathcal{E}} I(A) \leq \sup_{A \in \mathcal{E}} I(A) = I(\emptyset).$$

Kampé de Fériet[15] claims that the above inequality (1) is necessary and sufficient to build up an information theory; nevertheless, to attribute a universal value to $I(\Omega)$ and $I(\emptyset)$, the further conditions $I(\emptyset) = +\infty$ and $I(\Omega) = 0$ are given. The choice of these two values is obviously aimed at reconciling with the Wiener-Shannon theory. In general, condition (1) implies only that

$$I(A \vee B) \leq \min\{I(A), I(B)\};$$

we can specify the rule of composition by introducing a binary operation $\odot$ to compute $I(A \vee B)$ by means of $I(A)$ and $I(B)$.

Definition 2. An information measure defined on an additive set of events $\mathcal{A}$ is $\odot$-*decomposable* if there exists a binary operation $\odot$ on $[0, +\infty] \times [0, +\infty]$ such that, for every $A, B \in \mathcal{A}$ with $A \wedge B = \emptyset$, we have

$$I(A \vee B) = I(A) \odot I(B).$$

So "min" and the rule of Wiener-Shannon theory[a] are only two of the possible choices of $\odot$.

3. Conditional Events

An *event* can be singled-out by a (nonambiguous) *proposition E*, that is a statement that can be either *true* or *false* (corresponding to the two "values" 1 or 0). Since in general it is not known whether E is true or not, we are *uncertain* on E, in the sense that we do not have complete information on E.

In general, it is not enough to direct attention toward an event E in order to assess "convincingly" its measure of uncertainty or of information f, but it is also essential to take into account *other* events which may possibly contribute in determining the "information" on E. Then the fundamental tool must be *conditional measures*, since the true problem is not to assess $f(E)$, but rather to assess $f(E|H)$, taking into account all the relevant "information" carried by some other event H.

In order to deal adequately with *conditional measures*, we need to introduce the concept of *conditional event*, denoted by $E|H$, with $H \neq \emptyset$ (where $\emptyset$ is the *impossible* event): it is a *generalization* of the concept of event, and can be defined through its *truth–value* $T(E|H)$.

When we assume H true, we take $T(E|H)$ equal to 1 or 0 according to whether E or its contrary E^c is true, and *when we assume that H is false* we take $T(E|H)$ equal to a suitable function $t(E|H)$ with values in $[0, 1]$.

This truth–value $T(E|H)$ extends the concept of *indicator* $I_E = T(E|\Omega)$ concerning an (unconditional) event E. Moreover, notice that $H \neq \emptyset$ *does not mean* that I_H cannot take the value 0: it means only that I_H is not "constantly" equal to 0, i.e. (in other words) that *it is not known* that H is false (otherwise $H = \emptyset$).

This "definition" of conditional event (introduced in Ref. 8), differs from many seemingly "similar" 3-valued ones adopted in the relevant literature since 1935, starting with de Finetti.[13] In fact in this definition one does not assign the same third value u ("undetermined") to *all* conditional events, but make it suitably depend on $E|H$.

---

[a] $x \odot y = -c \log[e^{-x/c} + e^{-y/c}]$.

There is a "natural" interpretation of $T(E|H)$ in terms of a betting scheme, that may help in clarifying its meaning and in assigning its truth values: if an amount $t(E|H)$ — which suitably depends on $E|H$ — is paid to make a conditional bet on $E|H$, we get, *when H is true*, an amount 1 if also E is true (the bet is won) and an amount 0 if E is false (the bet is lost), and *we get back the amount $t(E|H)$ if H turns out to be false* (the bet is called off).

Since the conditional event $E|H$, or better its *boolean support* that is the (ordered) pair (E, H), induces a (unique) partition of the certain event Ω, that is $(E \wedge H, E^c \wedge H, H^c)$: one puts in fact

$$t(E|H) = t(E \wedge H, E^c \wedge H, H^c).$$

It follows $t(E|H) = t(E \wedge H|H)$, and so $T(E|H) = T((E \wedge H)|H)$.

In conclusion we require for $t(.|.)$ only the following conditions:

(i) the function $t(E|H)$ depends only on the partition $E \wedge H$, $E^c \wedge H, H^c$.

(ii) the function $t(\cdot|H)$ must be *not identically equal to zero*.

A useful representation of $T(E|H)$ (that will be denoted from now on by $I_{E|H}$) can be given by means of a discrete real random quantity

$$X = \sum_{h=1}^{\nu} x_h I_{E_h}$$

written in its "canonical" form (i.e. the E_h's are a *partition* of Ω): just take, in the above formula, $\nu = 3$, $E_1 = E \wedge H$, $E_2 = E^c \wedge H$, $E_3 = H^c$, and $x_1 = 1$, $x_2 = 0$, $x_3 = t(E|H)$, so that I_{H^c}.

$$I_{E|H} = 1 \cdot I_{E \wedge H} + 0 \cdot I_{E^c \wedge H} + t(E|H) \cdot I_{H^c}.$$

We recall that it is possible to give an interpretation in terms of betting scheme of $I_{E|H}$: if an amount p — which should suitably depend on $E|H$ — is paid to bet on $E|H$, we get, *when H is true*, either an amount 1 if also E is true (the bet is won) or an amount

0 if E is false (the bet is lost), and *we get back the amount p if H turns out to be false* (the bet is called off).

4. From Conditional Events to Conditional Information Measures

Since $t(E|H)$ can be thought as a measure of how much you believe in the truth of $E|H$, it turns out, introducing *partial* operations between conditional events, that it is the "natural" candidate to be a conditional *uncertainty measure*. Through particular different choices of these operations we get, for example, conditional *probability*, conditional *possibility* and conditional *belief functions*.

In the present context we necessarily follow a different line: consider a family $\mathcal{T} = \{I_{E_i|H_i}\}$ of *conditional events* $E|H$, represented as above by real random quantities, let λ be a decreasing function from $[0,1]$ to $[0,+\infty]$ such that $\lambda(1) = 0$ and $\lambda(0) = +\infty$. Consider now $\lambda(\mathcal{T}) = \{\lambda(I_{E_i|H_i})\}$ that is the family of random quantities representing the conditional events transformed by λ, whose range is $[0,+\infty]$.

We can give an interpretation in terms of betting scheme of

$$\lambda(I_{E|H}) = 0 \cdot I_{E\wedge H} + (+\infty) \cdot I_{E^c \wedge H} + \lambda(t(E|H)) \cdot I_{H^c}. \qquad (2)$$

If we have paid $\lambda(t(E|H))$ to obtain the following information: "under the hypothesis that H is true, E is also true", the random quantity $\lambda(I_{E|H})$ represents the amount which we get back when we know the truth values of E and H. In fact we get an amount 0, *when H and E are true*, an amount $+\infty$ if H is true and E is false (we receive the maximum danger and we obtain the maximum damage); finally *we get back the amount $\lambda(t(E|H))$ if H turns out to be false* (the information has no interest).

Given now two commutative, associative, and increasing operations $\odot$ and $\oplus$ from $[0,+\infty] \times [0,+\infty]$ to $[0,+\infty]$, having respectively $+\infty$ and 0 as neutral elements and with $\oplus$ distributive with respect to $\odot$ (for instance min and +), we define corresponding operations among the elements of $\lambda(\mathcal{T})$: the "result" is a random quantity, but it does not, in general, belong to $\lambda(\mathcal{T})$.

We have in fact, by (2), for any pair of conditional events $E|H$, $A|K$ (to improve readability of the two following formulas, for any event E we put $I_E = E$ and EA stands for $E \wedge A$ for any A):

$$\lambda(I_{(E|H)}) \odot \lambda(I_{(A|K)})$$
$$= [0 \odot 0]EHAK + [0 \odot +\infty]EHA^cK$$
$$+ [0 \odot +\infty]E^cHAK + [+\infty \odot +\infty]E^cHA^cK$$
$$+ [0 \odot \lambda(t(A|K))]EHK^c + [+\infty \odot \lambda(t(A|K))]E^cHK^c$$
$$+ [0 \odot \lambda(t(E|H))]AKH^c + [+\infty \odot \lambda(t(E|H))]A^cKH^c$$
$$+ [\lambda(t(E|H)) \odot \lambda(t(A|K))]H^cK^c,$$

and

$$\lambda(I_{(E|H)}) \oplus \lambda(I_{(A|K)})$$
$$= [0 \oplus 0]EHAK + [0 \oplus +\infty]EHA^cK$$
$$+ [0 \oplus +\infty]E^cHAK + [+\infty \oplus +\infty]E^cHA^cK$$
$$+ [0 \oplus \lambda(t(A|K))]EHK^c + [+\infty \oplus \lambda(t(A|K))]E^cHK^c$$
$$+ [0 \oplus \lambda(t(E|H))]AKH^c + [+\infty \oplus \lambda(t(E|H))]A^cKH^c$$
$$+ [\lambda(t(E|H)) \oplus \lambda(t(A|K))]H^cK^c.$$

It is easy to see that both right-hand sides of the latter two expressions are *not* of the kind (2), i.e. there does not exist a conditional event $A|B$ such that they can be written (using the simplified notation) as

$$0 \cdot AB + (+\infty) \cdot A^cB + \lambda(t(A|B)) \cdot B^c.$$

Nevertheless, if we operate by $\odot$ only on events $E|H$ and $A|K$ such that $H = K$ and $E \wedge A \wedge H = \emptyset$ then we have:

$$\lambda(I_{(E|H)}) \odot \lambda(I_{(A|H)}) = 0 \cdot EAH + (+\infty) \cdot E^cA^cH$$
$$+ [\lambda(t(E|H)) \odot \lambda(t(A|H))] \cdot H^c.$$

So, if $\mathcal{T}$ contains also $(E \vee A)|H$, necessarily we must have:

$$\lambda(t[(E \vee A)|H]) = \lambda(t(E|H)) \odot \lambda(t(A|H)).$$

Similarly, if for $\oplus$ we consider only events $E|H$ and $A|K$ such that $K = E \wedge H$, and if the family $\mathcal{T}$ containing $E|H$ and $A|(E \wedge H)$

contains also $(E \wedge A)|H$, we necessarily have:

$$\lambda(t[(E \wedge A)|H]) = \lambda(t(E|H)) \oplus \lambda(t(A|E \wedge H))$$

So, if we operate only with elements of $\lambda(\mathcal{T}) \times \lambda(\mathcal{T})$ such that the range of each operation is $\lambda(\mathcal{T})$, we "automatically" get conditions on $\lambda(t(E|H))$ that can be regarded as the "natural" axioms for a conditional information measure I, defined on $\mathcal{C} = \mathcal{E} \times \mathcal{H}$, with $\mathcal{E}$ a Boolean algebra, $\mathcal{H} \subseteq \mathcal{E}$ an additive set not containing $\{\emptyset\}$. Denoting $\lambda(t(\cdot)) = I(\cdot)$, we have:

(I1) $I(E|H) = I(E \wedge H|H)$, for every $E \in \mathcal{E}$ and $H \in \mathcal{H}^o$,

(I2) for any given $H \in \mathcal{H}^o$ $I(\cdot|H)$ is a $\odot$ "generalized decomposable measure of information", that is:

$$I(\Omega|H) = 0, \quad I(\emptyset|H) = +\infty,$$

and, for any $E, A \in \mathcal{E}$, with $A \wedge E \wedge H = \emptyset$, we have

$$I((E \vee A)|H) = I(E|H) \odot I(A|H)$$

(I3) for every $A \in \mathcal{E}$ and $E, H, E \wedge H \in \mathcal{H}^o$,

$$I((E \wedge A)|H) = I(E|H) \oplus I(A|(E \wedge H)).$$

Definition 3. We call $(\odot, \oplus)$-*conditional information measure* a function $I : \mathcal{C} \rightarrow [0, +\infty]$, with $\mathcal{C} = \mathcal{E} \times \mathcal{H}$, $\mathcal{E}$ a Boolean algebra, $\mathcal{H} \subseteq \mathcal{E}$ an additive set not containing $\{\emptyset\}$, satisfying conditions (I1), (I2), (I3).

Remark 1. We note that, if we fix $\odot$, then the choice of operation $\oplus$ is not free (for instance, in the case of Wiener-Shannon information measure, we can prove that *the only possible* choice for $\oplus$ is $+$). The constraints are given by the requirement of distributivity and, obviously, by the axioms. In fact we pretend that the following relation holds for every $A \vee E \subseteq H \subseteq K$:

$$[I(A|H) \odot I(E|H)] \oplus I(H|K) = [I(A|H) \oplus I(H|K)] \odot [I(E|H) \oplus I(H|K)].$$

Nevertheless, if for instance we choose $\odot = min$, then we have many different possible choices for $\oplus$.

In the literature there are some other axiomatizations for conditional information measures, we refer to that given by P. Benvenuti.[1]

Our axioms (I1), (I2) coincide respectively with (AII) and (AI), introduced in Ref. 1. In the quoted paper the author introduces the further following axiom:

(AIV): there exists a function ψ from $]0, +\infty] \times]0, +\infty] \times [0, +\infty] \times [0, +\infty]$ to $[0, +\infty]$, such that:

$$I(E|H \vee K) = \psi[I(H|\Omega), I(K|\Omega), I(E|H), I(E|K)].$$

This axiom in fact involves only conditional events whose conditioning events have strictly positive information, so it is not able to completely manage the conditional information, in the sense that we have no rules to assess $I(E|H)$ when $I(H|\Omega) = 0$.

Moreover, if we pretend to compute $I(E|H \vee K)$, involving only the values $I(H|\Omega), I(K|\Omega)$ and not also $I(H|H \vee K)$ and $I(K|H \vee K)$ we obtain the same difficulties as we would get when computing $P(H|H \vee K)$ and $P(K|H \vee K)$, in the case where $P(H|\Omega) = P(K|\Omega) = 0$.

Nevertheless, if $\oplus$ is strictly increasing in $]0, +\infty[$ and we restrict our attention to the events $E|H$ with $I(H|\Omega) \neq 0$, and $I(H|\Omega) \neq +\infty$, then it is easy to prove the following result:

Proposition 1. *Let I be a $(\odot, \oplus)$-conditional information measure, with $\oplus$ strictly increasing in $]0, +\infty[$, then, for events $E|H \vee K$, with $I(H|\Omega)$, $I(K|\Omega)$ in $]0, +\infty[$, condition AIV holds. On the other hand, if AIV holds, then I3 is satisfied.*

Condition I3 implies that a conditional information measure $I(\cdot|H)$ *is not singled-out (only) by the information measure of its conditioning event H, but its value is bound to the values of other conditional information measures $I(\cdot|E \wedge H)$, for suitable events E.*

Definition 4. Let $\mathcal{B}$ be a finite algebra and $\mathcal{C}_o$ the set of atoms in $\mathcal{B}$. The class $\mathcal{I} = \{I_o, \ldots, I_k\}$ of information measures, defined on $\mathcal{B}$, is said nested if (for $j = 1, \ldots, k$) the following conditions hold: for every $A \in \mathcal{B}$

- $I_0(A) = I(A|H_0^0)$ with $H_0^0 = \bigvee_{j=1}^n H_j$;
- $I_j(A) = I(A|H_0^j)$ with $H_0^j = \bigvee_r \{H_r : I_{j-1}(H_r) = +\infty\}$ $(j > 0)$;
- for any $C \in \mathcal{C}_o$ there exists a (unique) $j = j_C$ such that $I_{j_C}(C) < +\infty$.

Theorem 1. *Let $\mathcal{I} = \{I_o, \ldots, I_k\}$ be a nested class of information measures on $\mathcal{B}$. Let f be a function defined on $\mathcal{B} \times \mathcal{H}$ (with $\mathcal{H} \subseteq \mathcal{B}$ additive set not containing $\emptyset$) into $[0, +\infty]$, such that $f(A, B)$ is solution of all the equations*

$$I_\alpha(A \wedge B) = x \oplus I_\alpha(B), \tag{3}$$

$\alpha = 0, \ldots, k$ *and $f(A, B)$ is the* unique *solution of equation (3) related to j_B. Then, f is a $(\odot, \oplus)$-conditional information measure on $\mathcal{B} \times \mathcal{H}$.*

Proof. The proof of $I1$ and $I2$ is trivial.

To prove $I3$, consider a triple $I\big((E \wedge A)|H\big), I(E|H), I\big(A|(E \wedge H)\big)$ and let $\alpha = j_H$. We are interested in proving the equality $f((E \vee A)|H) = f(E|H) \oplus f\big(A|(E \wedge H)\big)$ or equivalently $I_\alpha(H) \oplus f((E \vee A)|H) = I_\alpha(H) \oplus f(E|H) \oplus f\big(A|(E \wedge H)\big)$.

By using equation (3) we have $f((E \vee A)|H) \oplus I_\alpha(H) = I_\alpha(E \wedge A \wedge H)$ and $f(E|H) \oplus I_\alpha(H) \oplus f\big(A|(E \wedge H)\big) = I_\alpha(E \wedge H) \oplus f\big(A|(E \wedge H)\big)$.

Now, if $I_\alpha(E \wedge H) = +\infty$, then necessarily also $I_\alpha(E \wedge A \wedge H) = +\infty$, and so the equality holds.

On the contrary, if $I_\alpha(E \wedge H) < +\infty$, then by equation (3) we have:

$$I_\alpha(E \wedge H) \oplus f\big(A|(E \wedge H)\big) = I_\alpha(E \wedge A \wedge H).$$

$\square$

5. Coherent Conditional Information Measures and Their Characterization

The concept of coherence, developed on uncertainty measures (starting from de Finetti relatively to probability), is the tool to manage partial assessments, that is functions defined in arbitrary sets of (conditional) events (i.e. sets without particular Boolean structure).

Coherence requires that some numbers attributed to some events are in fact the restriction of a specific uncertainty measure on a Boolean algebra or (for conditional events) on a product of an algebra and an additive set. The interest is obviously related to find necessary and sufficient conditions assuring coherence, possibly easily computable (see for instance Refs. 2, 5–7, 9, 11, 13, 14, 18–20 for precise and imprecise probabilities, Refs. 4 and 12 for possibilities and necessities). We extend the concept of coherence to (conditional) information measures.

Definition 5. Let $\mathcal{E}$ be an arbitrary set of conditional events and $I : \mathcal{E} \to [0, +\infty]$. The function I is a *coherent* $(\odot, \oplus)$-*conditional information measure* iff it can be extended on $\mathcal{B} \times \mathcal{H} \supset \mathcal{E}$ (with $\mathcal{B}$ a Boolean algebra, $\mathcal{H} \subseteq \mathcal{B}$ additive set not containing $\emptyset$) as a $(\odot, \oplus)$-conditional information measure.

The next theorem gives a characterization of a coherent $(\odot, \oplus)$-conditional information measure in terms of a class of unconditional $\odot$-decomposable information measures.

Theorem 2. *Let* $\mathcal{F} = \{E_1|H_1, \ldots, E_n|H_n\}$ *be a finite set of conditional events,* $\mathcal{C}_o$ *and* $\mathcal{B}$ *denote, respectively, the set of atoms and the algebra generated by* $\{E_1, H_1, \ldots, E_n, H_n\}$.

For a real function $I : \mathcal{F} \to [0, +\infty]$ *the following two statements are equivalent:*

(i) I *is a* $(\odot, \oplus)$-*coherent conditional information measure on* $\mathcal{F}$;
(ii) *there exists (at least) a nested class* $\mathcal{I} = \{I_o, \ldots, I_k\}$ *of information measures on* $\mathcal{B}$, *such that for any* $E_i|H_i \in \mathcal{F}$, $I(E_i|H_i)$ *is solution of all the equations*

$$I_\alpha(E_i \wedge H_i) = x \oplus I_\alpha(H_i) \qquad (4)$$

$\alpha = 0, \ldots, k$ *and* $I(E_i|H_i)$ *is the* unique *solution of equation (4) for* $\alpha = j_{H_i}$;
(iii) *there exists a sequence of compatible systems* S_α *(with* $\alpha = 0, \ldots, k$), *with unknowns* $x_r^\alpha = I_\alpha(C_r)$

$$S_\alpha = \begin{cases} \displaystyle\bigodot_{C_r \subseteq E_i \wedge H_i} x_r^\alpha = I(E_i|H_i) \oplus \bigodot_{C_r \subseteq H_i} x_r^\alpha \; \text{if} \; \mathbf{x}_r^{\alpha-1} = +\infty \\[4mm] \displaystyle\bigodot_{C_r \subseteq H_0^\alpha} x_r^\alpha = 0 \\[4mm] x_r^\alpha \in [0, +\infty] \end{cases}$$

where $\mathbf{x}^{\alpha-1}$ *(with rth component* $\mathbf{x}_r^{\alpha-1}$) *is solution of the system* $S_{\alpha-1}$ *and* $\mathbf{x}_r^{-1} = +\infty$ *for any* $C_r \in \mathcal{C}_o$.
Moreover $H_0^\alpha = \{\bigvee H_i : \bigodot_{C_r \subseteq H_i} \mathbf{x}_r^{\alpha-1} = +\infty\}$.

Proof. We only sketch the proof. It is easy to prove that the $\odot$-information measures obtained starting from the solutions of systems

S_α are a nested class (and so $(iii) \Rightarrow (ii)$). The proof of implication $(ii) \Rightarrow (i)$ has been essentially given in the previous Proposition. To prove $(i) \Rightarrow (iii)$ consider that coherence implies the existence of a $(\odot, \oplus)$-decomposable information measure on $\mathcal{A} \times \mathcal{B}$ where $\mathcal{A}$ is the algebra spanned by events E_i, H_i $(i = 1, \ldots, n)$ and $\mathcal{B}$ the additive set spanned by the events $H_i(i = 1, \ldots, n)$. Since $\mathcal{B}$ contains all the events H_α^0, the solution of any system S_α is given by $x_k^\alpha = P(\cdot|H_\alpha^0)$.

The previous result implies that the coherence of a given assignment I can be proved by finding a nested class agreeing with it, i.e. checking the compatibility of a sequence of systems S_α (with $\alpha = 0, \ldots, k$). $\qquad\square$

References

1. P. Benvenuti, Sur l'indépendance dans l'information. *Colloques internationaux du C.N.R.S.*, N.276 — Théorie de l'Information, pp. 44–55 (1977).
2. V. Biazzo and A. Gilio, A generalization of the fundamental theory of de Finetti for imprecise conditional probability assessments. *Int. J. of App. Reas.*, **24**, 251–272 (2000).
3. B. Bouchon-Meunier, G. Coletti and C. Marsala, Conditional possibility and necessity. *Technologies for Constructing Intelligent Systems* B. Bouchon-Meunier, J. Gutiérrez-Rios, L. Magdalena, R. R. and Yager eds, Vol. 1, Springer, Berlin, 2001 (Selected papers from IPMU 2000, Madrid) (2001).
4. B. Bouchon-Meunier, G. Coletti and C. Marsala, Independence and possibilistic conditioning. *Annals of Mathematics and Artificial Intelligence*, **35**, 107–124 (2002).
5. A. Capotorti and B. Vantagg, Locally strong coherence in inference processes. *Ann. Math. and Art. Int.*, **35**, 125–149 (2002).
6. G. Coletti, Coherent numerical and ordinal probabilistic assessments. *IEEE Transactions on Systems, Man, and Cybernetics*, **24**, 1747–1754 (1994).
7. G. Coletti and R. Scozzafava, Characterization of coherent probabilities as a tool for their assessment and extention. *J. of Uncertainty, Fuzziness and Knowledge Based Systems*, **44**(3), 101–132 (1996).
8. G. Coletti and R. Scozzafava, Conditioning and inference in intelligent systems. *Soft Computing*, **3**(3), 118–130 (1999).
9. G. Coletti and R. Scozzafava, The role of coherence in eliciting and handling "imprecise" probabilities and its application to medical diagnosis. *Information Sciences*, **130**, 41–65 (2000).
10. G. Coletti and R. Scozzafava, From conditional events to conditional measures: a new axiomatic approach. *Annals of Mathematics and Artificial Intelligence*, **32**, 373–392 (2001).
11. G. Coletti and R. Scozzafava, *Probabilistic Logic in a Coherent Setting*, trends in Logic n. 15, Kluwer, Dorbdrecht, Boston, London (2002).

12. G. Coletti and B. Vantaggi, Possibility theory: conditional independence. *J. of Fuzzy Sets and Systems*, **157**(11), 1491–1513 (2006). ·
13. B. de Finetti, La logique de la probabilité. *Actes du Congrès International de Philosophie Scientifique*, Hermann, Paris, IV, 1–9 (1935).
14. B. de Finetti, *Teoria della probabilità*. Einaudi, Torino (1970). (Engl. transl.: *Theory of Probability*, Vol. 1 and 2, Chichester, Wiley, 1974).
15. J. Kampé de Fériet, Measure de l'information. fournie par un événement. *Colloques Internationaux C.N.R.S.*, **186**, 191–221 (1969).
16. J. Kampé de Fériet, L'indépendance des événements dans la théorie géneralisée de l'information. *Journées Lyonnaises des questionnaires. C.N.R.S. Groupe de recherche* 22, n.1, 1–30 (1975).
17. J. Kampé de Fériet and B. Forte, Information et Probabilité. *Comptes Rendus Acad. Sci. Paris*, 265 A 110–114, 142–146, 350–353 (1967).
18. G. Regoli, Rational comparisons and numerical representation. *Decision Theory and Analysis: Trends and Challenges*. S. Rios ed., Kluwer, Boston, pp. 113–126 (1994).
19. P. Walley, *Statistical Reasoning with Imprecise Probabilities*, Chapman and Hall, London (1991).
20. P. M. Williams, Indeterminate probabilities. *Formal Methods in the Methodology of Empirical Sciences*, Riedel, Dordrecht, pp. 229–246 (1976).

Discourse Interpretation as Model Selection — A Probabilistic Approach

I. Zukerman

Faculty of Information Technology, Monash University
Clayton, VICTORIA 3800, Australia
ingrid@csse.monash.edu.au

Abstract

This paper presents a probabilistic approach to discourse interpretation that casts the selection of an interpretation as a model selection task. In selecting the best model, our formalism balances conflicting factors: model probability against data fit, and structural complexity against inference reasonableness. We first define an interpretation of discourse, and describe the process that generates an interpretation. We then discuss our basic probabilistic formalism, and show how it is extended to posit suppositions that account for beliefs stated in the discourse, and explanatory extensions that justify inferences in the discourse.

1. Introduction

Discourse interpretation may be viewed as a process whereby an addressee produces a representation of the speaker's or writer's discourse in terms of the addressee's own beliefs and inferences.[a] This process is fraught with uncertainty, as the concepts referenced by the speaker's words must be identified, the propositions built using these concepts must be understood, and the relations between these propositions must be determined. For example, consider the simple

---

[a] We will henceforth refer to the speaker or writer as "the speaker".

request "Can you please go to the bakery? We need some croissants." Here the addressee has to identify which bakery is intended, understand that he or she has to go to this bakery, and determine the relationship between going to the bakery and needing croissants (i.e. to purchase croissants).

Sometimes it is not possible to arrive at the interpretation intended by the speaker, e.g. when there are too many alternatives, insufficient information was provided, or there isn't enough time to think of all the options. However, even if the interpretation preferred by the addressee is not the intended one, it should be reasonable in the current context, thereby providing grounds for further interaction.

The interpretation preferred by the addressee often balances several factors, such as how well it matches the discourse, how reasonable it is in the current context, and how feasible it is. For instance, in the above example, the closest bakery may be generally preferred. However, if a special type of croissant had been requested, then a different bakery might better match the request. The bakery postulated in the preferred interpretation would reflect a balance of these factors.

In this paper, we cast discourse interpretation as a model selection problem, where the interpretation is the model and the discourse is the data. That is, we aim to select the model (interpretation) that best explains the observed data (discourse). This idea is inspired by the Minimum Message Length (MML) criterion — an operational form of Occam's Razor that balances model complexity against data fit.[1] According to this trade-off, *the simplest interpretation that fits the speaker's discourse well* is preferred. We implement this idea by means of a probabilistic approach which balances (prior) model probability against data fit, and structural model complexity against reasonableness of inference. For instance, an interpretation that postulates our usual bakery would have the highest prior probability, but not necessarily the best fit with the discourse, while a lower probability interpretation that postulates a different bakery may fit the discourse better. Also, people may prefer a more complex (lower probability) interpretation that contains explanations for some of its inferences, rather than a more concise (higher probability) interpretation that omits these explanations.

Our approach comprises three main elements, which are described in the following sections: (1) definition of an interpretation,

(2) algorithm for postulating interpretations, and (3) probabilistic formulation.

2. What is an Interpretation?

We define an interpretation of a piece of discourse as the tuple $\{IG, SC, EE\}$, where IG is an *interpretation graph*, SC is a *supposition configuration*, and EE are *explanatory extensions*.

- An **Interpretation Graph** is a structure comprising propositions and inferences from the system's knowledge base that connects between the propositions in the discourse. This structure bridges inferential leaps in the discourse.
- A **Supposition Configuration** is a set of suppositions attributed to the speaker (in addition to or instead of the beliefs shared with the system) to account for the beliefs expressed in the discourse.
- **Explanatory Extensions** consist of domain propositions that are connected to an interpretation graph in order to justify the consequent of an inference. Contrary to suppositions, the beliefs in explanatory extensions are shared by the speaker and the system.

In our initial work, our interpretations contained only interpretation graphs.[2,3] However, trials with users demonstrated the need for supposition configurations[4] and explanatory extensions.[5,6]

To illustrate these components, consider the sample argument at the top of Fig. 1 in relation to a murder mystery (the domain where we conducted our user trials), and the three segments under it. Each segment highlights one of these components for the preferred interpretation of this argument. Segment (a) shows the interpretation graph alone; Segment (b) adds a supposition to the interpretation; and Segment (c) adds an explanatory extension. Each segment shows the graphical form of the preferred interpretation and its textual rendition. The interpretation comprises propositions (stated by the speaker or postulated by the interpretation process), the beliefs in them,[b] and relationships between these propositions. The

---

[b] We use the following linguistic terms, which are similar to those used by Elsaesser,[7] to convey belief: *Very Probable, Probable, Possible* and their negations, and *Even Chance*. According to our surveys, these terms are most consistently understood by people.

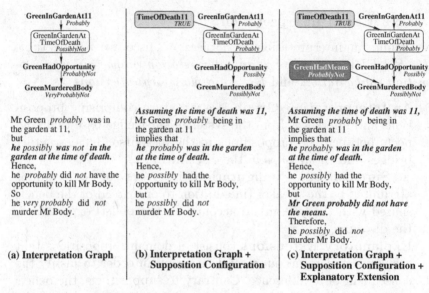

Fig. 1. Interpretation graph, supposition configuration and explanatory extension.

propositions that were postulated by the interpretation process are boxed in the graphical representations, and appear in boldface italics in the textual renditions. The propositions in an interpretation and the relationships between them are obtained from our domain knowledge, which in our system is represented by means of a Bayesian network (BN).[8] The system's beliefs in these propositions are obtained by means of Bayesian propagation from evidence encountered in the domain.

Let us now examine in more detail the three segments in Fig. 1. As mentioned above, the interpretation graph in Fig. 1(a) comprises propositions from the system's domain knowledge that appear in the argument or connect between the propositions in the argument (there is only one connecting proposition, GreenInGardenAtTimeOfDeath, which appears boxed). Note that the beliefs in this interpretation graph do not match those in the argument, as the system has no reason to believe that the time of death is 11. As a result, the argument antecedent GreenInGardenAt11 yields a belief of *PossiblyNot* in GreenInGardenAtTimeOfDeath, which in turn implies that Mr Green *ProbablyNot* had the opportunity to kill Mr Body, and *VeryProbablyNot* committed the murder.

To address this problem, the system *supposes* that the speaker believes that TimeOfDeath11 = TRUE. Figure 1(b) shows how this supposition (which appears boldfaced and gray boxed) fits in the interpretation graph, and depicts its impact on the beliefs in the interpretation. These beliefs now match those in the argument. However, one problem remains: the last inference in the argument goes from Mr Green *Possibly* having the opportunity to kill Mr Body to Mr Green *PossiblyNot* murdering Mr Body, but the reason for this "jump in belief" is not clear. The system addresses this problem by positing an *explanatory extension* that justifies the conclusion on the basis of beliefs shared with the speaker. In this case, the selected shared belief is that Mr Green *ProbablyNot* had the means to murder Mr Body. Figure 1(c) shows how this explanatory extension (which appears white boldfaced and dark-gray boxed) fits in the interpretation graph. Note that explanatory extensions don't affect the beliefs in an interpretation, as they simply state previously held beliefs.

3. Proposing Interpretations

The problem of finding the best interpretation is exponential, as there are many candidates for each component of an interpretation, and complex interactions between these components. For example, making a supposition could invalidate an otherwise sound line of reasoning. In order to generate reasonable interpretations in real time, we employ an *anytime* algorithm[9,10] that iteratively proposes interpretations until time runs out, i.e. until the system has to act upon a preferred interpretation or show the speaker one or more interpretations for validation.[11,12]

In each iteration, the algorithm generates an interpretation by first proposing a supposition configuration (which may be null), next an interpretation graph for this configuration, and last explanatory extensions for this supposition configuration and interpretation graph, if necessary. A supposition configuration is proposed first, because the beliefs in the domain affect the beliefs in the candidate interpretation graphs, which in turn affect the need for explanatory extensions. After a complete interpretation has been generated, its probability is estimated. Upon completion of the interpretation process (i.e. when time runs out), the K most probable interpretations are retained. At present, our interaction with the speaker stops when these interpretations are presented for validation. However, in a complete system, a dialogue module would have to determine a course of action based on the generated interpretation(s).

Owing to the different ways in which supposition configurations, interpretation graphs and explanatory extensions interact with each other, we employ different techniques to generate each of these components: a dynamic priority queue is used to generate interpretation graphs; supposition configurations are drawn from a static pool based on a dynamic priority queue; and a greedy search procedure is applied to generate explanatory extensions.

The generation of *interpretation graphs* is performed as follows. A priority queue is initialized with the smallest graph that connects a user's statements. An iterative process is then followed, where in each iteration, the candidate at the top of the queue is selected, its "children" (interpretation graphs based on the selected one) are generated, and their contribution to the probability of their interpretation is calculated. The newly generated children are then slotted in the queue according to their contribution. This process yields good results for interpretation graphs, as the order in which these graphs appear in the queue is indicative of their influence on the goodness of an interpretation (graphs that appear earlier are usually better).

However, this is not the case for *supposition configurations*, due to their complex interactions with interpretation graphs ("reasonable" suppositions may not necessarily yield beliefs that match those in the discourse). As a result, supposition configurations that are generated early may yield worse results overall than those that are generated later. In order to be able to access these later candidates and still achieve anytime performance, we created a static pool of promising candidates at the start of the interpretation process. This pool is populated by calling a priority queue of supposition configurations M times, and retaining the m best candidates $(M \gg m)$. During the interpretation process, a new component is probabilistically selected from this pool (the priority queue is never recalled).

Explanatory extensions are generated by a greedy search which selects the "best" explanatory extension for each inference that is deemed unacceptable. Such an approach is reasonable due to the simple interactions between explanatory extensions and interpretation graphs (explanatory extensions do not modify beliefs), and due to the nature of people's preferences regarding explanatory extensions.[6]

4. Probabilistic Formalism

The MML criterion,[1] on which our approach is based, requires the specification of three elements: *background knowledge, model* and *data.* **Background knowledge** is everything known to the system and the speaker prior to interpreting the speaker's discourse, e.g. domain knowledge, beliefs shared by the speaker and the system, and dialogue history; the **data** is the discourse itself; and the **model** is the interpretation.

We posit that the best interpretation is that with the highest posterior probability.

$$IntBest = \text{argmax}_{i=1,\ldots,q} \Pr(IG_i, SC_i, EE_i | Discourse),$$

where q is the number of interpretations.

After applying Bayes rule, this probability is represented as follows.[c]

$$\Pr(IG_i, SC_i, EE_i | Discourse)$$
$$\propto \Pr(IG_i, SC_i, EE_i) \times \Pr(Discourse | IG_i, SC_i, EE_i)$$

The first factor represents the prior probability of the model in the context of the background knowledge, and the second factor (known as data fit) represents how well the model fits the data.

- The prior probability of a model reflects how "easy" it is to construct the model (interpretation) from background knowledge. For instance, complex models (e.g. interpretations with larger interpretation graphs) usually have a lower prior probability than simpler models (e.g. interpretations with smaller graphs). Hence, this factor is also known as model complexity.
- Data fit measures how similar the data (discourse) is to the model (interpretation). The closer the data is to the model, the higher the probability of the data given the model (i.e. the probability that the speaker uttered the discourse when he or she intended the interpretation in question).

---

[c] In principle, $\Pr(IG_i, SC_i, EE_i | Discourse)$ can be calculated directly, but it is not clear how to incorporate the priors of an interpretation in the direct calculation.

Both the discourse and its interpretation contain numerical and structural information. The numerical portion of the discourse and the interpretation comprises the beliefs in their propositions (which include supposition configurations for the interpretation). The structural part of the discourse comprises the stated propositions and the relationships between them, while the structural part of the interpretation comprises the interpretation graph and explanatory extensions. The techniques employed to calculate the prior probability and data fit of both types of information are described below.

4.1.   *Prior probability of an interpretation*

The prior probability of the ***numerical*** information in an interpretation depends on the similarity between the beliefs in the interpretation and those in the background knowledge. The higher this similarity, the higher the probability of the interpretation. One of the functions we have used to calculate the probability of the beliefs in an interpretation is the Zipf distribution, where the parameter is the difference between beliefs,[3] e.g. between the beliefs in a supposition configuration SC and the beliefs in the corresponding propositions in the background knowledge.

The prior probability of the ***structural*** information in an interpretation is obtained from the probabilities of the elements in the structure (e.g. propositions and inferences in the interpretation graph) in light of the background knowledge. The simplest calculation assumes that the probability of including a proposition in an interpretation graph is uniform. That is, the probability of an interpretation graph comprising n propositions is $\binom{N}{n}^{-1}$, where N is the number of propositions in the domain. This calculation generally prefers small models to larger ones.[d] We have considered two additional factors to moderate the probability of an interpretation graph: *path validity* and *salience*. Reasoning paths through which evidence cannot propagate reduce the probability of an interpretation graph (in a BN these are *blocked paths*[8]) and salient propositions increase it.[3]

---

[d] In the rare cases where the number of propositions in an interpretation exceeds $N/2$, smaller models do not yield lower probabilities.

4.2. Data Fit Between the Discourse and an Interpretation

The similarity between the *numerical* information (beliefs) in the discourse and the corresponding information in an interpretation is calculated as described in Section 4.1 for the interpretation vis a vis the background knowledge. The closer the beliefs stated in the discourse are to the propagated beliefs in the interpretation, the higher the probability that the speaker presented the discourse when he or she intended this interpretation.

The similarity between the *structural* information in the discourse and the structural information in an interpretation is a function of the number and type of operations required to convert the interpretation graph into the discourse, e.g. insertions and deletions of propositions. In general, the more operations need to be performed, the lower the similarity between the discourse and the interpretation, and the lower the probability of the discourse given the interpretation.

4.3. Accounting for the Components of an Interpretation

We now discuss our basic probabilistic formalism, which accounts for interpretation graphs, followed by two enhancements: (1) a more complex model that accounts for suppositions; and (2) additional background knowledge that accounts for explanatory extensions.

Basic formalism: Interpretation graphs. Initially, our background knowledge consisted only of the facts known to the speaker and the system and the propositions and inference patterns in the system's domain knowledge (represented by a BN). Our model consisted only of an interpretation graph. As seen at the start of Sec. 4, smaller, simpler structures generally have a higher prior probability than larger, more complex ones. However, the smallest structure is not necessarily the best. For instance, the smallest possible interpretation for any discourse consists of a single proposition, but this interpretation has a very poor data fit with longer pieces of discourse. An increase in structural complexity (and corresponding reduction in probability) may reduce the discrepancy between the discourse structure and the structure of the interpretation graph, thereby improving data fit. If this improvement overcomes the reduction in probability due to the higher model complexity, we obtain a higher-probability

Table 1. Summary of trade-offs.

more complex structure	$\Rightarrow$	$\downarrow$ Pr model structure	$\rightsquigarrow$	$\uparrow$	Pr structural data fit
suppositions	$\Rightarrow$	$\downarrow$ Pr model beliefs	$\rightsquigarrow$	$\uparrow$	Pr belief data fit
explanatory extensions	$\Rightarrow$	$\downarrow$ Pr model structure	$\rightsquigarrow$	$\uparrow$	Pr model inferences (match with background)

interpretation overall. The first row in Table 1 illustrates this trade-off (read $\rightsquigarrow$ as "may cause").[e]

Extension 1: A more informed model. In order to address mismatches between the beliefs expressed in a piece of discourse and those in an interpretation, we extended the model to include supposition configurations. These configurations comprise beliefs attributed to the speaker in addition to or instead of the beliefs shared with the system, which are encoded in the background knowledge. Thus, making suppositions has a lower probability than not making suppositions (which has no discrepancy with the background knowledge). However, as seen in the example in Fig. 1(b), making a supposition that reduces or eliminates the discrepancy between the beliefs stated in the discourse and those in the interpretation increases considerably the data fit for beliefs. This trade-off is presented in the second row of Table 1.

Extension 2: Additional background knowledge. We conducted surveys to assess the influence of information included in probabilistic inferences on the acceptability of these inferences. Specifically, we focused on the relationship between the beliefs in the antecedents of an inference and the belief in its consequent. The main insights from our surveys are that people object to two types of inferences: (1) those which have more certainty regarding the consequent than regarding the antecedent(s) (e.g. *probably A* implies **very probably C**), and (2) those where there is a large change in certainty from the antecedent(s) to the consequent (e.g. *probably A* implies *even chance C*).[3,5]

---

[e] In this formalism, there is no belief discrepancy between an interpretation graph and the background knowledge, since the beliefs in interpretation graphs are obtained by Bayesian propagation from evidence in the background knowledge (the beliefs are the same in all the interpretation graphs). However, as seen in Fig. 1(a), there can be differences in belief between the interpretation graph and the discourse.

The complements of these objections were incorporated into our background knowledge as expectations for a range of acceptable beliefs in the consequents of inferences in light of their antecedents (e.g. *probably A* implies {*probably, possibly*} *C*). The farther the belief in the consequent of an inference is from these expectations, the lower the probability of this inference, and of the interpretation that contains it. These expectations add a new dimension to the background knowledge, which enables us to account for interpretations that include explanatory extensions. Interpretations with such extensions are more complex, and hence have a lower probability, than interpretations without such extensions. At the same time, as shown in the example in Fig. 1(c), an explanatory extension that overcomes an expectation violation regarding the consequent of an inference improves the acceptance of the interpretation, thereby increasing model probability. The third row in Table 1 illustrates this trade-off.

5. Conclusion

We have offered a probabilistic approach to discourse interpretation that casts the generation of an interpretation as a model selection task. In so doing, our approach balances the probability of the model in light of background knowledge against its data fit, and its structural model complexity against expectations in the background knowledge.

We have described the use of our basic formalism for the selection of an interpretation graph, and shown how extensions in the model and in background knowledge account respectively for the inclusion of suppositions and explanatory extensions in an interpretation. Our evaluations show that people found our interpretations generally acceptable, and our suppositions and explanatory extensions both necessary and reasonable.[6]

Although the approach presented in this paper has been implemented in a fairly restricted setting, we believe that our interpretation process and probabilistic formalism have wide applicability. Our approach is currently being extended in two main directions: dialogue modeling and spoken interactions with robots.

Dialogue modeling requires the inclusion of dialogue acts (e.g. REQUEST and INFORM) in interpretations, and the extension of background knowledge to incorporate expectations regarding dialogue acts.

Spoken interactions with robots pertain mainly to actions to be performed. Hence, feasibility plays an important role. In addition, these interactions present new challenges owing to the differences in open-endedness, granularity and certainty between the utterances in these interactions and the type of discourse considered in this paper. The discussion in this paper dealt with scenarios where all the propositions are explicitly represented, the smallest unit of representation is a proposition, relationships between propositions are causal or evidential, and there is no uncertainty regarding the propositions being mentioned. In spoken dialogue with robots, we have a complete representation of the actions in the domain and a partial representation of the objects in the domain, but there is no complete, explicit representation of the relationships between actions and objects. In addition, there can be a variety of relations between propositions, and the results produced both by automatic speech recognizers and scene analysis modules are probabilistic. Thus, our formalism must be extended to postulate "seen" and "heard" objects and actions, compose propositions from these objects and actions, and postulate different types of discourse relations between these propositions. It must also assess the plausibility and feasibility of these propositions and of the relations between them.

Finally, since robots must plan actions and execute their plans, we will investigate a mode of operation where the interpretation process continuously delivers "best so far" interpretations to a planner (instead of stopping after time has run out). This mode of operation enables a robot to continue thinking about an interpretation while it is formulating (and perhaps executing) a plan for the best interpretation produced so far.

Acknowledgments

The author thanks her collaborators on the research described in this paper: Sarah George and Michael Niemann. This research was supported in part by the ARC Centre for Perceptive and Intelligent Machines in Complex Environments.

References

1. C. Wallace, *Statistical and Inductive Inference by Minimum Message Length*, Springer, Berlin, Germany (2005).

2. I. Zukerman, S. George and M. George, Incorporating a user model into an information theoretic framework for argument interpretation. *UM03 — Proceedings of the 9th International Conference on User Modeling*, pp. 106–116, Johnstown, Pennsylvania (2003).

3. I. Zukerman and S. George, A probabilistic approach for argument interpretation. *User Modeling and User-Adapted Interaction, Special Issue on Language-Based Interaction*, **15** (1–2), 5–53 (2005).

4. S. George, I. Zukerman and M. Niemann, Modeling suppositions in users' arguments. *UM05 — Proceedings of the 10th International Conference on User Modeling*, pp. 19–29, Edinburgh, Scotland (2005).

5. I. Zukerman, M. Niemann and S. George, Balancing conflicting factors in argument interpretation. *Proceedings of the 7th SIGdial Workshop on Discourse and Dialogue*, pp. 134–143, Sydney, Australia (2006).

6. S. George, I. Zukerman and M. Niemann, Inferences, suppositions and explanatory extensions in argument interpretation. *User Modeling and User-Adapted Interaction*, **17**(5), 439–474 (2007).

7. C. Elsaesser, Explanation of probabilistic inference for decision support systems. *Proceedings of the AAAI-87 Workshop on Uncertainty in Artificial Intelligence*, pp. 394–403, Seattle, Washington (1987).

8. J. Pearl, *Probabilistic Reasoning in Intelligent Systems*. Morgan Kaufmann Publishers, San Mateo, California (1988).

9. T. Dean and M. Boddy, An analysis of time-dependent planning. *AAAI-88 — Proceedings of the 7th National Conference on Artificial Intelligence*, pp. 49–54, St. Paul, Minnesota (1988).

10. E. Horvitz, H. Suermondt and G. Cooper, Bounded conditioning: Flexible inference for decision under scarce resources. *UAI89 — Proceedings of the 1989 Workshop on Uncertainty in Artificial Intelligence*, pp. 182–193, Windsor, Canada (1989).

11. S. George, I. Zukerman and M. Niemann, An anytime algorithm for interpreting arguments. *PRICAI2004 — Proceedings of the 8th Pacific Rim International Conference on Artificial Intelligence*, pp. 311–321, Auckland, New Zealand (2004).

12. M. Niemann, S. George and I. Zukerman, Towards a probabilistic, multi-layered spoken language interpretation system. *Proceedings of the 4th IJCAI Workshop on Knowledge and Reasoning in Practical Dialogue Systems*, pp. 8–15, Edinburgh, Scotland (2005).

Elicitation of Expert Opinions for Constructing Belief Functions

Amel Ben Yaghlane[*], Thierry Denœux[†] and Khaled Mellouli[‡]

[*,‡]*LARODEC, Institut Supérieur de Gestion de Tunis*
41 rue de la liberté Cité Bouchoucha 2000 Le Bardo Tunisie
[*]amel.ben-yaghlane@hds.utc.fr

[*,†]*HeuDiaSyC, Université de Technologie de Compiègne, CNRS*
Centre de Recherches de Royallieu
B.P. 20529 F-60205 Compiègne Cedex France
[†]*Thierry.Denoeux@hds.utc.fr*

[‡]*Institut des Hautes Etudes Commerciales*
2016 Carthage Présidence Tunisie
[‡]*khaled.mellouli@ihec.rnu.tn*

Abstract

This paper presents a method for constructing belief functions from elicited expert opinions expressed in terms of qualitative preference relations. These preferences are transformed into constraints of an optimization problem whose resolution allows the generation of the least informative belief functions according to some uncertainty measures. Mono-objective and Multi-objective optimization techniques are used to optimize one or different uncertainty measures simultaneously.

1. Introduction

When dealing with real-world problems, uncertainty can rarely be avoided. In general, uncertainty emerges whenever information pertaining to the situation is incomplete, imprecise, contradictory or deficient in some other respect.[1]

In such situations and especially when data needed for the considered problem are not all available, a way to complement missing information is to use opinions elicitated from experts in the problem domain, i.e. individuals who have special skills in a subject area and are recognized as qualified to address the problem at hand. Expert opinions are statements, based on knowledge and experience, that experts provide in response to a given question.[2] Hence, the elicitation of expert opinions may be defined as the process of collecting and representing expert knowledge regarding the uncertainties of a problem.

For representing uncertainty, we can use appropriate frameworks such as probability theory, evidence theory or possibility theory. In this paper, we are interested in representing expert opinions in the evidence theory framework and precisely in the context of the Transferable Belief Model (TBM).[3] In the last twenty years, this theory, also known as the theory of belief functions (BFs) or Dempster-Shafer (DS) theory,[4] has attracted considerable interest as a rich and flexible framework for representing and reasoning with imperfect information. The concept of BFs subsumes those of probability and possibility measures, making the theory very general. The TBM is a recent variant of DS theory developed by Smets which is considered to be a coherent and axiomatically justified interpretation of BF theory.

For collecting expert opinions, we can proceed quantitatively or qualitatively. In a quantitative manner, we may ask the expert to provide his opinions as numbers according to the uncertainty theory that will be used to represent them. This approach supposes that the expert is familiar enough with the concepts of the theory framework to be able to correctly quantify his judgments. This is not always obvious. An alternative way is to elicit expert opinions qualitatively. This allows experts to express their opinions in a natural way, while deferring the use of numbers.

Recently, several authors have addressed the problem of eliciting qualitatively expert opinions and generating associated quantitative BFs.[5-7]

In this paper, we propose a new method for constructing BFs from elicited expert opinions. Our method consists in representing qualitatively expert opinions in terms of preference relations that will be transformed into constraints of an optimization problem. The resolution of this problem allows the generation of the least informative BFs according to some uncertainty measures (UMs). Mono-objective and Multiobjective optimization techniques are used and different optimization models are proposed and discussed.

The following section summarizes the background concepts related to the TBM, uncertainty measures, and the Least Commitment Principle (LCP). In Sec. 3, we summarize previous work addressing the problem considered in this paper. Section 4 presents the new method proposed for constructing BFs from qualitative expert opinions. The optimization models introduced in this section are illustrated by examples. Section 5 concludes the paper.

2. Background

2.1. *The transferable belief model*

The TBM is based on a two-level model: a credal level where beliefs are entertained, combined and updated, and a pignistic level where beliefs are converted to probabilities to make decisions.

2.1.1. *Credal level*

Let Ω denote a finite set called the frame of discernment. A basic belief assignment (bba) or mass function is a function $m : 2^{\Omega} \to [0, 1]$ verifying:

$$\sum_{A \subseteq \Omega} m(A) = 1. \tag{1}$$

$m(A)$ measures the amount of belief that is exactly committed to A. A bba m such that $m(\emptyset) = 0$ is said to be normal. Notice that this condition is relaxed in the TBM: the allocation of a positive mass to the empty set $(m(\emptyset) > 0)$ is interpreted as a consequence of the open-world assumption and can be viewed as the amount of belief allocated to none of the propositions of Ω. A bba verifying this condition is said to be subnormal, or unnormalized. The subsets A of Ω such that $m(A) > 0$ are called focal elements (FEs). Let $\mathcal{F}(m) \subseteq 2^{\Omega}$ denote the set of FEs of m.

The belief function induced by m is a function bel: $2^{\Omega} \to [0, 1]$, defined as:

$$\mathrm{bel}(A) = \sum_{\emptyset \neq B \subseteq A} m(B), \tag{2}$$

for all $A \subseteq \Omega$. bel(A) represents the amount of support given to A.

The plausibility function associated with a bba m is a function pl: $2^\Omega \to [0, 1]$ defined as:

$$\text{pl}(A) = \sum_{\emptyset \neq B \cap A} m(B). \qquad (3)$$

$\text{pl}(A)$ represents the total amount of potential specific support that could be given to A.

The commonality function associated with a bba m is a function q: $2^\Omega \to [0, 1]$ defined as:

$$\text{q}(A) = \sum_{B \supseteq A} m(B), \qquad (4)$$

where $A, B \subseteq \Omega$.

2.1.2. *Pignistic level*

At this level, beliefs are used to make decisions. When a decision must be made, the beliefs held at the credal level induce a probability measure at the pignistic level. This transformation is called the pignistic transformation. Let m be a bba defined on Ω, the probability function induced by m at the pignistic level, denoted by BetP and also defined on Ω is given by:

$$\text{BetP}(\omega) = \sum_{A: \omega \in A} \frac{m(A)}{|A|}, \qquad (5)$$

for all $\omega \in \Omega$ and where $|A|$ is the number of elements of Ω in A. This probability function can be used in order to make decisions using expected utility theory. Its justification is based on rationality requirements detailed by Smets and Kennes.[3]

2.2. *Uncertainty measures*

Several measures have been proposed to quantify the information content or the degree of uncertainty of a piece of information.[1] In this section we will focus on some of these measures proposed within the theory of evidence. For more details see Refs. 1, 8 and 9.

Klir[1] noticed that in BFs theory two types of uncertainty can be expressed: nonspecificity or imprecision on the one hand, and discord or strife on the other hand. Nonspecificity is connected with sizes (cardinalities) of FEs while discord expresses conflicts among the various FEs. Composite measures, referred to as global or total measures of uncertainty, have also been proposed. They attempt to capture both nonspecificity and conflict.

2.2.1. *Nonspecificity measures*

Dubois and Prade[1] proposed to measure the nonspecificity of a normal bba by a function N defined as:

$$N(m) = \sum_{A \in \mathcal{F}(m)} m(A) \log_2 |A|. \tag{6}$$

The bba m is all the more imprecise (least informative) that $N(m)$ is large. The minimum $(N(m) = 0)$ is obtained when m is a Bayesian BF (FEs are singletons) and the maximum $(N(m) = \log_2 |\Omega|)$ is reached when m is vacuous $(m(\Omega) = 1)$. The function N is a generalization of the Hartley function $(H(A) = \log_2 |A|$ where A is a finite set).

2.2.2. *Conflict measures*

Conflict measures are considered as the generalized counterparts of the Shannon's entropy $(- \sum_{\omega \in \Omega} p(\omega) \log_2 p(\omega)$ where p is a probability measure). Yager, Hohle, and Klir and Ramer[1,8,9] defined different conflict measures that may be expressed as follows:

$$Conflict(m) = - \sum_{A \in \mathcal{F}(m)} m(A) \log_2 f(A), \tag{7}$$

where f is, respectively, pl, bel or BetP. These conflict measures are called, respectively, Dissonance (E), Confusion (C) and Discord (D).

    Notice that different conflict measures that are not a generalization of the Shannon's entropy have been proposed by Smets[8] and George and Pal.[10]

2.2.3. *Composite measures*

Different global measures have been proposed by several authors.[1,8,9] Among them, the pignistic entropy (EP), and the total uncertainty (H) defined, respectively, as:

$$EP(m) = -\sum_{\omega \in \Omega} \mathrm{BetP}(\omega) \log_2 \mathrm{BetP}(\omega), \qquad (8)$$

$$H(m) = \sum_{A \in \mathcal{F}(m)} m(A) \log_2 \left(\frac{|A|}{m(A)} \right). \qquad (9)$$

The interesting feature of $H(m)$ is that it has a unique maximum.

2.3. *Least commitment principle*

The LCP,[11] also referred to as the principle of maximum uncertainty,[1] plays a central role in the TBM. It formalizes the idea that one should never presuppose more beliefs than justified. Given a family of BFs compatible with a set of constraints, depending on how their "information content" is compared, the LCP indicates that the most appropriate is the *least committed*. Dubois and Prade[11] have made three proposals to order BFs according to their informational content: pl-ordering, q-ordering, and s-ordering.[11] In this paper, however, we propose to apply the LCP using UMs for comparing the informational content of BFs. As pointed out by Klir [1], the degree of uncertainty of a piece of information is intimately connected to its information content. The LCP plays a role similar to the Maximum Entropy principle in Bayesian theory.

3. Previous Works

Methods for eliciting qualitatively expert opinions and generating associated quantitative BFs have been proposed by several authors.[5-7] In the sequel, some of these works are summarized.

3.1. *Wong and Lingras' method*

Wong and Lingras[5] proposed a method for generating BFs from qualitative preference relations. To express expert opinions, they defined two binary relations $\cdot >$ and $\sim$ defined on 2^Ω and called, respectively, the preference relation and the indifference relation. The idea behind this method is that given a pair of propositions A and B, an expert may express which of the propositions is more likely to be true using the preference relation $\cdot >$, or may judge the two propositions equally likely to be true using the indifference relation $\sim$ defined as:

$$A \sim B \Leftrightarrow (\neg(A \cdot > B), \neg(B \cdot > A)). \tag{10}$$

The objective of Wong and Lingras' method is to represent these preference relations by a BF *bel*, such that:

$$A \cdot > B \Leftrightarrow bel(A) > bel(B), \tag{11}$$

$$A \sim B \Leftrightarrow bel(A) = bel(B), \tag{12}$$

where $A, B \in 2^{\Omega}$.

Note that this method does not require that the expert supply the preference relations between all pairs of propositions in $2^{\Omega} \times 2^{\Omega}$. In fact, it allows the generation of BFs using *incomplete* qualitative preference relations. It has been shown that the existence of such BF depends on the structure of the preference relation $\cdot >$ that should satisfies the following axioms:

(1) *Asymmetry*: $A \cdot > B \Rightarrow \neg(B \cdot > A)$.
(2) *Negative Transitivity*: $\neg(A \cdot > B)$ and $\neg(B \cdot > C) \Rightarrow \neg(A \cdot > C)$.
(3) *Dominance*: For all $A, B \in 2^{\Omega}, A \supseteq B \Rightarrow A \cdot > B$ or $A \sim B$.
(4) *Partial monotonicity*: For all $A, B, C \in 2^{\Omega}$, if $A \supseteq B$ and $A \cap C \neq \emptyset$, then $A \cdot > B \Rightarrow (A \cup C) \cdot > (B \cup C)$.
(5) *Nontriviality*: $\Omega \cdot > \emptyset$.

Since the preference relation $\cdot >$ is asymmetric and negatively transitive, $\cdot >$ is a *weak order*.[12] It should be noted that Axioms 1 and 2 imply that $\cdot >$ is transitive. It has also been shown[13] that the binary relation $\sim$ defined by 10 is an *equivalence relation* on 2^{Ω}, i.e. it is reflexive, symmetric and transitive. Let $S = \cdot > \cup \sim$, defined on 2^{Ω}. S is a *complete preorder*[12] since $\cdot >$ is a weak order and $\sim$ is an equivalence relation.

To generate a BF from such preference relations, Wong and Lingras proceeded in two steps: determine the FEs, and compute the bba. The first step consists in considering that all the propositions that appear in the preference relations are potential FEs. Then, some of them are eliminated according to the following condition: if $A \sim B$ for some $B \subset A$, then A is not a FE. The second step enables the generation of a bba from the preference relations through the resolution of the system of equalities and inequalities defined by Eqs. (11)

and (12) using a perceptron algorithm. It should be noted that several BFs may be solutions of this system. However, the perceptron algorithm selects arbitrary only one of them.

It has been noted[6] that this method does not address the issue of inconsistency in the pairwise comparisons. In fact, the expert may provide inconsistent preference relations ($A\cdot > B$, $B\cdot > C$, and $C\cdot > A$).

3.2. *Bryson et al.' method*

Bryson, *et al.*[6] proposed a method called "Qualitative discrimination process" (QDP) for generating belief functions from qualitative preferences. The QDP is a multi-step process. First, it involves a qualitative scoring step in which the expert assign propositions first into a *Broad* category bucket, then to a corresponding *Intermediate* bucket, and finally to a corresponding *Narrow* category bucket. The qualitative scoring is done using a table where each *Broad* category is described by a linguistic quantifier in the sense of Parsons.[6,7] Hence, it allows the expert to progressively refine the qualitative distinctions in the strength of his beliefs in the propositions. In the second step, the qualitative scoring table from step 1 is used to identify and remove non-focal propositions by determining if the expert is indifferent in his strength of belief of any propositions and their subsets in the same or lower *Narrow* category bucket. It should be noted that this step is consistent with Wong and Lingras' approach presented in the previous section. Step 3 is called "imprecise pairwise comparisons" because the expert is required to provide numeric intervals to express his beliefs on the relative truthfulness of the propositions. In step 4, the consistency of the belief information provided by the expert is checked. Then, the belief function is generated in step 5 by providing a bba interval for each FE. Finally, in step 6, the expert examines the generated BF and stops the QDP if it is acceptable, otherwise the process is repeated.

It should be noted that the QDP, in spite of being proposed as a qualitative approach for generating BFs from qualitative information, involves numeric intervals in the elicitation process between all the pairs of propositions to provide BFs. Furthermore, Yaghlane *et al.*[14] showed that the QDP may violate the axiom of transitivity of the indifference relation.

4. Constructing Belief Functions from Qualitative Preferences

In this section we propose a new method for constructing BFs from qualitative expert opinions expressed in terms of preference relations. Our method allows the generation of *optimized* BFs in the sense of one or several UMs. We first present the main ideas behind our method, then we propose the optimization techniques and models used for deriving BFs along with illustrative examples. We also point out the main differences between our method and those presented in the previous section (see also Refs. 14 and 15).

4.1. *Main ideas*

Expressing expert opinions in terms of qualitative relations as proposed by Wong and Lingras[5] seems to be very attractive. In fact, it is natural and quite easy to make pairwise comparisons between propositions of a frame of discernment modeling a certain problem. Convinced of this motivation, we also propose to use the preference and indifference relations $(\cdot >, \sim)$ defined by Wong and Lingras to express expert judgments in our method. We assume that the preference relation satisfies axioms (1)–(5) introduced in Sec. 3.1.

Given such binary relations, we propose to convert them into constraints of an optimization problem whose resolution, according to some UMs, allows the generation of the *least informative* or the *most uncertain* BFs, as prescribed by the LCP recalled in Sec. 2.3.

Consequently, the criterion or objective function we optimize is an UM of the BF to be generated and the constraints are derived from the expert preferences, as defined in equations (11) and (12) as follows:

$$A \cdot > B \Leftrightarrow bel(A) - bel(B) \geq \varepsilon, \tag{13}$$

$$A \sim B \Leftrightarrow |bel(A) - bel(B)| \leq \varepsilon, \tag{14}$$

where $\varepsilon > 0$ is considered to be the smallest gap that the expert may discern between the degrees of belief in two propositions A and B. Note that ε is a constant specified by the expert before beginning the optimization process.

A crucial step for generating BFs before solving such optimization problem is to determine BF focal elements. We propose to consider that all the propositions existing in the preference and the indifference relations expressed by the expert are potential FEs. Furthermore, we assume that Ω should always be considered as a potential FE, which seems to us to be more coherent with BF theory.

Therefore, considering the problem of generating quantitative BFs from qualitative preference relations as an optimization problem, allows us to integrate the issue of the information content in the constructed BFs in our method. It should be noted that none of the methods presented in Sec. 3 address this issue. Furthermore, our method addresses the inconsistency of the preference relations provided by the expert. In fact, if these relations are consistent, then the optimization problem is feasible. Otherwise no solutions will be found. Thus, the expert may be guided to reformulate his preferences.

4.2. Mono-objective optimization model

According to the ideas presented above, we propose to formulate the problem by the following mono-objective optimization model. This model allows the construction of BFs that maximize one UM.

Model 1
$\text{Max}_m \, UM(m)$
s.t.
$bel(A) - bel(B) \geq \varepsilon \qquad \forall A \cdot > B$
$bel(A) - bel(B) \leq \varepsilon \qquad \forall A \sim B$
$bel(A) - bel(B) \geq -\varepsilon \qquad \forall A \sim B$
$\sum_{A \in \mathcal{F}(m)} m(A) = 1; \, m(A) \geq 0 \, \forall A \subseteq \Omega; \, m(\emptyset) = 0,$

where the first, second and third constraints are derived from Eqs. (13) and (14), representing the quantitative constraints corresponding to the qualitative preference relations.

Example 1. Let $\Omega = \{a, b\}$ be a frame of discernment and let $\{a\} \cdot > \{b\}$ be the preference relation given by an expert. To construct a BF from this preference relation, we first define the potential FEs of the BF, as proposed in Sec. 4.1. Hence, $\mathcal{F}(m_1) = \{\{a\}, \{b\}, \Omega\}$. Then, we formulate this problem according to Model 1. The UM we propose to optimize is the pignistic entropy (EP) given by Eq. (8). Assume that $\varepsilon = 0.01$.

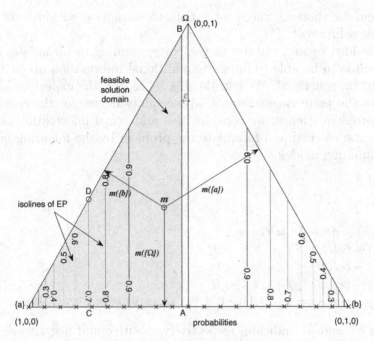

Fig. 1.   Graphical representation.

Notice that several BFs are solutions of this optimization problem. These BFs are plotted in Fig. 1 (segment AB). Each BF is represented as a point in an equilateral triangle using barycentric coordinates. The lower left corner, the lower right corner, and the upper corner correspond, respectively, to $\{a\}$, $\{b\}$, and Ω. The orthogonal distance to the lower side of the triangle is thus proportional to $m(\Omega)$, while the distances to the right-hand and the left-hand sides are, respectively, proportional to $m(\{a\})$ and $m(\{b\})$. The gray region corresponds to the domain of feasible solutions. Although this model allows the construction of BFs from qualitative preference relations, we consider that having only these preferences constitute too weak information to generate BFs.

4.3.   Multiobjective optimization models

As an alternative formulation of the BF generation problem, we propose to use multiobjective optimization techniques.[16] One of the well-known multiobjective methods is goal programming. This model allows to take into account simultaneously several objectives in a problem for choosing the most satisfactory solution within a set of feasible solutions.[17]

The idea behind the use of goal programming to formulate our problem is to be able to integrate additional information about the BFs to be generated. We can do this by asking the expert to give besides the preference relations, his certainty degree for the considered problem. Hence, we consider this additional information as a goal to be reached and formulate the problem by the following goal programming model:

Model 2

$\text{Min}_{m,\delta^+,\delta^-} \ (\delta^+ + \delta^-)$

s.t.

$UM(m) - \delta^+ + \delta^- = G$

$bel(A) - bel(B) \geq \varepsilon \qquad \forall A \cdot > B$

$bel(A) - bel(B) \leq \varepsilon \qquad \forall A \sim B$

$bel(A) - bel(B) \geq -\varepsilon \qquad \forall A \sim B$

$\sum_{A \in \mathcal{F}(m)} m(A) = 1; \ m(A) \geq 0 \ \forall A \subseteq \Omega; \ m(\emptyset) = 0; \ \delta^+, \delta^- \geq 0,$

where δ^+ and δ^- indicate, respectively, positive and negative deviations of the achievement level from aspirated level.[17] This model allows us to restrict the search space to the proximity of the goal G (level of aspiration) associated with the objective (UM).

Example 2. Let us consider the setting of Example 1. Suppose that the degree of certainty of the expert is equal to 70%. The problem is formulated according to Model 2.

Notice that, again we have several solutions, as the goal G may be attained in several points. Figure 1 (segment CD) shows that any bba such that $EP(m)$ are points of the isoline of EP equal to G are solutions of Model 2.

To overcome the problem encountered with the two previous models, we propose to integrate in the objective function of Model 2, the nonspecificity measure. So, the model is transformed as follows:

Model 3

$\text{Min}_{m,\delta^+,\delta^-} \ (\delta^+ + \delta^-) - N(m)$

s.t.

$UM(m) - \delta^+ + \delta^- = G$

$bel(A) - bel(B) \geq \varepsilon \qquad \forall A \cdot > B$

$bel(A) - bel(B) \leq \varepsilon \qquad \forall A \sim B$

$bel(A) - bel(B) \geq -\varepsilon \quad \forall A \sim B$

$\sum_{A \in \mathcal{F}(m)} m(A) = 1; \; m(A) \geq 0 \; \forall A \subseteq \Omega; \; m(\emptyset) = 0; \; \delta^+, \delta^- \geq 0.$

Solving this model allows us to generate a tradeoff solution. The BF constructed is the *least specific* and the *least informative* BF in the neighborhood of G. It is represented by the point D in Fig. 1. Notice that this point is the intersection of the isolines of $N(m)$ which are horizontal lines, and $EP(m) = 70\%$ (segment CD).

Detect inconsistencies

We also propose a different goal programming model allowing us to check the consistency of the preference relations provided by the expert. This is done by introducing slack variables in the constraints as follows:

Model 4

$\text{Min } (\delta^+ + \delta^-) + \sum_{A \cdot > B} \eta_{AB} + \sum_{C \sim D} \varphi_{CD} + \sum_{C \sim D} \varphi'_{CD} - N(m)$

s.t.

$UM(m) - \delta^+ + \delta^- = G$

$bel(A) - bel(B) + \eta_{AB} \geq \varepsilon \quad \forall A \cdot > B$

$bel(C) - bel(D) \leq \varepsilon + \varphi_{CD} \quad \forall C \sim D$

$bel(C) - bel(D) + \varphi'_{CD} \geq \varepsilon \quad \forall C \sim D$

$\sum_{A \in \mathcal{F}(m)} m(A) = 1; \; m(A) \geq 0 \; \forall A \subseteq \Omega; \; m(\emptyset) = 0; \; \delta^+, \delta^- \geq 0;$

$\eta_{AB} \geq 0 \; \forall A, B \text{ s.t. } A \cdot > B; \; \varphi_{CD} \geq 0, \varphi'_{CD} \geq 0 \; \forall C, D \text{ s.t. } C \sim D.$

Consequently, the inconsistencies are detected when the slack variables are positive.

5.   Conclusion

A new method for constructing BFs from elicited expert opinions expressed in terms of qualitative preference relations has been defined. It consists in transforming the preference relations provided by the expert into constraints of an optimization problem involving one or several uncertainty measures. Mono-objective and multi-objective optimization techniques were used to solve such constrained optimization problem. The BFs generated are the least informative ones. Further work is under way to extend our method to combine multi-expert qualitative opinions.

Acknowledgments

The authors would like to thank the CMCU (Le Comité Mixte franco-tunisien pour la Coopération Universitaire), which is supporting the first author in the preparation of her PhD thesis.

References

1. G. Klir and M. Wierman, *Uncertainty-Based Information: Elements of Generalized Information Theory*, Physica-Verlag, Heidelberg-New York (1998).
2. B. Ayyub, *Elicitation of Expert Opinions for Uncertainty and Risks*. CRC Press, Florida (2001).
3. P. Smets and R. Kennes, The transferable belief model artificial intelligence. *International Journal of Artificial Intelligence*, **66**, 191–234 (1994).
4. G. Shafer, *A Mathematical Theory of Evidence*. Princeton University Press (1976).
5. S. Wong and P. Lingras, Representation of qualitative user preference by quantitative belief functions. *IEEE Transactions on Knowledge and Data Engineering*, **6**, 72–78 (1994).
6. N. Bryson and A. Mobolurin, A process for generating quantitative belief functions. *European Journal of Operational Research*, **115**, 610–618 (1999).
7. S. Parsons, Some qualitative approaches to applying the dempster-shafer theory. *Information and Decision Technologies*, **19**, 321–337 (1994).
8. N. Pal, J. Bezdek and R. Hemasinha, Uncertainty measures for evidential reasoning I: A review. *International Journal of Approximate Reasoning*, **7**, 165–183 (1992).
9. N. Pal, J. Bezdek and R. Hemasinha, Uncertainty measures for evidential reasoning II: New measure of total uncertainty. *International Journal of Approximate Reasoning*, **8**, 1–16 (1993).
10. T. George and N. Pal, Quantification of conflict in dempster-shafer framework: A new approach. *European Journal of Operational Research*, **24**, 407–423 (1996).
11. D. Dubois, H. Prade and P. Smets, New semantics for quantitative possibility theory, *2nd International Symposium on Imprecise Probabilities and Their Applications*, Ithaca, New York (2001).
12. P. Vincke, Preferences and numbers. eds. M. P. A. Colorni and B. Roy, *A-MCD-A: Multiple Criteria Decision Aiding*, pp. 343–354 (2001).
13. S. Wong, Y. Yao, P. Bollmann and H. Burger, Axiomatization of qualitative belief structure. *IEEE Transactions on Systems, Man, and Cybernetics*, **21**, 726–734 (1991).
14. A. B. Yaghlane, T. Denoeux and K. Mellouli, Constructing belief functions from qualitative expert opinions, *Proceedings of IEEE ICTTA'06: International Conference on Information & Communication Technologies: From Theory to Applications*, Damascus, Syria (April 2006).
15. A. B. Yaghlane, T. Denoeux and K. Mellouli, Elicitation of expert opinions for constructing belief functions. *Proceedings of IPMU'2006: Information*

Processing and Management of Uncertainty in Knowledge-Based Systems, **I**, 403–411, Paris, France (July 2006).

16. Y. Collette and P. Siarry, *Multiobjective Optimization.* (Germany, 2003).
17. B. Aouni, F. B. Abdelaziz and J. Martel, Decision-maker's preferences modeling in the stochastic goal programming. *European Journal of Operational Research*, **162**, 624–633 (2003).

Managing Decomposed Belief Functions

Johan Schubert

Department of Decision Support Systems,
Division of Command and Control Systems,
Swedish Defence Research Agency,
SE-164 90 Stockholm, Sweden
schubert@foi.se

Abstract

In this paper we develop a method for clustering all types of belief functions, in particular non-consonant belief functions. Such clustering is done when the belief functions concern multiple events, and all belief functions are mixed up. Clustering is performed by decomposing all belief functions into simple support and inverse simple support functions that are clustered based on their pairwise generalized weights of conflict, constrained by weights of attraction assigned to keep track of all decompositions. The generalized conflict $c \in (-\infty, \infty)$ and generalized weight of conflict $J^- \in (-\infty, \infty)$ are derived in the combination of simple support and inverse simple support functions.

1. Introduction

In earlier papers[1,5,6] we developed methods within Dempster-Shafer theory[2,10,11] to manage simple support functions (SSFs) that concern different events where the SSFs were mixed up. This was the case when it was not known a priori to which event each SSF was related. The SSFs were clustered into subsets that should be handled independently. This was based on minimizing pairwise conflicts within each cluster where conflicts served as repellence, forcing conflicting SSFs into different clusters.

This method was extended[7,8] into also handling external information of an attracting nature, where attractions between SSFs suggested they belonged together.

In this paper we develop a method for managing non-consonant belief functions concerning different events where the belief functions are mixed up[a]. This is the general case where no a priori information is available regarding which event the belief functions refer to. This method is based on the extension introducing attractions and a decomposition method for belief functions.

In short, the method can be described as first decomposing all belief functions into a set of SSFs and inverse simple support functions (ISSFs).[12] Secondly, all SSFs and ISSFs are clustered, taking account of both the conflicts between every pair of SSFs and ISSFs as well as information regarding which SSFs and ISSFs were decomposed from the same belief function.

The number of clusters in the clustering process is an input parameter that needs to be known a priori. However, determination of number of clusters is outside the scope of this paper. It can be managed with other methods, e.g. the sequential estimation method proposed by Schubert and Sidenbladh.[9]

The methodology developed in this paper is intended to manage intelligence reports whose uncertainty is represented as belief functions with several alternative nonspecific propositions, i.e. nonsingleton focal elements. This can be the case when handling human intelligence (HUMINT) or for that matter sensor reports from some advanced type of sensor. Presumably, humans as information sources will also on average deliver fewer but more complex intelligence reports than simple sensor systems. Such complex intelligence or advanced sensor reports can be decomposed and managed with these methods.

For a recent overview of different alternatives to manage the combination of conflicting belief functions, see the article by Smets.[14]

We begin by describing the decomposition method for belief functions (Sec. 2). In Sec. 3 we study the characteristics of all types of combinations of SSFs and ISSFs and how generalized conflicts between SSFs and ISSFs are mapped onto weights. We demonstrate

---

[a] Consonant belief functions can be handled in the same way as SSFs without the method developed in this paper, by clustering the consonant belief functions without any decomposition using conflicts only.[1]

how to manage all SSFs and ISSFs using these weights together with logical constraints that keep track of the decomposition (Sec. 4). Finally, in Sec. 5, conclusions are drawn.

2.   Decomposition

Definition 1. An inverse simple support function on a frame of discernment Θ is a function $m : 2^\Theta \to (-\infty, \infty)$ characterized by a weight $w \in (1, \infty)$ and a focal element $A \subseteq \Theta$, such that, $m(\Theta) = w, m(A) = 1 - w$ and $m(X) = 0$ when $X \notin \{A, \Theta\}$.

Let us now recall the meaning of SSFs and ISSFs:[12] An SSF $m_1(A) \in [0, 1]$ represents a state of belief that "You have some reason to believe that the actual world is in A (and nothing more)". An ISSF $m_2(A) \in (-\infty, 0)$ on the other hand, represents a state of belief that "You have some reason *not* to believe that the actual world is in A". Equivalently, in the terminology of[12], A_1^w where $w \in [0, 1]$ and A_2^w where $w \in (1, \infty)$, respectively. Here, w is the mass assigned to Θ in m_1 and m_2. Note the notation used, where A_1^w and A_2^w represent the support for identical subsets A of the frame given by two different SSFs or ISSFs with index number 1 and 2. The lower index is the index number of the SSF or ISSF that lends support to this subset.

The ISSF A_2^w can be understood as some reason *not* to believe in A due to its absorbing belief. A simple example is one SSF $A_1^{3/4}$, i.e. $m_1(A) = 1/4$ and $m_1(\Theta) = 3/4$, and one ISSF $A_2^{4/3}$, i.e. $m_2(A) = -1/3$ and $m_2(\Theta) = 4/3$. Combining these two functions $A_1^{3/4} \oplus A_2^{4/3} = A_1^{3/4} \ominus A_2^{3/4} = A^1$ (i.e. $m_{1 \oplus 2}(\Theta) = 1$) yields a vacuous belief function. Here, $\text{Bel}_x \oplus A_1^y = \text{Bel}_x \ominus A_1^{1/y}$, where $\oplus$ is Dempster's rule, and $\ominus$ is the decombination operator absorbing belief.[12] Thus, the ISSF $A_2^{4/3}$ can be interpreted as $1/4$ reason *not* to believe in A, since it precisely eliminates the $1/4$ support in A expressed by $A_1^{3/4}$. It means that if you previously had some $1/4$ belief in A you should now delete it. That can not be achieved by supporting the complement of A. This makes $A_1^{3/4}$ and $A_2^{4/3}$ into two unique components called *confidence* and *diffidence*, respectively, by Smets.[12] Now, if you start out with only one ISSF $A^w, w > 1$, and nothing more, this is interpreted as if you have *no* reason to believe in A and that you need more than $1/w$ additional reason before you will start believing in it.

At precisely $1/w$ additional reason you will become completely igno-
rant $m(\Theta) = 1$. This is different than having some belief in A and
some in A^c whose combination can never be reduced to complete
ignorance.

All belief functions can be decomposed into a set of SSFs and
ISSFs using the method developed by Smets.[12] The decomposition
method is performed in two steps Eqs. (1) and (2). First, for any
non-dogmatic belief function Bel_0, i.e. where $m_0(\Theta) > 0$, calculate
the commonality number for all focal elements A by Eq. (1). We have

$$Q_0(A) = \sum_{B \supseteq A} m_0(B). \tag{1}$$

Secondly, calculate $m_i(C)$ for all decomposed SSFs and ISSFs, where
$C \subseteq \Theta$ including $C = \varnothing$, and i is the ith SFF or ISSF. There will
be one SSF or ISSF for each subset C of the frame unless $m_i(C)$
happens to be zero. In the general case we will have $|2^\Theta|$ SFFs and
ISSFs. We get for all $C \subseteq \Theta$ including $C = \varnothing$:

$$m_i(C) = 1 - \prod_{A \supseteq C} Q_0(A)^{(-1)^{|A|-|C|+1}}$$

$$m_i(\Theta) = 1 - m_i(C). \tag{2}$$

For dogmatic belief functions assign $m_0(\Theta) = \epsilon > 0$ and discount all
other focal elements proportionally.

For fast computation, take the logarithm of the product terms in
Eq. (2) and use the Fast Möbius Transform.[3]

3.   Combining Simple Support Functions and Inverse Simple Support Functions

When combining two decomposed parts from two different belief
function we face three different situations: the combination of two
SSFs, one SSF and one ISSF, or two ISSFs. These situations are
studied below.

3.1.   Two SSFs

In this situation we have two SSFs where $m_1(A) \in [0,1]$ and
$m_2(B) \in [0,1]$. When the two simple support functions are com-
bined we receive a conflict $c_{12} \in [0,1]$ whenever $A \cap B = \varnothing$. A weight

of conflict is calculated by

$$J_{ij}^- = -\log(1 - c_{ij}) \tag{3}$$

and $J_{ij}^- \in [0, \infty)$ but will be constrained to $J_{ij}^- \in [0, 5]$ in our neural clustering process[1,8] for computational reasons. This will ensure convergence. The weight J_{ij}^- will work as repellence between m_i and m_j in the clustering process. We use the notation J_{ij}^- for a weight of conflict to differentiate it from J_{ij}^+, a weight of attraction that will be introduced in Sec. 4.

This is the usual situation. It is proper that two propositions referring to different conflicting hypotheses are not combined when they are highly conflicting. Using the conflict we obtain such a graded measure (see Ref. 5).

3.2. *One SSF and one ISSF*

The situation when combining one SSF m_1 with one ISSF m_2 is interesting and unproblematic. Here, we have A_1^w where $w \in [0, 1]$ as usual, and B_2^w where $w \in (1, \infty)$, i.e. in terms of mass functions $m_2(B) \in (-\infty, 0)$.

Thus, when we combine a SSF A_1^w with an ISSF B_2^w we receive a generalized conflict $c_{12} \in (-\infty, 0]$ whenever $A \cap B = \varnothing$. Using Eq. (3) we get a generalized weight of conflict $J_{12}^- \in (-\infty, 0]$ which will serve as a weak attraction between m_1 and m_2. As before we will constrain the generalized weight of conflict for computational reasons, here to $J_{ij}^- \in [-5, 0]$.

The weak attraction is proper and rather immediate. If you believe in a proposition A ($A_1^w, 0 \leq w \leq 1$) and you receive further evidence indicating you have some reason *not* to believe in B ($B_1^w, w > 1$), $A \cap B = \varnothing$, that is an indirect weak support of A as some alternatives of the frame not supported by m_1 are disbelieved.

A simple example will demonstrate this. Suppose you have an SSF $A_1^{1/2}$ and an ISSF $B_2^{3/2}$ such that $A \cap B = \varnothing$. Combining them will result in a new type of object, henceforth called a *pseudo belief function*.[12]

In standard notation $A_1^{1/2}$ is

$$m_1(X) = \begin{cases} 1/2, X = A \\ 1/2, X = \Theta \end{cases}, \tag{4}$$

and $B_2^{3/2}$ is

$$m_2(X) = \begin{cases} -1/2, X = B \\ 3/2, X = \Theta \end{cases}. \tag{5}$$

A straightforward combination of m_1 and m_2 yields a pseudo belief function

$$m_{1\oplus 2}(X) = \begin{cases} 3/4, X = A \\ -1/4, X = B \\ 3/4, X = \Theta \\ -1/4, X = \varnothing \end{cases}, \tag{6}$$

without normalization and

$$m_{1\oplus 2}(X) = \begin{cases} 3/5, X = A \\ -1/5, X = B \\ 3/5, X = \Theta \end{cases} \tag{7}$$

after normalization. This is an increase of m_1's support for A from $1/2$ to $3/4$ and $3/5$, respectively, after combination with m_2. Note the interesting effect of normalization. Usually mass on the empty set is distributed proportionally among all focal elements by weighting up the support of the focal elements through normalization. When $m(\varnothing) < 0$, then instead the support for each focal element is weighted down to distribute support to the empty set so as to make $m(\varnothing) = 0$.

This support for the focal elements of $m_{1\oplus 2}$ is different from the one we would have if we instead had received support for B^c of $1/2$, $A \cap B = \varnothing$. Assume we have

$$m_3(X) = \begin{cases} 1/2, X = B^c \\ 1/2, X = \Theta \end{cases}, \tag{8}$$

then combining m_1 and m_3 yields

$$m_{1\oplus 3}(X) = \begin{cases} 1/2, X = A \\ 1/4, X = B^c \\ 1/4, X = \Theta \end{cases}, \tag{9}$$

i.e. support for A of $1/2$, or $3/4$ if $B^c \equiv A$.

When two conflicting belief functions are decomposed, each into several SSFs and ISSFs, the total conflict for all pairs of two SSFs originating from different belief functions will be higher than that between the two belief functions. This is because the SSFs have higher masses on their focal elements than the corresponding belief function, now that we also have ISSFs with negative mass.

A simple example will demonstrate the situation. Let us assume two belief functions m_a and m_b whose basic belief assignments are

$$m_a(X) = \begin{cases} 1/2, X = \{x, y\} \\ 3/10, X = \{x, z\} \\ 1/5, X = \Theta \end{cases}, \tag{10}$$

and

$$m_b(X) = \begin{cases} 1/2, X = \{x, y\} \\ 3/10, X = \{y, q\} \\ 1/5, X = \Theta \end{cases}. \tag{11}$$

The combination of m_a and m_b yields a conflict in the intersection of each function's second focal element $\{x, z\} \cap \{y, q\} = \varnothing$ of $m_{a \oplus b}(\varnothing) = 9/100$.

Using the decomposition algorithm, m_a can be decomposed into three functions. We get two SSFs $\{x, y\}_{a_1}^{2/7}$ and $\{x, z\}_{a_2}^{2/5}$, and one ISSF $\{x\}_{a_3}^{7/4}$, where $m_{a_1} \oplus m_{a_2} \oplus m_{a_3} = m_a$.

Similarly, m_b can be decomposed into two SSFs $\{x, y\}_{b_1}^{2/7}$ and $\{y, q\}_{b_2}^{2/5}$, and one ISSF $\{y\}_{b_3}^{7/4}$. Of the four pairs of SSFs (one from each decomposed belief function) only m_{a_2} and m_{b_2} are in conflict; $\{x, z\} \cap \{y, q\} = \varnothing$, see Fig. 1.

Combining m_{a_2} and m_{b_2} (or for that matter all four SSFs $m_{a_1}, m_{a_2}, m_{b_1}$ and m_{b_2}) yields a conflict $m_{a_2 \oplus b_2}(\varnothing) = 9/25$, i.e. four times as much conflict as in the combination $m_a \oplus m_b$. This will be

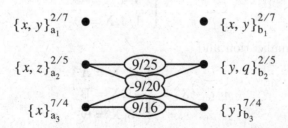

Fig. 1.   Generalized conflicts between SSFs and ISSFs originating from m_a and m_b.

compensated for by a negative generalized conflict when including the two ISSFs m_{a_3} and m_{b_3} in the picture. We observe (in Fig. 1) generalized conflicts between m_{a_2} and m_{b_3}, and between m_{a_3} and m_{b_2}, respectively, i.e. $m_{a_2 \oplus b_3}(\varnothing) = m_{a_3 \oplus b_2}(\varnothing) = -9/20$.

3.3. *Two ISSFs*

The situation when combining two inverse simple support functions (ISSFs) m_1 and m_2 is perhaps the most interesting case. Here, we have two ISSFs A_1^w and B_2^w where $w \in (1, \infty)$, i.e. in terms of mass functions $m_1(A) \in (-\infty, 0)$ and $m_2(B) \in (-\infty, 0)$.

Assuming $A \cap B = \varnothing$, we receive a generalized conflict $c_{12} \in (0, \infty)$ when combining m_1 and m_2 that will serve as a repellence. This is proper but perhaps not immediately intuitive. Let us again look at an example. Let us combine $A_1^{3/2}$ and $B_2^{3/2}$, i.e. $m_1(A) = m_2(B) = -1/2$ or in other terms you have some $(1/3)$ reason *not* to believe that the actual world is A and B, respectively, since $\text{Bel}_x \oplus A_1^{3/2} = \text{Bel}_x \ominus A_1^{2/3}$, where $\ominus$ is the decombination operator.[12] We have

$$m_1(X) = \begin{cases} -1/2, X = A \\ 3/2, X = \Theta \end{cases} \tag{12}$$

and

$$m_2(X) = \begin{cases} -1/2, X = B \\ 3/2, X = \Theta \end{cases}. \tag{13}$$

Combining m_1 and m_2 gives us

$$m_{1 \oplus 2}(X) = \begin{cases} -3/4, X = A \\ -3/4, X = B \\ 9/4, X = \Theta \\ 1/4, X = \varnothing \end{cases} \tag{14}$$

without normalization and

$$m_{1 \oplus 2}(X) = \begin{cases} -1, X = A \\ -1, X = B \\ 3, X = \Theta \end{cases} \tag{15}$$

after normalization.

The positive conflict $c_{12} = 1/4$ will serve to repel m_1 and m_2 which is proper since m_1 and m_2 contradict each other. This is observed in the decrease of belief in X = A and X = B where $m_{1 \oplus 2}(A) < m_1(A)$ and $m_{1 \oplus 2}(B) < m_2(B)$, i.e. the reason to doubt that X = A increases.

When the generalized conflict is greater than 1 we cannot use Eq. (3) to calculate a generalized weight of conflict as the logarithm is not defined for values less than 0. We call this *hyper conflicting*. We note, however, that the "1" in Eq. (3) is just a way to map a mass in the $[0, 1]$ interval to a weight in the $[0, \infty)$ interval. As there is nothing special about the "1" in Eq. (3) other than being an upper limit for a traditional conflict we can choose any other value greater than 1 to map hyper conflicts onto weights. One radical alternative would be to adjust the value to each application by choosing to map the interval $[0, \max\{c_{ij} | \forall i, j\}]$ to the interval $[0, \infty)$ in the case with two ISSFs or $(-\infty, \max\{c_{ij} | \forall i, j\}]$ to $(-\infty, \infty)$ in the general case. We could redefine Eq. (3) as

$$J_{ij}^- = -\log(\max\{c_{kl} | \forall k, l\} - c_{ij}). \qquad (16)$$

However, we will not do so. While this would work there are some drawbacks involved in choosing such a solution. First, if the maximum value is very high compared to most other generalized conflicts, most generalized weights of conflict would be very small which would lead to a slow convergence in the clustering process. Secondly, having a generalized conflict mapped into different generalized weights of conflict depending on the application is not attractive. Thirdly, we would like to maintain consistency with clustering only SSFs where two SSFs that flatly contradict each other for a conflict of 1 also receive a weight of conflict of ∞ and nothing less.

Thus, we will map any hyper conflicting generalized conflict greater than one to a weight of ∞. For generalized conflicts less than 0 there are of course no problems. From this we may redefine Eq. (3) as

$$J_{ij}^- = -\log(1 - \min\{1, c_{ij}\}), \qquad (17)$$

where $J_{ij}^- \in (-\infty, \infty)$. As before we will, however, for computational reasons restrict the generalized weight of conflict to $J_{ij}^- \in [-5, 5]$.

4.   Clustering SSFs and ISSFs

Having decomposed all belief functions into SSFs and ISSFs we may now cluster them using the Potts spin[15] neural clustering method extended with attractions.[8]

The Potts spin problem consists of minimizing an energy function

$$E = \frac{1}{2} \sum_{i,j=1}^{N} \sum_{a=1}^{K} (J_{ij}^{-} - J_{ij}^{+}) S_{ia} S_{ja} \qquad (18)$$

by changing the states of the spins S_{ia}'s, where $S_{ia} \in \{0, 1\}$ and $S_{ia} = 1$ means that m_i is in cluster a. N is the number of SSFs and ISSFs, K is the number of clusters and $J_{ij}^{+} \in [0, \infty)$ is a weight of attraction formally calculated as

$$J_{ij}^{+} = -\log(1 - p_{ij}), \qquad (19)$$

where p_{ij} is a basic belief assignment that m_i and m_j originate from the same belief function. This model serves as a clustering method if J_{ij}^{-} is used as a penalty factor when m_i and m_j are in the same cluster.

However, if m_i and m_j originate from the same belief function we assign $c_{ij} := 0$ and an attraction $p_{ij} := 1$, otherwise $p_{ij} := 0$. To assure smooth convergence of the neural network J_{ij}^{-} is restricted to $[-5, 5]$, while J_{ij}^{+} is restricted to $\{0, 5\}$ in this application.

Let us calculate the generalized weight of conflict between m_i and m_j, taking the restriction into account as

$$J_{ij}^{-} = \begin{cases} 0, & \exists x. m_i, m_j \in \mathrm{Bel}_x \\ -5, & \forall x. m_i, m_j \notin \mathrm{Bel}_x \\ & c_{ij} \leq 1 - e^5 \\ -\ln(1 - c_{ij}), & \forall x. m_i, m_j \notin \mathrm{Bel}_x, \\ & 1 - e^5 < c_{ij} < 1 - e^{-5} \\ 5, & \forall x. m_i, m_j \notin \mathrm{Bel}_x, \\ & c_{ij} \geq 1 - e^{-5} \end{cases} \qquad (20)$$

and assign weights of attraction as

$$J_{ij}^{+} = \begin{cases} 5, & \exists x. m_i, m_j \in \mathrm{Bel}_x \\ 0, & \forall x. m_i, m_j \notin \mathrm{Bel}_x \end{cases}, \qquad (21)$$

enforcing the constraint that SSFs and ISSFs originating from the same belief function end up in the same cluster.

The clustering of all SSFs and ISSFs is made using the Potts spin neural clustering method extended with attractions. The minimization of the energy function, Eq. (18), is carried out by simulated annealing. In simulated annealing temperature is an important parameter. The process starts at a high temperature where the S_{ia} change state more or less at random taking little account of the interactions (J_{ij}'s). The process continues by gradually lowering the temperature. As the temperature is lowered the random flipping of spins gradually comes to a halt and the spins gradually become more influenced by the interactions (J_{ij}'s) so that a minimum of the energy function is reached. This gives us the best partition of all evidence into the clusters with minimal overall conflict.

For computational reasons we use a mean field model in order to find the minimum of the energy function. Here, spins are deterministic with $V_{ia} = \langle S_{ia} \rangle \in [0, 1]$ where V_{ia} is the expectation value of S_{ia}. The Potts mean field equations are formulated[4] as

$$V_{ia} = \frac{e^{-H_{ia}[V]/T}}{\sum_{b=1}^{K} e^{-H_{ib}[V]/T}}, \tag{22}$$

where

$$H_{ia}[V] = \sum_{j=1}^{N} (J_{ij}^{-} - J_{ij}^{+}) V_{ja} - \gamma V_{ia}, \tag{23}$$

and T is a temperature variable that is initialized to the critical temperature T_c and then lowered step-by-step during the clustering process. We have $T_c = (1/K) \cdot \max(-\lambda_{\min}, \lambda_{\max})$, where $\lambda_{\min}$ and $\lambda_{\max}$ are the extreme eigenvalues of M, where $M_{ij} = J_{ij}^{-} - J_{ij}^{+} - \gamma \delta_{ij}$.

In order to minimize the energy function Eqs. (22) and (23) are iterated until a stationary equilibrium state has been reached for each temperature. Then, the temperature is lowered step-by-step by a constant factor until $\forall i, a. \; V_{ia} \in \{0, 1\}$ in the stationary equilibrium state.[8]

5. Conclusions

In this paper we have developed a methodology which makes it possible to cluster belief functions that are mixed up. The belief functions are first decomposed into simple support functions and inverse simple support functions. We then adopt a neural clustering algorithm intended for simple support functions to handle both SSFs and ISSFs while recording their decomposition for postclustering recomposing. With this method we may cluster any type of belief function, and in particular non-consonant belief functions.

Acknowledgment

I wish to express my sincere appreciation to the late Prof. Philippe Smets. The idea to decompose mixed up belief functions into SSFs and ISSFs in order to cluster all pieces was suggested by him.[13]

References

1. M. Bengtsson and J. Schubert, Dempster-Shafer clustering using Potts spin mean field theory. *Soft Computing*, **5**(3), 215–228 (2001).
2. A. P. Dempster, A generalization of Bayesian inference. *Journal of the Royal Statistical Society Series B*, **30**(2), 205–247 (1968).
3. R. Kennes, Computational aspects of the Möbius transformation of graphs. *IEEE Transactions on Systems, Man, and Cybernetics*, **22**(2), 201–223 (1992).
4. C. Peterson and B. Söderberg, A new method for mapping optimization problems onto neural networks. *International Journal of Neural Systems*, **1**(1), 3–22 (1989).
5. J. Schubert, On nonspecific evidence. *International Journal of Intelligent Systems*, **8**(6), 711–725 (1993).
6. J. Schubert, Specifying nonspecific evidence. *International Journal of Intelligent Systems*, **11**(8), 525–563 (1996).
7. J. Schubert, Clustering belief functions based on attracting and conflicting metalevel evidence. In *Intelligent Systems for Information Processing: From Representation to Applications*, B. Bouchon-Meunier, L. Foulloy, R.R. Yager (Eds.), pp. 349–360, Elsevier Science, Amsterdam.
8. J. Schubert, Clustering belief functions based on attracting and conflicting metalevel evidence using Potts spin mean field theory. *Information Fusion*, **5**(4), 309–318 (2004).
9. J. Schubert and H. Sidenbladh, Sequential clustering with particle filtering — estimating the number of clusters from data. *Proceedings of the Eighth International Conference on Information Fusion*, paper A4-3, pp. 1–8, Philadelphia, USA (July 2005).
10. G. Shafer, *A Mathematical Theory of Evidence*. Princeton University Press, Princeton, NJ (1976).
11. P. Smets and R. Kennes, The transferable belief model. *Artificial Intelligence*, **66**(2), 191–234 (1994).

12. P. Smets, The canonical decomposition of a weighted belief. *Proceedings of the 14th International Joint Conference on Artificial Intelligence*, **2**, pp. 1896–1901, Montréal, Canada (August 1995).
13. P. Smets, Personal communication (2000).
14. P. Smets, Analyzing the combination of conflicting belief functions. *Information Fusion*, **8**(4), 387–412 (2007).
15. F.Y. Wu, The Potts model. *Reviews of Modern Physics*, **54**(1), 235–268 (1982).

CLUSTERING, CLASSIFICATION AND SUMMARIZATION

Generalized Naive Bayesian Modeling

Ronald R. Yager

Machine Intelligence Institute
Iona College, New Rochelle,
NY 10801, USA
Yager@panix.com

Abstract

We provide an extension of the naive Bayesian classifier, introducing first a new class of OWA operators, called t-OWA operators, which are based on combining the OWA operators with t-norm's operators. We then show that the naive Bayesian classifier can be seen as a special case of this t-OWA operators. We then introduce an extended version of the naive Bayesian classifier which involves a weighted summation of products of the conditional probabilities. An algorithm is provided to obtain the weights associated with this extended naive Bayesian classifier.

1. The Naive Bayesian Classifier

The naive Bayesian classifier is a probabilistic approach to classifications.[1] Given an unclassified object $X = (x_1, \ldots, x_n)$ the classifier predicts that X belongs to the category having the highest posterior probability conditioned on X. Specifically, this classifies object X into category C_i if $P(C_i|X) > P(C_j|X)$ for all $j \neq i$. Using Bayes theorem, we can express

$$P(C_j|X) = \frac{P(X|C_j)P(C_j)}{P(X)}.$$

Since $P(X)$ is the same for all C_j the determination of the category is based on $P(X|C_j)P(C_j)$.

Training samples can be used to determine the required probabilities. The values $P(C_j)$ can be obtained as $P(C_j) = q_j/q$ where q is the number of training samples and q_j is the number of samples from category j. In some situations it is assumed that the classes are equally likely, here $P(C_j) = 1/m$.

The crucial part of the formulation of the Bayesian model is the determination of $P(X|C_j)$. The naive Bayesian model makes the simplifying assumption that $P(X|C_j) = \Pi_k P(x_k|C_j)$ which greatly reduces the complexity of determining the $P(X|C_j)$. This assumption, called **attribute conditional independence**, allows the independent determination of $P(x_k|C_j)$. If attribute A_k is discrete, then $P(x_k|C_j) = q_{jk}/q_j$ where q_j is the number of training samples in category j and q_{jk} is the number of these for which attribute A_k assumes the value x_k. If attribute A_k is continuous, it is typically assumed to be Gaussian. In this case $P(x_k|C_j) = \eta(\mu_{jk}, \sigma_{jk})$ Here, μ_{jk} is the mean value of attribute A_k for category j and σ_{jk} is the variance of attribute k for category j.

We now see the process of using the naive Bayesian classifier:

(i) **Construct the classifier 1**. Use the training data to determine the probabilities $P(C_j)$ and to determine the category conditional probabilities for discrete variable and the category means and variances for continuous variables.

(ii) **To classify new unclassified object** X (i) Calculate $P(X|C_j)P(C_j)$ for each C_j. (ii) Assign X to the category attaining the largest score.

Our goal here is to provide an extension of this basic Bayesian classifier.

2.   t-OWA Operators

We briefly review the OWA operators[2,3] and introduce a generalization of these operators called t-OWA operators. An OWA operator defined on the unit interval I and having dimension n, is a mapping $F : I^n \rightarrow I$ such that $F(a_1,\ldots,a_n) = \Sigma_j w_j b_j$ where b_j is the jth largest of the a_j and w_j are a collection of weights such that $w_j \in [0,1]$ and $\Sigma_j w_j = 1$.

Letting $id(j)$ be the index of the jth largest of a_i then $a_{id(j)} = b_j$ and we can express the OWA aggregation as $F(a_1,\ldots,a_n) =$

$\Sigma_j w_j a_{id(j)}$. We refer to the n vector W whose jth component is w_j OWA weighing vector. The OWA operator is parametrized by the weighing vector W. Different choices of W lead to different aggregation operators.

The attitudinal character[2] was introduced to characterize an OWA aggregation. The attitudinal character of an OWA aggregation with weighting vector W is defined as $A - C(W) = \Sigma_{j=1}^{n} \frac{n-i}{n-1} w_j$.

In Ref. 4, Yager suggested a new perspective on the OWA aggregation which lead to a generalization of the OWA operator. Consider the OWA aggregation using the weighting vector W, we denote this $F_W(a_1, \ldots, a_n)$. Let H_j be the collection of the j largest arguments, $H_j = \{a_{id(k)/k=1 \text{ to } j}\}$. Letting $\text{Min}[H_j]$ be the minimum of the elements in H_j we have $\text{Min}[H_j] = a_{id(j)}$. Using this we can express the OWA operators as

$$F_W(a_1, \ldots, a_n) = \sum_j w_j a_{id(j)} = \sum_j w_j \, \text{Min}[H_j]$$

Yager[4] pointed out that Min is an example of a t-norm operator,[5] a class of operators used to provide a generation of the logical "and" operator to the multivalued logic environment. We recall that the t-norm operators are associative, monotonic, symmetric operators on the unit interval that have one as an identity. With this in mind, he suggested a new general class of OWA operators in which Min is replaced by an arbitrary t-norm T. Following this suggestion we can have a general class of OWA aggregation operators $F_{W/T}(a_1, \ldots, a_n) = \Sigma_j w_j T(H_j)$ where $T(H_j) = \mathbf{T}_{i=1 \text{ to } j}(a_{id(i)})$. We refer to these as t-OWA operators.

We make some observations about this class of operators, Since for any t-norm $T(x_1, x_2, \ldots, x_k) \geq T(x_1, x_2, \ldots, x_k, x_{k+1})$ then $T(H_j) \geq T(H_j)$ when $j < i$. If we denote $d_j = T(H_j)$ then we can write $F_{W/T}(a_1, \ldots, a_n) = \Sigma_j w_j d_j$ where the d_j are ordered such that $d_j \geq d_k$ if $j < k$. We also observe that for any T we have $d_1 = T(H_1) = a_{id(1)} = \text{Max}_i[a_i]$ and $d_n = T(H_n) = T(a_1, \ldots, a_n)$.

3. An Extended Bayesian Classifier

In the preceding, we introduced the general class of t-OWA operators $F_{W/T}(a_1, \ldots, a_n) = \Sigma_j w_j T(H_j)$ where $H_j = \{a_{id(i)}/i = 1 \text{ to } j\}$ and where w_j are a set of OWA weights. A special case of the t-norm operator is the product, here $\Pi(a, b) = ab$. We now consider the class of t-OWA operators where $T = \Pi$. We call these Π-OWA operators. Here $F_{W/\Pi}(a_1, \ldots, a_n) = \Sigma_j w_j \Pi(H_j)$ where $\Pi(H_j)\Pi_{i=1 \text{ to } j}(a_{id(i)})$.

Some special, cases of this for notable examples of W are

$$F_{W^*/\Pi}(a_1, \ldots, a_n) = \text{Max}_i[a_i] \text{ when } w_1 = 1 \text{ and all other } w_j = 0,$$
$$F_{W/\Pi}(a_1, \ldots, a_n) = 1/n \Sigma_j \Pi(H_j) \text{ when } w_j = 1/n \text{ for all j}$$
$$F_{W_*/\Pi}(a_1, \ldots, a_n) = \Pi(Hn_j), \text{ the product of all the } a_i. \text{ Here}$$
$w_n = 1$ and all other $w_j = 0$.

We recall with the naive Bayesian classifier we are approximating the conditional probability of $P(X_k|C_i)$ by assuming independence and letting $P(X|C_i) = \prod_{k=1}^{n} P(X_k|C_i)$.

We observe that this formulation is a special case of our Π-OWA operator. In particular $P(X|C_i) = F_{W_*/\Pi}(P(x_1|C_i), \ldots, P(x_n|C_i)$. Thus $P(X|C_i)$ is a $\prod$-OWA aggregation with $W = W_*$ and arguments $P(X_k|C_i)$, the probability of x_k given category C_i.

This inspires us to consider a more general family of naive Bayesian classifiers, $P(X|C_i) = \Sigma_j w_j(\prod_{k=1}^{i} b_k)$. where b_k is the kth largest of the $P(x_1|C_i)$.

For simplicity, we shall denote $P(x_1|C_i)$ as P_1/i and let $id(k)$ be the index of the kth largest P_1/i then $b_k = p_{id(k)/i}$. With this notation $P(X|C_I) = \sum_{j=1}^{n} w_j(\prod_{k=1}^{i} P_{id(k)/i})$. Letting $d_j = (\prod_{k=1}^{i} P_{id(k)/i})$, the product of the jth largest probabilities under category C_i we have more succinctly $P(X|C_i) = \Sigma_j w_j d_j$. Here the w_j are a set of weights satisfying $w_j \in [0,1]$ and summing to one. Thus, with the introduction of this aggregation operator we have a more general formulation for the original naive Bayesian approach.

Let us look at this formulation for some special cases of the weights. In the case where $w_n = 1$ and $w_j = 0$ for $j \neq n$ we get the original naive Bayesian formula $P(X|C_i) = \prod_{k=1}^{n} P_{id(k)/i}$. At the other extreme is the case when $w_1 = 1$ and $w_j = 0$ for $j \neq 1$. In this case, $P(X|C_j) = P_{id(1)}|i$ here we are using the one feature value of the object X that most strongly supports it as being a member of the class C_i. This can be viewed as a kind of nearest neighbor type formulation. Another special case is when $w_j = \frac{1}{n}$. In the case $P(X|C_i) = 1/n \Sigma_j d_j$.

4. Algorithm for Learning Weights

The introduction of this more general classifier formulation provides us with additional degrees of freedom in the form of the associated weights. While the inclusion of the additional terms provides for a more general model it brings with it the problem of determining the values for these weights. We now turn to the question of obtaining the weights.

One natural approach to determining the OWA weights, the w_j, is to use the training set. In the pure naive Bayesian classifier, no attempt is made to assure that the training set itself will be correctly classified, the training set is just used to determine the probabilities. In the following, we suggest an approach to learning the weights based on teaching the model to appropriately classify the training data.

Consider our training set. Each element e in this set consists of a feature vector $X(e)$ of dimension n and a class, $C(e)$, to which it belongs. We shall denote $C(e) = i^*$ to indicate that this training object e is a member of class C_{i^*}. Furthermore, we will associate with each element e in the training set a collection of vectors, one corresponding to each of the categories. We denote these vectors as $D_1(e), \ldots, D_m(e)$. Each of these vectors is of dimension n, the number of features. The components of $D_i(e)$ are denoted $d_{ij}(e)$ where $d_{ij}(e) = \prod_{k=1}^{i} P_{id(k)/i}(e)$. Thus $d_{ij}(e)$ is the product of the j largest probabilities for the features of object e with respect to class i. Using these ideas, for the purpose of constructing an algorithm to learn the weights, we shall represent an object e in the training set as $e = (D_1(e), \ldots, D_m(e), C(e))$. For simplicity of notation we suppress the reference of the object and simply use $e = (D_1, \ldots, D_m, i^*)$.

Let $W = (W_1, \ldots, W_n)$ be our current estimate of weights. We now describe an algorithm for updating the w_i. Figure 1 provides the scheme of the updation.

The basic idea of this algorithm is as follows. We calculate the score $W^T D_i$ for each D_i. We recall that $W^T D_i = P(X(e)|C_i)$. If the largest of these $W^T D_i$ is D_{i^*} then we need make no change. If the largest is different from D_{i^*} we want to modify the weights so that we augment those weights that will improve the score of D_{i^*} with respect to the winner at the expense of those weights that contributed to its loss. Below is the formal implementation of this scheme.

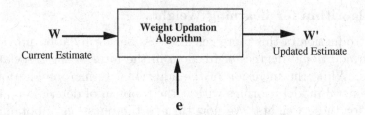

Fig. 1.   Weight updation scheme.

Updation Algorithm of W Based on Training Element e

(1) Input: Current training object $e = (D_1, \ldots, D_m, i^*)$
    Current weights estimate $w = (w_1, \ldots, w_n)$.
(2) For each D_i calculate the OWA aggregation: $f_i = W^T D_i = \sum_{j=1}^{n} w_j d_{ij}$.
(3) If (i) $f_{i^*} = \text{Max}_i[f_i]$ (No updation is necessary) STOP
    (ii) $f_{i^+} = \text{Max}_i[f_i]$ and if $i^+ \neq i^*$ then proceed to (4).
(4) For $j = 1$ to m calculate $\Delta_j = d_{i^* j} - di^+ j$.
(5) Sort the indexes $j = 1$ to n into three groups A, B and E
    $A = \{j/\Delta_j > 0\}, B = \{j/\Delta_j < 0\}. E = \{j/\Delta_j = 0\}.$
(6) Calculate $g = \alpha(f_{i^+} - f_{i^*})$ ($\alpha \in [0,1]$ is the learning rate).
(7) (a) For each $j \in A$ calculate: $\lambda_j = \dfrac{\delta_j}{\sum_{k \in A} \Delta_K}$.
    (b) For each $j \in B$ calculate: $\eta_j = \dfrac{\delta_j}{\sum_{k \in B} \Delta_k}$.
(8) (a) For each $j \in A$ calculate: $\gamma_j = w_j + \lambda_{jg}$
    (b) For each $j \in B$ calculate: $\gamma_j = w_j - \text{Min}(\eta_{jg}, w_j)$.
    (c) For each $j \in E$ set: $\gamma_j = w_j$
(9) Obtain the updated weights for $j = 1$ to n as.

$$w_j = \frac{\gamma_j}{\sum_{k=1}^{n} \gamma_k}.$$

5.   An Illustrative Example

The following example illustrates our updation algorithm

Example: We assume three categories: C_1, C_2 and C_3 and four features for each element V_1, V_2, V_3, V_4. The spaces of the feature values are: $V_1 \in \{h_1, h_2\}$, $V_2 \in \{s_1, s_2, s_3\}$, $V_3 \in \{t_1, t_2, t_3\}$ and $V_4 \in \{u_1, u_2\}$. The following table is the basic probability data for each feature value and each class.

DATA						
	V_1			V_2		
	h_1	h_2		s_1	s_2	s_3
C_1	0.6	0.4	C_1	0.5	0.3	0.2
C_2	0.7	0.3	C_2	0.2	0.6	0.2
C_3	0.5	0.5	C_3	0.2	0.4	0.4
	V_3				V_4	
	t_1	t_2	t_3		u_1	u_2
C_1	0.4	0.5	0.1	C_1	0.6	0.4
C_2	0.2	0.3	0.5	C_2	0.5	0.5
C_3	0.4	0.4	0.2	C_3	0.8	0.2

From this table we see that for feature V_2 an object in class C_1 has probability 0.3 of having the feature value s_2.

We consider the training object e which has feature values $X(e) = (h_1, s_2, t_3, u_1)$ and is in category C_3. For this object, we get for each C_j the probabilities associated with the corresponding feature value of e feature

$$\begin{bmatrix} 0.6 \\ 0.3 \\ 0.1 \\ 0.6 \end{bmatrix}_{C_1} \quad \begin{bmatrix} 0.7 \\ 0.6 \\ 0.5 \\ 0.5 \end{bmatrix}_{C_2} \quad \begin{bmatrix} 0.5 \\ 0.4 \\ 0.2 \\ 0.8 \end{bmatrix}_{C_3} .$$

Using this we get the vectors D_i

$$D_1 = \begin{bmatrix} 0.6 \\ 0.36 \\ 0.108 \\ 0.01 \end{bmatrix} \quad D_2 = \begin{bmatrix} 0.7 \\ 0.42 \\ 0.21 \\ 0.2 \end{bmatrix} \quad D_3 = \begin{bmatrix} 0.8 \\ 0.4 \\ 0.16 \\ 0.032 \end{bmatrix} .$$

For the initial value of the weights, the w_j, we assume we are at the start of the updation process and have started with the pure naive Bayesian classification. Hence, $w_4 = 1$ and $w_j = 0$ and $j = 1$ to 3.

Proceeding to step 2 in our algorithm we get

$$f_1 = 0.01, \quad f_2 = 0.1, \quad f_3 = 0.032.$$

Here then, $i^+ = 2$ while $i^* = 3$ and $i^+ = 2$. Proceeding to step four we must calculate $\Delta j = d_{3j} - d_{2j}$ for $j = 1$ to 4. This gives us

$$\Delta = \begin{bmatrix} 0.1 \\ -0.02 \\ -0.05 \\ -0.07 \end{bmatrix}. \quad \text{Using this we get in step 5 that}$$

$$A = \{1\}, \quad B = \{2, 3, 4\}, \quad E = \emptyset.$$

In step 6 we obtain, assuming our learning rate $\alpha = 0.1$, that $g = \alpha(f_2 - f_3)$ hence $g = 0.1(0.1 - 0.032) = 0.007$.

In step 7 we get for the elements in group A that $\lambda_1 = 1$ and for those in group B, we have $\eta_2 = 0.14$. $\eta_3 = 0.36$ and $\eta_4 = 0.5$. Using this in step 8 we get

$$\gamma_1 = 0 + 0.007 = 0.007, \quad \gamma_2 = 0 - 0 = 0, \quad \gamma_3 = 0 - 0 = 0$$
$$\gamma_4 = 1 - (0.5\,g\Lambda 1) = 1 - 0.0035 = 0.9965.$$

Finally in step 9 we get the updated weights

$$w_1 = \frac{0.007}{1.0035} = 0.007, \quad w_2 = 0. \quad w_3 = 0, \quad w_4 = \frac{0.9965}{1.0035} = 0.993.$$

The preceding algorithm is of course only part of a more global process in which we are trying to learn the weights to accommodate the appropriate classification of all elements in the training set. Here we must iteratively use all the elements in the training set until we are satisfied with the weights. As with all such gradient type learning processes[6] two issues must be addressed. The first issue is the initial values of the weights at the beginning of the process. Here one approach to this initialization issue is to assume we begin with a pure naive Bayesian classifier. This means we start with W such that $w_j = 0$ for $j \neq n$ and $w_n = 1$.

The second issue is when do we stop, for as in almost all these gradient type learning processes it is impossible to find weights that will allow the correct classification of all the training data. Here we can follow the usual the procedure used in these approaches.[6] We stop after we encounter a pass through all the training data which causes only some minimal change in the weights.

6. Retaining the Meanness

One feature of the ordinary OWA operator $F_W(a_1, \ldots, a_n) = \Sigma_j w_j a_{id(j)}$ is that it is a mean operator (averaging). It is monotonic, commutative and bounded, $\text{Min}_i[a_i] \leq F_W(a_1, \ldots, a_n) \leq \text{Max}_i[a_i]$. It is also idempotent $F_W(a_1, \ldots, a_n) = a$ if all $a_i = a$.

In the preceding we introduced the idea of the t-OWA operator $F_{W/T}(a_1, \ldots, a_n) = \Sigma_j w_j T(H_j)$ where $H_j = \{a_{id(k)}/k = 1 \text{to} j\}$, the j largest arguments, and T is an arbitrary t-norm. In this extension it is no longer the case that $F_{W/T}(a_1, \ldots, a_n)$ is a mean operator. In particular boundedness and idempotency are not generally guaranteed. In the following we suggest a slight modification of a special t-OWA operator that allows us to preserve the boundedness. In addition to providing a new interesting class of OWA operators this modification may help point the way of we can modify other t-OWA operators to preserve boundedness.

Consider the special t-OWA operator where T is Π, the product

$$F_{W/\Pi}(a_1, \ldots, a_n) = \sum_j w_j \Pi(H_j) \text{ where } \Pi(H_j) = \prod_{k=1}^{j} a_{id(k)}.$$

Consider the modification of this to

$$F_{W-\Pi}(a_1, \ldots, a_n) = \sum_j w_j (\Pi(H_j))^{1/j} = \sum_j w_j \left(\prod_{k=1}^{j} a_{id(k)} \right)^{1/j}.$$

Each product is raised to the reciprocal of the number of its terms

$$F_{W-\Pi}(a_1, \ldots, a_n) = w_1 b_1 + w_2 (b_1 b_2)^{1/2} + w_3 (b_1 b_2 b_3)^{1/3} + \cdots,$$

where we use $b_k = a_{id(k)}$ for notational simplicity.

We observe that if all $a_i = a$ then $(\prod_{k=1}^{i} a_{di(k)})^{1/j} = a$. This assures idempotency. More generally $a_{id(n)} \leq (\prod_{k=1}^{j} a_{id(k)})^{1/j} \leq a_{id(1)}$ and this guarantees boundedness.

7. Conclusion

We introduced a new class of operators by combining the OWA operators with t-norm's. We showed that the naive Bayesian classifier is a special case of this where the aggregate conditional feature probabilities using the product t-norm and $w_n = 1$. This inspired us to suggest an extended version of the naive Bayesian classifier which involves a weighted summation of products of probabilities. An algorithm was then suggested to obtain the weights associated with this extended naive Bayesian classifier.

References

1. R. O. Duda, P. E. Hart and D. G. Stork. Pattern Classification. Wiley Interscience: New York (2001).
2. R. R. Yager. On ordered weighted averaging aggregation operators in multicritcria decision making. *IEEE Transactions on Systems, Man and Cybernetics*, **18**, 183–190 (1988).
3. R. R. Yager and J. Kacprzyk. *The Ordered Weighted Averaging Operators: Theory and Applications*, Kluwer, Norwell, MA (1997).
4. R. R. Yager. Extending multicriteria decision making by mixing t-norms and OWA operators. *International Journal of Intelligent Systems*, **20**, 453–474 (2005).
5. E. P. Klement, R. Mesiar and E. Pap. *Traingular Norms*. Kluwer Academic Publishers, Dordrecht (2000).
6. J. M. Zaruda. *Introduction to Artificial Neural Systems*. West Publishing Co, St Paul, Mn (1992).

Gustafson-Kessel-like Clustering Algorithm Based on Typicality Degrees

Marie-Jeanne Lesot* and Rudolf Kruse†

FIN, Otto-von-Guericke Universität
Magdeburg, Germany
*lesot@iws.cs.uni-magdeburg.de
†kruse@iws.cs.uni-magdeburg.de

Abstract

Typicality degrees were defined in supervised learning as a tool to build characteristic representatives for data categories. In this paper, an extension of these typicality degrees to unsupervised learning is proposed to perform clustering. The proposed algorithm constitutes a Gustafson-Kessel variant and makes it possible to identify ellipsoidal clusters with robustness as regards outliers.

1. Introduction

Typicality degrees[1,2] were defined in a prototype building procedure, as a means to construct characteristic representatives of data categories: according to this approach, a point is typical of a category if it both resembles the other members of the category and differs from members of other categories. A prototype based on such typicality degrees then highlights the common features of the group members, but also their discriminative features compared to other categories. These properties make it a particularly appropriate data representative to characterize and summarize the category.

In this paper, typicality degrees are extended to the unsupervised learning framework, so as to perform clustering, i.e. to identify relevant subgroups in the data set. The underlying idea is that the characterization of a data subgroup using both common and discriminative features corresponds to the aim of identifying clusters that are both homogeneous and distinct one from another: compactness is directly related to the existence of common features and separability to existence of discriminative ones.

Therefore a typicality-based clustering algorithm, called TBC, is proposed. It relies on the Gustafson-Kessel principles,[3] which makes it possible to identify ellipsoidal clusters and not only spherical ones, through the automatic extraction of the cluster covariance matrices. TBC replaces the membership degrees used in the original Gustafson-Kessel algorithm by typicality degrees and relies on a method to compute the latter in the unsupervised learning framework.

Section 2 recalls the principles of some fuzzy clustering algorithms and justifies the typicality based approach. Section 3 recalls the typicality degree definition in the supervised learning framework and Section 4 extends it to the unsupervised case, describing the proposed clustering algorithm. Section 5 illustrates the results obtained on an artificial data set and Section 6 concludes the paper.

2.   Fuzzy Clustering

This section briefly discusses properties of some classic fuzzy clustering algorithms. We first recall the Gustafson-Kessel algorithm and then comment on some of its variants based on different definitions for the data weighting scheme. In the following, we denote $X = \{x_i, i = 1, \ldots, n\}$ the data set containing n data points, and c the number of clusters.

Gustafson-Kessel clustering algorithm

The Gustafson-Kessel algorithm[3] associates each cluster with both a point and a matrix, respectively representing the cluster center and its covariance. Whereas the original fuzzy c-means[4] make the implicit hypothesis that clusters are spherical, the Gustafson-Kessel algorithm is not subject to this constraint and can identify ellipsoidal clusters.

More precisely, denoting f_{ir} the influence of point i on cluster r (see below for some definitions for these coefficients), the cluster centers, w_r, $r = 1, \ldots, c$, and the covariance matrices, A_r, $r = 1, \ldots, c$, are computed as

$$w_r = \frac{\sum_{i=1}^{n} f_{ir}^m x_i}{\sum_{i=1}^{n} f_{ir}^m}, \quad A_r = \sqrt[p]{det(S_r)}S_r^{-1}, \qquad (1)$$

$$\text{with } S_r = \sum_{i=1}^{n} f_{ir}^m (x_i - w_r)(x_i - w_r)^T.$$

m is a user-defined parameter called fuzzifier. The cluster center is computed as a weighted mean of the data, the weights depending on the considered algorithm, as detailed in the following. The covariance matrix is defined as a fuzzy equivalent of classic covariance. Through Eq. (1), a size constraint is imposed on the covariance matrix whose determinant must be 1. As a consequence, the Gustafson-Kessel algorithm can identify ellipsoidal clusters having approximately the same size.

This cluster parameter updating step is alternated with the update of the weighting coefficients until a convergence criterion is met. In the following, we discuss some classic choices for these weights. They are based on comparison between data and cluster centers, and rely on the Mahalanobis distance defined as

$$d_{ir} = (x_i - w_r)^T A_r^{-1}(x_i - w_r). \qquad (2)$$

Fuzzy c-means (FCM) coefficient definition
In the FCM algorithm,[4] the f_{ir} coefficients, usually denoted u_{ir}, are defined as membership degrees

$$u_{ir} = \left(\sum_{s=1}^{c} \left(\frac{d_{ir}}{d_{is}} \right)^{\frac{2}{m-1}} \right)^{-1}, \qquad (3)$$

where m is a user-defined parameter. These membership degrees indicate the extent to which a point belongs to a cluster, or more precisely the extent to which it is shared between the clusters: the quantities involved in the definition are relative distances that compare the distance to a cluster center d_{ir} to the distance to other centers d_{is}.

Due to this relative definition, the influence of a point does not decrease with the absolute distance to the centers (see e.g. Ref. 5). This implies that FCM is sensitive to outliers: the latter are considered as equally shared between the clusters and can highly influence the cluster parameters.

Possibilistic c-means (PCM) coefficient definition

PCM[6] constitutes a more robust algorithm that relaxes the constraint causing the relative definition of membership degrees in FCM. The f_{ir} coefficients it is based on, usually denoted t_{ir}, measure the absolute resemblance between data points and cluster centers

$$t_{ir} = \left(1 + \left(\frac{d_{ir}^2}{\eta_r} \right)^{\frac{1}{m-1}} \right)^{-1}, \qquad (4)$$

where η_r is a parameter that evaluates the cluster diameter and can be defined *a priori* or defined from initializations.[7] Outliers, that are far away from all clusters are then associated with small weights for all clusters and thus do not influence their parameters.

PCM suffers from a coincident cluster problem (see e.g. Ref. 7): in some cases, clusters are confounded whereas natural subgroups in the data are overlooked. Moreover, it has been shown that the objective function global minimum is obtained when all clusters are coincident.[8] Satisfying results are obtained with PCM because the optimisation scheme leads to a local minimum and not the global minimum. This property is not satisfying from a theoretical point of view.

Possibilistic Fuzzy c-means

To solve the PCM coincident cluster problem, Pal *et al.*[5,9] propose to combine PCM and FCM: they argue that both possibilistic and membership coefficients are necessary to perform clustering, respectively to reduce the outlier influence and to assign data points to clusters. Therefore, they take into account both relative and absolute resemblance to cluster centers. In the PFCM[9] algorithm, the combination is performed through a weighted sum, in the form

$$f_{ir} = a u_{ir}^{m_1} + b t_{ir}^{m_2}, \qquad (5)$$

where u_{ir} are the membership degrees defined in Eq. (3) and t_{ir} the possibilistic coefficients defined in Eq. (4) with η_r replaced by η_r/b. a, b, m_1 and m_2 are user-defined parameters.

The algorithm proposed in this paper also takes into account two components to determine the importance of a data point: it considers the combination of other elements that provide more complementary information and considers a different aggregation scheme, as indicated in the following section, and thus leads to different results.

Other approaches

There exist many other approaches to solve the merging cluster problem or that of the outlier sensitivity: the cluster repulsion method[8] e.g. includes in the objective function an additional term to impose repulsion between clusters and prevent their merging. The noise clustering algorithm[10] has a rejecting process for outliers or noisy data, McLachlan and Peel[11] use t-student distributions to better model outliers thanks to heavier tailed distributions.

In this paper, we examine the solution provided when considering the typicality degree framework, whose principles appear relevant for clustering, as described in the next section.

3. Typicality Degrees

Principle

Typicality degrees were first introduced to build fuzzy prototypes to characterize categories:[1] a prototype is an element chosen to represent a data set and summarize it. The method proposed by Rifqi[1] to construct fuzzy prototypes uses the notion of typicality defined by Rosch:[12] according to this approach, the typicality of a point depends on its resemblance to other members of the category (internal resemblance) and its dissimilarity to members of other categories (external dissimilarity). The prototype derived from such typicality degrees then underlines both the common points of the category members and their discriminative features as opposed to other categories.

The prototype construction method can be decomposed into three steps: computation of (i) the internal resemblance and external dissimilarity, (ii) typicality degrees and (iii) the prototype itself.

Internal resemblance and external dissimilarity

For a given data point x belonging to a category C, its internal resemblance $R(x, C)$ and external dissimilarity $D(x, C)$ are respectively defined as its average resemblance to the other members of the category and its average dissimilarity to points belonging to other categories:

$$R(x, C) = avg(\rho(x, y), y \in C) \quad D(x, C) = avg(\delta(x, y), y \notin C). \quad (6)$$

ρ (resp. δ) is a resemblance (resp. dissimilarity) measure, i.e. a function that takes as input two data points and returns a value in the interval $[0, 1]$ that measures the similarity (resp. difference) between the two points.[13]

Typicality degree

The typicality degree of point x for category C is then defined as the aggregation of the internal resemblance and external dissimilarity, as

$$T(x, C) = \varphi(R(x, C), D(x, C)), \tag{7}$$

where φ denotes an aggregation operator such as the average mean or the symmetric sum for instance. It determines the semantics of the prototype, e.g. its being rather a central or discriminative element (see Ref. 2 for discussion).

Prototype computation

Lastly, the prototype is computed as the aggregation of the most typical data, as

$$p_C = \psi(\{x, T(x, C) > \tau\}), \tag{8}$$

where τ is a user-defined threshold and ψ an aggregation operator: for fuzzy data, it is a fuzzy aggregator that takes as input fuzzy sets and returns a fuzzy set.[1] For crisp data, it can be a weighted mean, or a more complex operator that aggregates crisp values into a fuzzy set, so as to build a prototype having an imprecise description.[2]

4. Typicality Degrees for Clustering

4.1. *Justification*

The previous definition of typicality degrees implies that, for specific choices of the aggregator φ, two kinds of points can have low typicality: (i) outliers, that are far away from the core points of the category and thus have low internal resemblance, (ii) points located in overlapping areas between categories, as they are not distinct enough from other categories and thus have low external dissimilarity.

Now these two cases correspond to points that should have low influence on cluster parameters in a clustering task: clusters are expected to be compact and separable, which means they should be robust against outliers and not concentrated in overlapping areas where the distinction between clusters may be difficult. Typicality degrees are directly related to these two desired properties, thus it seems justified to adapt them to unsupervised learning to perform clustering.

4.2. *Proposed algorithm architecture*

The underlying idea of the typicality-based clustering algorithm, TBC, is to use typicality degrees as weighting coefficients to determine the cluster parameters. TBC is not based on the optimisation of a cost function, but directly on update functions to be alternated: it consists in alternatively computing typicality degrees for each data point, and updating the cluster parameters according to Eq. (1) using these typicality degrees. These two steps are alternated until convergence of the center positions.

The cluster parameter update process is then the same as in the Gustafson-Kessel algorithm (cf. Eq. (1)). In the following, the typicality degree update process is described, as an adaptation of the previous methodology when the available information are cluster centers, covariance matrices and typicality degrees obtained from the previous step.

4.3. *Assignment computation*

Assignment computation role

The computation of typicality degrees relies on a crisp partition of the data: the typicality degree of a point is nonzero only for the category it belongs to; moreover assignment is necessary to compute internal resemblance and external dissimilarity.

In the clustering case, clusters must be questioned, thus typicality is computed with respect to all clusters and not only the one a point is assigned to.

Thus the assignment is only used for the computation of internal resemblance and external dissimilarity: for a given point x, and a cluster C, the internal resemblance is defined as the average resemblance between x and points assigned to C. When, in turn, typicality degrees are computed for points assigned to C, they are computed for all clusters and not only with respect to C. The assignment only remains a hypothesis.

Assignment definition

As seems natural, TBC assigns points to clusters according to their maximal typicality degree: a point is assigned to the cluster it is most typical of.

A special case is considered for points for which all typicality degrees are small (below 0.1 in our tests): such points, that correspond to outliers, should not be assigned to any cluster, as they are not typical of any. Indeed, if they were assigned to a cluster, they would arbitrarily lower the internal resemblance value for all points in the cluster: they would correspond to an especially low resemblance value and would thus distort the average value computation (see Eq. (6)), disturbing the whole process. It is to be noted that these points are still involved in the cluster parameter estimation, with low influence due to their low typicality degrees. Their special handling only concerns the assignment step.

4.4. *Comparison measure choice*

Having defined a crisp partition of the data according to previously obtained typicality degrees, internal resemblance and external dissimilarity can be computed for all points and all clusters. To that aim, comparison measures must be defined, they involve the available cluster covariance matrices.

Resemblance measure

Resemblance measures are normalized functions that indicate the extent to which two points are similar.[13] By analogy with PCM (see Eq. (4)), the Cauchy function is used

$$\rho(x, y) = \frac{1}{1 + \frac{d^2(x,y)}{\eta}}.$$

The resemblance measure is applied to points belonging to the same cluster, therefore it should be adapted to each cluster: one resemblance measure per cluster is considered by using for each cluster the distance associated to its covariance matrix (see Eq. (2)). The normalizing coefficient η is also determined locally: its square root corresponds to the distance from which the resemblance value is smaller than 0.5. Its value is chosen as being half the cluster diameter.

At the beginning of the process these cluster diameters are not known, as neither clusters nor their covariance matrices are known.

As inappropriate normalization factors could bias the resemblance measure and lead to inappropriate resemblance values, we apply the same process as for PCM: after convergence of the alternating scheme, the initial values for these parameters are updated and the alternating scheme is applied again with the new values.

Dissimilarity measure

Dissimilarity measures are normalized functions that indicate the extent to which two points are different one from another.[13] A measure also based on a Cauchy function is used

$$\delta(x,y) = 1 - \frac{1}{1 + \frac{d^2(x,y)}{\eta}}$$

with a different distance function d and another normalization coefficient η: the dissimilarity measure is used to compute external dissimilarities, i.e. it has an inter-cluster meaning. Therefore, d is here chosen to be the Euclidean distance, and η is defined so that the dissimilarity is 0.9 for couples whose distance equals half the data diameter.

4.5. *Aggregation operator choice*

Typicality degrees are then deduced from internal resemblance and external dissimilarity by aggregation. In the supervised case, many choices are possible, depending on the desired semantics of the prototype.[2]

In the clustering case, the aggregator should be a conjunctive operator, so that points are considered as typical only if they possess both high internal resemblance and external dissimilarity. Otherwise, outliers may have high typicality degrees for all clusters due to their high external dissimilarity (in the supervised case, this can be interesting if a discriminative prototype is desired). Therefore a t-norm is chosen (Lukasiewicz t-norm in the tests, $\varphi(a,b) = \max(a+b-1,0)$).

4.6. *Overall algorithm*

TBC can be summarized as follows. It only requires the user to set a single argument, the number of clusters. After an initialization step through a few iterations of FCM, initial values for the data partition and the cluster diameters are estimated and used for the computation of an initial typicality degree matrix. The iterating loop is then applied a first time. Cluster diameters are then updated, and the loop is applied a second time.

The iterating loop consists in alternatively computing typicality degrees and cluster parameters (centers and covariance matrices) until convergence of the center positions. Typicality degrees are computed as detailed above. The cluster parameter update equations are the same as in the Gustafson-Kessel algorithm (cf. Eq. (1)), using as influence coefficients the typicality degrees.

5. Numerical Experiments

5.1. *Considered setup*

Experiments were performed to compare the proposed TBC algorithm with the Gustafson-Kessel algorithm with fuzzy and possibilistic partitions (respectively denoted GKfcm and GKpcm) and the adaptation of the PFCM[9] algorithm to the detection of ellipsoidal clusters (denoted GKpfcm). The latter consists in applying the update equations for cluster parameters (Eq. (1)), using as weighting coefficients the coefficients as defined in Eq. (5).

The considered artificial dataset consists of two Gaussian distributed clusters and a small outlying group in the upper right corner (see Fig. 1). The lower and upper Gaussian clusters respectively have for centers and covariance matrices,

$$\begin{bmatrix} w_1 \\ w_2 \end{bmatrix} = \begin{bmatrix} 0 & 0 \\ 0 & 2.5 \end{bmatrix} \quad \Sigma_1 = \Sigma_2 = \begin{bmatrix} 4.47 & 0 \\ 0 & 0.22 \end{bmatrix}. \tag{9}$$

For the figures, points are assigned according to the maximal value of their coefficient (membership degree, possibilistic coefficient or typicality degree depending on the considered method). In the GKpfcm case, assignment is performed using the membership degrees. Each symbol depicts a different cluster, the plus sign represents the cluster centers, the ellipses represents the covariance matrix, the dashed one is the true covariance. In the case of GKpcm and TBC, stars represent points for which no assignment is relevant, i.e. points for which coefficients are smaller than 0.1 for both clusters.

Parameters were chosen as $c = 2$, $m = 2$ for GKfcm and GKpcm, $a = 1$, $b = 5$, $m = \eta = 1.5$ for GKpfcm, corresponding to values leading to the best results.

5.2. Obtained results

Figure 1(a) shows the results obtained using the fuzzy c-means to underline the necessity of extracting the covariance matrices to detect the expected subgroups: FCM cannot adapt to the elongated clusters and produces a counterintuitive result.

Figures 1(b–e) show the obtained partitions with the Gustafson-Kessel variants, Table 1 the values of the cluster parameters.

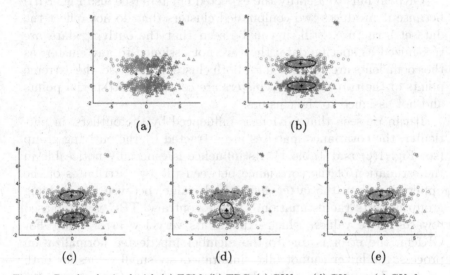

$$(a) \qquad (b)$$

$$(c) \qquad (d) \qquad (e)$$

Fig. 1.   Results obtained with (a) FCM, (b) TBC, (c) GKfcm, (d) GKpcm, (e) GKpfcm.

Table 1.   Cluster parameter error obtained by GKfcm, GKpcm, GKpfcm and TBC.

Algorithm	GKfcm	GKpcm	GKpfcm	TBC
Centers	$\begin{bmatrix} 0.15 & 0.03 \\ -0.08 & 2.56 \end{bmatrix}$	$\begin{bmatrix} 0.01 & 0.81 \\ 0.00 & 0.85 \end{bmatrix}$	$\begin{bmatrix} 0.06 & -0.01 \\ -0.11 & 2.54 \end{bmatrix}$	$\begin{bmatrix} 0.05 & -0.04 \\ -0.09 & 2.55 \end{bmatrix}$
Error	0.11	0.84	0.06	0.05
$\tilde{\Sigma}_1$	$\begin{bmatrix} 3.00 & 0.14 \\ 0.14 & 0.34 \end{bmatrix}$	$\begin{bmatrix} 1.07 & -0.10 \\ -0.10 & 0.94 \end{bmatrix}$	$\begin{bmatrix} 3.77 & 0.10 \\ 0.10 & 0.27 \end{bmatrix}$	$\begin{bmatrix} 4.45 & 0.04 \\ 0.04 & 0.23 \end{bmatrix}$
$\tilde{\Sigma}_2$	$\begin{bmatrix} 3.23 & 0.27 \\ 0.27 & 0.33 \end{bmatrix}$	$\begin{bmatrix} 1.08 & -0.10 \\ -0.10 & 0.94 \end{bmatrix}$	$\begin{bmatrix} 3.30 & 0.28 \\ 0.28 & 0.33 \end{bmatrix}$	$\begin{bmatrix} 5.19 & 0.13 \\ 0.13 & 0.20 \end{bmatrix}$
Cov. error	1.98	4.91	1.43	0.75

The indicated errors are computed as the square root sum of the square difference with the true parameters (w_i and Σ_i, $i = 1, \ldots, 2$, as indicated in Eq. (9)).

Table 1 shows that TBC is indeed competitive, it produces the best estimates for the cluster parameters. In particular, it leads to a clearly smaller error value for the covariance matrices: the estimates are very close to the true values for w_1 and Σ_1 and better for the second cluster than the ones provided by the other algorithms.

GKpcm fails to identify the expected clusters (see also Fig. 1(d)) because it produces two confounded clusters that do not reflect the dataset structure. Still, it can be seen that the outlying data are recognized as specific data: they are not assigned to any cluster, as the coefficients are very small for both clusters. Likewise, the extreme points of the two elongated clusters are considered as special points and not assigned to the clusters.

It can be seen that GKfcm is influenced by the outliers, in particular, the covariance matrices are attracted by the outlying group (see Fig. 1(c) and Table 1). Its influence is especially noticeable in the estimation of the covariance between the two attributes of the upper Gaussian: the latter gets a high value, because the outlying group distorts the estimation. On the contrary, TBC is not biased towards these values, which explains its very low error value. For GKfcm, the error is due to the membership degree normalization process: the latter cannot take simultaneously small values for both clusters. The outlying points have membership degrees around 0.6 and 0.4 for the upper and lower Gaussian cluster respectively.

In order to better interpret the results of the GKpfcm algorithm, Fig. 2(a) represents the weighting coefficient values for all data as a function of their position on the y-axis: it can be seen that, for GKpfcm, data in the outlying group have a weight comparable to the major part of the data in the bigger clusters. In TBC case (Fig. 2(b)), their typicality is significantly lower, which explains their lower influence.

As regards the comparison between GKpfcm and TBC, it is more-over to be noticed that the weighting coefficients can be exploited directly in the case of TBC, to characterize the data set further, whereas they do not have an intuitive interpretation in the case of GKpfcm. This is due to the fact that GKpfcm combines information about absolute and relative resemblance, whereas typicality degrees are based on more complementary components.

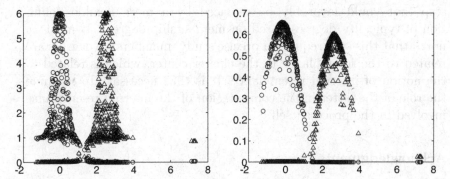

Fig. 2. Values of the weighting coefficients used in GKpfcm (Eq. (5)) and typicality degrees for all data points as a function of their position on the y-axis. Note that the scale differs from one graph to the other.

Figure 2 also shows that typicality degrees take into account both internal resemblance and external dissimilarity: the typicality degrees curves are not symmetric as compared to the mean of the clusters. Indeed, points located between the two clusters tend to have smaller typicality degrees, because they are not distinct enough from points belonging to other clusters. This is the reason why some points are not assigned (see Fig. 1(b)) in the area between the two Gaussian clusters. Globally unassigned points correspond to points having either a too low internal resemblance (outliers) or a too low external dissimilarity. This property can lead to a cluster repulsion effect: data located in such a way between clusters only apply a small attraction on the cluster centers that are thus not attracted towards overlapping areas. This effect is similar to that introduced by Timm and Kruse[8] in the objective function through an additional cluster repulsion term: in TBC, it follows from the definition of the weighting coefficient and it is not expressed in the cluster center definition.

6. Conclusion

This paper presented the extension of the typicality degree framework to unsupervised learning to perform clustering. First results indicate promising properties of the proposed algorithm and justify the proposed approach. A more comprehensive study of the algorithm is necessary to validate it.

One limitation of TBC comes from the fact that typicality degrees are based on a crisp partition of the data. This imposes an assignment step that could favorably be replaced by a more flexible definition of typicality degrees based on membership degrees. It must be noted that this step requires a precise study: membership degrees are related to the resemblance to the cluster center, which is related to the notion of internal resemblance. It is thus necessary to examine the role of the latter in the computation of the internal resemblance involved in the process itself.

Acknowledgments

This research was supported by a Lavoisier grant from the French Ministère des Affaires Etrangères.

References

1. M. Rifqi, Constructing prototypes from large databases. *Proc. of IPMU'96* (1996).
2. M.-J. Lesot, L. Mouillet and B. Bouchon-Meunier, Fuzzy prototypes based on typicality degrees. *8th Fuzzy Days*, pp. 125–138 (2004).
3. E. Gustafson and W. Kessel, Fuzzy clustering with a fuzzy covariance matrix. *Proc. of IEEE CDC* (1979).
4. J. Bezdek, *Fuzzy Mathematics in Pattern Classification*. PhD thesis, Applied Mathematical Center, Cornell University (1973).
5. N. Pal, K. Pal and J. Bezdek, A mixed c-means clustering model. *Fuzz-IEEE'97*, pp. 11–21 (1997).
6. R. Krishnapuram and J. Keller, A possibilistic approach to clustering. *IEEE Trans. on Fuzzy Systems*, **1**, 98–110 (1993).
7. F. Höppner, F. Klawonn, R. Kruse and T. Runkler, *Fuzzy Cluster Analysis, Methods for Classification, Data Analysis and Image Recognition*, Wiley (2000).
8. H. Timm and R. Kruse, A modification to improve possibilistic fuzzy cluster analysis. *Fuzz-IEEE'02*, pp. 1460–1465 (2002).
9. N. Pal, K. Pal, J. Keller and J. Bezdek, A new hybrid c-means clustering model. *Fuzz-IEEE'04*, pp. 179–184 (2004).
10. R. Davé, Characterization and detection of noise in clustering. *Pattern Recognition Letters*, **12**, 657–664 (1991).
11. G. McLachlan and D. Peel, Robust cluster analysis via mixtures of multivariate t-distributions. *Lecture Notes in Computer Science*, **1451**, 658–666 (1998).
12. E. Rosch, Principles of categorization. E. Rosch and B. Lloyd (eds). *Cognition and Categorization*, pp. 27–48. Lawrence Erlbaum Associates (1978).
13. B. Bouchon-Meunier, M. Rifqi and S. Bothorel, Towards general measures of comparison of objects. *Fuzzy Sets and Systems*, **84**(2), 143–153 (1996).

A Hierarchical Immune-Inspired Approach for Text Clustering

George B. Bezerra[*], Tiago V. Barra[†], Hamilton M. Ferreira[‡]
and Fernando J. Von Zuben[§]

Laboratory of Bioinformatics and Bio-Inspired Computing (LBiC)
Department of Computer Engineering and Industrial Automation,
University of Campinas, P.O. Box 6101,
13083-970 Campinas/SP, Brazil
[*] *bezerra@dca.fee.unicamp.br*
[†] *tbarra@dca.fee.unicamp.br*
[‡] *hmf@dca.fee.unicamp.br*
[§] *zonzuben@dca.fee.unicamp.br*

Abstract

Interpretation of human written language generally requires high levels of cognitive functionalities and computers are not originally designed for this task. However, with the fast development of information technology, computers are proving to be a fundamental tool for the analysis of electronic texts, given the huge quantity of information available. In this paper we present an effort in this direction and propose a novel hierarchical approach for text clustering. The method is based on an immune-inspired algorithm operating in conjunction with a semantic SOM adapted to deal with texts in the Portuguese language. The proposal is successfully applied to two clustering problems given rise to an automatic definition of the hierarchical configuration of clusters

1. Introduction

The necessity of automated ways of analyzing texts is more demanding than ever. The number of documents available in electronic format grows exponentially each year and manually analyzing or organizing such information is becoming prohibitive for most applications. As a consequence, there is a current race for developing text mining tools for effective clustering and classification of electronic text information.

The main difficulty associated with automated analysis of documents is that textual information is highly subjective. Although there are many efficient data mining tools available in the literature, converting such information into a rather objective and computer-interpretable codification is far from being straightforward. Invariably, this scenario imposes several limitations to the performance of the analytical tools. On the other hand, while this conversion step is still not entirely satisfactory, there must be an effort to enhance the clustering and classification techniques in order to handle the noisy and incomplete information generated by methods for semantic interpretation.

In this paper we propose a novel clustering algorithm for text mining applications, named ARIA (Adaptive Radius Immune Algorithm).[1] ARIA is an immune-inspired technique originally designed for density-based clustering. In order to enhance the applicability of ARIA to text mining, we adapted it to perform clustering in a hierarchical approach and used an alternative similarity metric, the correlation distance, rather than the usual Euclidean distance.

The main advantage of density-based clustering is that it is capable of detecting clusters with arbitrary shapes rather than predefined ones, making it possible to improve the identification of natural groups of documents. An automatic definition of the hierarchical configuration of clusters is highly desired in text mining, for it permits the identification of different levels of similarities between documents, and it organizes the texts into more complex structures and possibly more informative subcategories. In text clustering, few hierarchical methods have been proposed.[4,6,8,10] Furthermore, as we intend to indicate here the correlation distance metric, which is based on the Pearson correlation coefficient, makes more use of context information than the classic Euclidean distance.

The methodology adopted for transforming the documents into attribute vectors is the semantic SOM, proposed in Ref. 7. The semantic SOM is interesting for two main reasons. Firstly, rather than using one word per vector attribute, it performs dimensionality reduction by representing more than one word per neuron. Secondly, its vectorial representation can be used to handle some sort of context information of each word as an attempt to capture the subjective information present in the text. The semantic SOM, originally proposed to deal with English language, has been adapted to deal with texts in Portuguese. So, texts in both languages could be analyzed, depending on the choice of the version of the semantic SOM.

2. Semantic SOM

One of the challenges in text mining is how to properly represent each document in terms of a vector of attributes. In order to create this representation, it was used an implementation suggested in Ref. 12, which is based on Ref. 7. The proposal consists in representing a set of words (symbols) into a vector so that its meaning can be captured by a neural network, in which symbols semantically closer tends to be also closer in the topographic map.

However, representing words in a vector is a hard task, for identical words can have totally different meaning according to their context. The workaround of this issue is to tackle not only the symbol itself, but also the symbols on the neighborhood.

The methodology adopted consists of five steps:

(i) File pre-processing: The words repeated on most documents (common words) are removed as these words do not help to discriminate the subject of the documents. Besides, the suffixes of the words are also removed (stemming) to reduce the number of words;

(ii) Symbols (words) representation: The Random Projection suggested in Refs. 5 and 7 was adopted. According to this projection operator, all symbols remaining from the previous step are coded as a vector generated randomly. Identical words from different documents have the same symbol code. Random Projection performs dimensionality reduction;

(iii) Context vector definition: Two identical symbols can have different meaning when the context is taken into account. This issue is partially incorporated into the analysis if we adopt a context vector instead of the symbol code assigned to a word. As it is presented on Table 1, the context vector of the word w on position k denoted as $w(k)$, is composed of the symbol codes

Table 1. Example of context vectors assigned to two words $w(k)$.

$E(w(k-1))$	$E(w(k))$	$E(w(k+1))$
0.16 0.78 0.25	0.43 0.92 0.22	0.02 0.44 0.31
0.74 0.39 0.77	0.22 0.87 0.55	0.83 0.61 0.70

E of the words before $w(k-1)$ and after $w(k+1)$ the current word $w(k)$;

(iv) Semantic SOM: The context vectors are processed by a self-organizing map[7] and as the number of neurons is smaller than the number of context vectors a reduction in the number of dimensions is achieved. The number of context vectors mapped by each neuron should not vary too much;

(v) Static Signatures of the Document: All context vectors of all documents are presented to the semantic SOM generated in the previous step. Then a histogram of each document is generated according to the Best Matching Unit (BMU) and Second Best Match Unit (SBMU) activated by each context vector. Each attribute of the signature correspond to one neuron, and the value assigned to the attribute (i.e. the height of the attribute in the histogram) is determined according to Eq. (1), where $h_{m_i}^n$ corresponds to the height of attribute m_i in the static signature of document n;

$$h_{m_i}^n = \begin{cases} h_{m_i}^n + 1 & \text{if } m_i = BMU \\ h_{m_i}^n + 0.25 & \text{if } m_i = SBMU \end{cases}. \tag{1}$$

The result of the process above are documents converted into a set of vectors (Static Signatures), each of them is assigned to only one document. Since the documents are represented by a set of numerical vectors, it is now possible to analyze them by any numeric clustering technique that operates in $\Re^Q$, for arbitrary Q.

3. Adaptive Radius Immune Algorithm (ARIA)

Inspired by the natural immunological system, the algorithm interprets the input data set as antigens and generates antibodies (prototypes) capable of efficiently covering (recognizing) the antigenic space. ARIA puts a reduced number of antibodies, relative to the number of antigens, generating a network of prototypes that corresponds to a compact representation of the whole data, which possesses reduced levels of noise and redundancy.

Through mechanisms of clonal expansion and network suppression, together with the density information present in the data, ARIA tries to maximally preserve the relevant information from the original representation. It implements an adaptive mechanism, in which the suppression radius of the antibodies is inversely proportional to the local density, thus automatically putting more prototypes on the densest portions of the space. ARIA is a self-organizing and iterative procedure that can be summarized into three main steps[1]:

(i) Affinity maturation: the antigens (data points) are presented to the antibodies, which suffer hypermutation in order to better fit the antigens (antigen-antibody interactions);
(ii) Clonal expansion: those antibodies that are more stimulated are selected to be cloned, and the network grows;
(iii) Network suppression: the interaction between the antibodies is quantified and if one antibody recognizes another antibody, one of them is removed from the pool of cells (antibody-antibody interactions). This step is controlled by the parameter σ_s, which determines the size of the suppression radii of the antibodies;

After the final network is achieved, a tool from graph theory, the Minimum Spanning Tree (MST), is used. The MST is built on the resultant antibody network, and its inconsistent edges are then identified and removed, thus performing the network (data) separation into clusters. In this step, we use a discriminating criterion that takes into account the relative density of points in the space to determine the edges of the tree to be pruned.[11]

3.1. *The hierarchical approach*

Hierarchical clustering techniques provide a structured grouping of the input data set, going from all objects being members of the same cluster, to several clusters at the end of the process. The objects within these final clusters have high inter-document similarities. The hierarchical version of ARIA, denoted HARIA, operates similarly to another immune hierarchical approach described in Ref. 2. Firstly, a relative high value of σ_s is chosen to perform the first run (ARIA + MST). Generally, at this time the number of clusters is small. A decaying rate, previously set up, is applied to this parameter and for each cluster found a new instance of the algorithm is performed on the portion of data attributed to it. The following steps explain the hierarchical approach performed by HARIA:

(i) Parameter definition: define an initial value for σ_s (suppression threshold), and set up a decaying rate $0 < \alpha < 1$ for this parameter;

(ii) HARIA learning: run the ARIA learning algorithm with the given parameter;

(iii) Tree branching: each cluster detected by the MST constructed from the resultant network generates an offspring network in the next level of the tree, i.e. a new branch of the tree. The clusters already detected will indicate the portion of the data set to be attributed to each newly generated branch;

(iv) Parameters updating: reduce σ_s by geometrically decreasing it by the factor α;

(v) Offspring network evaluation: run each offspring network with the corresponding attributed portion of the data set;

(vi) Tree convergence: if the offspring network does not detect a novel cluster, the process is halted for that branch of the tree, and the tree expansion is completed at that branch. Each branch of the tree represents a cluster and a sequence of branches represents the hierarchy inherent to the data mapped into their corresponding clusters. Else, while a given offspring network (branch) of the tree is still capable of identifying more than one cluster, return to Step (iv) and the process continues until no new cluster can be identified in any active branch;

4. Similarity Metric

The correlation distance is based on the Pearson Correlation Coefficient, in which similarity of documents is measured in parallel; that is, it accounts for the shape of the static signature (histogram) of the texts, rather than the absolute values of each attribute. In this way, the pattern of variation in the use of words is taken into account, and the Euclidean measure ignores this feature. Let T_i be the value of attribute i of text T. For two texts A and B, the similarity measure S in a total of N attributes can be computed as follows:

$$S(A, B) = \frac{1}{N} \sum_{i=1}^{N} \left(\frac{A_i - A_{offset}}{\phi_A} \right) \left(\frac{B_i - B_{offset}}{\phi_B} \right).$$

$$\phi_T = \sqrt{\sum_{i=1}^{N} \frac{(T_i - T_{offset})^2}{N}}, \; T = A \; or \; B \tag{2}$$

The value T_{offset} was chosen zero in all cases. The value of S will range from -1 to 1. In order to work with distances, the following equation was used for the calculation of the distance D between two texts:

$$D(A, B) = 1 - S(A, B). \tag{3}$$

5. Computational Experiments

5.1. *Sport and cookery*

In the first computational experiment we analyzed 52 documents in Portuguese, previously labeled into two categories: one concerning 25 stock car news and the other 27 cookery recipes. This same data set was used in Ref. 12. The experiment is considered relatively simple, given that the two categories are too specific and also comprise of very dissimilar topics. The number of remaining symbols after stemming and removal of common words is 1326, of a total of 12 187 words originally present in the documents. A 20×20 semantic SOM was used, giving an average of 3.3 words per neuron and also document signatures with 400 attributes (one attribute for each neuron).

The hierarchical ARIA was applied to this data set and the dendrogram obtained is depicted in Fig. 1 (left). Note that the algorithm was able to correctly detect two largely distinct classes within the texts (clusters 1 and 2), corresponding to exactly the original predefined categories. Also, it detected several subcategories within each class. Take for instance, cluster 5. This cluster contains three cookery texts, all of them are recipes of cakes. The same can be observed in

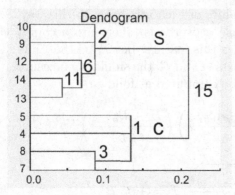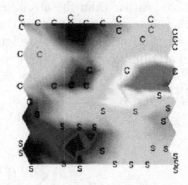

Fig. 1.   Left, Dendrogram obtained by ARIA. S and C represent the clusters for Sport and Cookery, respectively. Right, U-Matrix of the semantic SOM. Dark areas represent large distances, whereas light regions correspond to small distances among neighboring neurons.

cluster 10, which contains two stock car texts; both of them refer to the same pilot, Beto Giorgi, running at the speedway of Brasilia.

We compared these results with the performance of a standard self-organizing map. Figure 1 (right) shows the resulting U-matrix of a 20×20 SOM applied to the clustering of the documents. Note that the SOM was capable of mapping the two categories on distinct regions of the space, but the U-matrix[9] does not indicate a clear separation of the texts into two clusters. Also, as the ordinary SOM is not hierarchical, it is not capable of evidencing subcategories within the documents.

5.2.   *Brazilian newspaper*

The second experiment comprises the analysis of 60 documents divided into three main categories of 20 texts, and each of these contains two subcategories of 10 texts. The documents were taken from the Brazilian newspaper *Folha de S. Paulo* and the categories chosen correspond to sections of the newspaper: Money, Sport and Informatics. Sports news are labeled S and contains two subclasses, Car Racing (S_1) and Soccer (S_2). Money reports are labeled M and its subcategories are Oil (M_1) and International Commerce (M_2). The last class, Informatics, is labeled I and is divided into the subcategories Internet (I_1) and Technology (I_2).

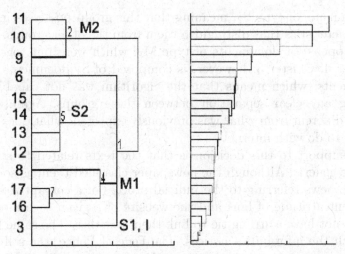

Fig. 2.   Dendrogram obtained by ARIA (left) and single-linkage hierarchical clustering algorithm.

A 30×30 semantic SOM was used for a total of 7456 remaining words after the preprocessing step, an average of 8.3 words per neuron. The original number of words is 14861. The results obtained by ARIA are depicted in Fig. 2 (left).

Notice that the algorithm firstly separated the dataset into two main clusters: cluster 2, which contains the texts of type M_2 and cluster 1, which contains all other texts. This means that the M_2 documents are considerably different from all other documents in the dataset, and were included in a separate branch of the tree. Note that, this hierarchical relationship is different from what should be expected, as M_1 and M_2 were originally taken to be subclasses of the same cluster. However, inspecting the documents it is possible to note that the nature of the M_2 texts is indeed very different from all other texts in the corpus. We observed that the type of information contained in M_2 is strongly statistic, i.e. the documents are full of numerical information regarding import and export taxes, prices for international and national products and economic rates in general. Although this outcome differs from our initial expectation, it seems to be very consistent with the observed features of the data.

Inside cluster 1, the dendrogram indicates the presence of four subcategories. Cluster 6 seems to be an outlier, composed of only four texts, two of type S and two of type I. Cluster 5 corresponds to the documents of type S_2, meaning that this group possesses inherent characteristics that distinguish them from the other groups. The same happens for documents of type M_1, which were put together in cluster 4. Cluster 3, however, is composed of S_1 documents and I documents, which means that the algorithm was not capable of detecting any clear separation between these groups. Again, this result is different from what was previously expected: what does soccer have to do with internet?

The support to this decision is that the texts related to soccer are quite generic. Although the newspaper classified them as soccer, there are news referring to the judicial process of a corrupt referee, the violent attitude of fans and the website of a given soccer team. They do not have a strong tie to link them together. The same happens with the informatics notices. The Federal Police, the sell of a telephone company and the hurricane Katrina, are some of the topics treated in these news. ARIA could not assign these documents to any other cluster, and, as a result, put them together into a larger miscellaneous cluster of generic themes.

To evaluate the consistency of our results, we also applied the K-means clustering to this problem. K-means was run for 2, 3, 5 and 10 as values of K, but the results were very poor for all cases. In all tests, there was one cluster with more than 80% of the texts, while the remaining of the texts were divided into very small clusters. The outcome suggests that the problem analyzed is far from being simple, otherwise a standard technique such as K-means would have obtained a considerable better performance.

Additionally to K-means, the well-known single-linkage hierarchical clustering algorithm[3] was applied to the same data set. The results obtained are shown in Fig. 2 (right).

The number in the x-axis represent the distance between clusters and the numbers in the y-axis denote the leaf clusters. Each leaf cluster is formed by the joining of two documents. Observe in the dendogram that there is no inherent cluster in the results produced by the techinique. Single-linkage was incapable of finding classes in the dataset, although these classes do exist, as HARIA was able to detect them. The problem with this method is that it is not able to identify clusters with arbitrary shape, which seems to be the case for the classes in the Brazilian Newspaper corpus.

6.   Discussion

In this paper we proposed a new method for text clustering based on an immune-inspired algorithm named ARIA. The proposal relies on three main features: (i) density-based clustering; (ii) hierarchical clustering; (iii) correlation distance.

We performed experiments with two datasets, concerning pre-labeled documents in the Portuguese language.

The results of the experiments evidenced several interesting characteristics of the functioning of the proposed method, as well as of the intrinsic structure of the documents analyzed. For the second experiment performed, the results presented differ from the original classification, but the clusters obtained do extract meaningful classes from the data. This means that there might be more then one possible consistent clustering of a single dataset, and that each one will be more or less adequate to a given purpose. The methodology proposed here can be regarded as one of such alternative clustering configurations, which although different from that presented in the newspaper, was indeed useful in revealing previously unknown characteristics of the texts.

Acknowledgments

The authors would like to thank to Universo Online S.A. (UOL) and CNPq for their financial support.

References

1. G. B. Bezerra, T. V. Barra, L. N. de Castro and F. J. Von Zuben, Adaptive radius immune algorithm for data clustering. C. Jacob, M. L. Pilat, P. J. Bentley, J. Timmis, (eds.). *Artificial Immune Systems, Lecture Notes in Computer Science*, **3627**, 290–303, Springer (August 2005).
2. G. B. Bezerra, L. N. de Castro and F. J. Von Zuben, A hierarchical immune network applied to gene expression data. G. Nicosia, V. Cutello, P. J. Bentley, J. Timmis, (eds.), *Artificial Immune Systems, Lecture Notes in Computer Science*, **3239**, 14–27, Springer (September 2004).
3. B. Everitt, S. Landau and M. Leese, *Cluster Analysis*. Fourth Edition, Oxford University Press (2001).
4. E. Gaussier, C. Goutte, K. Popat and F. Chen, A hierarchical model for clustering and categorizing documents. *Proceedings of ECIR-02, 24th European Colloquium on Information Retrieval Research*, Springer, **2291**, 229–247 (March 2002).

5. S. Kaski, Dimensionality reduction by random mapping: Fast similarity computation for clustering. *Proc. of the Int. Joint Conf. on Neural Networks* (IJCNN"98), **1**, 413–418 (1998).
6. E. M. Rasmussen, Clustering algorithms. *Information Retrieval: Data Structures & Algorithms*, pp. 419–442 (1992).
7. H. Ritter and T. Kohonen, Self-organizing semantic maps. *Biol. Cybernet.*, **61** 241–254 (1989).
8. A. Sun and E. P. Lim, Hierarchical text classification and evaluation. *International Conference on Data Mining (ICDM)*, pp. 521–528 (2001).
9. A. Ultsch, Knowledge acquisition with self-organizing neural networks. I. Aleksander and J. Taylor (eds.). *Artificial Neural Networks 2*, Vol. I, North-Holland, Amsterdam, Netherlands, pp. 735–738 (1992).
10. P. Willett, Recent trends in hierarchic document clustering: a critical review. *Information Processing and Management*, **24**(5), 577–597 (1988).
11. C. T. Zahn, Graph-theoretical methods for detecting and describing gestalt clusters. *IEEE Trans. Computer*, **20**(1), 68–86 (January 1971).
12. M. H. Zuchini, *Application of self-organizing maps in data mining and information retrieval* (in Portuguese). Master Thesis, School of Electrical and Computer Engineering, State University of Campinas (Unicamp) (2003).

An Incremental Hierarchical Fuzzy Clustering for Category-Based News Filtering

Gloria Bordogna[*], Marco Pagani[†] and G. Pasi[‡]

[*,†]CNR-IDPA, via Pasubio 5, Dalmine 24044 (BG), Italy
[*]gloria.bordogn@idpa.cnr.it
[†]marco.pagani@idpa.cnr.it

[‡]DISCo, Università di Milano Bicocca
via degli Arcimboldi 8, 20128 Milano, Italy
pasi@disco.unimib.itt

Abstract

An incremental and hierarchical fuzzy clustering algorithm based on the extension of the Fuzzy C-Means is proposed to support category based news filtering so as to offer users both an overview of the topics reported by media at different levels of granularity and the possibility of specifying flexible cut-offs of news within each cluster. The new fuzzy algorithm automatically determines the proper number of clusters to generate. Some experimental results are also reported.

1. Introduction

News filtering is an automatic process that has the objective of both monitoring news streams supplied by news agencies, and feeding users with relevant news to their interests. This process is performed based on the comparison of user's preferences represented in a user's profile with the available information about news contents, i.e. the news' representation based generally on meta-data and keywords.[2,3,15]

To improve both efficiency and effectiveness, some current filtering approaches apply clustering techniques to group incoming documents into categories dealing with homogeneous topics.[3,9,18]

Category-based filtering[17] can be seen as an extension to existing filtering strategies, when considering that user preferences are expressed not just for single items, but also for categories of similar items. The main characteristic of this approach is that filtering of incoming information is based on category ratings instead of single item rating.

When clustering techniques are applied in news filtering several crucial aspects have to be considered. First of all, the interests of users can have different granularity, referring to either general topics (such as "sport" news), or more specific topics (for instance news about "World cup football matches"). To deal with this problem, category-based filtering should be based on a hierarchical clustering technique capable to identify clusters corresponding with topics with different levels of granularity. A second problem is that news and categories of topics cannot be partitioned into well-defined disjoint groups. Further, when journalists browse into a category of news do not want to run the risk of missing potentially relevant news. A system that yields a ranked list of news in each group is much more flexible since it allows the user to select the desired number of news. For these reasons fuzzy clustering techniques are well suited to the purpose of news organization into overlapping clusters. The most popularly applied fuzzy clustering algorithm is the Fuzzy C Means (FCM).[8] However, this algorithm has several drawbacks when applied to document filtering. First of all it is not incremental and thus it is not adequate for supporting a dynamic process such as news filtering. Then, it does not yield a hierarchy and suffers from the need to specify some parameters in input that drastically influence the clustering results, such as the number of the clusters to generate, and the seeds where to start the grouping.

Several proposals of modification of the FCM[12] have been defined that tackle one of the above deficiencies, but, up to date there is not a proposal that faces all of them.

In this contribution we propose an incremental hierarchical fuzzy clustering algorithm for supporting news filtering that performs a grouping of news into fuzzy clusters allowing updating as new information is fed.

In the next section we synthetically introduce the problem of document clustering. In Sec. 3 the salient characteristics of the proposed algorithm are described and in Sec. 4 the definition of the clustering algorithm is provided. Section 5 illustrates the experiments and the conclusions summarize the main achievements.

2. History and Applications of Dissociative Recombination

A common approach to document categorization is based on the use of clustering algorithms.[9] Similarly to machine learning, clustering can be completely supervised or unsupervised. In supervised clustering, labeled documents are grouped into known pre-specified topic categories, while in unsupervised clustering both the number of the categories and the categories themselves are unknown and documents are grouped using some similarity measure (distance or density function). This last approach is the most feasible both in IR and in information filtering since a complete labeled collection is generally not available. The assumption of unsupervised clustering is that each cluster identifies a topic category, i.e. documents with similar contents. However, this arises the further problem of summarizing the cluster contents, i.e. to generate a textual description or a set of terms representing the topical content of the cluster.

In order to apply a clustering algorithm to a document collection D one needs to represent each document $d_i \in D$ as a feature vector in an N dimensional space[15]: $d_i = (w_{1i}, \ldots, w_{Ni})$ in which w_{ki} is a number expressing the significance of the descriptor k_i in synthesizing the content of document d_i.

Generally, a subset of the documents' index terms are used as descriptors and w_{ki} is automatically computed based on the classic product term frequency-inverse document frequency $tf*idf$.[15] A common approach is to generate a flat nonhierarchical partition of the documents into C distinct clusters.[20] This well known approach has been applied since long time at indexing phase for efficient retrieval purposes, or for implementing associate retrieval techniques for query expansion.[1] The most common partitioning clustering algorithm is the crisp K-means that needs as input the number C of clusters to generate.[7] It is relatively efficient and scalable, however, its application to news filtering is unsuited since news can hardly be partitioned into well defined and disjoint groups.[9–11]

This is the reason that motivates the application of fuzzy clustering techniques. By applying a fuzzy clustering news are associated with all clusters with a membership degree in $[0, 1]$. The Fuzzy C Means (FCM) is the most common fuzzy clustering algorithm.[8,13] It is based on the minimization of the J function defined as follows:

$$J(P, C) = \sum_{i=1}^{|C|} \sum_{k=1}^{|D|} \mu_{ik}^m \|d_k - c_i\|^2, \tag{1}$$

in which P is the matrix of the membership degrees of documents to the clusters, i.e. $\mu_{ik} \in [0, 1]$ is the membership degree of document k, represented by vector d_k, to the ith cluster, represented by the centroid vector $c_i = (c_{1i}, \ldots, c_{Mi})$; $m > 1$ is the fuzzification parameter, (for $m = 1$ we have the crisp clustering). $|C|$ is the number of the desired clusters (this is supplied as input to the FCM), and $|D| = N$ is the number of documents in the collection D; $\|*\|$ is the complement of the Euclidean distance in the N dimensional space of the indexes.

The optimization of J is achieved by an iterative process that computes the centroids of the $|C|$ clusters at each step by applying the following formula:

$$c_i = \frac{\sum_{k=1}^{|D|} \mu_{ik}^m d_k}{\sum_{k=1}^{|D|} \mu_{ik}^m} \quad \text{for } i = 1, \ldots, |C|, \tag{2}$$

and successively updates the membership degrees of documents to the fuzzy clusters by applying the following:

$$\mu_{ik} = \frac{\|d_k - c_i\|^2}{\sum_{i=1}^{|C|} \|d_k - c_i\|^2}, \tag{3}$$

for $i = 1, \ldots, |C|$ and $k = 1, \ldots, |D|$.

The iteration stops at step r when the value of J does not substantially change, i.e. when $(J(P_r, C_r) - J(M_r - 1, C_r - 1)) < \varepsilon$ at the iteration step r.

The application of the FCM in news filtering presents several drawbacks. The use of the Euclidean distance is not appropriate in IR where usually the cosine similarity is widely used. For this reason in Ref. 12 a modified FCM for documents' clustering has been defined based on the cosine similarity. Differently than in ad hoc retrieval where the collection is "static" in the news filtering task the collection is highly dynamic, so it would be desirable an incremental algorithm allowing to update the clusters. The number of clusters to generate is not known a priori. A typical approach to determine this number is to runs the clustering algorithm for a range of values and then to apply validity measures evaluated based on clusters' compactness and density to determine which value leads to the best partition.[19–21] However, in the news filtering one cannot expect to have all the clusters with comparable density and compactness. When a new story is started to be reported in the news the number of news about it grows for a period of time and then decreases when the story becomes obsolete.

3. The Rationale of the Proposal

In the following we introduce the distinguished characteristics of the proposed algorithm.

To proposed algorithm is a fuzzy agglomerative clustering algorithm based on the recursive application of the FCM. It works bottom up in building the levels of the fuzzy hierarchy. Once the centroids of the clusters in a level of the hierarchy are generated, the FCM is re-applied to group the newly identified centroids into new fuzzy clusters of the next upper level. The output is a fuzzy hierarchy of the news given in input. A membership degree in [0, 1] is computed for each item (news) to each generated fuzzy cluster. This allows to rank the news within a cluster and thus easily support the selection of the top ranked news within a cluster of interest.

The fuzzy hierarchy represents the topics from the most specific ones corresponding to the clusters of the bottom level, to the most general ones, corresponding with the clusters of the top level. It is fuzzy, thus allowing each cluster of a level to belong with distinct degrees to each cluster in the next upper level.

The clusters hierarchy can be easily and efficiently updated on-line when recent news arrive on the stream. This may possibly increase the number of the clusters already identified, and thus may require to compute the association of the old news to the new clusters. This has required the development of an incremental clustering modality. To achieve efficiency we assume that recent news do not alter the centroids of the pre-existing clusters. In fact, when a pre-fixed number of news is available on the stream, the clustering is applied in "reset" modality to build a completely new hierarchy. This number

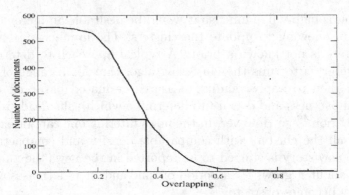

Fig. 1. Cumulative Histogram curve of the cardinalities of the sets of news with overlapping degrees.

is set depending on the desired efficiency required by the application. In the interval of time between two subsequent runs of the clustering in reset modality an existing hierarchy is updated by running the algorithm in incremental modality, thus possibly adding new clusters each time a news is available. Thus, the news added by the incremental modality should not alter too much an existing hierarchy, allowing at the same time to achieve efficiency. Since the optimal number of clusters to generate is unknown, the algorithm automatically determines this number $|C|$. The procedure is based on the analysis of the cumulative histogram curve of overlapping degrees between each pair of news vectors. It identifies the number of clusters $|C|$ corresponding with highest curve trend variation (see Fig. 1). For the upper hierarchical levels $L > 1$, the number of the clusters is set as a percentage reduction of number of clusters of the bottom level $|C| = N_1$. Thus, in climbing the hierarchy the clusters correspond with more general topics.

Finally, since the FCM is unstable with respect to the starting seeds, we select appropriate seeds by identifying in the feature space the $|C| = N_1$ points corresponding with highest local density of news favoring this way the convergence of the algorithm.

4. The Hierarchical Fuzzy Clustering Algorithm

4.1. *Feature selection*

The feature selection phase is aimed at selecting a proper set of the index terms for each item to cluster. Many research efforts have been proposed mainly based on the estimation of either the discrimination power of the features, that is a measure of the density of the index space, or the ability of the terms to decrease the entropy of the retrieval.[5,6] Previous works experimentally observed that the results of crisp document clustering remain stable in using 300 or even more significant index terms, with term significance defined by the classic *tf*idf* weighting scheme. By retaining these indications we applied indexing criteria so as to reduce as much as possible the set of indexes. After applying lexicographic analysis (Porter's stemming algorithm), and removal of stop words (using the stop word list from the SMART IR engine), we selected the top M index terms from the ranked list in decreasing order of their weights *tf*idf*. The cardinality M of the set of selected indexes is the minimum value guaranteeing that any news has at least a common index shared with other news.

4.2. *Generation of a hierarchy of fuzzy clusters*

Once the news vectors have been generated they are supplied in input to the clustering algorithm in form of a sparse vector representing a matrix I of dimensions $N \times M$ where $N = |D|$ is the cardinality of the starting collection and M the number of the features. Efficiency tests have estimated that the clustering can be applied in this "reset" modality every 5000 new incoming news. When running in "reset" modality the clustering rebuilds a new hierarchy. To manage in an efficient way the sparse matrix of feature vectors it adopts the Compressed Row Storage (CRS) format and relative methods. A fuzzy cluster of the hierarchical level L, indicated by C_{iL}, is represented in the M dimensional feature space $t_1, \ldots, t_M \in T$, by its centroid vector c_{iL}:

$$c_{iL} = (w_{1i}^L, \ldots, w_{Mi}^L). \qquad (4)$$

w_{ki}^L represents the significance of t_k in qualifying the subjects dealt with in all documents of cluster C_{iL}. To compute c_{iL} the FCM is applied to group the centroids of the next lower level $L-1$. Then the w_{ki}^L are computed by applying formula (2) in which the complement of the Euclidean distance is replaced by the cosine similarity and the vector d_k in formula (2) for $L > 1$ is the centroid c_{kL-1} of the next lower level $(L-1)$. For the first level $L = 1$ the I matrix of the documents vectors $d_1, \ldots, d_N$ constitutes the input of the algorithm.

To influence the grouping of the documents at level $L = 1$ we start the FCM with seeds corresponding to the points in the news space with highest local density. We identify as locally high dense points the mean vectors obtained by averaging the h news vectors with the lowest cumulative distance among them. In this way the fuzzy clusters grow around interesting regions of the news space coping with the instability caused by the use of random seeds.

For the levels greater than 1, $L > 1$, the matrix I_L of the centroids of the fuzzy clusters of that level is built in which each row is a vector of weights, i.e. the values w_{ki}^L in formula (4).

Another input parameter is the fuzziness parameter m indicating the desired fuzziness of the clusters that reduces to a crisp partition for $m = 1$. An appropriate value of m is estimated depending on the collection by performing a preliminary sensitivity analysis.

The number N_1 of clusters to generate at the bottom level $L = 1$ is estimated automatically as described in the next subsection.

4.3. *Determination of the number of clusters*

We first compute the degree of overlapping of each pairs of news vectors defined by the fuzzy Jaccard coefficient:

$$overlap(d_i, d_j) = \frac{\sum_{k=1}^{M} \min(w_{ki}, w_{kj})}{\sum_{k=1}^{M} \max(w_{ki}, w_{kj})}. \tag{5}$$

Second, the cumulative histogram $H : [0,1] \to \{1, \ldots, N\}$ of the cardinalities of the sets of news having an overlapping degree greater than σ with *at least k* other news is computed:

$$H(s) := \sum_{i=1}^{N} at\ least\ k \left(\sum_{j \neq i \wedge j=1}^{N} (overlap(d_j, d_i) > s) \right), \tag{6}$$

and

$$at\ least\ k(x) = \begin{cases} 1 & x \geq k \\ 0 & x < k \end{cases}. \tag{7}$$

By increasing k we increase the number of the news that must overlap each others to be grouped into a cluster.

Third we determine the overlapping value $\sigma \in [0,1]$ corresponding with the greatest variation of the histogram trend. Notice that the cumulative histogram curve is not increasing with σ (see Fig. 1).

σ is considered as a critical overlapping value that corresponds with the best partition of the news that deal with common topics with respect to those that are almost disjoint one another and thus deal with different topics. The value of N_1 is chosen as $N_1 = H(\sigma)$.

N_1 is the cardinality of the set of news which have an overlapping degree greater than σ with *at least* k other news.

For the levels $L > 1$, where the statistical analysis of the histogram curve is not significant due to the few data available, N_L is determined by specifying a percentage reduction x of N_{L-1}. When $N_L \leq 1$ we consider that the final level of the hierarchy has been reached. So, the hierarchy does not necessarily have a single node as root.

The output of the algorithm is the set of centroids of each level defined by formula (4) and the membership degrees η_{ik}^L, with $k = 1, \ldots, N_L$, of each cluster C_{iL-1} to the N_L clusters of the upper level L; they are computed by the applying formula (3).

Finally, the membership degree μ_{ik}^L of each single news d_k to the fuzzy clusters of the levels $L > 1$ are computed by applying again formula (3) in which we consider as centroids those of the cluster of the considered level L. In this way, we can rank the news with respect to the high level fuzzy clusters that, in this view, can be seen as fuzzy sets of news:

$$C_{iL} = \{(\mu_{ik}^L/d_k), \ k = 1, N\}. \tag{8}$$

4.4. *Updating a fuzzy hierarchy*

In the filtering task we may need to cluster the new news available through the continuous stream. However, it is not feasible to reapply the entire process to the increased collection that may grow to thousands of news in a week. Specifically, the cost of applying the algorithm is mainly due to the generation of the clusters of the bottom level. So we have designed an incremental clustering algorithm to update an existing fuzzy hierarchy by possibly adding new clusters as news become available.

The input to this phase is a matrix I_{update} in which each row is a news vector and, differently that in the reset mode, in update mode the existing hierarchy must be updated. This is achieved by processing one news vector d_k at a time and by clustering it with respect to the existing clusters of the first level.

First of all the similarities of the news d_k is computed with respect to every cluster's centroid of the first level $L = 1$: based on formula (3) for $i = 1, N_1$. If all these values are below the minimal membership degree of any news to any cluster of the level the news vector is instantiated as a centroid of a new fuzzy cluster of the level. In this case all news are associated with the new fuzzy cluster with a membership degree. The existing centroids are not updated since we assume that their position is not substantially affected by adding a few news to them. Once the clusters of the first levels have been updated, for the updating of the next upper levels clusters the FCM is reapplied by starting with the new clusters centroids of the first level. In this case since the number of the clusters is limited with respect to the number of news the procedure is efficient.

5.   Evaluation Results

We conducted the evaluations on two collections: a collection of 556 documents provided by the Open Directory Project (http://dmoz.org) and the RCV1 Reuters collection.[14] The DMOZ documents are classified into five categories with some documents labelled with multiple categories. The index vectors provided by Ref. 12 have a dimension of 620. We evaluated recall and precision of the category-based filter by considering the filtered clusters with respect to each a priori category, and then we averaged the results on all the categories. A fuzzy cluster is filtered with respect to a given a priori category if the label of the considered category is an index of its centroid vector. For estimating the recall measure we assumed as the relevant category for a fuzzy cluster the one that has the maximum frequency in the documents of the considered cluster; this frequency is computed by weighting the contribution of a document to a category by its membership degree. This way we identified a relevant category for each fuzzy cluster and computed an average precision of 98% and a recall of 50% for all a priori categories. Then we performed some evaluation using the classified Reuters collection RCV1.[14] We tested the algorithm for the automatic detection of the number of clusters to generate and observed a linear relation in scaling up the document set. We then evaluated average Recall and Precision of the filtered fuzzy clusters with respect to the available Reuters categories when running the algorithm in reset modality (with 3000 news and 900 indexes) and incremental modality (by adding 20%

news of the total already clustered) achieving an average precision of 81% and an average recall of 0,02 in reset modality against 83% of average precision and 0,04 of average recall in incremental modality. This is not surprising since the number of added news is limited (20% of the total) which is a reasonable assumption in a realistic setting where some thousands news arrive on the stream a day. Given that the algorithm in reset modality takes around 6 hours to cluster 3000 news on a PC with 1Gb Ram we can timestamp the reset modality to recluster everything every 6 hours, while running the updating in between on the pre-existing fuzzy hierarchy. Finally we compared the results produced by our algorithm an the probabilistic EM clustering implemented in WEKA observing a 15% greater average precision of the fuzzy clusters with respect to the probabilistic clusters.

6. Conclusions

The novelty of our approach is basically twofold: the proposal of a category-based news filtering model exploiting a fuzzy hierarchy of clusters so as to filter groups of news reflecting either general or specific topics. More technical innovations concern the definition of a novel incremental agglomerative fuzzy hierarchical clustering algorithm based on the FCM capable to automatically determine both the number of the clusters to generate and the seeds where to start the grouping.

References

1. R. Baeza-Yates and B. Ribeiro-Neto, *Modern Information Retrieval.* Addison-Wesley-Longman Publishing Co (1999).
2. M. Claypool, A. Gokhale, T. Miranda, P. Murnikov, D. Netes and M. Sartin, Combining content-based and collaborative filters in an online newspaper. *Proc. ACM SIGIR'99 Workshop on Recommender Systems-Implemenation and Evaluation*, Berkeley CA (1999).
3. M. Connor and J. Herlocker, Clustering for collaborative filtering. *Proc. of ACM SIGIR Workshop on Recommender Systems*, Berkeley CA (1999).
4. D. R. Cutting, D. R. Karger, J. O. Pedersen and J. W. Tukey, Scatter/Gather: A cluster-based approach to browsing large document collections. *Proc. of 15th Ann In. SIGIR'92* (1992).
5. F. Debole and F. Sebastiani, Supervised term weighting for automated text categorization. *Proc. SAC-03, 18th ACM Symposium on Applied Computing* (2003).

6. S. Dominich, J. Goth, T. Kiezer and Z. Szlavik, Entropy-based interpretation of retrieval status value-based retrieval. *Jour. of the American Society for Information Science and Technology.* John Wiley & Sons, **55**(7), 613–627 (2004).

7. V. Estivill-Castro. Why so many clustering algorithms: A position paper. *ACM SIGKDD Explorations Newsletter*, **4**(1) (2002).

8. R. J. Hathaway, J. C. Bezdek and Y. Hu, Generalized fuzzy C-means clustering strategies using Lp norm distances. *IEEE Transactions on Fuzzy Systems*, **8**(5), 576–582 (2000).

9. A. K. Jain, M. N. Murty and P. J. Flynn, Data clustering: A review. *ACM Computing Surveys*, **31**(3), 264–323 (1999).

10. J.-H. Lin and T.-F. Hu, Fuzzy correlation and support vector learning approach to multi-categorization of documents. *IEEE Int. Conf. on Systems, Man and Cybernetics*, **4**, 3735–3740 (2004).

11. K. Lin and K. Ravikuma, A similarity-based soft clustering algorithm for documents. *Proc. of the 7th International Conference on Database Systems for Advanced Applications*, pp. 40–47 (2001).

12. M. E. S. Mendes Rodrigues and L. Sacks, A scalable hierarchical fuzzy clustering algorithm for text mining. *Proc. of the 4th International Conference on Recent Advances in Soft Computing, RASC'2004,* Nottingham, UK, pp. 269–274 (2004).

13. W. Pedrycz, Clustering and fuzzy clustering, Chapter 1. *Knowledge-Based Clustering.* John Wiley and Son (2005).

14. http://www.daviddlewis.com/resources/testcollections/rcv1/.

15. G. Salton and M. J. McGill, *Introduction to Modern Information Retrieval.* McGraw-Hill Int. Book Co. (1984).

16. F. Sebastiani, *Text Categorization. Text Mining and its Applications,* Alessandro Zanasi (ed.), WIT Press, Southampton, UK (2005).

17. M. Sollenborn and P. Funk, Category-based filtering and user stereotype cases to reduce the latency problem in recommender systems. *6th European Conference on Case Based Reasoning, ECCBR2002*, 10 pages, in press, Springer Verlag Lecture Notes Series, Aberdeen, Scotland (2002).

18. L. H. Ungar and D. P. Foster, Clustering methods for collaborative filtering. *Proc. of the Workshop on Recommendation Systems*, AAAI Press, Menlo Park California (1998).

19. X. Xiong and K. L. Tan, Similarity-driven cluster merging method for unsupervised fuzzy clustering, *Proc. of the 20th ACM International Conference on Uncertainty in Artificial Intelligence*, pp. 611–618 (2004).

20. Y. Zhao and G. Karypis, Criterion functions for document clustering: Experiments and analysis. *Machine Learning* (2003).

21. Y. Zhao and G. Karypis, Empirical and theoretical comparisons of selected criterion functions for document clustering. *Machine Learning*, **55**, 311–331 (2004).

Soft Mapping Between Hierarchical Classifications

Trevor P. Martin* and Yun Shen†

Artificial Intelligence Group
Department of Engineering Mathematics
University of Bristol, UK
*Trevor.Martin@bris.ac.uk
†Yun.Shen@bris.ac.uk

Abstract

Indexing by means of a hierarchical classification is a common method of organizing information for subsequent ease of access. The semantic web makes use of this approach by allowing entities to be grouped into classes, with a sub-class/super-class structure. Frequently, different data sources use different hierarchical classification structures, which complicates the task of integrating information from multiple sources. In this paper, we outline a method for automatically determining a soft mapping between the classes in different hierarchies, using a previously described method for identifying equivalence instances. In turn, the identification of the correct category can improve the instance matching performance. A trial application mapping between genres in large movie databases is presented.

1. Introduction

According to recent estimates,[1] the amount of new information stored on paper, film, magnetic, and optical media increased by approximately 30% per annum in the period 1999–2002. At that time, the surface web was estimated to contain about 170 terabytes of data. Since then, it appears that the volume of information has continued to increase at a similar rate. The problem of information location is fundamental to the successful use of the worlds information resources, and the semantic web[2] is intended to address this issue by enabling the use of meta-data to classify and describe information, services, etc. The ability to create hierarchical classification structures is a core part of the semantic web knowledge representation (and indeed, a core part of many approaches to indexing and organizing information). However, there is no universal hierarchy of knowledge and hence different information sources will almost inevitably differ in the hierarchical classification scheme they adopt.[3] To take a very simple example, the set of tracks or albums classified in one online music store as

$$music > rock > classic\ rock > 70's\ classics$$

may correspond to another's

$$music > rock\&pop\ oldies$$

This is the basis of the ontology alignment or schema matching problem, when different sources classify the same set of objects according to two different hierarchies.

Music and film genres are an obvious application for soft category mapping — Aucouturier. and Pachet[4] state that

> music genre is an ill-defined notion, that is not founded on any intrinsic property of the music, but rather depends on cultural extrinsic habits.

They also comment that the intensional and extensional definitions of music genres frequently do not coincide, and they review various approaches to the representation and assignment of musical genre. They divide approaches into manual and automatic, with the latter further split into approaches which use various features of the music, typically extracted from signal processing, to decide class membership, and approaches which are based on measuring similarity to other tracks in a class.

Downie[5] investigates automatic association of genre tags with digital music, on the basis of sound samples, and Ref. 6 looked at the automatic creation of document genre in text libraries, also on the basis of measurable properties of the document. We take the view that genre (and in our view, most other useful hierarchical classifications) are subjective; at the same time, they are a very useful tool for organizing and retrieving instances in a collection. Although it is probably impossible to rigorously derive genre on the basis of simple features, the work reported here shows that a useful approximate classification method can be created.

In Refs. 7 and 8 we have used instance-matching to determine that objects from different sources are the same — for example, to deduce with a reasonable degree of certainty that an author known in one database as Lewis Carroll represents the same individual as the author known in a second database as C. L. Dodgson.

In this paper we briefly outline the SOFT method for instance matching and show its use in identifying when different news reports are concerned with the same underlying story. We go on to show how this leads to a method of finding correspondences between hierarchies, when instances are classified according to different categorizations (described by different meta-data schemata). We use the equivalence of instances from different sources to learn a soft mapping between categories in these hierarchies, allowing us to compare the hierarchical classification of instances as well as their attributes.

Such correspondences may in turn be used to improve the identification of equivalent instances. Some successful initial tests of the method on large movie databases are reported.

2. Instance Matching

We assume two sets of objects (also referred to as instances) $A = \{a_1, \ldots, a_n\}$ and $B = \{b_1, \ldots, b_m\}$, where we wish to establish an approximate relation

$$h : A \to B.$$

The SOFT method[7] determines which instances are equivalent by comparing their attributes. For example, if sets A and B refer to films, attributes could be title, director, year etc. Let the objects in A and B have attribute values taken from $C_1, C_2, \ldots, D_1, D_2$, with relations defined as

$$R_i : A \to C_i \ i = 1, \ldots, n_A$$
$$S_j : B \to D_j \ j = 1, \ldots, n_B$$

We do not assume that the information about A and B in relations R_i, S_j is identical or completely consistent, but we do assume that some of these relations reflect similar or identical properties of the objects in A and B. Thus for some choices of pairs of codomains (C_i, D_j) we assume an exact or approximate matching function h_{ij} which for each element of C_i returns a (possibly fuzzy) subset of D_j. As shown in Refs. 7 and 8, this can be converted to a mass assignment giving an estimate of the probability that the element corresponding to some C_i lies in a subset $\{d_1, \ldots, d_k\} \subseteq D_j$.

If

$$R_i(a_k) = C_{ik},$$

and

$$h_{ij}(C_{ik}) = \tilde{D}_{jk},$$

where $\tilde{D}_{jk}$ denotes a fuzzy subset of D_j, and

$$S_j(\tilde{B}_k) = \tilde{D}_{jk},$$

using the (inverse) extension principle then

$$h(a_k) = \tilde{B}_k,$$

i.e. a_k corresponds to a fuzzy subset $\tilde{B}_k$. We consider each h_{ij} to give a different observation of the true value,[a] and seek the fuzzy set most likely to give these observations. Let M_n be the mass assignment on B that makes the observed values most likely after n observations, i.e. choose the masses to maximize

$$Pr(M_n | o_1, o_2, \ldots, o_n).$$

---

[a] In an analogous way, to determine the bias of an unfair coin we could observe the results of several sequences of coin tosses and choose a bias to maximise the likelihood of the observations.

This gives a way of updating M after each observation o_i. Using a naive Bayes assumption[b]

$$Pr(M_n|o_1, o_2, \ldots, o_n) = \frac{Pr(o_1, o_2, \ldots, o_n|M_n) \times Pr(M_n)}{Pr(o_1, o_2, \ldots, o_n)}$$

$$Pr(o_1, o_2, \ldots, o_n|M_n) = Pr(o_1|M_n) \times Pr(o_2|M_n)$$
$$\times \cdots \times Pr(o_n|M_n)$$

Assuming each possible mass assignment M_n is equally likely,

$$M_n(B_k) = \frac{N_n(B_k)}{\sum_{X \subseteq B} N_n(X)}$$

where $N_n(X)$ is number of times the subset X has been observed.

2.1. *Example — news stories*

The SOFT algorithm was applied to 1701 stories from the BBC news archive (www.solutionsevenco.uk/bbc/ from May 19–31, 2005 inclusive) and 552 stories from the Sky news archive (www.sky.com/skynews/archive, same period). A manually produced ground truth established 353 true matches — this figure is low due to different editorial styles and content. An example is shown below, with matching attribute pairs as implied i.e. *Headline-Title*, etc.

The similarity between longer text sections (summary, content etc.) was computed as

$$\sum_{a \in doc_1} \sum_{b \in doc_2} f_a Sim(a, b) f_b,$$

where f is the relative frequency of a word in a document and Sim is the similarity of words measured using the word similarity matrix.[9] The similarity between short text sections is on the basis of the proportion of common words, with fuzzy matching for dates, currency, etc. Using the SOFT algorithm, we find 380 pairs of matching news stories when the similarity threshold between two stories is set to 0.15 to find a optimised balance point between the correct and wrong

---

[b] In common with many uses of naive Bayes, the independence assumption is hard to justify theoretically but appears to be valid in practice.

Table 1.   Example from BBC and SKY.

Attribute	Attribute Details
Source BBC:	
Headline	Oldest FA Cup sells for 420,000
Original Publication Date	2005/05/19 19:51:30
Summary	The oldest existing version of the FA Cup becomes the world's most expensive piece of football memorabilia.
Content	"The oldest existing version of the FA ..."
Source SKY:	
Title	FA CUP FETCHES 478,000
Last Updated	12:17 UK, Thursday May 19, 2005
Description	The oldest surviving FA Cup has been sold at auction for 478,400 — a world record for an item of football memorabilia.
Story	"Made in 1896 as a replacement for the stolen original, it ..."

matching pairs. Figures 1 and 2 illustrate the SOFT result, a recall of 100% and an average precision of 92%.

3.   Hierarchy Matching

Given two (or more) hierarchically organised sets of instances, we can use the SOFT method to determine which instances are equivalent by comparing their attributes. Having determined equivalent instances from the two sources, we can look for correspondences between the different classification structures. Repeating the earlier example, online music sources are typically organised hierarchically, but one site's "70's classics" section may correspond (or correspond mostly) to anothers "rock&pop oldies" because both contain mostly the same tracks (or albums) where the notion of same is determined by SOFT.

All elements in a sub-category belong to the broader parent category e.g. anything in classic rock also belongs to rock and hence to the category music. For convenience we define $X > X$ for all categories X. In general, we consider two sets of instances A and B with corresponding sets of labels L_A and L_B each of which has a hierarchical structure i.e. there is a partial order defined on the labels. Note that this does not imply that a hierarchy induces a partition on the instances — it may be that orthogonal attributes such as date

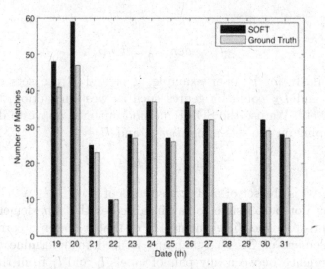

Fig. 1. The number of identified matches in the two data sources and the ground truth (per day). There are some false positives where SOFT wrongly identifies stories as the same but no false negatives.

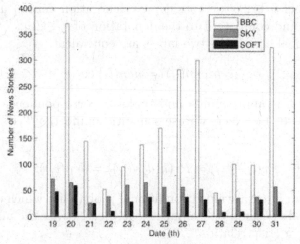

Fig. 2. The number of identified matches in the two news data sources compared to the total numbers of stories from the two sources.

and type of storytelling are represented within the same hierarchy. Each label $l_i \in L_A$ denotes a subset of A i.e. we have a denotation function

$$den : L_A \rightarrow A$$

such that

$$l_i > l_j \Leftrightarrow den(l_j) \subseteq den(l_i),$$

(and similarly for B). For example, if A and B are sets of films then L_A and L_B could be genres such as western, action, thriller, romance, etc. We use the SOFT method outlined above to derive a soft mapping on the sets of entities A and B

$$h : A \rightarrow \tilde{P}(B),$$

where $\tilde{P}(B)$ is the set of all fuzzy subsets of B.

It may not be possible to say in all cases that an element of A corresponds to a specific element of B or that it does not correspond to any element of B. This mapping is used to determine a (soft) correspondence between any pair of labels l_i and l_j from the label sets L_A and L_B

$$g : L_A \rightarrow \tilde{P}(L_B).$$

Given a label $l_i \in L_A$ we consider its denotation $den(l_i)$ under the mapping h and compare it to the denotation of $l_j \in L_B$.

In the ideal case if the two labels are equivalent,

$$h(den(l_i)) = den(l_j).$$

Given that h is approximate and that the correspondence between labels may not be exact, we use semantic unification[10] to compare the sets.

$$Pr(l_i \rightarrow l_j) = Pr(h(den(l_i)) = den(l_j)).$$

This gives an interval-valued conditional probability which expresses the relation between a pair of labels; we then extract the most likely pair to give a crisp relation

$$g_c : L_A \rightarrow L_B.$$

Ideally, it should be possible to map such categories into a user's personal hierarchy here, we concentrate on extracting rules from the overlap between categories in different classification structures based on a sample and use the derived rules to predict likely categorizations of new examples.

4. Application to Film Databases

The two film websites rotten tomatoes (http://www.rottentomatoes.com) and the internet movie data-base (http://www.imdb.com) are "user-maintained" datasets which aim to catalogue movie information. The databases denoted *dbT* and *dbI* below are derived from these sites, respectively containing 94 500 and 94 176 film records, and were used in experiments. Since *dbT* and *dbI* are produced by two different movie web sites, there is inevitable "noise" existing in the film data; i.e. different tag sets, different genre names and missing elements.

In order to match attributes, some very simple string matching functions were used as follows: (i) String S_1 is an approximate substring of S_2 if S_1 is shorter than S_2 and most words in S_1 are also in S_2. (ii) String S_1 is an approximate permutation of S_2 if they have a high proportion of common words, i.e. degree of match = proportion of common words, which must be at least two (typical strings are only a few words long). Both functions ignore stop words such as *the*, *and*, etc.

Clearly it is not useful to update with a pair of relations (R_i, S_j) whose codomains hardly match each other. The possible pairs of relations are ordered according to the maximum probability of matching (from the least prejudiced distribution), averaged over all elements of the codomain C_i:

$$AvMatch(h_{ij}) = \frac{\sum_{x \in C_i} \max_{y \in D_j}(Pr(y \in LPD(h_{ij}(x))))}{|C_i|}.$$

We use this in preference to the average maximum probability of matching, defined as

$$AvMatch(h_{ij}) = \frac{\sum_{x \in C_i} \max_{y \in D_j}(Pr(h_{ij}(x))}{|C_i|},$$

since the latter measure is not necessarily helpful if there is a large amount of uncertainty in the approximate mapping. We note also that it is possible to obtain better results for peoples names (attributes such as cast, director, etc.) using a more structured approach which extracts first name and surname and then matches

Table 2. Example from *dbI* and *dbT*.

Attribute	Attribute Details
Source dbI:	
Title	Gentleman B.
Year	2000
Directed_by	Jordan Alan
Genre	Thriller
Aka	Gentleman Bandit, The (2000) (USA: MIFED title)
Country	USA
Source dbT:	
Title	Gentleman Bandit
Year	2000
Director	Jordan Alan
Genre	Dramas, Film Noir, Blackmail
MPAA_rating	NOT Rated
Cast	Ed Lauter, Peter Greene, Justine Miceli, Ryan O'Neal

Table 3. Average degree of match between attributes in *dbI* and *dbT*.

dbI attributes	*dbT* attributes	average match
Year	Year	100%
Title	Title	41%
Directed_by	Director	27%
Aka	Title	21%

on that basis. The average matches between domains are given in Table 3. For example, *Year-Year* pair gives a 100% matching percentage because these two database maintain the correct release dates and it is less sensible to match Year against any other attributes, e.g. title, aka, etc.

On the basis of the three best attributes, the system identified movies from *dbI* dated 1976–1990 which were also in *dbT*, and compared the genre classification. The similarity threshold between two film records was set to an optimised value 0.5 giving a total of 14 124 movies which are found to be identical. The similarity between two genres is relatively hard to decide from text string matching. For example, animation is not similar to children from the point of view of text matching, but the extension of the sets

Table 4. Examples of matching genre pairs determined by the system.

dbT genre	*dbI* genre
Animation	Children
Comedy	Drama
Horror	Suspense
Sci-fi	Fantasy

of films in these two categories shows considerable overlap. Some examples of intuitively reasonable genre mappings are listed in Table 4.

4.1. *Results on unseen data*

The attribute and genre mappings were applied to a new set of 24 839 entries from *dbI* (calendar years 2000–2005), trying to find matches in *dbT*. For comparison, a manually produced ground truth established 1274 true matches — this figure is low due to the relatively large number of entries for TV series, foreign movies, etc. in *dbI* which are not included in *dbT*. Using the SOFT algorithm without genre mapping, we find 861 pairs of matching film entries when the similarity threshold between two films is set to an optimised value 0.44. With the presence of the ground truth, 261 film matching pairs out of 382 film pairs in 2000 are missing, 102 out of 364 in 2001 are missing, 87 out of 330 in 2002 are missing, 60 out of 142 in 2003 are missing, and 3 out of 8 in 2004 are missing (see Fig. 3). This represents a recall of 67 % and a precision of 100%. Incorporating the genre mapping as well produces a much better (100%) recall, at the expense of some loss in precision P see Figs. 3 and 4.

5. Summary

We see the availability of good meta-data as crucial to the development of intelligent information management systems, and the use of soft methods for approximate matching as a vital component in such systems. We have presented methods for determining similarity of content and for finding identifying similar categories within hierarchical classifications. Initial results are promising. Further

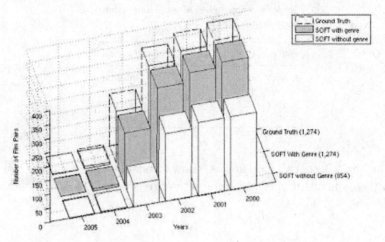

Fig. 3. The number of correctly identified matches in the two data sources, without and with genre mapping.

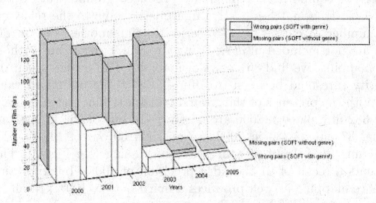

Fig. 4. The number of incorrectly identified matches when using genre information (white blocks) and the number of pairs not identified when not using genre information (shaded block) Instance and Genre Matching.

testing is necessary to fully establish the robustness of this work, involving a wider variety of datasets. The use of this method with a personal hierarchy would enable users to adapt source metadata to their own preferences and hence improve the retrieval process.

References

1. P. Lyman and H. R. Varian, How much information. URL: www.sims. berkeley.edu/how-much-info-2003 (2003).
2. T. Berners-Lee, J. Hendler and O. Lassila, The semantic web. *Scientific American*, **284**(5), 34–43 (May 2001).
3. T. P. Martin, Fuzzy sets in the fight against digital obesity. *Fuzzy Sets and Systems*, **156**(3), 411–417 (December 2005).
4. J. Aucouturier and F. Pachet, Representing musical genre: A state of art. *Journal of New Music Research*, **32**(1), 83–93 (2003).
5. J. S. Downie, A. F. Ehmann and D. Tcheng, Real-time genre classification for music digital libraries. *JCDL '05: Proceedings of the 5th ACM/IEEE-CS joint conference on Digital libraries*, pp. 377–377, New York, NY, USA, ACM Press. ISBN 1-58113-876-8 (2005).
6. A. Rauber and A. Müller-Kögler, Integrating automatic genre analysis into digital libraries. *JCDL '01: Proceedings of the 1st ACM/IEEE-CS joint conference on Digital libraries*, pp. 1–10, New York, NY, USA, ACM Press. ISBN 1-58113-345-6 (2001).
7. T. P. Martin, Soft integration of information with semantic gaps. *Fuzzy Logic and the Semantic Web*, pp. 150–180 (December 2005).
8. T. P. Martin and Y. Shen, Improving access to multimedia using multi-source hierarchical meta-data. *Adaptive Multimedia Retrieval: User, Context, and Feedback*, vol. LNCS3877, pp. 266–278. Springer-Verlag ISBN 3-540-32174-8 (2006).
9. T. P. Martin and M. Azmi-Murad, An incremental algorithm to find asymmetric word similarities for fuzzy text mining. *Soft Computing as Transdisciplinary Science and Technology*, pp. 838–847 (December 2005).
10. J. F. Baldwin, The management of fuzzy and probabilistic uncertainties for knowledge based systems. *Encyclopedia of AI* (1992).

On Linguistic Summarization of Time Series Using Fuzzy Logic with Linguistic Quantifiers

Janusz Kacprzyk[*], Anna Wilbik[†] and Sławomir Zadrożny[‡]

Systems Research Institute, Polish Academy od Sciences
ul. Newelska 6, 01-447 Warsaw, Poland
[*] kacprzyk@ibspan.waw.pl
[†] wilbik@ibspan.waw.pl
[‡] zadrozny@ibspan.waw.pl

Abstract

We discuss first the concept of a linguistic summary of a time series in the setting proposed by the authors[1] and then its extension to cover some additional types of summaries that concern the duration of (partial) trends identified here as straight line segments of a piece-wise linear approximation of a time series. Then, we use the features that characterize the trends: the slope of the line segment, the goodness of approximation and the length of the trend. The derivation of a linguistic summary of a time series is then related to a linguistic quantifier driven aggregation of trends. For this purpose we employ the classic Zadeh's calculus of linguistically quantified propositions in its basic form with the minimum operation. We present some results of a linguistic summarization of time series data on daily quotations of an investment fund over an eight year period, i.e. some best linguistic summaries with their associated degrees of truth (validity). The results obtained provide much insight into the very essence of the time series data, and prove to be promising.

1. Introduction

A linguistic data (base) summary is meant as a concise, human-consistent description of a (numerical) data set. This concept has been introduced by Yager[2] and then further developed by Kacprzyk and Yager[3], and Kacprzyk, Yager and Zadrożny[4]. In this approach the contents of a database is summarized via a natural language like expression semantics of which is provided in the framework of Zadeh's calculus of linguistically quantified propositions[5]. Since data sets are usually large, it is very difficult for a human being to capture and understand their contents. As natural language is the only fully natural means of articulation and communication for a human being, such linguistic descriptions are the most human consistent.

In this paper we consider a specific type of data, namely time series, i.e. a certain real valued function of time. For a manager, stock exchange players, etc. it might be convenient and useful to obtain a brief, natural language like description of trends present in the data on a company performance, stock exchange quotations, etc. over a certain period of time.

Though statistical methods exhibit their strength in such cases, and are often used, in our case we attempt to derive (quasi)natural language like descriptions that should be considered to be an additional form of data description of a remarkably high human consistency because — as we have already indicated — for a human being the only fully natural means of articulation, communication, etc. is natural language. Hence, our approach is not meant to replace the classical statistical analyses but rather serve as an additional form of data description characterized by its high human consistency.

The summaries of time series we propose refer in fact to the summaries of trends identified here with straight line segments of a piecewise linear approximation of time series. Thus, the first step is the construction of such an approximation. For this purpose we use a modified version of the simple, easy to use Sklansky and Gonzalez algorithm presented in Ref 6.

Then we employ a set of features (attributes) to characterize the trends such as the slope of the line, the fairness of approximation of the original data points by line segments and the length of a period of time comprising the trend.

Basically the summaries proposed by Yager are interpreted in terms of the number or proportion of elements possessing a certain property. In the framework considered here a summary might look like: "Most of the trends are short" or in a more sophisticated form: "Most long trends are increasing". Such expressions are easily interpreted using Zadeh's calculus of linguistically quantified propositions.

The most important element of this interpretation is a linguistic quantifier exemplified by "most". In Zadeh's[5] approach it is interpreted in terms of a proportion of elements possessing a certain property (e.g. a length of a trend) among all the elements considered (e.g. all trends).

In Kacprzyk, Wilbik and Zadrożny[1] we proposed to use Yager's linguistic summaries, interpreted in the framework of Zadeh's calculus of linguistically quantified propositions, for the summarization of time series. In our further papers (cf. Kacprzyk, Wilbik and Zadrożny[7-9])we proposed, first, another type of summaries that does not use the linguistic quantifier based aggregation over the number of trends but over the time instants they take altogether. For example, such a summary can be: "Trends taking most of the time are increasing" or "Increasing trends taking most of the time are of a low variability". Such summaries do not directly fit the framework of the original Yager's approach and to overcome this difficulty we generalize our previous approach by modeling the linguistic quantifier based aggregation both over the number of trends as well over the time they take using first the Sugeno integral and then the Choquet integral. All these approaches have been proposed using a unified perspective given by Kacprzyk and Zadrożny[10] that is based on Zadeh's[11] protoforms.

In this paper we will basically employ the classic Zadeh's calculus of linguistically quantified propositions in its basic form with the minimum operation. The method discussed is applied to time series data on daily quotations of an investment fund over an eight year period. The results give much insight into the very essence of what proceeds over time.

The paper is in line with some modern approaches to a human consistent summarization of time series. First of all, one should cite here the works of Batyrshin and his collaborators[12,13] or Chiang, Chow and Wang[14], but we use a different approach.

To see our approach in a proper perspective it may be expedient to refer to a interesting project coordinated by the University of Aberdeen, UK, SumTime, an EPSRC Funded Project for Generating Summaries of Time Series Data[a]. Its goal is to develop technology for producing English summary descriptions of a time-series data set by

---

[a] www.csd.abdn.ac.uk/research/sumtime/

integrating leading-edge time-series and natural language generation (NLG) technology".

Basically, the essence of this project is close in intent and spirit to our works. However, the type of summaries they generate is different, not accounting for an inherent imprecision of natural language. A good example is here the case of weather prediction that is one of the main application areas in that project. For instance, cf. Sripada et al.,[15] linguistic summaries related to wind direction and speed can be:

- WSW (West of South West) at 10–15 knots increasing to 17–22 knots early morning, then gradually easing to 9–14 knots by midnight,
- During this period, spikes simultaneously occur around 00:29, 00:54, 01:08, 01:21, and 02:11 (o'clock) in these channels.

They do provide a higher human consistency as natural language is used but they capture imprecision of natural language to a very limited extent. In our approach this will be overcome to a considerable extent.

2. Temporal Data and Trend Analysis

We deal with numerical data that vary over time, and a time series is a sequence of data measured at uniformly spaced time moments. We identify trends as linearly increasing, stable or decreasing functions, and therefore represent given time series data as piecewise linear functions. Evidently, the intensity of an increase and decrease (slope) will matter, too. These are clearly partial trends as a global trend in a time series concerns the entire time span of the time series, and there also may be trends that concern parts of the entire time span, but more than a particular window taken into account while extracting partial trends by using the Sklansky and Gonzalez[6] algorithm.

In particular, we use the concept of a uniform partially linear approximation of a time series. Function f is a uniform ε-approximation of a time series, or a set of points $\{(x_i, y_i)\}$, if for a given, context dependent $\varepsilon > 0$:

$$\forall i : \ |f(x_i) - y_i| \leq \varepsilon, \tag{1}$$

and, clearly, if f is linear, then such an approximation is a linear uniform ε-approximation.

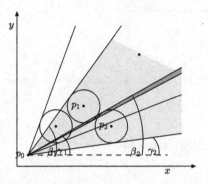
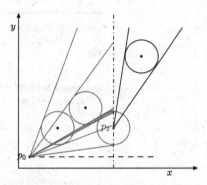

(a) the intersection of the cones is indicated by the dark gray area.

(b) a new cone starts in point p_2.

Fig. 1.   An illustration of the algorithm for the uniform ε-approximation.

We use a modification of the well known, effective and efficient Sklansky and Gonzalez[6] algorithm that finds a linear uniform ε-approximation for subsets of points of a time series. The algorithm constructs the intersection of cones starting from point p_i of the time series and including a circle of radius ε around the subsequent data points p_{i+j}, $j = 1, 2, \ldots$, until the intersection of all cones starting at p_i is empty. If for p_{i+k} the intersection is empty, then we construct a new cone starting at p_{i+k-1}. Figures 1(a) and 1(b) present the idea of the algorithm. The family of possible solutions is indicated as a gray area. Clearly other algorithms can also be used, and there is a lot of them in the literature (cg. Refs. 16 and 17).

First denote: `p_0` — a point starting the current cone, `p_1` — the last point checked in the current cone, `p_2` — the next point to be checked, `Alpha_01` — a pair of angles (γ_1, β_1), meant as an interval, that defines the current cone as shown in Fig. 1(a), `Alpha_02` — a pair of angles of the cone starting at the point `p_0` and inscribing the circle of radius ε around the point `p_2` (cf. (γ_2, β_2) in Fig. 1(a)), function `read_point()` reads a next point of data series, function `find()` finds a pair of angles of the cone starting at `p_0` and inscribing the circle of radius ε around `p_2`. A pseudocode of the algorithm that extracts trends is depicted in Fig. 2.

The bounding values of `Alpha_02` (γ_2, β_2), computed by function `find()` correspond to the slopes of two lines that: (1) are tangent to the circle of radius ε around $p_2 = (x_2, y_2)$ and (2) start at $p_0 = (x_0, y_0)$.

```
read_point(p_0);
read_point(p_1);
while(1)
{
  p_2=p_1;
  Alpha_02=find();
  Alpha_01=Alpha_02;
  do
  {

    Alpha_01 = Alpha_01 ∩ Alpha_02;

    p_1=p_2;
    read_point(p_2);
    Alpha_02=find();

  } while(Alpha_01 ∩ Alpha_02 ≠ ∅);

  save_found_trend();
  p_0=p_1;
  p_1=p_2;
}
```

Fig. 2.   Pseudocode of the modified Sklansky and Gonzalez[6] algorithm for extracting trends.

Thus, if $\Delta x = x_0 - x_2$ and $\Delta y = y_0 - y_2$ then

$$\beta_2, \gamma_2 = arctg\left[\left(\Delta x \cdot \Delta y \pm \varepsilon\sqrt{(\Delta x)^2 + (\Delta y)^2 - \varepsilon^2}\right)/\left((\Delta x)^2 - \varepsilon^2\right)\right].$$

The resulting linear ε-approximation of p_0, ... ,p_1 is either a single segment, chosen as, e.g. a bisector of the cone, or one that minimizes the distance (e.g. the sum of squared errors, SSE) from the approximated points, or the whole family of possible solutions, i.e. the rays of the cone.

3.   Dynamic Characteristics of Trends

In our approach, while summarizing trends in time series data, we consider the following three aspects: (1) dynamics of change, (2) duration, and (3) variability, and it should be noted that by trends we mean here global trends, concerning the entire time series (or some, probably a large, part of it), not partial trends concerning a small time span (window) taken into account in the (partial) trend extraction phase via the Sklansky and Gonzales[6] algorithm mentioned above.

Dynamics of change

Under the term *dynamics of change* we understand the speed of changes. It can be described by the slope of a line representing the trend, (cf. any angle η from the interval $\langle \gamma, \beta \rangle$ in Fig. 1(a)). Thus, to quantify dynamics of change we may use the interval of possible angles $\eta \in < -90; 90 >$.

For practical reasons we use a fuzzy granulation to meet the users' needs and task specificity, e.g.: *quickly decreasing, decreasing, slowly decreasing, constant, slowly increasing, increasing* and *quickly increasing*. Figure 3 illustrates the lines corresponding to those linguistic terms.

In fact, each term represents a fuzzy granule of directions. In Batyrshin *et al.*[12,13] there are presented many methods of constructing such a fuzzy granulation. The user may define a membership functions of particular linguistic terms depending on his or her needs.

We map a single value α (or the whole interval of angles corresponding to the gray area in Fig. 1(b)) characterizing the dynamics of change of a trend identified using the algorithm shown as a pseudocode in Fig. 2 into a fuzzy set (linguistic label) best matching a

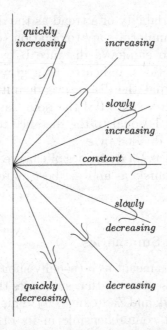

Fig. 3.   A visual representation of angle granules defining the dynamics of change.

given angle and we say that a given trend is, e.g. "decreasing to a degree 0.8".

Duration
Duration describes the length of a single trend, meant as a linguistic variable and exemplified by a "long trend" defined as a fuzzy set.

Variability
Variability refers to how "spread out" (in the sense of values) a group of data is. The following five statistical measures of variability are widely used in traditional analyses:

- The range (maximum — minimum).
- The interquartile range (IQR) calculated as the third quartile (the 75th percentile) minus the first quartile (the 25th percentile) that may be interpreted as representing the middle 50% of the data.
- The variance is calculated as $\frac{\sum_i (x_i - \bar{x})^2}{n}$, where $\bar{x}$ is the mean value.
- The standard deviation — a square root of the variance.
- The mean absolute deviation (MAD), calculated as $\frac{\sum_i |x_i - \bar{x}|}{n}$.

We measure the variability of a trend as the distance of the data points from its linear uniform ε-approximation (cf. Sec. 2). For this purpose we propose to employ a distance between a point and a family of possible solutions, indicated as a gray cone in Fig. 1(a). Equation (1) assures that the distance is definitely smaller than ε. The normalized distance equals 0 if the point lays in the gray area. In the opposite case it is equal to the distance to the nearest point belonging to the cone, divided by ε.

Similarly as in the case of dynamics of change, we find for a given value of variability obtained as above a best matching fuzzy set (linguistic label).

4. Linguistic Data Summaries

A linguistic summary is meant as a (usually short) natural language like sentence (or some sentences) that subsumes the very essence of a set of data (cf. Kacprzyk and Zadrożny[10,18]). This data set is numeric and usually large, not comprehensible in its original form by the human being. In Yager's approach (cf. Yager,[2] Kacprzyk and Yager,[3] and Kacprzyk, Yager and Zadrożny[4]) the following perspective is assumed:

- $Y = \{y_1, \ldots, y_n\}$ is a set of objects (records) in a database, e.g. the set of workers;
- $A = \{A_1, \ldots, A_m\}$ is a set of attributes characterizing objects from Y, e.g. salary, age, etc. in a database of workers, and $A_j(y_i)$ denotes a value of attribute A_j for object y_i.

/ A linguistic summary of a data set consists of:

- a summarizer P, i.e. an attribute together with a linguistic value (fuzzy predicate) defined on the domain of attribute A_j (e.g. "low" for attribute "salary");
- a quantity in agreement Q, i.e. a linguistic quantifier (e.g. most);
- truth (validity) T of the summary, i.e. a number from the interval $[0, 1]$ assessing the truth (validity) of the summary (e.g. 0.7); usually, only summaries with a high value of T are interesting;
- optionally, a qualifier R, i.e. another attribute together with a linguistic value (fuzzy predicate) defined on the domain of attribute A_k determining a (fuzzy subset) of Y (e.g. "young" for attribute "age").

Thus, a linguistic summary may be exemplified by

$$T(\text{most of employees earn low salary}) = 0.7, \tag{2}$$

or, in a richer (extended) form, including a qualifier (e.g. young), by

$$T(\text{most of young employees earn low salary}) = 0.9. \tag{3}$$

Thus, basically, the core of a linguistic summary is a *linguistically quantified proposition* in the sense of Zadeh[5] written, for (2) and (3), as

$$Qy\text{'s are } P, \tag{4}$$

$$QRy\text{'s are } P. \tag{5}$$

Then, T, i.e. the truth (validity) of a linguistic summary, directly corresponds to the truth value of (4) or (5). This may be calculated by using notably the original Zadeh's calculus of linguistically quantified propositions (cf. Ref. 5). In the former case, the truth values (from

$[0, 1])$ of (4) and (5) are calculated, respectively, as

$$T(Qy \text{ 's are } P) = \mu_Q \left(\frac{1}{n} \sum_{i=1}^{n} \mu_P(y_i) \right), \tag{6}$$

$$T(QRy \text{ 's are } P) = \mu_Q \left(\frac{\sum_{i=1}^{n}(\mu_R(y_i) \wedge \mu_P(y_i))}{\sum_{i=1}^{n} \mu_R(y_i)} \right), \tag{7}$$

where $\wedge$ is the minimum operation (more generally e.g. a t-norm), and Q is a fuzzy set representing the linguistic quantifier in the sense of Zadeh,[5] i.e. $\mu_Q : [0, 1] \longrightarrow [0, 1]$, $\mu_Q(x) \in [0, 1]$. We consider *regular non-decreasing monotone* quantifiers such that:

$$\mu(0) = 0, \quad \mu(1) = 1, \tag{8}$$

$$x_1 \leq x_2 \Rightarrow \mu_Q(x_1) \leq \mu_Q(x_2). \tag{9}$$

They can be exemplified by "most" given as in (10):

$$\mu_Q(x) = \begin{cases} 1 & \text{for } x \geq 0.8 \\ 2x - 0.6 & \text{for } 0.3 < x < 0.8 \\ 0 & \text{for } x \leq 0.3 \end{cases} \tag{10}$$

5.　Protoforms of Linguistic Trend Summaries

It was shown by Kacprzyk and Zadrożny[10] that Zadeh's[11] concept of a protoform is convenient for dealing with linguistic summaries. This approach is also employed here.

Basically, a protoform is defined as a more or less abstract prototype (template) of a linguistically quantified proposition. Then, the summaries mentioned above might be represented by two types of the protoforms:

* Frequency based summaries:
  — a protoform of a short form of linguistic summaries:

$$Q \text{ trends are } P. \tag{11}$$

  e.g. *Most* of trends are of a *large variability*
  — a protoform of an extended form of linguistic summaries:

$$QR \text{ trends are } P. \tag{12}$$

  e.g. *Most* of *slowly decreasing trends* are of a *large variability*

- Duration based summaries:
  - a protoform of a short form of linguistic summaries:

$$\text{Trends that took } Q \text{ time are } P \tag{13}$$

  e.g. Trends that took *most* of the time are of a *large variability*
  - a protoform of an extended form of linguistic summaries:

$$R \text{ trends that took } Q \text{ time are } P \tag{14}$$

  e.g. *Slowly decreasing trends* that took *most* of the time are of a *large variability*.

It should be noted that these summaries should be properly understood as, basicaly, that the (short, partial) trends that altogether took most of the time have a large variability.

The truth values of the above types and forms of linguistic summaries will be found using the classic Zadehs calculus of linguistically quantified propositions as it is effective and efficient, and provides the best conceptual framework within which to consider a linguistic quantifier driven aggregation of partial trends that is the crucial element of our approach.

6. The use of Zadeh's Calculus of Linguistically Quantified Propositions

Using Zadeh's[5] fuzzy logic based calculus of linguistically quantified propositions, a (proportional, nondecreasing) linguistic quantifier Q is assumed to be a fuzzy set defined in the unit interval $[0, 1]$ as, e.g. (10).

The truth values (from $[0,1]$) of (11) and (12) are calculated, respectively, as

$$T(Qy\text{'s are } P) = \mu_Q \left(\frac{1}{n} \sum_{i=1}^{n} \mu_P(y_i) \right), \tag{15}$$

$$T(QRy\text{'s are } P) = \mu_Q \left(\frac{\sum_{i=1}^{n} (\mu_R(y_i) \wedge \mu_P(y_i))}{\sum_{i=1}^{n} \mu_R(y_i)} \right), \tag{16}$$

where $\wedge$ is the minimum operation.

The computation of truth values of duration based summaries is more complicated and requires a different approach. While analyzing a summary "the trends that took Q time are P" we should compute the time which is taken by those trends for which "trend is P" is valid. It is obvious that when "trend is P" is to degree 1, then we can use the whole time taken by this trend. However, what should we do if "trend is P" is to some degree? We propose to take only a part of the time defined by the degree to which "trend is P". In other words we compute this time as $\mu(y_i)t_{y_i}$, where t_{y_i} is the duration of trend y_i. The obtained value (duration of those trends for which "trend is P") is then normalized by dividing it by the overall time T. Finally, we may compute to which degree the time taken by those trends which "trend is P" is Q. A similar line of thought might be followed for the extended form of linguistic summaries.

The truth value of the short form of duration based summaries (13) is calculated as

$$T(y \text{ that took } Q \text{ time are } P) = \mu_Q\left(\frac{1}{T}\sum_{i=1}^{n}\mu_P(y_i)t_{y_i}\right), \qquad (17)$$

where T is the total time of the summarized trends and t_{y_i} is the duration of the ith trend.

The truth value of the extended form of summaries based on duration (14) is calculated as

$$T(Ry \text{ that took } Q \text{ time are } P) = \mu_Q\left(\frac{\sum_{i=1}^{n}(\mu_R(y_i) \wedge \mu_P(y_i))t_{y_i}}{\sum_{i=1}^{n}\mu_R(y_i)t_{y_i}}\right)$$
$$(18)$$

where t_{y_i} is the duration of the ith trend.

Both the fuzzy predicates P and R are assumed above to be of a rather simplified, atomic form referring to just one attribute. They can be extended to cover more sophisticated summaries involving some confluence of various, multiple attribute values as, e.g. "slowly decreasing and short".

7. Numerical Experiments

The method proposed in this paper was tested on data coming from quotations of an investment fund that invests at most 50% of assets

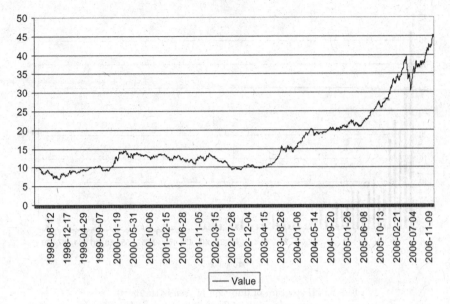

Fig. 4. A view of the original data.

in shares. Data shown in Fig. 4 were collected from April 1998 until December 2006 with the value of one share equal to PLN 10.00 in the beginning of the period to PLN 45.10 at the end (PLN stands for the Polish Zloty). The minimal value recorded was PLN 6.88 while the maximal one during this period was PLN 45.15. The biggest daily increase was equal to PLN 0.91, while the biggest daily decrease was equal to PLN 2.41.

Using the Sklansky and Gonzalez algorithm and $\varepsilon = 0.25$ we obtained 255 extracted trends. The shortest trend took 2 time units only, while the longest 71. The histogram of duration of trends is presented in Fig. 5.

Figure 6 shows the histogram of angles, which characterize dynamics of change. The histogram of variability of trends (in %) is in Fig. 7.

Some interesting summaries obtained by using the method proposed, and for different granulations of the dynamics of change, duration and variability, are:

- for seven labels for the dynamics of change (*quickly increasing, increasing, slowly increasing, constant, slowly decreasing,*

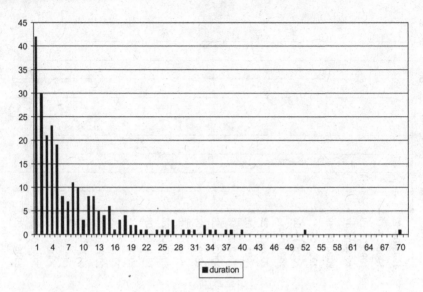

Fig. 5.   Histogram of duration of trends (in days).

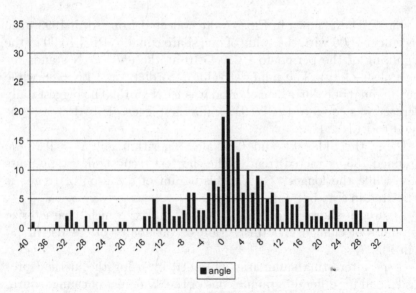

Fig. 6.   Histogram of angles describing dynamic of change.

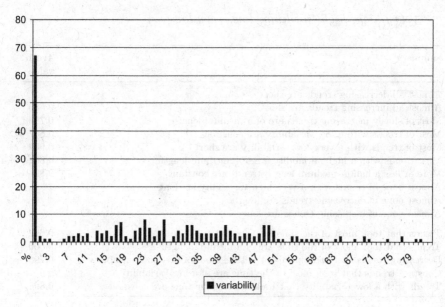

Fig. 7. Histogram of variability (IQR) of trends in %.

decreasing and quickly decreasing), five labels for the duration (*very long, long, medium, short, very short*) and the variability (*very high, high, medium, low, very low*):

Summary	Truth value
Almost all short trends are constant	1
Most trends are very short	0.78
Most trends with a low variability are constant	0.974
Most slowly decreasing trends are of a very low variability	0.636
Trends that took almost all of the time are constant	0.639
Trends that took more or less a half of the time are of a low variability	0.873
Decreasing trends that took most of the time are of a very low variability	0.989
Trends with a low variability that took almost all of the time are constant	1
Trends with a very high variability that took most of the time are constant	0.94

- Five labels for the dynamics of change (*increasing, slowly increasing, constant, slowly decreasing, decreasing*), three labels for the duration (*short, medium, long*) and five labels for the variability (*very high, high, medium, low, very low*):

Summary	Truth value
Almost all decreasing trends are short	1
Almost all increasing trends are short	0.580
Most of slowly increasing trends are of a medium length	0.798
Most of trends with a low variability are constant	0.567
Most of trends with a very low variability are short	0.909
Most trends with a high variability are of a medium length	0.801
More or less a half of medium length trends are constant	0.891
Almost none of trends with a very high variability are long	1
Almost none of decreasing trends are long	1
Almost none of increasing trends are long	1
Trends that took most of the time are constant	0.692
Trends that took most of the time are of a medium length	0.506
Decreasing trends that took most of the time are of a very low variability	0.798
Constant trends that took most of the time are of a low variability	0.5
Trends with a low variability that took most of the time are constant	0.898

The particular linguistic summaries obtained, and their associated truth values, are intuitively appealing. In addition, these summaries were found interesting by domain experts though a detailed analysis from the point of view of financial analyses is beyond the scope of this paper.

8. Concluding Remarks

We discussed the concept of a linguistic summary of a time series in the setting proposed by the authors[1] and its extension covering the duration of (partial) trends identified here as straight line segments of a piece-wise linear approximation of a time series. We used as the features that characterize the trends: the slope of the line segment, the goodness of approximation and the length of the trend. The derivation of a linguistic summary of a time series boiled down to the use of a linguistic quantifier driven aggregation of trends, and the classic Zadeh's calculus of linguistically quantified propositions in its basic form with the minimum operation was employed. Some results of a linguistic summarization of time series data on daily quotations of an investment fund over an eight year period, i.e. some best linguistic summaries with their associated degrees of truth (validity) were presented giving much insight into the very essence of the time series data, and proving to be promising. As a further step the use of various t-norms in Zadeh's calculus of linguistically quantified propositions was employed.

References

1. J. Kacprzyk, A. Wilbik and S. Zadrożny, Linguistic summarization of trends: a fuzzy logic based approach. *Proceedings of the 11th International Conference Information Processing and Management of Uncertainty in Knowledge-based Systems*, pp. 2166–2172, (2006). Paris, France, July 2–7, 2006.
2. R. R. Yager, A new approach to the summarization of data. *Information Sciences*, **28**, 69–86 (1982).
3. J. Kacprzyk and R. R. Yager, Linguistic summaries of data using fuzzy logic. *International Journal of General Systems*, **30**, 33–154 (2001).
4. J. Kacprzyk, R. R. Yager and S. Zadrożny, A fuzzy logic based approach to linguistic summaries of databases. *International Journal of Applied Mathematics and Computer Science*, **10**, 813–834 (2000).
5. L. A. Zadeh, A computational approach to fuzzy quantifiers in natural languages. *Computers and Mathematics with Applications*, **9**, 149–184 (1983).
6. J. Sklansky and V. Gonzalez, Fast polygonal approximation of digitized curves. *Pattern Recognition*, **12**(5), 327–331 (1980).
7. J. Kacprzyk, A. Wilbik and S. Zadrożny, On some types of linguistic summaries of time series. *Proceedings of the 3rd International IEEE Conference "Intelligent Systems"*, pp. 373–378. IEEE Press, London, UK (September 4–6, 2006).
8. J. Kacprzyk, A. Wilbik and S. Zadrożny, A linguistic quantifier based aggregation for a human consistent summarization of time series. eds. J. Lawry, E. Miranda, A. Bugarin, S. Li, M. A. Gil, P. Grzegorzewski and O. Hryniewicz. *Soft Methods for Integrated Uncertainty Modelling*, Springer-Verlag, Berlin and Heidelberg, pp. 186–190 (2006).
9. J. Kacprzyk, A. Wilbik and S. Zadrożny, Capturing the essence of a dynamic behavior of sequences of numerical data using elements of a quasi-natural language. *Proceedings of the 2006 IEEE International Conference on Systems, Man, and Cybernetics*, IEEE Press, Taipei, Taiwan, pp. 3365–3370 (2006).
10. J. Kacprzyk and S. Zadrożny, Linguistic database summaries and their protoforms: toward natural language based knowledge discovery tools. *Information Sciences*, **173**, 281–304 (2005).
11. L. A. Zadeh, A prototype-centered approach to adding deduction capabilities to search engines — the concept of a protoform. *Proceedings of the Annual Meeting of the North American Fuzzy Information Processing Society (NAFIPS 2002)*, pp. 523–525 (2002).
12. I. Batyrshin, On granular derivatives and the solution of a granular initial value problem. *International Journal Applied Mathematics and Computer Science*, **12**(3), 403–410 (2002).

13. I. Batyrshin and L. Sheremetov, Perception based functions in qualitative forecasting. eds. I. Batyrshin, J. Kacprzyk, L. Sheremetov and L. A. Zadeh. *Perception-based Data Mining and Decision Making in Economics and Finance*. Springer-Verlag, Berlin and Heidelberg (2006).

14. D.-A. Chiang, L. R. Chow and Y.-F. Wang, Mining time series data by a fuzzy linguistic summary system. *Fuzzy Sets and Systems*, **112**, 419–432 (2000).

15. S. Sripada, E. Reiter and I. Davy, Sumtime-mousam: Configurable marine weather forecast generator. *Expert Update*, **6**(3), 4–10 (2003).

16. E. Keogh and M. Pazzani, An enhanced representation of time series which allows fast and accurate classification, clustering and relevance feedback. *Proceedings of the 4th International Conference on Knowledge Discovery and Data Mining*, New York, NY, pp. 239–241 (1998).

17. E. Keogh, K. Chakrabarti, M. Pazzani and S. Mehrotra, Locally adaptive dimensionality reduction for indexing large time series databases. *Proceedings of ACM SIGMOD Conference on Management of Data*, Santa Barbara, CA, pp. 151–162 (2001).

18. J. Kacprzyk and S. Zadrożny, Fuzzy linguistic data summaries as a human consistent, user adaptable solution to data mining. eds. B. Gabrys, K. Leiviska, and J. Strackeljan, *Do Smart Adaptive Systems Exist?*, Springer, Berlin, Heidelberg, New York, pp. 321–339 (2005).

A Possible Worlds Interpretation of Label Semantics

Jonathan Lawry* and Van Nam Huynh†

*AI Group, Department of Engineering Mathematics
University of Bristol, Bristol, BS8 1TR, UK
j.lawry@bris.ac.uk

†School of Knowledge Science
Japan Advanced Institute of Science and Technology
Ishikawa 923-1292, Japan
huynh@jaist.ac.jp

Abstract

The label semantics linguistic representation framework is introduced as an alternative approach to computing and modelling with words, based on the concept of appropriateness rather than graded truth. A possible worlds interpretation of label semantics is then proposed. In this model it is shown that certain assumptions about the underlying possible worlds can result in appropriateness measures that correspond to well known t-norms and t-conorms for conjunctions and disjunctions of linguistic labels.

1. Introduction

The principle aim of the *computing with words* paradigm as proposed by Zadeh[18] is to increase the use of natural language for information and knowledge processing in computer systems. In practice this will require the development of a formal representation framework based on some restricted subset of natural language. Zadeh has suggested a form of *precisiated natural language*[19] based on the theory of generalized constraints and linguistic variables. *Label semantics*, introduced by Lawry,[11,12] provides an alternative representation for computing and modeling with words, which takes a somewhat different perspective than Zadeh on the processing of natural language information.

Zadeh's approach is based fundamentally on the notion of linguistic variables[17] where a semantic rule links natural language labels to an underlying graded vague concept as represented by a fuzzy set on the domain of discourse. Label semantics on the other hand, encodes the meaning of linguistic labels according to how they are used by a population of communicating agents to convey information. From this perspective it is important to consider the decision process an intelligent agent must go through in order to identify which labels or expressions can actually be used to describe an object or instance.

It cannot be denied that in their use of linguistic labels humans posses a mechanism for deciding whether or not to make assertions (e.g. Bill is *tall*) or to agree to a classification (e.g. Yes, that is a tree). Further, although the concepts concerned are vague this underlying decision process is fundamentally crisp (bivalent). For instance, you are either willing to assert that x is a *tree* given your current knowledge, or you are not. In other words, either tree is an appropriate label to describe x or it is not. As humans we are continually faced with making such crisp decisions regarding vague concepts as part of our every day use of language. Of course, we may be uncertain about labels and even express these doubts (e.g. I'm not sure whether you would call that a tree or a bush, or both) but the underlying decision is crisp.

Given this decision problem, we suggest that it is useful for agents to adopt what might be called an *epistemic stance*, whereby they assume the existence of a set of labelling conventions for the population governing what linguistic labels and expression can be appropriately used to describe particular instances. Of course, such linguistic conventions do not need to be imposed by some outside authority like the Oxford English Dictionary or the Academia Lengua Espanola, but instead would emerge as a result of interactions between agents each adopting the epistemic stance. Hence, label semantics does not attempt to link label symbols to fuzzy set concept extensions but rather to quantify an agent's subjective belief that a label L is appropriate to describe an object x and hence whether or not it is reasonable to assert that 'x is L'. In this respect it is close to the 'anti-representational' view of vague concepts proposed by Rohit

Parikh[15] which focuses on the notion of assertibility rather than that of truth; a view that is also shared by Alice Kyburg.[8]

Label semantics proposes two fundamental and inter-related measures of the appropriateness of labels as descriptions of an instance. Given a finite set of labels LA from which can be generated a set of expressions LE through recursive applications of logical connectives, the measure of appropriateness of an expression $\theta \in LE$ as a description of instance x is denoted by $\mu_\theta(x)$ and quantifies the agent's subjective belief that θ can be used to describe x based on its (partial) knowledge of the current labelling conventions of the population. From an alternative perspective, when faced with an object to describe, an agent may consider each label in LA and attempt to identify the subset of labels that are appropriate to use. Let this set be denoted by $\mathcal{D}_x$. In the face of their uncertainty regarding labelling conventions the agent will also be uncertain as to the composition of $\mathcal{D}_x$, and in label semantics this is quantified by a probability mass function $m_x : 2^{LA} \to [0, 1]$ on subsets of labels. The relationship between these two measures will be described in the following section.

This paper will propose an interpretation of the label semantics framework, where an agent evaluates $\mu_\theta(x)$ and m_x by considering different labelling scenarios, these being identified as possible worlds, and estimating their respective likelihoods. The latter would be based on the agent's past experience of labelling behaviour across the population. As a simplification it will be assumed that each possible world provides complete information as to which labels are and are not appropriate to describe every element in the universe. Clearly, this is unlikely to be the case in practice, not least because the underlying universe may be infinite, but as an idealization it provides a useful mechanism by which to study those calculi for the measures $\mu_\theta(x)$ and m_x consistent with a possible worlds model.

In probability theory the notion of *possible world* was used by Carnap[2] to explore the relationship between probability and logic. In fuzzy set theory a number of possible worlds semantics have been proposed. In particular, Gebhardt and Kruse[4] proposed the *context model* for integrating vagueness and uncertainty. In this approach possible worlds correspond to different contexts across which fuzzy concepts have different (crisp) extensions. For example, Huynh et al.[7] suggest that in the case where $LA = \{very\ short,\ short,\ medium, \ldots, tall,\ very\ tall\}$ the contexts (i.e. possible worlds) might correspond to nationalities such as Japanese, American, Swede, etc.

Another possible worlds model for fuzzy sets is the voting model, proposed by Gaines[3] and later extended by Baldwin[1] and Lawry.[9] Here possible worlds correspond to individual voters each of which is asked to identify the crisp extension of the concept under consideration. Alternatively, each voter is presented with each instance, one at a time, and asked to answer yes or no as to whether the instance satisfies the concept.

A somewhat different approach is adopted by Ruspini in Ref. 16 who defines a similarity measure between possible worlds and then defines an implication and consistency function in terms of this measure. These functions are then used to provide a foundation for reasoning with possibility and necessity measures, including Zadeh's generalized modus ponens law.

2.   The Label Semantics Framework

Unlike linguistic variables, which allow for the generation of new label symbols using a syntactic rule,[17] label semantics assumes a fixed finite set of labels LA. These are the basic or core labels to describe elements in a underlying domain of discourse Ω. Detailed arguments in favour of this assumption are given in Refs. 10 and 11. Based on LA, the set of label expression LE is then generated by recursive application of the standard logic connectives as follows:

Definition 1. Label Expressions
The set of label expressions of LA, LE, is defined recursively as follows:

- $L \in LE : L \in LA$
- If $\theta, \varphi \in LE$ then $\neg\theta, \theta \wedge \varphi, \theta \vee \varphi, \theta \rightarrow \varphi \in LE$

A mass assignment m_x on sets of labels then quantifies the agent's belief that any particular subset of labels contains all and only the labels with which it is appropriate to describe x.

Definition 2. Mass Assignment on Labels
$\forall x \in \Omega$ a mass assignment on labels is a function $m_x : 2^{LA} \rightarrow [0,1]$ such that $\sum_{S \subseteq LA} m_x(S) = 1$

The appropriateness measure, $\mu_\theta(x)$, and the mass m_x are then related to each other on the basis that asserting θ provides direct constraints on $\mathcal{D}_x$. For example, asserting 'x is $L_1 \wedge L_2$', for labels $L_1, L_2 \in LA$ is taken as conveying the information that both L_1 and L_2 are appropriate to describe x so that $\{L_1, L_2\} \subseteq \mathcal{D}_x$. Similarly, '$x$ is $\neg L$' implies that L is not appropriate to describe x so $L \notin \mathcal{D}_x$. In general we can recursively define a mapping $\lambda : LE \to 2^{2^{LA}}$ from expressions to sets of subsets of labels, such that the assertion 'x is θ' directly implies the constraint $\mathcal{D}_x \in \lambda(\theta)$ and where $\lambda(\theta)$ is dependent on the logical structure of θ. For example, if $LA = \{low, \ medium, \ high\}$ then $\lambda(medium \wedge \neg high) = \{\{low, medium\}, \{medium\}\}$ corresponding to those sets of labels which include *medium* but do not include *high*. Hence, the description $\mathcal{D}_x$ provides an alternative to Zadeh's linguistic variables in which the imprecise constraint 'x is θ' on x, is represented by the precise constraint $\mathcal{D}_x \in \lambda(\theta)$, on $\mathcal{D}_x$.

Definition 3. λ-mapping
$\lambda : LE \to 2^{2^{LA}}$ is defined recursively as follows: $\forall \theta, \ \varphi \in LE$

- $\forall L_i \in LA \ \lambda(L_i) = \{T \subseteq LA : L_i \in T\}$
- $\lambda(\theta \wedge \varphi) = \lambda(\theta) \cap \lambda(\varphi)$
- $\lambda(\theta \vee \varphi) = \lambda(\theta) \cup \lambda(\varphi)$
- $\lambda(\neg \theta) = \lambda(\theta)^c$
- $\lambda(\theta \to \varphi) = \lambda(\neg \theta) \cup \lambda(\varphi)$

Based on the λ mapping we then define $\mu_\theta(x)$ as the sum of m_x over those set of labels in $\lambda(\theta)$.

Definition 4. Appropriateness Measure

$$\forall \theta \in LE, \ \forall x \in \Omega \ \mu_\theta(x) = \sum_{S \in \lambda(\theta)} m_x(S)$$

Note that in label semantics there is no requirement for the mass associated with the empty set to be zero. Instead, $m_x(\emptyset)$ quantifies the agent's belief that none of the labels are appropriate to describe x. We might observe that this phenomena occurs frequently in natural language, especially when labelling perceptions generated along some continuum. For example, we occasionally encounter colours for which none of our available colour descriptors seem appropriate. Hence, the value $m_x(\emptyset)$ is an indicator of the describability of x in terms of the labels LA.

Example 1. If
$LA = \{small, \ medium, \ large\}$ then

$$\lambda(small \wedge medium) = \{\{small, medium\},$$
$$\{small, medium, large\}\}$$

hence,

$$\mu_{small \wedge medium}(x) = m_x(\{small, medium\})$$
$$+ m_x(\{small, medium, large\})$$

Also,

$$\lambda(small \to medium) = \{\{small, medium\}, \{small, medium, large\},$$
$$\{medium, large\}, \{medium\}, \{large\}, \emptyset\}$$

hence,

$$\mu_{small \to medium}(x) = m_x(\{small, medium\})$$
$$+ m_x(\{small, medium, large\})$$
$$+ m_x(\{medium, large\}) + m_x(\{medium\})$$
$$+ m_x(\{large\}) + m_x(\emptyset)$$

3. The Possible Worlds Model

In this section we introduce a possible worlds interpretation of label semantics and then investigate the relationship between different assumptions within this model and a number of standard t-norms and t-conorms for combining conjunctions and disjunctions of labels. Notice, as is typically the case in label semantics (see Lawry[12]), in such cases t-norms and t-conorms can only be applied at the label level (i.e. to elements of LA) and not arbitarily to label expressions from LE.

Let $\mathcal{W}$ be a finite set of possible worlds each of which identifies a set of valuations on LA, one for each value of $x \in \Omega$. More formally, for every x in Ω there is a valuation function $V_x : \mathcal{W} \times LA \to \{0, 1\}$ such that $\forall w \in \mathcal{W}$ and $\forall L \in LA$ $V_x(w, L) = 1$ means that, in world w, L is an appropriate label with which to describe x. Alternatively, $V_x(w, L) = 0$ means that, in world w, L is not an appropriate label with which to describe x. The valuation V_x can then be extended to a valuation $V_x : \mathcal{W} \times LE \to \{0, 1\}$ in the normal recursive manner. Let $P : \mathcal{W} \to [0, 1]$ be a probability measure on $\mathcal{W}$, where for $w \in \mathcal{W}$

$P(w)$ is the probability that w is the possible world corresponding to reality. Also we assume w.l.o.g that $P(w) > 0 \ \forall w \in \mathcal{W}$. Then in this model we can interpret appropriateness measures and mass assignments as follows:

$$\forall \theta \in LE \ \mu_\theta (x) = P(\{w \in \mathcal{W} : V_x(w, \theta) = 1\}),$$

and

$$\forall T \subseteq LA \ m_x(T) = P(\{w \in \mathcal{W} : \mathcal{D}_x^w = T\})$$
$$= P(\{w \in W : V_x(w, \alpha_T) = 1\})$$
$$= \mu_{\alpha_T}(x)$$

where $\forall x \in \Omega, \forall w \in \mathcal{W}$

$$\mathcal{D}_x^w = \{L \in LA : V_x(w, L) = 1\} \quad \text{and}$$

where $\forall T \subseteq LA$

$$\alpha_T = \left(\bigwedge_{L_i \in T} L_i \right) \wedge \left(\bigwedge_{L_i \notin T} \neg L_i \right).$$

Notice that as w varies then the set of appropriate labels corresponds to a random set $\mathcal{D}_x : \mathcal{W} \to 2^{LA}$ such that $\mathcal{D}_x(w) = \mathcal{D}_x^w$. This relates label semantics to the random set interpretation of fuzzy membership function as studied by Goodman,[5,6] and Nguyen.[13,14] The fundamental difference is that the latter defined random sets of the universe Ω whereas the former defines random sets of labels. This has a major impact on the resulting calculus allowing label semantics to be functional (although not truth-functional). See Lawry[11,12] for a discussion of the functionality of label semantics. A practical advantage of this approach is that while the universe Ω is often infinite the set of labels LA remains finite, and hence the underlying mathematics is considerably simplified.

Definition 5. Ordering on Worlds
For every $x \in \Omega$ the valuation V_x generates a natural ordering on $\mathcal{W}$ according to:

$$\forall w_i, w_j \in \mathcal{W} \ w_i \preceq_x w_j \ \text{iff} \ \forall L \in LA \ V_x(w_i, L) = 1 \Rightarrow V_x(w_j, L) = 1.$$

Theorem 1. *If $\forall x \in \Omega \preceq_x$ is a total (linear) ordering on $\mathcal{W}$ then $\forall S \subseteq LA$:*

$$\mu_{\bigwedge_{L \in S} L}(x) = \min\{\mu_L(x) : L \in S\} \quad and$$
$$\mu_{\bigvee_{L \in S} L}(x) = \max\{\mu_L(x) : L \in S\}.$$

Corollary 1. *If $\forall x \in \Omega \; V_x$ satisfies the conditions given in Theorem 1 then:*

$$\forall L, L' \in LA \; L \neq L' \; \mu_{L \to L'}(x) = \min(1, 1 - \mu_L(x) + \mu_{L'}(x)).$$

Interestingly, the implication operator in Corollary 1 corresponds to Lukasiewicz implication which, in fuzzy logic, is normally associated with the bounded sum t-conorm. More specifically, Lukasiewicz implication is the so called S-implication generated from $S(1 - a, b)$ where S is bounded sum. In fuzzy logic, it is not typical for Lukasiewicz implication to be associated with min and max as above.

A total ordering on words as assumed in Theorem 1 would naturally occur in those situations where for each $x \in \Omega$ there is a total ordering on the labels LA with regards to their appropriateness, and where this ordering is invariant across all possible worlds (i.e. for every x there is no doubt regarding the ordering of the labels in terms of their appropriateness). In this case the valuation V_x would be consistent with this ordering on labels in that if $V_x(w, L) = 1$ then $V_x(w, L') = 1$ for any L' which is at least as appropriate as L. Hence, the only variation in the possible worlds will be in terms of the generality of D_x^w; this then naturally generating a total ordering on $\mathcal{W}$. See[11] for more details.

Theorem 2. *If $\forall x \in \Omega$ and $\forall w \in \mathcal{W}$ it holds that:*

$$\forall L_i \in LA \; V_x(w, L_i) = 1 \Rightarrow V_x(w, L_j) = 0 \; \forall L_j \neq L_i,$$

then $\forall S \subseteq LA$

$$\mu_{\bigwedge_{L \in S} L}(x) = \max\left(0, \sum_{L \in S} \mu_L(x) - (|S| - 1)\right) \quad and$$

$$\mu_{\bigvee_{L \in S} L}(x) = \min\left(1, \sum_{L \in S} \mu_L(x)\right).$$

According to the conditions on $\mathcal{W}$ imposed in Theorem 2 all possible worlds are very conservative when identifying labels as appropriate descriptions of an instance $x \in \Omega$. In each world at most one label is identified as being appropriate with which to describe x. Notice that in the case that all worlds select one label so that $\forall w \in \mathcal{W} \; \mathcal{D}_x^w \neq \emptyset$ then $\mu_L(x) : L \in LA$ forms a probability distribution on LA.

Theorem 3. *If $\forall x \in \Omega$ and $\forall w \in \mathcal{W}$ it holds that:*

$$\forall L_i \in LA \; V_x\,(w, \neg L_i) = 1 \Rightarrow V_x\,(w, \neg L_j) = 0 \; \forall L_j \in LA : \; L_j \neq L_i$$

then $\forall S \subseteq LA$

$$\mu_{\bigwedge_{L \in S} L}(x) = \max\left(0, \sum_{L \in S} \mu_L(x) - (|S| - 1)\right) \quad and$$

$$\mu_{\bigvee_{L \in S} L}(x) = \min\left(1, \sum_{L \in S} \mu_L(x)\right).$$

The conditions in Theorem 3 are the dual of those in Theorem 2 such that in the former each world is conservative in ruling out the appropriateness of any label. For each possible world at most one label is ruled out as inappropriate with which to describe x. In the case where $\forall w \; \mathcal{D}_x^w \neq LA$ then $\mu_{\neg L}(x) : L \in LA$ forms a probability distribution on the set of negated labels $\{\, \neg L : L \in LA \}$.

Corollary 2. *If $\forall x \in \Omega \; V_x$ satisfies the conditions of either Theorem 2 or Theorem 3 then*

$$\forall L \neq L' \in LA \; \mu_{L \to L'}(x) = \max\left(1 - \mu_L(x), \mu_{L'}(x)\right).$$

The implication in Corollary 2 corresponds to the Kleene-Dienes implication operator. Again this is different from the fuzzy logic case where Kleene-Dienes is the S-implication operator generated by the max t-conorm.

Theorem 4. *Let $C_x = \{L \in LA : \forall w \in \mathcal{W} \; V_x(w, L) = 1\}$. If it holds that:*

$$\forall w \in \mathcal{W} \; \forall L_i \notin C_x V_x\,(w, L_i) = 1$$
$$\Rightarrow V_x\,(w, L_j) = 0 \,\forall\, L_j \notin C_x : L_j \neq L_i,$$

then

$$\mu_{\bigwedge_{L \in S} L}(x) = T_D\left(\mu_L(x) : L \in S\right),$$

where T_D is the drastic t-norm.

Corollary 3. *If $\forall x \in \Omega$ V_x satisfies the conditions of Theorem 4 then:*

$$\forall L \neq L' \in LA \ \mu_{L \to L'}(x) = \begin{cases} 1 : \mu_{L'}(x) = 1 \\ \mu_{L'}(x) : \mu_L(x) = 1, \ \mu_{L'}(x) \leq 1 \\ 1 - \mu_L(x) : \mu_L(x) < 1, \ \mu_{L'}(x) < 1 \end{cases}.$$

The implication in Corollary 3 does not correspond to the S-implication for the drastic t-conorm but it does correspond to the QL-implication for the drastic t-norm/t-conorm pair. In fuzzy logic the QL-implication operator is motivated by quantum logic and corresponds to $S(1 - a, T(a, b))$ for a t-norm T and dual t-conorm S. In effect this corresponds to the membership function for $L \to (L \wedge L')$.

The condition on $\mathcal{W}$ imposed in Theorem 4 means that for each x we can identify a set of labels $\mathcal{C}_x$ that are certainly appropriate as descriptions for x (i.e. they are judged appropriate in all possible worlds). Outside of $\mathcal{C}_x$ at most one other label is judged appropriate. Interestingly in the case where $\mathcal{C}_x = \emptyset$ then this condition is identical to that of Theorem 2 and hence in such cases the drastic and Lukasiewicz t-norms agree.

It is not the case that if $\forall x \in \Omega$ V_x satisfies the conditions of Theorem 4 that disjunctions can be combined using the Drastic t-conorm S_D as can be seen from the following counter-example:

Example 2. Let $LA = \{L_1, L_2, L_3, L_4\}$ and $\mathcal{W} = \{w_1, w_2, w_3\}$ with probability measure P defined such that $P(w_1) = 0.3$, $P(w_2) = 0.1$ and $P(w_3) = 0.6$. Also for some $x \in \Omega$ let $\mathcal{C}_x = \{L_1\}$ and $\mathcal{D}_x^{w_1} = \{L_1, L_2\}$, $\mathcal{D}_x^{w_1} = \{L_1, L_3\}$ and $\mathcal{D}_x^{w_3} = \{L_1\}$. This means that the mass assignment m_x is such that:

$$\{L_1, L_2\} : 0.3, \ \{L_1, L_3\} : 0.1, \ \{L_1\} : 0.6$$

Hence we have that

$$\mu_{L_2 \vee L_3 \vee L_4}(x) = 0.4 \text{ while } \mu_{L_2}(x) = 0.3, \mu_{L_3}(x) = 0.1 \text{ and } \mu_{L_4}(x) = 0$$
$$\text{Therefore } S_D\left(\mu_{L_2}(x), \mu_{L_3}(x), \mu_{L_4}(x)\right) = S_D\left(0.3, 0.1, 0\right) = 1$$

Label semantics is consistent with the Drastic t-conorm on disjunctions of labels when the possible worlds model is as given in the following theorem:

Theorem 5. *Let* $\mathcal{I}_x = \{L \in LA : \forall w \in W \; V_x(w, L) = 0\}$. *If it holds that:*

$$\forall w \in W \; \forall L_i \notin \mathcal{I}_x \; V_x(w, L_i) = 0$$
$$\Rightarrow V_x(w, L_j) = 1 \; \forall L_j \notin \mathcal{I}_x : L_j \neq L_i,$$

then

$$\forall S \subseteq LA \; \mu_{\bigvee_{L \in S} L}(x) = S_D(\mu_L(x) : L \in S).$$

Corollary 4. *If* $\forall x \in \Omega \; V_x$ *satisfies the conditions of Theorem 5 then:*

$$\forall L \neq L' \in LA \; \mu_{L \to L'}(x) = \begin{cases} 1 : \mu_L(x) = 0 \\ 1 - \mu_L(x) : \mu_L(x) > 0, \; \mu_{L'}(x) = 0 \\ \mu_{L'}(x) : \mu_L(x) > 0, \; \mu_{L'}(x) > 0 \end{cases}.$$

The conditions imposed on W in Theorem 5 means that $\forall x \in \Omega$ a set of definitely inappropriate labels $\mathcal{I}_x$ are identified (i.e. in all worlds the labels in $\mathcal{I}_x$ are deemed inappropriate to describe x). Then in each world, at most one other label not in $\mathcal{I}_x$ is judged inappropriate. In the case that $\mathcal{I}_x = \emptyset$ then this condition is equivalent to that in Theorem 3.

Theorem 6. *If* $\forall x \in \Omega \; V_x$ *is such that,* $\forall T \subseteq LA$

$$m_x(T) = P(\{w \in W : \mathcal{D}_x^w = T\})$$

$$= \left[\prod_{L \in T} P(\{w \in W : V_x(w, L) = 1\}) \right]$$

$$\times \left[\prod_{L \notin T} P(\{w \in W : V_x(w, L) = 0\}) \right]$$

$$= \left[\prod_{L \in T} \mu_L(x) \right] \times \left[\prod_{L \notin T} (1 - \mu_L(x)) \right],$$

then

$$\mu_{\bigwedge_{L \in S} L}(x) = \prod_{L \in S} \mu_L(x) \quad and$$

$$\mu_{\bigvee_{L \in S} L}(x) = \sum_{T \subseteq S} (-1)^{|T|-1} \prod_{L \in T} \mu_L(x).$$

The conditions on $\mathcal{W}$ imposed by Theorem 6 means that across the possible worlds the appropriateness of a particular label is not dependent on the appropriateness of any other label. This could be the case when different labels refer to different facets of x (e.g. $LA = \{tall, rich, blonde\}$).

Corollary 5. *If $\forall x \in \Omega$ V_x satisfies the conditions of Theorem 6 then $\forall L \neq L' \in LA$*

$$\mu_{L \to L'}(x) = 1 - \mu_L(x) + \mu_L(x)\mu_{L'}(x).$$

In Corollary 5 the operator is Reichenbach implication which is consistent with the fuzzy logic S-implication based on the product t-conorm.

4.   Conclusions

In this paper we have introduced the label semantics framework for modelling and reasoning with linguistic labels. This approach defines measures to quantify the appropriateness of a label as description of a given element of the underlying domain of discourse. We have also proposed a possible worlds model for this framework and have demonstrated that different assumptions result in different combination rules of labels, as characterized by different t-norms and t-conorms.

Acknowledgments

This research was carried out during exchange visits between JAIST and the University of Bristol, funded by a JAIST International Joint Research grant.

References

1. J. F. Baldwin, Support logic programming. *International Journal of Intelligent Systems*, **1**, 73–104 (1986).
2. R. Carnap, *The Logical Foundations of Probability*. University of Chicago Press, Chicago (1950).
3. B. R. Gaines, Fuzzy and probability uncertainty logics. *Journal of Information and Control* **38**, 154–169 (1978).
4. J. Gebhardt and R. Kruse, The context model: An integrating view of vagueness and uncertainty. *International Journal of Approximate Reasoning* **9**, 283–314 (1993).
5. I. R. Goodman, Fuzzy sets as equivalence classes of random sets. *Fuzzy Set and Possibility Theory* (ed. R. Yager), pp. 327–342 (1982).
6. I. R. Goodman, Some new results concerning random sets and fuzzy sets. *Information Science*, **34**, 93–113 (1984).
7. V. N. Huynh, Y. Nakamori, T. B. Ho and G. Resconi, A context model for fuzzy concept analysis based on modal logic. *Information Sciences*, **160**, 111–129 (2004).
8. A. Kyburg, When vague sentences inform: A model of assertability. *Synthese*, **124**, 175–192 (2000).
9. J. Lawry, A voting mechanism for fuzzy logic. *International Journal of Approximate Reasoning*, **19**, 315–333 (1998).
10. J. Lawry, A methodology for computing with words. *International Journal of Approximate Reasoning*, **28**, 51–89 (2001).
11. J. Lawry, A framework for linguistic modelling. *Artificial Intelligence*, **155**, 1–39 (2004).
12. J. Lawry, *Modelling and Reasoning with Vague Concepts*, Springer (in Press) (2006).
13. H. T. Nguyen, On random sets and belief functions. *Journal of Mathematical Analysis and Applications*, **65**, 531–542 (1978).
14. H. T. Nguyen, On modeling of linguistic information using random sets. *Information Science*, **34**, 265–274 (1984).
15. R. Parikh, Vague predicates and language games. *Theoria (Spain)*, **XI**(27), 97–107 (1996).
16. E. H. Ruspini, On the semantics of fuzzy logic. *International Journal of Approximate Reasoning*, **5** 54–99 (1991).
17. L. A. Zadeh, The concept of linguistic variable and its application to approximate reasoning Parts 1–3. *Information Sciences*, **8,9**, 199–249, 301–357, 43–80 (1975, 1976).
18. L.A. Zadeh, Fuzzy logic = Computing with words. *IEEE Transactions on Fuzzy Systems*, **4** 103–111 (1996).
19. L. A. Zadeh, Precisiated natural language (PNL). *AI Magazine*, **25**(3), 74–91 (2004).

DECISION MAKING AND
INFORMATION PROCESSING

Definition of an Importance Index for Bi-Capacities in Multi-Criteria Decision Analysis

C. Labreuche[*] and M. Grabisch[†]

[*]*Thales Research & Technology*
RD128 — 91767 Palaiseau Cedex, France
christophe.labreuche@thalesgroup.com

[†]*University of Paris I*
CERMSEM — 106–112, Bd de l'Hôpital
75647 Paris Cedex 13, France
michel.grabisch@lip6.fr

Abstract

The aim of this paper is to define an importance index for bi-capacities in the context of MCDA. We adopt an axiomatic approach. As for capacities the axioms are given in the context of cooperative game theory. The importance index is then derived from the parallel between MCDA and game theory.

1. Introduction

Multi-Criteria Decision Analysis (MCDA) aims at helping a decision maker (DM) in selecting the best option among several alternative options, on the basis of several decision criteria. The combination of the criteria is performed by an aggregation function. Such aggregation function has to be rich enough to represent all decision behaviors of the DM. Two types of behaviors are often encountered. Firstly, criteria may interact together. For instance, a bad score on a criterion can penalize highly well-satisfied criteria, yielding complementarity between these criteria. The Choquet integral w.r.t. a capacity has been proved to represent interaction among criteria. Another complexity is the possible existence of a special element on the scale, called neutral element, such that the decision behaviors are quite different for values above or below this element. Bipolar aggregation functions must then be used in such situations. Bi-capacities have been introduced in MCDA for taking into account both interaction between criteria and bipolarity.[3,6]

A bi-capacity contains many terms, which makes its interpretation not so easy for a DM. Hence several indices can be defined to describe various aspects of the decision behaviors embedded in the model. The most crucial one is the *importance index* that depicts the mean importance of each criterion. Even though it is a very basic index, its definition for bi-capacities is not so obvious. A proposal has already been made in Refs. 4 and 7. However, the expression of this index uses a very small subset of all terms of a bi-capacity, and its interpretation is not so convincing. The goal of this paper is to define a better definition of importance indices. Note that once this index has been defined all the interaction indices can be determined simply by using an induction axiom.[7]

Two approaches are basically possible for the definition of an index — an axiomatic approach deducing the expression of the index from a series of axioms and a constructive one describing an *ad hoc* technique for computing the index. The axiomatic approach is preferred since it provides a characterization of the concept. However a characterization with easily interpretable axioms (in MCDA) cannot always be readily obtained. For a capacity the importance index is classically the *Shapley value*[10] borrowed from *Cooperative Game Theory*. The axiomatization of this index has been done in the context of Game Theory.[12]

Our first attempt to define importance indices for bi-capacities was to construct two importance indices (one for the well-satisfied criteria and the other one for the ill-satisfied criteria) that are valid in all situations, i.e. whatever the value of the criteria.[7] This is very similar to *multi-choice games* in which a value is defined for each level of participation to the game irrespective of what is the real participation chosen by each player.[5] It turns out that this value lacks clear interpretation in Game Theory. Yet *cost allocation problems* are the main applications of multi-choice games by large.[9,11] The approach of cost allocation problems is different and consists in defining one single value (importance index) that is restricted to a given situation where the level of participation of players are known.[11] This is the approach we have adopted in Ref. 8. We extend this approach to bi-capacities in this paper.

Section 2 recalls the necessary definitions. The definition of the importance index in the context of Game Theory is given in Sec. 3. The application to MCDA is done in Sec. 4. Finally Sec. 5 gives an interpretation of the new importance index.

2. Preliminaries

The set of all criteria is denoted by $N = \{1, \ldots, n\}$. The problem of the determination of utility functions through a bi-capacity has already been addressed.[6] We focus here on the aggregation model so that all scores w.r.t. criteria are supposed to be given on the bipolar scale $\mathbb{R}^n$. Hence alternatives are elements of $X = \mathbb{R}^n$. Considering two acts $x, y \in X$ and $A \subseteq N$, we use the notation (x_A, y_{-A}) to denote the compound act $z \in X$ such that $z_i = x_i$ if $i \in A$ and y_i otherwise.

2.1. *Capacity and Choquet integral*

A *capacity*, also called fuzzy measure, is a set function $\nu : 2^N \to \mathbb{R}$ satisfying monotonicity condition "$S \subseteq T \Rightarrow \nu(S) \leq \nu(T)$", and boundary conditions $\nu(\emptyset) = 0$, $\nu(N) = 1$. $\nu(S)$ is interpreted as the overall assessment of the binary act $(1_S, 0_{-S})$.

The Choquet integral defined w.r.t. a capacity ν has the following expression :

$$C_\nu(x_1, \ldots, x_n) = \sum_{i=1}^n \left(x_{\pi(i)} - x_{\pi(i-1)} \right) \nu \left(S_{\pi(i)} \right), \tag{1}$$

where $x_{\pi(0)} := 0$, $x_{\pi(1)} \leq x_{\pi(2)} \leq \cdots \leq x_{\pi(n)}$, $S_{\pi(i)} = \{\pi(i), \ldots, \pi(n)\}$.

The Choquet has been introduced in MCDA for its ability to model decision behaviors ranging from tolerance to intolerance. It has been shown to represent the importance of criteria, the interaction between criteria and other decision strategies such as veto or favor.

2.2. *Bi-capacity*

Let $\mathcal{Q}(N) = \{(S,T) \in \mathcal{P}(N) \times \mathcal{P}(N) \mid S \cap T = \emptyset\}$. A bi-capacity is a function $v : \mathcal{Q}(N) \to \mathbb{R}$ satisfying[3]

- $S \subseteq S' \Rightarrow v(S,T) \leq v(S',T)$,
- $T \subseteq T' \Rightarrow v(S,T) \geq v(S,T')$,
- $v(\emptyset,\emptyset) = 0$, $v(N,\emptyset) = 1$, $v(\emptyset,N) = -1$.

The first two conditions depict monotonicity of v while the last condition corresponds to boundary conditions. Term $v(S,T)$ is interpreted as the overall assessment of the ternary act $(1_S, -1_T, 0_{-S\cup T})$.

The Choquet integral w.r.t. a bi-capacity has been proposed in Ref. 3. Let $x \in X$, $N^+ = \{i \in N, x_i \geq 0\}$ and $N^- = N \setminus N^+$. Define the capacity ν by $\nu(S) := v(S \cap N^+, S \cap N^-)$ for all $S \subseteq N$. Then the Choquet integral w.r.t. v is defined by:

$$BC_v(x) := C_\nu(x_{N^+}, -x_{N^-}).\qquad(2)$$

Note that N^+, N^- and ν depend on x.

3. Definition of a Value for Bi-Cooperative Games

A capacity or a bi-capacity quantifies the way the criteria interact each other. These concepts also exists in Cooperative Game Theory (known as *Transferable Utility (TU) game* and *bi-cooperative game* respectively) to quantify the way players cooperate when forming coalitions, where N denotes here the set of players.

In Cooperative Game Theory (CGT), a game is a capacity that is not necessarily monotone. For any $S \subseteq N$, $v(S)$ represents the wealth gained by the players of S if they form a coalition. After all, all players will finally form the grand coalition composed of all players N. The main question that arises then is how the players shall share the total wealth $v(N)$. A solution is a payoff vector $x \in \mathbb{R}^N$ that is accepted by all players as a fair share of $v(N)$. The Shapley value is a solution concept that evaluates the mean players' prospect.

A bi-cooperative game is a function $v : \mathcal{Q}(N) \longrightarrow \mathbb{R}$ with $v(\emptyset,\emptyset) = 0$. This model has been proved to be useful to represent some cost-allocation problems[9,11] such as the share of a water supply network among cities or the share of common heating costs.[8] Bi-cooperative games represent situations where, when players decide to cooperate, they can choose between two attitudes: the default one (called *positive attitude* hereafter) and the welfarist one (called *negative attitude* hereafter). By *default* attitude, we mean the attitude of collaboration that any player would adopt in the usual cooperative situation. By *welfarist* attitude, we mean an attitude that demands more commitment by the player but which allows a significant reduction of the total worth compared to the case where the player would have chosen the default attitude. This happens when the bi-cooperative game is monotone. The set of bi-cooperative games on N is denoted by $\mathcal{G}(N)$.

Unlike usual games where at the end, all players join the grand coalition, it is not assumed here that all players have decided to be positive contributors. We denote hereafter by S the set of players that have decided to be positive contributors, by T the set of players that have decided to be negative contributors. The remaining players $N\backslash(S \cup T)$ are abstentionist. Each player makes his decision in good faith.

Given a situation depicted by a bi-coalition (S,T), the worth that is obtained in this situation is $v(S,T)$. The players shall share this worth among themselves. Let us denote by $\phi^{S,T}(v) : \mathcal{G}(N) \to \mathbb{R}^N$ such a share in the situation of bi-coalition (S,T).

For classical value, it is assumed that all players finally participate to the game so that the grand coalition is formed. If it is not the case, a coalition structure has formed. Then the players of each coalition share the worth obtained by that coalition.[1] In this case, the players that do not belong to the coalition get zero from this coalition. So it is natural that the payoff for a player that does not participate vanishes. Hence

$$\forall i \in N \backslash (S \cup T), \quad \phi_i^{S,T}(v) = 0. \tag{3}$$

This holds also for cost allocation problems.[9,11]

Players of S contribute positively to the game (provided v is monotone) and deserve thus a non-negative payoff:

$$\forall i \in S, \quad \phi_i^{S,T}(v) \geq 0. \tag{4}$$

Players of T contribute negatively to the game (provided v is monotone) and deserve thus a nonpositive payoff:

$$\forall i \in T, \quad \phi_i^{S,T}(v) \leq 0. \tag{5}$$

Weber's characterization of the Shapley value is based on four axiom[12]: Linearity, Null player, Symmetry and Efficiency. We have generalized these axioms to characterize the Shapley value for bi-cooperative games.[8] We now describe the axioms we have defined for bi-cooperative games.

Consider first linearity. This axiom states that if several games are combined linearly then the values of each individual game shall be combined in the same way to obtain the value of the resulting game. This axiom is trivially extended to the case of bi-cooperative games.

Linearity (L): $\phi^{S,T}$ is linear on $\mathcal{G}(N)$.

The "null player" axiom says that if a player i is null, i.e. $\nu(S \cup \{i\}) = \nu(S)$ for any $S \subseteq N \setminus \{i\}$, then this player does not contribute at all to any coalition and thus the payoff for this player shall be zero. For bi-cooperative games, a player is said to be *null* if the asset is exactly the same if he joins the positive contributors or the negative contributors.

Definition 1. The player i is said to be *null* for the bi-cooperative game v if $v(S, T \cup \{i\}) = v(S, T) = v(S \cup \{i\}, T)$ for any $(S, T) \in \mathcal{Q}(N \setminus \{i\})$.

Null player (N): If a player i is null for the bi-cooperative game $v \in \mathcal{G}(N)$ then $\phi_i^{S,T}(v) = 0$.

We introduce a new axiom that is monotonicity in the following way. Let (N, v) and (N, v') be two TU games such that there exists $i \in N$ with $v'(K) = v(K)$ and $v'(K \cup \{i\}) \geq v(K \cup \{i\})$ for all $K \subseteq N \setminus \{i\}$. Then the contribution of player i to game v' is larger than that of player i to game v. Then the payoff of i in game v shall not be greater to that of i in v'.

Generalizing that to bi-cooperative games, we obtain

Monotonicity (M): Let v, v' be two bi-cooperative games such that there exists $i \in N$ with

$$\begin{cases} v'(S', T') = v(S, T) \\ v'(S' \cup \{i\}, T') \geq v(S' \cup \{i\}, T') \\ v'(S', T' \cup \{i\}) \geq v(S', T' \cup \{i\}) \end{cases}$$

for all $(S', T') \in \mathcal{Q}(N \setminus \{i\})$, then for all $i \in N$, $\phi_i^{S,T}(v') \geq \phi_i^{S,T}(v)$.

When i joins the positive coalition S', the added value for i is larger for game v' than for v. When i joins negative coalition T', the negative added value for i is smaller in absolute for v' than for v (the decrease of the value of the game when i joins the negative contributors is less important for v' than for v). Then the payoff of i in v shall not be greater to that of i in v'.

The next axiom that characterizes the Shapley value is symmetry with respect to the players which means that the rule for computing the share does not depend on the numbering of the players. It means that nothing special is done to one player compared to another one. In other words, the players are anonymous. This depicts fairness.

Let σ be a permutation on N. With some abuse of notation, we denote $\sigma(K) := \{\sigma(i)\}_{i \in K}$. The role of the players of S, T and $N \setminus (S \cup T)$ is different. So, for bi-cooperative games, symmetry holds only among players of S, players of T and players of $N \setminus (S \cup T)$.

Symmetry axiom (S): For any permutation σ of N such that $\sigma(S) = S$ and $\sigma(T) = T$,

$$\phi_{\sigma(i)}^{S,T}(v \circ \sigma^{-1}) = \phi_i^{S,T}(v) .$$

Positive Negative Symmetry (PNS): Let $i \in S$ and $j \in T$, and v_i, v_j be two bi-cooperative games such that for all $(S', T') \in \mathcal{Q}((S \cup T) \setminus \{i, j\})$

$$v_i(S' \cup \{i\}, T') - v_i(S', T') = v_j(S', T') - v_j(S', T' \cup \{j\})$$
$$v_i(S' \cup \{i\}, T' \cup \{j\}) - v_i(S', T' \cup \{j\})$$
$$= v_j(S' \cup \{i\}, T') - v_j(S' \cup \{i\}, T' \cup \{j\})$$

Then

$$\phi_i^{S,T}(v_i) = -\phi_j^{S,T}(v_j) .$$

We finally introduce the efficiency axiom. $\phi^{S,T}(v)$ is a share of the worth obtained by the bi-coalition (S, T).

Efficiency axiom (E): For every game in $\mathcal{G}(N)$,

$$\sum_{i \in N} \phi_i^{S,T}(v) = v(S,T).$$

We have proved the following result.[8]

Theorem 1. $\phi^{S,T}$ *satisfies axioms* **(L)**, **(N)**, **(M)**, **(S)**, **(PNS)** *and* **(E)** *if and only if one has for all* $i \in N$

$$\phi_i^{S,T}(v) = \sum_{K \subseteq (S \cup T) \setminus \{i\}} \frac{k!(s+t-k-1)!}{(s+t)!} \times [V(K \cup \{i\}) - V(K)],$$

where, for $K \subseteq S \cup T$, V *is defined by* $V(K) := v(S \cap K, T \cap K)$.

The indices in $\phi_i^{S,T}(v)$ coincides with the Shapley value of cooperative game V. Theorem 1 is essential since it proves that the only terms of a bi-cooperative game v that are used to determine $\phi^{S,T}(v)$ belong to

$$\mathcal{Q}_{S,T}(N) = \{(S',T') \in \mathcal{Q}(N), S' \subseteq S, T' \subseteq T\}$$

The payoff for a positive contributor depends only on his added-value from nonparticipation to positive contribution. The information regarding how this player behaves when he becomes negative contributor is not relevant. The same argument can be used symmetrically for negative contributors. From Theorem 1, it is not possible to define an allocation rule that looks at the contribution for the opposite action to the one chosen by each agent (positive vs. negative contribution). Hence for the computation of the value, one can restrict the bi-cooperative game to a usual game (namely V). Even though we have much more information than is contained in V, the remaining terms cannot be used in a coherent way.

4. Importance Index

Our final goal is actually to define an importance index for bi-capacities. The value defined for bi-cooperative games is a good candidate for this task.

4.1. Definition of the importance index in $\mathcal{Q}_{S,T}(N)$

Let us start with the importance index restricted to $\Sigma_{S,T}$, where

$$\Sigma_{S,T} = \left\{ x \in \mathbb{R}^N, x_S \geq 0, x_T \leq 0, x_{-(S \cup T)} = 0 \right\}.$$

We denote by $\omega_i^{S,T}(v)$ the wished importance index of criterion $i \in N$ w.r.t. bi-capacity v in the specific domain $\Sigma_{S,T}$.

Consider a usual capacity ν. For $x \in \mathbb{R}_+^n$ with $x_{N_0} = 0$ for some $N_0 \subseteq N$, it is easy to see from (1) that the terms of the capacity that are used to compute the Choquet integral $C_\nu(x)$ correspond to the subsets of $N \backslash N_0$. Consider now a bi-capacity v. From (2), for $x \in \Sigma_{S,T}$, the terms of v that are used to compute $BC_v(x)$ belongs to $\mathcal{Q}_{S,T}(N)$. We conclude that $\omega_i^{S,T}(v)$ shall depend only on the terms of v included in $\mathcal{Q}_{S,T}(N)$.

Theorem 1 showing that $\phi_i^{S,T}(v)$ is based only on terms of v in $\mathcal{Q}_{S,T}(N)$ suggests that $\omega_i^{S,T}(v)$ shall be derived from $\phi_i^{S,T}(v)$.

However, as we will see, the $\phi_i^{S,T}(v)$ value is not completely satisfactory for measuring the importance of criteria. This comes from the differences in interpretation between MCDA and Game Theory.

If $i \in N \setminus (S \cup T)$, then criterion i is discarded from the study. It has no importance within $\Sigma_{S,T}$. Hence (3) holds also for MCDA

$$\forall i \in N \setminus (S \cup T), \quad \omega_i^{S,T}(v) = 0. \tag{6}$$

Let now $i \in S$. If bi-capacity v is monotonic then the importance of criterion i shall be non-negative. Hence (4) holds

$$\forall i \in S, \quad \omega_i^{S,T}(v) \geq 0. \tag{7}$$

Finally consider $i \in T$. In Game Theory, this situation corresponds to a player that contributes negatively to the game since he goes to the negative contributor part. Hence the payoff for this player shall be nonpositive (see (5)). However, in MCDA, $\omega_i^{S,T}(v)$ represents the mean importance of this criterion in domain $\Sigma_{S,T}$. It is not possible to imagine a negative importance when the bi-capacity is monotonic. Hence (5) is not suitable and we should consider instead:

$$\forall i \in T, \quad \omega_i^{S,T}(v) \geq 0. \tag{8}$$

In Game Theory, the elementary contribution of player $i \in T$ is $v(K, L \cup \{i\}) - v(K, L)$ (which is nonpositive) whereas, in MCDA, the elementary contribution of criterion $i \in T$ is $v(K, L) - v(K, L \cup \{i\})$ (which is non-negative).

From Theorem 1, one has for $i \in S$

$$\phi_i^{S,T}(v) = \sum_{K \subseteq (S \cup T) \setminus \{i\}} \frac{k!(s + t - k - 1)!}{(s + t)!}$$
$$\times \ [v((K \cap S) \cup \{i\}, K \cap T) - v(K \cap S, K \cap T)]$$

and for $i \in T$

$$\phi_i^{S,T}(v) = \sum_{K \subseteq (S \cup T) \setminus \{i\}} \frac{k!(s + t - k - 1)!}{(s + t)!}$$
$$\times \ [v(K \cap S, (K \cap T) \cup \{i\}) - v(K \cap S, K \cap T)]$$

Following previous arguments, the expression of $\phi_i^{S,T}(v)$ is fine when $i \in S$, and opposite elementary contributions shall be considered in $\phi_i^{S,T}(v)$ when $i \in S$. This yields the following expression for $i \in S$

$$\omega_i^{S,T}(v) = \sum_{K \subseteq (S \cup T) \setminus \{i\}} \frac{k!(s + t - k - 1)!}{(s + t)!}$$
$$\times \ [v((K \cap S) \cup \{i\}, K \cap T) - v(K \cap S, K \cap T)] \qquad (9)$$

and for $i \in T$

$$\omega_i^{S,T}(v) = \sum_{K \subseteq (S \cup T) \setminus \{i\}} \frac{k!(s + t - k - 1)!}{(s + t)!}$$
$$\times \ [v(K \cap S, K \cap T) - v(K \cap S, (K \cap T) \cup \{i\})] \qquad (10)$$

One easily checks that (6), (7) and (8) hold. $\omega^{S,T}$ fulfills axioms **(L)**, **(N)** and **(S)**. Yet the efficiency axiom **(E)** is not satisfied for $\omega_i^{S,T}(v)$. Axioms **(M)** and **(PNS)** are not directly satisfied. However, slight modifications of these axioms are satisfied by $\omega^{S,T}$.

Monotonicity' (M'): Let v, v' be two bi-capacities such that there exists $i \in N$ with

$$\begin{cases} v'(S', T') = v(S, T) \\ v'(S' \cup \{i\}, T') \geq v(S' \cup \{i\}, T') \\ v'(S', T' \cup \{i\}) \leq v(S', T' \cup \{i\}) \end{cases}$$

for all $(S', T') \in \mathcal{Q}(N \setminus \{i\})$, then for all $i \in N$, $\omega_i^{S,T}(v') \geq \omega_i^{S,T}(v)$.

Positive Negative Symmetry' (PNS'): Let $i \in S$ and $j \in T$, and v_i, v_j be two bi-capacities such that for all $(S', T') \in \mathcal{Q}((S \cup T) \setminus \{i, j\})$

$$v_i(S' \cup \{i\}, T') - v_i(S', T') = v_j(S', T') - v_j(S', T' \cup \{j\})$$
$$v_i(S' \cup \{i\}, T' \cup \{j\}) - v_i(S', T' \cup \{j\})$$
$$= v_j(S' \cup \{i\}, T') - v_j(S' \cup \{i\}, T' \cup \{j\})$$

Then

$$\omega_i^{S,T}(v_i) = \omega_j^{S,T}(v_j) \ .$$

4.2. Mean importance value

In Ref. 4, two mean importance indices for criterion i were defined: one when i belongs to the positive part and one when i belongs to the negative part. These two indices are denoted by $\omega_i^+(v)$ and $\omega_i^-(v)$ respectively. More precisely $\omega_i^+(v)$ (resp. $\omega_i^-(v)$) is the mean importance of criterion i in the domain $\Sigma_i^+ := \{x \in \mathbb{R}^N, x_i \geq 0\}$ (resp. $\Sigma_i^- \{x \in \mathbb{R}^N, x_i \leq 0\}$). From the equality

$$\Sigma_i^+ = \bigcup_{S \subseteq N, i \in S} \Sigma_{S, N \setminus S},$$

one has the following relation between $\omega_i^+(v)$ and $\omega_i^{S,T}(v)$

$$\omega_i^+(v) = \frac{1}{2^{n-1}} \sum_{S \subseteq N, i \in S} \omega_i^{S, N \setminus S}(v)$$

We obtain

$$\omega_i^+(v) = \sum_{(K,L)\in\mathcal{Q}(N\setminus\{i\})} \frac{(k+l)!(n-k-l-1)!}{2^{k+l}\, n!}$$

$$\times\, (v(K\cup\{i\}, L) - v(K, L)).$$

Similarly, the mean importance in the negative part is

$$\omega_i^-(v) = \sum_{(K,L)\in\mathcal{Q}(N\setminus\{i\})} \frac{(k+l)!(n-k-l-1)!}{2^{k+l}\, n!}$$

$$\times\, (v(K, L) - v(K, L\cup\{i\})).$$

Finally, the mean importance in $\mathbb{R}^N$ is

$$\omega_i(v) = \frac{1}{2}\left(\omega_i^+(v) + \omega_i^-(v)\right) = \frac{1}{2^n}\sum_{S\subseteq N}\omega_i^{S,N\setminus S}(v)$$

$$= \sum_{(K,L)\in\mathcal{Q}(N\setminus\{i\})} \frac{(k+l)!(n-k-l-1)!}{2^{k+l}\, n!}$$

$$\times\, (v(K\cup\{i\}, L) - v(K, L\cup\{i\})).$$

5. Interpretation of the Importance Index

One can show the following result.

Theorem 2. *For a function* $h : \mathbb{R}^N \to \mathbb{R}$, *define the discrete bipolar derivative* $\Delta_i^b h(z_{-i}) = \frac{h(1_i, z_{-i}) - h(-1_i, z_{-i})}{2}$. *Then* $\omega_i(v)$ *is the mean value over* $[-1, 1]^{N\setminus\{i\}}$ *of the discrete bipolar derivative of* BC_v *w.r.t. criterion* i.

This result shows that $\omega_i(v)$ is the mean importance of criterion i, where the notion of importance is quantified by a discrete derivative. This shows that our new axiomatic approach leads exactly to the intuitive idea of importance in MCDA.

6. Conclusion

We have defined a new importance index for bi-capacities. The approach we have adopted is to define a value *à la* Shapley using an axiomatic approach in the context of Cooperative Game Theory. The game theoretical counterpart of bi-capacities is the concept of bi-cooperative games. Based on a cost allocation interpretation of bi-cooperative games, a new value has been defined. This value is restricted to a domain where the sign of collaboration of players is fixed. Besides, the payoff for negative players is negative, which does not fits with the interpretation of an importance index. As a result, in the context of multiple criteria decision analysis, the importance index for a bi-capacity in the domain where the sign of criteria is fixed, is defined as the absolute value of the value for the associated bi-cooperative game. The overall importance index is obtained after averaging over all possible domains. It turns out that the importance index so obtained is exactly the mean value of the discrete bipolar derivative of the Choquet integral w.r.t. the bi-capacity.

References

1. R. J. Aumann and J. H. Drèze, Cooperative games with coalition structures. *International Journal of Game Theory*, **3**, 217–237 (1974).
2. J. M. Bilbao, J. R. Fernandez, A. J. Losada and E. Lebrón, Bicooperative games. J. M. Bilboa (eds.) *Cooperative Game on Combinatorial Structures*. Kluwer, Acad. Publi. (2000).
3. M. Grabisch and Ch. Labreuche, Bi-capacities for decision making on bipolar scales. *EUROFUSE Workshop on Information Systems*. Varenna, Italy, pp. 185–190 (2002).
4. M. Grabisch and Ch. Labreuche, Bi-capacities. Part I: definition. *Möbius Transform and Interaction. Fuzzy Sets and Systems*, **151**, 211–236 (2005).
5. C. R Hsiao and T. E. S. Raghavan, Shapley value for multichoice cooperative games. *I. Games and Economic Behavior*, **5**, 240–256 (1993).
6. C. Labreuche and M. Grabisch, Generalized Choquet-like aggregation functions for handling ratio scales. *European Journal of Operational Research*, **172**, 931–955 (2006).
7. C. Labreuche and M. Grabisch, Bi-cooperative games and their importance and interaction indices. *Human Centered Process International Conference*, Kirchberg, Luxembourg, pp. 287–291 (2003).
8. C. Labreuche and M. Grabisch, *A Value for Bi-Cooperative Games*, preprint (2007).
9. H. Moulin, *Cooperative Microeconomics*. Princeton, NJ, Princeton University Press (1995).
10. L. S. Shapley, A value for n-person games. H. W. Kuhn and A. W. Tucker, (eds.), Contributions to the Theory of Games, Vol. II, Number 28 in *Annals of Mathematics Studies*, Princeton University Press, pp. 307–317 (1953).

11. Y. Sprumont, Coherent cost-sharing rules. *Games and Economic Behaviour* **33**, 126–144 (2000).
12. L. S. Weber, Probabilistic values for games. A. E. Roth (eds.) The Shapley value. *Essays in Honor of Lloyd S. Shapley*, Cambridge University Press, pp. 101–119 (1988).

A Fuzzy Constraint-Based Approach to the Analytic Hierarchy Process

Shin-ichi Ohnishi[*], Didier Dubois[†], Henri Prade[‡]
and Takahiro Yamanoi[§]

[*],[§] *Faculty of Engineerings, Hokkai-Gakuen University*
W11-1 S26 Chuo-ku, Sapporo 064-0926 Japan
[*]*ohnishi@eli.hokkai-s-u.ac.jp*
[§]*yamanoi@eli.hokkai-s-u.ac.jp*

[†],[‡]*IRIT, Universite Paul Sabatier*
118 route de Narbonne 31062 Toulouse cedex 9, France
[†]*dubois@irit.fr*
[‡]*prade@irit.fr*

Abstract

Analytic Hierarchy Process (AHP) is one of the most popular method in the field of decision-making today. While there exist many kinds of extensions of AHP using fuzzy measures or fuzzy sets, one of the most natural uses of fuzzy sets is to employ a reciprocal matrix with fuzzy-valued entries. Indeed, using classical AHP, there is often not enough consistency among the data due to strong conditions bearing on the reciprocal preference matrices. Fuzzy reciprocal matrices give us flexible specifications of pairwise preference. This paper presents an approach to using a fuzzy reciprocal matrix in AHP, as a way of specifying fuzzy restrictions on the possible values of the ratio judgments. Then, it can be computed to what extent there exists a consistent standard AHP matrix which is compatible with these restrictions. An optimal consistency index and optimal weights are derived using a fuzzy constraint satisfaction approach. Moreover we show an example of our approach in the last part of the paper.

1.   Introduction

The AHP methodology was proposed by T. L. Saaty in 1977,[9,10] and it has been widely used in the field of decision making. It elicits weights of criteria and alternatives through ratio judgments of relative importance. And finally the preference for each alternative can be derived. The classical method requires the decision-maker (DM) to express his or her preferences in the form of a precise ratio matrix encoding a valued preference relation. However, it can often be difficult for the DM to express exact estimates of the ratios of importance.

Therefore many kinds of methods employing intervals or fuzzy numbers as elements of a pairwise reciprocal data matrix have been proposed to cope with this problem. This allows for a more flexible specification of pairwise preference intensities accounting for the incomplete knowledge of the DM.

In practice, when interval-valued matrices are employed, the DM often gives ranges narrower than his or her actual perception would authorize, because he or she might be afraid of expressing information which is too imprecise. On the other hand, a fuzzy interval expresses rich information because the DM can provide (i) the core of the fuzzy interval as a rough estimate of his perceived preference and (ii) the support set of the fuzzy interval as the range that the DM believes to surely contain the unknown ratio of relative importance.

Usually, since components of the pairwise matrix are locally obtained from the DM by pairwise comparisons of activities or alternatives, its global consistency is not guaranteed. In classical AHP, consistency is usually measured by a consistency index (C.I.) based on the computation of an eigenvalue.

In the AHP, the transitivity of preferences between the elements to be compared is strongly related to the consistency of the matrix. Using intervals or fuzzy numbers as elements of the reciprocal matrices, strict transitivity is too hard to preserve in terms of equalities between intervals or fuzzy numbers. Therefore we only try to maintain consistency of precise matrices that fit the imprecise specifications provided by the DM. A new kind of consistency index for fuzzy-valued matrices is computed that corresponds to the degree of satisfaction of the fuzzy specifications by the best fitting consistent reciprocal preference matrices. Importance or priority weights are then derived based on these precise preference matrices.

2. Earlier Work

The earliest work in AHP using fuzzy sets as data was published by van Laarhoven and Pedrycz.[7] They compared fuzzy ratios described by triangular membership functions. Lootsma's logarithmic least square was used to derive local fuzzy priorities. Later using a geometric mean, Buckley[3,4] determined fuzzy priorities of comparison ratios whose membership functions were assumed trapezoidal. Modifying van Laarhoven and Pedrycz's method, Boender *et al.*[1] presented a more robust approach to the normalization of the local priorities.

The issue of consistency in AHP using fuzzy sets as elements of the matrix was first tackled by Salo.[11] Departing from the fuzzy arithmetic approach, he derived fuzzy weights using an auxiliary programming formulation, which described relative fuzzy ratios as constraints on the membership values of local priorities. Later Leung and Cao[8] proposed a notion of tolerance deviation of fuzzy relative importance that is strongly related to Saaty's consistency index C.I.

There also exist many other extensions of AHP using fuzzy measures and integrals.[12] These methods do not have to assume independence of activities and can avoid the rank reversal problems which the traditional AHP method may suffer from.

3. An Approach using a Fuzzy-valued Reciprocal Matrix

Since using fuzzy numbers as elements of a pairwise matrix is more expressive than using crisp values or intervals, we hope that the fuzzy approach allows a more accurate description of the decision making process. Rather than forcing the DM to provide precise representations of imprecise perceptions, we suggest using an imprecise representation instead. In the traditional method the obtained matrix does not exactly fit the AHP theory and thus must be modified so as to respect mathematical requirements. Here we let the DM be imprecise, and check if this imprecise data encompasses precise preference matrices obeying the AHP requirements.

3.1. *Fuzzy reciprocal data matrix*

In this paper, we employ a fuzzy pairwise comparison reciprocal $n \times n$ matrix $\tilde{R} = \{\tilde{r}_{ij}\}$ pertaining to n elements (criteria, alternatives). In the AHP model, entry r_{ij} of a preference matrix reflects the ratio of importance weights of element i over element j. In the fuzzy-valued matrix, diagonal elements are singletons ($= 1$) and the other entries $\tilde{r}_{ij}(i \neq j)$ have membership function μ_{ij} whose support is positive:

$$\tilde{r}_{ii} = 1, \quad \text{supp}(\mu_{ij}) \subseteq (0, +\infty), \quad i, j = 1, \ldots, n.$$

Moreover if element i is preferred to element j then supp (μ_{ij}) lies in $[1, +\infty)$, while $\text{supp}(\mu_{ij})$ lies in $(0, 1]$ if the contrary holds. The DM is supposed to supply the core (modal value) r_{ij} of $\tilde{r}_{ij}$ and its support set $[l_{ij}, u_{ij}]$ for $i < j$. The support set is the range that the DM believes surely contains the unknown ratio of relative importance. The DM may only supply entries above the diagonal like in the classical AHP.

We assume reciprocity $\tilde{r}_{ij} = 1/\tilde{r}_{ji}$ as follows[7]

$$\mu_{ij}(r) = \mu_{ji}(1/r). \tag{1}$$

Therefore

$$\text{core}(1/\tilde{r}_{ij}) = 1/r_{ij}, \tag{2}$$

$$\text{supp}(1/\tilde{r}_{ij}) = [1/u_{ij}, 1/l_{ij}]. \tag{3}$$

We may assume all entries whose core is larger than or equal to 1 form triangular fuzzy sets i.e. if $r_{ij} \geq 1$, we assume $\tilde{r}_{ij}$ is a triangular fuzzy number, denoted as

$$\tilde{r}_{ij} = (l_{ij}, r_{ij}, u_{ij})_\Delta, \tag{4}$$

but then the symmetric entry $\tilde{r}_{ji}$ is not triangular. Alternatively one may suppose that if $r_{ij} < 1$, $\tilde{r}_{ji}$ is $(1/u_{ij}, 1/r_{ij}, 1/l_{ij})_\Delta$. Therefore the following transitivity condition inherited from the AHP theory will not hold

$$\tilde{r}_{ij} \otimes \tilde{r}_{jk} = \tilde{r}_{ik} \tag{5}$$

in particular because multiplication of fuzzy intervals does not preserve triangular membership functions. However, even with intervals, this equality is too demanding (since it corresponds to requesting two usual equalities instead of one) and impossible to satisfy. For instance take $i = k$ in the above equality. On the left hand side is an interval, on the right-hand side is a scalar value ($=1$). So it makes no sense to consider a fuzzy AHP theory where fuzzy intervals would simply replace scalar entries in the preference ratio matrix.

3.2. Consistency

In our approach, a fuzzy-valued ratio matrix is considered to be a fuzzy set of consistent non-fuzzy ratio matrices. Each fuzzy entry is viewed as a flexible constraint. A ratio matrix is consistent in the sense of AHP (or AHP-consistent) if and only if there exists a set of weights $w_1, w_2, \ldots, w_n$, summing to 1, such that for all i, j, $r_{ij} = w_i/w_j$.

Using a fuzzy reciprocal matrix, some kind of consistency index of the data matrix is necessary. This index will not measure the AHP-consistency of a non-fully consistent matrix, but instead will measure the degree to which an AHP-consistent matrix R exists, that satisfies the fuzzy constraints expressed in the fuzzy reciprocal matrix $\tilde{R}$. More precisely this degree of satisfaction can be attached to a n-tuple of weights $\boldsymbol{w} = (w_1, w_2, \ldots, w_n)$ since this n-tuple defines an AHP-consistent ratio matrix. This degree is defined as

$$\alpha(\boldsymbol{w}) = \min_{i,j} \mu_{ij}(w_i/w_j). \tag{6}$$

It is the "degree of consistency" of the weight pattern $\boldsymbol{w}$ with the fuzzy ratio matrix $\tilde{R}$ in the sense of fuzzy constraint satisfaction problems (FCSPs).[5] The coefficient $\alpha(\boldsymbol{w})$ is in some sense an empirical validity coefficient measuring to what extent a weight pattern is close to, or compatible with, the DM revealed preference.

The best fitting weight patterns can thus be found by solving the following FCSP:

$$\text{maximize } \alpha \equiv \min_{i,j} \left\{ \mu_{ij} \left(\frac{w_i}{w_j} \right) \right\},$$

$$0 \leq w_i \leq 1, \quad i = 1, \ldots, n, \quad \sum_i^n w_i = 1,$$

where w_i is the weight of alternative i, and n is the total number of alternatives. Maximizing α corresponds to getting as close as possible to the ideal preference patterns of the DM (in the sense of the Chebychev norm). Let

$$\alpha^* \equiv \max_{w_1, \ldots, w_n} \min_{i,j} \left\{ \mu_{ij} \left(\frac{w_i}{w_j} \right) \right\}. \tag{7}$$

α^* is a degree of consistency different from Saaty's index, but it can be used as a natural substitute to the AHP-consistency index for evaluating the DM's degree of rationality when expressing his or her preferences.

Solving this flexible constraint satisfaction problem in terms of α enables the fuzzy ratio matrix to be turned into an interval-valued matrix defining crisp constraints for the main problem of calculating local weights, as shown in the next subsection.

As usual, the FCSP problem can be re-stated as follows

maximize α

$$\text{s.t.} \quad \mu_{ij}\left(\frac{w_i}{w_j}\right) \geq \alpha,$$

$$\sum_i^n w_i = 1, \quad i,j = 1,\ldots,n,$$

and we can express the first constraint as follows

$$w_i/w_j \in [\mu_{ij}^{-1}(\alpha), \overline{\mu_{ij}^{-1}(\alpha)}], \tag{8}$$

where $\mu_{ij}^{-1}(\alpha)$ and $\overline{\mu_{ij}^{-1}(\alpha)}$ are the lower and upper bound of the α-cut of $\mu_{ij}(w_i/w_j)$, respectively. This becomes

$$w_j\mu_{ij}^{-1}(\alpha) \leq w_i \leq w_j\overline{\mu_{ij}^{-1}(\alpha)}. \tag{9}$$

Here, if all $\mu_{ij}, i < j$, are triangular fuzzy numbers $(l_{ij}, r_{ij}, u_{ij})_\Delta$, the problem becomes a nonlinear programming problem as follows,

[NLP]

maximize α

$$w_j\{l_{ij} + \alpha(r_{ij} - l_{ij})\} \leq w_i \leq w_j\{u_{ij} + \alpha(r_{ij} - u_{ij})\}$$

$$i,j = 1,\ldots,n, \quad i < j, \quad \sum_i^n w_i = 1.$$

The problem is one of finding a solution to a set of linear inequalities if we fix the value of α. Hence we can solve it using dichotomy method.

3.3. *Unicity of the optimal weight pattern*

Results obtained by Dubois and Fortemps[6] on best solutions to maxmin optimization problems with convex domains can be applied here. Indeed, it is obvious that the set of weight patterns obeying (9), for all i, j is convex. Call this domain D_α. If $\boldsymbol{w}^1$ and $\boldsymbol{w}^2$ are in D_α, so is their convex combination $\boldsymbol{w} = \lambda \boldsymbol{w}^1 + (1 - \boldsymbol{w}^2)$. Note that the ratios w_i/w_j lie between w_i^1/w_j^1 and w_i^2/w_j^2. Hence, if for all w_i^1/w_j^1 differs from w_i^2/w_j^2, it is clear that

$$\mu_{ij}\left(\frac{w_i}{w_j}\right) > \min\left\{\mu_{ij}\left(\frac{w_i^1}{w_j^1}\right), \mu_{ij}\left(\frac{w_i^2}{w_j^2}\right)\right\}. \tag{10}$$

So in particular, suppose there are two optimal weight patterns $\boldsymbol{w}^1$ and $\boldsymbol{w}^2$ in the optimal α^*-cuts, whose ratio matrices differ for all nondiagonal components. It implies that for $\boldsymbol{w} = (\boldsymbol{w}^1 + \boldsymbol{w}^2)/2$,

$$\mu_{ij}\left(\frac{w_i}{w_j}\right) > \alpha^*, \quad i, j = 1, \ldots, n, \tag{11}$$

which is contradictory. In this case, there is only one weight pattern $\boldsymbol{w}$ coherent with the interval-valued matrix whose entries are intervals $(\tilde{r}_{ij})_{\alpha^*}$.

In the case when there are at least two optimal weight patterns $\boldsymbol{w}^1$ and $\boldsymbol{w}^2$ in the optimal α^*-cuts, their ratio matrices coincide for at least one nondiagonal component $(w_i^1/w_j^1 = w_i^2/w_j^2)$. It is shown[6] that in this case,

$$\mu_{ij}\left(\frac{w_i^1}{w_j^1}\right) = \mu_{ij}\left(\frac{w_i^2}{w_j^2}\right) = \alpha^*. \tag{12}$$

So the procedure is then iterated: For such entries of the matrix, the fuzzy numbers in place (i, j) must be replaced by the α^*-cut of $\tilde{r}_{ij}$. It can be done using the best weight pattern $\boldsymbol{w}^*$ obtained from the dichotomy method, checking for (i, j) such that

$$\mu_{ij}\left(\frac{w_i^*}{w_j^*}\right) = \alpha^*. \tag{13}$$

The problem [NLP] is solved again with the new fuzzy matrix. It yields an optimal consistency degree $\beta^* > \alpha^*$ (by construction). If the same lack of unicity phenomenon reappears, some fuzzy matrix entries are again turned into intervals, and so on, until all entries are interval. The obtained solution is called "discrimin"-optimal solution in Dubois and Fortemps' paper[6] and is provably unique from Theorem 5 in that paper.

4. An Example

In Table 1, a 4-dimensional fuzzy reciprocal matrix is presented; lower triangular components are omitted because they are reciprocal of their symmetric components and diagonals are singletons as in normal AHP.

For the data matrix found in Table 1, the degree of satisfaction can be calculated as $\alpha^* = 0.711$, and the fuzzy matrix can be turned into an interval-valued matrix presented in Table 2. At last, unique weights $w = (w_1, w_2, w_3, w_4)$ from the fuzzy data matrix are calculated as shown in Table 3. Also weights from the crisp data matrix (using the cores of Table 1) also appear in this table for comparison.

The optimal maxmin solution found in this example is unique. This is not surprising, because the situation of nonunicity is not common. In case this solution is not unique, the discrimin solution is unique[6] as pointed out above.

Table 1. Fuzzy reciprocal matrix.

1	$(1,3,5)_\triangle$	$(2,5,7)_\triangle$	$(6,8,9)_\triangle$
	1	$(1,2,4)_\triangle$	$(2,4,5)_\triangle$
		1	$(0.5,2,3)_\triangle$
			1

Table 2. Interval-valued matrix.

1	[2.42,3.58]	[4.13,5.58]	[7.42,8.29]
	1	[1.71,2.58]	[3.42,4.29]
		1	[1.57,2.29]
			1

Table 3. Weights from fuzzy and crisp matrix.

	fuzzy data	crisp data
w_1	0.581	0.590
w_2	0.240	0.228
w_3	0.110	0.119
w_4	0.070	0.063

5.   Evaluating Decisions

The global (aggregated) evaluation of a decision f is given by means of the unique (discrimin) optimal weight pattern $\boldsymbol{w}^*$ in D_α:

$$V_f = \sum_i w_i^* u_i(f), \tag{14}$$

where $u_i(f)$ is the utility of decision f under criterion i.

In order to account for the imprecision of the DM's inputs, we should also use weight patterns consistent with all α-cuts of the fuzzy ratio matrix, for $\alpha \in (0, \alpha^*]$, and obtain intervals as global evaluations of decision f:

$$[\underline{V_f^\alpha}, \overline{V_f^\alpha}] \tag{15}$$

by solving the following optimization problems,

$$\underline{V_f} = \min \sum_i w_i u_i(f), \tag{16}$$

$$\overline{V_f} = \max \sum_i w_i u_i(f), \tag{17}$$

$$\text{s.t.} \quad \frac{w_i}{w_j} \in (\tilde{r}_{ij})_\alpha, \quad \sum_i^n w_i = 1.$$

In theory, this problem should be solved for all $\alpha \in (0, \alpha^*]$. Noticing that all intervals $[\underline{V_f^\alpha}, \overline{V_f^\alpha}]$ are nested, we can compute a fuzzy evaluation of decision $\tilde{f}$, which is a fuzzy interval with height α^*. The subnormalization (which is the usual situation here) indicates some inconsistency between the best weight pattern in agreement with the fuzzy preference ratio matrix and the best local ratio evaluations provided by the DM (the cores of the fuzzy intervals $\tilde{r}_{ij}$).

In practice, we can approximate the fuzzy global evaluations of decisions as a triangular fuzzy number

$$\tilde{V} = (\underline{V_f}, V_f, \overline{V_f})_\Delta \tag{18}$$

with height α^* expressing the validity of the results, V_f being calculated from the optimal weight patterns, and $[\underline{V_f}, \overline{V_f}]$ being the widest interval calculated from the supports of the fuzzy entries $\tilde{r}_{ij}$. This representation is an approximation but it can be a useful compact way to show results. To refine it, it is enough to compute the interval-valued approximation for more cuts between 0 and α^*.

6. Conclusions

In classical AHP it is often difficult for the DM to provide an exact pairwise data matrix because it is hard to estimate ratios of importance in a precise way. Therefore we use fuzzy reciprocal matrices, and propose a new kind of consistency index. This index is considered as an empirical validity coefficient evaluating to what extent there is a weight pattern close to the DM revealed preference.

In the next step, we shall test the performance of the method on more extensive examples. Moreover we plan to implement these results on actual data. We will also try to refine the search for appropriate weights that employs the DM's subjective distance.

Here we maintained the idea of using numerical pairwise preference degrees as importance weight ratios, only acknowledging the idea that a DM cannot provide precise data. As a consequence, even if our method is more faithful to the poor precision of the data, the obtained ranking of decisions will suffer from all limitations of the AHP method (described in the book by Bouyssou *et al.*[2] for instance).

Another research direction would be to reconstruct a counterpart of Saaty's method on an ordinal scale such as a finite chain of preference levels, in order to get more robust results. This would imply giving up the weighted sum as a basis for decision evaluation.

Acknowledgments

This research is partly supported by the grant from the ministry of education, sports, science and technology to the national project of 'Advanced improvements of vision, image, speech and language information processing and the application to the technologies for the intelligent instrument and control' in the High-tech Research Center of Hokkai-Gakuen University.

References

1. C. G. E. Boender, J. G. de Graan and F. A. Lootsma, Multi criteria decision analysis with fuzzy pairwise comparisons. *Fuzzy Sets and Systems*, **29**, 133–143 (1989).

2. D. Bouyssou, T. Marchant, M. Pirlot, P. Perny, A. Tsoukias and P. Vincke, *Evaluation Models: A Critical Perspective.* Kluwer Acad. Pub., Boston. (2000).
3. J. J. Buckley, Ranking alternatives using fuzzy numbers. *Fuzzy Sets and Systems*, **15**, 21–31 (1985).
4. J. J. Buckley, Fuzzy hierarchical analysis. *Fuzzy Sets and Systems*, **17**, 233–247 (1985).
5. D. Dubois, H. Fargier and H. Prade, Possibility theory in constraint satisfaction problems: Handling priority, preference and uncertainty. *Applied Intelligence*, **6**, 287–309 (1996).
6. D. Dubois and P. Fortemps, Computing improved optimal solutions to max–min flexible constraint satisfaction problems. *European Journal of Operational Research*, **118**, 95–126 (1999).
7. P. J. M. van Laarhoven and W. Pedrycz, A fuzzy extension of Saaty's priority theory. *Fuzzy Sets and Systems*, **11**, 229–241 (1983).
8. L. C. Leung and D. Cao, On consistency and ranking of alternatives in fuzzy AHP. *European Journal of Operational Research*, **124**, 102–113 (2000).
9. T. L. Saaty, A scaling method for priorities in hierarchical structures. *J. Math. Psy.*, **15**(3), 234–281 (1977).
10. T. L. Saaty, *The Analytic Hierarchy Process.* McGraw-Hill, New York (1980).
11. A. A. Salo, On fuzzy ratio comparison in hierarchical decision models. *Fuzzy Sets and Systems*, **84**, 21–32 (1996).
12. T. Terano, K. Asai and M. Sugeno, *An Introduction to Applied Fuzzy System (in Japanese).* Ohm-sha, Tokyo (1989).

Using Different Transitivity Properties to Deal with Incomplete Fuzzy Preference Relations in Group Decision Making Environments

S. Alonso[*], E. Herrera-Viedma[†] F. Herrera[‡] and F. Chiclana[§]

[*,†,‡]*Department of Computer Science and Artificial Intelligence*
University of Granada, 18071, Granada, Spain
[*]*salonso@decsai.ugr.es*
[†]*viedma@decsai.ugr.es*
[‡]*herrera@decsai.ugr.es*
[§]*CCI — School of Computing*
DMU — Leicester LE1 9BH, UK
chiclana@dmu.ac.uk

Abstract

In Group Decision Making environments where experts have to express their preferences about a given set of alternatives by means of fuzzy preference relations, it is common to find incomplete information situations, that is, situations where not all the information that is expected from the experts is provided.

Based on a consistency principle characterized by the transitivity property, it is possible to make estimations for the unknown preference values in a fuzzy preference relation. In fact, in this paper we present a general procedure to complete fuzzy preference relations with missing values.

This procedure estimates those missing values of an incomplete fuzzy preference relation using different properties that have been proposed to model the concept of transitivity. For each one of these, we present a corresponding measure of consistency of the opinions provided by an expert.

1. Introduction

In Group Decision Making environments there are usually several challenges that have to be faced up in order to a solution for a problem. Some of these challenges are *consistency* and *lack of information*.

- *Consistency* refers to the capability of the experts to express their preferences in a consistent way, that is, avoiding self-contradiction.
- *Lack of information* situations appear when experts are not able to properly give all the information that they are asked for. There may be many different motives why an expert could not be able to give some of his or her preference opinions about the alternatives on a problem. For example, the expert may not have a precise or sufficient level of knowledge about some of the alternatives; the expert may not be able to discriminate the degree to which some options are better than others; or maybe there are too many alternatives and the expert cannot give his/her preferences in a consistent manner. In those situations an expert may have/want to give incomplete information.

There exist multiple possible characterizations for the consistency properties for preferences which allow to deal with consistency problems in decision making situations.[2,3,8] Additionally, it is usually desirable to have a *measurement* of consistency of the opinion expressed by the experts. As consistent information (without contradiction) is usually more valuable than contradictory one, these measures can enable us to develop models[6,9] to solve decision making problems where the most consistent information is better considered. In Refs. 1 and 9 we defined and used some consistency measures to develop complete models for group decision making problems that obtain solutions by giving different importance weights according to the level of consistency of the preferences. In these models the consistency measures were defined using the the additive transitivity property.[14]

In the literature we can find different approaches to deal with lack of information.[1,9,11,12,16–18] In particular, in Ref. 1 we developed a procedure which was able to estimate missing preference values in incomplete fuzzy preference relations. This procedure was also based on the additive transitivity property.

In this paper we generalize our procedure to estimate missing values in incomplete fuzzy preference relations. This general procedure is also guided by consistency, but with the main difference of being able to be characterized by using any of the different transitivity properties proposed in the literature. In such a way, we can freely choose the transitivity property that the preference relations should comply with, and present a more flexible estimation procedure.[1,8,9]

To do so, the paper is set out as follows: In Sec. 2 we present our preliminaries. In Sec. 3 we define consistency measures for incomplete fuzzy preference relations, each one of them associated to one of the known different transitivity properties. In Sec. 4 we present the general estimation procedure for incomplete fuzzy preference relations. Finally, in Sec. 5 we point out our conclusions and some future improvements for the procedure.

2. Preliminaries

In this section we present the concepts of *complete* and *incomplete fuzzy preference relations*, as well as those of *transitivity*, *consistency* and *completeness* for fuzzy preference relations that will be needed throughout the rest of the paper.

2.1. *Fuzzy preference relations*

In *Group Decision Making*, experts have to express their preferences about a set of given alternatives $X = \{x_1, \ldots, x_n\}$, $(n \geq 2)$ in order to find the best of those alternatives. There exist several different formats which can be used to represent experts' preferences, with *Fuzzy Preference Relations* being one the most widely used in the literature.

Definition 1 (Refs. 10 and 13). A fuzzy preference relation P on a set of alternatives X is a fuzzy set on the product set $X \times X$, i.e. it is characterized by a membership function

$$\mu_P \colon X \times X \longrightarrow [0, 1].$$

When cardinality of X is small, the preference relation may be conveniently represented by the $n \times n$ matrix $P = (p_{ik})$, being $p_{ik} = \mu_P(x_i, x_k)$ $(\forall i, k \in \{1, \ldots, n\})$ interpreted as the preference degree or intensity of the alternative x_i over x_k: $p_{ik} = 1/2$ indicates indifference between x_i and x_k ($x_i \sim x_k$), $p_{ik} = 1$ indicates that x_i is absolutely preferred to x_k, and $p_{ik} > 1/2$ indicates that x_i is preferred to x_k ($x_i \succ x_k$). Based on this interpretation we have that $p_{ii} = 1/2 \ \forall i \in \{1, \ldots, n\}$ ($x_i \sim x_i$).

Although fuzzy preference relations are very expressive and easy to use, and despite of the fact that individual fuzzy preference relations can be easily aggregated into group preferences,[5,8,10,14,15] they also present some drawbacks. One of them refers to the problem of *lack of information*. It is not unusual to find that some experts could have difficulties in expressing every preference degree between every pair of alternatives. These difficulties appear due to different reasons: the expert does not have a precise or sufficient level of knowledge about some of the alternatives, the expert is not able to discriminate the degree to which some options are better than others or maybe there are too many alternatives and the expert cannot give every preference degree in a consistent manner. In these situations the experts may choose not to provide every preference degree that they are required to, and thus, we have to deal with *incomplete fuzzy preference relations*:

Definition 2 A function $f: X \to Y$ is *partial* when not every element in the set X necessarily maps onto an element in the set Y. When every element from the set X maps onto one element of the set Y then we have a *total* function.

Definition 3. (Ref. 9). An Incomplete Fuzzy Preference Relation P on a set of alternatives X is a fuzzy set on the product set $X \times X$ that is characterized by a partial membership function.

When an expert does not provide a particular p_{ik} we will call it a *missing value* and we will represented it as $p_{ik} = x$. We also introduce the following sets:

$$A = \{(i,k) \mid i,k \in \{1, \ldots, n\} \wedge i \neq k\},$$
$$MV = \{(i,k) \in A \mid p_{ik} = x\},$$
$$EV = A \backslash MV,$$
$$EV_i = \{(i,k), (k,i) \in EV\},$$

where MV is the set of pairs of alternatives for which the preference degree of the first alternative over the second one is a missing value;

EV is the set of pairs of alternatives for which the expert provides preference values; and EV_i is the set of pairs of alternatives involving alternative x_i for which the expert provides preference values. We do not take into account the preference value of one alternative over itself as this is always assumed to be equal to 0.5.

2.2. *Transitivity, consistency and completeness concepts*

We define the *consistency* of a fuzzy preference relation as a degree to which the information on the relation is not contradictory. Because the preference degrees expressed in a preference relation can be freely chosen by the experts, we cannot directly assume that they comply with any particular consistency property. However, it is obvious that an inconsistent source of information should not be considered as useful as a consistent one. Therefore, to study the consistency of the preference relations to correctly solve decision problems we may face is quite important.

Consistency is usually characterized by *transitivity*, which represents the idea that the preference value obtained by directly comparing two alternatives should be equal to or greater than the preference value between those two alternatives obtained using an indirect chain of alternatives,[4] i.e. $x_i \succeq x_{j_1} \succeq \ldots \succeq x_{j_r} \succeq x_k \Rightarrow x_i \succeq x_k$.

In the literature, different properties to model the concept of transitivity have been suggested, as for example:[3]

- *Triangle Condition*

$$p_{ij} + p_{jk} \geq p_{ik} \quad \forall i, j, k,$$

- *Weak Transitivity*:

$$\min\{p_{ij}, p_{jk}\} \geq 0.5 \Rightarrow p_{ik} \geq 0.5 \quad \forall i, j, k,$$

- *Max-Min Transitivity*:

$$p_{ik} \geq \min\{p_{ij}, p_{jk}\} \quad \forall i, j, k,$$

- *Max-Max Transitivity*:

$$p_{ik} \geq \max\{p_{ij}, p_{jk}\} \quad \forall i, j, k,$$

- *Restricted Max-Min Transitivity*:

$$\min\{p_{ij}, p_{jk}\} \geq 0.5 \Rightarrow p_{ik} \geq \min\{p_{ij}, p_{jk}\} \quad \forall i, j, k,$$

- *Restricted Max-Max Transitivity*:

$$\min\{p_{ij}, p_{jk}\} \geq 0.5 \Rightarrow p_{ik} \geq \max\{p_{ij}, p_{jk}\} \quad \forall i, j, k,$$

- *Additive Transitivity*:

$$(p_{ij} - 0.5) + (p_{jk} - 0.5) = (p_{ik} - 0.5) \quad \forall i, j, k,$$

when for every three options in the problem $x_i, x_j, x_k \in X$ their associated preference degrees p_{ij}, p_{jk}, p_{ik} fulfil one of the previously presented transitivity properties we will consider the preference relation completely consistent. For example, a preference relation will be considered as *additive consistent* if its preference values comply with the additive transitivity property, or *Max-Min consistent* if it complies with the Max-Min transitivity property.

For every pair of alternatives x_i and x_k we define its *completeness measure* as

$$\alpha_{ik} = \frac{\#EV_i + \#EV_k - \#(EV_i \cap EV_k)}{4(n-1) - 2}.$$

$\alpha_{ik} = 1$ means that all the possible preference value involving alternatives x_i and x_k are provided by the expert. This value decreases as the number of missing preference values involving those alternatives in the fuzzy preference relation increases. If all the preference value involving both alternatives are missing then $\alpha_{ik} = 0$.

3. Consistency Measures Based on Different Transitivity Properties

In Ref. 9 we investigated and developed a complete decision making model which is able to handle incomplete information situations. In that investigation, we made use of the additive transitivity property to define consistency measures of fuzzy preference relations. Because additive transitivity may not be the most appropriate property to model consistency for certain problems (it can be a very restrictive property), in this section we will generalize our consistency measures to accommodate any of the above transitivity properties.

The transitivity properties presented in Sec. 2.2 can be used to test whether a fuzzy preference relation is consistent (according to that transitivity property) or not. However, they cannot directly be used to measure the level of consistency the preference relation is, i.e.

given two inconsistent fuzzy preference relations we cannot discern which one is the most inconsistent one.

As the preference relations that we are dealing with could be incomplete, it may be also necessary to rewrite the particular transitivity properties we are studying to be able to check that for every given p_{ik} in the preference relation the property is satisfied or not, and in the latter case, to measure how inconsistent every value is with respect to the rest of information in the relation.

Example 1. The *additive transitivity* property for a particular preference relation can be rewritten as:

$$p_{ik} = p_{ij} + p_{jk} - 0.5 \quad \forall i, j, k \quad (\text{exp}. 1) \tag{1}$$

and from that expression, and knowing that additive transitivity implies reciprocity ($p_{ik} = 1 - p_{ki}$) we can also deduce that:

$$p_{ik} = p_{jk} - p_{ji} + 0.5 \quad \forall i, j, k \quad (\text{exp}. 2) \tag{2}$$

and that:

$$p_{ik} = p_{ij} - p_{kj} + 0.5 \quad \forall i, j, k \quad (\text{exp}. 3) \tag{3}$$

Example 2. Max-Min *transitivity* property:

$$p_{ik} \geq \min\{p_{ij}, p_{jk}\} \quad \forall i, j, k \quad (\text{exp}. 1) \tag{4}$$

cannot be rewritten in any other form.

In order to check whether a particular value p_{ik} given by the expert is consistent or not, preference values relating both alternatives x_i and x_k with other different alternatives are to be known or provided by the expert. The sets of alternatives (x_j) that can be used to check the consistency of a preference value p_{ik} are represented as H_{ik}^l (l is the number of expressions that a particular transitivity property implies):

Example 3. The H_{ik}^l sets for the additive transitivity property are:

- For (exp. 1) (1):

$$H_{ik}^1 = \{j \neq i, k \mid (i, j), (j, k) \in EV\}$$

- For (exp. 2) (2):

$$H_{ik}^2 = \{j \neq i, k \mid (j, i), (j, k) \in EV\}$$

- For (exp. 3) (3):

$$H_{ik}^3 = \{j \neq i, k \mid (i,j), (k,j) \in EV\}$$

Example 4. For Max-Min transitivity property there is only one H_{ik}^l set corresponding to (exp. 1) (4):

$$H_{ik}^1 = \{j \neq i, k \mid (i,j), (j,k) \in EV\}.$$

Once that we know the alternatives that can be used to check the consistency of a preference value p_{ik} we define a partial consistency degree according to every expression l as follows:

$$cl_{ik}^l = \begin{cases} \dfrac{\displaystyle\sum_{j \in H_{ik}^l} cl_{ik}^{jl}}{\#H_{ik}^l} & if \ (\#H_{ik}^l \neq 0), \\ 0 & otherwise \end{cases}$$

where cl_{ik}^{jl} is a normalized distance function between the value p_{ik} and the value that would be obtained by applying expression l. Note that if $H_{ik}^l = \emptyset$ then expression l cannot be applied, and we assign $cl_{ik}^{jl} = 0$).

Example 5. If the additive transitivity property is used we have:
For (exp. 1) (1):

$$cl_{ik}^{j1} = (2/3) \cdot |p_{ik} - (p_{ij} + p_{jk} - 0.5)|,$$

For (exp. 2) (2):

$$cl_{ik}^{j2} = (2/3) \cdot |p_{ik} - (p_{jk} - p_{ji} + 0.5)|,$$

For (exp. 3) (3):

$$cl_{ik}^{j3} = (2/3) \cdot |p_{ik} - (p_{ij} - p_{kj} + 0.5)|.$$

Example 6. For Max-Min transitivity property we have:
For (exp. 1) (4):

$$cl_{ik}^{j1} = \begin{cases} |p_{ik} - mm| & if \ (p_{ik} < mm) \\ 0 & otherwise \end{cases},$$

with $mm = \min\{p_{ij}, p_{jk}\}$.

Finally, the consistency level of the preference value p_{ik} is obtained as a combination of the partial consistency degrees and the completeness measure presented in Sec. 2.2:

$$CL_{ik} = \alpha_{ik} \cdot (1 - \phi(cl_{ik}^l)),$$

where ϕ corresponds to the arithmetic mean.

$CL_{ik} = 1$ means that the preference value p_{ik} is completely consistent with the other information in the preference relation.

4. Generalized Procedure to Estimate Missing Values

In Refs. 1 and 9, we developed an iterative procedure that allows the estimation of missing values in incomplete fuzzy preference relations by means of the application of the additive transitivity property. In this section we will generalize that procedure to be able to use any of the transitivity properties in the estimation process, and thus to provide a more flexible procedure in terms of its applicability.

In order to develop the procedure two different tasks have to be carried out:

(A) Establish the elements that can be estimated in each step of the procedure, and
(B) produce the particular expression that will be used to estimate a particular missing value.

(A) *Elements to be estimated in step h*

The subset of missing values MV that can be estimated in step h of our procedure is denoted by EMV_h (*estimated missing values*) and defined as follows:

$$EMV_h = \{(i,k) \in RMV_h \mid \exists j \in \{H_{ik}^h\}\},$$

where $EMV_0 = \emptyset$ (by definition), RMV_h stands for Remaining Missing Values

$$RMV_h = MV \setminus \bigcup_{l=0}^{h-1} EMV_l,$$

and where $H_{ik}^h = \bigcup_{l=0}^{h-1} H_{ik}^l$ where the H_{ik}^l sets are computed in every iteration as in Sec. 3 with the known and estimated values in the relation from the previous iteration.

Example 7. For the Max-Min transitivity property, in iteration h of the procedure the H_{ik} set is:

$$H_{ik} = H_{ik}^1 = \{j \mid (i,j),(j,k) \in A \setminus RMV_h\}.$$

When $EMV_{maxIter} = \emptyset$ with $maxIter > 0$ the procedure will stop as there will not be any more missing values to be estimated.

(B) *Expression to estimate a particular value p_{ik} in step h*

In order to estimate a particular value p_{ik} with $(i,k) \in EMV_h$, we propose the application of the following function:

```
function estimate_p(i,k)
```

(1) $\mathcal{K} = 0$
(2) for every expression l to evaluate:
(3) $\quad cp_{ik}^l = 0$

(4) $\quad$ if $\#H_{ik}^l \neq 0 \Rightarrow cp_{ik}^l = \dfrac{\sum\limits_{j \in H_{ik}^l} cp_{ik}^{jl}}{\#H_{ik}^l}$; $\mathcal{K}++$

(5) end for
(6) Calculate $cp_{ik} = \frac{1}{\mathcal{K}} \cdot \sum\limits_{l} cp_{ik}^l$

```
end function
```

cp_{ik}^{jl} is the *minimum* value that would be obtained by the application of expression l and cp_{ik} is the final estimated value.

Example 8. For the additive transitivity property we have that:

$$cp_{ik}^{j1} = p_{ij} + p_{jk} - 0.5,$$

$$cp_{ik}^{j2} = p_{jk} - p_{ji} + 0.5,$$

$$cp_{ik}^{j3} = p_{ij} - p_{kj} + 0.5.$$

Example 9. For the Max-Min transitivity property we have that:

$$cp_{ik}^{j1} = \min\{p_{ij}, p_{jk}\}.$$

Finally, the *iterative estimation procedure pseudo-code* is as follows:

```
   ESTIMATION PROCEDURE
0.  EMV_0 = ∅
1.  h = 1
2.  while EMV_h ≠ ∅ {
3.     for every (i, k) ∈ EMV_h {
4.        estimate_p(i,k)
5.     }
6.     h + +
7.  }
```

5. Conclusions and Future Works

In this paper we have presented a general consistency based procedure which allows the estimation of missing values in incomplete fuzzy preference relations. This procedure, which generalizes those presented in Refs. 1 and 9 can be used in group decision making environments to handle incomplete information situations and avoiding the introduction of contradictions in the information provided by the experts.

The procedure allows the use of different transitivity properties to model the consistency concept to implement in the particular decision making problem to solve. Additionally, different consistency measures for the different transitivity properties have been defined which could be used in several decision making models to weight the preferences of the experts according to their consistency (consistent information is usually more valuable than contradictory information).

In future works we will extend this procedure to be able to handle other kinds of preference relations (linguistic, multiplicative and interval-valued preference relations) to be able to use it in richer decision models where experts would have the possibility of giving their preferences using multiple preference representation formats.[7]

Acknowledgments

This paper has been partially funded by the EPSRC research project "EP/C542215/1".

References

1. S. Alonso, F. Chiclana, F. Herrera, E. Herrera-Viedma and J. Alcalá-Fdez, A consistency based procedure to estimate missing pairwise preference values. *International Journal of Intelligent Systems*, in press (2007).
2. F. Chiclana, F. Herrera and E. Herrera-Viedma, A Note on the internal consistency of various preference representations. *Fuzzy Sets and Systems*, **131**(1), 75–78 (2002).
3. F. Chiclana, F. Herrera and E. Herrera-Viedma, Reciprocity and consistency of fuzzy preference relations. (eds) B. De Baets and J. Fodor. *Principles of Fuzzy Preference Modelling and Decision Making*, Academia Press, pp. 123–142 (2003).
4. D. Dubois and H. Prade, *Fuzzy Sets and Systems, Theory and Application*. Academic Press, New York (1980).
5. J. Fodor and M. Roubens, *Fuzzy Preference Modelling and Multicriteria Decision Support*. Kluwert Academic Publichers, Dordrecht (1994).
6. E. Herrera-Viedma, S. Alonso, F. Chiclana and F. Herrera, A consensus model for group decision making with incomplete fuzzy preference relations. *IEEE Transactions on Fuzzy Systems*, in press (2007).
7. E. Herrera-Viedma, F. Herrera and F. Chiclana, A consensus model for multiperson decision making with different preference structures. *IEEE Transactions on Systems, Man and Cybernetics. Part A: Systems and Man*, **32**(3), 394–402 (2002).
8. E. Herrera-Viedma, F. Herrera, F. Chiclana and M. Luque, Some issues on consistency of fuzzy preference relations. *European Journal of Operational Research*, **154**, 98–109 (2004).
9. E. Herrera-Viedma, F. Chiclana, F. Herrera and S. Alonso, A group decision-making model with incomplete fuzzy preference relations based on additive consistency. *IEEE Transactions on Systems, Man and Cybernetics, Part B, Cybernetics*, **37**(1), 176–189 (2007).
10. J. Kacprzyk, Group decision making with a fuzzy linguistic majority. *Fuzzy Sets and Systems*, **18**, 105–118 (1986).
11. S. H. Kim and B. S. Ahn, Interactive group decision making procedure under incomplete information. *European Journal Of Operational Research*, **116**, 498–507 (1999).
12. S. H. Kim, S. H. Choi and J. K. Kim, An interactive procedure for multiple attribute group decision making with incomplete information: Range-based approach. *European Journal of Operational Research*, **118**, 139–152 (1999).
13. S. A. Orlovski, Decision-making with fuzzy preference relations. *Fuzzy Sets and Systems*, **1**, 155–167 (1978).
14. T. Tanino, Fuzzy preference orderings in group decision making. *Fuzzy Sets and Systems*, **12**, 117–131 (1984).
15. T. Tanino, Fuzzy preference relations in group decision making. (eds.) J. Kacprzyk and M. Roubens. *Nonconventional Preference Relations in Decision Making*, Springer-Verlag, Berlin, pp. 54–71 (1988).

16. Z. S. Xu, Goal programming models for obtaining the priority vector of incomplete fuzzy preference relation. *International Journal of Approximate Reasoning*, **36**(3), 261–270 (2004).

17. Z. S. Xu, An approach to group decision making based on incomplete linguistic preference relations. *International Journal of Information Technology & Decision Making*, **4**(1), 153–160 (2005).

18. Z. S. Xu, A practical procedure for group decision making under incomplete multiplicative linguistic preference relations. *Group Decision and Negotiation*, **15**, 581–591 (2006).

A Bargaining Agent Models Its Opponent with Entropy-Based Inference

John Debenham

Faculty of Information Technology
University of Technology, Sydney
NSW, Australia
debenham@it.uts.edu.au

Abstract

A negotiating agent engages in multi-issue bilateral negotiation in a dynamic information-rich environment. The agent strives to make informed decisions. It may assume that the integrity of some of its information decays with time, and that a negotiation may break down under certain conditions. The agent makes no assumptions about the internals of its opponent — it focuses only on the signals that it receives. It constructs two probability distributions over the set of all deals. First the probability that its opponent will accept a deal, and second that a deal will prove to be acceptable to it in time.

1. Introduction

A *Negotiating Agent*, *NA*, engages in bilateral bargaining with an opponent, *OP*. It strives to make informed decisions in an information-rich environment that includes information drawn from the Internet by bots. Its design was provoked by the observation that agents are not always utility optimizers. *NA* attempts to fuse the negotiation with the information generated both by and because of it. It reacts to information derived from its opponent and from the environment, and proactively seeks missing information that may be of value.

243

This work is based on the notion that when an intelligent agent buys a hat, a car, a house or a company she does so because she feels comfortable with the general terms of the deal. This "feeling of comfort" is achieved as a result of information acquisition and validation. Negotiation is as much of an information acquisition and exchange process as it is an offer exchange process — one feeds off the other.

NA draws on ideas from information theory. Game theory tells us what to do, and what outcome to expect, in many well-known negotiation situations, but these strategies and expectations are derived from assumptions about the internals of the opponent. Game theoretic analyses of bargaining are founded on the notion of agents as utility optimizers in the presence of complete and incomplete information about their opponents.[1]

Two probability distributions form the foundation of both the offer evaluation and the offer making processes. They are both over the set of all deals and are based on all information available to the agent. The first distribution is the probability that any deal is acceptable to *OP*. The second distribution is the probability that any deal will prove to be acceptable to *NA* — this distribution generalizes the notion of utility.

NA may not have a von Neumann-Morgerstern utility function. *NA* makes no assumptions about the internals of *OP* in particular whether it has a utility function. *NA* does make assumptions about: the way in which the integrity of information will decay, preferences that its opponent may have for some deals over others, and conditions that may lead to breakdown. It also assumes that unknown probabilities can be inferred using *maximum entropy probabilistic logic*[2] that is based on random worlds.[3] The maximum entropy probability distribution is "the least biased estimate possible on the given information; i.e. it is maximally noncommittal with regard to missing information".[4] In the absence of knowledge about *OP*'s decision-making apparatus, *NA* assumes that the "maximally noncommittal" model is the correct model on which to base its reasoning.

A *preference relation* is an assumption that *NA* makes about *OP*'s preferences for some deals over others. For example, that she prefers to pay a lower price to a higher price. A *single-issue preference relation* assumes that she prefers deals on the basis of one issue alone, independent of the values of the other issues. A preference relation may be assumed prior to the negotiation, or during it based on the offers made. For example, the opponent may display a preference for items of a certain color[5]; describes a basis for ordering colors. The preference relations illustrated here are single-issue orderings, but the agent's reasoning operates equally well with any preference relation as long as it may be expressed in Horn clause logic.

Under some circumstances bilateral bargaining has questionable value as a trading mechanism. Bilateral bargaining is known to be inherently inefficient.[6,7] shows that a seller is better off with an auction that attracts $n + 1$ buyers than bargaining with n individuals, *no matter what* the bargaining protocol is. Reference 8 shows that the weaker bargaining types will fare better in exchanges leading to a gradual migration. These results hold for agents who aim to optimize their utility and do limit the work described here.

2. The Negotiating Agent: *NA*

NA operates in an information-rich environment. The integrity of its information, including information extracted from the Internet, will decay in time. The way in which this decay occurs will depend on the type of information, and on the source from which it is drawn. Little appears to be known about how the integrity of information, such as news-feeds, decays.

One source of *NA*'s information is the signals received from *OP*. These include offers to *NA*, and the acceptance or rejection of *NA*'s offers. If *OP* rejected *NA*'s offer of \$8 two days ago then what is *NA*'s belief now in the proposition that *OP* will accept another offer of \$8 now? Perhaps it is around 0.1. A linear model is used to model the integrity decay of these beliefs, and when the probability of a decaying belief approaches 0.5[a] the belief is discarded. This choice of a linear model is independent of the bargaining method. The model of decay could be exponential, quadratic or what ever.

2.1. *Interaction protocol*

The agents communicate using sentences in a first-order language $\mathcal{L}$. This includes the exchange, acceptance and rejection of offers. $\mathcal{L}$ contains the following predicates: $\mathit{Offer}(\delta)$, $\mathit{Accept}(\delta)$, $\mathit{Reject}(\delta)$

---

[a] A sentence probability of 0.5 represents "maybe, maybe not".

and $Quit(.)$, where $Offer(\delta)$ means "the sender is offering you a deal δ", $Accept(\delta)$ means "the sender accepts your deal δ", $Reject(\delta)$ means "the sender rejects your deal δ" and $Quit(.)$ means "the sender quits — the negotiation ends".

Two negotiation protocols are described. First, negotiation *without decay* in which all offers stand for the the entire negotiation. Second, with *with decay* in which offers stand only if accepted by return — *NA* represents *OP*'s offers as beliefs with sentence probabilities that decay in time.

NA and *OP* each exchange offers alternately at successive discrete times.[9] They enter into a commitment if one of them accepts a standing offer. The protocol has three stages:

(1) Simultaneous, initial, binding offers from both agents;
(2) A sequence of alternating offers, and
(3) An agent quits and walks away from the negotiation.

The negotiation ceases *either* in the second round if one of the agents accepts a standing offer *or* in the final round if one agent quits and the negotiation breaks down.

In the first stage the agents simultaneously send $Offer(.)$ messages to each other. These initial offers are taken as limits on the range of values that are considered possible. This is crucial to the method described in Sec. 3 where there are domains that would otherwise be unbounded. The exchange of initial offers "stakes out the turf" on which the subsequent negotiation will take place. In the second stage an $Offer(.)$ message is interpreted as an implicit rejection, $Reject(.)$, of the opponent's offer on the table.

2.2. *Agent architecture*

Incoming messages from all sources are time-stamped and placed in an "In Box", $\mathcal{X}$, as they arrive. *NA* has a knowledge base $\mathcal{K}$ and a belief set $\mathcal{B}$. Each of these two sets contains statements in $\mathcal{L}$. $\mathcal{K}$ contains statements that are generally true, such as $\forall x(Accept(x) \leftrightarrow \neg Reject(x))$ — i.e. an agent does one thing or the other. The belief set $\mathcal{B} = \{\beta_i\}$ contains statements that are each qualified with a *given sentence probability*, $\mathbf{B}(\beta_i)$, that represents an agent's belief in the truth of the statement. These sentence probabilities may decay in time.

The distinction between the knowledge base $\mathcal{K}$ and the belief set $\mathcal{B}$ is simply that $\mathcal{K}$ contains unqualified statements and $\mathcal{B}$ contains statements that are qualified with sentence probabilities. $\mathcal{K}$ and $\mathcal{B}$ play different roles in the method described in Sec. 3

NA's actions are determined by its "strategy". A *strategy* is a function $\mathbf{S} : \mathcal{K} \times \mathcal{B} \to \mathcal{A}$ where $\mathcal{A}$ is the set of actions. At certain distinct times the function $\mathbf{S}$ is applied to $\mathcal{K}$ and $\mathcal{B}$ and the agent does something. The set of actions, $\mathcal{A}$, includes sending *Offer(.)*, *Accept(.)*, *Reject(.)* and *Quit(.)* messages to *OP*. The way in which $\mathbf{S}$ works is described in Sec. 5. Momentarily before the $\mathbf{S}$ function is activated, a "revision function" $\mathbf{R}$ is activated:

$\mathbf{R} : (\mathcal{X} \times \mathcal{K} \times \mathcal{B}) \to (\mathcal{K} \times \mathcal{B})$

$\mathbf{R}$ clears the "In Box", and stores the messages *either* in $\mathcal{B}$ with a given sentence probability *or* in $\mathcal{K}$.

A *deal*, δ, is a commitment for the sender to do something, τ (the sender's "terms"), subject to the receiver committing to do something, ω (the receiver's "terms"): $\delta = (\tau, \omega)$. *NA* may have a real-valued *utility* function: $\mathbf{U} : \mathcal{T} \to \Re$, where $\mathcal{T}$ is the set of terms. If so, then for any deal $\delta = (\tau, \omega)$ the expression $\mathbf{U}(\omega) - \mathbf{U}(\tau)$ is called the *surplus* of δ. An agent may be unable to specify a utility function either precisely or with certainty.[b] Section 4 describes a predicate *NAAcc(.)* that represents the "acceptability" of a deal.

NA uses three things to make offers: an estimate of the likelihood that *OP* will accept any offer [Sec. 3], an estimate of the likelihood that *NA* will, in hindsight, feel comfortable accepting any particular offer [Sec. 4], and an estimate of when *OP* may quit and leave the negotiation.

Let $\mathcal{G}$ be the set of all positive ground literals that can be constructed using the predicate, function and constant symbols in $\mathcal{L}$. A *possible world* is a valuation function $\mathbf{v} : \mathcal{G} \to \{\top, \bot\}$. $\mathbf{V}$ denotes the set of all possible worlds, and $\mathbf{V}_\mathcal{K}$ denotes the set of possible worlds that are consistent with a knowledge base $\mathcal{K}$.[3]

A *random world* for $\mathcal{K}$ is a probability distribution $\mathbf{W}_\mathcal{K} = \{p_i\}$ over $\mathbf{V}_\mathcal{K} = \{\mathbf{v}_i\}$, where $\mathbf{W}_\mathcal{K}$ expresses an agent's degree of belief that

---

[b] The often-quoted oxymoron "I paid too much for it, but its worth it." attributed to Samuel Goldwyn, movie producer, illustrates that intelligent agents may choose to negotiate with uncertain utility.

each of the possible worlds is the actual world. The *derived sentence probability* of any $\sigma \in \mathcal{L}$, *with respect to* a random world $\mathbf{W}_\mathcal{K}$ is:

$$\mathbf{P}_{\mathbf{W}_\mathcal{K}}(\sigma) \triangleq \sum_n \{p_n \; : \; \sigma \; is \; \top \; in \; \mathbf{v}_n\}. \tag{1}$$

A random world $\mathbf{W}_\mathcal{K}$ is *consistent* with the agent's beliefs $\mathcal{B}$ if: $(\forall \beta \in \mathcal{B})(\mathbf{B}(\beta) = \mathbf{P}_{\mathbf{W}_\mathcal{K}}(\beta))$. That is, for each belief its derived sentence probability as calculated using Eq. (1) is equal to its given sentence probability.

The *entropy* of a discrete random variable X with probability mass function $\{p_i\}$ is:[2]

$$H(X) = -\sum_n p_n \log p_n, \quad \text{where } p_n \geq 0 \text{ and } \sum_n p_n = 1.$$

Let $\mathbf{W}_{\{\mathcal{K},\mathcal{B}\}}$ be the "maximum entropy probability distribution over $\mathbf{V}_\mathcal{K}$ that is consistent with $\mathcal{B}$". Given an agent with $\mathcal{K}$ and $\mathcal{B}$, its *derived sentence probability* for any sentence, $\sigma \in \mathcal{L}$, is:

$$(\forall \sigma \in \mathcal{L})\mathbf{P}(\sigma) \triangleq \mathbf{P}_{\mathbf{W}_{\{\mathcal{K},\mathcal{B}\}}}(\sigma). \tag{2}$$

Using Eq. (2), the derived sentence probability for any belief, β_i, is equal to its given sentence probability. So the term *sentence probability* is used without ambiguity.

3. Estimating $\mathbf{P}(OPAcc(.))$

NA does two different things. First, it reacts to offers received from *OP* — that is described in Sec. 4. Second, it sends offers to *OP*. This section describes the estimation of $\mathbf{P}(OPAcc(\delta))$ where the predicate $OPAcc(\delta)$ means "the deal δ is acceptable to *OP*".

When a negotiation commences *NA* may have no information about *OP* or about prior deals.[10] If so then the initial offers may only be based on past experience or circumstantial information.[c] So the opening offers are simply taken as given.

---

[c] In rather dire circumstances King Richard III of England is reported to have initiated a negotiation with remarkably high stakes: "A horse! a horse! my kingdom for a horse!" [William Shakespeare]. Fortunately for Richard, a person named Catesby was nearby, and advised Richard to retract this rash offer "Withdraw, my lord", and so Richard's intention to honor his commitments was not put to the test.

In the four sub-sections following, NA is attempting to sell something to OP. In Secs. 3.1 and 3.2 NA's terms τ are to supply a particular good, and OP's terms ω are money — in those examples the amount of money ω is the subject of the negotiation. In Secs. 3.3 and 3.4 NA's terms are to supply a particular good together with some negotiated warranty period, and OP's terms are money — in those examples the amount of money p and the period of the warranty period w are the subject of the negotiation.

3.1. *One issue — Without decay*

The unary predicate $OPAcc(x)$ means "the amount of money \$$x$ is acceptable to OP". NA is interested in whether the unary predicate $OPAcc(x)$ is true for various values of \$$x$. NA assumes the following preference relation on the $OPAcc$ predicate:

$$\kappa_1 : \forall x, y((x > y) \rightarrow (OPAcc(x) \rightarrow OPAcc(y))).$$

Suppose that NA's opening offer is $\overline{\omega}$, and OP's opening offer is $\underline{\omega}$ where $\underline{\omega} < \overline{\omega}$. Then $\mathcal{K}$ now contains two further sentences: $\kappa_2 :$ $\neg OPAcc(\overline{\omega})$ and $\kappa_3 : OPAcc(\underline{\omega})$. There are now $\overline{\omega} - \underline{\omega}$ possible worlds, and the maximum entropy distribution is uniform.

Suppose that NA knows its true valuation for the good, u_{na}, and that NA has decided to make an "expected-utility-optimizing" offer: $x = \frac{\overline{\omega} + u_{na}}{2}$. This offer is calculated on the basis of the preference ordering κ_1 and the two signals that NA has received from OP. The response is in terms of only NA's valuation u_{na} and the signal $Reject(\overline{\omega})$ — it is independent of the signal $Offer(\underline{\omega})$ which implies that $\underline{\omega}$ is acceptable.

In the standard game theoretic analysis of bargaining,[1] NA assumes that OP has a utility, u_{op}, that it lies in some interval $[\underline{u}, \overline{u}]$, and that the expected value of u_{op} is uniformly distributed on that interval. On the basis of these assumptions NA then derives the expected-utility-optimizing offer: $\frac{\overline{u} + u_{na}}{2}$. These two offers differ by $\overline{u}$ in the game-theoretic result and $\overline{\omega}$ in the maximum entropy result. The game theoretic approach relies on estimates for $\underline{u}$ and $\overline{u}$:

$$\mathbf{E}([\underline{u}, \overline{u}] | Reject(\overline{\omega}) \wedge Accept(\underline{\omega})).$$

If OP has a utility, and it may not, then if OP is rational: $\underline{u} \leq \underline{\omega} \leq \overline{u}$. The inherent inefficiency of bilateral bargaining[6] shows for an economically rational OP that u_{op}, and so consequently $\bar{u}$, may be greater than $\bar{\omega}$. There is no reason to suspect that $\bar{u}$ and $\bar{\omega}$ will be equal.

3.2. One issue — With decay

As in the previous example, suppose that the opening offers at time t_0 are taken as given and are $\underline{\omega}$ and $\bar{\omega}$. Then $\mathcal{K}$ contains κ_1, κ_2 and κ_3. Suppose $\mathcal{L}$ contains n consecutive, integer constants in the interval $[\underline{\omega}, \bar{\omega}]$, where $n = \bar{\omega} - \underline{\omega} + 1$, that represent various amounts of money. κ_1 induces a total ordering on the sentence probabilities for $OPAcc(x)$ on the interval $[\underline{\omega}, \bar{\omega}]$, where the probabilities are ≈ 0 at $\bar{\omega}$, and ≈ 1 at $\underline{\omega}$.

Suppose that at time t_1 NA makes an offer ω_{na} which is rejected by OP, who has replied at time t_2 with an offer of ω_{op} where $\underline{\omega} \leq \omega_{op} \leq \omega_{na} \leq \bar{\omega}$. At time t_3 $\mathcal{B}$ contains $\beta_1 : OPAcc(\omega_{na})$ and $\beta_2 : OPAcc(\omega_{op})$. Suppose that there is some level of integrity decay on these two beliefs: $0 < \mathbf{B}(\beta_1) < 0.5 < \mathbf{B}(\beta_2) < 1$. Then $\mathbf{V}_\mathcal{K}$ contains $n + 1$ possible worlds ranging from "all false" to "all true" each containing n literals. So a random world for $\mathcal{K}$ will consist of $n + 1$ probabilities $\{p_i\}$, where, say, p_1 is the probability of "all true", and p_{n+1} is the probability of "all false". $\mathbf{P}_{\{\mathcal{K},\mathcal{B}\}}$ will be the distribution that maximizes $-\sum_n p_n \log p_n$ subject to the constraints: $p_n \geq 0$, $\sum_n p_n = 1$, $\sum_{n=1}^{\bar{\omega}-\omega_{na}+1} p_n = \mathbf{B}(\beta_1)$ and $\sum_{n=1}^{\bar{\omega}-\omega_{op}+1} p_n = \mathbf{B}(\beta_2)$.

The optimization of entropy, H, subject to linear constraints is described in Sec. 3.2.1 below. $\mathbf{P}_{\{\mathcal{K},\mathcal{B}\}}$ is:

$$p_n = \begin{cases} \frac{\mathbf{B}(\beta_1)}{\bar{\omega}-\omega_{na}+1} & \text{if } 1 \leq n \leq \bar{\omega} - \omega_{na} + 1 \\ \frac{\mathbf{B}(\beta_2)-\mathbf{B}(\beta_1)}{\omega_{na}-\omega_{op}} & \text{if } \bar{\omega} - \omega_{na} + 1 < n < \bar{\omega} - \omega_{op} + 2 \\ \frac{1-\mathbf{B}(\beta_2)}{\omega_{op}-\underline{\omega}+1} & \text{if } \bar{\omega} - \omega_{op} + 2 \leq n \leq \bar{\omega} - \underline{\omega} + 2 \end{cases}.$$

Using Eq. (2), for $\omega_{op} \leq x \leq \omega_{na}$:

$$\mathbf{P}(OPAcc(x)) = \mathbf{B}(\beta_1) + \frac{\omega_{na} - x}{\omega_{na} - \omega_{op}}(\mathbf{B}(\beta_2) - \mathbf{B}(\beta_1)). \qquad (3)$$

These probability estimates are used in Sec. 5 to calculate NA's next offer.

The values for $\mathbf{P}(OPAcc(x))$ in the region $\omega_{op} \leq x \leq \omega_{na}$ are derived from only two pieces of information that are the two signals

Reject(ω_{na}) and *Offer*(ω_{op}) each qualified with the time at which they arrived, and the decay rate on their integrity. The assumptions in the analysis given above are: the choice of values for $\underline{\omega}$ and $\overline{\omega}$ — which do not appear in Eq. (3) in any case — and the choice of the "maximally noncommittal" distribution.

If the agents continue to exchange offers then new beliefs will be acquired and the integrity of old beliefs will decay. If the next pair of offers lies within the interval $[\omega_{op}, \omega_{na}]$ and if the integrity of β_1 and β_2 decays then the sentence probabilities of β_1 and β_2 will be inconsistent with those of the two new beliefs due to the total ordering of sentence probabilities on $[\underline{\omega}, \overline{\omega}]$ induced by κ_1. This inconsistency is resolved by the revision function **R** that here discards inconsistent older beliefs, β_1 and β_2, in favor of more recent beliefs. If the agents continue in this way then the sentence probabilities for the *OPAcc* predicate are given simply by Eq. (3) using the most recent values for ω_{na} and ω_{op}.

The analysis given above requires that values be specified for the opening offers $\underline{\omega}$ and $\overline{\omega}$. The only part of the probability distribution that depends on the values chosen for $\underline{\omega}$ and $\overline{\omega}$ are the two "tails" of the distribution. So the choice of values for these two opening offers is unlikely to effect the estimates. The two tails are necessary to "soak up" the otherwise unallocated probability.

3.2.1. *Maximizing entropy with linear constraints*

If X is a discrete random variable taking a finite number of possible values $\{x_i\}$ with probabilities $\{p_i\}$ then the *entropy* is the average uncertainty removed by discovering the true value of X, and is given by $H = -\sum_n p_n \log p_n$. The direct optimization of H subject to a number, θ, of linear constraints of the form $\sum_n p_n g_k(x_n) = \overline{g}_k$ for given constants $\overline{g}_k$, where $k = 1, \ldots, \theta$, is a difficult problem. Fortunately this problem has the same unique solution as the *maximum likelihood problem* for the Gibbs distribution.[11] The solution to both problems is given by:

$$p_n = \frac{\exp(-\sum_{k=1}^{\theta} \lambda_k g_k(x_n))}{\sum_m \exp(-\sum_{k=1}^{\theta} \lambda_k g_k(x_m))} \tag{4}$$

for $n = 1, 2, \ldots$, where the constants $\{\lambda_i\}$ may be calculated using Eq. (4) together with the three sets of constraints: $p_n \geq 0$, $\sum_n p_n = 1$

and $\sum_n p_n g_k(x_n) = \bar{g}_k$. The distribution in Eq. (4) is known as *Gibbs distribution*.

Calculating the expressions for the values of $\{p_n\}$ given in the example above in Sec. 3.2 does not require the full evaluation of the expressions in Eq. (4). That equation shows that there are just three different values for the $\{p_n\}$. Applying simple algebra to that fact together with the constraints yields the expressions given.

3.3.   *Two issues — Without decay*

The above approach to single-issue bargaining generalizes without modification to multi-issue bargaining, it is illustrated with two issues only for ease of presentation. The problem considered is the sale of an item with $0, \ldots, 4$ years of warranty. The terms being negotiated specify an amount of money p and the number of years warranty w. The predicate $OPAcc(w, p)$ now means "*OP* will accept the offer to purchase the good with w years warranty for $\$p$".

NA assumes the following two preference orderings, and $\mathcal{K}$ contains:

$$\kappa_{11} : \forall x, y, z((x > y) \to (OPAcc(y, z) \to OPAcc(x, z)))$$

$$\kappa_{12} : \forall x, y, z((x > y) \to (OPAcc(z, x) \to OPAcc(z, y))).$$

As in Sec. 3.1 these sentences conveniently reduce the number of possible worlds. The number of possible worlds will be finite as long as $\mathcal{K}$ contains two statements of the form: $\neg OPAcc(4, a)$ and $OPAcc(0, b)$ for some a and b. Suppose that *NA*'s initial offer was "4 years warranty for $\$21$" and *OP*'s initial offer was "no warranty for $\$10$". $\mathcal{K}$ now contains:

$$\kappa_{13} : \neg OPAcc(4, 21) \quad \kappa_{14} : OPAcc(0, 10).$$

These two statements, together with the restriction to integers only, limit the possible values of w and p in $OPAcc(w, p)$ to a 5×10 matrix.

Suppose that *NA* knows its utility function for the good with $0, \ldots, 4$ years warranty and that its values are: $\$11.00$, $\$11.50$, $\$12.00$, $\$13.00$ and $\$14.50$ respectively. Suppose that *NA* uses the strategy $\mathbf{S}^{(n)}$ — the details of that strategy are not important now. If *NA* uses that strategy with $n = 2$, then *NA* offers $Offer(2, \$16)$ which suppose *OP* rejects and counters with $Offer(1, \$11)$. Then with $n = 2$ again,

NA offers *Offer*(2, $14) which suppose *OP* rejects and counters with *Offer*(3, $13). $P(OPAcc(w, p))$ now is:

	$w = 0$	$w = 1$	$w = 2$	$w = 3$	$w = 4$
$p = 20$	0.0000	0.0000	0.0000	0.0455	0.0909
$p = 19$	0.0000	0.0000	0.0000	0.0909	0.1818
$p = 18$	0.0000	0.0000	0.0000	0.1364	0.2727
$p = 17$	0.0000	0.0000	0.0000	0.1818	0.3636
$p = 16$	0.0000	0.0000	0.0000	0.2273	0.4545
$p = 15$	0.0000	0.0000	0.0000	0.2727	0.5454
$p = 14$	0.0000	0.0000	0.0000	0.3182	0.6364
$p = 13$	0.0455	0.0909	0.1364	1.0000	1.0000
$p = 12$	0.0909	0.1818	0.2727	1.0000	1.0000
$p = 11$	0.1364	1.0000	1.0000	1.0000	1.0000

and the expected-utility-optimizing offer is: *Offer*(4, $18). If *NA* makes that offer then the expected surplus is $0.95. The matrix above contains the "maximally noncommittal" values for $P(OPAcc(w, p))$; those values are recalculated each time a signal arrives. The example demonstrates how the *NA* is able to conduct multi-issue bargaining in a focussed way without making assumptions about *OP*'s internals, in particular, whether *OP* is aware of a utility function.[12]

3.4.   *Two issues — With decay*

Following from the previous section, suppose that $\mathcal{K}$ contains κ_{11}, κ_{12}, κ_{13} and κ_{14}. The two preference orderings κ_{11} and κ_{12} induce a partial ordering on the sentence probabilities in the $P(OPAcc(w, p))$ array [as in Sec. 3.3] from the top-left where the probabilities are ≈ 0, to the bottom-right where the probabilities are ≈ 1. There are 51 possible worlds that are consistent with $\mathcal{K}$.

Suppose that $\mathcal{B}$ contains: $\beta_{11} : OPAcc(2, 16)$, $\beta_{12} : OPAcc(2, 14)$, $\beta_{13} : OPAcc(1, 11)$ and $\beta_{14} : OPAcc(3, 13)$ — this is the same offer sequence as considered in Sec. 3.3 — and with a 10% decay in integrity for each time step: $\mathbf{P}(\beta_{11}) = 0.4$, $\mathbf{P}(\beta_{12}) = 0.2$, $\mathbf{P}(\beta_{13}) = 0.7$ and $\mathbf{P}(\beta_{14}) = 0.9$. Belief β_{11} is inconsistent with $\mathcal{K} \cup \{\beta_{12}\}$ as together they violate the sentence probability ordering induced by κ_{11} and κ_{12}. Resolving this issue is a job for the belief revision function $\mathbf{R}$ which discards the older, and weaker, belief β_{11}.

Equation (4) is used to calculate the distribution $\mathbf{W}_{\{\mathcal{K}, \mathcal{B}\}}$ which has just five different probabilities in it. The resulting values for the three λ's are: $\lambda_{12} = 2.8063$, $\lambda_{13} = -2.0573$ and $\lambda_{14} = -2.5763$. $P(OPAcc(w, p))$ now is:

	$w = 0$	$w = 1$	$w = 2$	$w = 3$	$w = 4$
$p = 20$	0.0134	0.0269	0.0286	0.0570	0.0591
$p = 19$	0.0269	0.0537	0.0571	0.1139	0.1183
$p = 18$	0.0403	0.0806	0.0857	0.1709	0.1774
$p = 17$	0.0537	0.1074	0.1143	0.2279	0.2365
$p = 16$	0.0671	0.1343	0.1429	0.2849	0.2957
$p = 15$	0.0806	0.1611	0.1714	0.3418	0.3548
$p = 14$	0.0940	0.1880	**0.2000**	0.3988	0.4139
$p = 13$	0.3162	0.6324	0.6728	**0.9000**	0.9173
$p = 12$	0.3331	0.6662	0.7088	0.9381	0.9576
$p = 11$	0.3500	**0.7000**	0.7447	0.9762	0.9978

In this array, the derived sentence probabilities for the three sentences in $\mathcal{B}$ are shown in bold type; they are exactly their given values.

4. Estimating $\mathbf{P}(NAAcc(.))$

The proposition $NAAcc(\delta)$ means: "δ is acceptable to NA". This section describes how NA attaches a conditional probability to the proposition: $\mathbf{P}(NAAcc(\delta) \mid \mathcal{I}_t)$ in the light of information $\mathcal{I}_t$. The meaning of "acceptable to NA" is described below. This is intended to put NA in the position "looking back on it, I made the right decision at the time" — this is a vague notion but makes sense to the author. The idea is for NA to accept a deal δ when $\mathbf{P}(NAAcc(\delta) \mid \mathcal{I}_t) \geq \alpha$ for some threshold value α that is one of NA's mental states.

$\mathbf{P}(NAAcc(\delta)|\mathcal{I}_t)$ is derived from conditional probabilities attached to four other propositions:

$\mathbf{P}(Suited(\omega)|\mathcal{I}_t)$,
$\mathbf{P}(Good(OP)|\mathcal{I}_t)$,
$\mathbf{P}(Fair(\delta)|\mathcal{I}_t \cup \{Suited(\omega), Good(OP)\})$ and
$\mathbf{P}(Me(\delta)|\mathcal{I}_t \cup \{Suited(\omega), Good(OP)\})$,

meaning respectively: "terms ω are perfectly suited to my needs", "OP will be a good agent for me to be doing business with", "δ is generally considered to be a good deal for NA", and "on strictly subjective grounds, δ is acceptable to NA". The last two of these four probabilities factor out both the suitability of ω and the appropriateness of the opponent OP. The difference between the third and fourth is that the third captures the concept of "a good market deal" and the fourth a strictly subjective "what ω is worth to NA". The "$Me(.)$" proposition is related to the concept of a private valuation in game theory.

5. Negotiation Strategies

Section 3 estimated the probability distribution, $\mathbf{P}(OPAcc)$, that OP will accept an offer, and Sec. 4 estimated the probability distribution, $\mathbf{P}(NAAcc)$, that NA should be prepared to accept an offer. These two probability distributions represent the opposing interests of the two agents NA and OP. $\mathbf{P}(OPAcc)$ will change every time an offer is made, rejected or accepted. $\mathbf{P}(NAAcc)$ will change as the background information changes. This section discusses NA's strategy $\mathbf{S}$.

Bargaining can be a game of bluff and counter-bluff in which an agent may even not intend to close the deal if one should be reached. A basic conundrum in any offer-exchange bargaining is: it is impossible to force your opponent to reveal information about their position without revealing information about your own position. Further, by revealing information about your own position you may change your opponents position — and so on.[d] This infinite regress, of speculation and counter-speculation, is avoided here by ignoring the internals of the opponent and by focussing on what is known for certain — that is: *what* information is contained in the signals received and *when* did those signals arrive.

A fundamental principle of competitive bargaining is "never reveal your best price", and another is "never reveal your deadline — if you have one".[15] It is not possible to be prescriptive about what an agent *should* reveal. All that can be achieved is to provide strategies that an agent may choose to employ. The following are examples of such strategies.

An agent's strategy $\mathbf{S}$ is a function of the information $\mathcal{I}_t$ that is has at time t. That information will be represented in the agent's $\mathcal{K}$ and $\mathcal{B}$, and will have been used to calculate

---

[d] This a reminiscent of Werner Heisenberg's indeterminacy relation, or *unbestimmtheitsrelationen*: "you can't measure one feature of an object without changing another" — with apologies.

$\mathbf{P}(OPAcc)$ and $\mathbf{P}(NAAcc)$. Simple strategies choose an offer only on the basis of $\mathbf{P}(OPAcc)$, $\mathbf{P}(NAAcc)$ and α. The greedy strategy $\mathbf{S}^+$ chooses $\arg\max_\delta\{\mathbf{P}(NAAcc(\delta))|\mathbf{P}(OPAcc(\delta)) \gg 0\}$, it is appropriate for an agent that believes OP is desperate to trade. The *expected-acceptability-to-NA-optimizing strategy* $\mathbf{S}^*$ chooses $\arg\max_\delta\{\mathbf{P}(OPAcc(\delta)) \times \mathbf{P}(NAAcc(\delta))|\mathbf{P}(NAAcc(\delta)) \geq \alpha\}$, it is appropriate for a confident agent that is not desperate to trade. The strategy $\mathbf{S}^-$ chooses $\arg\max_\delta\{\mathbf{P}(OPAcc(\delta))|\mathbf{P}(NAAcc(\delta)) \geq \alpha\}$, it optimizes the likelihood of trade — it is a good strategy for an agent that is keen to trade without compromising its own standards of acceptability.

An approach to issue-tradeoffs is described in Ref. 5. The bargaining strategy described there attempts to make an acceptable offer by "walking round" the iso-curve of NA's previous offer (that has, say, an acceptability of $\alpha_{na} \geq \alpha$) towards OP's subsequent counter offer. In terms of the machinery described here, an analogue is to use the strategy $\mathbf{S}^-$: $\arg\max_\delta\{\mathbf{P}(OPAcc(\delta))|\mathbf{P}(NAAcc(\delta)|\mathcal{I}_t) \gtrsim \alpha_{na}\}$ for $\alpha = \alpha_{na}$. This is reasonable for an agent that is attempting to be accommodating without compromising its own interests. Presumably such an agent will have a policy for reducing the value α_{na} if her deals fail to be accepted. The complexity of the strategy in Ref. 5 is linear with the number of issues. The strategy described here does not have that property, but it benefits from using $\mathbf{P}(OPAcc)$ that contains foot prints of the prior offer sequence — see Sec. 3.4 — in that distribution more recent offers have stronger weights.

6. Conclusions

The negotiating agent achieves its goal of reaching informed decisions whilst making no assumptions about the internals of its opponent. This agents has been implemented in Java[e] incorporating a modified version of tuProlog that handles the Horn clause logic including the belief revision and the identification of those random worlds that are consistent with $\mathcal{K}$. Existing text and data mining bots have been used to feed information into NA in experiments including a negotiation

---

[e] http://e-markets.org.au

between two agents in an attempt to swap a mobile phone for a digital camera with no cash involved.

Reference 3 discusses problems with the random-worlds approach, and notes particularly representation and learning. Representation is particularly significant here — for example, the logical constants in the price domains could have been given other values, and, as long as they remained ordered, and as long as the input values remained unchanged, the probability distributions would be unaltered. Learning is not an issue now as the distributions are kept as simple as possible and are re-computed each time step. The assumptions of maximum entropy probabilistic logic exploit the agent's limited rationality by attempting to assume "precisely no more than is known".

References

1. A. Muthoo, *Bargaining Theory with Applications*. Cambridge UP (1999).
2. D. MacKay, *Information Theory, Inference and Learning Algorithms*. Cambridge University Press (2003).
3. J. Halpern, *Reasoning about Uncertainty*. MIT Press (2003).
4. E. Jaynes, Information theory and statistical mechanics. Part I. *Physical Review*, **106**, 620–630 (1957).
5. P. Faratin, C. Sierra and N. Jennings, Using similarity criteria to make issue trade-offs in automated negotiation. *Journal of Artificial Intelligence*, **142**(2), 205–237 (2003).
6. R. Myerson and M. Satterthwaite, Efficient mechanisms for bilateral trading. *Journal of Economic Theory*, **29**, 1–21 (1983).
7. J. Bulow and P. Klemperer, Auctions versus negotiations. *American Economic Review*, **86**(1), 180–194 (March 1996).
8. Z. Neeman and N. Vulkan, *Markets Versus Negotiations*. Technical report, Center for Rationality and Interactive Decision Theory, Hebrew University, Jerusalem (2000).
9. S. Kraus, *Strategic Negotiation in Multiagent Environments*. MIT Press (2001).
10. C. Sierra and J. Debenham, Information-based agency. *Proceedings of Twentieth International Joint Conference on Artificial Intelligence IJCAI-07*, pp. 1513–1518, Hyderabad, India (January 2007).
11. S. D. Pietra, V. D. Pietra and J. Lafferty, Inducing features of random fields. *IEEE Transactions on Pattern Analysis and Machine Intelligence*, **19**(2), 380–393 (1997).
12. M. J. Osborne and A. Rubinstein, *Bargaining and Markets*. Academic Press (1990).
13. J. Castro-Schez, N. Jennings, X. Luo and N. Shadbolt, Acquiring domain knowledge for negotiating agents: A case study. *International Journal of Human-Computer Studies*, **61**(1), 3–31 (2004).

14. S. Ramchurn, N. Jennings, C. Sierra and L. Godo, A computational trust model for multi-agent interactions based on confidence and reputation. *Proceedings 5th Int. Workshop on Deception, Fraud and Trust in Agent Societies* (2003).

15. T. Sandholm and N. Vulkan, Bargaining with deadlines. *Proceedings of the National Conference on Artificial Intelligence (AAAI)* (1999).

16. J. Debenham, An eNegotiation Framework. *The 23rd International Conference on Innovative Techniques and Applications of Artificial Intelligence, AI'2003*, Springer Verlag, pp. 79–92 (2003).

17. C. Sierra and J. Debenham, Trust and honour in information-based agency. (eds.) P. Stone and G. Weiss. *Proceedings 5th International Conference on Autonomous Agents and Multi Agent Systems AAMAS-2006*, Hakodate, Japan. ACM Press, New York, pp. 1225–1232 (May 2006).

Comparison of Spatiotemporal Difference of Brain Activity Between Correct and Approximation Answer Choices on Addition

Takahiro Yamanoi[*,†], Yuta Fujiwara[*], Hisashi Toyoshima[*],
Michio Sugeno[‡] and Elie Sanchez[§]

[*]Faculty of Engineering, Hokkai-Gakuen University
W 11-1-1, S 26, Central Ward, Sapporo, 064-0926, Japan
[†]yamanoi@eli.hokkai-s-u.ac.jp
[‡]Faculty of Information Science, Doshisha University
Tataramiyakodani 1-3, Kyotanabe, 610-0394, Japan
msugeno@mail.doshisha.ac.jp
[§]Faculty of Medicine, University of Aix-Marseille II
27 Bd. Jean Moulin, 13385 Marseille Cedex5, France
elie.sanchez@medecine.univ-mrs.fr

Abstract

We recorded event-related potentials (ERPs) by electroencephalograms (EEGs) while subjects were performing selections of an answer. The subjects were seven normal university students. They were asked to add double figures and select an answer from the two choices. Choices were of two types; Type1 was correct choice including the correct answer, and Type2 was approximation choice without the correct answer. Moreover, we classified the Type2 into the following cases according to presentation types. The cases were Type2A: the answer was smaller than choices, Type2B: the answer was between choices, and Type2C: the answer was bigger than choices. We analyzed by using the equivalent current dipole source localization (ECDL) to compare brain activities in the meantime. ECDs were localized at the left middle frontal gyrus (MFG), the left inferior frontal gyrus (IFG) and the left lateral postcentral gyrus (PstCG) between latencies from 150 ms to 250 ms after presentation of choices (PRC) which is 1000 ms after the beginning of EEG measurement. Until 250 ms after the PRC, ECDs were localized at the same parts in both type, Correct and Approximation. After 250 ms from the PRC, the ERP of the approximation answer had delays from 60 to 100 ms for the ERP of the correct answer. In the case of approximation answer only, the ECDs were localized at the right MFG.

1. Introduction

In the human brain, the logical process is performed in the left hemisphere and the intuitive process is performed in the right hemisphere. Precisely, the left hemisphere is dominant for speech and language functions. It is also dominant for motor planning skills. The right hemisphere, on the other hand, is dominant for spatial abilities and for some aspects of music. There is also some evidence that it is more involved in various aspects of emotional behavior than the left hemisphere.[1]

With respect to arithmetic calculations, it is said that the crisp calculation is done at the left lower frontal lobe and that the approximation is done at the parietal lobe.[2,3]

On the other hand, the visual disparity detection for the stereopsis was discovered at the visual area 1 (V1) and the visual area 2 (V2) from neurophysiological research.[4] Yamanoi *et al.* have clarified the process of stereopsis, after a subject received visual stimuli, especially after V1,[5] by observing event-related potentials (ERPs).[6-8]

The present authors have used the same methodology as the preceding research.[10,11] By presenting correct and approximate calculations to the subjects, the authors recorded ERPs under these calculations. Summing these ERPs of correct and approximate calculations respectively, we subtracted these two ERPs to get the essential difference of ERPs between correct and approximate calculations. Generally the latencies of the two are different, but it is natural to suppose that latencies are around the peaks of subtracted ERPs. From this point of view, each peak latency of ERP is detected and analyzed by the equivalent current dipole source localization (ECDL)[9] at that latency. And resulting ECDs are analyzed by use of the discriminant analysis.[10] This paper deals with the brain process of selection after presenting two possible choices of answer of addition that are composed of two types. One type includes the correct answer (Type1) and the other includes only an approximate answer (Type2).

2. Experiments

2.1. *Experimental apparatus and method*

Subjects are seven university students from 21 to 22 years old and have normal visual acuity (four males and three females; six right-handed and one left-handed). The subjects put on an electrode cap and watched the 21 inch CRT 30 cm in front of them. Their heads were fixed on a chin rest on the table. Each question was displayed on the CRT. Questions had been stored on the disk of PC as a file and they were presented in random order.

Positions of electrodes on the cap were according to the International 10–20 system and others two electrodes were fixed on the upper and lower eyelids on dominant eye for eye movement monitoring. Impedances were adjusted to the range from 2 to 5 kΩ. Reference electrodes were put on both earlobes and the ground electrode was on the base of the nose. Electroencephalograms (EEGs) were recorded on the digital EEG measuring system (Japan GE Marquette, Synafit EE2500); the amplitude is $5\mu V/V$, the frequency band is between 0.5 and 60 Hz. Analog outputs were sampled at a rate of 1 kHz and stored on the hard disk of server PC (Fig. 1).

2.2. *Stimulus conditions and presentations*

In order to verify the results of Dehaene *et al.*,[2] questions to add double figures with two types of calculations were presented to the subjects. One type includes correct answer (Type1) and the other includes only approximate answer (Type2). Further, we divided the type2 into three sub types according to inequality relationship among choices and the correct answer (CA). Type2A is CA < choice1 < choice2, Type2B is choice1 < CA < choice2, and Type2C is choice1 < choice2 < CA.

We have attempted the above four experiments in a similar way. One second after the presentation of a question on the adding on natural numbers, for example as "$27 + 21 =$" (Fig. 2), the two choices of answer appeared on the CRT. The subjects were asked to choose one answer from the two. The real answer was included in the choice in

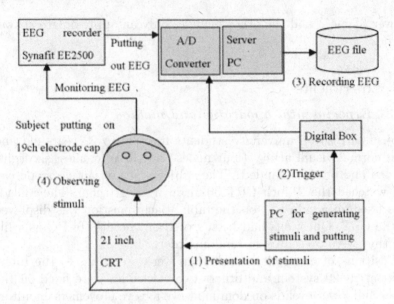

Fig. 1.   Experimental apparatus for stimulus.

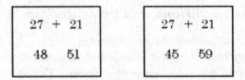

Fig. 2.   Example for addition (Answer: 48).

27 + 21	27 + 21
48 51	45 59

Fig. 3.   Choices are presented one second after the question is presented. Left. Correct answer is included (Type1). Right. Correct answer is not included (Type2B).

the experiment (Type Correct: Fig. 3 left). But for the Type Approximation experiment, two choices to be approximated were displayed (Fig. 3 right).

Two seconds after the choices were displayed the choices, a prompting mark "?" was presented for an answer. The procedure is the same in four types of experiment after the prompting mark (Fig. 4).

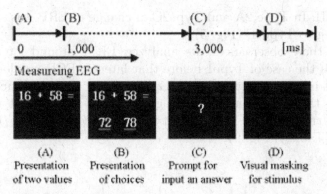

Fig. 4. Experimental time chart; A. Presentation of two values to be added, start to measure EEG; B. Presentation of choice, stop measuring EEG after 3000 ms; C. Prompting for input an answer; D. Visual masking for stimulus in 2000 ms after decision, then return to the next experimental cycle.

3. Experimental Results

We had measured EEGs of the Type1, Type2A, 2B and 2C; each data was summed and averaged according to the type of choices and the subjects in order to get ERPs. Summing these ERPs of the four types respectively, we subtracted these ERPs to get the essential difference of ERPs between the Type1 and the Type2 (2A, 2B and 2C). Generally the latencies of these ERPs are different, but it is natural to suppose main activations are around the peak potentials of subtracted ERPs. From this point of view, each peak potential of the subtracted ERPs was detected and analyzed by the ECDL at that latency. And then we analyzed the process after presentation of choices (PRC). To each ERP by each subject, the ECDL method was applied. Because the number of the recording electrodes was 19, at most three ECDs were estimated by PC-based ECDL analysis software "SynaPointPro"[9] (Japan GE Marquette). The goodness of fit (GOF) of ECD was over 99.8%.

Before latency of 300 ms, no remarkable difference was observed. From 300 ms to 400 ms, difference appeared gradually, and a remarkable difference was observed after 400 ms, between Type1 and each of Type2.

In the case of Type1, change of ERP is smooth after 300 ms, although slight change was observed around 420 ms. On the contrary, change was rapid around 450 ms, 520 ms, 580 ms and 640 ms in Type2B. In Type 2A and Type2C, a change of ERP was smooth comparing to Type2B (Fig. 5).

From these observances, we analyzed ERPs around latency at 400 ms, in the case of Type1 before that latency, ECD was localized at the left inferior frontal gyrus (IFG) (Fig. 6), at the left rectus gyrus (RG), at the left superior frontal gyrus (SFG), at the left middle frontal gyrus (MFG) (Fig. 7) and at the left precentral gyrus (PrCG) (Fig. 8) (Table 1; Fig. 9).

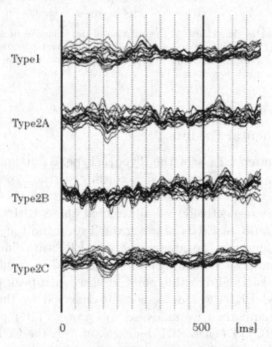

Fig. 5.   Grand-averages of ERPs after PRC.

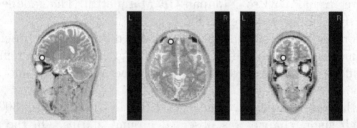

Fig. 6.   ECDs localized at the left IFG at 273 ms (subject: KN), Type1.

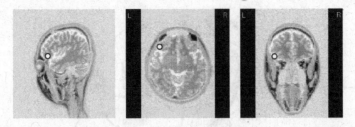

Fig. 7. ECDs localized at the left MFG at 361 ms (subject: KN), Type1.

Fig. 8. ECDs localized at the left PrCG at 426 ms (subject: KN), Type1.

Table 1. Relationship between estimated source and latency from the left IFG to the left PrCG (Type1).

Subject	Left IFG1	Right MFG	Left IFG2	Left RG	Left SFG	Left MFG	Left PrCG
KN	273			288	299	361	426
HT	255			271	297	362	419
MH	259			289	311	353	423
YM	259			294	316	357	418
KA	266			283	313	356	420
ED	273			290	338	363	432
MT	274			303	317	365	441

In the case of Type2, ECDs were localized at the left IFG (Fig. 10), at the right MFG (Fig. 11), at the left RG, at the left SFG and at the left PrCG (Fig. 12) (Table 2; Fig. 13).

In the case of Type 2B, ECDs were localized at the left PrCG, at the left intraparietal sulcus (IPS), at the right IPS (Fig. 14), at the right superior parietal lobulus (SPL), at the left MFG, at the right precentral sulcus (PrCS), at the right MFG (Fig. 15), at the left MFG and at the right PrCG after latency 400 ms (Fig. 16; Table 3, Table 4).

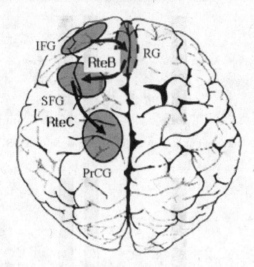

Fig. 9.   Spatiotemporal activities from left IFG to left PrCG before 400 ms (Type1).

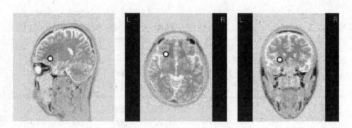

Fig. 10.   ECDs localized at the left IFG at 258 ms (subject: KN), Type2B.

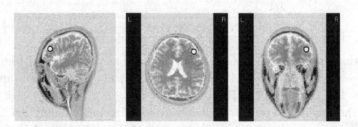

Fig. 11.   ECDs localized at the right MFG at 305 ms (subject: KN), Type2B.

Fig. 12.   ECDs localized at the left PrCG at 408 ms (subject: KN), Type2B.

Table 2.   Relationship between estimated source and latency from
the left IFG to the left PrCG (Type2B).

Subject	Left IFG1	Right MFG	Left IFG2	Left RG	Left SFG	Left MFG	Left PrCG
KN	258	305	327	355	384		408
HT	266	278	329	368	380		383
MH	259	298	308	323	361		376
YM	257	312	335	367	385		394
KA	262	303	333	359	371		391
ED	250	302	322	358	370		412
MT	254	286	320	346	369		392

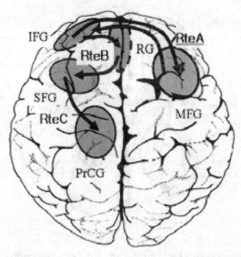

Fig. 13.   Spatiotemporal activities from left IFG to left PrCG before 400 ms (Type2A,
2B and 2C).

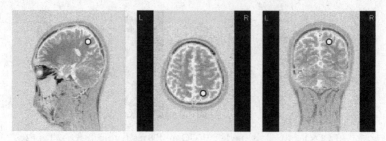

Fig. 14. ECDs localized at the right IPS at 455 ms (subject: KN), Type2B.

Fig. 15. ECDs localized at the right MFG at 594 ms (subject: KN), Type2B.

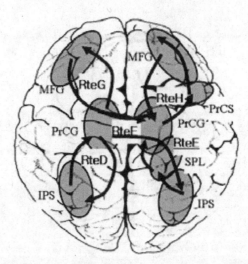

Fig. 16. Spatiotemporal activities from the left PrCG to the right PrCG after 400 ms (Type2B).

Table 3. Relationship between estimated source and latency from the left PrCG after 400 ms (Type2B).

Subject	Left PrCG	Left IPS	Right IPS	Right SPL	Left PrCG	Right PrCG
KN	408	437	455	487	488	518
HT	383	417	455	483	509	522
MH	376	433	472	477	483	511
YM	394	420	451	482	483	523
KA	391	425	471	487	492	526
ED	412	425	455	464	482	527
MT	392	417	447	467	484	537

Table 4. Relationship between estimated source and latency from the left MFG after Table 3 (Type2B).

Subject	Left MFG1	Right PrCS	Right MFG1	Right MFG2	Left MFG2	Right PrCG
KN	557	559	574	594	599	661
HT	553	570	592	608	629	671
MH	539	550	585	615	626	671
YM	561	577	609	625	633	667
KA	547	559	592	608	619	655
ED	559	559	591	613	621	678
MT	556	566	589	618	634	666

On the other hand, in the case of Type2A and Type2C, numbers of areas, where ECDs were localized, were rather smaller than Type2B (Fig. 17), no such tendency was observed in Type1.

ECDs were also localized to the corpus callosum (CoC) between translation of the area from the left hemisphere and the right hemisphere.

4. Discussion

In comparison after PRC, ECDs were localized at almost the same area in the case of Type1 and Type2, however, some ECDs were localized at the right hemisphere in Type2. And after the right MFG, delays more than 50 ms were observed in Type2.

In the case of Type2 after latency of 400 ms, translation of activities on the left parietal lobe, the right parietal lobe, the left frontal

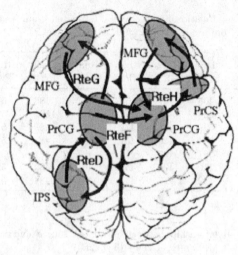

Fig. 17. Spatiotemporal activities from the left PrCG to the right PrCG after 400 ms (Type2A and 2C).

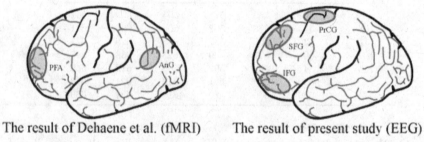

The result of Dehaene et al. (fMRI)　　　The result of present study (EEG)

Fig. 18. Comparison between estimated brain activities in the case of Type1. Left. The result of Dehaene et al.,[2] Right. The result of the present study.

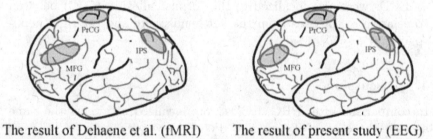

The result of Dehaene et al. (fMRI)　　　The result of present study (EEG)

Fig. 19. Comparison between estimated brain activities in the case of Type2. Left. The result of Dehaene et al.,[2] Right. The result of the present study.

lobe and the right frontal lobe were observed in Type2B, on the contrary no translation to the right hemisphere was observed in the case of Type2A and Type2C. Further, consideration of the grand-average of EEG, we could find activities in the right hemisphere where the wave from changed drastically.

From these results, before latency of 400 ms, the subjects were supposed to be searching for the correct answer in both cases; in Type1 and Type2, however, they had been using the right hemisphere in search for the approximation answer. Further, in Type2A and Type2C it was easy to compare the correct answer between two choices, so there was a remarkable difference in latency of activities.

In comparison with the results of Dehaene *et al.*, although they showed results on the left hemisphere, in case of the Type1, they had higher activities also on the MFG and the IPS (Fig. 18), however they had no activities to the SFG, the IFG and the PrCG that we found. In the case of the Type2, the results almost coincide on the MFG ad the IPS (Fig. 19), however, they had activities on the upper part of the Broca's area and the posterior part of the postcentral gyrus (PstCG) that were not observed in our results. We suppose that the difference between the results of Dehaene *et al.* and ours is caused by experimental equipment. Dehaene *et al.* measured activity in the brain by functional MRI (fMRI). The time resolution of fMRI is more than five seconds, although that of EEG we used is less than one millisecond. This means that measurement and analysis by use of EEG for detecting the activity in the brain is more precise.

Acknowledgments

This research is partly supported by the grant from the ministry of education, sports, science and technology to the national project in the High-tech Research Center of Hokkai-Gakuen University.

References

1. N. Geschwind and A. M. Galaburda, *Cerebral Lateralization, The Genetical Theory of Natural Selection.* Oxford. Clarendon Press (1987).
2. S. Dehaene, E. Spelke, P. Pinel, R. Stanescu and S. Tsickin, Source of mathematical thinking: Behavioral and brain-imaging evidence. *Science*, **284**(5416), 970–974 (1999).
3. B. Butterworth, A head for figures. *Science*, **284**(5416), 928–929 (1999).

4. R. Hayashi, Y. Miyawaki, Y. Yanagida, T. Maeda and S. Tachi, VEPs to dynamic random dot stereograms in different visual fields — influence of stimulus location on peak latency-(in Japanese). *Proceedings of the 14th Symposium on Biological and Physiological Engineering*, pp. 205–208 (1999).
5. M. Saito, T. Yamanoi, S. Ohnishi and T. Yamazaki, Event-related potentials and information processes in brain during binocular stereoscopic vision (in Japanese). *Proceedings of the 16th Symposium on Biological and Physiological Engineering*, pp. 81–84 (2001).
6. Y. Kuroiwa and M. Sonou (eds.), *Clinical Evoked Potential Handbook* (in Japanese). Reed Education and Professional Publishing Ltd. (1994).
7. J. R. Hunghes, *EEG in Clinical Practice*. 2nd ed. Medical Science International Press (1998).
8. S. Niwa and N. Tsuru (eds.), *Event Related Potentials* (in Japanese). Shinko Medical Press (1997).
9. T. Yamazaki, K. Kamijo, T. Kiyuna, Y. Takaki, Y. Kuroiwa, A. Ochi and H. Otsubo, PC-based multiple equivalent current dipole source localization system and its applications. *Res. Adv. in Biomedical Eng.* **2**, 97–109 (2001).
10. T. Yamanoi, M. Saito, M. Sugeno and E. Sanchez, Difference in areas of the brain for fuzzy and crisp calculation. *Journal of Advanced Computational Intelligence*, **6**(1), 51–55 (2001).
11. T. Yamanoi, T. Yamazaki, J.-L. Vercher, E. Sanchez and M. Sugeno, Dominance of recognition of words presented on right or left eye. Comparison of Kanji and Hiragana. To appear in *Modern Information Processing, From Theory to Applications*, B. Bouchon-Meunier, G. Coletti and R.R. Yager (eds.), Elsevier Science B.V., pp. 407–416 (2006).

Overabundant Answers to Flexible Queries — A Proximity-Based Intensification Approach

Patrick Bosc[*], Allel Hadjali[†] and Olivier Pivert[‡]

IRISA/ENSSAT, Univeristé de Rennes 1
6, rue de Kerampont, 22305 Lannion Cedex, France
[*]bosc@enssat.fr
[†]hadjali@enssat.fr
[‡]pivert@enssat.fr

Abstract

One of the common problems that users might be confronted with in their web search is overabundant answers, that is, being provided with an avalanche of responses that satisfy their query. Most users are overwhelmed by such responses since it is difficult to examine them. In this paper, we attempt to address this issue in the context of flexible queries. The basic idea behind the solution proposed consists in modulating the fuzzy conditions involved in the user query by applying an appropriate transformation. This operation aims at intensifying the constraints of the query. A transformation that relies on a convenient parameterized proximity relation is introduced. The predicates of the modified query are obtained by means of fuzzy arithmetic. The main features of our proposal are investigated and a comparison with other approaches is outlined.

1. Introduction

Retrieving desired data from large databases available online in the Web is becoming a ubiquitous challenge for ordinary users. Exploiting Web-based information sources is nontrivial because the user has no direct access to the data (one cannot for instance browse the whole target database). Users in general accomplish the search by queries that the Web search engines provide. A majority of Web search queries are Boolean and an item from the database simply either matches or it does not. Moreover, users are often confronted with the following two common problems: *no data* or a *very large amount of data* is returned.

In the first case, the problem is called the *empty answer problem*, that is, the problem of not being able to provide the user with any data fitting his/her query. Users are frustrated by such a kind of answers since they do not meet their expectations and interests. Several approaches have been proposed to deal with this issue. Some of them are based on a *relaxation paradigm* that expands the scope of the query so that more information can be gathered in the answers.[9,12] The second problem arises when the user query results in *overabundant answers*, i.e. there is a huge number of data that satisfy the query. In this case, users are overwhelmed by the hugeness of answers since it is pragmatically impossible to sift through them.

To the best of our knowledge, only little attention, however, has been paid to the overabundant answers problem in the literature. Ozawa and Yamada have addressed this issue in Refs. 13 and 14. In Ref. 13, they suggest a method based on generating macro expressions of the queried database. Those expressions allow for providing the user with information about the *data distribution*. Then, the system identifies the appropriate attribute on which a new condition can be added to reconstruct another query. In Ref. 14, Ozawa and Yamada propose a cooperative approach that provides the user with *linguistic answers* using knowledge discovery techniques. From this information, the user can easily understand what kinds of data were retrieved and can then express a new query that shrinks the data set according to his/her interests. Let us also mention the work done by Godfrey[10] in which he discusses the sources of the two above described problems. He claims that finding a *balancing specificity* in a query plays a central role in avoiding such problems.

In the context of flexible queries (i.e. queries that contain gradual predicates represented by means of fuzzy sets and whose satisfaction is a matter of degree), similar problems could still arise. In this context, the *empty answer problem* is defined in the same way as in the Boolean case. Namely, there is no available data in the database that *somewhat satisfies* the user query. Let us now introduce the *fuzzy counterpart* of the *overabundant answer problem*. It can be stated as follows: there are too many data in the database that *fully satisfy* the user query. This means that *satisfaction degrees* of all retrieved data are *equal to 1*. Facing this problem, users' desires are mainly to reduce this very large set of answers and keep a manageable subset that can be easily examined and exploited.

Let Q be a flexible query that contains one or several predicates. In the fuzzy literature, only few works[1-3,5] have addressed the empty answer problem. They mainly aim at relaxing the fuzzy requirements involved in the failing query. *Query relaxation* can be achieved by applying an appropriate transformation to gradual predicates of a failing query. Such a transformation aims at modifying a given predicate into an enlarged one by *widening its support*. For instance, Bosc *et al.*[2,3] have shown how a *tolerance relation* modeled by an appropriate *parameterized proximity relation* can provide a basis for a transformation that is of interest for the purpose of query weakening.

Now to cope with the issue of overabundant answers to Q, the idea is to carry on like above by transforming the fuzzy constraints contained in Q. This transformation basically aims at intensifying the query Q to make it less permissive. *Shrinking the core* of the fuzzy set associated to a predicate in Q is the basic required property of this transformation. This property allows for reducing the wideness of the core and then effectively decreasing the number of answers to Q with degree 1. In this paper, a particular transformation to intensify the meaning of a gradual predicate P is proposed. It also relies on the notion of a *parameterized proximity relation*. Applied to P, it aims at eroding the fuzzy set representing P by the parameter underlying the semantics of the considered proximity relation. The resulting predicate is *semantically not too far* from the original one but it is *more precise* and *more restrictive*. As will be seen, the desirable property of reducing the core is satisfied.

The paper is structured as follows. Section 2 introduces a fuzzy modeling of a proximity relation and describes a particular operation that is the key tool in our approach dedicated to query intensification. In Sec. 3, we present in details the problem of overabundant answers on the one hand, and discuss how it can be solved in the case of single-predicate queries on the other hand. Section 4 provides a comparison of our proposal with other approaches. Intensification strategy to deal with this problem in case of flexible conjunctive queries is investigated in Sec. 5. Last, we briefly recall the main features of our proposal and conclude the paper.

2.   Background

The purpose of this section is twofold. First, the notion of a *parameterized absolute proximity relation* is introduced. Then, we present an operation on fuzzy sets that is of interest for our problem.

2.1.   *Absolute proximity relation*

Definition 1 (Ref. 6).   An *absolute proximity relation* is an approximate equality relation E which can be modeled by a fuzzy relation of the form:

$$\mu_E(x, y) = \mu_Z(x - y), \tag{1}$$

which only depends on the value of the difference $x - y$.

The parameter Z, called a *tolerance indicator*, is a fuzzy interval centered in 0, such that: (i) $\mu_Z(r) = \mu_Z(-r)$ (i.e. $Z = -Z$): this property ensures the *symmetry* of the approximate equality relation E (i.e. $\mu_E(x, y) = \mu_E(y, x)$); (ii) $\mu_Z(0) = 1$: expresses that x is *approximately equal* to itself to a degree 1; (iii) the support $\mathcal{S}(Z) = \{r, \mu_Z(r) > 0\}$ is *bounded* and is of the form $[-\Omega, \ \Omega]$ where Ω is a positive real number. In terms of trapezoidal membership function $(t.m.f.)$, Z can be represented by $(-z, z, \ \delta, \delta)$ with $\Omega = z + \delta$ and $[-z, z]$ denotes the core $\mathcal{C}(Z) = \{r, \mu_Z(r) = 1\}$ of Z. Classical equality is recovered for $Z = 0$ defined as $\mu_0(x - y) = 1$ if $x = y$ and $\mu_0(x - y) = 0$ otherwise. Other interesting properties of the relation E are given in Ref 6. Furthermore, we shall write $E[Z]$ to denote the proximity relation E parameterized by Z and $(E[Z])_r = \{s, \mu_{E[Z]}(s, r) > 0\}$ to represent the set of elements that are close to r in the sense of $E[Z]$.

2.2.   *Dilation and erosion operations*

Let us consider a fuzzy set F on the scalar universe U and an absolute proximity $E(Z)$, where Z is a tolerance indicator. The set F can be associated with a nested pair of fuzzy sets when using $E(Z)$ as a tolerance relation. Indeed, we can build a fuzzy set: (i) F^Z close to

F, such that $F \subseteq F^Z$, this is the *dilation operation*; (ii) F_Z close to F, such that $F_Z \subseteq F$, this is the *erosion operation*.

2.2.1. *Dilation operation*

Dilating the fuzzy set F by Z will provide a fuzzy set F^Z defined by

$$
\begin{aligned}
\mu_{F^Z}(r) &= \sup_s \min \left(\mu_{E[Z]}(s, r), \mu_F(s) \right) \\
&= \sup_s \min \left(\mu_Z(r - s), \mu_F(s) \right), \text{ since } Z = -Z \\
&= \mu_{F \oplus Z}(r), \text{ observing that } s + (r - s) = r. \quad (2)
\end{aligned}
$$

Hence, $F^Z = F \oplus Z$, where $\oplus$ is the addition operation extended to fuzzy sets.[8] F^Z gathers the elements of F and the elements outside F which are somewhat *close to* an element in F.

Lemma 1. $F \subseteq F^Z$.

Thus, F^Z can be viewed as a relaxed variant of F. In terms of *t.m.f.* if $F = (A, B, a, b)$ and $Z = (-z, z, \delta, \delta)$ then $F^Z = (A - z, B + z, a + \delta, b + \delta)$, see Fig. 1. This operation can provide a basis for relaxing flexible queries involving gradual predicates as shown in Refs. 2 and 3. In practice, relaxation technique is often used to support approaches for addressing the *empty answer problem*.

2.2.2. *Erosion operation*

Let $Z \oplus X = F$ be an equation where X is the unknown variable. It has been demonstrated that the greatest solution of this equation

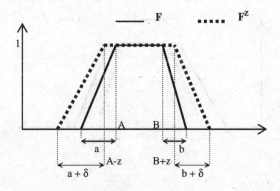

Fig. 1. Dilation operation.

is given by $\overline{X} = F~)+(~(-Z) = F~)+(~Z$ since $Z = -Z$ and where $)+($ is the extended Minkowski subtraction defined by[7,8]:

$$\mu_{F~)+(~Z}(r) = \inf_s(\mu_Z(r-s)\mathcal{I}_\mathbb{T}(\mu_F(s))) = \inf_s(\mu_{E[Z]}(s,r)\mathcal{I}_\mathbb{T}\mu_F(s)) \tag{3}$$

where $\mathbb{T}$ is a t-norm, and $\mathcal{I}_\mathbb{T}$ is the implication induced by $\mathbb{T}$ defined by $\mathcal{I}_\mathbb{T}(u,v) = \sup\{\lambda \in [0,1]/\mathbb{T}(u,\lambda) \leq v\}$, for $u,v \in [0,1]$. We make use of the same t-norm $\mathbb{T} = min$ as in the dilation operation which implies that $\mathcal{I}_\mathbb{T}$ is the so-called *Gödel implication*. Formula (3) can be regarded as the degree of inclusion of $(E[Z])_r$ in F. This means that r belongs to $F~)+(~Z$ if all the elements s that are close to r are F. Hence, the semantic entailment $F~)+(~Z \subseteq F$ holds. Now, eroding the fuzzy set F by Z results in the fuzzy set F_Z defined by $F_Z = F~)+(~Z$.

Lemma 2. $F_Z \subseteq F$.

Hence, F_Z is more precise than the original fuzzy set F but it still remains not too far from F semantically speaking. If $F = (A,B,a,b)$ and $Z = (-z,z,\delta,\delta)$ then $F~)+(~Z = (A+z, B-z, a-\delta, b-\delta)$ provided that $a \geq \delta$ and $b \geq \delta$, see Fig. 2. In the crisp case, $F~)+(~Z = [A,B]~)+(~[-z,z] = [A+z, B-z]$ (while $F \oplus Z = [A-z, B+z]$).

Lemma 3. $F_Z \subseteq F \subseteq F^Z$.

In practice it may happen that one requires that the erosion operation should affect only one constituent part of a fuzzy set F (either the core or the support). Denoting by *core erosion* (resp. *support erosion*) the eroding transformation that modifies only the core (resp.

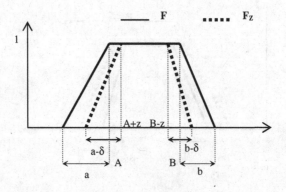

Fig. 2.   Erosion operation.

support) of F, the following proposition shows how to obtain such desirable results.

Proposition 1. Let F be a fuzzy set and $E[Z]$ a proximity relation,

(i) *Core erosion* is obtained using the family of tolerance indicators of the form $Z = (-z, z, 0, 0)$[a].

(ii) *Support erosion* is obtained using the family of tolerance indicators of the form $Z = (0, 0, \delta, \delta)$.

By this proposition, if $F = (A, B, a, b)$ the core erosion (resp. support erosion) leads to $F_Z = (A + z, B - z, a, b)$ (resp. $F_Z = (A, B, a - \delta, b - \delta)$).

3.   Overabundant Answers

Let Q be a *flexible* query and let Σ_Q be the set of answers to Q when addressed to a regular database. Σ_Q contains the items of the database that *somewhat* satisfy the fuzzy requirements involved in Q. Let now Σ_Q^* denotes the set of answers that *fully* satisfy Q, i.e. each item has a satisfaction degree equal to 1. Obviously, $\Sigma_Q^* \subseteq \Sigma_Q$ holds. Let now introduce the problem of overabundant answers and show how it can be approached by means of the parameterized proximity $E[Z]$.

3.1.   *Problem definition*

Definition 2.   We say that Q results in *overabundant answers* if the cardinality of Σ_Q^* is too large.

This is what we will call the **Overabundant Answers Problem** (**OAP**). It is worthy to note that definition 2 is specific to fuzzy queries and does not make sense in the Boolean setting since fuzzy queries express preferences and the notion of satisfaction is a matter of degree. In the case of too many items that partially satisfy the query (i.e. whose degrees lie in $]0, 1[$), the solution is simple and it consists in considering just an $\alpha - cut$ of the retrieved data with an appropriate *high level*. This is why our definition only concerns retrieved data with degree 1.

---

[a] In *t.m.f.* if the bounds of the core change, the support will also change. Here, only the left-hand and the right-hand spreads are unchanged.

This problem often stems from the specificity of the user query
that is too general. In other terms, fuzzy requirements involved in the
query are not restrictive enough. To counter this problem, one can
refine the query to make it more specific, so as to return a reasonable
set of items. This refinement consists in intensifying the fuzzy constraints of the query in order to reduce the set Σ_Q^*. To achieve this
task, a fundamental required property of the intensification mechanism is to significantly shrink the cores of the fuzzy sets associated
with the conditions of the query.

A way to perform query intensification is to apply a *basic transformation* $T^\downarrow$ on all or some predicates involved in the query. This
transformation can be applied iteratively if necessary. Some properties are required for any transformation $T^\downarrow$ when applied to a predicate P ($T^\downarrow(P)$ representing the intensified predicate):

- $\mathcal{C}_1 : T^\downarrow$ does not increase the membership degree for any element
  of the domain, i.e. $\forall u, \mu_{T^\downarrow(P)}(u) \leq \mu_P(u)$;
- $\mathcal{C}_2 : T^\downarrow$ must shrink the core $\mathcal{C}(P)$ of P, i.e. $\mathcal{C}(T^\downarrow(P)) \subset \mathcal{C}(P)$;
- $\mathcal{C}_3 : T^\downarrow$ preserves the left-hand (resp. right-hand) spread of P,
  i.e. if
  $P = (A, B, a, b)$, then $T^\downarrow(P) = (A', B', a', b')$ with $a = a'$ and b
  $= b'$, and $A'-A < a$ and $B-B' < b$.

The second property allows for reducing the cardinality of the core
and then effectively decreasing the number of answers with degree 1.
The last property guarantees that the data excluded from the core
of P remain in its support.

3.2.   *Intensifying atomic queries*

Let P be a fuzzy predicate and $E[Z]$ be a proximity relation parameterized by a tolerance indicator Z of the form $(-z, z, 0, 0)$. Making
use of the erosion operation, P can be transformed into a *restricted*
fuzzy predicate P' defined as follows:

$$P' = T^\downarrow(P) = P_Z = P \;)+(\; Z.$$

This transformation allows for reinforcing the meaning of the vague
concept expressed by P. As previously mentioned, the resulting predicate P' contains elements r such that all elements that are close
to r are in P. Hence, this transformation is not simply a technical

operator acting on the membership degrees but it is endowed with a clear semantics as well. Now, if $P = (A, B, a, b)$ then $T^{\downarrow}(P) = (A + z, B - z, a, b)$, see Fig. 2. As can be checked, the properties $\mathcal{C}_1$ to $\mathcal{C}_3$ hold.

Principle of the Approach. Let $\mathcal{Q} = P$ be an atomic query (i.e. containing a single fuzzy predicate P). Assume that $\Sigma_{\mathcal{Q}}^*$ is too large. In order to reduce $\Sigma_{\mathcal{Q}}^*$, we transform $\mathcal{Q}$ into $\mathcal{Q}_1 = T^{\downarrow}(P) = P$)+(Z. This intensification mechanism can be applied iteratively until the database returns a manageable set of answers to the modified query $\mathcal{Q}_n = T^{\downarrow(n)}(P) = P) + (n \cdot Z$. This strategy provides an implicit measure of nearness such as: $\mathcal{Q}_k$ is nearer to $\mathcal{Q}$ than $\mathcal{Q}_l$ if $k < l$. Let us take a look at the subset of $\Sigma_{\mathcal{Q}}^*$ resulting from the intensification process. The items in that subset represent the typical values of the concept expressed by the fuzzy set associated with $\mathcal{Q}$.

Controlling the intensification. We claim that semantic limits[b] of an intensification process are not as crucial as in the case of query relaxation. Indeed, the intensification process only aims at reducing the large set of answers; not at finding alternative answers. It is worthy, however, to emphasize that the query refinement must stop when the upper bound and the lower bound of the core (of the modified query $\mathcal{Q}_i$) are equal to $(A + B)/2$. Indeed, the *t.m.f.* associated to $\mathcal{Q}_i$ is $(A + i \cdot z, B - i \cdot z, a, b)$. Now, since $A + i \cdot z \leq B - i \cdot z$ holds we have $i \leq (B - A)/2z$. This means that the maximal query refinement is obtained when the core is reduced to a *singleton*. Let us note that the risk to obtain empty answers ($\Sigma_{\mathcal{Q}} = \emptyset$) during the process is excluded when $a > z$ and $b > z$ (since the data that have been eliminated from $\Sigma_{\mathcal{Q}_{i-1}}^*$ related to $\mathcal{Q}_{i-1}$ still belong to the support of $\mathcal{Q}_i$). Now if a too specific query arises and returns $\Sigma_{\mathcal{Q}}^* = \emptyset$, one can back up and try another variation (for instance, adjust the tolerance parameter Z).

Intensification Algorithm. Algorithm 1 formalizes this intensification approach (where $\Sigma_{\mathcal{Q}_i}^*$ stands for the set of answers to $\mathcal{Q}_i$).

Particular case. Let us note that for some kinds of atomic queries to be intensified, the *property of symmetry* of the tolerance indicator

---

[b] In query relaxation, semantic limits stand for the maximum number of relaxation steps that can be performed such that the final modified query $\mathcal{Q}_n$ is *not too far*, semantically speaking, from the original one.[2]

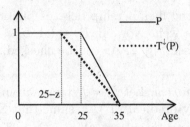

Fig. 3.   Fuzzy predicate "*young*".

Z is not required. Consider, for instance, the query $Q = P$ where $P = (0, 25, 0, 10)$ which expresses the concept "*young*" as illustrated in Fig. 3. Intensifying P comes down to reducing the cardinality of the core $\mathcal{C}(P)$ and thus to come closer to the typical values of P. As can be seen, the left part of $\mathcal{C}(P)$ contains the typical values of the concept "*young*". Then, the intensification transformation must only affect the right part of $\mathcal{C}(P)$ and preserve entirely its left part. The appropriate form of Z allowing this operation is $(0, z, 0, 0)$ which leads to $T^{\downarrow}(P) = (0, 25 - z, 0, 10)$.

Algorithm 1. Atomic query Intensification.

---

let $Q := P$;
let $Z = (-z, z, 0, 0)$ be a tolerance indicator;
$i := 0$; $Q_i := Q$;
compute $\Sigma^*_{Q_i}$;
while ($|\Sigma^*_{Q_i}|$ is too large **and** $i \leq (B - A)/2 \cdot z$) **do**
begin
$i := i + 1$;
$Q_i := T^{\downarrow(i)}(P) := P) + (i \cdot Z$;
compute $\Sigma^*_{Q_i}$;
end
return $\Sigma^*_{Q_i}$;

3.3. *Basic features of the approach*

In this section, we investigate the main features of our intensification approach. To do this, we point out three criteria that seem to be of

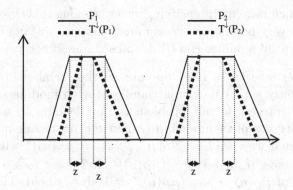

Fig. 4. Impact of the slopes and the relative position of the membership functions.

a major importance from a user point of view:

(i) *Intensification nature.* Taking a look at the *t.m.f.* of $T^{\downarrow}(P)$, it is easy to see that the effect of the intensification over the core of P in the right and the left parts is the same and amounts to z. This means that the resulting intensification is of a *symmetrical* nature.

(ii) *Impact of the domain and the predicate.* As illustrated in Fig. 4 where P_1 and P_2 are two predicates related to the same attribute, the *relative position* of the membership function (in the domain of the attribute) has no impact on the intensifying effect. However, the *attribute domain* is identified as a major factor affecting the intensification because the parameter z is an absolute value which is added and subtracted (for instance, z will be different for the attribute "*age*" and the attribute "*salary*").

(iii) *Applicability to the crisp case.* It can be easily checked that our transformation $T^{\downarrow}$ is still valid for crisp predicates. For example, if $P = (22, 30, 0, 0)$, then $T^{\downarrow}(P)$ writes $(22 + z, 30 - z, 0, 0)$.

4. Comparison with Other Modifier-Based Approaches

In the fuzzy set framework, modifying a linguistic term P can be also achieved by fuzzy modifiers.[11] Such operators are used either to weaken or to intensify a linguistic term P. Here, we only focus on modifiers which have an intensifying effect. Among this class of modifiers two are very popular: *powering modifiers* and *shifting modifiers*. Let m be a fuzzy modifier ($m(P)$ denotes the modified predicate):

(i) *Powering modifiers:* They operate on the membership degrees of the fuzzy set. A particular family of such modifiers which is of great interest to our problem is that leading to a decrease in the degrees of membership (called *the restrictive modifiers*). In a formal way, we have $\forall u, \mu_{m(P)}(u) = (\mu_P(u))^n$ with $n > 1$. For instance, $\mu_{very(P)}(u) = (\mu_P(u))^2$. It is easy to see that the entailment $\mu_P(u) = 1 \Rightarrow (\mu_P(u))^n = 1$ always hold. This means that the core of P is never affected by the modification, i.e. C_2 is not satisfied. Hence, such modifiers are inappropriate for our problem.

(ii) *Shifting modifiers:* They shift the membership function n units to the left or to the right in the universe of discourse. Formally, we have $\forall u, \mu_{m(P)}(u) = \mu_P(u - n)$ with n in $\mathbb{R}$. If P is partially increasing and partially decreasing, $m(P)$ can never be a subset of P. Then, the property C_1 does not hold.

In Ref. 4, another interesting family of linguistic modifiers m_γ (such as *"really"*) has been proposed to reinforce the meaning of P. Such modifiers are defined in the following way:

$$\mu_{m\gamma(P)} = \max(0, \min(1, (u - A + a)/\gamma \cdot a, (u - B - b)/\gamma \cdot b)),$$

with $\gamma \in]1, (B - A + a + b)/(b + a)[$ and $P = (A, B, a, b)$. Let us take a look at the modified predicate $m_\gamma(P)$. It is easy to check that $S(m_\gamma(P)) = S(P)$ (support preserving) and $C(m_\gamma(P)) \subset C(P)$ (core reducing). This means that both properties C_1 and C_2 are satisfied by the transformation induced by this modifier. Hence, one could use this approach to deal with the problem at hand. But a major shortcoming of this approach lies in the lack of semantics whereas semantics is our starting point.

5. Case of Conjunctive Flexible Queries

A conjunctive fuzzy query Q is of the form $P_1 \wedge \ldots \wedge P_k$, where the symbol '$\wedge$' stands for the connector '*and*' (which is interpreted by the '*min*' operator) and P_i is a fuzzy predicate. Our strategy to solve the OAP problem in this case is still based on reinforcing the fuzzy requirements involved in Q. Let us first consider the following proposition.

Proposition 2. *If $Q = P_1 \wedge \ldots \wedge P_k$ results in overabundant answers, then each subquery of Q results also in overabundant answers.*

Lemma 4. *If $Q = P_1 \wedge \ldots \wedge P_k$ results in overabundant answers, then each atomic query Q_i (i.e. $Q_i = P_i$) of Q results also in overabundant answers.*

As solving the OAP problem comes down to reducing the cardinality of the retrieved data set Σ_Q^*, it suffices then to reduce the cardinality of values (in Σ_Q^*) associated with one predicate P_s (with $1 \leq s \leq k$). To do so, we apply the intensification transformation only to P_s. In practice, the question is about the predicate (i.e. attribute) to select for intensification (since a judicious choice could lead to an efficient fast intensification strategy).

Several ways can be used for selecting the predicate to be considered for intensification: one can exploit the data distribution of the queried database, or call for user intervention. In the following, we advocate another way of selecting that only exploits the retrieved data set Σ_Q^* to the user query Q. The main idea is to take a look at the distribution of values in Σ_Q^* of each predicate P_i (with $1 \leq i \leq k$) with respect to its core (for instance, examine the location of those values regarding the bounds of the core). Let $P_i = (A_i, B_i, a_i, b_i)$, we compute the average value, $aver(P_i)$, of its values in Σ_Q^* and then the distance d_i between $aver(P_i)$ and the bounds of its core. The predicate P_s to select is such that the distance d_s is minimal. This means that the retrieved values related to P_s are closer to the bounds of the core than the other values associated with the other predicates. It is then more efficient to apply the intensification process to P_s rather to other predicates. This method can be formalized as follows:

- **Step 1:** calculus of the average value
  for each i **in** $[1 \ldots k]$
      compute $aver(P_i)$
- **Step 2:** distance-based index of values distribution
  for each i **in** $[1 \ldots k]$
      compute $d_i = \min(|aver(P_i) - A_i|, (|aver(P_i) - B_i|)$
- **Step 3:** selecting the predicate P_s
  select s such that $d_s = \min_{i=1,k} d_i$.

6. Conclusion

In this paper, we have addressed the problem of overabundant answers in the fuzzy querying setting. We have shown how it can be automatically dealt with. The key tool of the proposed approach is a tolerance relation expressed by a convenient parameterized proximity relation. Such a fuzzy relation can provide the basis to achieving query intensification of the user query. The main advantage of our proposal is the fact that it operates only on the conditions involved in the query without adding new conditions or performing any summarizing operation. Such an approach can be useful to construct intelligent information retrieval systems that provide the user with cooperative answers.

References

1. T. Andreasen and O. Pivert, On the weakening of fuzzy relational queries. *8th Int. Symp. on Meth. for Intell. Syst.*, Charlotte, USA, pp. 144–151 (1994).
2. P. Bosc, A. HadjAli and O. Pivert, Towards a tolerance-based technique for cooperative answering of fuzzy queries against regular databases. *7th Int. Conf. CoopIS, LNCS 3760*, pp. 256–273 (2005).
3. P. Bosc, A. HadjAli and O. Pivert, Weakening of fuzzy relational queries: An absolute proximity relation-based approach. To appear in *Journal of Mathware and Soft Computing*.
4. B. Bouchon-Meunier, Stability of linguistic modifiers compatible with a fuzzy logic. *Uncertainty in Intelligent Systems, LNCS 313*, pp. 63–70 (1988).
5. M. de Calmès, D. Dubois, E. Hullermeier, H. Prade and F. Sedes, Flexibility and fuzzy case-based evaluation in querying: An illustration in an experimental setting. *Int. J. of Uncertainty, Fuzziness and Knowledge-based Systems*, **11**(1), 43–66 (2003).
6. D. Dubois, A. HadjAli and H. Prade, Fuzzy qualitative reasoning with words, in: *Computing with Words* (P. P. Wang, (ed).). John Wiley & Son, *Series of Books on Intelligent Systems*, pp. 347–366 (2001).
7. D. Dubois and H. Prade, Inverse operations for fuzzy numbers. *Proc. of IFAC Symp. on Fuzzy Info., Knowledge Repre. and Decision Analysis*, pp. 391–395 (1983).
8. D. Dubois and H. Prade, *Possibility Theory*, Plenum Press (1988).
9. T. Gaasterland, Cooperative answering through controlled query relaxation. *IEEE Expert*, **12**(5), 48–59 (1997).
10. P. Godfrey, Relaxation in Web Search: A new paradigm for search by Boolean queries. *Personal Communication* (March 1998).
11. E. E. Kerre and M. de Cock, Linguistic modifiers: An overview. *Fuzzy Logic and Soft Computing*, (Chen, Ying, Cai, (eds).), pp. 69–85 (1999).

12. I. Muslea, Machine learning for online query relaxation. *10th Int. Conf. of Knowledge and Discovery and Data Mining, KDD'2004*, pp. 246–255 (2004).
13. J. Ozawa and K. Yamada, Cooperative answering with macro expression of a database. *5th Int. Conf. IPMU*, Paris 4–8 July, pp. 17–22 (1994).
14. J. Ozawa and K. Yamada, Discovery of global knowledge in database for cooperative answering. *5th IEEE Int. Conf. on Fuzzy Systems*, pp. 849–852 (1995).

SYSTEMS MODELING
AND APPLICATIONS

Words or Numbers, Mamdani or Sugeno Fuzzy Systems: A Comparative Study

Sylvie Galichet[*], Reda Boukezzoula[†] and Laurent Foulloy[‡]

University of Savoie, Polytech'Savoie/LISTIC
BP80439, 74944 Annecy le Vieux Cedex, France
[*] *Sylvie.Galichet@univ-savoie.fr*
[†] *Reda.Boukezzoula@univ-savoie.fr*
[‡] *Laurent.Foulloy@univ-savoie.fr*

Abstract

In Sugeno's rules, conclusions are usually considered as being crisp numerical values. On the other hand, in Mamdani's rules, conclusions are viewed as fuzzy numbers or more rarely as words. This paper makes an attempt at smoothing out this distinction by proposing to handle fuzzy rules with conclusions of the three different types using Mamdani's reasoning as well as Sugeno's interpolation mechanism. The extension of Sugeno's fuzzy systems is carried out using fuzzy arithmetic operators for implementing the weighted mean of fuzzy numbers or words. Concerning Mamdani's systems, the compositional rule of inference is applied indifferently at the numerical and linguistic levels. After the presentation of the different possible implementations of a rule-based system, the developed ideas are illustrated using a fuzzy rulebase that approximates the arithmetic mean of two quantities.

1. Introduction

Fuzzy rule-based systems are usually categorized into two families: Sugeno's systems and Mamdani's systems. Both types of systems are often distinguished according to the way the rule conclusions are expressed. On one hand the family of Sugeno's systems is based on conclusions that can be numerically computed for given input

variables. On the other hand, Mamdani's rules use a linguistic specification of the conclusions with fuzzy subsets. Both families are associated with specific computation mechanisms. Concerning Sugeno's
systems, a numerical interpolation is carried out to fill the gap
between the identified behaviors expressed by the rule conclusions
when Mamdani's systems are based on fuzzy reasoning. Hence, in
most applications of Mamdani's systems a defuzzification step is
achieved for computing a crisp numerical output. By doing so, it
becomes possible to compare the input-output mapping associated
with both families of fuzzy systems. In this framework, different
studies showed that there exists particular configurations for which
both families of fuzzy systems are equivalent. The major aim of this
paper is to extend the usual interpolation mechanism implemented
in Sugeno's systems for dealing with Mamdani's rules, that is rules
whose conclusions are linguistically expressed. Actually, two different interpretations of such conclusions are considered. In the first
one, the symbol C_k involved in the conclusion "z is C_k" is associated
with a specific fuzzy subset, namely a fuzzy number. In the second
one, C_k is viewed as a word, i.e. a crisp element belonging to some
dictionary. These two points of view result in two different implementations of the interpolation mechanism inherent to Sugeno's systems.
The same distinction is proposed for Mamdani's systems, leading also
to two distinct inference mechanisms. To sum up the paper content
at a glance, six computation techniques are presented according to
Table 1. Each cell contains the number of the section where the corresponding computation mechanism is detailed. The gray cells are
associated with the conventional implementation of both families of
fuzzy systems.

The paper is organized according to Table 1. Section 2 aims
at presenting the usual Sugeno's interpolation mechanism and its
extension for handling fuzzy numbers and words. Section 3 is devoted

Table 1. Paper content.

C_k is	Computation	
	Interpolation (Sugeno)	Reasoning (Mamdani)
A crisp number	2.1	3.1
A fuzzy number	2.2	3.1
A word	2.3	3.2

to Mamdani's fuzzy systems with an insight into its possible use for computing with words. Section 4 gives an illustration of the developed ideas using a simple rulebase that implements a fuzzy arithmetic mean of two quantities. The final section contains a brief discussion about future works and a conclusion.

2. Sugeno-Like Fuzzy Systems

2.1. *Computation mechanism*

Sugeno's fuzzy systems are based on a collection of "**If** ... **then** ..." rules whose antecedent part is linguistically expressed but whose conclusion part is numeric (real value, linear or polynomial equation...). Without loss of generality we restrict ourselves to rules with two inputs of the form:

$$\mathrm{R^S}_{(i,j,k)} : \textbf{If } x \text{ is } A_i \quad \textbf{and} \quad y \text{ is } B_j \quad \textbf{then } z = c_k, \tag{1}$$

where A_i and B_j are linguistic values with fuzzy triangular membership functions and c_k a real value. For precise inputs x_0 and y_0, the output z is computed according to the following mechanism:

$$z = \mathrm{SUG}(x_0, y_0) = \sum_{(i,j,k) \in I} w_{i,j} \cdot c_k / \sum_{(i,j) \in J} w_{i,j} \tag{2}$$

with $w_{i,j} = \mu_{A_i}(x_0) \cdot \mu_{B_j}(y_0)$. For the sake of simplicity, a strict triangular partitioning of the input universes of discourse is assumed, that is we have $\Sigma_{(i,j) \in J} w_{i,j} = 1$, which leads to:

$$z = \mathrm{SUG}(x_0, y_0) = \sum_{(i,j,k) \in I} w_{i,j} \cdot c_k. \tag{3}$$

The idea developed in this paper consists in extending the Sugeno's computational mechanism for dealing with rules of the form:

$$\mathrm{R^M}_{(i,j,k)} : \textbf{If } x \text{ is } A_i \quad \textbf{and} \quad y \text{ is } B_j \quad \textbf{then } z = C_k, \tag{4}$$

where the conclusion C_k is now a linguistic value with a fuzzy triangular membership function. The direct extension of Eq. (3) leads to:

$$z_L = \mathrm{LSUG}(x_0, y_0) = \left(\sum_{(i,j,k) \in I} \right) w_{i,j} \otimes C_k, \tag{5}$$

where $z_L = \text{LSUG}(x_0, y_0)$ denotes the linguistic output of the fuzzy system. It is worth noting that Eq. (5) involves specific operators for handling addition and product by a scalar in a linguistic framework. In other words, the operators $\oplus$ and $\otimes$ represent the linguistic counterpart of the real-valued operators $+$ and $\times$.

2.2. Computing with fuzzy numbers

One possible interpretation of Eq. (5) consists in making no distinction between symbol C_k and its fuzzy meaning, that is its membership function. In this case, fuzzy numbers have to be combined using a weighted fuzzy mean operator which can be implemented according to fuzzy arithmetics. The application of the extension principle leads to the following definition of the operators $\otimes$ and $\oplus$:

$$\mu_{w \otimes C}(z) = \mu_C(z/w), w \neq 0, \tag{6}$$

$$\mu_{C_1 \oplus C_2}(z) = \sup_{v \in \Re}(\min(\mu_{C_1}(z - v), \mu_{C_2}(z))). \tag{7}$$

Using a parametric representation where $C = (l, m, r)$ denotes the triangular fuzzy subset C with modal value m and support $[l, r]$, the development of Eqs. (6) and (7) leads to the following exact results:

$$w \otimes C = w \otimes (l, m, r) = (w.l, w.m, w.r), \tag{8}$$

$$C_1 \oplus C_2 = (l_1, m_1, r_1) \oplus (l_2, m_2, r_2) = (l_1 + l_2, m_1 + m_2, r_1 + r_2). \tag{9}$$

Finally, according to Eqs. (8) and (9), the output of the implemented Sugeno-like fuzzy system (Eq. (5)) is a triangular fuzzy subset whose parameters are computed using a weighted mean. For example, the modal value of z_L is given by $m = \Sigma_{(i,j,k) \in I} \, w_{i,j} \cdot m_k$, where m_k is the modal value of the symbols C_k involved in the conclusion of the rules (4). The same equation holds for dealing with the left and right parameters, i.e. l and r. Comparing with Eq. (3), it appears clear that the modal value of the computed result is equal to the result obtained using a usual Sugeno's system with constant conclusions. The difference between both implementations resides in the imprecision attached to the computed result determined from the one associated with the combined conclusions.

2.3. Computing with words

Another possible implementation of Eq. (5) consists in defining linguistic operators $\oplus$ and $\otimes$ for directly dealing with symbols C_k. In this framework, the "addition" of two words should provide another word. In this case, the $\oplus$ operator is defined by a function from $LZ \times LZ$ to LZ where $LZ = \{C_1, C_2, \ldots, C_K\}$ is the set of words used for describing the numeric variable $z \in Z$. According to this approach, essentially used for dealing with qualitative equations, it is not possible to model any gradual behavior without defining a large number of words, which is prejudicial to the system interpretability. An alternative proposal consists in expressing the result of the "addition" of two words as a fuzzy linguistic set, that is a fuzzy set defined on a set of words, i.e. LZ in the present case. Such an approach is developed in the remainder of this section.

2.3.1. Notations

Let us first introduce the notations used for expressing fuzzy linguistic subsets defined on LZ. Let E be such a fuzzy subset, with extensional definition:

$$E = \alpha_1/C_1 + \alpha_2/C_2 + \cdots + \alpha_K/C_K = \sum_{k=1,\ldots,K} \alpha_k/C_k. \qquad (10)$$

In others words, any symbol C_k belongs to E with the degree α_k, i.e. $\mu_E(C_k) = \alpha_k$. For the sake of simplicity, any symbol associated with a zero membership degree is usually removed from Eq. (10). Finally, let $F(LZ)$ be the set of all fuzzy linguistic subsets defined on LZ. Any word C_k can be viewed as the singleton $\{C_k\}$ whose extensional definition is simply $1/C_k$. It means that any word can be assimilated with a degenerated fuzzy linguistic subset, i.e. an element in $F(LZ)$. In this framework, both operators $\oplus$ and $\otimes$ involved in Eq. (5) will be defined for handling fuzzy linguistic subsets. It means that the addition will induce a relation from $F(LZ) \times F(LZ)$ to $F(LZ)$ while the product by a degree will generate a relation from $[0, 1] \times F(LZ)$ to $F(LZ)$. The methodology further proposed for defining these two relations makes use of the assumption that all processed symbols have a numerical meaning. In this context, it is possible to define linguistic operations so as to guarantee coherence with corresponding numerical operations. With this aim in view, it is important to clarify the links existing between linguistic and numerical worlds and to define a mapping between objects of both universes. That is the purpose of the next section.

2.3.2. Mapping between words and numbers

Interfaces are here proposed for transforming numbers into words and conversely. More precisely, links between numbers and fuzzy linguistic subsets are considered and specified by means of two functions:

- The first one D is in charge of converting a number into a fuzzy linguistic subset. An element z in Z is thus associated with a fuzzy subset of terms in LZ, that is an element in F(LZ). D(z), called descriptor by Zadeh, can be deduced from the fuzzy meaning of used terms, namely:

$$D : Z \to F(LZ)$$
$$z \to D(z) = \sum_{k=1,...,K} \mu_{C_k}(z)/C_k \qquad (11)$$

  Actually, the description mapping D implements a special kind of *fuzzification*, called *linguistic* or *symbolic fuzzification*.[3]
- The second function H produces a crisp numerical value, i.e. an element in Z, from a fuzzy linguistic subset, i.e. an element in F(LZ). In the same way that the description D implements a symbolic fuzzification, the mapping H carries out a *linguistic* or *symbolic defuzzification*.[3] Several methods of symbolic defuzzification can be chosen. Here, we restrict ourselves to the *height* method defined as:

$$\forall E \in F(LZ), \quad H(E) = \sum_{k=1}^{K} \mu_E(C_k) \cdot m_k \bigg/ \sum_{k=1}^{K} \mu_E(C_k), \qquad (12)$$

where m_k represents a significative value associated with symbol C_k, usually the modal value.

In Ref. 1, it is shown that under the condition of a strict triangular partitioning of the numeric universe of discourse Z, the pair of interfaces (D, H) satisfies the following equation $\forall z \in Z$, $H(D(z)) = z$, which characterizes *optimal interfaces*. It is worth noting that the image of Z under D is not F(LZ) but only a subset of F(LZ). Otherwise expressed, the description function D is not surjective. It means that $\exists F \in F(LZ), D(H(F)) \neq F$. For example, an element F in F(LZ) that contains more than two words

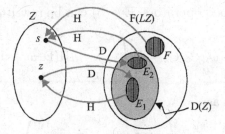

Fig. 1. Optimal interfaces.

with a non-null membership degree cannot be mapped to using the description D. Actually, by restricting the definition domain of H to those fuzzy linguistic subsets that can be obtained by the description function D, it can be verified that $\forall E \in D(Z), D(H(E)) = E$, where $D(Z) \subset F(LZ)$ is the image of Z under D. Properties of the defined *optimal interfaces* are illustrated in Fig. 1. In the case of strict triangular partitioning of Z, the restricted definition domain of H is given by $D(Z) = \{\alpha/C_{k-1} + (1 - \alpha)/C_k; k = 2, \ldots, K, \alpha \in [0, 1]\}$.

2.3.3. *Linguistic operations*

Having laid down functions for transforming numbers into fuzzy linguistic subsets and conversely, it becomes possible to proceed with the definition of the linguistic operators $\oplus$ and $\otimes$ according to the three following steps:

- Fuzzy linguistic arguments are transformed into numbers using the function H.
- The arithmetic operation is carried out with the so-obtained numeric operands.
- The result is retransformed into a fuzzy linguistic subset by means of the description function H.

It follows:

$$\forall E_1, E_2 \in F(LZ), \quad E_1 \oplus E_2 = D(H(E_1) + H(E_2)), \qquad (13)$$

$$\forall E \in F(LZ), \forall w \in [0, 1], \quad w \otimes E = D(w \cdot H(E)). \qquad (14)$$

Using the so-defined operators, Eq. (5) can be rewritten in the form:

$$z_L = \sum_{(i,j,k) \in I} w_{i,j} \otimes C_k = D\left(\sum_{(i,j,k) \in I} H(D(w_{i,j} \cdot H(1/C_k))) \right)$$

and reformulated as:

$$z_L = D\left(\sum_{(i,j,k) \in I} w_{i,j} \cdot H(1/C_k) \right). \tag{15}$$

Assuming that m_k is the modal value of the triangular fuzzy meaning of C_k, it follows $z_L = D(\Sigma_{(i,j,k) \in I} w_{i,j} \cdot m_k)$. Comparing with Eq. (3), it appears that the proposed linguistic computation leads to the linguistic description of the result that would be obtained with a usual Sugeno system with constant numeric conclusions, provided that the modal values of the involved symbols C_k, i.e. m_k, correspond with the constant conclusions c_k in (1).

3. Mamdani-Like Fuzzy Systems

3.1. *Reasoning with fuzzy numbers*

The usual way for dealing with Mamdani's fuzzy rules (4) consists in using the compositional rule of inference. Considering fuzzy observed data E_x and E_y, the conclusion concerning z is the element F in $F(Z)$ given by:

$$\forall z \in Z \quad \mu_F(z) = \sup_{(x,y) \in X \times Y} T_1(T_2(\mu_{E_x}(x), \mu_{E_y}(y)), \mu_\Gamma(x,y,z)), \tag{16}$$

where T_1 and T_2 represent fuzzy t-norms and Γ the graph of the fuzzy relation built from the rules. Choosing a conjunctive interpretation of the rules, it follows:

$$\mu_\Gamma(x,y,z) = \perp_{(i,j,k) \in I} T_3(T_4(\mu_{A_i}(x), \mu_{B_j}(y)), \mu_{C_k}(z)), \tag{17}$$

where T_3 and T_4 represent fuzzy t-norms and $\perp$ a fuzzy t-conorm. In the particular case considered here, observed data x_0 and y_0 are crisp, which induces that Eq. (16) is reduced to:

$$\forall z \in Z \, \mu_F(z) = \mu_\Gamma(x_0, y_0, z). \tag{18}$$

In the original Mamdani's work, the fuzzy operators min/max were chosen as t-norm and t-conorm. In that case, the inferred fuzzy result

F is given by:

$$\forall z \in Z \quad \mu_F(z) = \max_{(i,j,k) \in I} \min(\mu_{A_i}(x_0), \mu_{B_j}(y_0), \mu_{C_k}(z)). \quad (19)$$

Another choice that guarantees some linearity properties is based on the use of the *t*-norm product and the *t*-conorm bounded sum, i.e. $T_3(a, b) = T_4(a, b) = a.b$ and $\perp(a, b) = \min(1, a + b)$. Equations (17) and (18) are then rewritten as:

$$\forall z \in Z \quad \mu_F(z) = \min\left(1, \sum_{(i,j,k) \in I} \mu_{A_i}(x_0) \cdot \mu_{B_j}(y_0) \cdot \mu_{C_k}(z)\right).$$
$$(20)$$

In the specific case where the rule conclusions are real values c_k (a type-II system for Sugeno[8]), symbols C_k are defined as singletons, which leads to:

$$\mu_F(z) = \perp_{(i,j,k) \in I} T_4(\mu_{A_i}(x_0), \mu_{B_j}(y_0)) \quad \text{if } z = c_k, \quad = 0 \text{ otherwise.}$$
$$(21)$$

In this context, the *bounded sum/product* inference and the center of gravity defuzzification allows an exact equivalence with Sugeno's formalism.

3.2. *Reasoning with words*

Considering now that symbols C_k are words, the compositional rule of inference can be directly applied at the linguistic level. It means that the crisp observations x_0 and y_0 have also to be expressed at the linguistic level. One way of handling the required numeric-to-linguistic transformation consists in using the fuzzy description D over the defined sets of terms. It follows:

$$\forall C_k \in LZ \quad \mu_F(C_k) = \sup_{(A_i, B_j) \in LX \times LY}$$
$$T_1(T_2(\mu_{D(x_0)}(A_i), \mu_{D(y_0)}(B_j)), \mu_\Gamma(A_i, B_j, C_k)), \quad (22)$$

where Γ is now the graph of a linguistic relation built from the rules. Actually, each rule (4) defines an element in Γ. In other words, the 3-tuple (A_i, B_j, C_k) belongs to Γ, i.e. $\mu_\Gamma(A_i, B_j, C_k) = 1$, when there exists a rule linking input symbols A_i and B_j with output symbol C_k. As the input linguistic domain $LX \times LY$ is a countable set, the supremum coincides with the maximal element and Eq. (22) can be generalized by using any *t*-conorm instead of *max*. This formalism can also be used to handle weighted linguistic rules of the form "**If** x is A_i **and** y is B_j **then** $z = C_k$ with weight α_{ijk}". In this case, α_{ijk} represents the strength of the link between involved symbols, i.e. $\mu_\Gamma(A_i, B_j, C_k) = \alpha_{ijk}$.

4. Illustration

The purpose of this section is to compare the different possible implementations of a rule-based system. With this aim in view, a unique target function is chosen for testing both families of fuzzy systems and their variants:

Sugeno's systems

a. *with constant conclusions*
b. *with symbolic conclusions viewed as fuzzy numbers*
c. *with symbolic conclusions viewed as words*

Mamdani's systems

d. *with symbolic conclusions viewed as singletons*
e. *with symbolic conclusions viewed as fuzzy numbers*
f. *with symbolic conclusions viewed as words*

The comparative study aims at focusing on the manner in which the imprecision inherently present in the rule based system is transmitted to the computed result. In this context, a *bounded sum/product* inference is considered in all Mamdani's system implementations with the purpose of avoiding undesirable nonlinearities. Furthermore, a simple target function is chosen so as to suppress approximation problems. A linear system that implements the arithmetic mean[5] of two numbers x and y is thus considered. Moreover, the use of the implemented mean operator is restricted to a specific case for which it makes sense to describe numbers with symbols. The numeric variables x and y are thus viewed as being student marks. In the french education system, the corresponding universe of discourse X and Y are usually $[0, 20]$. A possible alternative consists in marking with letters, i.e. $LX = LY = \{F, E, D, C, B, A\}$. The meaning generally attributed to each symbol is given in Fig. 2. Applying the modal equivalence principle[4] allows an automatic synthesis of a Sugeno's system that exactly implements any linear function. Considering the target function $f(x, y) = (x + y) / 2$, the rulebase given in Table 2 is obtained.

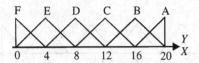

Fig. 2.   Input partitions.

Table 2.   Sugeno's rulebase.

x	y					
	F	E	D	C	B	A
A	10	12	14	16	18	20
B	8	10	12	14	16	18
C	6	8	10	12	14	16
D	4	6	8	10	12	14
E	2	4	6	8	10	12
F	0	2	4	6	8	10

All along this section, the crisp numerical observations $x_0 = 15$ and $y_0 = 8.8$ are considered. According to the defined partitions, the resulting fuzzy descriptions are given by $D(x_0) = 0.75/B + 0.25/C$ and $D(y_0) = 0.8/D + 0.2/C$.

Case a. The Sugeno's system output z is computed according to Eq. (2), where the single fired rules are the four rules framed in Table 2. It follows $z = (0.75*0.8*12) + (0.75*0.2*14) + (0.25*0.8*10) + (0.25*0.2*12) = 11.9$ which, as expected, is the exact arithmetic mean of $x_0 = 15$ and $y_0 = 8.8$.

Case b. Viewing rule conclusions as fuzzy numbers previously requires the definition of appropriate fuzzy subsets. With this aim in view, it is reasonable to transform each real value c_k involved in a rule conclusion into a fuzzy subset called "around c_k". According to Table 2, eleven fuzzy numbers are defined. However, instead of using generic terms such as "around 10", a naming related to student marks is preferred. Thus, the term set LZ associated with the output variable z is chosen as $LZ = \{F, \mathbf{F\_E}, E, \mathbf{E\_D}, D, \mathbf{D\_C}, C, \mathbf{C\_B}, B, \mathbf{B\_A}, A\}$. For example, the symbol $\mathbf{E\_D}$ corresponds to a mark between E and D. The corresponding fuzzy partition of the domain Z is illustrated in Fig. 3. It is important to be aware that a linguistic mark, for example C, has

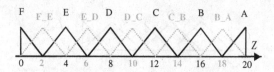

Fig. 3. Output partition.

Table 3. Linguistic rulebase.

x	y					
	F	E	D	C	B	A
A	D_C	C	C_B	B	B_A	A
B	D	D_C	C	C_B	B	B_A
C	E_D	D	D_C	C	C_B	B
D	E	E_D	D	D_C	C	C_B
E	F_E	E	E_D	D	D_C	C
F	F	F_E	E	E_D	D	D_C

different meaning depending on the underlying variable, x, y on the first hand, z on the other one. The linguistic rulebase derived from Table 2 is given in Table 3.

The fuzzy mean of $x_0 = 15$ and $y_0 = 8.8$ is computed using Eq. (5), that is $z_L = (0.6 \otimes C) \oplus (0.15 \otimes \mathbf{C\_B}) \oplus (0.2 \otimes \mathbf{D\_C}) \oplus (0.05 \otimes C) = (l, m, r)$. According to fuzzy arirthmetics, z_L is the fuzzy triangular number plotted in Fig. 4 whose parameters are $(9.9, 11.9, 13.9)$.

Case c. The linguistic arithmetic mean of $x_0 = 15$ and $y_0 = 8.8$ is still computed using Eq. (5), that is: $z_L = (0.6 \otimes C) \oplus (0.15 \otimes \mathbf{C\_B}) \oplus (0.2 \otimes \mathbf{D\_C}) \oplus (0.05 \otimes C)$. However, the operators $\otimes$ and $\oplus$ are now interpreted as linguistic operators as proposed in Sec. 2.3.3. It follows: $z_L = D(11.9) = 0.05/\mathbf{D\_C} + 0.95/C$.

Case d. Symbolic conclusions involved in Table 3 are now viewed as singletons. Considering inputs $x_0 = 15$ and $y_0 = 8.8$, the inferred

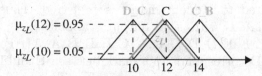

Fig. 4. Arithmetic mean computed as an interpolated fuzzy number.

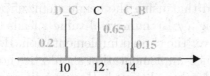

Fig. 5.   Inferred result with singleton conclusions.

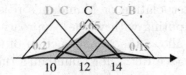

Fig. 6.   Mamdani's inference.

fuzzy set F is computed using Eq. (21) with product as t-norm and bounded sum as t-conorm. The obtained result is plotted in Fig. 5.

Case e. This case corresponds to usual Mamdani's systems as described in Sec. 3.1. The fuzzy arithmetic mean of $x_0 = 15$ and $y_0 = 8.8$, computed using Eq. (20), is given in Fig. 6.

Case f. This last case corresponds to the use of the compositional rule of inference at the linguistic level. According to Eq. (22), the linguistic arithmetic mean is $F = 0.2/\mathbf{D\_C} + 0.65/\mathbf{C} + 0.15/\mathbf{C\_B}$.

All results obtained are regrouped in Table 4.

Table 4.   Fuzzy arithmetic mean of $x_0 = 15$ and $y_0 = 8.8$.

	Interpolation (Sugeno)	Reasoning (Mamdani)
Crisp number	11.9 *Case a.*	*Case d.*
Fuzzy number	*Case b.*	*Case e.*
Word	*Case c.*	*Case f.*

It can be verified that using the height defuzzification method H for finally computing a crisp numerical value z leads to equal results, i.e. $z = 11.9$, whatever the chosen implementation. Hence, there is no means to decide which implementation should be chosen considering only the defuzzified value obtained. However, it appears clear that the uncertainty inherent to the representation of the target function f by means of fuzzy rules is propagated differently depending on whether Sugeno's interpolation or Mamdani's reasoning is used. In both cases, the "computing with words" approach provides a fuzzy linguistic result that allows the reconstruction of the corresponding fuzzy numeric subset (see Ref. 2 for Mamdani's rules).

5. Conclusion

Six different computation mechanisms have been investigated for implementing rule-based systems and illustrated using a simple example. From a computational point of view, each solution is feasible when triangular membership functions are considered. Furthermore, all obtained results are coherent with presently used rule-based systems, most of the time artificially precisiated (implicitly in usual Sugeno's systems, explicitly in Mamdani's systems where a defuzzification step is often included). Of course, the practical use of suggested implementations required that further work be developed. For Sugeno's interpolation, it is important to identify to which systems the proposed approach can be applied. In this framework, recent studies on fuzzy arithmetic (for example Refs. 6 and 7) will probably be useful for handling nontriangular fuzzy conclusions. For "computing with words" implementations, an important point concerns the assessment of the information content. Indeed, if reasoning at a linguistic level does not induce any loss of information, the symbolic implementation ($case f$) is probably the most efficient one for chaining fuzzy systems.

References

1. J.V. de Oliveira. Semantic constraints for membership function optimization. *IEEE Trans. on Systems, Man, and Cybernetics, Part A*, **29**(1), 128–138 (1999).

2. D. Dubois, L. Foulloy, S. Galichet and H. Prade. Performing approximate reasoning with words? *Computing with Words in Information/Intelligent Systems 1-Foundations*. L.A. Zadeh, J. Kacprzyk (eds). Physica-Verlag, pp. 24–49 (1999).

3. L. Foulloy and S. Galichet, Typology of Fuzzy Controllers. *Theoretical Aspects of Fuzzy Control*. H.T. Nguyen, M. Sugeno, R. Tong and R. Yager (eds). John Wiley & Sons, pp. 65–90 (1995).

4. S. Galichet and L. Foulloy. Fuzzy controllers: synthesis and equivalences. *IEEE Trans. on Fuzzy Systems*, **3**(2), 140–148 (1995).

5. L.S. Gao. The fuzzy arithmetic mean. *Fuzzy Sets and Systems*, **107**(3), 335–348 (1999).

6. M.L. Guerra and L. Stefanini. Approximate fuzzy arithmetic operations using monotonic interpolations. *Fuzzy Sets and Systems*, **150**(1), 5–33 (2005).

7. A. Piegat. Cardinality approach to fuzzy number arithmetic. *IEEE Trans. on Fuzzy Systems*, **13**(2), 204–215 (2005).

8. M. Sugeno. On stability of fuzzy systems expressed by fuzzy rules with singleton consequents. *IEEE Trans. on Fuzzy Systems*, **7**(2), 201–224 (1999).

A New Method to Compare Dynamical Systems Modeled Using Temporal Fuzzy Models

Juan Moreno-Garcia*, Jose Jesus Castro-Schez† and Luis Jimenez‡

Universidad de Castilla-La Mancha
Escuela Universitaria de Ingenieria Tecnica Industrial,
Toledo, Spain
Juan.Moreno@uclm.es
†*Escuela Superior de Informatica*
Ciudad Real, Spain
JoseJesus.Castro@uclm.es
‡*Escuela Superior de Informatica*
Ciudad Real, Spain
Luis.Jimenez@uclm.es

Abstract

The aim of this work is to present a new method to compare dynamical systems by using Temporal Fuzzy Models (TFMs). To do that, first two TFMs are generated, after that, they are compared. The output obtained is the similarity of the two dynamical systems. This output is given by means of linguistic labels. Our method is checked by using two human steps.

1. Introduction

Dynamical Systems[1] (*DS*) are *systems that change over time*, understand *system* as a set of elements with some relations between them. We have worked with MISO DSs (Multiple In, Simple Out), and found that the values of the system variables at a time t_i depend on the values of variables in times $t_{i-1}, \ldots, t_1$ in the

307

DSs. They verify the *continuity* feature, i.e. the variable evolution is continued in time, at a time t_{i+1} the variable value $v_{t_{i+1}}$ is *similar* to the variable value v_{t_i} at a time t_i. We assume this hypothesis when we define that the TFMs.[2] DSs are modeled by using different traditional techniques.[1] They are modeled to explain and to predict its behavior, and to analyze their dynamical properties. There are some previous works that propose the use of the fuzzy logic, for example Refs. 3 and 4. TFMs are used to represent the evolution of the DS. TFMs simulate the DS behavior by using the input variables. In this work, we use the TFMs to compare the *dynamism* between two DSs. For this purpose, the TFM of the two DSs are generated, and later on, the two obtained models are compared to obtain their differences. The aim of this work is to present a method to compare TFMs. The remainder of the paper is organized as follows. Section 2 presents an introduction to TFMs. Afterwards, the proposed method is shown. A real example of the behavior of the algorithm is explained in Sec. 4. Finally, the obtained conclusions are presented.

2. Introduction to TFMs

Firstly, the two inputs of the algorithm are explained (a time series and an ordered set of labels). A **time series** E is a sequence of data that is ordered in the time and represents the DS, $E = \{e_1, \ldots, e_n\}$ being $e_i = (x_1^i, \ldots, x_m^i, s^i, t_i)$ with x_j^i, s^i and t_i being the input and the output values and the instant of e_i respectively. Each example e_i of E contains the values of the input and output x_j^i and s_i variables in an instant t_i. TFMs work with linguistic variables with some restrictions in its domain named continuous linguistic variables (from now on variables) that can take values from an ordered set of labels. X_j is a **continuous linguistic variable** if it has associated a semantic to each A_j^i defined by itself that verifies: (1) Each label A_j^i is defined by an ordered domain; (2) The labels defined on X_j are sorted by means of the *middle of maximum MOM*[5]; (3) The sum of the membership grade of a value x to all labels defined in a continuous variable must be 1, $\sum_{A_j^i \in A_j} \mu_{A_j^i}(x) = 1$.[6] Linguistic labels (from now on labels) of the variables are defined before the TFM is obtained. An **ordered set of linguistic labels** is defined for each input variable X_j. Its structure is $A_j = \{A_j^1, \ldots, A_j^{|A|}\}$. An ordered set of linguistic labels $B = \{B^1, \ldots, B^{|B|}\}$ is defined for the output variable. The index i is the position of the label in these sets. The order of the labels is based on the MOM.[5]

A **temporal fuzzy model (TFM)** is an ordered set of *Temporal Fuzzy Rules (TFRs)*, that is, $TFM = \{R_1, \ldots, R_{|TFM|}\}$ with R_i being a *TFR*. *TFRs* have two components: an antecedent and an output label. The antecedent is a conjunction of disjunctions of expressions like the following: X_j *is* A_j^i. The antecedent has associated **a set of consecutive examples** denoted as $E_{p,u}$. A set of consecutive examples $E_{p,u}$ is a set of examples that verifies: (1) $p \leq u$ and $E_{p,u} \subset E$; (2) $\forall k \in [p, u], \exists e_k \in E_{p,u}$; (3) $\forall e_a, e_b \in E_{p,u}, a \neq b$, with E is the set of examples; p, u, k, a and b are the indexes to the examples of E. The linguistic intervals are used to represent the disjunctions, and the set of m linguistic intervals to represent the conjunctions of a TFR. **A linguistic interval** $I_j^{p,q}$ [6] is a sequence of consecutive labels defined on A_j that begins in the label p and finishes in q. It is represented as $I_j^{p,q} = \{A_j^p, \ldots, A_j^q\}$, where $A_j = \{A_j^1, \ldots, A_j^{|A|}\}$ is an ordered set of $|A|$ labels on X_j, p is the position on A_j of the first label of the linguistic interval and q is the last label of the interval. An **ordered set of m intervals** SI_m is a sequence of m intervals defined on m variables. It is represented as $SI_m = \{I_1^{p_1, q_1}, \ldots, I_m^{p_m, q_m}\}$ where p_j is the position in A_j of the first label of the interval j and q_j is the last label of the interval j. SI_m are used to represent linguistically the values range of the m input variables. Formally, a **temporal fuzzy rule** $R_{p,u}$ is a fuzzy rule that verifies: (1) Its antecedent is a SI_m; (2) Its consequent is a label $B^w \in B$; (3) Its SI_m has associated a set of consecutive examples $E_{p,u}$. $E_{p,u}$ indicates the times that the TFR represents.

To finish this section, Algorithm 1 shows the TFMs inference method. The membership function of $I_j^{p,q}$ is studied to understand the TFMs behavior. The following equation defines the $I_j^{p,q}$ membership function: $\mu_{I_j^{p,q}}(a_j) = \sum_{A_j^z \in I_j^{p,q}} \mu_{A_j^z}(a_j)$, where a_j is a discrete value defined on the domain of the variable X_j, $z \in [p \cdot q]$. The membership function of a SI_m is the following equation: $\mu_{SI_m}(e_i) = *(\mu_{I_j^{p_j, q_j}}(x_j))$, where e_i is an example of the set E, $j \in [1, \ldots, m]$ and $*$ is a t-norm.

Algorithm 1 Inference method

$j \leftarrow 1$
  for $i = 1$ to $|E|$ **do**
    if $\mu_{SI_m^j}(e_i) > \mu_{SI_m^{j+1}}(e_i)$ **then**
      $s \leftarrow Cons(R_j)$
    else
      $s \leftarrow Cons(R_{j+1})$
      $j \leftarrow j + 1$
    end if
  end for

The inference algorithm has a set of examples as input. The current example and rule are indicated by means of the indexes i and j respectively. The loop *for* is used to go across the set of examples E by using the index i. If the membership grade of e_i to SI_m of R_j (SI_m^j) is greater than the membership grade of e_i to SI_m of R_{j+1} (SI_m^{j+1}) the output is the output label of R_j ($s \leftarrow Cons(R_j)$), in other case the output is the output label of R_{j+1} ($s \leftarrow Cons(R_{j+1})$) and the new current rule is R_{j+1} ($j \leftarrow j + 1$). A defuzzification process is needed to obtain a discrete output value.[5,7]

Algorithm 2 TFMs comparison

$TFM_1 \leftarrow InduceTFM(E_1, A_1 \ldots A_n, B)$
$TFM_2 \leftarrow InduceTFM(E_2, A_1 \ldots A_n, B)$
$ST_1 \leftarrow GetSetTendencies(TFM_1)$
$ST_2 \leftarrow GetSetTendencies(TFM_2)$
$[S_1, S_2] \leftarrow GetSections(ST_1, ST_2)$
$L \leftarrow CompareSections(S_1, S_2)$

---

3. The Proposed Method of DSs Comparison

The proposed method carries out the comparison of the temporal evolution by means of the creation and the later comparison of TFMs. In Ref. 2, it is explained how a TFM is induced from a time series. Lines 1 and 2 of Algorithm 2 obtain the two TFMs TFM_1 and TFM_2. There after the comparison of TFM_1 and TFM_2 is carried out. To do that, the lines from 3 to 6 are used. In the following subsections we explain how the set of tendencies are obtained (Sec. 3.1), the sections of each tendency (Sec. 3.2) and how these sections are compared (Sec. 3.3).

3.1.   *Obtaining the set of tendencies*

Lines 3 and 4 of Algorithm 2 obtain the *sets of tendencies* from each *TFM*. A tendency is a set of consecutive TFM rules that represents an increment or a decrement of the output variable values (an increasing tendency or a decreasing tendency respectively). Two consecutive tendencies indicate a different direction. For example, let [1,2,4,3,2,3,5,6] be the TFRs output labels, where each number represents the label position in the ordered set of labels. The obtained set of tendencies is the following: [[1,2,4],[3,2],[3,5,6]], where the first tendency, [1,2,4], is an increasing tendency (the antecedent of the rules are omitted due to the page number limitation, but a tendency is a set of rules, not only its consequents); the second one [3,2] is a decreasing tendency; and finally we find a third tendency [3,5,6] that is increasing.

Algorithm 3 obtains the tendencies of a TFM (GetSetTendencies). Initially the set of tendencies are empty ($ST \leftarrow \theta$) and the current tendency to be calculated is initialized to empty ($T \leftarrow \theta$). After that, it is checked if the first tendency is increasing or decreasing. To do that, it is used the *if* sentence that is before of the loop *for*. This sentence uses the variable *direction* to indicate if is an increasing (*direction* $\leftarrow$ '+') or decreasing (*direction* $\leftarrow$ '$-$'). Later, the output labels of the consecutive rules are compared. When tendency is increasing the algorithm groups consecutive rules on T if the output label of the next rule is greater than the output label of the previous rule ($Cons(R_1) < Cons(R_2)$). This is carried out until a change of tendency occurs, then the *else* sentence is done. This sentence changes the direction of the tendency by means of the sentence *direction* $\leftarrow$ '$-$', the calculated tendency is added to ST and the new current tendency is initialized to empty ($T \leftarrow \theta$). The second *if* of the loop *for* is used when the tendency is decreasing, and the process is similar.

3.2.   *Obtaining the sections of a tendency*

Now it is obtained what we have denominated *sections of a tendency* (line 5 of Algorithm 2). A *section* is a group of consecutive rules

---

Algorithm 3 Obtaining the set of tendencies (GetSetTendencies)

$ST \leftarrow \theta$
$T \leftarrow \theta$
if $Cons(R_1) < Cons(R_2)$ **then**
  direction $\leftarrow$ '+'
else
  direction $\leftarrow$ '−'
end if
for $i = 1$ to $|TFM| - 1$ **do**
  if *direction* = '+' **then**
    if $Cons(R_i) < Cons(R_{i+1})$ **then**
      $T \leftarrow T + R_i$
    else
      direction $\leftarrow$ '−'
      $ST \leftarrow ST + T$
      $T \leftarrow \theta$
    end if
  end if
  if *direction* = '−' **then**
    if $Cons(R_i) > Cons(R_{i+1})$ **then**
      $T \leftarrow T + R_i$
    else
      direction $\leftarrow$ '+'
      $ST \leftarrow ST + T$
      $T \leftarrow \theta$
    end if
  end if
end for

---

belonging to a tendency that they will be compared with a section of another tendency, i.e. a group of consecutive rules of a tendency to compare with another group of consecutive rules of another tendency. These two sections represent the same temporal zone. The algorithm compares the output label of the tendencies T_1 and T_2 rule to rule to obtain the sections. The rules are grouped until two rules have the same output. We show an example to explain the process. If we have two TFMs with the following output labels: ST_1=[[VN, N, NR, FP, P, VP], [P, NR, FN, N, VN], [N], [VN]] and ST_2=[[VN, FN,

NR, P, VP], [P, FP, NR, FN, N, VN], [N], [VN]], where ST_1 and ST_2 are the sets of tendencies with the output labels of the rules in the tendencies of the two TFMs, and the set of labels $LABELS = \{VN, N, FN, NR, FP, P, VP\}$ where VN is *Very Negative*, N is *Negative*, FN is *Few Negative*, NR is *Norm*, FP is *Few Positive*, P is *Positive* and VP is *Very Positive*. These partitions of the variables domains are done a priori. This set is used for all examples shown in this work. Now, the tendencies i of ST_1 (T_i^1) and ST_2 (T_i^2) are compared between them to obtain the sections. In our example the tendencies comparisons are the following: T_1^1 =[VN, N, NR, FP, P, VP] with T_1^2 =[VN, FN, NR, P, VP], T_2^1 =[P, NR, FN, N, VN] with T_2^2 =[P, FP, NR, FN, N, VN], T_3^1 =[N] with T_3^2 =[N] and T_4^1 =[VN] with T_4^2 =[VN].

Algorithm 4 (*GetSections*) is used to compare each pair of tendencies. It obtains the following sections for both tendencies:

- The sections [[VN], [N, NR], [FP, P], [VP]] for T_1^1 and [[VN], [FN, NR], [P], [VP]] for T_1^1. It means that the section $[VN]$ is compared with $[VN]$, $[N, NR]$ is compared with $[FN, NR]$ and so on ...
- Sections [[P], [NR], [FN], [N], [VN]] and [[P], [FP, NR], [FN], [N], [VN]] for the second tendencies (T_2^1 and T_2^2).
- Sections [[N]] and [[N]] for the third tendency (T_3^1 and T_3^2).
- Sections [[VN]] and [[VN]] for the fourth tendency (T_4^1 and T_4^2).

We explain an example in order to clarify the process from how the sections are obtained. Algorithm 4 is applied to the first tendency. In this algorithm T_1^1 and T_1^2 are represented as T_1 and T_2 respectively to simplify the notation. Initially S_1, S_2, A_1 and A_2 are initialized to θ; and j_1 and j_2 to 1 (they point to the first element of the first tendency). There after that, the direction of the first tendency is calculated, so the consequents of the first and second rules of T_1 are obtained (the label VN is compared with the label N), then the direction is incremented ('+'). Now, the groups are created, T_1 and T_2 are traveled by using the indexes j_1 and j_2. This is made in the algorithm by means of the loop *while*. In the first iteration the first *if* is done like the direction is '+'. The consequent of the first rule of T_1 (R_{1,j_1}) is compared with the consequent of the first rule of T_2 (R_{2,j_2}), that is, VN with VN, like they are equals the condition if $Cons(R_{1,j_1}) = Cons(R_{2,j_2})$ ($Cons(R_{1,j_1})$ represents the j_1 rule

---

Algorithm 4 Obtaining the sections of the tendencies

$S_1 \leftarrow \theta$
$A_1 \leftarrow \theta$
$j1 \leftarrow 1$
$S_2 \leftarrow \theta$
$A_2 \leftarrow \theta$
$j2 \leftarrow 1$
if $Cons(T_{1,1}) < Cons(T_{1,2})$ **then**
    $direction \leftarrow$ '+'
else
    $direction \leftarrow$ '−'
end if
while $j_1 < |T_1|$ and $j_2 < |T_2|$ **do**
    if $direction =$ '+' **then**
        if $Cons(R_{1,j_1}) = Cons(R_{2,j_2})$ **then**
            $S_1 \leftarrow S_1 + R_{1,j_1}$
            $A_1 \leftarrow A_1 + S_1$
            $j_1 \leftarrow j_1 + 1$
            $S_1 \leftarrow \theta$
            $S_2 \leftarrow S_2 + R_{2,j_2}$
            $A_2 \leftarrow A_2 + S_2$
            $j_1 \leftarrow j_1 + 1$
            $S_2 \leftarrow \theta$
        else
            if $Cons(R_{1,j_1}) < Cons(R_{2,j_2})$ **then**
                $S_1 \leftarrow S_1 + R_{1,j_1}$
                $j_1 \leftarrow j_1 + 1$
            else
                $S_2 \leftarrow S_2 + R_{2,j_2}$
                $j_2 \leftarrow j_2 + 1$
            end if
        end if
    end if
    if $direction =$ '−' **then**
        if $Cons(R_{1,j_1}) = Cons(R_{2,j_2})$ **then**
            $S_1 \leftarrow S_1 + R_{1,j_1}$
            $A_1 \leftarrow A_1 + S_1$
            $j_1 \leftarrow j_1 + 1$
            $S_2 \leftarrow S_2 + R_{2,j_2}$
            $A_2 \leftarrow A_2 + S_2$
            $j_1 \leftarrow j_1 + 1$
        else
            if $Cons(R_{1,j_1} > Cons(R_{2,j_2})$ **then**
                $S_1 \leftarrow S_1 + R_{1,j_1}$
                $j_1 \leftarrow j_1 + 1$
            else
                $S_2 \leftarrow S_2 + R_{2,j_2}$
                $j_2 \leftarrow j_2 + 1$
            end if
        end if
    end if
end while
if $j_1 < |T_1|$ **then**
    $S_1 \leftarrow S_1 + R_{1,j_1}$
end if
if $S_1 \neq \theta$ **then**
    $A_1 \leftarrow A_1 + S_1$
end if
if $j_2 < |T_2|$ **then**
    $S_2 \leftarrow S_2 + R_{2,j_2}$
end if
if $S_2 \neq \theta$ **then**
    $A_2 \leftarrow A_2 + S_2$

end if

---

consequent of T_1) is verified, the actions associated to the *if* sentence are made:

- $S_1 \leftarrow S_1 + R_{1,j_1}$, the first rule of T_1 is added to S_1; $A_1 \leftarrow A_1 + S_1$, like the first section is totally constructed, the calculated section (S_1) is added to the set of sections A_1 ($A_1 = [[VN]]$); $j_1 \leftarrow j_1+1$, j_1 is increased, then it points to the next rule; $S_1 \leftarrow \theta$, S_1 is assigned to θ with the aim of calculating the second section.

- $S_2 \leftarrow S_2 + R_{2,j_2}$, the first rule of T_2 is added to S_2; $A_2 \leftarrow A_2 + S_2$, the calculated section S_2 is added to the set of sections, then $A_2 = [[VN]]$; $j_2 \leftarrow j_2 + 1$, j_2 is increased, it points to the second rule; $S_2 \leftarrow \theta$, S_2 is initialized to θ with the aim of calculating the next section.

After that, the *second loop iteration* is run. The comparison of the consequents of the rules pointed by the indexes j_1 and j_2 is carried out, i.e. the label N ($Cons(R_{1,j_1})$) is compared with the label FN ($Cons(R_{2,j_2})$). Like these two labels are different, it is verified that $Cons(R_{1,j_1}) < Cons(R_{2,j_2})$, since $N < FN$, then the two sentences associated to the *if* sentence are done: S_1 takes the value $[N]$ ($S_1 \leftarrow S_1 + R_{1,j_1}$) and j_1 is incremented ($j_1 \leftarrow j_1 + 1$) taking the value 3. In the *third loop iteration* the third rule consequent of T_1 is compared with the second rule consequent of T_2 (NR with FN), then the sentences associated to the *else* sentence of the second *if* are carried out. The first sentence ($S_2 \leftarrow S_2 + R_{2,j_2}$) does $S_2 = [FN]$ and the second one makes that $j_2 = 3$. The rules consequents pointed by the indexes j_1 and j_2 are compared in the *next loop iteration* (NR with NR). Like these two labels are equals, the second sections of both tendencies are completed, then A_1 changes its value to $[[VN],[N,NR]]$, A_2 to $[[VN],[FN,NR]]$, $j_1 = 4$ and $j_2 = 4$. In the *fifth iteration* the consequent of the fourth rule is compared with the consequent of the rule fourth of the second tendency (FP is compared with P). Then the second *if* sentence is executed because $FP < P$: S_1 takes the value $[FP]$ and j_1 is increased taking the value 5. In the *following loop iteration* the rules consequents pointed by j_1 and j_2 are compared (P with P). Like these two labels are equals, the second sections of both tendencies are completed, A_1 takes the value $[[VN],[N,NR],[FP,P]]$, $A_2 = [[VN],[FN,NR],[P]]$, $j_1 = 6$ and $j_2 = 5$. Finally, the *last loop iteration* is run. The label VP is compared with VP, then $A_1 = [[VN],[N,NR],[FP,P],[VP]]$, $A_2 = [[VN],[FN,NR],[P],[VP]]$, $j_1 = 7$ and $j_2 = 7$. These values results in the final part of the *while* sentence. The algorithm compares the section $[VN]$ with $[VN]$, $[N, NR]$ with $[FN, NR]$, $[FP, P]$ with $[P]$ and $[VP]$ with $[VP]$ for the first tendencies. We want to highlight that the last label of each pair of sections is the same label. The other sections of the other tendencies are calculated in the same way.

3.3. *Comparing sections*

The last line of the Algorithm 2 makes the comparison of the tendencies section to section. This is carried out in two phases:

(1) Making a rule union over each section, then it is obtained a structure formed by two components. The first one is a SI_m obtained as the union of the SI_m of the rules to unite. The second one is a set of labels obtained as a labels union of the output labels of each rule to unite. We represent this structure as $UNION$: $U_i = <Ant_i, CE_i>$, where Ant_i is a SI_m and CE_i is a set of labels.

(2) Comparison of U_1 and U_2. To do that, Ant_1 is compared with Ant_2 and CE_1 is compared with CE_2, after that, it is made a t-norm between the obtained values (Eq. (1)). We will present the equations to measure the similarity later (Eqs. (1), (2) and (3)).

To perform the union of two SI_m, SI_m^1 and SI_m^2, we do the union of the intervals of SI_m^1 and SI_m^2 one to one.[2] For example, let be a section that is compounded by the two following rules: (1) IF ((VP) and (N) and (NR or FP)) THEN VN; (2) IF ((P) and (N) and (FP)) THEN FN. $SI_m^1 = [[VP], [N], [NR, FP]]$ and $SI_m^2 = [[P], [N], [FP]]$ are united. Its union is $Ant_i = [[P, VP], [N], [NR, FP]]$. Regarding the set of labels we observe that $CE_i = [VN] \bigcup [FN] = [VN, FN]$. Then, for these two rules it is obtained that $U_i = <[[P, VP], [N], [NR, FP]], [VN, FN]>$

The similarity between two $UNION$ U_1 and U_2 is calculated by using Eq. (1).

$$*(*(S(I_j^{p_1, f_1}, I_j^{p_2, f_2})), R(CE_1, CE_2)), \tag{1}$$

where $*$ is a t-norm, $S(I_j^{p_1, f_1}, I_j^{p_2, f_2})$ calculates the similarity between intervals Eq. (2) and Eq. (3) is used to compare the sets of labels

CE_1 and CE_2.

$$S(I_j^{p_1,f_1}, I_j^{p_2,f_2}) = 1 - \left| \frac{M(I_j^{p_1,f_1}) - M(_j^{p_2,f_2})}{Max_j - Min_j} \right|, \qquad (2)$$

where $M(I_j^{p_i,f_i})$ is the central value of the interval, Max_j and Min_j are the maximum and minimum values of X_j support.

$$R(CE_1, CE_2) = \frac{support(CE_1 \cap CE_2)}{Max\{CE_1 \cup CE_2\} - Min\{CE_1 \cup CE_2\}}. \qquad (3)$$

As it can be observed, this equation represents a fraction between the support length of $CE_1 \cap CE_2$ and difference between the minimum and maximum values of the support of measurement $CE_1 \cup CE_2$. As a consequence of the calculate of the similarity between the sections an ordered set of sections similarities denoted as $simil = <s_1, s_2 \ldots s_n>$ where n is the number of sections (a measure for each section) is obtained.

We are interested to obtain the similarity of two TFMs in a linguistic way. To do that, we define an ordered set of labels named P that defines how a model resembles another one. We calculate the membership grade of each measure of similarity (s_i of $simil$) to the labels of P. Thereafter we select the label with more membership grade in P.

4. A Real Example

To check the algorithm we have used two time series that represents two human steps. TFMs obtained are similar because all the people without pathologies walk in a similar way. For this reason, we aleatorily eliminate some examples of the two time series. Thus, there are differences between the two obtained TFMs. The time series have three input variables and one output variable. The first input variable is hip angle of the right leg (RH variable), the second refers to the flexion and extension angle of the right knee (RK variable) and the later to the ankle angle of the right leg (RA variable). The flexion and extension angle of the left knee (LK variable) is used as output variable. To obtain the TFMs we use the ordered sets of labels defined in Sec. 3.2 for each input and output variable. TFMs show in Table 1 are obtained by using the TFMs induction algorithm presented in Ref. 2.

Table 1. TFM_1 and TFM_2 obtained.

TFM_1				TFM_2			
RH	RK	RA	LK	RH	RK	RA	LK
$\{VP\}$	$\{VN\}$	$\{FP,P\}$	VN	$\{VP\}$	$\{VN\}$	$\{P\}$	VN
$\{VP\}$	$\{N\}$	$\{FP\}$	N	$\{VP\}$	$\{N\}$	$\{NR,FP\}$	FN
$\{P\}$	$\{N\}$	$\{FP\}$	NR	$\{VP\}$	$\{N\}$	$\{FP\}$	NR
$\{P\}$	$\{N\}$	$\{FP,P\}$	FP	$\{P\}$	$\{N\}$	$\{P\}$	P
$\{P\}$	$\{N\}$	$\{P\}$	P	$\{FN..FP\}$	$\{VN,N\}$	$\{P,VP\}$	VP
$\{NR,FP\}$	$\{VN,N\}$	$\{P,VP\}$	VP	$\{FN\}$	$\{VN\}$	$\{VP\}$	P
$\{FN,NR\}$	$\{VN\}$	$\{VP\}$	P	$\{N,FN\}$	$\{VN\}$	$\{VP\}$	FP
$\{N,FN\}$	$\{VN\}$	$\{VP\}$	NR	$\{N\}$	$\{VN\}$	$\{VP\}$	NR
$\{N\}$	$\{VN\}$	$\{VP\}$	FN	$\{N\}$	$\{VN\}$	$\{VP\}$	FN
$\{VN,N\}$	$\{VN\}$	$\{VP\}$	N	$\{VN,N\}$	$\{VN\}$	$\{VP\}$	N
$\{VN\}$	$\{VN\}$	$\{P,VP\}$	VN	$\{VN\}$	$\{VN,N\}$	$\{P,VP\}$	VN
$\{VN..FP\}$	$\{VN..VP\}$	$\{VN..FP\}$	N	$\{VN..FP\}$	$\{VN..VP\}$	$\{VN..FP\}$	N
$\{P,VP\}$	$\{VN..VP\}$	$\{NR..P\}$	VN	$\{P,VP\}$	$\{VN..VP\}$	$\{NR..P\}$	VN

Algorithm 3 is used to obtain the sets of tendencies ST_1 and ST_2: $ST_1 = [[VN, N, NR, FP, P, VP], [P, NR, FN, N, VN], [N], [VN]]$ and $ST_2 = [[VN, FN, NR, P, VP], [P, FP, NR, FN, N, VN], [N], [VN]]$. Algorithm 4 calculates the sections into the tendencies: $A_1 = [[VN], [N, NR], [FP, P], [VP], [P], [NR], [FN], [N], [VN], [N], [VN]]$ and $A_2 = [[VN], [FN, NR], [P], [VP], [P], [FP, NR], [FN], [N], [VN], [N], [VN]]$.

Latter A_1 and A_2 are compared sections by sections obtaining the sequence of similarities $simil$: [0.93, 0.33, 0.5, 0.935, 0.93, 0.5, 1.0, 1.0, 0.93, 0.93, 0.93]. Equation 1 is applied to calculate each one of these values (similarity between two $UNION$).

Finally, the label that define the similarity for each value of similarity of a section is calculated. For this purpose, an ordered set of 5 trapeziodal labels P is defined, its labels are as follow: $ANYTHING = [0, 0, 0.10, 0.15]$, $LITTE = [0.10, 0.15, 0.35, 0.40]$, $MEDIUM = [0.35, 0.40, 0.60, 0.65]$, $A\ LOT = [0.60, 0.65, 0.85, 0.90$ and $EQUAL = [0.85, 0.90, 1, 1]$. The following sequence of labels are obtained: $LABELS =$['EQUAL', 'LITTLE', 'MEDIUM', 'EQUAL', 'EQUAL', 'MEDIUM', 'EQUAL', 'EQUAL', 'EQUAL', 'EQUAL', 'EQUAL']. To finish this section, we want to highlight that we can describe linguistically the "similarities of the two TFMs" using the obtained sections (A_1 and A_2) and the sequence $LABELS$ in the following way:

> Human step 1 (TFM_1) and human step 2 (TFM_2) are
> EQUAL in the first section $[VN]$, they look like each other
> a LITTLE from N to NR, they have a MEDIUM resem-
> blance in the section from FP to P and they are EQUALS
> in the section VP.

5. Conclusions

A method to compare TFMs is presented. We can compare linguistically DSs by using this method as we have explained in Sec. 4. We
want to emphasize that the proposed method is totally automatic
and produces linguistic outputs that are easier to understand. Our
method is suggested to compare DSs of the same kind, for example when we want to compare a "perfect model" with other models
to detect errors. Our method can be used in automatic sport train-
ers, or to detect pathologies (for example, in the human walk). This
method can be also used in others fields like economy. We must equip
the method with more flexibility so that the expert can select the
variables to compare, time intervals to study.... As future works we
want to improve and use this method in sport training to check its
efficiency and possible improvements. Currently we are working with
biomechanics experts.

Acknowledgments

This work was supported by the Spanish Ministry of Science and
Technology Research Project DEVLENA TIN2007-62568, and Junta
de Comunidades de Castilla-La Mancha Research Projects PBC06-
0064-4504 and PAC-06-0141.

References

1. D. G. Luenberger, *Introduction to Dynamic Systems: Theory, Models and
   Applications.* John Wiley and Sons (1979).
2. J. Moreno-Garcia, L. Jimenez and J. J. Castro-Schez, A direct induction algorithm of temporal fuzzy models. *Proceeding IEEE International Conference on
   Fuzzy Systems (FUZZIEEE'2004)*, Budapest, pp. 635–640 (July 2004).

3. J. Moreno-Garcia, L. Jimenez, J. J. Castro-Schez and L. Rodriguez, A direct linguistic induction method for systems. *Fuzzy Sets and Systems*, **146**, 79–96 (2004).

4. J. L. Castro, J. J. Castro-Schez and J. M. Zurita, Learning maximal structure rules in fuzzy logic for knowledge acquisition in expert systems. *FSS*, **101**(7), 331–342 (1999).

5. W. V. Leekwijck and E. E. Kerre, Defuzzification: Criteria and classification. *Fuzzy Sets and Systems*, **108**(2), 159–178 (1999).

6. J. Moreno-Garcia, J. J. Castro-Schez and L. Jimenez, A fuzzy inductive algorithm for modeling dynamical systems in a comprehensible way. *To be published in IEEE Transactions on Fuzzy Systems* **15**(4), 652–672 (2007).

7. K. Tanaka, *An Introduction to Fuzzy Logic for Practical Aplications*. Springer (1998).

Improvement of Approximation Properties of a First-Order Takagi-Sugeno Fuzzy System[a]

Felipe Fernández[*], Julio Gutiérrez[†], Gracián Triviño[‡]
and Juan Carlos Crespo[§]

D. T. F., Facultad de Informática
Universidad Politécnica de Madrid
28660 Madrid, Spain
[*]felipe.fernandez@es.bosch.com
[†]jgr@dtf.fi.upm.es
[‡]gracian.trivino@softcomputing.es
[§]crespozj@dtf.fi.upm.es

Abstract

First-order Takagi-Sugeno models are mainly based on the interpolation between several local affine functions usually defined on trapezoidal fuzzy partitions. The standard computational model presents some shape-failures: the approximation does not preserve the positivity, monotony or convexity of the data that belong to the corresponding antecedent term cores. Moreover the standard output does not have a continuous derivative. This paper presents an improved model that primarily transforms the original first-order trapezoidal TS system into an equivalent zero-order triangular TS one. Furthermore, for each univariate transition region: two equidistant triangular labels are added, one at each end of the corresponding interval, to capture the information of derivatives of the affine functions. Finally in each transition region, a local even box filter is applied to the corresponding four triangular labels in order to obtain a local uniform quadratic B-spline partition. This transform preserves the original affine

---

[a]This research has been supported by CICYT TIC 2006-2009 HiSCoP.

functions in the reduced cores of the original fuzzy partition and converts the intermediate C^0 piecewise linear-multilinear output function into a C^1 piecewise linear-multiquadratic one.

1. Introduction

Models usually have a limited range of validity and to emphasize this aspect, they are called "local models" on an "operating regime", as opposed to "global models" that are valid in the full range of operation. However, by means of a piecewise approach, the full range of operation is covered by a number of possibly overlapping regimes. Within each operating regime the system is modeled by a local model, and they can be blended in the transition regions using suitable weighting functions, taken into account that he operating regimes are not hard boundaries regions. This means that there will be a gradual transition between local models when the system is in intermediate regimes.

Piecewise affine functions are powerful tool to describe nonlinear systems. Affine Takagi-Sugeno (ATS) models extend the capability of piecewise based modelling to fuzzy systems and give a simple formal language to characterize and analyze complex systems.

ATS models can exploit fuzzy partitions and piecewise affine systems by combining simple local models, each valid within a certain operating regime. Each rule antecedent defines a fuzzy local region and the associated rule consequent describes the corresponding affine function that specifies the corresponding local model.

The rest of the paper is organized as follows: Section 2 reviews ATS model, Sec. 3 analyses the shape failure of standard ATS model. Section 4 presents the main characteristics of the fuzzy partition transformations introduced. Sections 5 and 6 respectively depict the linear-multilinear and linear-multiquadratic ATS models, and Sec. 7 describes the local uniform linear-quadratic B-spline partitions obtained. A practical example is shown in Sec. 8, and finally Sec. 9 concludes the paper.

2. Review of ATS Model

The considered ATS rules of a standard MISO system are on the conjunctive canonical form:

$$R_r: \text{If } x_1 \text{ is } A_{r,1} \text{ and } \dots \text{and } x_n \text{ is } A_{r,n} \text{ then } z = \mathbf{p}_r^T \mathbf{x} + q_r, \quad (1)$$

where $\mathbf{x} = (x_1, \ldots, x_n)^T$ is the multivariate input variable, $(A_{r1}, \ldots, A_{rn})$ are trapezoidal membership functions that belong to the corresponding univariate partition of unity or Ruspini fuzzy partition[2,4,8] and $z = \mathbf{p}_r^T \mathbf{x} + q_r$ is the corresponding multivariate affine output function.

Each univarate trapezoidal partition is defined by a knot sequence $(t_0, t_1, t_2, \ldots, t_m)$.

Multivariate ATS rules can also be written in a multivariate-closed form as

$$R_r: \text{If } \mathbf{x} \text{ is } \mathbf{A}_r \quad \text{then} \quad z = \mathbf{p}_r^T \mathbf{x} + q_r, \tag{2}$$

where $\mathbf{A}_r = \mathbf{A}_r(\mathbf{x}) = A_{r1}(x_1) \times \cdots \times A_{rn}(x_n)$ is the corresponding multivariate tensor product. The corresponding multivariate partition of unity satisfies the following constraints:

$$0 \leq \mathbf{A}_r(\mathbf{x}) \leq 1 \quad \text{and} \quad \Sigma_r \mathbf{A}_r(\mathbf{x}) = 1. \tag{3}$$

The global approximator obtained by the inference mechanism gives a blending procedure of the corresponding local affine models.

Using the standard product-sum method, the output function can be written in matrix form as

$$z = \sum_{r=1}^{R} \mathbf{A}_r(x) \times (\mathbf{p}_r^T \mathbf{x} + q_r), \tag{4}$$

where $\mathbf{A}_r(\mathbf{x}) = A_{r1}(x_1) \times \cdots \times A_{rn}(x_n)$ is the referred multivariate tensor product of rule r, $R = (m_1 + 1)(m_2 + 1), \ldots, (m_n + 1)$ is the number rules, and $((m_1 + 1), (m_2 + 1), \ldots, (m_n + 1))$ are the corresponding numbers of trapezoidal fuzzy terms.

Therefore, in the cores of multivariate tensor-product trapezoidal membership function where $\mathbf{A}_r(\mathbf{x}) = 1$, the global output function z is equal to the corresponding local affine function $z = \mathbf{p}_r^T \mathbf{x} + q_r$. We call these multivariate regions: multivariate *affine intervals* of an ATS model. The corresponding univariate components are called univariate affine intervals $AI_i = [t_{2i}, t_{2i+1}]$.

In the multivariate regions where the tensor-product $0 < \mathbf{A}_r(\mathbf{x}) < 1$, the global output function z is given by a local convex combination of the corresponding local affine functions $z = \Sigma_r \mathbf{A}_r(\mathbf{x}) \times (\mathbf{a}_r \mathbf{x} + b_r)$. We call such regions multivariate *transition intervals* of an ATS model. The corresponding univariate components are called univariate transition intervals $TI_i = (t_{2i+1}, t_{2i+2})$.

3. Analysis of Shape-Failures of ATS Models

The output function of a standard ATS model does not have continuous derivatives and is not shape preserving[9] since it exhibits wild wiggles that are not inherent in the core data.[1,2] In this section we briefly analysed these undesirable properties of standard ATS systems.

For this purpose, the following basic SISO ATS is considered (see a particular example in Fig. 1):

$$R_0: \text{If } x \text{ is } A_0 \text{ then } z = 0; \quad R_1: \text{If } x \text{ is } A_1 \text{ then } z = a_1(x-1) + b_1,$$
(5)

where the trapezoidal fuzzy partition $\{A_0, A_1\}$ is defined by the knot sequence $(t_0, \mathbf{0}, \mathbf{1}, t_3)$. The standard output function z of this system in the transition interval $TI_0 = (0, 1)$ is given by

$$z(x) = (1-x)0 + (x)(a_1(x-1) + b_1) = a_1 x^2 + (b_1 - a_1)x,$$
(6)

its derivative is given by

$$z'(x) = 2a_1 x + b_1 - a_1 = 2a_1(x - 1/2(1 - b_1/a_1)),$$
(7)

which is not equal in the corners of the transition interval ($z'(0) = (b_1 - a_1); z'(1) = (b_1 + a_1)$) to the corresponding derivatives of the specified affine functions ($z_0' = 0, z_1' = a_1$). This derivative becomes

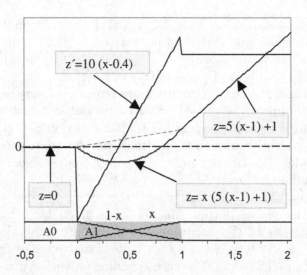

Fig. 1.   Example of output function and its derivative of a standard ATS system.

negative in the interval [0,1] when $x < 1/2(1 - b_1/a_1))$. If $(-1 < (b_1/a_1) < -1)$ then the output derivative is negative in the interval $[0, 1/2(1 - b_1/a_1))]$, even though the slopes of the local affine models considered are non-negative.

Therefore, the global output function of an ATS system does not have continuous derivative and it is not shape preserving[9] since it does not conserve the positivity, monotony and convexity of the defined data by the corresponding multidimensional antecedent term cores. A general reason of this objectionable behavior is that the same membership functions are used to blend the constant part b_i and linear part $a_i x$ of the affine function $a_i x + b_i$. Notice that classical Hermite spline interpolation[5] uses completely different types of blending functions for these two components. The approach presented in this paper is in a sense analogous to Bezier splines approximators,[5] i.e. we transform the information of the slopes (derivatives) of the affine output functions into new additional control points.

Next section presents an equivalent linear-multilinear ATS model, which has a shape-preserving behavior.

4. Fuzzy Partition Transformations Portfolio

In order to avoid the shape failures of standard ATS schema, this paper presents a transformational process that primarily converts the original first-order trapezoidal TS system into an equivalent zero-order triangular TS one. To accomplish this process, each original univariate trapezoidal antecedent fuzzy partitions here considered are first transformed into equivalent triangular one, in order to obtain a shape-preserving C^0 piecewise linear-multilinear approximator.

In this paper it is taken into account the usual practical hypothesis that the lengths of affine intervals are longer than the lengths addition of the adjacent transition intervals: $\|AI_i\| \geq \|TI_{i-1}\| + \|TI_i\|$. This consideration allows a subsequent local independent filtering that greatly simplifies the corresponding analysis and involved computations.

In order to obtain an output function with C^1 continuity, we need to capture the information of derivatives of the affine functions in the corners of each multivariate transition interval. To accomplish this target, in this paper, two equidistant triangular labels are added, one at each end of each univariate transition interval. The corresponding expanded transition regions are called in this paper, *enlarged transition intervals*.

Finally, to improve the smoothness and continuity order of the corresponding output function, an even box filter is locally applied to the four triangular labels of each univariate transition region in order to obtain a local uniform quadratic B-spline partition.[3] This filtering transform (more deeply described in Secs. 6 and 7) preserves the original affine functions in the reduced cores of the original multivariate fuzzy partition and converts the intermediate C^0 piecewise linear-multilinear function into a C^1 piecewise linear-multiquadratic one.

The computational complexity of the filtered ATS systems in the transition regions is augmented, since the increase in one unit of the antecedent-overlapping factor. Within each local univariate filter interval, the overlapping factor changes from two to three. This is the involved penalty paid for augmenting the continuity order and smoothness of the corresponding output function. However, the definition of local uniform quadratic B-spline partitions in the transition regions also makes easier the corresponding computation.

The obtained output function is a piecewise linear-multiquadratic approximator that preserves the affine functions on the reduced cores of the initial multivariate antecedent terms.

Standard B-spline partitions have also been used in different fuzzy models[6,7,10,11] as a high-level hybridization between fuzzy and spline techniques. In this paper a low-level hybridization is presented that deeply combines synergies between crisp and B-spline partitions, in order to obtain a shape-preserving fuzzy model. Moreover, the obtained quadratic B-splines are locally uniform within each transition intervals, which imply less computational load than the referred approaches in the corresponding fuzzy algorithms.

5.   Linear-Multilinear ATS Model

In the previous section, in order to improve the ATS model and to obtain a shape-preserving piecewise output function, each original univariate *trapezoidal* antecedent fuzzy partitions $\{A_{ji}\}$ of a domain U_j, defined by the knots sequence $T_i = (t_{j0}, t_{j1}, \ldots, t_{jm})$, has been first transformed into an equivalent univariate *triangular* one $\{B_{jk}\}$ using the same knots sequence.

In the SISO example of Fig. 1, the output function is defined by the rule:

$$\text{If } x \text{ is } A_1 \text{ then } z = 5(x - 1) + 1 \text{ else } z = 0. \tag{8}$$

For the antecedent knots sequence $T = (-1, 0, 1, 2)$, the corresponding outputs of triangular antecedent rules are respectively $c_0 = 0 \; c_1 = 0$, $c_2 = 1 \; c_3 = 6$. The global output of this system is a piecewise affine function also shown by a dashed line in Fig. 1.

In a general MIMO case, the derived zero-order TS model has a rule for each corner of the original multidimensional antecedents core intervals. The new equivalent zero-order TS system gives the following nonsmooth C^0 linear-multilinear output function:

$$z = \sum_{r=1}^{R'} B_r(x) \times c_r, \tag{9}$$

where $R' = (m_1' m_2' \ldots m_n')$ is the number of new derived rules, $(m_1', m_2', \ldots, m_n')$ are the corresponding numbers of triangular fuzzy terms, $m_i' = 2(m_i + 1)$, and c_r are the constant output functions of the corresponding rules. This output function is a C^0 shape-preserving piecewise linear-multilinear interpolator.

6. Linear-Multiquadratic ATS Model

For each transition interval $(t_j, \; t_{j+1})$ of each input variable, two additional transformations are carried out:

(1) The referred enlargement of each transition interval using two extra equidistant knots, one at each end of the transition interval:

$$(t_j, t_{j+1}) \rightarrow (t_j - w, t_j, t_{j+1}, t_{j+1} + w), \tag{10}$$

where $w = \|t_j, t_{j+1}\| = (t_{j+1} - t_j)$ is the width of the original transition interval. To simplify the analysis, in each enlarged transition interval, a local variable u is defined:

$$u = (x - t_j)/(t_{j+1} - t_j) = (x - t_j)/w. \tag{11}$$

In this transformed local domain, the corresponding uniform triangular partition is defined by the knots sequence $(-1, 0, 1, 2)$.

(2) Each previous univariate triangular fuzzy partition $\{B_j^2 : j = -1, 0, 1, 2\}$ (uniform B-spline partition of order two[3]) is transformed

into a linear-quadratic spline fuzzy partition $\{B_j^3 \colon j = -1, 0, 1, 2\}$ (spline partition of order three) using the corresponding local filter. For each univariate triangular term B_j^2 the following box filter is applied

$$B_j^3(u) = \int_{Uj} B_j^2(v) \cdot N^1(u - v) \, dv, \qquad (12)$$

where $N^1(\cdot)$ is a even box filter or first-order B-spline.[3]

This box filter has a unit width in the local transformed domain and a width w in the original domain.

The considered box filter is not applied in the whole interval $(t_j - w, t_{j+1} + w)$ but in a reduced one $(t_j - w/2, t_{j+1} + w/2)$ called filter *interval*, which is defined by the interval $(-0.5, 1.5)$ in the transformed local domain of variable u. Outside this filter interval the corresponding output affine function is preserved.

The local uniform box filter described increases the smoothness and continuity order of the corresponding generated output function and transforms the intermediate C^0 piecewise multilinear function into a C^1 piecewise multiquadratic one.

Next section analyzes the main characteristics of the local B-spline partitions obtained.

7. Local Linear-Quadratic B-Spline Partitions

In each local transformed interval $(-1, 2)$, linear-quadratic B-spline partitions $\{B_j^3 \colon j = -1, 0, 1, 2\}$ are derived by means of the referred even box (first-order B-spline) filter N^1 applied to each uniform triangular fuzzy partition $\{B_j^2\}$:

$$N^1 * \{B_j^2\} = \{B_j^3\} \quad j = -1, 0, 1, 2. \qquad (13)$$

Figure 2 depicts this linear-quadratic partition in the transformed domain, which is uniform and piecewise quadratic in the filter interval $(-0.5, 1.5)$, and symmetrical in relation to the value 0.5. This local B-spline partition is linear outside this filter interval.

To compute the quadratic B-splines $\{B_j^3 \colon j = -1, 0, 1, 2\}$, we apply the corresponding box filter:

$$B_j^3(u) = \int_{u-1/2}^{u+1/2} B_j^2(v) \, dv \qquad (14)$$

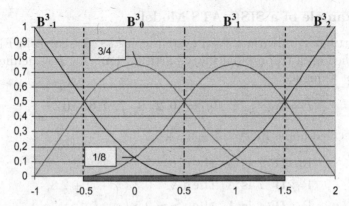

Fig. 2.   Piecewise linear-quadratic B-spline partition $\{B_j^3: j = -1, 0, 1, 2\}$ defined over the enlarged transition interval $(-1, 2)$.

within the filter interval $[-0.5, 1.5]$. Outside this filter interval, the resultant splines overlap the original triangular splines B_j^2.

Over this filter interval, the concerned overlapping quadratic splines have the following expressions:

If $(-0.5 \le u < 0.5)$ then

$$B_{-1}^3(u) = (u - 0.5)^2/2$$
$$B_1^3(u) = (u + 0.5)^2/2$$
$$B_0^3(u) = 1 - B_{-1}^3 - B_{+1}^3 = 3/4 - u^2. \tag{15}$$

If $(-0.5 \le u < 0.5)$ then

$$B_0^3(u) = (u - 1.5)^2/2$$
$$B_2^3(u) = (u + 0.5)^2/2$$
$$B_1^3(u) = 1 - B_0^3 - B_2^3 = 3/4 - (u - 1)^2. \tag{16}$$

These formulas give the three quadratic segments of the corresponding uniform quadratic B-splines over the intervals $[-0.5, 0.5]$ and $[0.5, 1.5]$.

Outside the filter interval $[-0.5, 1.5]$ the corresponding local uniform triangular splines are not filtered, because they belong to the same affine region, and therefore an even box filter has no influence on the output function (affine invariance property).

8. Example of a SISO ATS Model

The particular univariate ATS system considered, shown in Fig. 3, is specified on a trapezoidal fuzzy partition $\{A_0, A_1, A_2\}$ defined by the knot sequence:

$$T = (t_0, t_1, \ldots, t_5) = (0, \mathbf{2}, \mathbf{3}, \mathbf{7}, \mathbf{7.6}, \mathbf{10}). \tag{17}$$

The specified affine fuzzy rules are:

$$R_0: \textbf{IF } x \textbf{ is } A_0 \textbf{ then } z = 3\,(x - 2) + 3,$$
$$R_1: \textbf{IF } x \textbf{ is } A_1 \textbf{ then } z = 0.2\,(x - 7) + 2.8,$$
$$R_2: \textbf{IF } x \textbf{ is } A_2 \textbf{ then } z = 2.5\,(x - 7.6) + 3. \tag{18}$$

Using the augmented knot sequence $(0, 1, \mathbf{2}, \mathbf{3}, 4, 6.4, \mathbf{7}, \mathbf{7.6}, 8.2, 10)$, a triangular fuzzy partition $\{B_0, B_1, B_2, B_3, B_4, B_5, B_6, B_7, B_8, B_9\}$ is derived.

The corresponding equivalent zero-order TS fuzzy rules are:

R_0: **If** x **is** B_0 **then** $z = 9$ R_5: **If** x **is** B_5 **then** $z = 2.68$
R_1: **If** x **is** B_1 **then** $z = 6$ R_6: **If** x **is** B_6 **then** $z = 2.8$
R_2: **If** x **is** B_2 **then** $z = 3$ R_7: **If** x **is** B_7 **then** $z = 3$
R_3: **If** x **is** B_3 **then** $z = 2$ R_8: **If** x **is** B_8 **then** $z = 4.5$
R_4: **If** x **is** B_4 **then** $z = 2.2$ R_9: **If** x **is** B_9 **then** $z = 9$ (19)

The two filter intervals are shown in Fig. 3, where the corresponding box filter widths are 1 and 0.6. Figure 3 also depicts

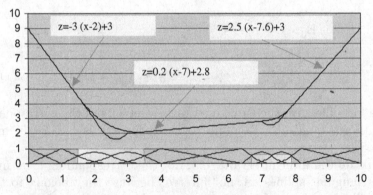

Fig. 3.   Example of a SISO Shape-preserving ATS system using local uniform quadratic B-splines.

the piecewise affine function C^0 obtained using the standard ATS model, with shape-failures, and the piecewise linear-quadratic output function C^1 computed using the uniform local filter previously described.

The obtained output function provides a suitable shape-preserving smooth approximation and has a local affine behavior outside the filter intervals.

9. Conclusions

In this paper an approximation improvement of an affine Takagi-Sugeno fuzzy system has been introduced based on the local use of uniform quadratic B-spline partitions in the transition regions, automatically derived from the original trapezoidal partition.

The stability of the corresponding ATS controllers can also be improved taking into account the shape-preserving nature of the described model.

The deduced piecewise linear-quadratic fuzzy model provides a new fuzzy tool that can be applied to system identification, signal processing and control design problems.

References

1. R. Babuska, C. Fantuzzi, U. Kaymak and H. B. Verbrunggen, Improved inference for Takagi-Sugeno models. *Proc. 5th IEEE International Conference on Fuzzy Systems*, New Orleans, USA, pp. 701–706 (1996).
2. R. Babuska, *Fuzzy Modeling for Control.* Kluwer Academic Publisher (1998).
3. C. K. Chui, Wavelets: A mathematical tool for signal analysis. *SIAM* (1997).
4. Driankov, H. Hellendoorn and M. Reinfrank, *An Introduction to Fuzzy Control.* Springer-Verlag (1993).
5. G. Farin, *Curves and Surfaces for Computer-Aided Geometric Design.* 4th edn. Academic Press (1998).
6. F. Fernández and J. Gutiérrez, Structured design of an extended TS controller using global fuzzy parameters and fuzzification transform. *Proc. of 8th International Conference IPMU 2000*, **II**, 724–731 (2000).
7. F. Fernández and J. Gutiérrez, A Takagi-Sugeno model with fuzzy inputs viewed from multidimensional interval analysis. *Fuzzy Sets and Systems*, **135**(1), 39–61 (2003).
8. G. Klir and B. Yuan, *Fuzzy Sets and Fuzzy Logic.* Prentice Hall (1995).
9. B. I. Kvasov, *Methods of Shape-Preserving Spline Approximation.* Word Scientific (2000).

10. J. Zhang and A. Knoll, Constructing fuzzy controllers with B-spline models. *IEEE Intern. Conference on Fuzzy Systems*, **I**, 416–421 (1996).
11. J. Zhang and A. Knoll, Unsupervised learning of control surfaces based on B-spline models. *IEEE International Conference on Fuzzy Systems*, pp. 1725–1730 (1997).

Knowledge and Time: A Framework for Soft Computing Applications in PHM

Piero P. Bonissone* and Naresh Iyer[†]

General Electric Global Research
One Research Circle, Niskayuna NY 12309, USA
*bonissone@crd.ge.com
†iyerna@crd.ge.com

Abstract

We analyze the issue of decision-making within the context of Prognostics and Health Management (PHM). We address PHM requirements by developing Soft Computing (SC) models, such as fuzzy sets, evolutionary algorithms, neural nets, statistics, and information theory. We define a natural framework as the cross product of the decision's *time-horizon* and the *domain knowledge* type used by the SC models. Within this framework, we analyze the progression from simple to annotated lexicon, morphology, syntax, semantics, and pragmatics. We compare such progression with the injection of domain knowledge in SC to perform anomaly detection, anomaly identification, failure mode analysis (diagnostics), estimation of remaining useful life (prognostics), on-board control, and off board logistics actions. We illustrate this framework with a selected PHM case study.

1. Introduction

To address real-world problems that are usually ill defined, difficult to model, and exhibiting large solution spaces, we often resort to approximate solutions based on available domain knowledge and field data. Unfortunately, both knowledge and data are marred with imperfect (uncertain and incomplete) information. The relevant domain knowledge tends to be a combination of first principles and empirical knowledge, while the data are usually a noisy, incomplete collection of input-output measurements representing instances of the system's behavior. Soft Computing (SC) techniques, leveraged in combination with more traditional disciplines such as statistics, AI, and information theory, have proven to be an extremely valuable toolkit to address these problems, as they offer a broad spectrum of design choices to integrate knowledge and data in the construction of approximate models.

Within the range of SC applications, we will focus on Prognostics and Health Management (PHM) for assets such as locomotives, medical scanners, aircraft engines, etc. PHM's main goal is to maintain these assets' performance over time, improving their utilization while minimizing their maintenance cost. This tradeoff is typical of long-term service agreements offered by OEM's to their valued customers.

2.   PHM Functional Architecture

Figure 1 illustrates the major PHM functions and their relationships. The first block depicts the typical tasks of sensor validation, data segmentation, scrubbing, filtering, and smoothing that usually precede data compression and sometimes, features extraction. The second block (*anomaly detection and identification*) leverages unsupervised learning techniques, such as clustering. Its goal is to extract the underlying structural information from the data, define normal structures and identify departures from such *normal* structures. The third block (*diagnostic analysis*) leverages supervised learning techniques, such as classification. Its goal is to extract potential signatures from the data, which could be used to recognize different failure modes. These two blocks produce information related to the time and type of the anomaly/failure, which is an input for the fourth block (*prognostics*) to produce estimates of Remaining Useful Life (RUL). The goal of this block is to maintain and forecast the asset health index. Originally, this index reflects the expected deterioration under normal operating conditions. Later the index is modified by the occurrence of an anomaly or failure, reflecting faster RUL reductions.

All these functions interpret the system's stat and could lead to an *on-board control* action, as illustrated by the fifth block, or an *off-board maintenance*, repair and planning action, as illustrated by the sixth block. On-board control actions usually focus

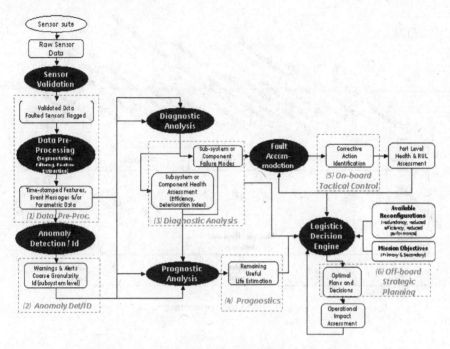

Fig. 1.   PHM functional architecture.

on preserving performance or safety margins, and are executed in real-time. Off-board maintenance/repair actions cover more complex offline decisions. They require a decision support system (DSS) performing multi-objective optimizations, exploring Pareto frontiers of corrective actions, and combining them with preference aggregations to generate the best decision tradeoffs. All functions depicted in Fig. 1 require different types of data and knowledge, and have rather different temporal requirements and decision horizons, which we will discuss next.

3.   Decisions and Time Horizons

We want to define a framework for PHM functionalities by analyzing the temporal horizon and the domain knowledge needed by SC models to produce such PHM decisions. The decision horizon determines requirements for data quality and size, domain knowledge, problem complexity, and crispness of performance evaluation needed to automate the PHM decision-making process. To cope with such variety of

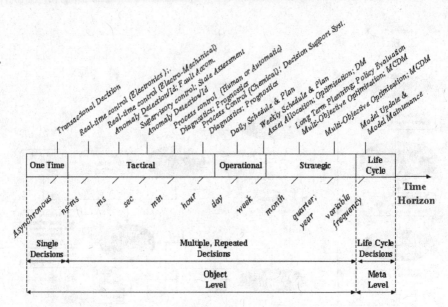

Fig. 2.   Temporal segmentation.

requirements, we propose a temporal segmentation along the decision time horizon, as illustrated in Fig. 2. We can identify the following segments:

(i) **Single Decisions.** These are situations in which data are collected only once and decisions are made on that basis. This is typical of transactional applications, such as insurance underwriting.

(ii) **Multiple, Repeated Decisions.** These are situations in which data are collected synchronously and decisions are taken multiple times, usually within a similar time frame. Depending on their frequency, we can distinguish among three types of decisions:

    (a) **Tactical** decisions range from microseconds (for real-time control of electronics) to hours (for process control of chemical plants). The time scale of the underlying system dynamics determines the required decision frequency.

    (b) **Operational** decisions can be taken daily or weekly (such as production schedule).

(c) **Strategic** decisions, such as company-wide maintenance policy evaluation, have a horizon ranging from months to quarters.

(iii) **Life Cycle Decisions.** Finally we have a different type of temporal requirements to support the *life cycle* of these models. Unlike the previous decisions, which are made at the object-level, these decisions belong to the meta-level, as they try to assess and maintain the validity of the object-level models. These lifecycle issues have been discussed before by the authors.[1-3]

4. A Linguistics Metaphor

One of soft computing main characteristic is the ability to integrate domain knowledge with field data.[4,5] While it is relatively easy to quantify the amount of available field data, it is not as simple to measure and characterize the type and quality of domain knowledge that can be used to build a SC model. To this end, we propose a *linguistics* metaphor, using its structure as a paradigm for characterizing the type of domain knowledge exploited by a SC system. The correspondence between linguistic and PHM concepts is illustrated in Fig. 3.

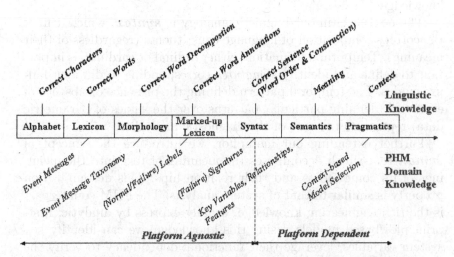

Fig. 3.   Correspondence between linguistics and PHM knowledge types.

In formal languages, the lowest level of information is the **alphabet**, representing the set of legal characters that compose each word in the language. The next level, which is our starting point in the metaphor, is the **lexicon**, i.e. the set of terminals in the language. This set represents the collection of all possible legal words that could appear in a sentence of the language. In PHM, the lexicon counterpart is the set of possible (normal or abnormal) *event codes* that could be recorded in an asset log. Without any additional knowledge about their relationships, order, meaning, etc. they are simply words that are recorded over time. This is the case of analyzing event logs without a data dictionary. Let us now introduce the concept of **morphology**, which describes the structures of words. Among these structures, the most common is that of word stem or root. The PHM counterpart of this concept is the taxonomy of event codes, which might indicate that all codes sharing the same initial symbol combinations refer to components belonging to the same system.

As we extend our metaphor, we observe that an annotated or **marked-up lexicon** provide us with a coarse classification of the words. Similarly, by labeling certain event codes or event logs (e.g. normal, type-1 abnormal, etc.) we produce the references required to label different types of anomalies. This can be used for training classifiers, such as neural networks, fuzzy-based classifiers, etc. As we increase the problem complexity, we need to leverage deeper domain knowledge.

The next level in our linguistic analogy is **syntax**, which defines the correct composition of language constituents (regardless of their meaning). Temporal information, either ordinal or cardinal, is important to define and identify *signatures* corresponding to different failure modes. The temporal pattern defining the presence or absence of events (or defining particular patterns over the values of parametric data) represents the core of the diagnostic analysis.

Further extending our metaphor, we introduce the concept of **semantics**, which decomposes the meaning of text into the meanings of its components and their relationships. This decomposition property is similar to that of system analysis. The PHM counterpart is the rich engineering knowledge, usually express by analytic, first-principles based models. Using this knowledge, we can identify key system variables, leverage their functional dependency to verify the correctness of other variables, extract the most informative features to create more compact representations, etc.

We conclude our metaphor with the use of **pragmatics**, which uses external, contextual knowledge to fully understand the meaning of our communication. While all prior levels dealt with information contained in the message itself (object-level), pragmatics requires higher-level knowledge (meta-level) to provide the contextual information needed to disambiguate a sentence, correctly interpret its meaning, etc. In John Searle's speech acts,[6] the speaker's communicative intentions, the social distance between the speaker and the listener, and other factors are leveraged to refine the meaning. The PHM counterpart of pragmatics consists in leveraging contextual information (such as operational regimes, environmental conditions, health deterioration) to determine the degree of applicability of local models and to select the best (or the best mixture). For example, fuzzy supervisory control[7] analyzes the region of the state space in which the system is operating and, based on performance, efficiency, and safety tradeoffs, selects the mixture of low-level controllers to compute the control action.

The selection of the most appropriate SC techniques, in conjunction with *sibling* disciplines, such as AI, Statistics, and Information Theory, depends on the type of available domain knowledge. Table 1 depicts the most useful SC approaches for different knowledge types (labeled according to our linguistic metaphor).

Table 1. SC techniques and domain knowledge.

SC/Stat/AI Techniques	Domain Knowledge
Self-Organizing Maps (SOM) Kolmogorov Complexity, One-class SVM, NN, Unsupervised ML techniques, fuzzy clustering, nonparametric statistics	Lexicon and Morphology
Supervised Machine Learning techniques, NN, Fuzzy Classifiers, CART, Random Forest, MARS	Marked-up Lexicon
Automated Kernel Splitting, Grammatical Inference, EA	Syntax
Feature extraction/selection, fuzzy models, 1st Principle based simulations, temporal reasoners, Case-based Reasoners, planners, Evolutionary Algorithms (EA)	Semantics
Model Selection/Mixing, EA, MOEA, Fuzzy models for preference aggregation and tradeoffs	Pragmatics

5. Knowledge and Time: A Framework

Having described the two dimensions (temporal and cognitive), we can now propose a decision framework for PHM functions based on the product space of *time horizon* and *domain knowledge,* as illustrated in Fig. 4. We observe that only for tactical horizon applications we can develop models that are based on relatively shallow knowledge. In these cases, it is also common to construct an ensemble of such models, ensuring their diversity (in the sense of errors' uncorrelation[8]) and performing a fusion to increase the output's reliability.

We recently described[9] a representative subset of this framework, discussed selected PHM applications in anomaly detection and prognostics, and illustrated their associated Soft Computing based solutions. In the last section of this paper we will focus on the last stage of the PHM problem described in Fig. 1, the logistics decision engine and its underlying Decision Support System (DSS).

Time Horizon

Time Horizon / Domain Knowledge	One Time	Tactical	Operational	Strategic	Meta
Lexicon		Anomaly Detection			
Morphology		Anomaly Detection			
Marked-up Lexicon		Anomaly Identification			
Syntax		Anomaly Id. Diagnostics	Scheduling		
Semantics	Transactional Decision	Anomaly Id. Diagnostics Prognostics Control	Scheduling Planning Readiness Assessment Asset Allocation Optimization DM	Long-Term Planning Contingency Planning Asset Management MOO Tradeoffs MCMD	Model Update & Maintenance
Pragmatics					

Domain Knowledge

Fig. 4.　Framework: *Domain Knowledge* × *Time Horizon.*

6. Decision Support for Maintenance and Logistics

6.1. *Problem formulation and SC solution*

We describe a decision support system (DSS) for operational and maintenance decision making with PHM-specific data. Challenges arise from the large amount of information pieces that a decision maker needs to consider. The DSS enables the decision maker (DM) to make optimal decisions based on his/her expression of trade-offs through a guided evaluation of different optimal decision alternatives under operational boundary conditions using user-specific and interactive collaboration.

The need for a SC solution arises from the search complexity associated with this decision-making problem. Given the multiple ways in which assets can be allocated to missions and repairs can be performed to assets, the size of potential set of decisions that can be enacted at any given moment is exponential with respect to the number of repair actions. Hence, we propose the use of Evolutionary Multi-Objective Optimization (EMOO) to perform this search efficiently and generate a Pareto frontier formed by *nondominated* alternatives.

The use of EMOO results in the identification of alternative mission allocations and maintenance plans that are nondominated along PHM-specific objectives (overall mission success, safety, maintenance cost).[10]

After generating a set of nondominated alternatives, the DM can employ constraint-based approaches or *interactive* tools[11] to select the operational plan that best meets his field requirements to iteratively select a small subset of alternatives. The DM can also select a portion of a solution (for instance 4 out of 12 tail numbers assigned to a flight schedule) and ask the DSS to find alternative selections for the remaining portion of the problem. The EMOO can re-run a reduced version of the problem to represent a solution that incorporates the user's handpicked selections. If there are feasible nondominated solutions, the EMOO will generate the corresponding Pareto set and complete the assignments. In addition, an interactive module better addresses many decision-making elements in an operational environment, like interactions between user and system, state representation and awareness, preference elicitation, query answering, and uncertainty representation.

6.2. Results

For a 2-asset, 2-mission, 7 maximum parts per asset problem, with
only one available unit per part on the inventory, we find that 2135 (of
the exhaustive 32 768) allocations (each being a simultaneous assignment of repair actions resources to assets and assets to missions that
is logically possible) are both feasible and optimal (for 4 objectives).
To down-select from this subset to a single solution, however, could
be a daunting task.

In one mode of interaction, the DM expresses desired levels of
performance for each of the current missions, such as maximum time
within which to dispatch mission, minimum reliability required to
fly mission, and so on. The DSS looks through the feasible set of
allocations to find the ones that satisfy the specified constraints and
presents them to the DM. In the absence of any allocation that satisfies the constraints, the DSS additionally tries to find a currently
infeasible allocation that could potentially satisfy the expressed constraints. Upon finding such an allocation, it indicates to the decision-
maker the infeasible allocation as well as the requirements in terms of
additional parts that would make this allocation feasible. Thus the
DSS translates currently unattainable goals of the decision-maker
into a set of actions for the decision-maker by virtue of which those
goals could be attained. If none of the infeasible plans can satisfy
the currently expressed constraints, then the DSS indicates that
to the decision-maker and communicates the need to weaken some of
the constraints. In an alternative mode of operation, the DM is presented with all available feasible allocations in a fashion that allows
him to identify the levels of performance that are attainable across
multiple missions simultaneously and select from the available set.

In Fig. 5, each point represents a potential *plan* that prescribes
the repair actions for an asset in the repair-shop as well as the asset
to be allocated to a mission. Each plan is feasible only if the repair
actions are achievable, given the part availability in the shop. The
plot shows the intrinsic trade-offs present in the real-world when trying to satisfy multiple missions (e.g. mission i and mission j) which
compete for the same resources (parts, time, man-power). Figure 5
shows that repair-plans with very high values of predicted reliability
for mission i are also plans that result in low predicted reliability
values for competing mission j (and vice-versa). Presenting the DM
with such plots confronts them with the need to understand the

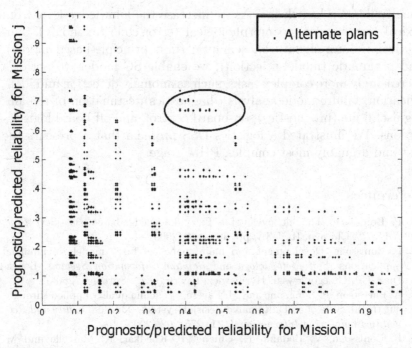

Fig. 5. Interactive decision-making for selection of best repair and mission allocations.

competing/conflicting nature of the metrics they are trying to simultaneously maximize, and thereby presents them also with the opportunity to locate feasible plans that can potentially optimize along all such metrics simultaneously. For example, the set of points inside the ellipse represent a subset of plans with reasonable values of predicted reliability for both competing missions. Such an interaction gives the decision-maker an opportunity to identify what is globally attainable in the space of feasible allocations/plans. By using interactive features like cross-linked plots,[11] heat-maps and other interactive tools, the user can further explore allocations of interest in the set of visible plots and select the best plan to implement.

7. Conclusions

We proposed a framework based on the cross product of decision time and domain knowledge to analyze various PHM-related tasks. We categorized time according to three different scales (tactical, operational, and strategic), while we used a linguistic metaphor to classify domain knowledge. As we increase the knowledge level from lexical (error-codes) to morphological (error-code taxonomy), syntactical (failure signature), semantic (first principle-based model), and pragmatic (model selection), we enable SC models to perform increasingly more complex tasks, such as anomaly detection and identification, failure mode analysis (diagnostics), estimation of remaining useful life (prognostics), on-board control, and off board logistics actions. We illustrated a logistics DSS problem that represents the last and arguably most complex PHM stage.

References

1. P. Bonissone, The life cycle of a fuzzy knowledge-based classifier. *Proc. NAFIPS*. Chicago, IL, USA, pp. 488–494 (2003).
2. P. Bonissone, Development and maintenance of fuzzy models in financial applications. *Soft Methodology and Random Information Systems*. Lopez-Diaz, Gil, Grzegorzewski, Hyrniewicz, Lawry (eds.). Springer (2004).
3. A. Patterson, P. Bonissone and M. Pavese, Six sigma quality applied throughout the lifecycle of and automated decision system. *Journal Quality and Reliability Engineering International*, **21**, 275–292 (2005).
4. P. Bonissone, V. Badami, K. Chiang, P. Khedkar, K. Marcelle and M. Schutten, Industrial applications of fuzzy logic at GE., *Proc. IEEE*, **83**(3), 450–465 (1995).
5. P. Bonissone, A. Varma, K. Aggour and F. Xue, Design of local fuzzy models using evolutionary algorithms. *CSDA Journal*, **51**, 398–416 (2006).
6. J. Searle, *Speech Acts. An Essay in the Philosophy of Language*. Cambridge (1969).
7. P. Bonissone, Y-T. Chen, K. Goebel and P. Khedkar, Hybrid soft computing systems: Industrial and commercial application. *Proceedings IEEE*, **87**(9), 1641–1667, (1999).
8. L. Kuncheva and C. J. Whitaker, Measures of diversity in classifier ensembles. *Machine Learning*, **51**, 181–207 (2003).
9. A. Varma, P. Bonissone, W. Yan, N. Eklund, K. Goebel, N. Iyer and S. Bonissone, Anomaly detection using nonparametric information. *ASME Turbo Expo* (2007).
10. N. Iyer, K. Goebel and P. Bonissone, Framework for post-prognostic decision support. *IEEE Aerospace Conf. 11.0903* (2006).
11. J. Josephson, B. Chandrasekaran, M. Carroll, N. Iyer, B. Wasacz, G. Rizzoni, Q. Li and D. A. Erb, An architecture for exploring large design spaces. *AAAI*, pp. 143–150 (1998).

A Multi-Granular Model for Direct E-Commerce Services

Vincenzo Loia*, Sabrina Senatore†, Maria I. Sessa‡
and Mario Veniero§

Dipartimento di Matematica e Informatica
Universitá degli Studi di Salerno
via Ponte Don Melillo 84084 Fisciano (SA), Italy
*loia@unisa.it
†ssenatore@unisa.it
‡misessa@unisa.it
§mveniero@unisa.it

Abstract

E-commerce marketers conduct their business through various advertising messages which do not often reflect the user interest. The necessity of tailoring responses to individual customer requirements asks for opportune advertising systems able to capture user attention, proposing banner ads or messages which meet their real needs. Starting from this key point, this work describes a system for e-commerce services, which proposes selected on-line advertisements to users during their navigation. Focus is the use of the fuzzy multiset as formal model to profile the user and enterprise interests. Through an agent-based architecture and fuzzy clustering techniques, the system provides a straightforward support to e-commerce market mediation.

1. Introduction

E-commerce marketing has assumed a primary role for transacting business in a wide range of interactions. Banner ads, chat or communities, sponsorships and push technology are the most popular forms of on-line advertising. Web enterprises, commercial web sites attire the user interest launching advertising on their products: the effectiveness is achieved "if the pertinent message is delivered to the right visitor at the right time". Web sites must present appropriate customized banner ads to different users, taking into account their preferences and tastes.[1] Retailers are also interested in the users which are potentially viewing the banner ads. Several issues in the e-commerce domain drive to the "intelligent" enhancements: computational intelligence and fuzzy technology play an important role for improving the e-commerce activities (i.e. searching and trading of information, services, products, etc.).[2-7]

Our work proposes an agent-based architecture which tracks the profiles of presumed customers during their web navigation, in order to deliver advertising messages targeted to respond to their needs. At the same time, the system analyzes the asset marketing of the web enterprises in order to address their advertising activities to the interested customers. The approach defines profiles of both enterprises and users exploiting the fuzzy multiset modeling. It allows, on the one hand, the managing of different kinds of information, by means of the same formal model, on the other hand, the use of fuzzy clustering to select the asset advertising closer to the user profile. The chapter is organized as follows: the whole architecture and the main modules are described in Sec. 2. Section 3 focuses on the modeling details of the e-commerce context, introducing the formal description of the adopted model and its data representation, detailed in Sec. 4. Then, the clustering method is presented in Sec. 5, whereas Sec. 6 illustrates the agent-based interactions of the system, showing the agents activities, aimed at satisfying enterprise and user expectations. Finally, conclusions close the paper.

2. Architecture Overview

The system (shown in Fig. 1) is designed as a multi-tiered web-centric application implementing a typical server-initiated web advertising process. The main components are described as follows:

- *User's Activity Spooner*: tracks all the activities of the user web navigation, allowing the *Targeted Advertising Application Server* to create and maintain user profiles.

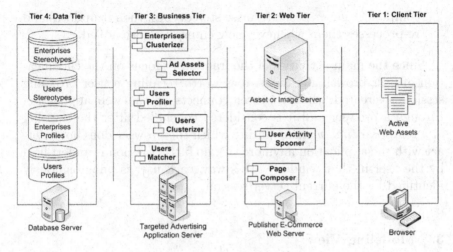

Fig. 1.   Logical architecture.

- *Page Composer*: creates a customized web content, targeted on the user's interest, exploiting the results returned by the *Ad Assets Selector*.
- *Users Profiler*: maintains and updates user's browsing session profiles, according to the data model (shown in the following).
- *Users Clusterizer*: builds the clustering of collected user profiles and updates the set of behavioral prototypes.
- *Enterprises Clusterizer*: discovers the best set of market segments (or clusters) to which the enterprises belong to.
- *Users Matcher*: finds the optimal correspondence between user profiles and market segments.
- *Ad Assets Selector*: performs the selection of the advertising assets which better matches the user's inferred interests.
- *Users Profiles*: stores a historical view of significant user browsing sessions into the comprehensive user profiles. It is dynamically updated according to the users' browsing activities.
- *Users Stereotypes*: maintains the current behavioral stereotypes of the user browsing sessions. It is updated during the data mining process.
- *Enterprises Stereotypes*: stores and classifies the current market segments of information. It is updated whenever a new enterprise affiliates the web marketing services of the portal.
- *Enterprises Profiles*: stores significant enterprise data into the comprehensive enterprise profiles. At system startup, this

component generates enterprise stereotypes, then it updates and re-processes them whenever new enterprises are added.

Since the main activities of the framework focus on the classification of user browsing sessions, it is worth recalling a user browsing session is created when the user connects to the web application through a browser and it is considered concluded after the elapsing of a temporal *time window* during which the browser does not interact with the application anymore (i.e. no further action is undertaken by the user in that window). This way, each user is unambiguously identified by the current server session.

3. Modeling View

The proposed approach aims at defining a suitable user/enterprise model which responds to the binomial "demand/offering" requirement, through market requests such as "if a user is interested in the item X, she/he could be also likely interested in the items Y and Z". In our framework X, Y and Z represent retailers which can be considered a community of sellers whose profiles are similar enough to constitute a market segment. Our approach focuses on the following goals:

- Evaluation of the similarity between the user's interests and the enterprise target in order to assemble the users into a set of stereotypes and the enterprises into a set of market segments.
- Analysis of the market segment closer to the user profile, dynamically defined through his navigation activity.

The user profile is built by analyzing associated browsing actions during the entire navigation session. The "searching scope" of a user is represented by the delineated profile. In fact, the user interest is measured by evaluating relevant terms (collected from the navigated web pages), according to a given number of different indicators, each one related to a user action, which typically occurs within a web session. Examples are "user click on a hyperlink topic", "request of a web page", "user permanence time on a web-page", etc. These measures of interest are used to create the current user profile. In the following, we will use the term "user" to denote a "user profile", except when a context disambiguation is required.

Similarly, the profile of an enterprise is evaluated on the terms of the dictionary, associated to the enterprise description. This evaluation is carried out exploiting some fixed proper indicators, corresponding to enterprise features. Some examples are "bidder identification", "advertised assets", etc.. More formally, a set P of entities (i.e. a set of users, a set of enterprises) are described through a formal model (named "profile"), by exploiting heterogeneous factors in a set A of indicators. The goal is to produce an appropriate classification of these individual "profiles". A common data representation is exploited, driven by the following idea:

the fuzzy multiset based formalism provides a flexible tool to represent a measure of membership taking into account a set of heterogeneous and complex indicators. This model exploits a set T of selected terms, named "topics" or "patterns", by associating a sequence of numeric values in $[0,1]$ with each term. These values provide a sort of "multi-component" measure of "interest" of the considered term, with respect to the characterization of the given entity.

In our context, the "searching scope" and "market segment" represent the characterizations of the user and the enterprise, respectively. Let us recall the formal definition of multiset:[8]

Definition 1. Let $P = \{p_1, \ldots, p_m\}$ be a set of elements and $\mathcal{FM}(T)$ the collection of all fuzzy multiset on the set $T = \{t_1, \ldots, t_n\}$. Let $\mathcal{S} : P \to \mathcal{FM}(T)$ be a function such that $\forall\, p_i \in U$, with $i = 1, \ldots, m$, $\mathcal{S}(p_i)$ is the fuzzy-multiset on T defined as:

$$\mathcal{S}(p_i) = \{(\mu_1(t_1), \ldots, \mu_{n_1}(t_1))/t_1, \ldots, (\mu_1(t_n), \ldots, \mu_{n_n}(t_n))/t_n\},$$

where $\mu_r(t_j) \in [0,1]$ with $r \leq |A|$ is the membership value for the element t_j $(1 \leq j \leq n)$ with respect to the rth indicator in the set A, and $(\mu_1(t_j), \ldots, \mu_{n_j}(t_j))$ is the *membership sequence* associated to the element t_j.

In the sequel we shall only consider *normalized* multisets, i.e. fuzzy multisets with nonincreasing ordering in the membership sequence, denoted by angular brackets. It is worth noting that the definition of membership sequence allows us to qualitatively manage the heterogeneous information provided by the indicators regarding a common topic. Moreover, the fuzzy multiset formalism provides a natural tool to manage vague and incomplete information and represents an enhancement of the usual fuzzy set formalism.

To better explain these assertions, let us provide the "profile" $p_j \in P$ of a user, by considering his browsing actions performed during the web navigation. Let us assume that the profile is defined by the sequence of terms t_i $(i = 1, \ldots, n)$ from a given dictionary T that is extracted from the navigated web pages. Then, a measure of the interest of the user p_j in a given term t_i is required. Such an interest is evaluated via various indicators which assume values in the range $[0, 1]$. For instance, let us consider the following measures:

- $\mu_{clk}(t_i)$: measure of the customer's interest in the term t_i evaluated on direct *click on a hyperlink* related to t_i;
- $\mu_{req}(t_i)$, measure of the customer's interest in the term t_i evaluated on the *user's request of a web page* related to t_i;
- $\mu_{ban}(t_i)$, measure of the customer's interest in the term t_i evaluated on a *direct click on a banner* related to t_i.

The relationships diagram of Fig. 2 explains the intended correlation among given indicators. Each term $t_{i,x}$ represents a "qualitative specialization" of the term t_i, and the indicator x emphasizes its role in the evaluation of the measure of the interest. This way, the fuzzy set associated to the user p_j is represented such as: $F(p_j) = \{\ldots, \mu(t_{i,clk})/t_{i,clk}, \mu(t_{i,req})/t_{i,req}, \mu(t_{i,ban})/t_{i,ban}, \ldots\}$, where $\mu(t_{i,x}) = \mu_x(t_i) \in [0, 1]$ provides the membership contribution of the specialized term $t_{i,x}$ to the representation of the relevance of the term t_i on the "user profile" p_j. Assuming the ordering relationship $\mu(t_{i,req}) \geq \mu(t_{i,clk}) \geq \mu(t_{i,ban})$, the user's measure of interest induced by the term t_i is given as a normalized fuzzy membership sequence, by moving from the fuzzy set $F(p_j)$ to the multiset $S(p_j)$ through the transformation of the fuzzy membership values into the

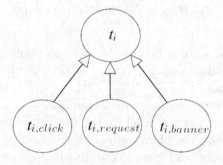

Fig. 2. Term relationship.

fuzzy multi-membership sequence:

$$F(p_j) = \{\ldots, \ \mu(t_{i,clk})/t_{i,clk}, \ \mu(t_{i,req})/t_{i,req}, \ \mu(t_{i,ban})/t_{i,ban}, \ldots\} \rightarrow$$
$$S(p_j) = \{\ldots, \ (\mu_{req}(t_i), \ \mu_{clk}(t_i), \ \mu_{ban}(t_i))/t_i, \ldots\},$$

or generally (with respect to the ordering):

$$S(p_j) = \{\ldots, \ \langle \mu_1(t_i), \ \mu_2(t_i), \ \mu_3(t_i) \rangle / t_i, \ldots\}.$$

In other words, the measure of the membership of the term t_i relative to the "user profile" is composed of a multi-membership sequence evaluated for each indicator. The same approach is used to represent the "marketing target" of an enterprise. The formal details are explained in the next section.

4. Data Representation

The collected information, regarding users and enterprises must be adapted to the clustering phase. Classical clustering algorithms act on input vectors describing suitable features. In our approach the vector-based representation of patterns exploits fuzzy multisets. This mathematical model permits a simple and concise representation of both the enterprises and the user profiles, emphasizing some characteristics observed and/or acquired during the activities of system interaction and web browsing.

Let us stress that the multiset formalism allows us to consider as granular information the collection of the different contributions provided by the considered indicators.

The *Business Tier* activities of Fig. 1 give the extracted profiles (vectors of features) as input to the clustering processes. Both profiles are collected in order to reflect the relationships the system has with the involved entities (users and enterprises).

In summary, when enterprises want to advertise their services or assets, according to a specific business process, a commercial interaction (leading to a business contract underwriting) will be conducted. Structured information (i.e. bidder identification, goods category, marketing target meta-keywords, etc.) is acquired and off-line processed in order to define the enterprise features. These features will constitute the "enterprise profile".

The acquisition process relative to users is quite different and based on the activity of the publisher's e-commerce web portal

(*Web Tier* in Fig. 1). At first, the portal notifies to the targeted advertising system the access of a new user and makes him insert generality and preliminary information (keywords of an input query, his preferences on a registration form, etc.). In its turn, the targeted advertising application layer (*Business Tier*) initializes the user profile with the received information. Then, the portal starts a server-side activity to gather the user in-site browsing information. This collected information allows the updating of the corresponding user profile. The collected information regarding both users and enterprises compose two reference sets of terms (dictionaries), T_1, T_2. Although two different typologies of information are shown, the fuzzy multiset model allows us to exploit a common data structure.

Definition 2. Let P_1 and P_2 be, respectively, collections of users and enterprises, i.e. $P_1 = \{p_{1_1}, p_{1_2}, \ldots, p_{1_k}\}$ and $P_2 = \{p_{2_1}, p_{2_2}, \ldots, p_{2_l}\}$, and let $T_1 = \{t_{1_1}, t_{1_2}, \ldots, t_{1_m}\}$ and $T_2 = \{t_{2_1}, t_{2_2}, \ldots, t_{2_n}\}$ be the terms in the reference dictionaries, respectively, for users and enterprises. A fuzzy multiset, called "entity profile", is associated to each entity p_{u_i}. Each element (feature) in the fuzzy multiset is a term $t_{u_j} \in T_u$, with $u = 1, 2$ and the related sequence of membership values is computed according to some suitable indicators.

Let $\mathcal{S} : P_u \to \mathcal{FM}(T_u)$ be a function where $\mathcal{FM}(T_u)$ is the collection of all fuzzy multiset in T_u. Then $\forall\ p_{u_i} \in P_u$, with $u = 1, 2$ and $i = 1, \ldots, |P_u|$, $\mathcal{S}(p_{u_i})$ is the fuzzy-multiset on T_u defined as:

$$\mathcal{S}(p_{u_i}) = \{\langle \mu_{\alpha_{u_1}}(t_{u_1}), \ldots, \mu_{\alpha_{u_q}}(t_{u_1}) \rangle / t_{u_1}, \ldots,$$
$$\langle \mu_{\alpha_{u_1}}(t_{u_r}), \ldots, \mu_{\alpha_{u_q}}(t_{u_r}) \rangle / t_{u_r} \},$$

where $r \leq |T_u|$, $\alpha_{u_h} \in \mathcal{A}_u$ represents a given indicator in a predefined set $\mathcal{A}_u$ of evaluation parameters, and $\mu_{\alpha_{u_h}}(t_{u_j}) \in [0, 1]$, $h \leq |\mathcal{A}_u|$, is the membership value for term t_{u_j} $(1 \leq j \leq r)$ evaluated according to the specific indicator $\alpha_{u_h} \in \mathcal{A}_u$.

In particular, considering the user profile, the set $\mathcal{A}_1$ represents some typical actions associated to a user web browsing activity. The generic membership value $\mu_{\alpha_{1_h}}(t_{1_j}) \in [0, 1]$ measures the *interest degree* of the user (with respect to his searching scope) in the term (feature) $t_{1_j} \in T_1$, estimated either as normalized evaluation of quantities related to the indicators (e.g. $\frac{observed\ quantity}{max\ threshold}$) or as binary evaluation (1 if is present, 0 otherwise), according to the observation parameter α_{1_h}. Examples of measures of user interest degree with respect to some indicators are the following:

- $\mu_{clk}(t_i)$ evaluates clicks on a direct link anchoring t_i.
- $\mu_{ban}(t_i)$ evaluates clicks on an advertising banner referring to t_i;
- $\mu_{req}(t_i)$ considers the requested web page, whose content presents meaningful occurrences of t_i;
- $\mu_{page}(t_i)$ computes the time spent (over a given threshold) on a web page whose content presents meaningful occurrences of t_i;

In the case of enterprise profiles the set $\mathcal{A}_2$ contains different indicators. For instance:

- $\mu_{bid}(t_i)$ evaluates the bidder identification including t_i;
- $\mu_{ast}(t_i)$ evaluates advertised assets description containing t_i;
- $\mu_{trg}(t_i)$ evaluates marketing target meta-keywords including t_i;
- $\mu_{cat}(t_i)$ evaluates the selling catalogue of the enterprise containing t_i;
- $\mu_{con}(t_i)$ evaluates t_i as an enterprise characterization given from a third-part expert consultant;

where the value $\mu_{\alpha_{2_h}}(t_{2_j}) \in [0, 1]$ represents the *pertinency degree* of the enterprise (with respect to its "marketing target") related to the term $t_{2_j} \in T_2$, according to the indicator α_{2_h}.

5. The Clustering

The clustering activity exploits the well-known Fuzzy C-Means algorithm.[9] It is an unsupervised approach, except for the setting of the parameters of the algorithms, the number K of clusters and the distance function which is exploited. In general, the FCM algorithm accepts a vector-based representation of entities of a universe U in the form of a data matrix and produces a fuzzy partitioning of them.

Each multiset describes a vector where each component is the membership sequence, associated to a given term (i.e. feature). Then the input to the clustering algorithm can be given in a matrix form where each row represents a normalized multiset.

For instance, let us suppose $T = \{t_1, t_2, t_3\}$ is a set of terms and $P = \{p_1, p_2\}$ the universe of entities.

$$S(p_1) = \{\langle 1.0, 0.5\rangle/t_1, \ \langle 0.7, 0.5, 0.2\rangle/t_2, \ \langle 1.0, 0.5, 0.2\rangle/t_3\},$$
$$S(p_2) = \{\langle 0.5, 0.2\rangle/t_1, \ \langle 1.0, 0.7, 0.5, 0.2\rangle/t_2, \ \langle 0.2\rangle/t_3\}.$$

The corresponding matrix I_p, can be represented as follows:

$$\mathcal{I}_P = \begin{array}{c} \\ p_1 \\ p_2 \end{array} \begin{pmatrix} \overset{t_1}{(1.0, 0.5)} & \overset{t_2}{(0.7, 0.5, 0.2)} & \overset{t_3}{(1.0, 0.5, 0.2)} \\ (0.5, 0.2) & (1.0, 0.7, 0.5, 0.2) & (0.2) \end{pmatrix}.$$

More formally, the FCM algorithm aims at minimizing an objective function in the universe U. Exploiting the notation introduced in Sec. 3, let us consider $P_u = \{p_{u_1}, \ldots, p_{u_L}\}$. Fixed a number K of clusters, we use the following standard objective function:[8,9]

$$J(M, V) = \sum_{i=1}^{K} \sum_{j=1}^{L} a_{i,j}^2 d(C_i, S(p_{u_j})) \tag{1}$$

where $u = 1, 2$, $M = (a_{i,j})$ is a $K \times L$ matrix of cluster memberships satisfying the constraint:

$$M = \left\{ a_{i,j} : \sum_{i=1}^{K} a_{i,j} = 1; a_{i,j} \geq 0, \forall i, j \right\}, \tag{2}$$

$V = (C_1, \ldots, C_K)$ is the ordered collections of cluster centers.

Finally, $d(C_i, S(p_{u_j}))$ represents the distance evaluation function between the two fuzzy multiset C_i and $S(p_{u_j})$, defined as follows.[8]

Definition 3. Given two normalized fuzzy multisets $A, B \in \mathcal{FM}(T)$ where $A = \{\langle \mu_A^1(x_1), \ldots, \mu_A^{n_{x_1}}(x_1)\rangle/x_1, \ldots\}$ and $B = \{\langle \mu_B^1(x_1), \ldots, \mu_B^{n_{x_1}}(x_1)\rangle/x_1, \ldots\}$

$$d(A, B) = \sum_{x \in T} \sum_{j=1}^{L(x)} |\mu_A^j(x) - \mu_B^j(x)|, \tag{3}$$

where:[8]

$$L(X) = \max\{L(x : A), L(x : B)\}, \tag{4}$$
$$L(x : A) = \max\{j : \mu_A^j(x) \neq 0 \ \ j = 1, \ldots, n_x\}. \tag{5}$$

$L(x : A)$ represents the length of the membership sequence $\langle \mu_A^1(x),$ $\mu_A^2(x), \ldots, \mu_A^{n_x}(x) \rangle$ related to $x \in T$.

Observe that d satisfies the axiom of metrics.[8] Let us note two entities $p_{u_1}, p_{u_2} \in P_u$ $(u = 1, 2)$ such that $d(S(p_{u_1}), S(p_{u_2})) = 0 \not\Rightarrow$ $p_{u_1} = p_{u_2}$ since different entities p_{u_i} may produce the same fuzzy multiset $S(p_{u_i})$.

6. Agents and the Data Mining Step

The agent paradigm has been pervasively used in the system architecture. The whole framework has been already implemented by exploiting the JADE framework.[10] Let us emphasize the agent-based component *Users Matcher* is strictly related to the data mining step. Figure 3 focuses on the agent-based structure of the system dataflow (depicted in Fig. 1); particularly the diagram shows the data mining process implemented by the system. The *Users Clusterizer* and the *Enterprises Clusterizer* modules are in charge of computing user/enterprise prototypes using, respectively, the users' and the enterprises' prototypes (refer to Fig. 3). Prototypes and user profiles are the information exploited by the decision procedure to identify the most suitable advertising assets. This process is performed through the "matcher" procedure/unit/agency (i.e. *Users Matcher*) that associates closer enterprise profiles to each user profile (computed by exploiting the distance measure). When a user requires web content to the site, the *Page Composer* forwards a request of advertising assets to the *Ad Assets Selector*. The latter one, in its turn, sends the request to the *Users Matcher* agency where there are two distinct task-oriented agents, the *Enterprises Direct Matcher* and *User Stereotype Matcher* agents (respectively, *EDM* and *USM* in Fig. 3). These agents, separately, try to locate their own best assets and successively cooperate to find the optimal trade-off between direct association to a market and deferred association by computing the user profile similarity to the user stereotypes. The result of this trade-off represents the best user classification into the market segments space.

Summarizing, the system performs some activities of pattern discovery:

- "if a user is interested in item X then it is likely interested in Y, Z and ...";

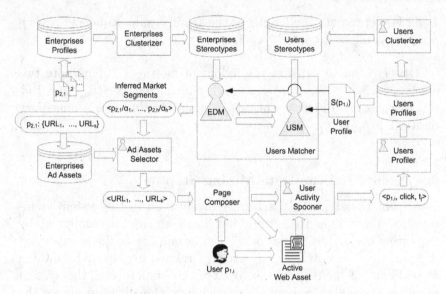

Fig. 3.   Data flow of the e-commerce services framework.

- "if a user belongs to stereotype S much likely he is interested in products from enterprise X and enterprise Y ... (i.e. which compose the prototype)";
- "if a user is interested in X or belongs to stereotype S then he is likely a "satisfiable" user".

Moreover, the system replies to questions such as "Which and how many are the unsatisfiable users for the portal?". This added value represents a further service the system is able to offer to the portal, allowing it to better fidelize users.

7.   Conclusions

This work presents a suitable user/enterprise model which responses the "demand/offering" requirement: marketing products are proposed to users through attractive on-line advertising which guess their interests and preferences. Focus is the use of the fuzzy multiset as one formal model to represent multi-granular contributes of information coming from different sources in the e-commerce marketing context. This model can properly profile both users and enterprises, exploiting a unique formal tool able to detail heterogeneous information. Additional enhancements have been taken into account in order to avoid a loss of information that may occur during the matching procedure. In fact, a drawback could arise for the evaluation of the distance between user and enterprise profiles: syntactically different topics t and t' (even though semantically equivalent) could be not taken into account by the Matcher module. A set of built-in similarity relations $\mathcal{R}$ has been analyzed and defined on the set of terms, by considering semantic and lexicographic relationships among the terms. As future work, the relation $\mathcal{R}$ could be a suitable similarity providing values in $[0, 1]$.

References

1. S. M. Bae, S. Park and S. H. Ha, Fuzzy web ad selector based on web usage mining. *IEEE Intelligent Systems*, **18**(6), 62–69 (2003).
2. C. Allen, D. Kania and B. Yaeckel, *Internet World Guide to One-To-One Web Marketing*. John Wiles and Sons (1998).
3. M. Eirinaki and M. Vazirgiannis, Web mining for web personalization. *ACM Trans. Inter. Tech.*, **3**(1), 1–27 (2003).
4. M. He and H. Leung, Agents in e-commerce: State of the art. *Knowledge and Information Systems*, **4**(3), 257–282 (2002).
5. M. Shyu, C. Haruechaiyasak and S. Chen, Category cluster discovery from distributed WWW directories. *Inf. Sci. Inf. Comput. Sci.*, **155**(3–4), 181–197 (2003).
6. V. Jain and R. Krishnapuram, Applications of fuzzy sets in personalization for e-commerce. *IFSA World Congress and 20th NAFIPS International Conference*, **1**, 263–268, Vancouver, BC.
7. R. R. Yager, Targeted E-commerce marketing using fuzzy intelligent agents. *IEEE Intelligent Systems*, **15**(6), 42–45 (2000). ISSN 1094–7167.
8. S. Miyamoto, Information clustering based on fuzzy multisets. *Information Processing and Management*, **39**, 197–213 (2003).
9. J. C. Bezdek, *Pattern Recognition and Fuzzy Objective Function Algorithms*. Plenum Press, N. York (1981).
10. JADE. Java Agent DEvelopment Framework. URL: http://jade.tilab.com/.

Using the Fuzzy Spatial Relation "Between" to Segment the Heart in Computerized Tomography Images

Antonio Moreno[*], Isabelle Bloch[†], Celina Maki Takemura[‡],
Olivier Colliot[§] and Oscar Camara[¶]

[*,†] GET-ENST, TSI Department
CNRS UMR 5141 LTCI Paris, France
[*] Antonio.Moreno@enst.fr
[†] Isabelle.Bloch@enst.fr
[‡] Department of Computer Science
Institute of Mathematics and Statistics (IME)
University of São Paulo (USP), São Paulo, Brazil
[§] Cognitive Neuroscience and Brain Imaging Laboratory
CNRS UPR 640-LENA, Université Pierre et Marie Curie — Paris 6
Hôpital de la Pitié-Salpêtrière, Paris, France
[¶] Computational Imaging Lab, Department of Information
and Communication Technologies, Universitat Pompeu Fabra
Passeig Circumval-lació 8, 08003 Barcelona, Spain

Abstract

Segmenting the heart in medical images is a challenging and important task
for many applications. Most heart segmentation methods proposed in the
literature deal with cardiac internal structures, but there is a real interest in
segmenting the heart as a whole. In this paper, we address this problem and
propose an automatic method, based on the modeling of spatial relations of

---

[*]A. Moreno is currently at INSERM U.562 — Cognitive Neuroimaging Unit,
CEA/SAC/DSV/I2BM/NeuroSpin, Bâtiment 145, Point Courrier 156, F-91191 Gif-sur-
Yvette CEDEX, France.

the heart with the lungs. The main a priori anatomical knowledge we use
in this work is expressed by the spatial relation "the heart is between the
lungs" and we propose a fuzzy representation of this anatomical knowledge,
which then drives the segmentation process.

1. Introduction

Segmenting the heart in medical images such as noncontrast computerized tomography (CT) images is a challenging task due to their low
contrast and the similar gray-level values of the surrounding structures (liver, tumors). Many clinical applications could benefit from a
reliable heart segmentation procedure, such as the study of cancer in
the thoracic region or other cardiac and vascular diseases. The delin-
eation of the heart is important in oncological applications such as
dose estimation in radiotherapy: it may be used in treatment planning in order to define a security margin around this organ to prevent
it from being irradiated. It can also be useful as a preliminary step
for registration of multimodal images.

Most heart segmentation methods proposed in the literature deal
with segmentation of internal structures (in particular the left ventricle)[1,2] and are focused on MRI modality or ultrasound but rarely
on CT. However, in particular for the aforementioned applications
(where CT is one of the most common anatomical imaging modalities), there is also a need to segment the heart as a whole in order to
distinguish its limits and the separations with surrounding structures
(as the liver). Among the existing methods for segmenting the heart
as a whole, Gregson[3] works on MR images where he manually selects
a 2D slice containing the heart and then uses a hierarchical algorithm
to segment other structures in this slice (torso, lungs, background).
Once the heart is recognized in the selected slice, the segmentation
is propagated to adjacent slices. Lelieveldt et al.[4] proposed another
method based on a fuzzy atlas of thoracic structures. Their method is
applied on MR data and the fuzzy model must be built beforehand,
which is a strong limitation, in particular for the segmentation of
pathological images that may have a different structural configuration than the ones used for the atlas construction. The segmentation
method proposed by Jolly,[5] developed to segment the left ventricle in
2D MR slices, has been extended to CT with minimal adjustments.
Her method proceeds in two steps. First, a global localization step
roughly localizes the left ventricle and then a local deformation step

combines EM-based (Expectation-Maximization) region segmentation and Dijkstra active contours. This method furnishes very satisfactory results for high-resolution contrast CT images. The work of Funka-Lea *et al.*[6] deals with the segmentation of the heart as a whole in CT. Their goal is to isolate the outer surface of the entire heart in order to easily visualize the coronary vessels. They make use of graph-cuts for the segmentation. Their method is fast and robust for contrast CT studies with sub-millimeter resolution where the brightest regions are bone and blood. The recent work of Ecabert *et al.*[7] describes a multi-compartment mesh of both atria, both ventricles, the myocardium around the left ventricle and the trunks of the great vessels and it is adapted to an image volume. The adaptation is performed in a coarse-to-fine manner by progressively relaxing constraints on the degrees of freedom of the allowed deformations. Their method is largely validated and it furnishes very satisfactory results. However, these methods are not directly applicable to noncontrast and low resolution 3D CT images and major adaptations and extensions would be needed.

In addition to their low contrast and the similar gray-level values of the surrounding structures, noncontrast CT images present specific difficulties for the segmentation of the heart due to their low resolution (compared to existing submillimetric CT data) and their anisotropy. For these reasons, there exist few methods for the segmentation of the heart for noncontrast CT images and the existing methods for other modalities cannot deal with this type of images.

In this paper, we propose an automatic method based on the modeling of spatial relations of the heart with surrounding structures. In this particular case, the main a priori anatomical knowledge we use is expressed by the spatial relation "the heart is between the lungs". Several definitions of this knowledge are presented and we discuss which one is more adapted to our problem. This work extends a preliminary version.[8] Since the segmentation of the lungs is generally straightforward in CT scans due to their high contrast with respect to surrounding structures, we first segment them in order to obtain the region of interest (ROI) of the heart. Then we add the anatomical knowledge to the evolution of a deformable model to precisely segment the heart.

In Sec. 2, we introduce the basis of our approach: the spatial relation "between". In Sec. 3, the main steps of our approach are detailed.

Next, in Sec. 4 some results are shown and discussed. Finally, in Sec. 5 we conclude and evoke some future work.

2.   The Spatial Relation "Between"

Usual anatomical descriptions of the heart include a common statement: "the heart is between the lungs". Our method relies on modeling this statement.

A complete study of the spatial relation "between" has been made by Bloch et al.:[9] different definitions of this spatial relation were proposed, compared and discussed according to different types of situations. The main ones are discussed here in light of the specificities of the addressed problem. We restrict ourselves to definitions designed for objects having similar spatial extensions.

Crisp Definitions — The most intuitive crisp definition is based on the convex hull of the union of the objects. However this approach is not appropriate to find the ROI of the heart because some parts of the heart are not included in this convex hull as shown in Fig. 1. A more flexible definition is therefore required. This is a strong argument in favor of one of the following fuzzy definitions.

Fuzzy Dilations — The region between A_1 and A_2 is defined as a fuzzy set in the image domain. Our problem involves nonconvex shapes (the lungs) which have important concavities facing each other (the cavity of the heart). For this reason, the fuzzy directional dilation definitions of the relation "between" are adapted to this case. The simplest definition is:

$$\beta_{FDil1}(A_1, A_2) = D_{\nu_2}(A_1) \cap D_{\nu_1}(A_2) \cap A_1^C \cap A_2^C, \qquad (1)$$

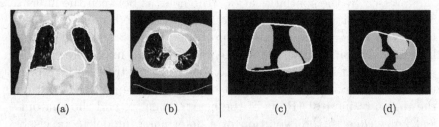

(a)   (b)   (c)   (d)

Fig. 1.   Coronal (a, c) and axial (b, d) views of an example of the segmentation of the lungs and the heart. The contours of these organs are superimposed on the original image (on the left) and the convex hull is superimposed on the segmented lungs and heart (on the right): Some parts of the heart are not contained in this region.

where A_1 and A_2 represent the objects (the lungs in our case), A^C represents the (fuzzy) complementation of A and $D_{\nu_i}(A_j)$, $i, j \in \{1, 2\}$, is the fuzzy dilation of A_j with the fuzzy structuring element ν_i: $D_\nu(\mu)(x) = \sup_y t[\mu(y), \nu(x - y)]$ where μ denotes the (fuzzy) set to be dilated, ν the structuring element, t a t-norm and x and y points of space.[10]

The structuring elements are derived from the angle histogram between the objects.[11] For instance, if object A_2 is mainly to the right of object A_1, then Eq. (1) defines the region which is both to the right of A_1 and to the left of A_2 (excluding A_1 and A_2). This definition is illustrated in Fig. 2(a).

Another definition of "between", which removes the concavities of the objects which are not facing each other, is:

$$\beta_{FDil2}(A_1, A_2) = D_{\nu_2}(A_1) \cap D_{\nu_1}(A_2) \cap A_1^C \cap A_2^C$$
$$\cap [D_{\nu_1}(A_1) \cap D_{\nu_1}(A_2)]^C \cap [D_{\nu_2}(A_1) \cap D_{\nu_2}(A_2)]^C. \tag{2}$$

In this case, if object A_2 is mainly to the right of object A_1, then Eq. (2) defines the region which is both to the right of A_1 and to the left of A_2 (excluding A_1 and A_2), but which is not to the left of both A_1 and A_2 nor to the right of both. Figure 2(b) shows the region between the lungs obtained with this definition.

Admissible segments — The notion of visibility plays an important role in the definition of "between" as illustrated by Bloch

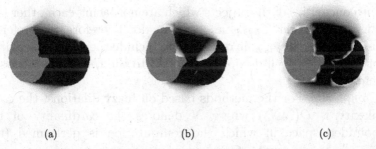

(a)   (b)   (c)

Fig. 2. Fuzzy regions between the lungs, superimposed on an axial slice of the segmented lungs (in gray and dark gray): (a) β_{FDil1}, (b) β_{FDil2} and (c) β_{FVisib}. Their membership values vary from 0 (white) to 1 (black). It can be observed that β_{FDil1} does not remove the concavities of the objects which are not facing each other.

et al.[9] The visible points are those which belong to admissible segments[a] and the region $\beta_{Adm}(A_1, A_2)$ between A_1 and A_2 can then be defined as the union of admissible segments. However, the definition of admissible segments may be too strict in some cases, in a similar manner as the convex hull definition (see Fig. 1). For this reason, the notion of approximate (or fuzzy) visibility has been introduced. Thus, a segment $]a_1, P]$ with $a_1 \in A_1$ (respectively $[P, a_2[$ with $a_2 \in A_2$) is said semi-admissible if it is included in $A_1^C \cap A_2^C$. At each point P of space, we compute the angle the closest to π between two semi-admissible segments from P to A_1 and A_2 respectively. This is formally defined as:

$$\theta_{\min}(P) = \min\{|\pi - \theta|, \theta$$
$$= \angle([a_1, P], [P, a_2]),]a_1, P] \text{ and } [P, a_2[\text{ semi-admissible}\}. \tag{3}$$

The region between A_1 and A_2 is then defined as the fuzzy region of space with membership function:

$$\beta_{FVisib}(A_1, A_2)(P) = f(\theta_{\min}(P)), \tag{4}$$

where f is a function from $[0, \pi]$ to $[0, 1]$ such that $f(0) = 1$, f is decreasing, and becomes 0 at the largest acceptable distance to π (this value can be tuned according to the context). The result obtained with this definition is illustrated in Fig. 2(c).

Selected Definition — In order to decide which definitions better match our problem, we have compared them with respect to two criteria:

(1) *Concavities.* The fuzzy dilation definition β_{FDil1} does not remove the concavities of the objects which are not facing each other (see Fig. 2). However, β_{FDil2} and β_{FVisib} do. Therefore, we prefer to use β_{FDil2} or β_{FVisib}, in order not to include the small concavities of the lungs which do not correspond to the heart but to vessels and bronchi.
(2) *Complexity.* For the methods based on fuzzy dilations, the complexity is $O(NN_\nu)$ where N denotes the cardinality of the bounded space in which the computation is performed (the

---

[a] A segment $]x_1, x_2[$, with x_1 in A_1 and x_2 in A_2, is said to be admissible if it is included in $A_1^C \cap A_2^C$.

image) and N_ν is the cardinality of the support of the structuring element used in the fuzzy dilations. The morphological approach additionally requires the computation of the angle histogram which has a complexity of $O(N_1 N_2)$, where N_i denotes the cardinality of A_i. The computation of $\beta_{Adm}(A_1, A_2)$ for the admissible segments method is of the order of $N_1 N_2 \sqrt{N}$. Finally, the fuzzy visibility approach has a complexity of $O(N N_1 N_2)$.

As β_{FDil2} and β_{FVisib} furnish comparable results with respect to concavities, we prefer β_{FDil2} due to its lower complexity. In order to reduce computing time, images can be under-sampled to obtain the region between the lungs, since a very precise result is not necessary at this stage. In this case, the small concavities may be removed by the under-sampling and therefore the differences between β_{FDil1} and β_{FDil2} are notably reduced.

Finally, we define: $\beta_{btw}(A_1, A_2) = \beta_{FDil2}(A_1, A_2)$. The interest of the selected fuzzy definitions is that the between region extends smoothly outside the convex hull of the union of both objects which is a required feature for our application (see Fig. 1).

3. Using "Between" to Segment the Heart

The main feature of our approach is to include the anatomical knowledge "the heart is between the lungs" in the segmentation process of the heart in CT images. This knowledge is modeled by the spatial relation "between" as explained in Sec. 2.

As detailed in our previous work,[8] we proceed in two steps:

(1) we select the region of interest (ROI) by combining the spatial relation "between" and the distance to the lungs;
(2) we introduce the spatial relation "between" in the evolution scheme of a deformable model to find the boundaries of the heart.

In our approach, we lean on the segmentation of the lungs, which relies on previous work.[12] An example of the segmentation of the lungs is illustrated in Fig. 1.

3.1. *Definition of the region of interest*

First, we want to find the region of interest where the heart is contained. The heart is in the space between the lungs, more precisely, in the widest part of this region, where the lungs are the farthest from each other. For this reason, we propose to combine the spatial relation "between" and the distance to the lungs in order to find the ROI.

In 2D, as explained by Gregson,[3] the maximum of the distance function to the lungs (on a previously selected slice containing the heart) is a good candidate to be the center of a disk containing this organ (the radius of this disk being 110% of the value of the distance at the center point).

We extend this idea to 3D and improve it in order to avoid failure cases by combining the distance to the lungs with the spatial relation "between". This distance function is computed using a chamfer algorithm.[13] However, the maximum of the distance to the lungs is not necessarily contained inside the heart.

To solve this problem, we combine the distance with the spatial relation "between". The goal is to find a robust candidate to be the center of a sphere that will contain the whole heart. Obviously this point (as it is inside the heart) will be in the region between the lungs with a high value of the membership function β_{btw} (see Fig. 3(a)), and it should be one of the points with a maximum distance to both lungs. The normalized distance function can be interpreted as a fuzzy set which represents the region "far from the lungs". Its membership function β_{ffl} is shown in Fig. 3(b).

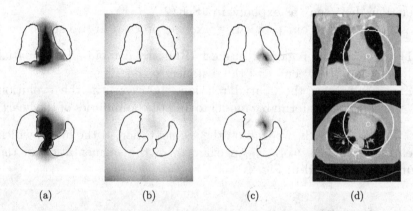

(a)   (b)   (c)   (d)

Fig. 3.   (a) The spatial relation "between" β_{btw} calculated with Eq. (2). (b) The distance map to the lungs β_{ffl} and (c) the conjunctive fusion of both β_R. (d) Image shows the obtained ROI of the heart and the initial contour of the deformable model superimposed on the original image. Coronal views are in the top row and axial views in the bottom one.

Thus, the algorithm to find the center of the heart has two different steps:

(1) *Combination of anatomical knowledge.* Let us denote by β_R the fusion of β_{btw} and β_{ffl}:

$$\beta_R(x) = \beta_{btw}(x) \cdot \beta_{ffl}(x). \tag{5}$$

This is the combination of the distance to the lungs and the "between" function defined by Eq. (2). This combination is done with a conjunctive fusion with the t-norm "product", which means that the points with higher values will fulfill both spatial constraints. The result of this combination is shown in Fig. 3(c).

(2) *Calculation of the sphere-ROI.* The center of the sphere is defined as the point having the maximum value in the previous result. The radius is simply defined as 110% of the value of the distance at this point.

This stage provides a restricted ROI for the heart (not too many surrounding structures included) and it is robust as it uses two stable characteristics of the center of the heart. The resulting ROI is used to constrain a deformable model to remain inside this region and to define the initialization for the deformable model as a small sphere centered in this ROI (see Fig. 3(d)).

3.2. *Segmentation using a deformable model*

Once we have selected the region of interest and the initialization, we use a deformable model to segment precisely the heart. Deformable models were introduced by Kass *et al.*[14] and are often used for segmentation in image processing. They consist in defining an initial surface (in 3D) that evolves under the effect of some forces towards a final state that should correspond to the object we want to segment. The evolution of the deformable surface $\mathbf{X}$ can be described using a dynamic force formulation and written as follows:

$$\gamma \frac{\partial \mathbf{X}}{\partial t} = \mathbf{F}_{int}(\mathbf{X}) + \mathbf{F}_{ext}(\mathbf{X}), \tag{6}$$

where $\mathbf{F}_{int}$ is the *internal* force related to the physical properties or constraints of the model that specifies the regularity of the surface,[14] and $\mathbf{F}_{ext}$ is the *external* force that drives the surface towards the desired features in the image (in general image edges) and sometimes includes forces interactively introduced by the user. The solution is the steady state of the previous equation.

The external force can be defined with the Gradient Vector Flow (GVF)[15] as also used in previous work.[12,16,17] The GVF defines a vector field towards the previously calculated contours of the image (the edge map). As proposed in our previous work[18] the external force can also include spatial relations in order to constraint the segmented object to stay in a region where given spatial relations are satisfied.

We introduce the spatial relation "between" combined with "far from the lungs" in the external force $\mathbf{F}_{ext}$ (Eq. (6)). Thus, this force describes both edge information (GVF) and structural constraints:

$$\mathbf{F}_{ext} = \lambda \, \mathbf{F}_{gvf} + (1 - \lambda) \, \mathbf{F}_R, \tag{7}$$

where $\mathbf{F}_{gvf}$ is a classical data term that drives the model towards the edges,[15] $\mathbf{F}_R$ is a force associated to the spatial relations and λ is a weighting coefficient. The force $\mathbf{F}_R$ must constrain the model to evolve towards the regions with high values of $\beta'_R = 1 - \beta_R$, i.e. regions closer to the lungs and "less between" them than the center. When the relation β'_R is completely satisfied (not between and inside the lungs), the model should only be driven by edge information ($\mathbf{F}_{gvf}$) and we should have $\mathbf{F}_R = 0$ if $\beta'_R = 1$. This illustrates an important advantage of using fuzzy spatial relations to guide the model, as we can define a vector field towards the regions where the relations are more satisfied. Several methods for external forces that fulfill these properties are described in our previous work.[18] We have chosen the one using a gradient diffusion technique because of the smoothness and the wide attraction range of the vector field calculated this way. This is detailed in our previous work.[8]

Finally, we add a pressure term to Eq. (7) in order to reinforce the effect of spatial relations and to improve convergence:

$$\mathbf{F}_{ext} = \lambda \, \mathbf{F}_{gvf} + (1 - \lambda) \, \mathbf{F}_R + \mathbf{F}_p, \tag{8}$$

where $\mathbf{F}_p$ represents a pressure force,[19] normal to the surface and of module $w_p(x)$ defined as:

$$w_p(x) = k \, \beta_R, \tag{9}$$

where k is a constant. This means that the pressure force is stronger at the points between the lungs which are the farthest from them (where β_R takes higher values), and it decreases when getting closer to them (where β_R takes lower values because the chosen spatial relations are less fulfilled).

4. Results and Discussion

We have applied our algorithm on 10 different cases of CT images coded on 8 bits, with sizes $512 \times 512 \times Z$ voxels with Z varying from 63 to 122 and resolutions typically around $2\,\text{mm} \times 2\,\text{mm} \times dz\,\text{mm}$ for the three directions of the space (X, Y and Z respectively), with dz varying from 4.5 to 7.5 mm.

In our experiments, we have used the following parameters:

- The initial mesh for the deformable model is a sphere with a small enough radius (10 mm) to ensure that the starting surface is completely contained inside the contours of the heart.
- The value of λ in Eq. (8) is 0.7, which gives a more important weight to the GVF force. Obviously, the weight of $\mathbf{F}_{gvf}$ should be more important because it guides the deformable model precisely towards the contours, whereas $\mathbf{F}_R$ represents a more general evolution. However, the spatial relation force remains necessary for the evolution of the deformable model.
- The constant k for the pressure force weight in Eq. (9) is $k = 0.05$. This constant balances the pressure force in order to prevent the deformable model from inflating too much or too little.
- The number of iterations for the evolution of the deformable model (simplex mesh) is 10000, which is sufficient for convergence of the model. The internal force coefficients are $\alpha = 0.2$ and $\beta = 0.1$ which provide a good trade-off between tension and rigidity.

These parameters were set experimentally. The algorithm has been applied to the 10 different cases obtaining good results. The comparison with manual segmentations provides mean distances varying from 3.9 to 9.3 mm, which is perfectly acceptable with voxel resolutions in Z between 4.5 and 7.5 mm. As explained and illustrated in our previous work,[8] all the terms in Eq. (8) are necessary to obtain correct results, and the addition of the spatial relations significantly improves the accuracy and the robustness of the heart segmentation algorithm. Some results for different patients are illustrated in Fig. 4.

Figure 5 shows some results of the segmentation of the heart with different definitions of the spatial relation "the heart is between

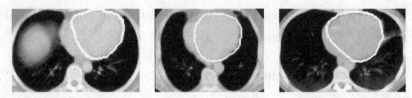

Fig. 4.   Axial views of some results of the automatic segmentation of the heart using our method for three other patients.

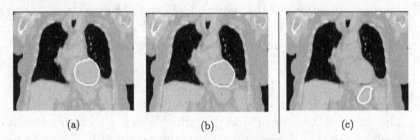

(a)   (b)   (c)

Fig. 5.   Coronal views of some results of heart segmentation with different definitions of the spatial relation "between": (a) using β_{FDil1} and (b) using β_{FDil2}. A similar result is obtained with β_{FVisib}. (c) Result of heart segmentation using β_{FVisib}, when the acceptable distance to π is not tuned correctly.

the lungs". The results obtained using any of the fuzzy definitions β_{FDil1}, β_{FDil2} or β_{FVisib} are very satisfactory and very similar in all cases.

For the use of β_{FVisib}, however, the acceptable distance to π (i.e. the shape of the function f in Eq. (4)) has to be tuned appropriately in order to obtain a correct result. Otherwise, incorrect results of heart segmentation can be obtained as illustrated in Fig. 5(c). This value could vary for different anatomies. The definitions of "between" that use fuzzy dilations do not have this limitation as the shape of the structuring element is computed from the angle histogram, which is adapted automatically to each particular case.

5.   Conclusion and Future Work

We propose an approach that uses fuzzy structural knowledge coming from the spatial relations "between the lungs" and "far from the lungs" to segment the heart in CT images in a robust way. First, spatial relations are used to define the region of interest of the heart and then we derive, from the fuzzy sets representing the spatial relations, a new external force that is introduced in the evolution scheme of a deformable model. In this paper, several definitions of the spatial relation "between" are presented. The discussion of the results shows that a fuzzy dilation definition with removes concavities is best adapted to our problem. The proposed method substantially improves the segmentation of the heart compared to classical approaches which use only a pressure force and GVF, and it avoids the surrounding structures to be included in the final segmentation of the heart. The results still have to be validated on larger databases with medical experts. However, preliminary quantitative results based on the comparison with manual segmentations performed by an expert show a strong agreement between the manual segmentations and the ones obtained by our approach. This confirms the potential of the proposed method.

Future work will aim at applying our algorithm to other imaging modalities such as positron emission tomography (PET) images.

Further applications include the use of the segmentation of the heart in registration algorithms based on structures[20] and, subsequently, in radiotherapy planning procedures.

Acknowledgments

The authors would like to thank Liège, Lille, Louisville and Val de Grâce Hospitals for the images and the members of Segami Corporation for their contribution to this project. This work was partially supported by the French Ministry of Research, by the CAPES (BEX3402/04-5) and by a "ParisTech/Région Ile-de-France" Fellowship.

References

1. H. C. van Assen, M. G. Danilouchkine, A. F. Frangi, S. Ordás, J. J. M. Westenberg, J. H. C. Reiber and B. P. F. Lelieveldt, SPASM: A 3D-ASM for segmentation of sparse and arbitrarily oriented cardiac MRI data. *Medical Image Analysis*, **10**(2), 286–303 (2006).
2. J. S. Suri, Computer vision, pattern recognition and image processing in left ventricle segmentation: The last 50 years. *Pattern Analysis & Applications*, **3**(3), 209–242 (2000).
3. P. H. Gregson, Automatic segmentation of the heart in 3D MR images. *Canadian Conference on Electrical and Computer Engineering*, **2**, 584–587 (1994).

4. B. P. F. Lelieveldt, R. J. van der Geest, M. R. Rezaee, J. G. Bosch and J. H. C. Reiber, Anatomical model matching with fuzzy implicit surfaces for segmentation of thoracic volume scans. *IEEE Transactions on Medical Imaging*, **18**(3), 218–230 (1999).
5. M.-P. Jolly, Automatic segmentation of the left ventricle in cardiac MR and CT images. *International Journal of Computer Vision*, **70**(2), 151–163 (2006).
6. G. Funka-Lea, Y. Boykov, C. Florin, M.-P. Jolly, R. Moreau-Gobard, R. Ramaraj and D. Rinck, Automatic heart isolation for CT coronary visualization using graph-cuts. *IEEE International Symposium on Biomedical Imaging (ISBI)*, Arlington, Virginia, USA, pp. 614–617 (2006).
7. O. Ecabert, J. Peters, M. J. Walker, J. von Berg, C. Lorenz, M. Vembar, M. E. Olszewski and J. Weese, Automatic whole heart segmentation in CT images: Method and validation. (eds.) J. Pluim and J. Reinhardt, *SPIE Medical Imaging*, San Diego, California, USA **6512** (2007).
8. A. Moreno, C. M. Takemura, O. Colliot, O. Camara and I. Bloch, Heart segmentation in medical images using the fuzzy spatial relation "Between". *Information Processing and Management of Uncertainty in Knowledge-Based Systems (IPMU)*, Paris, France, pp. 2052–2059 (2006).
9. I. Bloch, O. Colliot and R. M. Cesar, On the ternary spatial relation "Between". *IEEE Transactions on Systems, Man, and Cybernetics SMC-B*, **36**(2), 312–327 (2006).
10. I. Bloch and H. Maître, Fuzzy mathematical morphologies: A comparative study. *Pattern Recognition*, **28**(9), 1341–1387 (1995).
11. K. Miyajima and A. Ralescu, Spatial organization in 2D segmented images: Representation and recognition of primitive spatial relations. *Fuzzy Sets and Systems*, **65**(2/3), 225–236 (1994).
12. O. Camara, O. Colliot and I. Bloch, Computational modeling of thoracic and abdominal anatomy using spatial relationships for image segmentation. *Real-Time Imaging*, **10**(4), 263–273 (2004).
13. G. Borgefors, Distance transformations in digital images. *Computer Vision, Graphics, and Image Processing (CVGIP)*, **34**(3), 344–371 (1986).
14. M. Kass, A. Witkin and D. Terzopoulos, Snakes: Active contour models. *International Journal of Computer Vision*, **1**(4), 321–331 (1987).
15. C. Xu and J. L. Prince, Gradient vector flow: A new external force for snakes. *IEEE Computer Society Conference on Computer Vision and Pattern Recognition*, Los Alamitos, San Juan, Puerto Rico, pp. 66–71 (1997).
16. O. Colliot, O. Camara, R. Dewynter and I. Bloch, Description of brain internal structures by means of spatial relations for MR image segmentation. *SPIE Medical Imaging*, San Diego, California, USA **5370**, pp. 444–455 (2004).
17. O. Colliot, O. Camara and I. Bloch, Integration of fuzzy spatial relations in deformable models — Application to brain MRI segmentation. *Pattern Recognition*, **39**(8), 1401–1414 (2006).
18. O. Colliot, O. Camara and I. Bloch, Integration of fuzzy structural information in deformable models. *Information Processing and Management of Uncertainty in Knowledge-Based Systems (IPMU)*, Perugia, Italy **2**, pp. 1533–1540 (2004).

19. L. D. Cohen, On active contour models and balloons. *Computer Vision, Graphics, and Image Processing: Image Understanding (CVGIP:IU)*, **53**(2), 211–218 (1991).
20. O. Camara, G. Delso, O. Colliot, A. Moreno-Ingelmo and I. Bloch, Explicit incorporation of prior anatomical information into a nonrigid registration of thoracic and abdominal CT and 18-FDG whole-body emision PET images. *IEEE Transactions on Medical Imaging*, **26**(2), 164–178 (2007).

Neurofuzzy Network with On-Line Learning in Fault Detection of Dynamic Systems

Walmir Caminhas* and Fernando Gomide[†]

*Department of Electrical Engineering
Federal University of Minas Gerais
Belo Horizonte, MG, Brazil
caminhas@eee.ufmg.br
†Department of Computer Engineering and Automation
State University of Campinas
Campinas, SP, Brazil
gomide@dca.fee.unicamp.br

Abstract

This study introduces an approach for fault detection and diagnosis of dynamic systems based on a neurofuzzy network structure with on-line learning. Experiments with a direct current driving system suggest that, due its adaptive and simple network structure, the approach is reliable, robust, fast, and requires low computational resources. These are essential ingredients of fault detection and diagnosis systems, especially for real-time applications.

1. Introduction

Fault detection and diagnosis is a major and growing industry concern because it provides safer plants and operation environments, reducing maintenance and operation costs. During the last decade, dynamic systems have received an increasing attention and brought considerable challenges to researchers and practitioners of the field.[1]

There are two major approaches to detect faults in dynamic systems: hardware and software (analytic) redundancy. The focus of this paper is on the second approach, namely, software (analytic) redundancy. Analytic redundancy needs either a quantitative or a qualitative, knowledge-based model of the plant. In practice, qualitative and qualitative models are combined to assemble a workable methodology.[1] Examples of fault detection and diagnosis approaches that use quantitative models include those based on Luenberger state observers, Kalman filters,[2,3] robust observers[4,5] parameter estimation methods,[6,7] neural networks and learning.[8,9] Qualitative model-based approaches use classic logic[10] or fuzzy logic.[11]

In this paper we introduce a new approach based on an adaptive, on-line learning neural fuzzy network approach to model the plant and generate residues for fault detection, and a neural fuzzy pattern classifier for fault diagnosis. A direct current driving system platform is used to test and validate the adaptive neurofuzzy structure. Experimental results show that the approach is reliable and computationally efficient, essential characteristics for successful fault detection and diagnosis in industrial real-time applications.

2. Fault Detection and Diagnosis

Figure 1 overviews the fault detection and diagnosis approach suggested in this work. The main idea is to consider fault detection and diagnosis as a pattern classification problem. The classifier uses

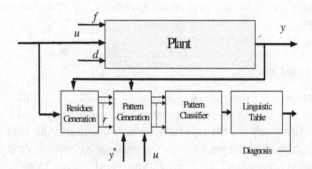

Fig. 1. Fault detection and diagnosis system.

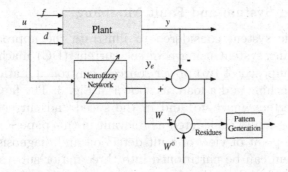

Fig. 2.   Residues generation.

plant inputs u, plant output y, reference output y^*, and residues r generated by the neurofuzzy plant model.

The residues are generated using parameters estimated by the neurofuzzy network model as shown in Fig. 2. The topology of the network is the same as the one suggested in Ref. 12. The parameters of the neurofuzzy model are the synaptic weights. Fault detection and diagnosis uses an on-line learning procedure whose basis has been introduced in Ref. 14. Before the network is put to operate on-line, an off-line learning phase is executed to determine a set of weights W_0, using plant input and output data under normal operation. Next the network starts to operate learning on-line. Whenever a fault occurs new weights W are computed and the difference between W and W_0 is used to generate the residues and the corresponding fault patterns. The fault patterns are inputs for the pattern classifier.

The pattern classifier uses a pattern recognition mechanism composed of a neural fuzzy network that, differently from the one used to model the plant, uses fuzzy set-based models of neurons modeled via triangular norms.[13,15] The pattern classifier outputs are numbers that encode the type of fault. These numbers are converted into linguistic expressions in the form *if* the pattern is i *then* the faulty device is j. These expressions are easily captured from the neural fuzzy network classifier structure after learning the relevant types of faults. See Ref. 13 for a detailed description of the classifier structure and its learning algorithm. Relevant faults, denoted by f in Fig. 1, are used to train the pattern classifier to recognize the corresponding residues patterns they generate.

3. Driving System and Fault Modeling

The dynamic system considered to illustrate the approach is an electric driving system using a direct current (DC) machine. This system is composed of two power sources, controlled static converters, a DC machine and a load, as shown in Fig. 3. The faults occurs in the converters, machine, and in the speed and current sensors. These are the faults considered as relevant in this paper.

From the point of view of fault detection and diagnosis, the DC driving system can be partitioned into three major subsystems: the actuators (field and armature converters), the plant (machine and load) and instruments (speed and current sensors). The relevant faults are summarized in Table 1. These faults are simulated to generate learning data using the dynamic model described by the equations below, assuming that $x_1 = i_a, x_2 = i_{fd}$ and $x_3 = \omega_r$ are the measured variables:

$$
\begin{bmatrix} \dot{x}_1 \\ \dot{x}_2 \\ \dot{x}_3 \end{bmatrix} = \begin{bmatrix} -k_{aa}\dfrac{r_a}{L_a} & -k_{aa}\dfrac{L_{afd}}{L_a} & 0 \\ 0 & -k_{afd}\dfrac{r_{fd}}{L_{fd}} & 0 \\ \dfrac{L_{afd}}{J_m}x_2 & 0 & -\dfrac{B_m}{J_m} \end{bmatrix} \begin{bmatrix} x_1 \\ x_2 \\ x_3 \end{bmatrix}
$$

$$
+ \begin{bmatrix} \dfrac{1}{L_a} & 0 \\ 0 & \dfrac{1}{L_{fd}} \\ 0 & 0 \end{bmatrix} \begin{bmatrix} k_{aa}\bar{k}_{cca}v_a \\ k_{afd}\bar{k}_{ccfd}v_{fd} \end{bmatrix} + \begin{bmatrix} 0 \\ 0 \\ -1 \end{bmatrix} \cdot [T_L],
$$

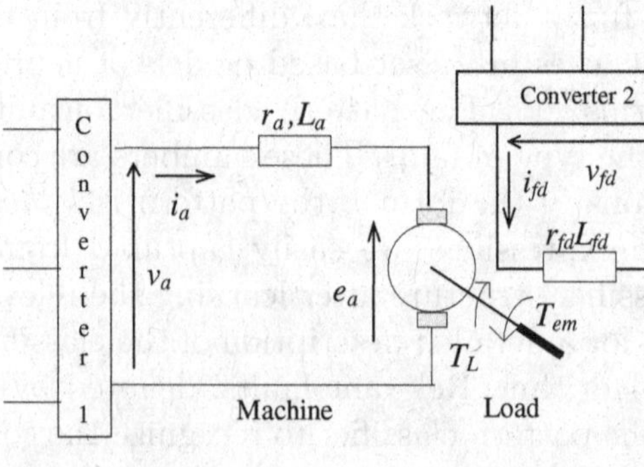

Fig. 3.   DC driving system.

Table 1.   Fault types and the corresponding parameters.

Fault type	Fault parameter	Parameter values
Armature coil open	k_{aa}	$\{0, 1\}$
Field coil open	k_{afd}	$\{0, 1\}$
Armature converter short circuit	k_{cca}	$\{0, 1\}$
Field converter short circuit	k_{ccfd}	$\{0, 1\}$
Armature current sensor fault	$k_{i_a}^{f}$	$\{0, 1\}$
Field current sensor fault	$k_{i_a}^{f}$	$\{0, 1\}$
Speed sensor fault	$k_{i_a}^{f}$	$\{0, 1\}$

$$\begin{bmatrix} y_1(k) \\ y_2(k) \\ y_2(k) \end{bmatrix} = \begin{bmatrix} \bar{k}_{i_a}^{f} & 0 & 0 \\ 0 & \bar{k}_{i_{fd}}^{f} & 0 \\ 0 & 0 & \bar{k}_{\omega_r}^{f} \end{bmatrix} \cdot \begin{bmatrix} x_1 \\ x_2 \\ x_3 \end{bmatrix}$$

where $\bar{k}_i = 1 - k_i$ and $T_L = C_0 + C_1\omega_r + C_2\omega_r^2$

In the model above, v_a is the armature voltage source, v_{fd} is the field voltage source, i_a the armature current, i_{fd} the field current, ω_r the mechanical speed (rad/s), r_a the armature resistance, r_{fd} the field resistance, L_a the armature inductance, L_{fd} the field inductance, L_{afd} the armature/field mutual inductance, T_L the load torque, B_m the dumping coefficient, and J_m the motor/load inertia. The values of the parameters k_{aa}, k_{afd}, k_{cca}, k_{ccfd}, $k_{i_a}^{f}$, $k_{i_a}^{f}$, $k_{i_a}^{f}$ are set to unity when a fault occur and zero under normal operating conditions (see Table 1).

4.   Neurofuzzy Network

The topology of the neurofuzzy network (NFN) is depicted in Fig. 4. Each synapse processes its inputs through fuzzy inference and defuzzification whose effect corresponds to a nonlinear function $f_i(x_i)$. The result is aggregated adding their respective outputs.

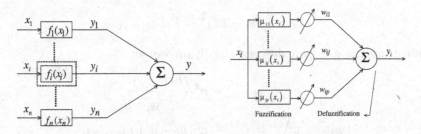

Fig. 4.   Topology of the neurofuzzy network.

This means that if a squared error criterion is used to guide learning, the resulting error function will be a quadratic and convex function with respect to the neurofuzzy network weights w_{ij}. This is highly desirable because, since learning is formulated as an optimization problem, local optima are also global. The output of the NFN is computed as follows:

$$y = \sum_{i=1}^{n} y_i(x_i) = \sum_{i=1}^{n} f_i(x_i).$$

Note that the values of y_i are determined similarly as in a rule-based fuzzy system.[15] In particular, considering complementary triangular membership functions to partition the input variables universes, we note that, for any input, only two membership function values are not null. This means that for each value of input x_i, at most two neighbors, among p membership functions, denoted by k_i and $k_i + 1$, are activated. Thus, using the max-min inference procedure and center of gravity defuzzification,[15] we find that the values of $f_i(x_i)$ are:

$$f_i(x_i) = \frac{\sum_{j=1}^{p} \mu_{ij}(x_i)\, w_{ij}}{\sum_{j=1}^{p} \mu_{ij}(x_i)} = \frac{\mu_{ik_i}(x_i)\, w_{ik_i} + \mu_{ik_i+1}(x_i)\, w_{ik_i+1}}{\mu_{ik_i}(x_i) + \mu_{ik_i+1}(x_i)}.$$

Since the membership functions are complementary, only two neighbors are active for any input. Thus the sum of the membership degrees is one and the equation above becomes

$$f_i(x_i) = \mu_{ik_i}(x_i)\, w_{ik_i} + \mu_{ik_i+1}(x_i)\, w_{ik_i+1}.$$

The learning procedure updates the neurofuzzy network weights to minimize a squared error function. In other words, for each pair of training data (y_t, y_t^d), where y_t and y_t^d are the tth network and actual system output, respectively, the network weights w_{ij} are changed until E_t achieves its minimum. A way to do that is to use a gradient descent algorithm. Therefore we have

$$E_t = \frac{1}{2}\left(y_t - y_t^d\right)^2 = E_t(w_{ij}),$$

and using the gradient descent algorithm we get:

$$w_{ik_i}^{t+1} = w_{ik_i}^t - \alpha^t \frac{\partial E_t(w_{ik_i}^t)}{\partial w_{ik_i}^t}$$

that is, $w_{ik_i}^{t+1} = w_{ik_i}^t - \alpha^t\left(y_t - y_t^d\right)\mu_{ik_i}(x_{ti}).$

In general, the step size α^t, the learning rate, is found either experimentally or using direct (quadratic approximation) or indirect (golden section, Fibonacci, etc.) unidirectional search procedures. However, since the error function is quadratic and convex, we can easily compute, as detailed in the appendix, the optimal step size. Thus, for each training data pair we find the optimal value of the error function in one step. The value of the optimal step size is (see Appendix)

$$\alpha^t = 1 \left/ \left(\sum_{i=1}^{n} \mu_{ik_i}(x_{ti})^2 + \mu_{ik_i+1}(x_{ti})^2 \right) \right. .$$

5. Identification of DC Driver System

The first step to construct the fault detection and diagnosis system is to get the neurofuzzy model of the plant. This is needed to obtain the network weights W_0 that correspond to normal plant operation. In the case of the DC driver system, modeling proceeds as follows. Model inputs and outputs are $[\hat{i}_a(k-1)\ \hat{i}_{fd}(k-1)$ $\hat{w}_{k-1}(k-1)\ v_a(k)\ v_{fd}]$, equivalently, $[\hat{y}_1(k-1)\ \hat{y}_2(k-1)\ \hat{y}_3(k-1)$ $u_1(k)\ u_2(k)]$, and $[\hat{y}_1(k)\ \hat{y}_2(k)\ \hat{y}_3(k)]$, respectively. Figures 5 and 6 depict the estimated and actual values of y_1 (armature current) as well as the value of weight w_{121} of the NFN at the first and 10th off-line training cycle, respectively. We note that, despite the network model approximate the plant dynamics with null error, the

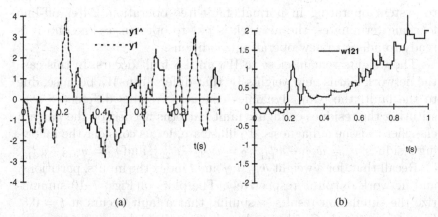

(a)   (b)

Fig. 5. Estimated and actual output y_1 (a) and weight w_{121} of the NFN (b) after the first training cycle.

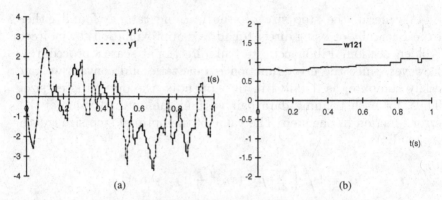

Fig. 6.   Estimated and actual output y_1 (a) and weight w_{121} of the NFN (b) after the 10th training cycle.

weights still present significant variations. After a few cycles of learning iterations, weights variations decrease until the values remain approximately constant. The neurofuzzy network has each of its input granulated with three membership functions. During learning, the system inputs u_1 e u_2 were generated randomly.

6.   Fault Detection and Diagnosis

As shown in Fig. 2, the fault detection and diagnosis system uses the variations in the weights of the NFN to generate the residues. Weights W^0 of the NFN, as discussed before, are determined during the off-line training phase. In this phase, training data correspond to system operating in normal, fault-free operation. After off-line learning terminates, the network is put to operate on-line and it is ready to adapt to new operating conditions.

The weights remain close to W_0 until a fault occurs. In this case the network learns new weights W that differs from W_0 because, due to the fault, the plant dynamics changes. Weights differences constituting the residues configure fault patterns needed by the pattern classifier to issue a diagnosis. To illustrate, let us consider the following residues: $r_1 = w_{121} - w_{121}^0$, $r_2 = w_{222} - w_{222}^0$, and $r_3 = w_{313} - w_{313}^0$.

Recall that, for a weight w_{ijl}, i, j and l index the inputs, partitions, and network outputs, respectively. The plots of Figs. 7–10 summarize the simulation results, assuming that a fault occurs at $t = 0.5$. Figure 7 shows the residues values for a fault in the speed sensor. In this case, speed information values becomes zero after $t = 0.5$ and

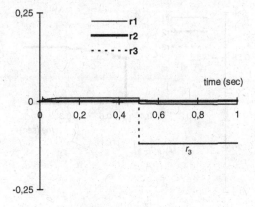

Fig. 7.   Residues for speed sensor fault.

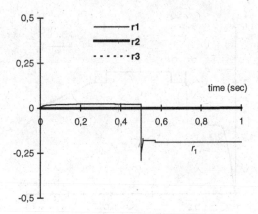

Fig. 8.   Residues of armature source fault.

new neurofuzzy network weights are identified, especially those that correspond to output y_3, the system speed. When the fault is in the armature power source, we note significant variations in the weights that correspond to outputs y_1, as shown in Fig. 8. For a short-circuit fault in field power source, the weight that varies most correspond to field current y_2, Fig. 9. In this case we also note in Fig. 10 that the load conjugate curve is robust to load disturbances. This is an interesting characteristic of the neurofuzzy model acquired through learning. During off-line learning random load disturbances values are input to excite system dynamics under disturbances that do not correspond to faults.

Clearly, residues information provides an effective way for fault detection. Diagnosis, however, requires further information to classify

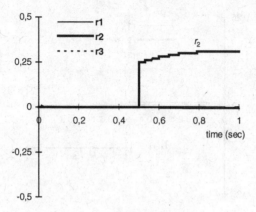

Fig. 9. Residues short-circuit fault in the field power source.

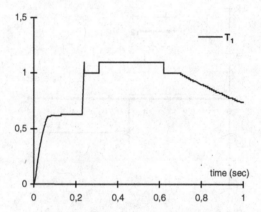

Fig. 10. Load conjugate curve during short-circuit in the field power source.

the faults, currents and speed values in the DC driving system case. That is, the pattern classifier needs r_1, r_2, r_3, x_1, x_1, and x_1 as inputs. Since system designer has found seven relevant faults, the classifier has eight outputs, to include plant operating under normal conditions. We refer the reader to Ref. 13 for details of the neural fuzzy classifier adopted in this paper, but in principle different forms of pattern recognition schemes can be used.

To fully evaluate the performance of the approach proposed in this paper, a set of two thousand simulations have been performed during a time horizon of 1 sec with 2 msec sampling period. The fault index has been randomly generated for each simulation. The time instant at which fault occurs was also randomly generated. Random loads disturbances with a maximum of 50% of the system nominal value were taken into account. Random measurement noise within 2% of the nominal variable value has been added. Under these conditions, the fault detection and diagnosis system performed satisfactorily once all faults have been successfully detected and diagnosed within 8 msec, that is, within four sampling periods, at most.

7. Conclusion

This paper has introduced a fault detection and diagnosis system for dynamic systems that uses a neurofuzzy network with an effective and fast on-line learning algorithm. To convey the main ideas and an application example, a DC driver system has been presented and discussed. The system exploits the idea of using the neurofuzzy network to model the plant under normal operating conditions and use the network weights variation as a residue generation mechanism. The residues values are used to detect faults and to generate its associated patterns for diagnosis purposes. The main advantage of the system proposed herein when compared with classic approaches[6] is its simplicity. It is easy to design and to develop, once most of the design effort is managed via learning techniques. In addition, the number of operations performed by the NFN is low, the on-line learning algorithm proceeds with optimal step-sizes and is fast. Therefore, any structural plant variation that occurs due to faults is detected almost instantaneously. This is essential for real-time, industrial and safety-critical systems.

Acknowledgment

The second author is grateful to CNPq, the Brazilian National Research Council, for its support via grant 304857/2006-8, and to the State University of Campinas, Unicamp, for grant PRP-FAEPEX.

References

1. P. Frank and R. Seliger, Fault detection and isolation in automatic process. *Control and Dynamic Systems*, **49**, 241–287 (1991).
2. R. Clark, A simplified instruments failure detection scheme. *IEEE Trans. Aerospace Electron. Syst.*, **14**, 558–563 (1978).
3. P. Frank and L. Keller, Sensitivity discriminating observer design for instrument failure detection. *IEEE Trans. Aerospace Electron. Syst.*, **AES-16**, 460–467 (1980).

4. W. Ge and C. Fang, Detection of faulty components via robust observation. *Int. J. Control*, **47**, 581–599 (1988).
5. P. Frank and J. Wünnenberg, Robust fault diagnosis using unknown input observer schemes, *Fault Diagnosis in Dynamic Systems, Theory and Applications*, R. Patton, P. Frank and R. Clark (eds.), 47–98 (1989).
6. R. Iserman, Process fault detection based on modeling and estimation methods — A survey. *Automatica*, **20**, 387–404 (1984).
7. H. Camargo, *Detecção e Isolação de Falhas Utilizando Estimação de Parâmetros de Modelos Contínuos e Limites de Confiança Adaptativos, Aplicação a uma Planta Piloto.* MSc. Thesis, PPGEE/UFMG (in Portuguese) (1997).
8. M. Pistauer, Neural network design for a process fault-diagnosis module with fuzzy system. *Proceedings of the 6th International Fuzzy Systems Association World Congress, IFSA'95.* São Paulo, Brazil, **2**, 591–594 (1995).
9. M. Polycarpou and A. Vemuri, Learning methodology for failure detection and accommodation. *IEEE Control Systems*, June, 16–24 (1995).
10. R. Milne, Artificial intelligence for online diagnosis. *IEE Proceedings*, **134**(4), 238–244 (1987).
11. U. Mihaela, Diagnosis by approximate reasoning on dynamic fault trees. *Proc. 3rd IEEE International Conference on Fuzzy Systems.* Orlando, Florida, USA, pp. 2051–2056 (1994).
12. T. Yamakwa, E. Uchino and T. Miki, A neo fuzzy neuron and its applications to system identification and predictions to system behavior. *Proc. of the 2nd IZUKA.* Izuka-Japan, pp. 477–483 (1992).
13. W. Caminhas, H. Tavares, F. Gomide and W. Pedrycz, Fuzzy set based neural networks: Structure, learning and application. *Journal of Advanced Computational Intelligence*, **3**(3), 151–157 (1999).
14. W. Caminhas and F. Gomide. A fast learning algorithm for neofuzzy networks. *Proc. of the 8th IPMU, 2000.* Madrid, Spain, **1**(1), 1784–1790 (2000).
15. W. Pedrycz and F. Gomide, *An Introduction to Fuzzy Sets: Analysis and Design.* MIT Press, Cambridge, USA (1998).

Appendix

In this appendix we show that, given a pattern $X_t = (x_{ti}, x_{t2}, \ldots, x_{ti}, \ldots, x_{tn})$ and y_t^d, the corresponding value for the mapping $y = f(X)$, a closed expression for the learning rate α^t can be found such that the error is null at a step. Thus, given W^t, the aim is to obtain α^t such that the error is null, that is:

$$E_t = \frac{1}{2}(y_t - y_t^d)^2 = \frac{1}{2}(e_t)^2 = 0$$

$$e_t = \left(\left(\sum_{i=1}^n w_{ik_i}^t \mu_{k_i}(x_i) + w_{ik_i}^t \mu_{k_i+1}(x_{ti}) \right) - y_t^d \right), \tag{A1}$$

for

$$w_{ik_i}^{t+1} = w_{ik_i}^t - \alpha^t e_t \mu_{ik_i}(x_{ti}) \text{ and } w_{ik_i+1}^{t+1} = w_{ik_i+1}^t - \alpha^t e_t \mu_{ik_i+1}(x_{ti}).$$
(A2)

(A1) holds if $\sum_{i=1}^{n} w_{ik_i}^t \mu_{k_i}(x_{ti}) + w_{ik_i+1}^t \mu_{k_i+1}(x_{ti}) = y_t^d$.

Multiplying both sides of (A2) by $\mu_{ik_i}(x_i)$ and $\mu_{ik_i+1}(x_i)$ we get:

$$w_{ik_i}^{t+1}\mu_{ik_i}(x_{ti}) = w_{ik_i}^t \mu_{ik_i}(x_{ti}) - \alpha^t e_t [\mu_{ik_i}(x_{ti})]^2$$
$$w_{ik_i+1}^{t+1}\mu_{ik_i+1}(x_{ti}) = w_{ik_i+1}^t \mu_{ik_i+1}(x_{ti}) - \alpha^t e_t [\mu_{ik_i+1}(x_{ti})]^2$$
(A3)

Adding the $2n$ expressions above gives:

$$\sum_{i=1}^{n} [w_{ki_i}^{t+1} \mu_{ik_i}(x_{ti}) + w_{ki_i+1}^{t+1} \mu_{ik_i+1}(x_{ti})]$$

$$= \sum_{i=1}^{n} [w_{ki_i}^t \mu_{ik_i}(x_{ti}) + w_{ki_i+1}^t \mu_{ik_i+1}(x_{ti})]$$

$$- \alpha^t e_t \left[\sum_{i=1}^{n} \mu_{ik_i}(x_{ti})^2 + \mu_{ik_i+1}(x_{ti})^2 \right].$$
(A4)

From (A4) we note that the left side is y_t^d. Therefore

$$\alpha^t e_t \left[\sum_{i=1}^{n} \mu_{ik_i}(x_{ti})^2 + \mu_{ik_i+1}(x_{ti})^2 \right] = e_t \quad \text{or}$$

$$\alpha^t = \frac{1}{\sum_{i=1}^{n} \mu_{ik_i}(x_{ti})^2 + \mu_{ik_i+1}(x_{ti})^2}.$$

A New Hybrid Fusion Method for Diagnostic Systems

A. Zemirline, L. Lecornu and B. Solaiman

ITI Department, ENST Bretagne
29285 Brest, France

Abstract

In this study, we present a new fusion method based on fuzzy set theory. This method consists of combining several data and knowledge bases of diagnostic systems. It is characterized by a hybrid fusion, which combines base fusion of data and knowledge of the Case-Based Reasoning diagnostic systems. The fusion method relies on a distortion measure of various diagnostic systems (of case and knowledge bases). This distortion measure is integrated into the diagnostic system in order to improve its performance. It is defined by confidence degrees associated to each parameter that contitutes the case and knowledge bases of diagnostic systems. The confidence degrees are then integrated into the diagnostic system procedure.

1. Introduction

Nowadays, several institutions and organizations combine homogeneous data coming from different systems and/or produced at different instants. This situation is faced, in particular, by medical institutions, where a new set of data is to be stored regularly which is used, on the one hand, to extract new information and, on the other hand, to update the older versions of data.

There are three main types of fusion methods which can be distinguished according to the conceptual level of information[1]: data fusion, decision fusion and model fusion.

389

- Data fusion is a fusion process operated on the first conceptual level of information. It consists of combining raw data resulting from several sources or various primitive levels extracted from only one source in order to obtain less noisy data.

- Decision fusion is the solution of problem modeling applied to a specific data set. Several data sources and several types of processing can respectively provide a decision for the same problem. Thus, when several sensors observe the same scene or when several independent approaches make it possible to provide a solution then, the decision fusion consists of a comparison of solutions suggested by various systems in order to choose only the most realistic one or to combine these decisions in order to make a more reliable or considered decision.

- Model fusion is a concept which combines data processing and artificial intelligence. This model characterizes and represents in a more or less complex way the knowledge that makes up the advanced systems. The model fusion either builds the new knowledge model or adopts a compromise of the precedents.

There are some fusion procedures that combine data bases of systems[2] and there are others which combine decisions of systems.[3] However, no fusion procedure exists that combines the knowledge bases and/or data bases of several systems in order to obtain a more powerful system.

In this work, we have several diagnostic systems depending on case-based reasoning and we want to combine them to obtain a better diagnostic system. The objectives of our fusion method are not limited to enriching the diagnostic system case base by increasing the number of cases, rather it also allows the diagnostic system to have more accurate and relevant results for the recognition of the new cases. This is possible by taking into account the distortion measure of various diagnostic systems (of case and knowledge bases).

The fusion type that we propose in this article is the hybrid fusion that combines two fusion types: data fusion and knowledge fusion. This hybrid fusion consists of merging several case and knowledge bases of diagnostic systems to obtain only one case base and one knowledge base.

In this work, we have tackled the regularly confronted problem of integrating new medical case bases into a diagnostic system. As an example, we take a diagnostic system which applies to medical bases.

These medical bases are homogeneous and they contain descriptions of endoscopic lesions. However, each one of these bases has its own features to describe the lesions.

This article is organized in the following way: in the second section, we describe the diagnostic system to which our method of fusion is applied. In section three, we describe our fusion method. In the fourth section, we analyze the results obtained through our method. We finally conclude in the fifth section.

2. Diagnostic System

The diagnostic system depends on case-based reasoning (CBR) and is made up of two bases (Fig. 1): the internal knowledge base and the external knowledge base. Thanks to the internal knowledge, the diagnostic system predicts the classes corresponding to the new case and retrieves the most similar cases.[4] This knowledge base is deduced from the case base.

The external knowledge base contains the information describing the significance of parameters in the definition of different classes which should be recognized by the diagnostic system.

2.1. *The internal knowledge base*

This is a knowledge base designed from the case base; no data or external information at the base is introduced for the definition of this knowledge base. The diagnostic systems relies on the internal knowledge base for the classification of the cases and the measure

Fig. 1.   Diagnostic system with the internal and external knowledge bases.

of similarity of the two cases. This knowledge base is made up of membership functions for each class.

The procedure for setting up the external knowledge base comprises of 3 steps: The first step brings together the cases of the diagnostic case base according to their class, then it generates a group of cases for each class. The second measures the frequency of the parameters which constitute the cases for each group (i.e. for each class). In the last step, for each class, the membersip functions are generated. These membership functions attribute a membership degree of the specific class to a parameter.

The membership functions to a specific class are built by a histogram of the normalized frequencies method:[5]

- $B = \{X_1, \ldots, X_n\}$ is a set of n cases.
- $\Omega = \{\omega_1, \ldots, \omega_m\}$ is a set of m parameters which constitute the cases of B.
- $C = \{c_1, \ldots, c_p\}$ is a set of p class labels which also constitute the cases of B.
- A case $X \in B$ is the $k + 1 - tuple$ and its representation is $X = \{x_1, \ldots, x_k, c\}$ where $x_i \in \{x_{i1}, \ldots, x_{il}\}$ or $x_i \in \emptyset$, $x_{ij} \in \Omega$ and $c \in C$.
- A query case $X' \in B$ is the $k - tuple$ and its representation is $X' = \{x_1, \ldots, x_k\}$ where $x_i \in \{x_{i1}, \ldots, x_{il}\}$ or $x_i \in \emptyset$ and $x_{ij} \in \Omega$.
- f_{c_i} is the function which gives the standardized frequency of the ω_j to the label class c_i:

$$f_{c_i}(\omega_j) = \frac{g_{c_i}(\omega_j)}{max_{\omega_k \in \Omega}(g_{c_i}(\omega_k))},$$

where

$$g_{c_i}(\omega_j) = \frac{|\{X \in B | c_i \in X, \ \omega_j \in X\}|}{|\{X \in B | c_i \in X\}|}.$$

Using this membership function, we can calculate the membership degree of a case to a specific class by using the compromise operator such as the geometric mean:

$$Deg_{c_i}(X') = \frac{\sqrt[|X'|]{\prod_{\omega_j \in X'} \mu_{c_i}(\omega_j)}}{\sum_{c_k \in C} \sqrt[|X'|]{\prod_{\omega_j \in X'} \mu_{c_k}(\omega_j)}}, \tag{1}$$

where

$$\mu_{c_i} : \Omega \to [0, 1]$$
$$\omega_j \to f_{c_i}(\omega_j) / \sum_{c_k \in C}(f_{c_k}(\omega_j)).$$

These functions of membership are used to measure the similarity between two cases. The measure of similarity is made up of diagnostic systems which use case base reasoning. The similarity measure gives the similarity degree between the query case X' and the case X. The latter takes into account the common parameters and their degree memberships to the class c_i such as $c_i \in X$.

$$sim_A(X', X) = \frac{\sum_{\omega_k \in X' \cap X} \mu_A(\omega_k)}{\sum_{\omega_k \in X' \cup X} \mu_A(\omega_k)}. \tag{2}$$

2.2. The external knowledge base

The external knowledge base is generated from the diagnostic system case base. It is designed to be a fusion interface to a diagnostic system and is used to estimate the divergence of different sources of a diagnostic system. The external knowledge base attributes a linguistic value of uncertainty to each parameter that constitutes the case base in order to define the importance of these items in the characterization of different classes of the diagnostic system case base.

The linguistic characterization is, in general, less specific than the numerical one and is more significant.

The procedure for setting up the external knowledge base is made up of 3 steps: The first step brings together the parameters according to their class and then generates a group of parameters for each class. The second step measures the frequency of the parameters which constitute the cases for each group (i.e. for each class). In the last step, for each class, the membership functions for several frequency terms are generated. These membership functions attribute a degree of membership of the specific frequency term to each parameter. For each parameter, this step assigns a frequency term to each class. To define these membership functions, we denote the linguistic variable which is characterized by a quintuple:[6] $(x, T(x), U, G, M)$

- x is the name of the linguistic variable. In our application x is equal to the linguistic variable frequency.

- $T(x)$ is the set of terms associated with the linguistic value, in which the frequency is represented according to the following set {*Never, Exceptional, Rare, Usual, Frequent, Very Frequent, Always*}.
- U is the universe of discourse and $U = \{\forall \omega_j \in \Omega | f_{c_i}(\omega_j)\}$.

The terms of $T(x)$ are characterized by fuzzy subsets defined by the following functions of membership:[7]

- K: is the set of centroids of fuzzy sets obtained by the algorithm of fuzzy c-means (FCM)[8] which is applied to U such as $K = \{0, \ldots, C_{i-1}, C_i, C_{i+1}, \ldots, 1\}$.
- $\mu_{c_i,\alpha}$: corresponds to $\mu_{c_i,\alpha}(\omega_j) = \nu_{c_i,\alpha}(f_{c_i}(\omega_j))$.
- $\nu_{i,\alpha}$: corresponds to the membership function in the linguistic term α. It is built from a set of instance frequencies which belong to the class label i.

$$
\nu_{c_i,\alpha}(f_{c_i}(\omega_j)) = \begin{cases} 1 - (f_{c_i}(\omega_j) - C_i)/(C_i - C_{i-1}) \\ \quad \text{if } C_{i-1} < f_{c_i}(\omega_j) \leq C_i \\[2mm] 1 - (f_{c_i}(\omega_j) - C_i)/(C_{i+1} - C_i) \ . \\ \quad \text{if } C_i \leq f_{c_i}(\omega_j) < C_{i+1} \\[2mm] 0 \quad \text{otherwise} \end{cases}
$$

3. Fusion Method

Our fusion method involves comparing the importance of parameter characterization of the classes in each diagnostic system.

Thereafter, the new knowledge base is produced by merging the external knowledge bases of each diagnostic system. This new knowledge base is called confidence knowledge base and it results from the disparity measure between the various external knowledge bases. It is constituted by attributing a confidence degree to each parameter. Then, the diagnostic system combines this information with the information extracted from the internal knowledge base. This procedure is represented in Fig. 2.

Before passing on to the presentation of the fusion method, we illustrate an example of divergence. We take a parameter ω which is contained in source A (diagnostic system A). It has a high frequency of appearance in the representation of class c which is expressed

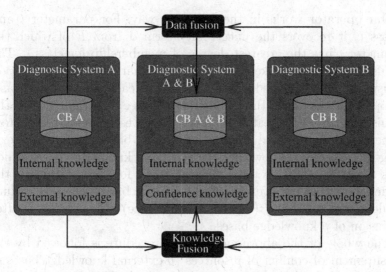

Fig. 2.   Hybrid fusion integrated in a diagnostic system.

Table 1.   Appearance frequency of the parameter ω in
the representation of a class c for Source A and B.

	Source A	Source B
parameter ω	*"very-frequent"*	*"exceptional"*

by a strong degree of membership of the *"very-frequent"* subset for
this class (Table 1). In source B (diagnostic system B), the same
parameter has a very low frequency of appearance in the representation of the same previously mentioned class which is expressed by a
strong degree of membership of the *"exceptional"* subset for class c
(Table 1). We note a great disparity in the consideration of a parameter in the definition of same class of two distinct sources. This
term can be regarded as ambiguous in the description class c.

In order to measure the distortion of k bases, we define a global
measurement operator of conflict between p sources. This operator applies to p External Knowledge Bases (EKB) deduced from
p sources and to another knowledge base which is deduced from
the coupling of the aforementioned p external knowledge bases. This
external knowledge base is called F for simplification and the p external knowledge bases are henceforth called p knowledge bases.

Our operator works in the following way: For parameter t and a class c, it recovers the uncertainty term α from F of which the parameter t has the greatest degree of membership for class c. The linguistic term α is taken as a reference mark for the calculation of disparity of p knowledge bases. Then for each p knowledge base, the operator calculates the membership degree of parameter t to the linguistic term α. Thereafter, we keep the lowest value of the degrees of membership obtained from p knowledge bases. In this context, the goal is to find a knowledge base in the p knowledge bases which gives the representation level of parameter t for class c which is the farthest one from the average of p knowledge bases. Then we deduce the degree of reliability (degree of confidence) of a parameter after the fusion of p knowledge bases.

The whole of the above-mentioned procedure is followed by the measurement of conflict of p sources (p external knowledge bases of diagnostic system). This measurement is inspired by the method proposed by Dubois and Prade.[9] In this study, a conflict is defined as the distance that separates the classification of a parameter between the new external knowledge base F (corresponds to the external knowledge base deduced from p external knowledge bases) and p external knowledge bases.

In the following sections, we present how the new external knowledge base is set up (Sec. 3.1). Thereafter, we define how the referent linguistic term is selected (Sec. 3.2). Then we define the conflict operator (Sec. 3.3) and finally we present the measurement of confidence (Sec. 3.4).

3.1. *Definition of the new external knowledge base which is deduced from the p source coupling*

- $B = \{B_1, \ldots, B_p\}$ is set of p case bases.
- $B_i = \{X_1^i, \ldots, X_n^i\}$ is the case base of n cases.
- $\Omega = \{\omega_1, \ldots, \omega_m\}$ is a set of m parameters which constitute the cases of $B_i \in B$.
- $C = \{c_1, \ldots, c_l\}$ is a set of l class labels which also constitute the cases of $B_i \in B$.
- A case $X_j^i \in B_i$ is the $k + 1 - tuple$ and its representation is $X_j^i = \{x_1, \ldots, x_k, c\}$ where $x_i \in \{x_{i1}, \ldots, x_{il}\}$ or $x_i \in \emptyset$, $x_{ij} \in \Omega$ and $x \in C$.

- f_{c_i} is the function that gives the standardized frequency of ω_j to label class c_i in all case bases of B:

$$f_{c_i}(\omega_j) = \frac{g_{c_i}(\omega_j)}{max_{\omega_k \in \Omega}(g_{c_i}(\omega_k))},$$

where

$$g_{c_i}(\omega_j) = \frac{|\{X \in B_1 \,|\, c_i \in X \text{ and } \omega_j \in X\}|}{|\{X \in B_1 \,|\, c_i \in X\}|}$$
$$+ \cdots +$$
$$\frac{|\{X \in B_l \,|\, c_i \in X \text{ and } \omega_j \in X\}|}{|\{X \in B_l \,|\, c_i \in X\}|}.$$

The membership functions of this new external knowledge base have the same definition as given in Sec. 2.2. Nevertheless, some notations are modified in order to integrate the notion of multisource.

- $\nu_{c_i,\alpha}^l$ represents the function of membership in the linguistic term α for class c_i of the knowledge base l.
- $\mu_{c_i,\alpha}^l$ corresponds to $\mu_{c_i,\alpha}^l(\omega_j) = \nu_{c_i,\alpha}^l(f_{c_i}(\omega_j))$.
- F corresponds to the knowledge base deduced from p knowledge bases.

3.2. Selecting the referent linguistic term

As we defined previously, the linguistic term α is considered as a reference mark of base F to measure the disparity between p bases. The linguistic term of frequency α for the parameter ω_j in class c_i is selected as referent if $\mu_{c_i,\alpha}^f(\omega_k)$ presents the greatest value such as:

$$\mu_{c_i,\alpha}^F(\omega_k) = max_{j \in T(x)}(\mu_{c_i,j}^F(\omega_k)).$$

3.3. Operator of the conflict measure

In p bases, the operator of conflict seeks the lowest value of membership degrees of ω_j to the linguistic reference α for class c_i. It is based on the *T-norm* $\mathcal{I}$:

$$h_{c_i}^\alpha(\omega_j) = \mathcal{I}(\mu_{c_i,\alpha}^1(\omega_j), \dots, \mu_{c_i,\alpha}^p(\omega_j)). \tag{3}$$

We note that this operator is strict, i.e. if one base of p bases has the value of membership of ω_j to the linguistic referent α equal to zero, we can induce that the value given by operator of conflict is also equal to zero even if this base has the membership value of ω_j to the linguistic neighbor at the linguistic referent α which is different from zero. In certain cases, it is necessary to be less strict so we modified the conflict operator in order to integrate the tolerance parameter that is parametrized according to our needs.

$$h_{c_i}^{\alpha}(\omega_j) = \mathcal{I}(max_{\alpha-d \leq k \leq \alpha+d \text{ and } k \in [0,|T(x)|-1]}(\mu_{c_i,k}^1(\omega_j)),$$
$$\cdots,$$
$$max_{\alpha-d \leq k \leq \alpha+d \text{ and } k \in [0,|T(x)|-1]}(\mu_{c_i,k}^p(\omega_j))).$$

- d is the tolerance index. It is used by the conflict operator in order to take into account the membership of ω_j to the referent linguistic term α and also the d linguistic terms close to the referent linguistics term. d is an integer and $\in [0, |T(x)| - 1]$.
- $\alpha - d$ indicates the linguistic term that is at position d on the left of the referent linguistic term α. Example: if α is equivalent to the linguistic *frequent* and $T(x) = \{never, exceptional, habitual, very frequent, always\}$ then $\alpha - 2$ indicates the linguistic term *"rare"*.
- $\alpha + d$ indicates the linguistic that is at position d on the right of the referent linguistic term α.

3.4. *Confidence measure*

We define a confidence measurement function of all parameters in the new base:

$$\mu_{conf,c_i}(\omega_j) = \begin{cases} 1 & \text{if } h_{c_i}^{\alpha}(\omega_j) \in [0,\varepsilon] \\ 1 - h_{c_i}^{\alpha}(\omega_j)/(1-\varepsilon) & \text{if } h_{c_i}^{\alpha}(\omega_j) \in [\varepsilon, 1[\end{cases},$$

where $\varepsilon \in]0, 1[$, which is used as a threshold in order to estimate the confidence of a parameter from the conflict value. $\mu_{conf,c_i}(\omega_j)$ considers the agreement measurement and is completely reliable if the agreement degree is higher than a certain threshold, i.e. the parameter is reliable if its appearance frequencies in the various bases belong to the same linguistic term or a linguistic term close to the referent linguistic which is obtained from F.

The integration of the index of confidence into the calculation of the degree of membership makes it possible to take into account certain parameters whose index of confidence is higher than a certain value:

$$Deg_{c_i}(X') = \frac{{}^{2|X'|}\sqrt{\prod_{w_j \in X'} \mu_{conf,c_i}(w_j)\mu_{c_i}(w_j)}}{\sum_{c_k \in C} {}^{2|X'|}\sqrt{\prod_{w_j \in X'} \mu_{conf,c_i}(w_j)\mu_{c_i}(w_j)}}. \tag{4}$$

The integration of the index of confidence into the calculation of the similarity of cases:

$$sim_{c_i}(X', X) = \frac{\sum_{w_k \in X' \cap X} \sqrt{\mu_{conf,c_i}(w_k)\mu_{c_i}(w_k)}}{\sum_{w_k \in X' \cup X} \sqrt{\mu_{conf,c_i}(w_k)\mu_{c_i}(w_k)}}. \tag{5}$$

4. Evaluation

In this section, we evaluate our knowledge fusion approach on 7 databases from an endoscopic image analysis system.[10] This system is an assistant system for decision-making of the endoscopic lesion diagnosis. These bases are made up of endoscopic image description via symbolic terms which are defined by the minimal standard terminology of the SEGE (European Company of Gastro-Enterology). A case in a base represents a description (a set of parameters) of an endoscopic lesion. In all bases, there are 206 parameters and 89 types of lesions, (i.e. 89 label classes).

Figure 3 gives the results of three types of fusion methods applied to a diagnostic system:

- Data fusion method: It is a very simple grouping of data from distinct sources.
- Decision fusion Method: This method combines the results of the diagnostic system applied to various sources and takes the result having the greatest reliability.
- Hybrid method: This is our method applied to a diagnostic system which takes into account the degree of confidence calculated through our fusion method.

The test that we carried out to assess the diagnostic systems, which are based on various fusion methods, consists of amalgamating 1000 cases at the starting base at each stage.

Our method is the one that presents the best estimates. We note that at the beginning, the three methods present almost the same estimates but immediately after the first fusion, the difference between the estimates increases. In fact, all estimation rates

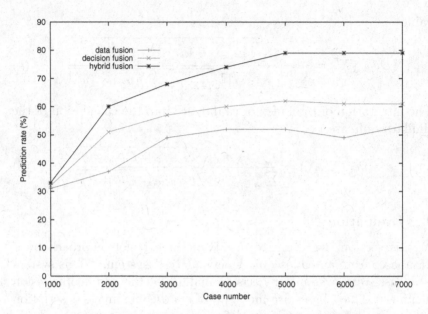

Fig. 3.   Results of accurate estimates of various case bases.

increase and our method gives the highest estimation rate. The progression of the estimation rates slows down during the sixth stage. However, our method remains unaffected.

5.   Conclusion

In this article, we suggest a new fusion method which is applied to the case-based reasoning diagnostic system. This fusion method combines two fusion types: the knowledge base fusion and the data base fusion. The data base fusion merges the case bases of the several diagnostic systems. The knowledge bases refer to the diagnostic system knowledge base and are used in order to measure the conflict of the diagnostic system case bases. Thereafter, the conflict measure is integrated into the new diagnostic system processes. We have presented experimental results, showing that the proposed method always outperforms the decision fusion method and the data fusion method. The performance gap increases with the problem size.

Our fusion method can be extended to measure the distortion of distributed homogeneous systems before they are brought together into one. Then, only the system with the lowest distorsion are brought together. Our method is original as it presents the possibility of its application to any case base.

References

1. B. Solaiman and B. Dasarathy, Information fusion concepts from information elements definition to the application of fusion approaches. *SPIE proceedings Series (SPIE Proc. Ser.) International Society for Optical Engineering Proceedings Series*, **385**, 205–212 (2001).
2. G. Saporta, Data fusion and data grafting. *International meeting on Nonlinear Methods and Data Mining*, **38** (2000).
3. D. Dubois, M. Grabisch, H. Prade and P. Smets, Using the transferable belief model and a qualitative possibility theory approach on an illustrative example: The assessment of the value of a candidate. *International Journal of Intelligent Systems*, **16**(11), 1245–1272 (Novembre 2001). BB.
4. A. Zemirline, L. Lecornu and B. Solaiman, Data mining system applied in endoscopic image base. *Proceedings of ICTTA'06: International Conference on Information and Communication Technologies: From Theory to Applications* (2006).
5. S. Chauvin, *Evaluation des théories de la décision appliquées à la fusion de capteurs en image satellitaire*. PhD thesis. Thèse de Doctorat d'Université Nantes (1995).
6. L. Zadeh, The concept of a linguistic variable and its application to approximate reasoning — ii. *Information Sciences (Part 2)*, **8**(4), 301–357 (1975).
7. L. Zadeh, Fuzzy sets. *Informations and Control*, **8**, 338–353 (1965).
8. J. Bezdek, *Pattern Recognition with Fuzzy Objective Function Algorithms (Advanced Applications in Pattern Recognition)*. Springer, July (1981) URL. http://www.amazon.co.uk/exec/obidos/ASIN/0306406713/citeulike-21.
9. D. Dubois and H. Prade, Combination of fuzzy information in the framework of possibility theory. *In Data Fusion in Robotic and Machine Intelligence*, pp. 481–505 (1992).
10. J. Cauvin, C. L. Guillou, B. Solaiman, M. Robaszkiewicz, P. L. Beux and C. Roux, Computer-assisted diagnosis system in digestive endoscopy. *IEEE Transactions on Information Technology in Biomedicine*, **7**, 256–262 (2003).

LOGIC AND MATHEMATICAL
STRUCTURES

Fuzzy Description Logic Programs

Umberto Straccia

ISTI- CNR, Pisa, Italy,
straccia@isti.cnr.it

Abstract

Description Logic Programs (DLPs), which combine the expressive power
of classical description logics and logic programs, are emerging as an
important ontology description language paradigm. In this study, we
present fuzzy DLPs, which extend DLPs by allowing the representation
of vague/imprecise information.

1. Introduction

Rule-based and object-oriented techniques are rapidly making their
way into the infrastructure for representing and reasoning about the
Semantic Web: combining these two paradigms emerges as an important objective.

Description Logic Programs (DLPs),[1-7] which combine the
expressive power of classical *Description Logics* (DLs) and classical *Logic Programs* (LPs), are emerging as an important ontology
description language paradigm. DLs capture the meaning of the most
popular features of structured representation of knowledge, while LPs
are powerful rule-based representation languages.

In this work, we present *fuzzy* DLPs, which is a extension of DLPs
towards the representation of vague/imprecise information.

We proceed as follows. We first introduce the main notions related
to fuzzy DLs and fuzzy LPs, and then show how both can be

integrated, defining fuzzy DLPs in Sec. 3. Section 4 concludes and outlines future research.

2.   Preliminaries

Fuzzy DLs. DLs[8] are a family of logics for representing structured knowledge. Each logic is identified by a name made of labels, which identify the operators allowed in that logic. Major DLs are the so-called logic $\mathcal{ALC}$[9] (*A*ttributive *L*anguage with *C*omplement) and is used as a reference language whenever new concepts are introduced in DLs, $\mathcal{SHOIN}(D)$, which is the logic behind the ontology description language OWL DL and $\mathcal{SHIF}(D)$, which is the logic behind OWL LITE, a slightly less expressive language than OWL DL (see Refs. 10 and 11).

Fuzzy DLs[12,13] extend classical DLs by allowing to deal with *fuzzy/imprecise concepts*. While in classical DLs concepts denotes sets, in fuzzy DLs fuzzy concepts denote fuzzy sets.[14]

Syntax. While the method we rely on in combining fuzzy DLs with fuzzy LPs does not depend on the particular fuzzy DL of choice, to make the paper self-contained, we shall use here fuzzy $\mathcal{ALC}(D)$,[15] which is fuzzy $\mathcal{ALC}$[12] extended with explicit represent membership functions for modifiers (such as "very") and vague concepts (such as "Young").[15] We refer to Ref. 13 for fuzzy OWL DL and related work on fuzzy DLs.

Fuzzy $\mathcal{ALC}(D)$ allows explicitly to represent membership functions in the language via fuzzy concrete domains. A *fuzzy concrete domain* (or simply *fuzzy domain*) is a pair $\langle \Delta_D, \Phi_D \rangle$, where Δ_D is an interpretation domain and Φ_D is the set of *fuzzy domain predicates* d with a predefined arity n and an interpretation $d^D \colon \Delta_D^n \to [0,1]$, which is a n-ary fuzzy relation over Δ_D. To the ease of presentation, we assume the fuzzy predicates have arity one, the domain is a subset of the rational numbers $\mathbb{Q}$ and the range is $[0,1]_{\mathbb{Q}} = [0,1] \cap \mathbb{Q}$. Concerning fuzzy predicates, there are many membership functions for fuzzy sets membership specification. However (see Fig. 1), for $k_1 \le a < b \le c < d \le k_2$ rational numbers, the *trapezoidal* $trz(a,b,c,d,[k_1,k_2])$, the *triangular* $tri(a,b,c,[k_1,k_2])$, the *left-shoulder* $ls(a,b,[k_1,k_2])$, the *right-shoulder* $rs(a,b,[k_1,k_2])$ and the *crisp function* $cr(a,b,[k_1,k_2])$ are simple, yet most frequently used to specify membership degrees and are those we are considering in this paper. To simplify the notation, we may omit the domain range, and write, e.g. $cr(a,b)$ in place of $cr(a, b, [k_1, k_2])$, whenever the domain range is not important. For instance, the concept "less than 18 year old" can be defined as a crisp concept $cr(0, 18)$, while Young, denoting the degree of youngness of a person's age, may be defined as Young $= ls(10, 30)$. We also consider fuzzy modifiers in fuzzy $\mathcal{ALC}(D)$. Fuzzy modifiers, like very, more_or_less and slightly, apply to fuzzy sets to change their membership function. Formally, a *modifier* is a function $f_m : [0, 1] \to [0, 1]$. For instance, we may define $\text{very}(x) = \text{lm}(0.7, 0.49, 0, 1)$, while define $\text{slightly}(x)$ as $\text{lm}(0.7, 0.49, 1, 0)$, where $lm(a, b, c, d)$ is the *linear modifier* in Fig. 1.

Now, let C, R_a, R_c, I_a, I_c and M be nonempty finite and pair-wise disjoint sets of *concepts names* (denoted A), *abstract roles names* (denoted R), *concrete roles names* (denoted T), *abstract constant names* (denoted a), *concrete constant names* (denoted c) and *modifiers* (denoted m). R_a contains a nonempty subset F_a of *abstract feature names* (denoted r), while R_c contains a nonempty subset F_c of *concrete feature names* (denoted t). Features are functional roles. The set of fuzzy $\mathcal{ALC}(D)$ *concepts* is defined by the syntactic rules (d is a unary fuzzy predicate) in Fig. 2. A *TBox* $\mathcal{T}$ consists of a finite set of *terminological axioms* of the form $C_1 \sqsubseteq C_2$ (C_1 is sub-concept of C_2) or $A = C$ (A is defined as the concept C), where A is a concept

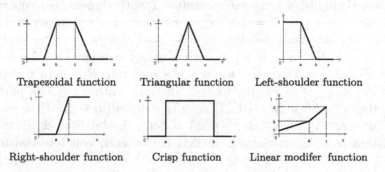

Trapezoidal function   Triangular function   Left-shoulder function

Right-shoulder function   Crisp function   Linear modifer function

Fig. 1.   Membership functions and modifiers.

$$C \longleftrightarrow \top \mid \bot \mid A \mid C_1 \sqcap C_2 \mid C_1 \sqcup C_2 \mid \neg C \mid \forall R.C \mid \exists R.C \mid \forall T.D \mid \exists T.D \mid m(C)$$
$$D \to d \mid \neg d$$
$$m \to \text{lm}(a, b, c, d)$$
$$d \to \text{trz}(a, b, c, d) \mid \text{tri}(a, b, c) \mid \text{ls}(a, b) \mid \text{rs}(a, b) \mid \text{cr}(a, b)$$

Fig. 2. $\mathcal{ALC}(D)$ concepts.

name and C is concept. Using axioms we may define the concepts of a minor and young person as

$$\text{Minor} = \text{Person} \sqcap \exists \text{age.} \leq_{18}, \tag{1}$$
$$\text{YoungPerson} = \text{Person} \sqcap \exists \text{age.Young}. \tag{2}$$

We also allow to formulate statements about constants. A *concept-*, *role-assertion axiom* and an *constant (in)equality axiom* has the form $a: C$ (a is an instance of C), $(a, b): R$ (a is related to b via R), $a \approx b$ (a and b are equal) and $a \not\approx b$, respectively, where a, b are abstract constants. For $n \in [0, 1]_{\mathbb{Q}}$, an *ABox* $\mathcal{A}$ consists of a finite set of constant (in)equality axioms, and *fuzzy concept* and *fuzzy role assertion axioms* of the form $\langle \alpha, n \rangle$, where α is a concept or role assertion. Informally, $\langle \alpha, n \rangle$ constrains the truth degree of α to be greater or equal to n. A fuzzy $\mathcal{ALC}(\mathbf{D})$ *knowledge base* $\mathcal{K} = \langle \mathcal{T}, \mathcal{A} \rangle$ consists of a TBox $\mathcal{T}$ and an ABox $\mathcal{A}$.

Semantics. We recall here the main notions related to fuzzy DLs (for more on fuzzy DLs, see Refs. 12 and 13). The main idea is that an assertion $a: C$, rather being interpreted as either true or false, will be mapped into a truth value $c \in [0, 1]_{\mathbb{Q}}$. The intended meaning is that c indicates to which extend 'a is a C'. Similarly for role names. Formally, a *fuzzy interpretation* $\mathcal{I}$ with respect to a concrete domain $\mathbf{D}$ is a pair $\mathcal{I} = (\Delta^{\mathcal{I}}, \cdot^{\mathcal{I}})$ consisting of a nonempty set $\Delta^{\mathcal{I}}$ (called the *domain*), disjoint from $\Delta_{\mathbf{D}}$, and of a *fuzzy interpretation function* $\cdot^{\mathcal{I}}$ that assigns (i) to each abstract concept $C \in \mathbf{C}$ a function $C^{\mathcal{I}}: \Delta^{\mathcal{I}} \to [0, 1]$; (ii) to each abstract role $R \in \mathbf{R}_a$ a function $R^{\mathcal{I}}: \Delta^{\mathcal{I}} \times \Delta^{\mathcal{I}} \to [0, 1]$; (iii) to each abstract feature $r \in \mathbf{F}_a$ a partial function $r^{\mathcal{I}}: \Delta^{\mathcal{I}} \times \Delta^{\mathcal{I}} \to [0, 1]$ such that for all $u \in \Delta^{\mathcal{I}}$ there is an unique $w \in \Delta^{\mathcal{I}}$ on which $r^{\mathcal{I}}(u, w)$ is defined; (iv) to each abstract constant $a \in \mathbf{I}_a$ an element in $\Delta^{\mathcal{I}}$; (v) to each concrete constant $c \in \mathbf{I}_c$ an element in $\Delta_{\mathbf{D}}$; (vi) to each concrete role $T \in \mathbf{R}_c$ a function $T^{\mathcal{I}}: \Delta^{\mathcal{I}} \times \Delta_{\mathbf{D}} \to [0, 1]$; (vii) to each concrete feature $t \in \mathbf{F}_c$ a partial function $t^{\mathcal{I}}: \Delta^{\mathcal{I}} \times \Delta_{\mathbf{D}} \to [0, 1]$ such that for all $u \in \Delta^{\mathcal{I}}$ there is an unique $o \in \Delta_{\mathbf{D}}$ on which $t^{\mathcal{I}}(u, o)$ is defined; $(viii)$ to each modifier $m \in \mathbf{M}$ the function $f_m: [0, 1] \to [0, 1]$; (ix) to each unary concrete predicate d the fuzzy relation $d^{\mathbf{D}}: \Delta_{\mathbf{D}} \to [0, 1]$ and to $\neg d$ the negation of $d^{\mathbf{D}}$. To extend the interpretation function to complex concepts, we use so-called *t-norms* (interpreting conjunction), *s-norms* (interpreting disjunction), *negation function* (interpreting negation), and

	Lukasiewicz Logic	Gödel Logic	Product Logic	"Zadeh semantics"
$\neg x$	$1 - x$	if $x = 0$ then 1 else 0	if $x = 0$ then 1 else 0	$1 - x$
$x \wedge y$	$\max(x + y - 1, 0)$	$\min(x, y)$	$x \cdot y$	$\min(x, y)$
$x \vee y$	$\min(x + y, 1)$	$\max(x, y)$	$x + y - x \cdot y$	$\max(x, y)$
$x \Rightarrow y$	if $x \leq y$ then 1 else $1 - x + y$	if $x \leq y$ then 1 else y	if $x \leq y$ then 1 else y/x	$\max(1 - x, y)$

Fig. 3. Typical connective interpretation.

implication function (interpreting implication).[16] In Fig. 3 we report most used combinations of norms.

The mapping $\cdot^{\mathcal{I}}$ is then extended to concepts and roles as follows (where $u \in \Delta^{\mathcal{I}}$): $\top^{\mathcal{I}}(u) = 1$, $\bot^{\mathcal{I}}(u) = 0$,

$$(C_1 \sqcap C_2)^{\mathcal{I}}(u) = C_1^{\mathcal{I}}(u) \wedge C_2^{\mathcal{I}}(u) \qquad (C_1 \sqcup C_2)^{\mathcal{I}}(u) = C_1^{\mathcal{I}}(u) \vee C_2^{\mathcal{I}}(u)$$
$$(\neg C)^{\mathcal{I}}(u) = \neg C^{\mathcal{I}}(u) \qquad (m(C))^{\mathcal{I}}(u) = f_m(C^{\mathcal{I}}(u))$$
$$(\forall R.C)^{\mathcal{I}}(u) = \inf_{w \in \Delta^{\mathcal{I}}} R^{\mathcal{I}}(u, w) \Rightarrow C^{\mathcal{I}}(w) \qquad (\exists R.C)^{\mathcal{I}}(u) = \sup_{w \in \Delta^{\mathcal{I}}} R^{\mathcal{I}}(u, w) \wedge C^{\mathcal{I}}(w)$$
$$(\forall T.D)^{\mathcal{I}}(u) = \inf_{o \in \Delta_{\mathbf{D}}} T^{\mathcal{I}}(u, o) \Rightarrow D^{\mathcal{I}}(o) \qquad (\exists T.D)^{\mathcal{I}}(u) = \sup_{o \in \Delta_{\mathbf{D}}} T^{\mathcal{I}}(u, o) \wedge D^{\mathcal{I}}(o) .$$

The mapping $\cdot^{\mathcal{I}}$ is extended to assertion axioms as follows (where $a, b \in \mathbf{I}_a$): $(a \colon C)^{\mathcal{I}} = C^{\mathcal{I}}(a^{\mathcal{I}})$ and $((a, b) \colon R)^{\mathcal{I}} = R^{\mathcal{I}}(a^{\mathcal{I}}, b^{\mathcal{I}})$. The notion of *satisfiability* of a fuzzy axiom E by a fuzzy interpretation $\mathcal{I}$, denoted $I \models E$, is defined as follows: $I \models C_1 \sqsubseteq C_2$ iff for all $u \in \Delta^{\mathcal{I}}, C_1^{\mathcal{I}}(u) \leq C_2^{\mathcal{I}}(u)$; $I \models A = C$ iff for all $u \in \Delta^{\mathcal{I}}, A^{\mathcal{I}}(u) = C^{\mathcal{I}}(u)$; $I \models \langle \alpha, n \rangle$ iff $\alpha^{\mathcal{I}} \geq n$; $\mathcal{I} \models a \approx b$ iff $a^{\mathcal{I}} = b^{\mathcal{I}}$; and $\mathcal{I} \models a \not\approx b$ iff $a^{\mathcal{I}} \neq b^{\mathcal{I}}$. The notion of *satisfiability* (is *model*) of a knowledge base $\mathcal{K} = \langle \mathcal{T}, \mathcal{A} \rangle$ and *entailment* of an assertional axiom is straightforward. Concerning terminological axioms, we also introduce degrees of subsumption. We say that $\mathcal{K}$ *entails* $C_1 \sqsubseteq C_2$ to degree $n \in [0, 1]$, denoted $\mathcal{K} \models \langle C_1 \sqsubseteq C_2, n \rangle$ iff for every model $\mathcal{I}$ of $\mathcal{K}$, $[\inf_{u \in \Delta^{\mathcal{I}}} C_1^{\mathcal{I}}(u) \Rightarrow C_2^{\mathcal{I}}(u)] \geq n$.

Example 1.[13] Consider the following simplified excerpt from a knowledge base about cars:

SportsCar $= \exists$speed.very(High), $\quad \langle$mg_mgb $\colon \exists$speed.$\leq_{170}, 1 \rangle$,
$\langle$ferrari_enzo $\colon \exists$speed.$>_{350}, 1 \rangle$, $\quad \langle$audi_tt $\colon \exists$speed. $=_{243}, 1 \rangle$.

speed is a concrete feature. The fuzzy domain predicate High has membership function High $= rs(80, 250)$. It can be shown that $\mathcal{K}$ entails the following three fuzzy axioms:

$\langle$mg_mgb $\colon \neg$SportsCar$, 0.72 \rangle$, $\langle$ferrari_enzo $\colon$ SportsCar$, 1 \rangle$, $\langle$audi_tt $\colon$ SportsCar$, 0.92 \rangle$.

Similarly, consider $\mathcal{K}$ with terminological axioms Eqs. (1) and (2). Then under Zadeh logic $\mathcal{K} \models \langle$Minor $\sqsubseteq$ YoungPerson$, 0.5 \rangle$ holds.

Finally, given $\mathcal{K}$ and an axiom α, it is of interest to compute its best lower degree bound. The *greatest lower bound* of α w.r.t. $\mathcal{K}$, denoted $glb(\mathcal{K},\alpha)$, is $glb(\mathcal{K},\alpha) = \sup\{n\colon \mathcal{K} \models \langle \alpha,n \rangle\}$, where $\sup \emptyset = 0$. Determining the *glb* is called the *Best Degree Bound* (BDB) problem. For instance, the entailments in Example 1 are the best possible degree bounds. Note that, $\mathcal{K} \models \langle \alpha,n \rangle$ iff $glb(\mathcal{K},\alpha) \geq n$. Therefore, the BDB problem is the major problem we have to consider in fuzzy $\mathcal{ALC}(\mathtt{D})$.

Fuzzy LPs. The management of imprecision in logic programming has attracted the attention of many researchers and numerous frameworks have been proposed. Essentially, they differ in the underlying truth space (e.g. *Fuzzy set theory*,[17–23] *Multi-valued logic*[24–40])and how imprecision values, associated to rules and facts, are managed.

Syntax. We consider here a very general form of the rules[39,40]: $A \leftarrow f(B_1,\ldots,B_n)$, where $f \in \mathcal{F}$ is an n-ary computable monotone function $f : [0,1]_\mathbb{Q}^n \to [0,1]_\mathbb{Q}$ and B_i are atoms. Each rule may have a different f. An example of rule is $s \leftarrow \min(p,q) \cdot \max(\neg r,0.7) + v$, where p,q,r,s and v are atoms. Computationally, given an assignment I of values to the B_i, the value of A is computed by stating that A is at least as true as $f(I(B_1),\ldots,I(B_n))$. The form of the rules is sufficiently expressive to encompass all approaches to fuzzy logic programming we are aware of. We assume that the standard functions $\wedge$ (meet) and $\vee$ (join) belong to $\mathcal{F}$. Notably, $\wedge$ and $\vee$ are both monotone. We call $f \in \mathcal{F}$ a *truth combination function*, or simply *combination function*.[a] We recall that an *atom*, denoted A, is an expression of the form $P(t_1,\ldots,t_n)$, where P is an n-ary predicate symbol and all t_i are terms, i.e. a *constant* or a *variable*. A *generalized normal logic program*, or simply *normal logic program*, denoted with $\mathcal{P}$, is a finite set of rules. The *Herbrand universe* $H_\mathcal{P}$ of $\mathcal{P}$ is the set of constants appearing in $\mathcal{P}$. If there is no constant symbol in $\mathcal{P}$ then consider $H_\mathcal{P} = \{a\}$, where a is an arbitrary chosen constant. The *Herbrand base* $B_\mathcal{P}$ of $\mathcal{P}$ is the set of ground instantiations of atoms appearing in $\mathcal{P}$ (ground instantiations are obtained by replacing all variable symbols with constants of the Herbrand universe). Given $\mathcal{P}$, the generalized normal logic program $\mathcal{P}^*$ is constructed as follows: (i) set $\mathcal{P}^*$ to the set of all ground instantiations of rules in

---

[a] Due to lack of space, we do not deal with non-monotonic negation here, though we can managed is as in Ref. 40.

$\mathcal{P}$; (ii) if an atom A is not head of any rule in $\mathcal{P}^*$, then add the rule $A \leftarrow 0$ to $\mathcal{P}^*$ (it is a standard practice in logic programming to consider such atoms as *false*); (iii) replace several rules in $\mathcal{P}^*$ having same head, $A \leftarrow \varphi_1$, $A \leftarrow \varphi_2$, ... with $A \leftarrow \varphi_1 \vee \varphi_2 \vee \ldots$ (recall that $\vee$ is the join operator of the truth lattice in infix notation). Note that in $\mathcal{P}^*$, each atom appears in the head of *exactly one* rule.

Semantics. An *interpretation I of a logic program* is a mapping from atoms to members of $[0,1]_\mathbb{Q}$. I is extended from atoms to the interpretation of rule bodies as follows: $I(f(B_1, \ldots, B_n)) = f(I(B_1), \ldots, I(B_n))$. The ordering $\leq$ is extended from $[0,1]_\mathbb{Q}$ to the set of all interpretations point-wise: (i) $I_1 \leq I_2$ iff $I_1(A) \leq I_2(A)$, for every ground atom A. With $\mathtt{I}_\perp$ we denote the bottom interpretation under $\leq$ (it maps any atom into 0).

An interpretation I is a *model* of a logic program $\mathcal{P}$, denoted by $I \models \mathcal{P}$, iff for all $A \leftarrow \varphi \in \mathcal{P}^*$, $I(\varphi) \leq I(A)$ holds. The semantics of a logic program $\mathcal{P}$ is determined by the least model of $\mathcal{P}$, $M_\mathcal{P} = \min\{I : I \models \mathcal{P}\}$. The *existence and uniqueness* of $M_\mathcal{P}$ is guaranteed by the fixed-point characterization, by means of the *immediate consequence operator* $\Phi_\mathcal{P}$. For an interpretation I, for any ground atom A, $\Phi_\mathcal{P}(I)(A) = I(\varphi)$, where $A \leftarrow \varphi \in \mathcal{P}^*$. We can show that the function $\Phi_\mathcal{P}$ is monotone, the set of fixed-points of $\Phi_\mathcal{P}$ is a complete lattice and, thus, $\Phi_\mathcal{P}$ has a least fixed-point and I is a model of a program $\mathcal{P}$ iff I is a fixed-point of $\Phi_\mathcal{P}$. Therefore, the minimal model of $\mathcal{P}$ coincides with the least fixed-point of $\Phi_\mathcal{P}$, which can be computed in the usual way by iterating $\Phi_\mathcal{P}$ over $\mathtt{I}_\perp$.[39,40]

Example 2.[23] In Ref. 23, Fuzzy Logic Programming is proposed, where rules have the form $A \leftarrow f(A_1, \ldots, A_n)$ for some specific f. Reference 23 is just a special case of our framework. As an illustrative example consider the following scenario. Assume that we have the following facts, represented in the tables below. There are hotels and conferences, their locations and the distance among locations.

HasLocationH		HasLocationC		Distance		
HotelID	HasLocationH	ConferenceID	HasLocationC	HasLocationH	HasLocationC	Distance
h1	hl1	c1	cl1	hl1	cl1	300
h2	hl2	c2	cl2	hl1	cl2	500
⋮	⋮	⋮	⋮	hl2	cl1	750
				hl2	cl2	750
				⋮	⋮	

Now, suppose that our query is to find hotels close to the conference venue, labeled c1. We may formulate our query as the rule:

$$\texttt{Query}(h) \leftarrow \min(\texttt{HasLocationH}(h, hl), \texttt{HasLocationC}(\texttt{c1}, cl), \texttt{Distance}(hl, cl, d), \texttt{Close}(d)),$$

where $\texttt{Close}(x)$ is defined as $\texttt{Close}(x) = \max(0, 1 - x/1000)$. As a result to that query we get a ranked list of hotels.

3. Fuzzy DLPs

In this section we introduce fuzzy *Description Logic Programs* (fuzzy DLPs), which are a combination of fuzzy DLs with fuzzy LPs. In the classical semantics setting, there are mainly three approaches (see Refs. 41 and 42, for an overview), the so-called axiom-based approach (e.g. [6, 7]) and the DL-log approach (e.g. Refs. 2–4) and the autoepistemic approach (e.g. Refs. 1 and 5). We are not going to discuss in this section these approaches. The interested reader may see Ref. 43. We just point out that in this paper we follow the DL-log approach, in which rules may not modify the extension of concepts and DL atoms and roles appearing the body of a rule act as procedural calls to the DL component.

Syntax. We assume that the description logic component and the rules component share the same alphabet of constants. Rules are as for fuzzy LPs except that now atoms and roles may appear in the rule body. We assume that no rule head atom belongs to the DL signature. For ease the readability, in case of ambiguity, DL predicates will have a DL superscript in the rules. Note that in Ref. 3 a concept inclusion may appear in the body of the rule. We will not deal with this feature. A *fuzzy Description Logic Program* (fuzzy DLP) is a tuple $\mathcal{DP} = \langle \mathcal{K}, \mathcal{P} \rangle$, where $\mathcal{K}$ is a fuzzy DL knowledge base and $\mathcal{P}$ is a fuzzy logic program. For instance, the following is a fuzzy DLP:

$$\texttt{LowCarPrize}(x) \leftarrow \min(\texttt{made\_by}(x, y), \texttt{ChineseCarCompany}^{DL}(y)), \texttt{has\_prize}(x, z), \texttt{LowPrize}^{DL}(z)$$
$$\texttt{made\_by}(x, y) \leftarrow \texttt{makes}^{DL}(y, x),$$
$$\texttt{LowPrize} = \texttt{ls}(5.000, 15.000)$$
$$\texttt{ChineseCarCompany} = (\exists\texttt{has\_location.China}) \sqcap (\exists\texttt{makes.Car})$$

meaning: A chinese car company is located in china, makes cars, which are sold as low prize cars. Low prize is defined as a fuzzy concept with left-shoulder membership function.

Semantics. We recall that in the DL-log approach, a DL atom appearing in a rule body acts as a query to the underlying DL knowledge base (see Ref. 3). So, consider a fuzzy DLP $\mathcal{DP} = \langle \mathcal{K}, \mathcal{P} \rangle$. The

Herbrand universe of $\mathcal{P}$, denoted $H_\mathcal{P}$ is the set of constants appearing in $\mathcal{DP}$ (if no such constant symbol exists, $H_\mathcal{P} = \{c\}$ for an arbitrary constant symbol c from the alphabet of constants). The *Herbrand base* of $\mathcal{P}$, denoted $\mathcal{B}_\mathcal{P}$, is the set of all ground atoms built up from the non-DL predicates and the Herbrand universe of $\mathcal{P}$. Then, the definition of $\mathcal{P}^*$ is as for fuzzy LPs. An *interpretation* I w.r.t. $\mathcal{DP}$ is a function $I \colon B_\mathcal{P} \to [0,1]_\mathbb{Q}$ mapping non-DL atoms into $[0,1]_\mathbb{Q}$. We say that I is a *model* of a $\mathcal{DP} = \langle \mathcal{K}, \mathcal{P} \rangle$ iff $I^\mathcal{K} \models_\mathcal{K} \mathcal{P}$, where

(1) $I^\mathcal{K} \models \mathcal{P}$ iff for all $A \leftarrow \varphi \in \mathcal{P}^*$, $I^\mathcal{K}(\varphi) \leq I^\mathcal{K}(A)$;
(2) $I^\mathcal{K}(f(A_1, \ldots, A_n)) = f(I^\mathcal{K}(A_1), \ldots, I^\mathcal{K}(A_n))$;
(3) $I^\mathcal{K}(P(t_1, \ldots, t_n)) = I(P(t_1, \ldots, t_n))$ for all ground non-DL atoms $P(t_1, \ldots, t_n)$;
(4) $I^\mathcal{K}(A(a)) = glb(\mathcal{K}, a \colon A)$ for all ground DL atoms $A(a)$;
(5) $I^\mathcal{K}(R(a,b)) = glb(\mathcal{K}, (a,b) \colon R)$ for all ground DL roles $R(a,b)$.

Note how in Points (4) and (5) the interpretation of a DL-atom and role depends on the DL-component only. Finally, we say that $\mathcal{DP} = \langle \mathcal{K}, \mathcal{P} \rangle$ *entails* a ground atom A, denoted $\mathcal{DP} \models A$, iff $I \models A$ whenever $I \models \mathcal{DP}$.

For instance, assume that together with the $\mathcal{DP}$ about low prize cars we have the following instances, where $\mathtt{l1}$ and $\mathtt{l2}$ are located in China and $\mathtt{car1}$ and $\mathtt{car2}$ are cars.

CarCompany		Makes		Prize		LowPrizeCar	
CarCompany	has_location	CarCompany	makes	Car	prize	Car	LowPrizeDegree
c1	l1	c1	car1	car1	10.000	car1	0.5
c2	l2	c2	car2	car2	7.500	car2	0.75
⋮	⋮	⋮	⋮	⋮	⋮	⋮	⋮

If the prizes are as in the table above then the degree of the car prizes is depicted in the right table. Note that due to the definition of chinese car companies, $\mathtt{c1}$ and $\mathtt{c2}$ are chinese car companies.

Interestingly, it is possible to adapt the standard results of Datalog to our case, which say that a satisfiable description logic program $\mathcal{DP}$ has a minimal model $M_{\mathcal{DP}}$ and entailment (logical consequence) can be reduced to model checking in this minimal model.

Proposition 1. *Let* $\mathcal{DP} = \langle \mathcal{K}, \mathcal{P} \rangle$ *be a fuzzy DLP. If* $\mathcal{DP}$ *is satisfiable, then there exists a unique model* $M_{\mathcal{DP}}$ *such that* $M_{\mathcal{DP}} \leq I$

for all models I of $\mathcal{DP}$. Furthermore, for any ground atom A, $\mathcal{DP} \models A$ iff $M_{\mathcal{DP}} \models A$.

The minimal model can be computed as the least fixed-point of the following monotone operator. Let $\mathcal{DP} = \langle \mathcal{K}, \mathcal{P} \rangle$ be a fuzzy DLP. Define the operator $T_{\mathcal{DP}}$ on interpretations as follows: for every interpretation I, for all ground atoms $A \in B_{\mathcal{P}}$, given $A \leftarrow \varphi \in \mathcal{P}^*$, let $T_{\mathcal{DP}}(I)(A) = I^{\mathcal{K}}(\varphi)$. Then it can easily be shown that $T_{\mathcal{DP}}$ is monotone, i.e. $I \leq I'$ implies $T_{\mathcal{DP}}(I) \leq T_{\mathcal{DP}}(I')$, and, thus, by the Knaster-Tarski Theorem $T_{\mathcal{DP}}$ has a least fixed-point, which can be computed as a fixed-point iteration of $T_{\mathcal{DP}}$ starting with $\mathtt{I}_{\perp}$.

Reasoning. From a reasoning point of view, to solve the entailment problem we proceed as follows. Given $\mathcal{DP} = \langle \mathcal{K}, \mathcal{P} \rangle$, we first compute for all DL atoms $A(a)$ occurring in $\mathcal{P}^*$, the greatest truth lower bound, i.e. $n_{A(a)} = glb(\mathcal{K}, a\colon A)$. Then we add the rule $A(a) \leftarrow n_{A(a)}$ to $\mathcal{P}$, establishing that the truth degree of $A(a)$ is at least $n_{A(a)}$ (similarly for roles). Finally, we can rely on a theorem prover for fuzzy LPs only either using a usual bottom-up computation or a top-down computation for logic programs.[23,24,39,40] Of course, one has to be sure that both computations, for the fuzzy DL component and for the fuzzy LP component, are supported. With respect to the logic presented in this paper, we need the reasoning algorithm described in Ref. 15 for fuzzy DLs component[b] or the *fuzzy DL* system available from Straccia's home page, while we have to use Refs. 39 and 40 for the fuzzy LP component.

We conclude by mentioning that by relying on Ref. 40, the whole framework extends to fuzzy description normal logic programs as well (nonmonotone negation is allowed in the logic programming component).

4. Conclusions

We integrated the management of imprecision into a highly expressive family of representation languages, called fuzzy Description

---

[b] However, sub-concept specification in terminological axioms are of the form $A \sqsubseteq C$ only, where A is a concept name and neither cyclic definitions are allowed nor may there be more than one definition per concept name A.

Logic Programs, resulting from the combination of fuzzy Description Logics and fuzzy Logic Programs. We defined syntax, semantics, declarative and fixed-point semantics of fuzzy DLPs. We also detailed how query answering can be performed by relying on the combination of currently known algorithms, without any significant additional effort.

Our motivation is inspired by its application in the Semantic Web, in which both aspects of structured and rule-based representation of knowledge are becoming of interest.[44,45]

There are some appealing research directions. At first, it would certainly be of interest to investigate about reasoning algorithm for fuzzy description logic programs under the so-called axiomatic approach. Currently, very few is known about that. Secondly, while there is a huge literature about fuzzy logic programming and many-valued programming in general, very little is known in comparison about fuzzy DLs. This area may deserve more attention.

References

1. F. M. Donini, M. Lenzerini, D. Nardi, W. Nutt and A. Schaerf, An epistemic operator for description logics. *Artificial Intelligence.* **100**(1–2), 225–274 (1998). ISSN 0004-3702. doi: http://dx.doi.org/10.1016/S0004-3702(98)00009-5.
2. F. M. Donini, M. Lenzerini, D. Nardi and A. Schaerf, AL-log: Integrating datalog and description logics. *Journal of Intelligent Information Systems.* **10**(3), 227–252 (1998).
3. T. Eiter, T. Lukasiewicz, R. Schindlauer and H. Tompits, Combining answer set programming with description logics for the semantic web. *Proceedings of the 9th International Conference on Principles of Knowledge Representation and Reasoning (KR-04).* AAAI Press (2004).
4. T. Eiter, T. Lukasiewicz, R. Schindlauer and H. Tompits, Well-founded semantics for description logic programs in the semantic web. *Proceedings RuleML 2004 Workshop, International Semantic Web Conference.* Number 3323 in Lecture Notes in Computer Science, Springer Verlag, pp. 81–97 (2004).
5. A. L. Enrico Franconi, Gabriel Kuper and L. Serafini, A robust logical and computational characterization of peer-to-peer database systems. *Proceedings of the VLDB International Workshop on Databases, Information Systems and Peer-to-Peer Computing (DBISP2P-03),* (2004).
6. I. Horrocks and P. F. Patel-Schneider, A proposal for an OWL rules language. *Proceeding of the Thirteenth International World Wide Web Conference (WWW-04).* ACM (2004). URL download/2004/HoPa04a.pdf.
7. A. Y. Levy and M.-C. Rousset, Combining horn rules and description logics in CARIN. *Artificial Intelligence,* **104**, 165–209 (1998).

8. F. Baader, D. Calvanese, D. McGuinness, D. Nardi and P. F. Patel-Schneider, (eds.). *The Description Logic Handbook: Theory, Implementation, and Applications.* Cambridge University Press (2003).

9. M. Schmidt-Schauß and G. Smolka, Attributive concept descriptions with complements. *Artificial Intelligence,* **48**, 1–26 (1991).

10. I. Horrocks and P. Patel-Schneider, Reducing OWL entailment to description logic satisfiability. *Journal of Web Semantics* (2004). ISSN 1570-8268. To Appear.

11. I. Horrocks, P. F. Patel-Schneider and F. van Harmelen, From SHIQ and RDF to OWL: The making of a web ontology language. *Journal of Web Semantics,* **1**(1), 7–26 (2003).

12. U. Straccia, Reasoning within fuzzy description logics. *Journal of Artificial Intelligence Research,* **14**, 137–166 (2001).

13. U. Straccia, A fuzzy description logic for the semantic web. (ed.) E. Sanchez. *Fuzzy Logic and the Semantic Web,* Capturing Intelligence. Elsevier, Chapter 4, 73–90 (2006).

14. L. A. Zadeh, Fuzzy sets. *Information and Control,* **8**(3), 338–353 (1965).

15. U. Straccia, Description logics with fuzzy concrete domains. (eds.) F. Bachus and T. Jaakkola. *21st Conference on Uncertainty in Artificial Intelligence (UAI-05),* Edinburgh, Scotland, AUAI Press, pp. 559–567 (2005).

16. P. Hájek, *Metamathematics of Fuzzy Logic.* Kluwer (1998).

17. T. H. Cao, Annotated fuzzy logic programs. *Fuzzy Sets and Systems,* **113**(2), 277–298 (2000).

18. R. Ebrahim, Fuzzy logic programming. *Fuzzy Sets and Systems,* **117**(2), 215–230 (2001).

19. M. Ishizuka and N. Kanai, Prolog-ELF: incorporating fuzzy logic. *Proceedings of the 9th International Joint Conference on Artificial Intelligence (IJCAI-85),* Los Angeles, CA, pp. 701–703 (1985).

20. S. Krajči, R. Lencses and P. Vojtáš, A comparison of fuzzy and annotated logic programming. *Fuzzy Sets and Systems,* **144**, 173–192 (2004).

21. E. Y. Shapiro, Logic programs with uncertainties: A tool for implementing rule-based systems. *Proceedings of the 8th International Joint Conference on Artificial Intelligence (IJCAI-83),* pp. 529–532 (1983).

22. M. van Emden, Quantitative deduction and its fixpoint theory. *Journal of Logic Programming,* **4**(1), 37–53 (1986).

23. P. Vojtáš, Fuzzy logic programming. *Fuzzy Sets and Systems,* **124**, 361–370 (2001).

24. C. V. Damásio, J. Medina and M. Ojeda Aciego, A tabulation proof procedure for residuated logic programming. *Proceedings of the 6th European Conference on Artificial Intelligence (ECAI-04),* (2004).

25. C. V. Damásio, J. Medina and M. Ojeda Aciego, Termination results for sorted multi-adjoint logic programs. *Proceedings of the 10th International Conference on Information Processing and Managment of Uncertainty in Knowledge-Based Systems, (IPMU-04),* pp. 1879–1886 (2004).

26. C. V. Damásio and L. M. Pereira, Antitonic logic programs. *Proceedings of the 6th European Conference on Logic Programming and Nonmonotonic*

Reasoning (LPNMR-01). Number 2173 in Lecture Notes in Computer Science. Springer-Verlag (2001).

27. M. C. Fitting, Fixpoint semantics for logic programming — a survey. *Theoretical Computer Science*, **21**(3), 25–51 (2002).

28. M. Fitting, A Kripke-Kleene-semantics for general logic programs. *Journal of Logic Programming*, **2**, 295–312 (1985).

29. M. Kifer and V. Subrahmanian, Theory of generalized annotated logic programming and its applications. *Journal of Logic Programming*, **12**, 335–367 (1992).

30. L. V. Lakshmanan and N. Shiri, A parametric approach to deductive databases with uncertainty. *IEEE Transactions on Knowledge and Data Engineering*, **13**(4), 554–570 (2001).

31. Y. Loyer and U. Straccia, The approximate well-founded semantics for logic programs with uncertainty. *28th International Symposium on Mathematical Foundations of Computer Science (MFCS-2003)*. Number 2747 in Lecture Notes in Computer Science, Bratislava, Slovak Republic, Springer-Verlag, pp. 541–550 (2003).

32. Y. Loyer and U. Straccia, Default knowledge in logic programs with uncertainty. *Proc. of the 19th Int. Conf. on Logic Programming (ICLP-03)*. Number 2916 in Lecture Notes in Computer Science, Mumbai, India, Springer Verlag, pp. 466–480 (2003).

33. Y. Loyer and U. Straccia, Epistemic foundation of the well-founded semantics over bilattices. In *29th International Symposium on Mathematical Foundations of Computer Science (MFCS-2004)*. Number 3153 in Lecture Notes in Computer Science, Bratislava, Slovak Republic, Springer Verlag, pp. 513–524 (2004).

34. Y. Loyer and U. Straccia, Any-world assumptions in logic programming. *Theoretical Computer Science*, **342**(2–3), 351–381 (2005).

35. C. Mateis, Extending disjunctive logic programming by t-norms. *Proceedings of the 5th International Conference on Logic Programming and Nonmonotonic Reasoning (LPNMR-99)*. Number 1730 in Lecture Notes in Computer Science, Springer-Verlag, pp. 290–304 (1999).

36. C. Mateis, Quantitative disjunctive logic programming: Semantics and computation. *AI Communications*, **13**, 225–248 (2000).

37. J. Medina, M. Ojeda-Aciego and P. Vojtáš, A procedural semantics for multi-adjoint logic programming. *Proceedings of the 10th Portuguese Conference on Artificial Intelligence on Progress in Artificial Intelligence, Knowledge Extraction, Multi-agent Systems, Logic Programming and Constraint Solving*, Springer-Verlag, pp. 290–297 (2001). ISBN 3-540-43030-X.

38. J. Medina, M. Ojeda-Aciego and P. Vojtáš, Multi-adjoint logic programming with continuous semantics. *Proceedings of the 6th International Conference on Logic Programming and Nonmonotonic Reasoning (LPNMR-01)*, Vol. 2173, *Lecture Notes in Artificial Intelligence*, Springer Verlag, pp. 351–364 (2001). URL citeseer.ist.psu.edu/medina01multiadjoint.html.

39. U. Straccia, Uncertainty management in logic programming: Simple and effective top-down query answering. (eds.) R. Khosla, R. J. Howlett and L. C. Jain.

9th International Conference on Knowledge-Based & Intelligent Information & Engineering Systems (KES-05), Part II. Number 3682 in Lecture Notes in Computer Science, Springer Verlag, Melbourne, Australia, pp. 753–760 (2005).

40. U. Straccia, Query answering in normal logic programs under uncertainty. In *8th European Conferences on Symbolic and Quantitative Approaches to Reasoning with Uncertainty (ECSQARU-05)*. Number 3571 in Lecture Notes in Computer Science, Springer Verlag, Barcelona, Spain, pp. 687–700 (2005).

41. P. *et al. Specification of Coordination of Rule and Ontology Languages*. Technical report, Knowledge Web Network of Excellence, EU-IST-2004-507482, (2004). Deliverable D2.5.1.

42. E. Franconi and S. Tessaris, Rules and queries with ontologies: A unified logical framework. *Workshop on Principles and Practice of Semantic Web Reasoning (PPSWR-04)*, (2004).

43. U. Straccia, Uncertainty and description logic programs over lattices. (ed.) E. Sanchez. *Fuzzy Logic and the Semantic Web*. Capturing Intelligence, Elsevier, Chapter 7, pp. 115–133 (2006).

44. B. N. Grosof, I. Horrocks, R. Volz and S. Decker, Description logic programs: Combining logic programs with description logic. *Proceedings of the 12th international conference on World Wide Web*, ACM Press, pp. 48–57 (2003). ISBN 1-58113-680-3. doi: http://doi.acm.org/10.1145/775152.775160.

45. I. Horrocks and P. F. Patel-Schneider, Three theses of representation in the semantic web. *Proceedings of the 12th International Conference on World Wide Web*, ACM Press, pp. 39–47 (2003). ISBN 1-58113-680-3. doi: http://doi.acm.org/10.1145/775152.775159.

Imperfect Information Representation
Through Extended Logic Programs
in Bilattices

Daniel Stamate

Department of Computing
Goldsmiths College, University of London, UK
d.stamate@doc.gold.ac.uk

Abstract

The basis of (default) negative information in the well-founded semantics is given by the so-called unfounded sets, used to complete missing information from a program through a kind of pessimistic assumption. We extend this concept by considering optimistic, pessimistic, skeptical and inconsistent assumptions in the context of multivalued logics given by bilattices. The extended well-founded semantics defined here for extended logic programs in bilattices is capable to express imperfect information considered to be missing/incomplete, uncertain and/or inconsistent. We provide a method of computing the semantics and show that, for different assumptions, it captures the Kripke-Kleene semantics, the well-founded semantics and Fitting's least multivalued stable model. We show also that the complexity of the computation of our semantics is polynomial time in a useful class of so-called limited bilattices.

1. Introduction

One of the most used assumptions in logic programming and deductive databases is the so-called Closed World Assumption (CWA), according to which atoms that cannot be inferred with the rules are considered to be false (i.e. a pessimistic assumption). Such assumptions are needed as the conventional logic programs with negation can be seen as incomplete logic theories, i.e. we cannot always infer any ground atom A or its negation from a logic program. In order to enrich such a theory we can make assumptions on the logical values of atoms that cannot be inferred from the rules. This is similar to the process of reasoning by default.

One of the most successful semantics of conventional logic programs based on the CWA is the well-founded semantics.[13] However, the CWA is not applicable in all circumstances when information is handled, as for example in a legal case, where a person should be considered innocent unless the contrary is proved (i.e. an optimistic assumption). That is, all the semantics based on the CWA, in particular the well-founded semantics, would behave inadequately in such a case.

In this work we extend the well-founded semantics definition in order for it to be based also on alternative assumptions, in particular on an optimistic assumption, according to which, if in doubt then assume true.

Let us illustrate this using the following legal case example represented through the set of rules and facts P:

$$
\begin{array}{lll}
\text{charge(X)} & \leftarrow & \text{suspect(X)} \land \neg\text{innocent(X)} \\
\text{free(X)} & \leftarrow & \text{suspect(X)} \land \text{innocent(X)} \\
\text{innocent(X)} & \leftarrow & \exists Y(\text{alibi(X,Y)} \land \neg\text{relatives(X,Y)}) \\
\text{suspect(John)} & \leftarrow & true
\end{array}
$$

The only assertion made in the program is that John is suspect, but we know nothing as to whether he is innocent.

If we consider the pessimistic assumption, then we are led to assume that John is not innocent, and we can infer that John must not be freed, and must be charged. If, on the other hand, we consider the skeptical assumption, i.e. we assume nothing about the innocence of John, then we can infer nothing as to whether he must be freed or charged.

If we consider the optimistic assumption then *innocent(John)* is true and we can infer that John must be freed, and must not be charged.

If we choose the (less intuitive) inconsistent assumption then we get *suspect(John)* is true, *innocent(John)*, *free(John)*, *charge(John)* and all the other ground atoms are all inconsistent.

The basis of (default) negative information in the well-founded semantics is given by the so-called unfounded sets.[13] We extend this concept by considering as default value for underivable atoms any element of Belnap's four-valued logic:[2] true, false, unknown and inconsistent. Thus we make an optimistic, pessimistic, skeptical and inconsistent assumption, respectively, that will be incorporated elegantly in the definition of the well-founded semantics. Apart the generalization, the difference between the definition in[13] and ours is that the first one has rather a syntactic flavour, while the second has a semantic flavour. Expressing this concept in a semantic manner allows an elegant extension.

As our previous discussion shows, the logic we will consider contains at least four logical values, corresponding to the four mentioned assumptions. However, in fact many real life situations require processing of imperfect information, that is incomplete, inconsistent, and/or uncertain/imprecise. The use of multivalued logics to express the imperfection of information may be needed. In order to illustrate this idea we use the following example.

Suppose we combine information from two sources that are the experts E_1 and E_2 which express their opinion on a statement A. It may be that the two experts are not sure about the truthness of A, due to the imperfection of the available knowledge. The first expert may believe that A is true with a degree of 0.6 of confidence (so there is a degree of 0.4 of doubt), while the second expert may believe that A is true with a degree of 0.8 of confidence (so there is a degree of 0.2 of doubt). If we want to combine the information obtained from the two experts, a natural way would be to consider the consensus of their beliefs: A is true with a degree of confidence of 0.6, and a degree of doubt of 0.2. That is, the pair $\langle 0.6, 0.2 \rangle$ would express the maximal confidence and doubt the two experts agree on. We see such pairs of reals between 0 and 1, expressing degrees of confidence and doubt (note that they are not necessarily complementary w.r.t. 1), as logical values, and we call the space of these logical values the *confidence-doubt logic* — let us denote it by $\mathcal{L}^{\mathcal{CD}}$. We have two orders on $\mathcal{L}^{\mathcal{CD}}$, namely the truth and knowledge orders denoted $\leq_t$ and $\leq_k$, respectively, defined as follows: $\langle x, y \rangle \leq_t \langle z, w \rangle$ iff $x \leq z$ and $w \leq y$, and $\langle x, y \rangle \leq_k \langle z, w \rangle$ iff $x \leq z$ and $y \leq w$, where $\leq$ is the usual order between reals. Intuitively speaking, an increase in the truth order corresponds to an increase in the degree of confidence and a decrease in the degree of doubt, while an increase in the knowledge order corresponds to an increase in both the degree of confidence and the degree of doubt. The least and greatest elements under $\leq_t$ are $\langle 0, 1 \rangle$ and $\langle 1, 0 \rangle$, representing no confidence, full doubt, and full confidence, no doubt, respectively. They may be identified with the classical logical values *false* and *true*. The least and greatest elements under $\leq_k$ are $\langle 0, 0 \rangle$ and $\langle 1, 1 \rangle$, representing no confidence, no doubt, and full confidence, full doubt, respectively. They may be identified with the logical values *unknown* (denoted $\perp$) and *inconsistent* (denoted $\top$).

Note that $\mathcal{L}^{\mathcal{CD}}$ has an interesting double algebraic structure of complete lattice (given by the two orders). Such a structure is captured by the concept of bilattice.[9] Bilattices will be used here as multivalued logics in which we define the extended well-founded semantics of extended logic programs. The four assumptions to be considered correspond to a parameter α whose value can be *true*, *false*, $\perp$ or $\top$ (which, as we have seen in the example of the confidence-doubt logic, are the extreme values of the bilattice). Once fixed, the value of α represents the "default value" for those atoms of a program that cannot be inferred from the rules. If we want to work under a particular assumption, we choose the appropriate value for α, namely *true* for the optimistic assumption, *false* for the pessimistic assumption, $\perp$ for the skeptical assumption and $\top$ for the inconsistent assumption.

We show that, for the pessimistic assumption our extended well-founded semantics captures the conventional well-founded semantics[13] and one of the Fitting's multivalued stable models,[5] while for the skeptical assumption our semantics captures the Kripke-Kleene semantics.[3]

The work is organized as follows. In Sec. 2 we define the extended programs in multivalued logics expressed as bilattices. In Sec. 3 we define our extended well-founded semantics providing a method to compute it, and we show that it can be obtained in polynomial time with respect to the size of the set of facts from the program. Finally we present related work and concluding remarks in Sec. 4.

2. Preliminaries

2.1. *Bilattices*

If we consider the four extreme logical values from the confidence-doubt logic $\mathcal{L}^{\mathcal{CD}}$ presented in Introduction, then we get Belnap's

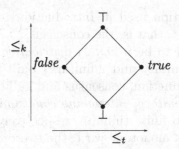

Fig. 1.   The logic $\mathcal{FOUR}$.

four-valued logic,[2] called $\mathcal{FOUR}$, which is depicted in Fig. 1. The horizontal axis shows an increase in the degree of truth, while the vertical axis shows an increase in the degree of knowledge. As seen above, the confidence-doubt and Belnap's logics have an interesting algebraic structure of double complete lattice w.r.t. the truth and knowledge orders. This structure is captured by the concept of bilattice introduced in Ref. 9 defined as follows.

Definition 1. A bilattice is a triple $\langle \mathcal{B}, \leq_t, \leq_k \rangle$, where $\mathcal{B}$ is a nonempty set, and $\leq_t$ and $\leq_k$ are partial orders each giving $\mathcal{B}$ the structure of a complete lattice.

For the bilattice $\mathcal{B}$, join and meet under $\leq_t$ are denoted $\vee$ and $\wedge$ (called extended disjunction and conjunction), and join and meet under $\leq_k$ are denoted $\oplus$ and $\otimes$ (called gullibility and consensus). The greatest and least elements under $\leq_t$ are denoted *true* and *false*, and the greatest and least elements under $\leq_k$ are denoted $\top$ and $\bot$.

A bilattice has a negation, denoted $\neg$, if $\neg$ is a unary operation which is antimonotone w.r.t. the truth order and monotone w.r.t. the knowledge order. In addition $\neg true = false$, $\neg false = true$, $\neg \bot = \bot$ and $\neg \top = \top$. Note that $\neg$ is an extension of the negation in the two-valued logic.

Taking into account the two orders in the case of the bilattice $\mathcal{L}^{\mathcal{CD}}$, the binary operations and, independently, the negation are given as follows:

$$\langle x, y \rangle \wedge \langle z, w \rangle = \langle min(x, z), max(y, w) \rangle,$$
$$\langle x, y \rangle \vee \langle z, w \rangle = \langle max(x, z), min(y, w) \rangle,$$
$$\langle x, y \rangle \otimes \langle z, w \rangle = \langle min(x, z), min(y, w) \rangle,$$
$$\langle x, y \rangle \oplus \langle z, w \rangle = \langle max(x, z), max(y, w) \rangle \quad \text{and} \quad \neg \langle x, y \rangle = \langle y, x \rangle.$$

Note that the operation used in Introduction to combine the two experts' opinions is $\otimes$, that is, the consensus.

A bilattice is said to be *infinitely distributive* if all the distributive laws (that is, finitary and infinitary) built with the extended conjunction and disjunction, consensus and gullibility, hold. We say that the *finitary* (*infinitary*) *interlacing conditions hold* if the above operations applied to finite (infinite, respectively) sets of elements from the bilattice are monotone w.r.t. the two orders.

We introduce the concept of *limited* bilattice, used when we evaluate the complexity of the evaluation of the semantics we will define.

Definition 2. The bilattice $\mathcal{B}$ is limited if there exists a polynom p such that for any set of elements $A = \{a_1, \ldots, a_n\}$ from $\mathcal{B}$, the closure of A w.r.t. the bilattice operations has no more than $p(n)$ elements.

A trivial subclass of limited bilattices is that of the finite bilattices, obviously. However, the limited bilattices class contains also infinite bilattices, as the following proposition shows:

Proposition 1. *The confidence-doubt logic $\mathcal{L}^{\mathcal{CD}}$ is a limited bilattice.*

In the remaining of the paper we assume that any bilattice is infinitely distributive, that all finitary and infinitary interlacing conditions hold, and that it has a negation. Note that $\mathcal{FOUR}$ and $\mathcal{L}^{\mathcal{CD}}$ are exactly of this type.

We use bilattices as spaces of logical values for the extended programs we define in the next subsection. For illustration purposes we use the logics $\mathcal{L}^{\mathcal{CD}}$ and $\mathcal{FOUR}$ in our examples.

2.2. *Extended programs*

Conventional logic programming has the set $\{false, true\}$ as its intended space of truth values, but since not every query may produce an answer, partial models are often allowed (i.e. $\perp$ is added). If we want to deal with inconsistency as well, then $\top$ must be added. Fitting extended the notion of logic program, that we will call *extended program*, to bilattices as follows. Let $\mathcal{B}$ be a bilattice.

Definition 3[4]

- A formula is an expression built up from literals and elements of $\mathcal{B}$, using $\wedge, \vee, \otimes, \oplus, \neg, \exists, \forall$.
- A clause or rule r is of the form $P(x_1, \ldots, x_n) \leftarrow \phi(x_1, \ldots, x_n)$ where the atomic formula $P(x_1, \ldots, x_n)$ is the head, denoted by $head(r)$, and the formula $\phi(x_1, \ldots, x_n)$ is the body, denoted by $body(r)$. It is assumed that the free variables of the body are among $x_1, \ldots, x_n$.
- A program is a finite set of clauses with no predicate letter appearing in the head of more than one clause (this apparent restriction causes no loss of generality).

The following set P of three rules is an example of program considered in the context of the confidence-doubt logic $\mathcal{L}^{\mathcal{CD}}$, where all the atoms are ground. Note that the last rule may be seen as a fact definition. Here the atom F will be assigned the logical value expressing the grades of confidence of 0.7 and of doubt of 0.1:

$$\text{P: } A \leftarrow (C \oplus D) \vee B; \quad D \leftarrow D \otimes \neg A; \quad F \leftarrow \langle 0.7, 0.1 \rangle.$$

A *conventional logic program*[4] is one whose underlying truth-value space is the bilattice $\mathcal{FOUR}$ and which does not involve $\otimes, \oplus, \forall, \perp, \top$.

3. Extended Well-Founded Semantics of Extended Programs

In the remaining of this paper, in order to simplify the presentation, we assume that all extended programs are instantiated programs, called simply programs.

3.1. *Interpretations*

We can extend the two orders on bilattice $\mathcal{B}$ to the set of all interpretations over $\mathcal{B}$, denoted by $\mathcal{V}(\mathcal{B})$. An interpretation I of a program P is defined as a partial function over the Herbrand base $\mathcal{HB}_P$, and a completion of I is any total interpretation I' such that $I(A) = I'(A)$, for any atom A in the domain of definition of I, denoted by $def(I)$. When comparing interpretations, we consider their least completion. The least completion of an interpretation I is defined to be the completion J of I such that $J(A) = \perp$, for every atom A not defined under I. Now, if I_1 and I_2 are two interpretations having the least completions I_1' and I_2', respectively, then $I_1 \leq_t I_2$ if $I_1'(A) \leq_t I_2'(A)$ for all ground atoms A (and similarly for $\leq_k$).

The total interpretations can be extended from atoms to formulas as follows: $I(X \wedge Y) = I(X) \wedge I(Y)$ (and similarly for the other bilattice operations), $I((\exists x)\phi(x)) = \bigvee_{t \in GT} I(\phi(t))$, and $I((\forall x)\phi(x)) = \bigwedge_{t \in GT} I(\phi(t))$, where GT stands for the set of all ground terms.

However we are interested to see now how *partial* interpretations can be used to evaluate formulas. If B is a closed formula then we say that B evaluates to the logical value β with respect to a partial interpretation I, denoted by $B \equiv \beta$ w.r.t. I, or by $B \equiv_I \beta$, if $J(B) = \beta$ for any completion J of I. The following lemma provides an efficient method of testing whether $B \equiv_I \beta$ by computing the logical value of the formula B w.r.t. only two completions of the interpretation I.

Lemma 1. *Let $I_\perp$ and $I_\top$ be two completions of I defined as follows: $I_\perp(A) = \perp$ and $I_\top(A) = \top$ for every atom A of $\mathcal{HB}_P$ not in $def(I)$. Then $B \equiv_I \beta$ iff $I_\perp(B) = I_\top(B) = \beta$.*

We use also the concept of compatibility of interpretations in the sense that two interpretations I and J are said to be compatible if, for any atom A, $I(A)$ and $J(A)$ are both defined implies $I(A) = J(A)$.

3.2. *Semantics of extended programs*

Given a program P, we consider two ways of inferring new information from P. First by activating the rules of P and deriving new information through an immediate consequence operator T. Second, by a kind of default reasoning based on the assumption we make in each of the optimistic, pessimistic, skeptical and inconsistent approaches, respectively.

The immediate consequence operator T that we use takes as input an interpretation I and returns an interpretation $T(I)$, defined as follows: for all ground atoms A,

$$T(I)(A) = \beta \text{ if } (A \leftarrow B \in P \text{ and } B \equiv_I \beta),$$

and is undefined, otherwise.

Each assumption is expressed as a hypothesis H^α which formally is an interpretation I that assigns the value α (for $\alpha = true, false, \perp$ and $\top$) to every atom of its domain of definition $def(I)$. Roughly speaking, the hypothesis concerns some of the atoms of the Herbrand base whose logical values cannot be inferred by rule activation.

Definition 4. Let P be a program and I a partial interpretation. A hypothesis H^α is called sound (w.r.t. P and I) if the following hold:

(1) H^α is compatible with I and
(2) for every atom A in $def(H^\alpha)$, if there is a rule r of P with $head(r) = A$ then $body(r) \equiv \alpha$ w.r.t. $I \cup H^\alpha$.

Intuitively the above definition says that a sound hypothesis must succeed in being tested against the sure knowledge provided by the rules of P (condition (2)) and by a given fixed interpretation I (condition (1)). Note also that if we restrict our attention to conventional logic programs, then the concept of sound hypothesis for $\alpha = false$ reduces to that of unfounded set of Van Gelder *et al.*,[13] used in the definition of the well-founded semantics. The difference is that the definition in Ref. 13 has rather a syntactic flavour, while ours has a semantic flavour. We should also note that our sound hypotheses correspond only to unfounded sets which do not contradict the interpretations from which they are built.[a] Moreover, our definition not only extends the concept of unfounded set to multivalued logics, but also generalizes its definition w.r.t. the optimistic, pessimistic, skeptical and inconsistent assumptions (corresponding to $\alpha = true, false, \bot$ and $\top$, respectively).

We note that, for any given P, I and α, there is at least one sound hypothesis H^α (the everywhere undefined interpretation), thus the class of sound hypotheses is nonempty. The following proposition shows that the class of sound hypotheses has a greatest element which is obtained by the union of all sound hypotheses H^α w.r.t. I, that we denote by $H^\alpha_{max}(I)$.

Proposition 2. *Let P, I and α be fixed. Then there is a sound hypothesis $H^\alpha_{max}(I)$ such that: $T(I) \cup H^\alpha \leq_k T(I) \cup H^\alpha_{max}(I)$, for all sound hypotheses H^α w.r.t. I.*

We have seen that there are two ways of deriving information from a program: by applying the rules and by using sound hypotheses (namely the maximal ones, in order to derive maximal information

---

[a] Note that all the other unfounded sets do not prove to be useful anyway, as they may not be used in the construction of the well-founded semantics of a program.[13]

from the program). Hence the idea to build the following sequence of interpretations, where I^u is the everywhere undefined interpretation:

$$I_0 = I^u; \quad I_{i+1} = T(I_i) \cup H^\alpha_{\max}(I_i); \quad I_j = \bigcup_{i<j} I_i \text{ if j is a limit ordinal.}$$

It can be proved that the sequence $I_{i \geq 0}$ is increasing w.r.t. the knowledge order, and has a limit, denoted by $lfp^\alpha(P)$. Note that, intuitively speaking, $lfp^\alpha(P)$ represents all the information that can be inferred from the program P. Obviously it is a fixpoint of the operator $T \cup H^\alpha_{max}$. Moreover, we can show that $lfp^\alpha(P)$ has an important property namely that it satisfies the rules of the program P. Formally, an interpretation I satisfies an instantiated rule $A \leftarrow B$ if $I(B) \leq_t I(A)$. This notion comes from the intuitive remark that, as the consequence is derived from a premise, the degree of truth of the consequence should be at least the degree of truth of the premise. We have:

Proposition 3. *The interpretation $lfp^\alpha(P)$ satisfies any rule of P.*

This justifies the following definition of semantics for P.

Definition 5. The interpretation $lfp^\alpha(P)$ is defined to be the *extended well-founded semantics of P* w.r.t. the logical value α, that we denote by $ewfs^\alpha(P)$.

Considering the four different assumptions, we have the following relationships between the semantics obtained:

Proposition 4. *If P is a program then: $ewfs^\perp(P) \leq_k ewfs^\alpha(P) \leq_k ewfs^\top(P)$ for $\alpha \in \mathcal{FOUR}$.*

Fitting[5] introduced the (multivalued) stable models for extended programs in bilattices. This concept extends that of stable model in the conventional two-valued logic.[8] We show that if we consider the pessimistic approach, our semantics coincides with Fitting's multivalued stable model that has the least degree of information.

Theorem 1. *Let P be a program and $mstable_k(P)$ be its least multivalued stable model w.r.t. $\leq_k$, as defined in Ref. 5 Then $ewfs^{false}(P) = mstable_k(P)$.*

This equality may seem surprising since $ewfs^{false}(P)$ advantages the negative information while $mstable_k(P)$ prefers the lack of information, as it is minimal in the knowledge order. However, as Fitting shows in Refs. 5 and 6, in the definition of the multivalued stable models there exists a preference for falsehood, in the sense that, whenever possible, the truth value *false* is assigned to atoms. See Ref. 6 for an approach of building a theory that prefers falsehood.

The last result of the subsection compares our semantics with the well-founded semantics[13] and Kripke-Kleene semantics[3] of a conventional program P, denoted $wfs(P)$ and $kks(P)$, respectively.

Theorem 2. *If P is a conventional program and the bilattice is $\mathcal{FOUR}$ then $ewfs^{false}(P) = wfs(P)$ and $ewfs^{\perp}(P) = kks(P)$.*

3.3. *Computing the extended well-founded semantics*

In order to compute the extended well-founded semantics we need a method for computing the greatest sound hypothesis $H^{\alpha}_{\max}$ used in the definition of the semantics. We provide it by considering the following sequence of instantiated atoms $PF_i(I)_{i \geq 0}$, for a given interpretation I: $PF_0(I) = \emptyset$;

$$PF_{i+1}(I) = \{A \mid A \leftarrow B \in P \text{ and } B \not\equiv \alpha \ w.r.t. \ J_{i,I}\}, \quad \text{for } i \geq 0,$$

where $J_{i,I}$ is the interpretation defined by:

$$J_{i,I}(A) = \begin{cases} I(A) \text{ if } A \in def(I), \\ \alpha \text{ if } A \in (\mathcal{HB}_P \backslash PF_i) \backslash def(I), \\ undefined, \quad otherwise. \end{cases}$$

One can prove that the sequence $PF_i(I)_{i \geq 0}$ is monotone with respect to set inclusion, so it has a limit denoted by $PF(I)$.

Theorem 3. *Let P, I and α be fixed. If J is an interpretation defined by: $J(A) = \alpha$ for any $A \in (\mathcal{HB}_P \backslash PF(I))$ and $J(A) = undefined$ for any other ground atom A, then $H^{\alpha}_{\max}(I) = J$.*

If we compute the semantics of the program P provided in Introduction in the context of the bilattice $\mathcal{FOUR}$, for each of the pessimistic, optimistic, skeptical and inconsistent approaches respectively, we get the following table, where we have included on the first row only the instantiated atoms built with predicates defined by the program rules:[b]

---

[b] All the other instantiated atoms are assigned the corresponding logical value α, and have been omitted.

Table 1. $ewfs^\alpha(P)$

α	s(John)	i(John)	f(John)	c(John)
false	*true*	*false*	*false*	*true*
true	*true*	*true*	*true*	*false*
$\perp$	*true*	$\perp$	$\perp$	$\perp$
$\top$	*true*	$\top$	$\top$	$\top$

We conclude this section with a complexity result showing that our semantics can be computed in polynomial time with respect to the size of the set of facts from the program. Formally, let $\mathcal{B}$ be a limited bilattice and let $P = P_{Rules} \cup P_{Facts}$ be a program with no function symbol,[c] where P_{Facts} is the set of facts (i.e. the set of rules of the form $A \leftarrow c$ where c is a logical value from the bilattice $\mathcal{B}$) and P_{Rules} is the set of rules (i.e. the remaining part of P).

Theorem 4. *The time complexity of the computation of the extended well-founded semantics of the program P in a limited bilattice is polynomial w.r.t.* $|P_{Facts}|$.

4.   Related Work and Concluding Remarks

We have proposed an approach for handling imperfect information through extended logic programs by defining the extended well-founded semantics. We consider imperfect information to be missing/incomplete, uncertain and/or inconsistent information. In our semantics, missing information is completed by using *optimistic*, *pessimistic*, *skeptical* and *inconsistent* assumptions. Imperfect information is handled by using bilattices as multivalued logics. We provide a method of computation of our semantics and show that, for the pessimistic assumption our extended well-founded semantics captures the conventional well-founded semantics and Fitting's least multivalued stable model having the least degree of information, while for the skeptical assumption our semantics captures the Kripke-Kleene semantics.

The conventional logic program semantics are mostly based on pessimistic and skeptical approaches,[3,8,12,13] which is also the case

---

[c] Note that the fixpoint computation of our semantics terminates in a finite number of steps in this case.

with the most extended semantics expressing uncertainty.[5,7,10,15] Although useful — as we have shown through our example in Introduction, the optimistic approach has been uncommon. In Ref. 6 Fitting proposes a mechanism of building a theory of truth that prefers falsehood, that is, the logical value *false* is assigned to atoms whenever possible. It is suggested that this mechanism, used also for defining the multivalued stable models for extended programs,[5] can be straightforwardly extended to build a theory that prefers truthhood, which would correspond, in our terms, to using an optimistic assumption. We have shown the connection between our semantics defined in the pessimistic approach and the least multivalued stable model that has the least degree of information.

We have also shown that the complexity of the evaluation of the extended well-founded semantics with respect to the size of the set of program facts is polynomial time for the useful class of limited bilattices.

References

1. O. Arieli, Paraconsistent declarative semantics for extended logic programs. *Annals of Mathematics and Artificial Intelligence*, **36**(4), 381–417 (2002).
2. N. D. Belnap, Jr. A useful four-valued logic, J. M. Dunn and G. Epstein (eds.). *Modern Uses of Multiple-Valued Logic*, D. Reichel, Dordrecht (1977).
3. M. C. Fitting, A kripke/kleene semantics for logic programs. *J. Logic Programming*, **2**, 295–312 (1985).
4. M. C. Fitting, Bilattices and the semantics of logic programming. *J. Logic Programming*, **11**, 91–116 (1991).
5. M. C. Fitting, The family of stable models. *J. Logic Programming*, **17**, 197–225 (1993).
6. M. C. Fitting, A theory of truth that prefers falsehood. *Journal of Philosophical Logic*, **26**, 477–500 (1997).
7. M. C. Fitting, Fixpoint semantics for logic programming — a survey. *Theoretical Computer Science*, **278**, 25–51 (2002).
8. M. Gelfond and V. Lifschitz, The Stable Model semantics for logic programming. *Proc. of the 5th International Conference on Logic Programming* (1988).
9. M. L. Ginsberg, Multivalued logics: A uniform approach to reasonning in artificial intelligence. *Computationnal Intelligence*, **4**, 265–316 (1988).
10. V. S. Lakshmanan and F. Sadri, On a theory of probabilistic deductive databases. *J. Theory and Practice of Logic Programming*, **1**(1) (2001).
11. Y. Loyer, N. Spyratos and D. Stamate, Hypothesis-based semantics of logic programs in multivalued logics *ACM Transactions on Computational Logic*, **15**(3), 508–527 (2004).

12. T. C. Przymusinski, The well-founded semantics coincides with the three-valued stable semantics. *Fundamenta Informaticae*, **13**(4), 445–464 (1990).
13. A. Van Gelder, K. A. Ross and J. S. Schlipf, The well-founded semantics for general logic programs. *J. ACM*, **38**, 620–650 (1991).
14. K. M. Sim, Bilattices and reasoning in artificial intelligence: Concepts and Foundations. *Artificial Intelligence Review*, **15**(3), 219–240 (2001).
15. V. S. Subrahmanian, Probabilistic databases and logic programming. *Proc. of 17th International Conference of Logic Programming* (2001).

On n-Contractive Fuzzy Logics: First Results

Carles Noguera* and Francesc Esteva[†]

Artificial Intelligence Research Institute IIIA — CSIC
Campus de la UAB, 08193 Bellaterra, Catalonia, Spain
*cnoguera@iiia.csic.es
†esteva@iiia.csic.es

Joan Gispert

Department of Logic, University of Barcelona
Gran Via de les Corts Catalanes 585
08007 Barcelona, Catalonia, Spain
jgispertb@ub.edu

Abstract

In order to reach a deeper understanding of the structure of fuzzy logics, some very general new logics are defined. Namely, we consider the extensions of MTL by adding the generalized contraction and excluded middle laws introduced in Ref. 4 and we enrich this family by means of the axiom of weak cancellation and the Ω operator defined in Ref. 19. The algebraic counterpart of these logics is studied characterizing the subdirectly irreducible, the semisimple and the simple algebras. Finally, some important algebraic and logical properties of the considered logics are discussed: local finiteness, finite embedding property, finite model property, decidability and standard completeness.

*The authors acknowledge partial support of the Spanish projects MULOG TIN2004-07933-C03-01 and TIN2004-07933-C03-02.

1.   Introduction

The research on formal systems for fuzzy logic has been growing rapidly during the last years. The origin of this development can be traced back to Hájek's works (see Ref. 12) when he defined the *basic fuzzy logic* BL in order to capture the common fragment of the three main fuzzy logics known at that time: Łukasiewicz logic, Product logic and Gödel logic. These three logics were proved to be standard complete, i.e. complete with respect to the semantics where the set of truth values is the real unit interval $[0, 1]$, the conjunction is interpreted by a continuous t-norm (Łukasiewicz t-norm, the product t-norm and the minimum t-norm, respectively) and the implication is interpreted by the residuum of the t-norm. In Ref. 5 it was proved that BL is, in fact, complete with respect to the semantics given by all continuous t-norms and their residua. Nevertheless, the necessary and sufficient condition for a t-norm to be residuated is not the continuity, but only the left-continuity. For this reason it makes perfect sense to consider a more general fuzzy logic system whose semantic completeness would be the class of all left-continuous t-norm and their residua. This logic, MTL, was introduced by Esteva and Godo in Ref. 7 and its standard completeness was proved in Ref. 15. Therefore, if we understand fuzzy logic systems as those that are complete with respect to some class of t-norms and their residua, then MTL becomes the weakest fuzzy logic and the research on fuzzy logic systems becomes research on extensions of MTL. Moreover, since it is an algebraizable logic whose equivalent algebraic semantics is the variety of all MTL-algebras, then there is a one-to-one correspondence between axiomatic extensions of MTL and subvarieties of MTL-algebras. Some of them are already known (see for instance Refs. 6, 9–11, 13, 16, 19 and 21–23) but a general description of the structure of all these extensions is still far from being known. In this paper we make some new steps in this direction by considering some very general varieties of MTL-algebras, namely the varieties of n-contractive MTL-algebras. Some of them were already introduced in Ref. 4.

After some necessary general preliminaries about axiomatic extensions of MTL and their algebraization, we consider in Sec. 3 some equations introduced by Kowalski and Ono in Ref. 17 to define n-contractive fuzzy logics. Section 4.1 deals with the algebraic counterpart of these logics, the n-contractive MTL-algebras; subdirectly irreducible, semisimple and simple algebras are characterized. In

Sec. 4.2 we add some other logics to the hierarchy of n-contractive fuzzy logics by means of the weak cancellation law and the Ω operator and we show that all of them are finitely axiomatizable. Finally, Sec. 4.3 collects the obtained results regarding some relevant logical and algebraic properties of the considered logics, namely local finiteness, finite embedding property, finite model property, decidability and standard completeness. Most of the problems are solved, but some are still open.

2. Axiomatic Extensions of MTL and their Algebraization

In Ref. 7 Esteva and Godo define MTL (Monoidal T-norm based Logic) as the sentential logic in the language $\mathcal{L} = \{\&, \to, \wedge, \overline{0}\}$ of type $\langle 2, 2, 2, 0 \rangle$ given by a Hilbert-style calculus with the inference rule of *Modus Ponens* and the following axioms (using implication as the least binding connective):

(A1) $(\varphi \to \psi) \to ((\psi \to \chi) \to (\varphi \to \chi))$

(A2) $\varphi \& \psi \to \varphi$

(A3) $\varphi \& \psi \to \psi \& \varphi$

(A4) $\varphi \wedge \psi \to \varphi$

(A5) $\varphi \wedge \psi \to \psi \wedge \varphi$

(A6) $\varphi \& (\varphi \to \psi) \to \varphi \wedge \psi$

(A7a) $(\varphi \to (\psi \to \chi)) \to (\varphi \& \psi \to \chi)$

(A7b) $(\varphi \& \psi \to \chi) \to (\varphi \to (\psi \to \chi))$

(A8) $((\varphi \to \psi) \to \chi) \to (((\psi \to \varphi) \to \chi) \to \chi)$

(A9) $\overline{0} \to \varphi$

Other usual connectives are defined by:

$$\varphi \vee \psi := ((\varphi \to \psi) \to \psi) \wedge ((\psi \to \varphi) \to \varphi);$$

$$\varphi \leftrightarrow \psi := (\varphi \to \psi) \& (\psi \to \varphi);$$

$$\neg \varphi := \varphi \to \overline{0}; \overline{1} := \neg \overline{0}.$$

We denote by $Fm_{\mathcal{L}}$ the set of $\mathcal{L}$-formulae (built using a countable set of variables). If $\Gamma \cup \{\varphi\} \subseteq Fm_{\mathcal{L}}$, we write $\Gamma \vdash_{\text{MTL}} \varphi$ if, and only if, φ is derivable from Γ in the given calculus. We write $\vdash_{\text{MTL}} \varphi$ instead of $\emptyset \vdash_{\text{MTL}} \varphi$.

Definition 1. [7] Let $\mathcal{A} = \langle A, *, \rightarrow, \wedge, \vee, \overline{0}^{\mathcal{A}}, \overline{1}^{\mathcal{A}} \rangle$ be an algebra of type $\langle 2, 2, 2, 2, 0, 0 \rangle$. $\mathcal{A}$ is an MTL-algebra iff it is a bounded integral commutative residuated lattice satisfying the prelinearity equation: $(x \rightarrow y) \vee (y \rightarrow x) \approx \overline{1}$. The negation operation is defined as $\neg a = a \rightarrow \overline{0}^{\mathcal{A}}$. If the lattice order is total we will say that $\mathcal{A}$ is an MTL-chain. The MTL-chains defined over the real unit interval $[0, 1]$ (with the usual order) are those where $*$ is a left-continuous t-norm and they are called standard MTL-chains. $[0, 1]_*$ will denote the standard chain given by a left-continuous t-norm $*$. The class of all MTL-algebras is a variety and it is denoted by $\mathbb{MTL}$. The $\overline{0}$-free subreducts of MTL-algebras are called *prelinear semihoops* and they are defined in Ref. 8.

Definition 2. Given $\Gamma \cup \{\varphi\} \subseteq Fm_{\mathcal{L}}$ and a class $\mathbb{K}$ of MTL-algebras, we define: $\Gamma \vDash_{\mathbb{K}} \varphi$ iff for all $\mathcal{A} \in \mathbb{K}$ and for all evaluation v in $\mathcal{A}$, we have $v(\varphi) = \overline{1}^{\mathcal{A}}$ whenever $v(\psi) = \overline{1}^{\mathcal{A}}$ for every $\psi \in \Gamma$.

Then, it is proved that for every $\Gamma \cup \{\varphi\} \subseteq Fm_{\mathcal{L}}$, $\Gamma \vdash_{\mathrm{MTL}} \varphi$ iff $\Gamma \vDash_{\mathrm{MTL}} \varphi$. Moreover, it is not difficult to prove that MTL is an algebraizable logic in the sense of Blok and Pigozzi (see Ref. 2) and $\mathbb{MTL}$ is its equivalent algebraic semantics. This implies much more than the algebraic completeness. In particular, there is an order-reversing isomorphism between axiomatic extensions of MTL and subvarieties of $\mathbb{MTL}$:

- If $\Sigma \subseteq Fm_{\mathcal{L}}$ and L is the extension of MTL obtained by adding the formulae of Σ as schemata, then the equivalent algebraic semantics of L is the subvariety of $\mathbb{MTL}$ axiomatized by the equations $\{\varphi \approx 1 : \varphi \in \Sigma\}$. We denote this variety by $\mathbb{L}$ and we call its members *L-algebras*.
- Let $\mathbb{L} \subseteq \mathbb{MTL}$ be the subvariety axiomatized by a set of equations Λ. Then the logic associated to $\mathbb{L}$ is the axiomatic extension L of MTL given by the axiom schemata $\{\varphi \leftrightarrow \psi : \varphi \approx \psi \in \Lambda\}$.

In the study of these subvarieties the chains play a crucial role because each MTL-algebra is isomorphic to a subdirect product of MTL-chains, as proved in Ref. 7. This implies that MTL is complete with respect the semantics given by MTL-chains. The same kind of result is true for every axiomatic extension of MTL. In some cases, it is also possible to restrict the semantics to the algebras defined in the real unit interval by a left-continuous t-norm and its residuum, obtaining the so-called standard completeness results. If a logic L is an axiomatic extension of MTL, we say that L enjoys *(finite) strong standard completeness* if, and only if, for every (finite) set of formulae $T \subseteq Fm_{\mathcal{L}}$ and every formula φ, $T \vdash_L \varphi$ iff $T \models_{\mathcal{A}} \varphi$ for every standard L-algebra $\mathcal{A}$. We will call this property (F)SSC, for short. We say that L enjoys the *standard completeness* (SC, for short) if, and only if, the equivalence is true for $T = \emptyset$. Tables 1 and 2 collect several axiom schemata and important axiomatic extensions of MTL that are defined by adding them to the Hilbert-style calculus given above for MTL. Table 2 also collects the standard completeness properties that they satisfy.

However, we are not only interested in the standard completeness properties of the logics. We will also consider several other properties which are interesting both from the algebraic and the logical point of view.

Table 1. Some usual axiom schemata in fuzzy logics.

Axiom schema	Name
$\neg\neg\varphi \rightarrow \varphi$	(Inv)
$\neg\varphi \vee ((\varphi \rightarrow \varphi\&\psi) \rightarrow \psi)$	(C)
$\varphi \rightarrow \varphi\&\varphi$	(C$_2$)
$\varphi \vee \neg\varphi$	(S$_2$)
$\varphi \wedge \psi \rightarrow \varphi\&(\varphi \rightarrow \psi)$	(Div)
$(\varphi\&\psi \rightarrow \overline{0}) \vee (\varphi \wedge \psi \rightarrow \varphi\&\psi)$	(WNM)

Table 2. Some important axiomatic extensions of MTL and their standard completeness properties. Ł is Łukasiewicz logic, Π is product logic, G is Gödel logic, and CPC is the classical propositional calculus.

Logic	Additional axiom schemata	SC	FSSC	SSC
MTL		Yes	Yes	Yes
IMTL	(Inv)	Yes	Yes	Yes
WNM	(WNM)	Yes	Yes	Yes
NM	(Inv), (WNM)	Yes	Yes	Yes
BL	(Div)	Yes	Yes	No
Ł	(Div), (Inv)	Yes	Yes	No
Π	(Div), (C)	Yes	Yes	No
G	(C$_2$)	Yes	Yes	Yes
CPC	(S$_2$)	No	No	No

Definition 3. Let $\mathbb{K}$ be a class of algebras of the same type. Then,

- $\mathbb{K}$ is locally finite (LF, for short) if for every $\mathcal{A} \in \mathbb{K}$ and for every finite set $B \subseteq A$, the subalgebra generated by B, is also finite.
- $\mathbb{K}$ has the finite embeddability property (FEP, for short) if, and only if, every finite partial subalgebra of some member of $\mathbb{K}$ can be embedded in some finite algebra of $\mathbb{K}$.
- $\mathbb{K}$ has the strong finite model property (SFMP, for short) if, and only if, every quasiequation that fails to hold in every algebra of $\mathbb{K}$ can be refuted in some finite member of $\mathbb{K}$.
- $\mathbb{K}$ has the finite model property (FMP, for short) if, and only if, every equation that fails to hold in every algebra of $\mathbb{K}$ can be refuted in some finite member of $\mathbb{K}$.

A variety has the FMP if, and only if, it is generated by its finite members and a quasivariety has the SFMP if, and only if, it is generated (as a quasivariety) by its finite members. In Ref. 3 it is proved that for classes of algebras of finite type closed under finite products (hence, in particular, for varieties of MTL-algebras) the FEP and the SFMP are equivalent. Moreover, it is clear that for every class of algebras $\mathbb{L}$ which is the equivalent algebraic semantics of a recursively axiomatizable logic L, we have:

- If $\mathbb{L}$ is locally finite, then it has the FEP.
- If $\mathbb{L}$ has the FEP, then it has the FMP.
- If $\mathbb{L}$ has the FMP, then L is decidable.

Table 3 shows which of these properties are true for the above mentioned axiomatic extensions of MTL.

Table 3.   Algebraic and logical properties.

Logic	LF	FEP	FMP	Decidable
MTL	No	Yes	Yes	Yes
IMTL	No	Yes	Yes	Yes
WNM	Yes	Yes	Yes	Yes
NM	Yes	Yes	Yes	Yes
BL	No	Yes	Yes	Yes
L	No	Yes	Yes	Yes
Π	No	No	No	Yes
G	Yes	Yes	Yes	Yes
CPC	Yes	Yes	Yes	Yes

Our aim is to classify axiomatic extensions of MTL and study their relevant properties as it has been done with the so far mentioned logics. In the case of BL and its extensions the study strongly relied on the following structure theorem for BL-chains:

Theorem 1.[1] *For every* BL-*chain* $\mathcal{A}$, *there is a set of Wajsberg hoops* $\{\mathcal{A}_i \mid i \in I\}$ *such that* $\mathcal{A}$ *is their ordinal sum; in symbols:* $\mathcal{A} = \bigoplus_{i \in I} \mathcal{A}_i$.

This result is a generalization of the well-known theorem proved in Ref. 20 that states that all continuous t-norms (i.e. BL-chains over $[0, 1]$) are decomposable as ordinal sum of their Archimedean components, which are the three basic t-norms: Łukasiewicz, product and minimum t-norms. However, in Theorem 1 the decomposition is done by means of Wajsberg hoops, i.e. the $\bar{0}$-free subreducts of the MV-chains. This is not true in general in all MTL-chains; nevertheless in Ref. 19 some results in this direction are proved.

Definition 4. Let $\mathcal{A}$ be an MTL-chain or a totally ordered semi-hoop. We define a binary relation $\sim$ on A by letting for every $a, b \in A$, $a \sim b$ if, and only if, there is $n \geq 1$ such that $a^n \leq b \leq a$ or $b^n \leq a \leq b$. It is easy to check that $\sim$ is an equivalence relation. Its equivalence classes are called *Archimedean classes*. Given $a \in A$, its Archimedean class is denoted as $[a]_\sim$.

Definition 5.[19] A totally ordered semihoop is indecomposable if, and only if, it is not isomorphic to any ordinal sum of two non-trivial totally ordered semihoops.

Theorem 2.[19] *For every* MTL-*chain* $\mathcal{A}$, *there is the maximum decomposition as ordinal sum of indecomposable totally ordered semi-hoops, with the first one bounded.*

Corollary 1.[19] *Let* $\mathcal{A}$ *be an* MTL-*chain. If the partition* $\{[a]_\sim : a \in A \setminus \{\bar{1}^{\mathcal{A}}\}\}$ *given by the Archimedean classes gives a decomposition as ordinal sum, then it is the maximum one. In this case we say that* $\mathcal{A}$ *is totally decomposable.*

One can produce varieties where the chains are decomposable as ordinal sum of Archimedean components. Indeed, the Ω operator is introduced to produce new logics from the known ones by considering the ordinal sums of their corresponding semihoops. Namely, given any axiomatic extension L of MTL, $\Omega(\mathbb{L})$ is defined as the variety of MTL-algebras generated by all the ordinal sums of $\bar{0}$-free subreducts of L-chains with the first bounded. $\Omega(L)$ denotes its corresponding logic.

3. The n-Contraction

In Ref. 17 Kowalski and Ono studied some varieties of bounded integral commutative residuated lattices. In particular, they considered for every $n \geq 2$ the varieties defined by the following equations:

$$(E_n)\, x^n \approx x^{n-1}$$
$$(EM_n)\, x \vee \neg x^{n-1} \approx \bar{1}.$$

(E_2) corresponds, in fact, to the law of contraction, which defines the variety of Heyting algebras. Therefore, for every $n \geq 3$ the equation (E_n) corresponds to a weak form of contraction that we will call n-contraction. Notice that (EM_2) is the algebraic form of the law of the excluded middle, and for every $n \geq 3$ (EM_n) corresponds to a weak form of this law. In Ref. 4 Ciabattoni, Esteva and Godo brought the equations (E_n) to the framework of fuzzy logics. Indeed, for each $n \geq 2$, they defined the n-contraction axiom as: $\varphi^{n-1} \rightarrow \varphi^n$ (C_n), and they called C_nMTL (resp. C_nIMTL) the extension of MTL (resp. IMTL) obtained by adding this axiom. Given $n \geq 2$, the equivalent algebraic semantics of C_nMTL (resp. C_nIMTL) is the class of n-contractive MTL-algebras (resp. IMTL-algebras), i.e. the subvariety of MTL (resp. IMTL) defined by the equation: $x^{n-1} \approx x^n$. Strong standard completeness for these logics was also proved in Ref. 4. It is easy to see that C_2MTL is Gödel logic and C_2IMTL is the classical propositional calculus CPC. Moreover, for every $n \geq 3$, WNM is a strict extension of C_nMTL, NM is a strict extension of C_nIMTL, C_nMTL is a strict extension of C_{n+1}MTL and C_nIMTL is a strict extension of C_{n+1}IMTL.

We say that an axiomatic extension of MTL L is n-contractive if $\vdash_L (C_n)$. Of course, given any L we can make it n-contractive by adding the schema (C_n). We call the resulting logic C_nL.

Theorem 3. *If* L *is an* n-contractive *axiomatic extension of* MTL, *then for every* $\Gamma \cup \{\varphi, \psi\} \subseteq Fm_{\mathcal{L}}$ *we have:*

$$\Gamma, \varphi \vdash_L \psi \text{ if, and only if, } \Gamma \vdash_L \varphi^{n-1} \rightarrow \psi.$$

Proposition 1 (Prop. 1.1^{17}). *Let* $\mathbb{K}$ *be a variety of residuated lattices. Then,* $\mathbb{K}$ *has the property EDPC (equationally definable principal congruences) if, and only if,* $\mathbb{K} \models (E_n)$, *for some* $n \geq 2$.

According to a bridge theorem of Abstract Algebraic Logic, an algebraizable logic has the global deduction-detachment theorem if, and only if, its equivalent algebraic semantics has the EDPC. Therefore, in our framework of fuzzy logics as axiomatic extensions of MTL, the contractive logics are a good choice in the sense that they are the only finitary extensions of MTL enjoying the global deduction-detachment theorem. Moreover, in Ref. 3 the authors prove that for varieties of finite type enjoying the EDPC property (equationally definable principal congruences) the FEP and the FMP are equivalent.

We will consider also the axioms corresponding to (EM_n): $\varphi \vee \neg\varphi^{n-1} (S_n)$. Given any axiomatic extension L of MTL, S_nL will be its extension with (S_n).

4. New Results

4.1. *n-contractive chains*

In this section we will study some basic properties of the n-contractive chains. Observe that this is an important and big class of chains since it contains all the finite MTL-chains (clearly, every finite MTL-chain is n-contractive for some n). Given an MTL-algebra $\mathcal{A}$, $a \in A$ is idempotent iff $a^2 = a$. It is easy to see that in n-contractive chains, the idempotent elements are those of the form a^{n-1}. As in standard BL-chains, they determine the Archimedean components:

Proposition 2. *Let* $\mathcal{A}$ *be an* n-*contractive MTL-chain. Then, for every* $a, b \in A$:

(i) $a \sim b$ *if, and only if,* $a^{n-1} = b^{n-1}$, *and*
(ii) $a^{n-1} = \min[a]_\sim$.

Corollary 2. *Let* $\mathcal{A}$ *be an* n-*contractive MTL-chain and let* $a \in A$. *If* $[a]_\sim$ *has supremum, then it is the maximum.*

Therefore, Archimedean classes with supremum in n-contractive chains are always intervals of the form $[b^{n-1}, b]$. Moreover, this implies that given a standard n-contractive chain $\mathcal{A}$, the idempotent elements have neither predecessor nor successor. In particular, 1 is an accumulation point of idempotent elements.[a] Next proposition characterizes the subdirectly irreducible n-contractive algebras.

Proposition 3. *An n-contractive MTL-chain is subdirectly irreducible if, and only if, its set of idempotent elements has a coatom. Therefore, there are no subdirectly irreducible standard n-contractive MTL-chains.*

An important subclass of subdirectly irreducible algebras is the class of simple algebras, those without non-trivial congruences.

Proposition 4. *Let $\mathcal{A}$ be an MTL-chain. Then, $\mathcal{A} \models (EM_n)$ if, and only if, $\mathcal{A}$ is n-contractive and simple.*

Corollary 3. *For each $n \geq 2$, the class of semisimple n-contractive MTL-algebras is the variety $\mathbb{S}_n$MTL.*

For every $n \geq 2$, $\mathbb{S}_n$MTL $\cap$ MV $=$ $\mathbb{C}_n$MTL $\cap$ MV. However, in MTL and in IMTL the situation is not so easy. In the first level the varieties corresponding to (E_n) and (EM_n) are still easy to compute. Indeed, $\mathbb{S}_2$MTL $=$ $\mathbb{S}_2$IMTL $=$ $\mathbb{C}_2$IMTL $=$ BA and $\mathbb{C}_2$MTL $=$ G. For $n = 3$, we have $\mathbb{S}_3$MTL $\subsetneqq$ WNM, in fact, the $\mathbb{S}_3$MTL-chains are those where the product of two non-one elements is always zero, i.e. the so-called drastic product. When $n = 3$, we also have $\mathbb{S}_3$IMTL $=$ $\mathbb{V}(Ł_3) = $ NM $\cap$ MV $\subsetneqq$ NM $\subseteq$ $\mathbb{C}_3$IMTL. Therefore for each $n \geq 3$, $\mathbb{S}_n$IMTL $\subsetneqq$ $\mathbb{C}_n$IMTL and $\mathbb{S}_n$MTL $\subsetneqq$ $\mathbb{C}_n$MTL. The variety $\mathbb{S}_4$IMTL and its lattice of subvarieties have been fully studied in Ref. 11.

Proposition 5. *Every simple n-contractive non-trivial MTL-chain $\mathcal{A}$ has a coatom, i.e. there exists the maximum of $A\backslash\{\overline{1}^{\mathcal{A}}\}$.*

This implies that the n-contractive MTL-chains defined by a left-continuous t-norm are not simple, i.e. there are no standard $\mathbb{S}_n$MTL-chains.

4.2. *Combining weakly cancellative and n-contractive fuzzy logics*

In Ref. 19 the variety WCMTL of weakly cancellative MTL-algebras was defined to provide examples of indecomposable MTL-chains.

---

[a] These remarks on n-contractive left-continuous t-norms are already available in Ref. 18.

Besides, the Ω operator gave rise to the variety $\Omega(\text{WCMTL})$ which was a kind of analogue of $\mathbb{BL}$ in the sense that here all the chains were also decomposable as ordinal sums of weakly cancellative semihoops. Now it seems natural to consider the intersection of these varieties with the classes of n-contractive algebras (or equivalently the supremum of the corresponding logics) in order to obtain some new kinds of algebras with a nice and simpler structure. Therefore, we will consider for every $n \geq 2$ the logics $S_n\text{WCMTL}$ and $C_n\text{WCMTL}$.

Proposition 6. *For every* $n \geq 2$, $\{(WC), (C_n)\} \vdash_{\text{MTL}} (S_n)$. *Thus, given any axiomatic extension* L *of WCMTL and* $n \geq 2$, *the extensions obtained by* (S_n) *and* (C_n) *coincide. In particular,* $S_n\text{WCMTL} = C_n\text{WCMTL}$.

It is straightforward to prove that the Ω operator and the schemata (C_n) commute:

Proposition 7. *Let* L *be an axiomatic extension of* MTL. *For every* $n \geq 2$, $\Omega(\mathbb{C}_n L) = C_n\Omega(L)$.

Finally, we will consider for every $n \geq 2$ the logic $\Omega(S_n\text{MTL})$ and we will show that it is also finitely axiomatizable.

Proposition 8. *Let* $\mathcal{A}$ *be an* n-*contractive* MTL-*chain. The following are equivalent:*

(i) $\mathcal{A}$ *is totally decomposable (in the sense of Corollary 1).*
(ii) $\mathcal{A}$ *is an ordinal sum of simple* n-*contractive chains.*
(iii) $\mathcal{A} \models (y^{n-1} \to x) \lor (x \to x\&y) \approx \overline{1}$.

Corollary 4. $\Omega(\mathbb{S}_n\text{MTL})$ *is the variety generated by the totally decomposable* n-*contractive chains, and it is axiomatized by* $(y^{n-1} \to x) \lor (x \to x\&y) \approx \overline{1}$.

Therefore $\Omega(S_n\text{MTL})$-chains are an analogue of the standard BL-chains in the class of n-contractive MTL-algebras in the sense that they are also decomposable as ordinal sum of their Archimedean classes.

4.3. *Some properties of n-contractive fuzzy logics*

We are currently studying some logical and algebraic properties of the considered logics. The obtained results are collected in Table 4. The table also shows which problems still remain open.

Table 4.   Standard completeness properties of n-contractive fuzzy logics.

Logic	FEP = FMP	Decidable	SC	FSSC	SSC
C_nMTL	Yes	Yes	Yes	Yes	Yes
C_nIMTL	Yes	Yes	Yes	Yes	Yes
S_nMTL	Yes	Yes	No	No	No
S_nIMTL	?	?	No	No	No
$\Omega(S_n$MTL$)$	Yes	Yes	Yes	Yes	Yes
S_nWCMTL	Yes	Yes	No	No	No
$\Omega(C_n$WCMTL$)$	Yes	Yes	?	?	?

As mentioned above, the SSC was proved in Ref. 4 for C_nMTL and C_nIMTL for every $n \geq 2$. For $\Omega(S_n$MTL$)$ we have used the *real embedding method* introduced in Ref 15. The logics satisfying some (S_n) schema do not enjoy any standard completeness property because there are no standard algebras in the corresponding varieties. The FEP can be proved directly using an easy semantical construction and the decidability just follows. As regards to local finiteness, we can prove that n-contractivity is a necessary condition for it; however the sufficiency remains an open problem, so local finiteness of varieties of n-contractive MTL-algebras is still unkown in general.*

References

1. P. Aglianò and F. Montagna, Varieties of BL-algebras I: General properties. *Journal of Pure and Applied Algebra*, **181**, 105–129 (2003).
2. W. J. Blok and D. Pigozzi, Algebraizable logics. *Mem. Amer. Math. Soc.*, **77**, 396 (1989).
3. W. J. Blok and C. J. Van Alten, The finite embeddability property for residuated lattices, pocrims and BCK-algebras. *Algebra Universalis*, **48**, 253–271 (2002).
4. A. Ciabattoni, F. Esteva and L. Godo, T-norm based logics with n-contraction. *Neural Network World*, **5**, 441–452 (2002).
5. R. Cignoli, F. Esteva, L. Godo and A. Torrens, Basic fuzzy logic is the logic of continuous t-norms and their residua. *Soft Computing*, **4**, 106–112 (2000).
6. F. Esteva, J. Gispert, L. Godo and F. Montagna, On the standard and rational completeness of some axiomatic extensions of monoidal t-norm based logic. *Studia Logica*, **71**, 199–226 (2002).
7. F. Esteva and L. Godo, Monoidal t-norm based logic: Towards a logic for left-continuous t-norms. *Fuzzy Sets and Systems*, **124**, 271–288 (2001).

*The research on the properties of n-contractive fuzzy logics has been continued after the submission of this paper in Ref. 15, where some of our open problems are solved.

8. F. Esteva, L. Godo, P. Hájek and F. Montagna, Hoops and fuzzy logic. *Journal of Logic and Computation*, **13**(4), 531–555 (2003).

9. F. Esteva, L. Godo and F. Montagna, Equational characterization of the subvarieties of BL generated by t-norm algebras. *Studia Logica*, **76**, 161–200 (2004).

10. J. Gispert, Axiomatic extensions of the nilpotent minimum logic. *Reports on Mathematical Logic*, **37**, 113–123 (2003).

11. J. Gispert and A. Torrens, Axiomatic extensions of IMT3 logic. *Studia Logica*, **81**, 311–324 (2005).

12. P. Hájek, *Metamathematics of fuzzy logic, Trends in Logic*, Vol. 4 Kluwer (1998).

13. R. Horčík, Standard Completeness Theorem for ΠMTL. *Archive for Mathematical Logic*, **44**, 413–424 (2005).

14. R. Horčík, C. Noguera and M. Petrík, On *n*-contractive fuzzy logics, *Mathematical Logic Quarterly*, **53**, 268–288 (2007).

15. S. Jenei and F. Montagna, A proof of standard completeness for Esteva and Godo's logic MTL. *Studia Logica*, **70**, 183–192 (2002).

16. Y. Komori, Super Łukasiewicz propositional logics, *Nagoya Mathematical Journal*, **84**, 119–133 (1981).

17. T. Kowalski and H. Ono, Residuated lattices: An algebraic glimpse at logics without contraction (preliminary report), (2001).

18. A. Mesiarová, A note on the structure of *n*-contractive t-norms. *Proceedings of IFSA 2003*, pp. 69–72.

19. F. Montagna, C. Noguera and R. Horčík, On weakly cancellative fuzzy logics. *Journal of Logic and Computation*, **16**, 423–450 (2006).

20. P. S. Mostert and A. L. Shields, On the structure of semigroups on a compact manifold with boundary. *Annals of Math.*, **65**, 117–143 (1957).

21. C. Noguera, *Algebraic Study of Axiomatic Extensions of Triangular Norm Based Fuzzy Logics*, PhD. dissertation. Universitat de Barcelona (2006).

22. C. Noguera, F. Esteva and J. Gispert, Perfect and bipartite IMTL-algebras and disconnected rotations of prelinear semihoops. *Archive for Mathematical Logic*, **44**, 869–886 (2005).

23. C. Noguera, F. Esteva and J. Gispert, On some varieties of MTL-algebras. *Logic Journal of the IGPL*, **13**, 443–466 (2005).

Geometric Representations of Weak Orders

Sergei Ovchinnikov

Mathematics Department
San Francisco State University
San Francisco, CA 94132, USA
sergei@sfsu.edu

Abstract

The paper presents geometric models of the set **WO** of weak orders on a finite set X. In particular, **WO** is modeled as a set of vertices of a cubical subdivision of a permutahedron. This approach is an alternative to the usual geometric representation of **WO** by means of a weak order polytope.

1. Introduction

Let $\mathcal{B}$ be a family of binary relations on a finite set X. This set can be endowed with various structures which are important in applications. One particular way to represent $\mathcal{B}$ is to embed it into a cube $\{0,1\}^N$ of sufficiently large dimension ($N = |X|^2$ would always work) by using characteristic functions of relations in $\mathcal{B}$, and consider a convex hull of the set of corresponding points. Then $\mathcal{B}$ is treated as a polytope with rich combinatorial and geometric structures. There are many studies of *linear order polytopes, weak order polytopes, approval–voting polytopes*, and *partial order polytopes*, and their applications. (See, for instance, Refs. 1, 2 and 3.)

In this paper we study the set **WO** of all weak orders on X from a different point of view. We model the Hasse diagram of **WO** as a 1-skeleton of a cubical subdivision of a permutahedron. Our motivation has its roots in media theory[4–6] where it is shown that the graph of a medium is a partial cube.[6]

Section 2 presents some basic facts about weak orders and the Hasse diagram of **WO**. In Sec. 3 we describe various geometric models of **WO**. They are combinatorially equivalent under the usual connection between zonotopes, polar zonotopes, and hyperplane arrangements.

2. The Hasse Diagram

In the paper, X denotes a finite set with $n > 1$ elements. A binary relation W on X is a *weak order* if it is transitive and strongly complete. Antisymmetric weak orders are *linear orders*. The set of all weak orders (resp. linear orders) on X will be denoted **WO** (resp. **LO**).

For a weak order W, the *indifference* relation $I = W \cap W^{-1}$ is an equivalence relation on X. Equivalence classes of I are called *indifference* classes of W. These classes are linearly ordered by the relation W/I. We will use the notation $W = (X_1, \ldots, X_k)$ where X_i's are indifference classes of W and $(x, y) \in W$ if and only if $x \in X_i$, $y \in X_j$ for some $1 \le i \le j \le k$. Thus our notation reflects the linear order induced on indifference classes by W.

We distinguish weak orders on X by the number of their respective indifference classes: if $W = (X_1, \ldots, X_k)$, we say that W is a *weak k-order*. The set of all weak k-orders will be denoted **WO**(k). In particular, weak n-orders are linear orders and there is only one weak 1-order on X, namely, $W = (X) = X \times X$, which we will call a *trivial* weak order. Weak 2-orders play an important role in our constructions. They are in the form $W = (A, X \setminus A)$ where A is a nonempty proper subset of X. Clearly, there are $2^n - 2$ distinct weak 2-orders on a set of cardinality n.

The set **WO** is a partially ordered set with respect to the set inclusion relation $\subseteq$. We denote the Hasse diagram of this set by the same symbol **WO**. The following figure shows, as an example, the Hasse diagram **WO** for a 3-element set $X = \{a, b, c\}$.

In Fig. 1 the maximal element corresponds to the trivial weak order, the six vertices in the layer below correspond to weak 2-orders,

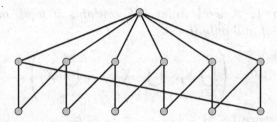

Fig. 1.   The Hasse diagram of **WO** ($|X| = 3$).

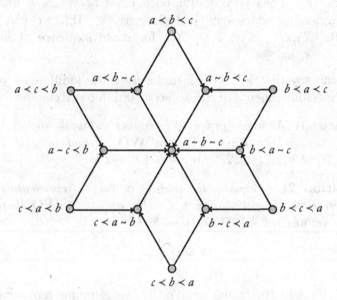

Fig. 2.   Another form of the Hasse diagram.

and the vertices in the lowest layer correspond to the linear orders on X.

We find it more intuitive to represent the Hasse diagram **WO** by a directed graph as shown in Fig. 2. (Similar diagrams were introduced in Refs. 7 and 8.)

Here the arrows indicate the partial order on **WO** and, for instance, the weak order $(\{ab\}, \{c\})$ is represented as $a \sim b \prec c$.

In the rest of this section we establish some properties of **WO**. The following proposition is Problem 19 on p. 115 in Ref. 9.

Proposition 1. *A weak order W' contains a weak order $W = (X_1, \ldots, X_k)$ if and only if*

$$W' = \left(\bigcup_{j=1}^{i_1} X_j, \bigcup_{j=i_1+1}^{i_2} X_j, \ldots, \bigcup_{j=i_m}^{k} X_j \right),$$

for some sequence $1 \leq i_1 < i_2 < \cdots < i_m \leq k$.

Proof. Let $W \subset W'$. Then the indifference classes of W form a subpartition of the partition of X defined by the indifference classes of W'. Thus each indifference class of W' is a union of some indifference classes of W. Since $W \subset W'$, we can write $W' = (\cup_1^{i_1} X_j, \cup_{i_1+1}^{i_2} X_j, \ldots, \cup_{i_m}^{k} X_j)$ for some sequence of indexes $1 \leq i_1 < \cdots < i_m \leq k$. $\square$

One can say that $W \subset W'$ if and only if the indifference classes of W' are "enlargements of the adjacent indifference classes"[9] of W.

Corollary 1. *A weak order W' covers a weak order $W = (X_1, \ldots, X_k)$ in the Hasse diagram* **WO** *if and only if $W' = (X_1, \ldots, X_i \cup X_{i+1}, \ldots, X_k)$ for some $1 \leq i < k$.*

Proposition 2. *A weak order admits a unique representation as an intersection of weak 2-orders, i.e. for any $W \in$ **WO** there is a uniquely defined set $J \subseteq$ **WO**(2) such that*

$$W = \bigcap_{U \in J} U. \tag{1}$$

Proof. Clearly, the trivial weak order has a unique representation in the form (1) with $J = \emptyset$.

Let $W = (X_1, \ldots, X_k)$ with $k > 1$ and let J_W be the set of all weak 2–orders containing W. By Proposition 1, each weak order in J_W is in the form

$$W_i = (\cup_1^i X_j, \cup_{i+1}^k X_j), \quad 1 \leq i < k.$$

Let $(x, y) \in \bigcap_{i=1}^{k-1} W_i$. Suppose $(x, y) \notin W$. Then $x \in X_p$ and $y \in X_q$ for some $p > q$. It follows that $(x, y) \notin W_q$, a contradiction. This proves (1) with $J = J_W$.

Let $W = (X_1, \ldots, X_k)$ be a weak order in the form (1). Clearly, $J \subseteq J_W$. Suppose that $W_s = (\cup_1^s X_j, \cup_{s+1}^k X_j) \notin J$ for some s. Let $x \in X_{s+1}$ and $y \in X_s$. Then $(x, y) \in W_i$ for any $i \neq s$, but

$(x, y) \notin W$, a contradiction. Hence, $J = J_W$ which proves uniqueness of representation (1). $\qquad\square$

Let J_W, as in the above proof, be the set of all weak 2-orders containing W, and let $\mathcal{J} = \{J_W\}_{W \in \mathbf{WO}}$ be the family of all such subsets of $\mathbf{WO}(2)$. The set $\mathcal{J}$ is a poset with respect to the inclusion relation.

The following theorem is an immediate consequence of Proposition 2.

Theorem 1. *The correspondence $W \mapsto J_W$ is a dual isomorphism of posets $\mathbf{WO}$ and $\mathcal{J}$.*

Clearly, the trivial weak order on X corresponds to the empty subset of $\mathbf{WO}(2)$ and the set $\mathbf{LO}$ of all linear orders on X is in one-to-one correspondence with maximal elements in $\mathcal{J}$. The Hasse diagram $\mathbf{WO}$ is dually isomorphic to the Hasse diagram of $\mathcal{J}$.

Theorem 2. *The set $\mathcal{J}$ is a combinatorial simplicial complex, i.e. $J \in \mathcal{J}$ implies $J' \in \mathcal{J}$ for all $J' \subseteq J$.*

Proof. Let $J' \subseteq J = J_W$ for some $W \in \mathbf{WO}$, i.e. $W = \bigcap_{U \in J_W} U$. Consider $W' = \bigcap_{U \in J'} U$. Clearly, W' is transitive. It is complete, since $W \subseteq W'$. By Proposition 2, $J' = J_{W'} \in \mathcal{J}$. $\qquad\square$

It follows that $\mathcal{J}$ is a complete graded meet-semilattice (cf. Ref. 10). Therefore the Hasse diagram $\mathbf{WO}$ is a complete join-semilattice with respect to the join operation $W \vee W' = \overline{W \cup W'}$, the transitive closure of $W \cup W'$.

3. Geometric Models of WO

A weak order polytope $\mathbf{P}_{WO}^n$ is defined as the convex hull in $\mathbb{R}^{n(n-1)}$ of the characteristic vectors of all weak orders on X (see, for instance, Ref. 3). Here we suggest different geometric models for $\mathbf{WO}$. For basic definitions in the area of polytopes and complexes, the reader is referred to Ziegler's book.[11]

Definition 1. A *cube* is a polytope combinatorially equivalent to $[0, 1]^m$. A *cubical complex* is a polytopal complex $\mathcal{C}$ such that every $P \in \mathcal{C}$ is a cube. The *graph* $G(\mathcal{C})$ of a cubical complex $\mathcal{C}$ is the 1-skeleton of $\mathcal{C}$.

Thus the vertices and the edges of $G(\mathcal{C})$ are the vertices and the edges of cubes in $\mathcal{C}$, and $G(\mathcal{C})$ is a simple undirected graph.

Let $d = 2^n - 2$, where $n = |X|$, be the number of elements in $\mathbf{WO}(2)$. We represent each $W \in \mathbf{WO}$ by a characteristic function $\chi(J_W)$ of the set J_W. These characteristic functions are vertices of the cube $[0, 1]^d$. Let $L \in \mathbf{LO}$ be a linear order on X. Then J_L is a maximal element in $\mathcal{J}$ and, by Theorem 2, the convex hull of $\{\chi(J_W)\}_{W \supseteq L}$ is a subcube C_L of $[0, 1]^d$. The dimension of C_L is $n - 1$. The collection of all cubes C_L with $L \in \mathbf{LO}$ and all their subcubes form a cubical complex $\mathcal{C}(\mathbf{WO})$ which is a subcomplex of $[0, 1]^d$. Clearly, $\mathcal{C}(\mathbf{WO})$ is a pure complex of dimension $n - 1$ and the graph of this complex is isomorphic to the graph (that we denote by the same symbol, $\mathbf{WO}$) of the Hasse diagram of $\mathbf{WO}$.

The above construction yields an isometric embedding of the graph $\mathbf{WO}$ into the graph of $[0, 1]^d$. Thus the graph $\mathbf{WO}$ is a partial cube.

The dimension $\dim \mathcal{C}(\mathbf{WO}) = n - 1$ is much smaller than the dimension $d = 2^n - 2$ of the space $\mathbb{R}^d$ in which $\mathcal{C}(\mathbf{WO})$ was realized. Simple examples indicate that $\mathcal{C}(\mathbf{WO})$ can be realized in a space of a much smaller dimension.

For instance, for $n = 3$ we have a realization of $\mathcal{C}(\mathbf{WO})$ in $\mathbb{R}^3$ as shown in Fig. 3. (This is a "flat" analog of the popular smooth surface $z = x^3 - 3xy^2$.) One can compare this picture with the picture shown in Fig. 2.

It turns out that there is a cubical complex, which is combinatorially equivalent to $\mathcal{C}(\mathbf{WO})$, and such that its underlying set is a polytope in $\mathbb{R}^{n-1}$.

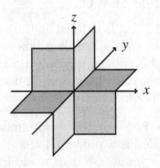

Fig. 3.   "Monkey Saddle."

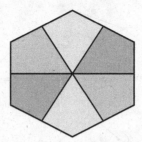

Fig. 4. A cubical complex associated with Π_2.

We begin with a simple example. Let $X = \{1, 2, 3\}$ and let Π_2 be the 2-dimensional permutahedron. Consider a subdivision of Π_2 shown in Fig. 4.

Clearly, this subdivision defines a cubical complex which is combinatorially isomorphic to the cubical complex shown in Fig. 3. (Compare it also with the diagram in Fig. 2.)

In general, let Π_{n-1} be a permutahedron of dimension $n - 1$, where $n = |X|$. According to (Ref. 11, p. 18), "k-faces (of Π_{n-1}) correspond to ordered partitions of (the set X) into $n - k$ nonempty parts" (see also Ref. 12, p. 54). In other words, each face of Π_{n-1} represents a weak order on X. Linear orders on X are represented by the vertices of Π_{n-1} and the trivial weak order on X is represented by Π_{n-1} itself. Weak 2-orders are in one-to-one correspondence with the facets of Π_{n-1}. Let L be a vertex of Π_{n-1}. Consider the set of barycenters of all faces of Π_{n-1} containing L. A direct computation shows that the convex hull C_L of these points is a (combinatorial) cube. This is actually true for any simple zonotope (Π_{n-1} is a simple zonotope). The following argument belongs to Günter Ziegler.[13]

Let Z be a simple zonotope. By Corollary 7.18 in Ref. 11, C_L is the intersection of the vertex cone of L (which is a simplicial cone) with the dual facet cone of the dual of Z (which is again a simplicial cone). This intersection is an $(n - 1)$-dimensional (combinatorial) cube.

Cubes in the form C_L form a subdivision of Π_{n-1} and, together with their subcubes, form a cubical complex isomorphic to $\mathcal{C}(\mathbf{WO})$. One of these cubes is shown in Fig. 5.

Another geometric model for the set $\mathbf{WO}$ of all weak orders on X can be obtained using the polar polytope Π_{n-1}^{Δ}. Let $L(\Pi_{n-1})$ be the face lattice of the permutahedron Π_{n-1}. The joint-semilattice $\mathbf{WO}$ is isomorphic to the joint-semilattice $L(\Pi_{n-1})\backslash\{\emptyset\}$ (Fig. 1). By duality,

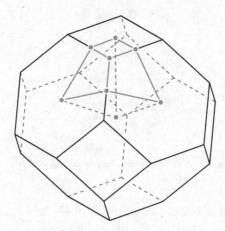

Fig. 5.   A maximum cube of the cubical subdivision of the permutahedron Π_3.

the Hasse diagram **WO** is dually isomorphic to the meet-semilattice $L(\Pi_{n-1}^{\Delta})\backslash\{\Pi_{n-1}^{\Delta}\}$ of all proper faces of Π_{n-1}^{Δ}. Under this isomorphism, the linear orders on X are in one-to-one correspondence with facets of Π_{n-1}^{Δ}, the weak 2-orders on X are in one-to-one correspondence with vertices of Π_{n-1}^{Δ}, and the trivial weak order on X corresponds to the empty face of Π_{n-1}^{Δ}. Note that Π_{n-1}^{Δ} is a simplicial polytope. The set of its proper faces is a simplicial complex which is a geometric realization of the combinatorial simplicial complex $\mathcal{J}$ (cf. Theorem 2).

Other geometric and combinatorial models of **WO** can be constructed by using the usual connections between zonotopes, hyperplane arrangements, and oriented matroids.[11] One particular model utilizes the following well known facts about weak orders on X.

Let f be a real-valued function on X and, as before, let $n = |X|$. Then W_f defined by

$$(x, y) \in W_f \Leftrightarrow f(x) \le f(y),$$

for all $x, y \in X$, is a weak order. On the other hand, for a given weak order W there exists a function f such that $W = W_f$. Two functions f and g are said to be equivalent if $W_f = W_g$. Clearly, equivalent functions form a cone C_W in $\mathbb{R}^n$ and the union of these cones is $\mathbb{R}^n$. Thus there is a natural one-to-one correspondence between the set **WO** and the family $\{C_W\}_{W \in \mathbf{WO}}$. The cones in the form C_W arise from the braid arrangement $\mathcal{B}_n$ defined by the hyperplanes $H_{ij} = \{x \in \mathbb{R}^n : x_i = x_j\}$ for $i < j$ (see Fig. 6).

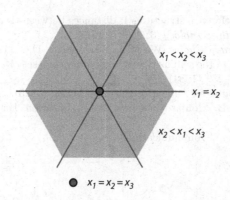

Fig. 6. The braid arrangement $\mathcal{B}$ and its cones.

The braid arrangement $\mathcal{B}_n$ is the hyperplane arrangement associated with the zonotope Π_{n-1}. Following the standard steps,[11] one can also construct an oriented matroid representing **WO**.

Geometric objects introduced in this section, the cubical complex $\mathcal{C}(\mathbf{WO})$, the simplicial complex $\mathcal{J}$ of proper faces of the polar zonotope Π_{n-1}^{Δ}, and the braid arrangement $\mathcal{B}_n$, all share the combinatorial structure of the Hasse diagram **WO**.

Acknowledgments

The author wishes to thank Jean-Paul Doignon and Jean-Claude Falmagne for their careful reading of the original draft of the paper.

References

1. J.-P. Doignon and M. Regenwetter, On the combinatorial structure of the approval-voting polytope. *J. Math. Psych.*, **46**, 554–563 (2002).
2. S. Fiorini, A combinatorial study of partial order polytopes. *European Journal of Combinatorics*, **24**, 149–159 (2003).
3. S. Fiorini and P. C. Fishburn, Weak order polytopes. *Discrete Math.*, **275**, 111–127 (2004).
4. J.-Cl. Falmagne, Stochastic token theory, *J. Math. Psych.*, **41**(2), 129–143 (1997).
5. J.-Cl. Falmagne and S. Ovchinnikov, Media theory. *Discrete Appl. Math.*, **121**, 103–118 (2002).
6. S. Ovchinnikov and A. Dukhovny, Advances in media theory. *Int. J. of Uncertainty, Fuzziness and Knowledge-Based Systems*, **8**(1), 45–71 (2000).
7. J. G. Kemeny and J. L. Snell, *Mathematical Models in the Social Sciences*. The MIT Press, Cambridge, MA (1972).

8. K.P. Bogart, Preference structures I: distances between transitive preference relations. *J. Math. Sociology*, **3**, 49–67 (1973).

9. B.G. Mirkin, *Group Choice*. Winston, Washington, D.C. (1979).

10. M.L. Janowitz, On the semilattice of weak orders of a set. *Mathematical Social Sciences*, **8**, 229–239 (1984).

11. G. Ziegler, *Lectures on Polytopes*. Springer-Verlag (1995).

12. M. Barbut and B. Monjardet, *Ordre et Classification*. Hachette Université (1970).

13. G. Ziegler, personal communication.

Lexicographic Composition of Similarity-Based Fuzzy Orderings

Ulrich Bodenhofer

Institute of Bioinformatics
Johannes Kepler University Linz
Altenberger Str. 69, A-4040 Linz, Austria
bodenhofer@bioinf.jku.at

Abstract

The paper introduces an approach to construct lexicographic compositions of similarity-based fuzzy orderings. This construction is demonstrated by means of nontrivial examples. As this is a crucial feature of lexicographic composition, the preservation of linearity is studied in detail. We obtain once again that it is essential for meaningful results that the t-norm under consideration induces an involutive (strong) negation.

1. Introduction

Lexicographic composition is a fundamental construction principle for ordering relations. The most important feature of this construction is that the composition of two linear orderings again yields a linear ordering. Given two orderings $\leq_1$ and $\leq_2$ on nonempty domains X_1 and X_2, respectively, the lexicographic composition is an ordering $\leq'$ on the Cartesian product $X_1 \times X_2$, where $(x_1, x_2) \leq' (y_1, y_2)$ if and only if

$$(x_1 \neq y_1 \wedge x_1 \leq_1 y_1) \vee (x_1 = y_1 \wedge x_2 \leq_2 y_2). \tag{1}$$

Rewriting $x_1 \neq y_1 \wedge x_1 \leq_1 y_1$ as $x_1 <_1 y_1$ (i.e. the strict ordering induced by $\leq_1$) and taking into account that $x_1 = y_1 \vee x_1 \neq y_1$ is a tautology and that $\leq_1$ is reflexive, we obtain that (1) is equivalent to

$$(x_1 \leq_1 y_1 \wedge x_2 \leq_2 y_2) \vee x_1 <_1 y_1. \tag{2}$$

The study of fuzzy orderings can be traced back to the early days of fuzzy set theory.[1-4] Partial fuzzy orderings in the sense of Zadeh,[1] however, have severe shortcomings that were finally resolved by replacing the crisp equality by a fuzzy equivalence relation, thereby maintaining the well-known classical fact that orderings are obtained from preorderings by factorization.[5-9]

In previous works of the author,[7,10] several methods for constructing fuzzy orderings are presented, including Cartesian products. How to transfer lexicographic composition to the fuzzy framework, however, remained an open problem. The reason why this remained an open issue for a relatively long time is that there was no meaningful concept of strict fuzzy ordering in the similarity-based framework so far. As this issue is solved now,[11] we are able to give a solution in this paper. For proof details, the reader is referred to upcoming publications.

2.   Preliminaries

For simplicity, we consider the unit interval $[0,1]$ as our domain of truth values in this paper. Note that most results, with only minor and obvious modifications, also hold for more general structures.[5,9,12,13] The symbols T, $\tilde{T}$, etc., denote left-continuous t-norms.[14] Correspondingly, $\vec{T}$ denotes the unique residual implication of T. Furthermore, we denote the residual negation of T with $N_T(x) = \vec{T}(x,0)$.

Definition 1. A binary fuzzy relation $E : X^2 \to [0,1]$ is called *fuzzy equivalence relation*[a] with respect to T, for brevity *T-equivalence*, if the following three axioms are fulfilled for all $x, y, z \in X$:

(1) Reflexivity: $E(x,x) = 1$
(2) Symmetry: $E(x,y) = E(y,x)$
(3) T-transitivity: $T(E(x,y), E(y,z)) \leq E(x,z)$

---

[a] Note that various diverging names for this class of fuzzy relations appear in literature, like similarity relations, indistinguishability operators, equality relations, and several more.[1,13,15,16]

Definition 2. A binary fuzzy relation $L : X^2 \to [0,1]$ is called *fuzzy ordering* with respect to T and a T-equivalence $E : X^2 \to [0,1]$, for brevity *T-E-ordering*, if it fulfills the following three axioms for all $x, y, z \in X$:

(1) *E*-reflexivity: $E(x,y) \le L(x,y)$
(2) *T-E*-antisymmetry: $T(L(x,y), L(y,x)) \le E(x,y)$
(3) *T*-transitivity: $T(L(x,y), L(y,z)) \le L(x,z)$

Definition 3. A fuzzy relation $R : X^2 \to [0,1]$ is called *strongly complete* if $\max(L(x,y), L(y,x)) = 1$ for all $x, y \in X$.[2,4,17] R is called T-linear if $N_T(L(x,y)) \le L(y,x)$ for all $x, y \in X$.[5,17]

Definition 4. A binary fuzzy relation $S : X^2 \to [0,1]$ is called *strict fuzzy ordering* with respect to T and a T-equivalence $E : X^2 \to [0,1]$, for brevity *strict T-E-ordering*, if it fulfills the following axioms for all $x, x', y, y', z \in X$:

(1) Irreflexivity: $S(x,x) = 0$
(2) *T*-transitivity: $T(S(x,y), S(y,z)) \le S(x,z)$
(3) *E*-extensionality: $T(E(x,x'), E(y,y'), S(x,y)) \le S(x',y')$

As already mentioned above, it is of vital importance for lexicographic composition how to "strictify" a given fuzzy ordering. The following theorem summarizes the most important facts.

Theorem 1.[11] *Consider a T-equivalence $E : X^2 \to [0,1]$ and a T-E-ordering $L : X^2 \to [0,1]$. Then the following fuzzy relation is a strict T-E-ordering on X:*

$$S(x,y) = \min(L(x,y), N_T(L(y,x))).$$

Moreover, S is monotonic with respect to L in the following sense (for all $x, y, z \in X$).

$$T(L(x,y), S(y,z)) \le S(x,z)$$
$$T(S(x,y), L(y,z)) \le S(x,z).$$

S is the largest strict T-E-ordering contained in L that fulfills this kind of monotonicity.

For intersecting T-transitive fuzzy relations, the concept of dominance of t-norms is of vital importance.[14,18,19]

Definition 5. A t-norm T_1 is said to *dominate* another t-norm T_2 if, for every quadruple $(x, y, u, v) \in [0, 1]^4$, the following holds:

$$T_1\big(T_2(x, y), T_2(u, v)\big) \geq T_2\big(T_1(x, u), T_1(y, v)\big)$$

Lemma 1.[18] *Consider two t-norms T_1 and T_2. The T_1-intersection of any two arbitrary T_2-transitive fuzzy relations is T_2-transitive if and only if T_1 dominates T_2.*

3. Starting the Easy Way: One Crisp and One Fuzzy Ordering

Let us first consider the case where the primary ordering is crisp and the secondary ordering is fuzzy. As the strict ordering is only needed for the primary ordering, we do not need to take any strict fuzzy ordering into account.

Proposition 1. *Let us consider a crisp ordering $L_1 : X_1^2 \to \{0, 1\}$, a T-equivalence $E_2 : X_2^2 \to [0, 1]$, and a T-E_2-ordering $L_2 : X_2^2 \to [0, 1]$. Then the fuzzy relation $L : (X_1 \times X_2)^2 \to [0, 1]$ defined as*

$$L((x_1, x_2), (y_1, y_2)) = \begin{cases} 1 & \text{if } x_1 \neq y_1 \text{ and } L_1(x_1, y_1) = 1, \\ L_2(x_2, y_2) & \text{if } x_1 = y_1, \\ 0 & \text{otherwise,} \end{cases}$$

is a fuzzy ordering with respect to T and the T-equivalence $E : (X_1 \times X_2)^2 \to [0, 1]$ defined as

$$E((x_1, x_2), (y_1, y_2)) = \begin{cases} E_2(x_2, y_2) & \text{if } x_1 = y_1, \\ 0 & \text{otherwise.} \end{cases}$$

Note that, if both components L_1 and L_2 are crisp orderings, then L as defined above is equivalent to the constructions (1) and (2). Moreover, E as defined above is nothing else but the Cartesian product of the crisp equality with E_2.

Example 1. Consider $X_1 = X_2 = [0, 4]$, let L_1 be the classical linear ordering of real numbers, and assume that L_2 is defined as follows:

$$L_2(x, y) = \max(\min(1 - x + y, 1), 0).$$

It is easy to see that L_2 is a strongly complete fuzzy ordering with respect to the Łukasiewicz t-norm $T_{\mathbf{L}}(x, y) = \max(x + y - 1, 0)$ and

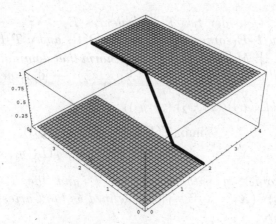

Fig. 1.   Cut view of a lexicographic composition of a crisp linear ordering and a fuzzy ordering according to Proposition 1.

the $T_{\mathbf{L}}$-equivalence $E_2(x,y) = \max(1 - |x-y|, 0)$. Figure 1 shows a cut view of the fuzzy ordering L that is obtained when applying the construction from Proposition 1. The cut view has been obtained by plotting the value $L((2,2),(y_1,y_2))$ as a two-dimensional function of y_1 and y_2.

The following proposition clarifies in which way linearity of the two component orderings L_1 and L_2 is preserved by the construction in the previous proposition.

Proposition 2. *Let us make the same assumptions as in Proposition 1. If L_1 is a crisp linear ordering and L_2 is strongly complete, then L is also strongly complete. If L_1 is a crisp linear ordering and L_2 is T-linear, then L is also T-linear.*

4.   Lexicographic Composition of Two Nontrivial Fuzzy Orderings

The results of the previous section have been known to the author since 1998, but they were not published so far, as they cannot be considered a full-fledged solution of the problem. So let us now consider the general case, where both components are fuzzy orderings without any further assumptions. The following theorem gives a general construction inspired by the classical construction (2).

Theorem 2. *Consider two T-equivalences $E_1 : X_1^2 \to [0,1]$, $E_2 : X_2^2 \to [0,1]$, a T-E_1-ordering $L_1 : X_1^2 \to [0,1]$, and a T-E_2-ordering $L_2 : X_2^2 \to [0,1]$. Moreover, let $\tilde{T}$ be a t-norm that dominates T. Then the fuzzy relation $\text{Lex}_{\tilde{T},T}(L_1, L_2) : (X_1 \times X_2)^2 \to [0,1]$ defined as*

$$\text{Lex}_{\tilde{T},T}(L_1, L_2)((x_1, x_2),(y_1, y_2)) =$$
$$\max(\tilde{T}(L_1(x_1, y_1), L_2(x_2, y_2)),$$
$$\min(L_1(x_1, y_1), N_T(L_1(y_1, x_1)))) \quad (3)$$

is a fuzzy ordering with respect to T and the T-equivalence $\text{Cart}_{\tilde{T}}(E_1, E_2) : (X_1 \times X_2)^2 \to [0,1]$ defined as the Cartesian product of E_1 and E_2:

$$\text{Cart}_{\tilde{T}}(E_1, E_2)((x_1, x_2), (y_1, y_2)) = \tilde{T}(E_1(x_1, y_1), E_2(x_2, y_2)).$$

Note that, if L_1 is a crisp ordering, then $\text{Lex}_{\tilde{T},T}(L_1, L_2)$ defined as in Theorem 2 coincides with the fuzzy relation L defined in Proposition 1. Consequently, if both components L_1 and L_2 are crisp orderings, then $\text{Lex}_{\tilde{T},T}(L_1, L_2)$ is equivalent to the constructions (1) and (2).

Construction (3) is based on one specific formulation of lexicographic composition, namely (2). This is just one possible way of defining lexicographic composition. It is unknown whether there are other meaningful ways to define lexicographic composition on the basis of a different formulation that is equivalent to (2) in the classical Boolean case.

Example 2. Consider again the domain $X = [0, 4]$ and consider the following three fuzzy relations on X:

$$L_3(x,y) = \max\left(\min\left(1 - \frac{1}{2}(x - y), 1\right), 0\right)$$
$$L_4(x,y) = \min(\exp(y - x), 1)$$
$$L_5(x,y) = \min(\exp(3(y - x)), 1)$$

L_3 is a $T_{\mathbf{L}}$-E_3-ordering with $E_3(x,y) = \max(1 - \frac{1}{2}|x - y|, 0)$. L_4 is a $T_{\mathbf{P}}$-E_4-ordering[b] with $E_4(x,y) = \exp(-|x - y|)$ and, since $T_{\mathbf{L}} \leq T_{\mathbf{P}}$, a $T_{\mathbf{L}}$-E_4-ordering as well. L_5 is a $T_{\mathbf{P}}$-E_5-ordering with $E_4(x,y) =$

---

[b] Here $T_{\mathbf{P}}$ denotes the product t-norm; note that $T_{\mathbf{P}}$ dominates $T_{\mathbf{L}}$.[19]

$\exp(-3|x-y|)$ and a $T_\mathbf{L}$-E_5-ordering as well. Thus we can define the following fuzzy relations from the fuzzy orderings L_2 (from Example 1), L_3, L_4, and L_5:

$$\mathbf{L}_a = \operatorname{Lex}_{T_\mathbf{M}, T_\mathbf{L}}(L_2, L_2)$$
$$\mathbf{L}_b = \operatorname{Lex}_{T_\mathbf{L}, T_\mathbf{L}}(L_3, L_2)$$
$$\mathbf{L}_c = \operatorname{Lex}_{T_\mathbf{P}, T_\mathbf{L}}(L_4, L_2)$$
$$\mathbf{L}_d = \operatorname{Lex}_{T_\mathbf{P}, T_\mathbf{L}}(L_5, L_5)$$

Theorem 2 then ensures that all these four fuzzy relations are fuzzy orderings with respect to the Łukasiewicz t-norm $T_\mathbf{L}$ and $T_\mathbf{L}$-equivalences defined as the corresponding Cartesian products. Figure 2 shows cut views of the four lexicographic compositions, where we keep the first argument vector constant (we choose $(x_1, x_2) = (2, 2)$) and plot the value $\mathbf{L}_*((2, 2), (y_1, y_2))$ as a two-dimensional function of y_1 and y_2.

Now the question arises whether the lexicographic composition of two linear fuzzy orderings is again linear. Note that there are several notions of linearity of fuzzy orderings.[17] Let us first consider strong completeness.

Example 3. All fuzzy orderings considered in Examples 1 and 2 are strongly complete. Note, however, that none of the lexicographic compositions defined in Example 2 is strongly complete. To demonstrate that, consider the plots in Fig. 3. These two plots show the values:

$$\max(\mathbf{L}_a((2, 2), (y_1, y_2)), \mathbf{L}_a((y_1, y_2), (2, 2)))$$
$$\max(\mathbf{L}_d((2, 2), (y_1, y_2)), \mathbf{L}_d((y_1, y_2), (2, 2)))$$

as two-dimensional functions of y_1 and y_2. If $\mathbf{L}_a$ and $\mathbf{L}_d$ were strongly complete, these two functions would have to be the constant 1, which is obviously not the case. The same is true for the two other lexicographic compositions $\mathbf{L}_b$ and $\mathbf{L}_c$.

After this negative answer, let us relax the question a bit and attempt the question whether the lexicographic composition of two strongly complete fuzzy orderings is T-linear.

Proposition 3. *Let us make the same assumptions as for Theorem 2. If L_1 and L_2 are strongly complete fuzzy orderings and*

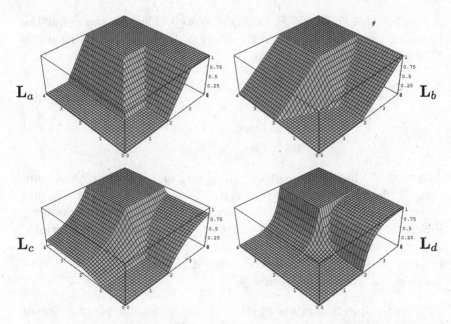

Fig. 2.   Cut views of the four lexicographic compositions from Example 2.

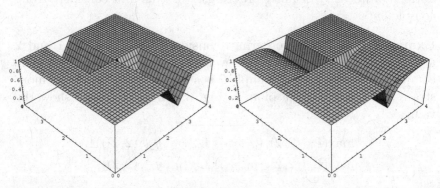

Fig. 3.   Plots of the functions $\max\left(\mathbf{L}_a((2,2),(y_1,y_2)),\mathbf{L}_a((y_1,y_2),(2,2))\right)$ (left) and $\max\left(\mathbf{L}_d((2,2),(y_1,y_2)),\mathbf{L}_d((y_1,y_2),(2,2))\right)$ (right).

the residual negation N_T is involutive (i.e. $N_T(N_T(x)) = x$ holds for all $x \in [0,1]$), then the fuzzy ordering $\mathrm{Lex}_{\tilde{T},T}(L_1,L_2)$ is T-linear.

Note that Proposition 3 also proves that all the four lexicographic compositions defined in Example 2 are $T_{\mathbf{L}}$-linear.

The proof of Proposition 3 does not work if we do not assume that N_T is an involution. The question arises, of course, whether this condition is not only sufficient, but also necessary. The answer is that this is the case, as the following example demonstrates.

Example 4. Consider a left-continuous t-norm for which a value $z \in {]0,1[}$ exists such that $N_T(N_T(z)) \neq z$. Since $N_T(N_T(z)) \geq z$ always holds, we can infer, in this case, that $N_T(N_T(z)) > z$ must hold. Now let us consider two simple strongly complete fuzzy orderings on the sets $X_1 = \{a, b\}$ and $X_2 = \{c, d\}$, respectively:

$$
\begin{array}{c|cc}
L_6 & a & b \\
\hline
a & 1 & 1 \\
b & z & 1
\end{array}
\qquad
\begin{array}{c|cc}
L_7 & c & d \\
\hline
c & 1 & 1 \\
d & 0 & 1
\end{array}
$$

Then we can infer the following for any choice of $\tilde{T}$:

$$
\mathrm{Lex}_{\tilde{T},T}(L_6, L_7)((a,d),(b,c)) = N_T(L_6(b,a)) = N_T(z)
$$
$$
\mathrm{Lex}_{\tilde{T},T}(L_6, L_7)((b,c),(a,d)) = L_6(b,a) = z.
$$

Hence we obtain that

$$
N_T\big(\mathrm{Lex}_{\tilde{T},T}(L_6, L_7)((a,d),(b,c))\big) = N_T(N_T(z))
$$
$$
> z = \mathrm{Lex}_{\tilde{T},T}(L_6, L_7)((b,c),(a,d)),
$$

which shows that $\mathrm{Lex}_{\tilde{T},T}(L_6, L_7)$ is not T-linear.

Note that the condition of involutiveness of N_T in particular excludes all t-norms without zero divisors. Therefore, lexicographic compositions of nontrivial (i.e. noncrisp) fuzzy orderings with respect to the popular minimum and product t-norms are problematic, if not meaningless. The reason for this is simple. It is known[11] that the only strict fuzzy ordering included in a fuzzy ordering that is strictly greater than zero (e.g. like L_4 and L_5 from Example 2) is the trivial zero relation. When it comes to lexicographic composition, the strict fuzzy ordering induced by the first component relation plays a crucial role. If it vanishes, no meaningful lexicographic composition that preserves linearity properties can be expected. As an example, see Fig. 4. It shows a cut view of the fuzzy ordering $\mathrm{Lex}_{T_P,T_P}(L_5, L_4)$. It is easy to see that $\mathrm{Lex}_{T_P,T_P}(L_5, L_4)$ is nothing else but the Cartesian product of L_5 and L_4, which is of course not T_P-linear.

The final and most important question is whether the lexicographic composition of two T-linear fuzzy orderings is again T-linear.

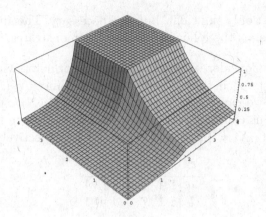

Fig. 4.   A cut view of $\mathrm{Lex}_{T_\mathbf{P},T_\mathbf{P}}(L_5, L_4)$.

Strong completeness always implies T-linearity,[17] thus, strongly complete fuzzy orderings are a sub-class of T-linear fuzzy orderings (no matter which T we choose). If the involutiveness of N_T is a necessary condition for meaningful results in Proposition 3, there is no point in considering a t-norm that does not induce an involutive negation any further.

Theorem 3. *Let us again make the same assumptions as for Theorem 2. If L_1 and L_2 are T-linear fuzzy orderings and the residual negation N_T is involutive, then the following fuzzy ordering is T-linear:*

$$\mathrm{Lex}_{T_\mathbf{M},T}(L_1, L_2)((x_1, x_2),(y_1, y_2)) = \\ \max(\min(L_1(x_1, y_1), L_2(x_2, y_2)), \\ \min(L_1(x_1, y_1), N_T(L_1(y_1, x_1)))).$$

Obviously, Theorem 3 does not allow any choice of the aggregating t-norm $\tilde{T}$ as in the original construction in Theorem 2, but enforces the choice of the minimum t-norm (i.e. $\tilde{T} = T_\mathbf{M}$). This is not an arbitrary restriction, but a necessary condition, as the following example demonstrates.

Example 5. Consider an arbitrary left-continuous t-norm T that induces an involutive negation N_T and assume that $\tilde{T} < T_\mathbf{M}$. Then there exists a $y \in \,]0, 1[$ such that $\tilde{T}(y, y) < y$. Now let us consider the following two fuzzy relations:

$$
\begin{array}{c|cc}
L_8 & a & b \\
\hline
a & 1 & y \\
b & 1 & 1
\end{array}
\qquad
\begin{array}{c|cc}
L_9 & c & d \\
\hline
c & 1 & y \\
d & N_T(y) & 1
\end{array}
$$

It is easy to see that L_8 and L_9 are T-linear fuzzy orderings with respect to T and some T-equivalences (the exact definition of them is not important at this point). Now we can compute:

$$\text{Lex}_{\tilde{T},T}(L_8, L_9)((a,c),(b,d)) = \max(\tilde{T}(y,y), \min(y, N_T(1)) = \tilde{T}(y,y)$$

$$\text{Lex}_{\tilde{T},T}(L_8, L_9)((b,d),(a,c)) = \max(\tilde{T}(1, N_T(y)), \min(1, N_T(y))$$
$$= N_T(y)$$

If $\text{Lex}_{\tilde{T},T}(L_8, L_9)$ was linear, the following inequality would be fulfilled:

$$N_T(\text{Lex}_{\tilde{T},T}(L_8, L_9)((b,d),(a,c))) \leq \text{Lex}_{\tilde{T},T}(L_8, L_9)((a,c),(b,d))$$

However, we obtain:

$$N_T(\text{Lex}_{\tilde{T},T}(L_8, L_9)((b,d),(a,c))) = N_T(N_T(y))$$
$$= y > \tilde{T}(y,y)$$
$$= \text{Lex}_{\tilde{T},T}(L_8, L_9)((a,c),(b,d)).$$

Therefore, $\text{Lex}_{\tilde{T},T}(L_8, L_9)$ can never be T-linear if $\tilde{T} < T_{\mathbf{M}}$. This example, therefore, justifies the assumptions of Theorem 3.

5. Conclusion

In this paper, we have introduced an approach to lexicographic composition of similarity-based fuzzy orderings. This construction, in principle, works for all choices of t-norms. However, *the* essential property of lexicographic compositions — that the lexicographic composition of linear orderings is again a linear ordering on the product domain — is only maintained if the underlying t-norm T induces an involutive negation (in particular, including nilpotent t-norms and the nilpotent minimum). This once more confirms the viewpoint that such t-norms are most adequate choices in fuzzy relations theory, fuzzy preference modeling and related fields.[11,17,20–22]

Acknowledgments

When this paper was mainly written, the author was affiliated with Software Competence Center Hagenberg, A-4232 Hagenberg, Austria. Therefore, he thanks for support by the Austrian Government, the State of Upper Austria, and the Johannes Kepler University Linz in the framework of the K*plus* Competence Center Program. Furthermore, the partial support of COST Action 274 "TARSKI" is gratefully acknowledged.

References

1. L. A. Zadeh, Similarity relations and fuzzy orderings. *Inform. Sci.*, **3**, 177–200 (1971).
2. S. V. Ovchinnikov, Similarity relations, fuzzy partitions, and fuzzy orderings. *Fuzzy Sets and Systems*, **40**(1), 107–126 (1991).
3. S. V. Ovchinnikov and M. Roubens, On strict preference relations. *Fuzzy Sets and Systems*, **43**(3), 319–326 (1991).
4. J. Fodor and M. Roubens, *Fuzzy Preference Modelling and Multicriteria Decision Support*, Kluwer Academic Publishers, Dordrecht (1994).
5. U. Höhle and N. Blanchard, Partial ordering in *L*-underdeterminate sets. *Inform. Sci.*, **35**, 133–144 (1985).
6. U. Bodenhofer, A similarity-based generalization of fuzzy orderings preserving the classical axioms. *Int. J. Uncertain. Fuzziness Knowledge-Based Systems*, **8**(5), 593–610 (2000).
7. U. Bodenhofer, Representations and constructions of similarity-based fuzzy orderings. *Fuzzy Sets and Systems*, **137**(1), 113–136 (2003).
8. R. Bělohlávek, *Fuzzy Relational Systems. Foundations and Principles*. IFSR Int. Series on Systems Science and Engineering, Kluwer Academic/Plenum Publishers, New York (2002).
9. M. Demirci, A theory of vague lattices based on many-valued equivalence relations—I: general representation results, *Fuzzy Sets and Systems*, **151**(3), 437–472 (2005).
10. U. Bodenhofer, *A Similarity-Based Generalization of Fuzzy Orderings*. Vol. C 26. *Schriftenreihe der Johannes-Kepler-Universität Linz*. Universitätsverlag Rudolf Trauner (1999).
11. U. Bodenhofer and M. Demirci, Strict fuzzy orderings in a similarity-based setting. *Proc. Joint 4th Conf. of the European Society for Fuzzy Logic and Technology and 11 Recontres Francophones sur la Logique Floue et ses Applications*, pp. 297–302, Barcelona (September, 2005).
12. P. Hájek, *Metamathematics of Fuzzy Logic*. Vol. 4. *Trends in Logic*. Kluwer Academic Publishers, Dordrecht (1998).
13. F. Klawonn and J. L. Castro, Similarity in fuzzy reasoning. *Mathware Soft Comput.*, **3**(2), 197–228 (1995).
14. E. P. Klement, R. Mesiar and E. Pap, *Triangular Norms*. Vol. 8. *Trends in Logic*, Kluwer Academic Publishers, Dordrecht (2000).

15. E. Trillas and L. Valverde, An inquiry into indistinguishability operators. In eds. H. J. Skala, S. Termini and E. Trillas. *Aspects of Vagueness*, Reidel, Dordrecht, pp. 231–256 (1984).

16. D. Boixader, J. Jacas and J. Recasens, Fuzzy equivalence relations: Advanced material. In eds. D. Dubois and H. Prade, *Fundamentals of Fuzzy Sets*. Vol. 7. *The Handbooks of Fuzzy Sets*, Kluwer Academic Publishers, Boston, pp. 261–290 (2000).

17. U. Bodenhofer and F. Klawonn, A formal study of linearity axioms for fuzzy orderings. *Fuzzy Sets and Systems*, **145**(3), 323–354 (2004).

18. B. De Baets and R. Mesiar, *T*-partitions. *Fuzzy Sets and Systems*, **97**, 211–223 (1998).

19. S. Saminger, R. Mesiar and U. Bodenhofer, Domination of aggregation operators and preservation of transitivity. *Int. J. Uncertain. Fuzziness Knowledge-Based Systems*, **10**(Suppl.), 11–35 (2002).

20. B. De Baets and J. Fodor, Towards ordinal preference modelling: the case of nilpotent minimum. *Proc. 7th Int. Conf. on Information Processing and Management of Uncertainty in Knowledge-Based Systems* Paris I, 310–317 (1998).

21. B. De Baets, B. Van de Walle and E. E. Kerre, A plea for the use of Łukasiewicz triplets in the definition of fuzzy preference structures. (II). The identity case. *Fuzzy Sets and Systems*, **99**(3), 303–310 (1998).

22. B. Van de Walle, B. De Baets and E. E. Kerre, A plea for the use of Łukasiewicz triplets in the definition of fuzzy preference structures. (I). General argumentation. *Fuzzy Sets and Systems*, **97**(3), 349–359 (1998).

Efficiently Updating and Tracking the Dominant Normalized Kernel Principal Components

Geert Gins[*], Ilse Y. Smets[†] and Jan F. Van Impe[‡]

BioTeC, Department of Chemical Engineering
Katholieke Universiteit Leuven
W. de Croylaan 46, B-3001 Leuven (Belgium)
[*]geert.gins@cit.kuleuven.be
[†]ilse.smets@cit.kuleuven.be
[‡]jan.vanimpe@cit.kuleuven.be

Abstract

Various state-of-the-art machine learning problems rely on kernel based methods. These kernel methods have the ability to solve highly nonlinear problems by reformulating them in a linear context. Hereto, the dominant eigenspace of a (normalized) kernel matrix is often required. Unfortunately, due to the computational requirements of the existing kernel methods, this eigenspace can only be obtained for relatively small data sets.

This paper focuses on a kernel based method for large data sets. More specifically, a *tracking* algorithm for the dominant eigenspace of a normalized kernel matrix is proposed. This tracking algorithm consists in an *updating* step followed by a *downdating* step, and allows to estimate the evolution of the dominant eigenspace over time.

1. Introduction

Kernel based methods have become increasingly popular in various state-of-the-art machine learning problems, such as, e.g. classification, function estimation, pattern recognition, signal processing and system identification problems.[7,9] These kernel based methods are capable of solving highly nonlinear problems by implicitly mapping all data points in an often high-dimensional space, in which linear techniques are used for solving the reformulated problem.

The majority of the currently employed kernel based methods, such as, e.g. kernel principal component analysis (KPCA),[8] fixed size least squares support vector machines (LS-SVM),[9] and spectral clustering,[5,10] rely, either directly or indirectly, on the eigenvectors of the $n \times n$ symmetric kernel Gram matrix K, which provides a similarity measure for the n available data points. Typically, only the dominant m eigenvectors of the $n \times n$ kernel matrix K are needed, where m is much smaller than n.

The eigenspace of the kernel matrix is often computed by means of the singular value decomposition (SVD).[a] Even though the SVD has a high numerical precision and stability, the computational demands (typically $O(n^3)$ operations with an $O(n^2)$ memory requirement) represent a substantial drawback. Furthermore, the mapping (or embedding) is only obtained for existing data points. All computations must be performed all over again if new data points are added to the set, or if old points are removed (such as, e.g. when *tracking* the dominant eigenspace of the kernel matrix, where new data points are continuously added to the data set while old points are removed). The applicability of these otherwise well performing kernel methods is, therefore, limited to relatively small data sets and off-line problems.

Algorithms that try to alleviate these problems are currently being developed.[4,6] To the best of the authors' knowledge, however, a truly on-line algorithm has not been reported so far, although Hoegaerts *et al.*[3] proposed an algorithm for tracking the dominant subspace for solving KPCA problems quasi-online. Based on the SVD of the kernel matrix K, their proposed algorithm solves the problem of the matrix expanding in both row and column dimension when a new point is added to the data set, a situation conventional SVD updating schemes are unable to handle. The method is, however, not applicable to *normalized* kernels, which are often used in, e.g. spectral clustering[5,10] and typically yield better results than non-normalized kernels.[10]

---

[a] Because the kernel matrix is positive (semi-)definite, the singular value decomposition (SVD) is identical to a standard eigenvalue decomposition (EVD). SVD is preferred over EVD because of its numerical precision and stability.

Using the algorithm of Hoegaerts *et al.*[3] as a reference framework, this paper proposes an algorithm capable of dynamically tracking the eigenspace of a *normalized* kernel with satisfying accuracy, while requiring substantially less computation time ($O(nm^2)$ operations) and memory space ($O(nm)$). The algorithm starts by *updating* the kernel matrix when a new data point is added to the data set, after which an old data point is removed from the set in a *downdating* step.

2. The Laplacian Kernel Matrix

Given the data set $S = \{\mathbf{x}_1, \mathbf{x}_2, \ldots, \mathbf{x}_n\}$, with $\mathbf{x}_i \in \mathbb{R}^p$, the $n \times n$ symmetric kernel Gram matrix K is defined as $[K]_{ij} = k(\mathbf{x}_i, \mathbf{x}_j)$, where the kernel function k provides a pairwise similarity measure between data points. Commonly used kernel functions k are the linear, polynomial and Gaussian kernels.

$$k_{\mathrm{L}}(\mathbf{x}_i, \mathbf{x}_j) = \mathbf{x}_i \cdot \mathbf{x}_j, \tag{1}$$

$$k_{\mathrm{P}}(\mathbf{x}_i, \mathbf{x}_j) = (a + \mathbf{x}_i \cdot \mathbf{x}_j)^b, \tag{2}$$

$$k_{\mathrm{G}}(\mathbf{x}_i, \mathbf{x}_j) = \exp\left(-\frac{\|\mathbf{x}_i - \mathbf{x}_j\|^2}{2\sigma^2}\right), \tag{3}$$

where a, b and σ are problem-specific, user-defined parameters.

When working with a normalized kernel, a transformation of the kernel Gram matrix is used. An example of such a transformation is the *divisive normalization* which substitutes the Laplacian L for the kernel matrix K.[5,10]

$$L = D^{-1/2} K D^{-1/2}, \tag{4}$$

$$[D]_{ij} = \begin{cases} 0 & \text{if } i \neq j \\ \sum_{k=1}^{n} [K]_{ik} & \text{if } i = j \end{cases}. \tag{5}$$

Notice that the normalization matrix D is usually defined slightly differently, i.e. $[D]_{ii} = \sum_{k \neq i} [K]_{ik}$. This definition often leads to better embeddings of the data points, but has no significant impact upon the algorithm presented in Secs. 3, 4 and 5.

3. Updating the Eigenspace

When a new data point is added to the data set, the new $(n+1) \times m$ eigenspace $U_{(n+1)m}$ of the new Laplacian L_{n+1} must be computed. While the eigenspace can be calculated directly from the new data set using batch SVD calculations, this computation typically requires $O(n^3)$ operations and becomes inefficient and slow as n increases. Instead of performing the calculations from scratch, an approximation of the desired eigenspace can be computed requiring only $O(nm^2)$ operations, assuming that the $n \times m$ dominant eigenspace U_{nm} and corresponding $m \times m$ diagonal eigenvalue matrix Σ_n of L_n, and the $n \times n$ diagonal normalization matrix D_n are known.

When adding a new data point to an existing data set of size n, the set's size increases to $n + 1$, requiring the $n \times n$ non-normalized kernel matrix K_n to be updated. This is achieved by adding a new row and column to the existing kernel matrix K_n.

$$K_{n+1} = \begin{bmatrix} K_n & \mathbf{a}_u \\ \mathbf{a}_u^T & b_u \end{bmatrix}. \tag{6}$$

Here, $\mathbf{a}_u$ is an $n \times 1$ vector defined as $[\mathbf{a}_u]_i = k(\mathbf{x}_i, \mathbf{x}_{n+1})$ and $b_u = k(\mathbf{x}_{n+1}, \mathbf{x}_{n+1})$ is a scalar.

The non-normalized kernel matrix K_n can be computed from the normalized kernel matrix L_n using (4), because the normalizing matrix D_n is known.

$$K_n = D_n^{1/2} L_n D_n^{1/2}. \tag{7}$$

Substituting (7) in (6) and factorizing the resulting matrix yields

$$K_{n+1} = \begin{bmatrix} D_n^{1/2} & \mathbf{0}_n \\ \mathbf{0}_n^T & 1 \end{bmatrix} \begin{bmatrix} L_n & D_n^{-1/2} \mathbf{a}_u \\ \mathbf{a}_u^T D_n^{-1/2} & b_u \end{bmatrix} \begin{bmatrix} D_n^{1/2} & \mathbf{0}_n \\ \mathbf{0}_n^T & 1 \end{bmatrix}, \tag{8}$$

where $\mathbf{0}_n$ is an $n \times 1$ null vector. Thus, an expression for the updated non-normalized kernel matrix K_{n+1} is obtained.

The normalization matrix D_{n+1} is used to find a recursive expression for the Laplacian matrix L, after block-partitioning the normalization matrix D_{n+1} in its $n \times n$ upper block $D_{n+1,U}$ and the scalar $d_{n+1,L}$.

$$L_{n+1} = \begin{bmatrix} D_{n+1,U}^{-1/2} & \mathbf{0}_n \\ \mathbf{0}_n^T & d_{n+1,L}^{-1/2} \end{bmatrix} \begin{bmatrix} D_n^{1/2} & \mathbf{0}_n \\ \mathbf{0}_n^T & 1 \end{bmatrix} \cdot$$

$$\cdots \begin{bmatrix} L_n & D_n^{-1/2}\mathbf{a}_u \\ \mathbf{a}_u^T D_n^{-1/2} & b_u \end{bmatrix} \begin{bmatrix} D_n^{1/2} & \mathbf{0}_n \\ \mathbf{0}_n^T & 1 \end{bmatrix} \begin{bmatrix} D_{n+1,U}^{-1/2} & \mathbf{0}_n \\ \mathbf{0}_n^T & d_{n+1,L}^{-1/2} \end{bmatrix}.$$

$$(9)$$

Because the central matrix still contains the unknown matrix L_n, its known rank-m approximation $L_n \approx U_{nm}\Sigma_n U_{nm}^T$ is used, in accordance to Hoegaerts *et al.*[3] to obtain

$$L_{n+1} \approx D_{n+1}^{*1/2} \begin{bmatrix} U_0 & A \end{bmatrix} \begin{bmatrix} \Sigma_n & O_m \\ O_m^T & D_u \end{bmatrix} \begin{bmatrix} U_0^T \\ A^T \end{bmatrix} D_{n+1}^{*1/2}, \qquad (10)$$

$$D_{n+1}^* \triangleq \begin{bmatrix} D_{n+1,U}^{-1} D_n & \mathbf{0}_n \\ \mathbf{0}_n^T & d_{n+1,L}^{-1} \end{bmatrix}, \qquad (11)$$

$$U_0 \triangleq \begin{bmatrix} U_{nm} \\ \mathbf{0}_m^T \end{bmatrix}, \qquad (12)$$

$$A \triangleq \begin{bmatrix} D_n^{-1/2}\mathbf{a}_u & D_n^{-1/2}\mathbf{a}_u \\ \dfrac{b_u}{2}+1 & \dfrac{b_u}{2}-1 \end{bmatrix}, \qquad (13)$$

$$D_u \triangleq \begin{bmatrix} \dfrac{1}{2} & 0 \\ 0 & -\dfrac{1}{2} \end{bmatrix}. \qquad (14)$$

Here, O_m is an $m \times 2$ null matrix.

$D_{n+1,U}^{-1}D_n$, the $n \times n$ upper block of D_{n+1}^*, is a diagonal matrix. The nonzero elements of this block can be formulated as

$$\left[D_{n+1,U}^{-1}D_n \right]_{ii} = \frac{d_{ii,n}}{d_{ii,n+1}}, \qquad (15)$$

where $d_{ii,n}$ and $d_{ii,n+1}$ are the ith diagonal elements of D_n and D_{n+1}, respectively.

Assuming the number of data points n is large enough,[b] $d_{ii,n}$ and $d_{ii,n+1}$ can be expressed as

$$d_{ii,n} = \bar{d}_{ii}\, n, \tag{16}$$

$$d_{ii,n+1} \approx \bar{d}_{ii}\, (n+1), \tag{17}$$

where $\bar{d}_{ii}$ is defined as the average of d_{ii} over all n (or $n-1$) data points.[c]

Based on these relations, (15) is reformulated and substituted in (11), yielding

$$D_{n+1,U}^{-1} D_n \approx \frac{n}{n+1}\, I_n, \tag{18}$$

$$D_{n+1}^* \approx \begin{bmatrix} \dfrac{n}{n+1}\, I_n & \mathbf{0}_n \\ \mathbf{0}_n^T & \dfrac{1}{d_{n+1,L}} \end{bmatrix}. \tag{19}$$

In a next step, the matrix D_{n+1}^* is folded into the eigenspace $[U_0\ A]$ by using (19).

$$D_{n+1}^{*1/2} \begin{bmatrix} U_0 & A \end{bmatrix} \triangleq \begin{bmatrix} U_0^* & A^* \end{bmatrix}. \tag{20}$$

$$U_0^* \approx \begin{bmatrix} \sqrt{\dfrac{n}{n+1}}\, U_{nm} \\ \mathbf{0}_m^T \end{bmatrix} = \sqrt{\dfrac{n}{n+1}}\, U_0, \tag{21}$$

$$A^* \approx \begin{bmatrix} \sqrt{\dfrac{n}{n+1}}\, D_n^{-1/2} \mathbf{a}_u & \sqrt{\dfrac{n}{n+1}}\, D_n^{-1/2} \mathbf{a}_u \\ \dfrac{b_u + 2}{2\sqrt{d_{n+1,L}}} & \dfrac{b_u - 2}{2\sqrt{d_{n+1,L}}} \end{bmatrix}. \tag{22}$$

A new eigenspacè $[U_0^*\ A^*]$ is obtained. As can be seen from (21), the folding of D_{n+1}^* does not influence the orthogonality of the m

---

[b] This assumption is valid because only large data sets are considered.

[c] When working with the alternative normalization $[D]_{ii} = \sum_{i \neq k} K_{ik}$, the average $\bar{d}$ must be defined over $n-1$ data points. However, the results remain virtually unchanged, with $(n-1)/n$ being used instead of $n/(n+1)$ in further steps of the algorithm.

eigenvectors in U_0^*, but merely alters their length.[d] The $(n+1) \times 2$ matrix A^* contains two vectors which are not orthogonal to the eigenspace. Therefore, A^* is decomposed into an orthogonal $(A_\perp^*)$ and a parallel component $(A_\parallel^*)$ with respect to the space spanned by U_0^* (and thus U_0), in a way similar to Hoegaerts *et al.*[3]

$$A^* = A_\perp^* + A_\parallel^*, \tag{23}$$

$$= (I_{n+1} - U_0 U_0^T)A^* + U_0 U_0^T A^*, \tag{24}$$

$$\overset{\triangle}{=} Q_A R_A + U_0 U_0^T A^*. \tag{25}$$

where the QR-factorization of $A_\perp^* = Q_A R_A$ has been used to make the columns of $A_\perp^*$ mutually orthogonal, resulting in the $(n+1) \times 2$ matrix Q_A and the 2×2 matrix R_A. The computation of Q_A and R_A only requires $O(nm)$ operations, which is an affordable amount.

The updated eigenspace can now easily be obtained using (21) and (25). Factorizing the result yields

$$\begin{bmatrix} U_0^* & A^* \end{bmatrix} \approx \sqrt{\frac{n}{n+1}} \begin{bmatrix} U_0 & Q_A \end{bmatrix} \begin{bmatrix} I_m & \sqrt{\dfrac{n+1}{n}}\, U_0^T A^* \\ O_m^T & \sqrt{\dfrac{n+1}{n}}\, R_A \end{bmatrix}, \tag{26}$$

$$\overset{\triangle}{=} \sqrt{\frac{n}{n+1}}\, Q_u R_u. \tag{27}$$

Using (27), the recursive formulation of the Laplacian L (10) can be reformulated as

$$L_{n+1} \approx \frac{n}{n+1} Q_u \left(R_u \begin{bmatrix} \Sigma_n & O_n \\ O_n^T & D_u \end{bmatrix} R_u^T \right) Q_u^T, \tag{28}$$

where O_n is an $n \times 2$ matrix of zeroes.

---

[d] Strictly speaking, U_0^* does not contain eigenvectors because $U_0^{*T} U_0^* \neq I_n$. This issue will be addressed in a later stage of the algorithm by introducing the same factor in the QR-decomposition of $A_\perp^*$.

Then, the eigenvalue decomposition of the three middle matrices is performed using the SVD,[e] requiring $O(m^3)$ operations.

$$R_u \begin{bmatrix} \Sigma_n & O_n \\ O_n^T & D_u \end{bmatrix} R_u^T = V' \Sigma'_{n+1} V'^T. \tag{29}$$

Finally, the last (smallest) two eigenvectors are discarded, and the factor $n/(n+1)$ is included in the central matrix. This yields the final result

$$L_{n+1} \approx U_{(n+1)m} \Sigma_{n+1} U_{(n+1)m}^T, \tag{30}$$

where the $(n+1) \times m$ updated eigenspace is obtained as

$$U_{(n+1)m} \overset{\triangle}{=} Q_u V' \tag{31}$$

together with the $m \times m$ eigenvalue matrix

$$\Sigma_{n+1} \overset{\triangle}{=} \frac{n}{n+1} \Sigma'_{n+1}. \tag{32}$$

This updated eigenspace $U_{(n+1)m}$ is obtained in $O(nm^2)$ operations, and the updating of the eigenvalues Σ_{n+1} requires the negligible amount of $O(m)$ operations. Hence, the global algorithm is capable of computing the embedding of a new data point in $O(nm^2)$ operations while using $O(nm)$ memory space.

4. Downdating the Eigenspace

After every update the dimension of the eigenspace increases, resulting in higher memory requirements and slower computations. Even though the updating scheme proposed in Sec. 3, reduces the computational requirements, it is still impractical in on-line applications and subspace trackers, where the dimension of the studied eigenspace needs to remain constant. Therefore, every update of the data set and its kernel eigenspace must be followed by a downsize, a step during which the oldest data point is removed from the data set, reducing the data set size from $n+1$ to n.

---

[e] SVD and EVD are only equal if the matrix is positive (semi-)definite. This requirement can be relaxed by using the properties $\lambda(A) + x = \lambda(A + xI_n)$ and $u(A) = u(A + xI_n)$ to *lift* the matrix into the positive semi-definite region before performing the SVD.

As in Sec. 3, the non-normalized kernel matrix K_{n+1} is partitioned. However, this time the first row and first column are separated from the rest of the matrix.

$$K_{n+1} = \begin{bmatrix} b_d & \mathbf{a}_d^T \\ \mathbf{a}_d & K_n' \end{bmatrix}. \tag{33}$$

K_n' is the $n \times n$ non-normalized kernel matrix of the data set containing only the last n data points. The $n \times 1$ vector $\mathbf{a}_d$ and scalar b_d contain all information pertaining to the first (oldest) data point, which is to be removed from the data set.

Pre- and postmultiplying K_{n+1} with an expanded version of D_n', the rescaling matrix for K_n', the kernel matrix associated with the last n data points, yields the matrix L_n^*,

$$L_n^* \triangleq \begin{bmatrix} \alpha & \mathbf{0}_n^T \\ \mathbf{0}_n & D_n'^{-1/2} \end{bmatrix} K_{n+1} \begin{bmatrix} \alpha & \mathbf{0}_n^T \\ \mathbf{0}_n & D_n'^{-1/2} \end{bmatrix}, \tag{34}$$

which, using (33) and (7), becomes

$$L_n^* = \begin{bmatrix} \alpha^2 b_d & \alpha \mathbf{a}_d^T D_n'^{-1/2} \\ \alpha D_n'^{-1/2} \mathbf{a}_d & L_n' \end{bmatrix}. \tag{35}$$

As can clearly be seen, the lower block of the $(n+1) \times (n+1)$ matrix L_n^* contains the $n \times n$ downdated Laplacian L_n'. The parameter α in (35) can be freely chosen because it only influences the first row and column of L_n^*.

The normalization matrix D_{n+1}, associated with the expanded data set kernel matrix K_{n+1}, is block-partitioned in the scalar $d_{n+1,U}$ and the $n \times n$ lower block $D_{n+1,L}$, and used to reformulate (34).

$$D_{n+1} = \begin{bmatrix} d_{n+1,U} & \mathbf{0}_n^T \\ \mathbf{0}_n & D_{n+1,L} \end{bmatrix}. \tag{36}$$

$$L_n^* = \begin{bmatrix} \alpha & \mathbf{0}_n^T \\ \mathbf{0}_n & D_n'^{-1/2} \end{bmatrix} D_{n+1}^{1/2} L_{n+1} D_{n+1}^{1/2} \begin{bmatrix} \alpha & \mathbf{0}_n^T \\ \mathbf{0}_n & D_n'^{-1/2} \end{bmatrix}. \tag{37}$$

Because all matrices except L_{n+1} are diagonal, the above expression is reformulated as

$$L_n^* = D_n^{*1/2} L_{n+1} D_n^{*1/2}, \tag{38}$$

$$D_n^* \triangleq \begin{bmatrix} \alpha d_{n+1,U} & \mathbf{0}_n^T \\ \mathbf{0}_n & D_n'^{-1} D_{n+1,L} \end{bmatrix}. \tag{39}$$

Selecting the parameter α to be equal to $\frac{n+1}{n} d_{n+1,U}$ and under the assumption that n is large enough to drive $d_{ii,n+1}/d_{ii,n}$ towards the $(n+1)/n$ ratio,[f] D_n^* can be approximated as

$$D_n^* \approx \frac{n+1}{n} I_{n+1}. \tag{40}$$

Substituting (40) in (38) and exploiting the known SVD of $L_{n+1} = U_{(n+1)m} \Sigma_{n+1} U_{(n+1)m}^T$ results in

$$L_n^* \approx \frac{n+1}{n} U_{(n+1)m} \Sigma_{n+1} U_{(n+1)m}^T. \tag{41}$$

To obtain the downdated Laplacian L_n' from L_n^*, the first row of $U_{(n+1)m}$, represented by the $1 \times m$ vector $\mathbf{u}^T$, must be discarded, thus retaining the $n \times m$ matrix U_{nm}'', which contains all other rows of $U_{(n+1)m}$.

$$L_n^* \approx \frac{n+1}{n} \begin{bmatrix} \mathbf{u}^T \Sigma_{n+1} \mathbf{u} & \mathbf{u}^T \Sigma_{n+1} U_{nm}''^T \\ U_{nm}'' \Sigma_{n+1} \mathbf{u} & U_{nm}'' \Sigma_{n+1} U_{nm}''^T \end{bmatrix}. \tag{42}$$

Retaining only the lower $n \times n$ block of L_n^*, which contains the downdated Laplacian L_n', results in an approximate decomposition of L_n',

$$L_n' \approx \frac{n+1}{n} U_{nm}'' \Sigma_{n+1} U_{nm}''^T, \tag{43}$$

where the columns of U_{nm}'' are not mutually orthonormal. Instead of performing a computationally expensive QR-decomposition of U_{nm}'

---

[f] Or towards $n/(n-1)$, depending on the definition of the normalization matrix D.

to restore orthonormality, a transformation matrix M is used, as proposed by Hoegaerts *et al.*[3] This $m \times m$ matrix M is defined as

$$M \triangleq \begin{bmatrix} \overline{\mathbf{u}} & \overline{\mathbf{u}}_\perp \end{bmatrix} \begin{bmatrix} \dfrac{1}{\sqrt{1 - \|\mathbf{u}\|^2}} & \mathbf{0}_{m-1}^T \\ \mathbf{0}_{m-1} & I_{m-1} \end{bmatrix} = \begin{bmatrix} \dfrac{\overline{\mathbf{u}}}{\sqrt{1 - \|\mathbf{u}\|^2}} & \overline{\mathbf{u}}_\perp \end{bmatrix}, \quad (44)$$

where $\overline{\mathbf{u}} = \mathbf{u}/\|\mathbf{u}\|$ is the vector $\mathbf{u}$ divided by its length. The $m \times (m - 1)$ matrix $\overline{\mathbf{u}}_\perp$ is the right null space of $\overline{\mathbf{u}}^T$.

The matrix Σ_{n+1} is adjusted to compensate for the effects of this transformation, and decomposed into its eigenvalues and -vectors.

$$M^{-1} \Sigma_{n+1} M^{-T} = U_\Sigma \Sigma_n'' U_\Sigma^T. \quad (45)$$

Instead of inverting the transformation matrix M directly, its particular structure is exploited to compute the inverse transformation matrix M^{-1} more rapidly and with higher numerical accuracy.

$$M^{-1} = \begin{bmatrix} \overline{\mathbf{u}}^T \sqrt{1 - \|\mathbf{u}\|^2} \\ \overline{\mathbf{u}}_\perp^T \end{bmatrix}. \quad (46)$$

Finally, the eigenvalue decomposition of L_n' is obtained.

$$L_n' \approx U_{nm}' \Sigma_n' U_{nm}'^T, \quad (47)$$

where the $n \times m$ downdated eigenspace and the $m \times m$ downdated eigenvalue matrix are respectively defined as

$$U_{nm}' \triangleq U_{nm}'' M U_\Sigma, \quad (48)$$

$$\Sigma_n' \triangleq \frac{n+1}{n} \Sigma_n''. \quad (49)$$

The dominant term in the downsizing cost is the M-transformation, which requires $O(nm^2)$ operations.

When the downsizing is preceded by an updating, the SVD of the updating step may be postponed until after downdating.

5. Tracking the Eigenspace

When the updating scheme from Sec. 3 is combined with the downdating scheme from Sec. 4, a tracking algorithm is obtained, where at each step a new data point is added to the data set, and an old point is removed. Using this algorithm, the dominant eigenspace of the normalized Laplacian kernel can be tracked dynamically, requiring only $O(nm^2)$ operations and $O(nm)$ memory space per iteration step. The complete tracking algorithm is summarized in Appendix A.

The proposed algorithm also applies to the tracking of the dominant eigenspace of a *non-normalized* kernel matrix, as proposed by Hoegaerts *et al.*[3] By adjusting the formulae of the tracking algorithm proposed in this work with a few assumptions, the algorithm of Hoegaerts *et al.*[3] is recovered.

$$\lim_{n\to\infty} \frac{n+1}{n} = 1, \qquad \lim_{n\to\infty} [D]_{ii} = 1.$$

6. Performance Assessment

The performance of the proposed algorithm is tested on the well-known Abalone data set,[1] which is often used as a benchmark in various machine learning problems. The Abalone set has a size n of 3000, and the dimension p of each sample is equal to 7. The employed kernel function is the Gaussian kernel; the parameter σ is set equal to 10. The normalization is performed using the alternative definition $[D]_{ii} = \sum_{i \neq j} [K]_{ik}$.

The $500 \times m$ eigenspace of the Abalone data set is tracked during 2000 iteration steps. In each step, a new point is added, and the oldest point is removed from the data set. After each iteration step, $||\hat{L} - L||_F / ||L||_F$, the relative deviation of the approximations obtained through the tracking scheme and batch SVD calculations from the full rank Laplacian is calculated. The evolution of these errors is depicted in Fig. 1 for the case where m equals 10.

The algorithm does not reach the exceptional quality level of batch SVD calculations when m increases, but nevertheless has a more than acceptable performance. The batch SVD calculations reach this exceptional accuracy by recalculating the eigenspace from scratch whenever a data point is added to the set. The updating algorithm sacrifices some of this accuracy in order to obtain results quickly.

Another important observation is that the relative error of the updating algorithm reaches a stationary value after about 250 iteration steps. This is a valuable result, as it implies that the algorithm is an appropriate tool for tracking the eigenspace during a large number of iteration steps before retraining is required. Table 1 summarizes these stationary approximation errors for various values of m.

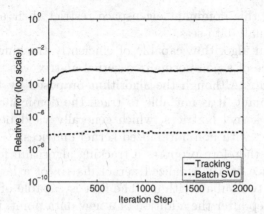

Fig. 1. Relative error versus iteration step for the 500×10 eigenspace resulting from the updating algorithm and batch SVD computations.

Table 1. Mean value of the stationary relative error, averaged over the final 1500 iteration steps of the tracking experiment, for a data set size n equal to 500.

m	Updating	Batch SVD	m	Updating	Batch SVD
8	$7.291 \cdot 10^{-4}$	$1.392 \cdot 10^{-6}$	20	$7.295 \cdot 10^{-4}$	$5.474 \cdot 10^{-10}$
10	$7.203 \cdot 10^{-4}$	$1.192 \cdot 10^{-7}$	40	$7.380 \cdot 10^{-4}$	$6.956 \cdot 10^{-12}$

7. Numerical Stability and Further Benchmarking

A detailed discussion of the numerical stability of the proposed tracking algorithm can be found in Gins *et al.*[2] In addition, the performance of the proposed tracking algorithm for the dominant eigenspace of a normalized kernel matrix is benchmarked against more state of the art batch computation algorithms.

8. Conclusions

Kernel based methods are frequently exploited in classification, function estimation, pattern recognition, system identification and signal processing problems. They are very powerful tools, because of their capability of solving highly nonlinear problems by reformulating them in a linear context. Often, the dominant eigenspace of a (normalized) kernel matrix is needed to perform this reformulation. Unfortunately, the computational requirements of current methods for computing this dominant eigenspace restrict their applicability to relatively small data sets.

Recently, an algorithm capable of efficiently tracking the dominant eigenspace of a non-normalized kernel matrix was proposed by Hoegaerts *et al.*[3] Although the algorithm proposed by the authors is very performant, it is not able to track the dominant eigenspace of normalized kernel matrices, which generally yield better results when compared with non-normalized kernel matrices.[10]

This paper therefore proposes a tracking algorithm for the dominant eigenspace of a normalized kernel matrix of a large data set by combining two subalgorithms. The first is capable of computing an *updating* step after the addition of a new data point, inducing an extension of the Laplacian matrix in both its row and column dimension while all matrix elements are rescaled. The second subalgorithm performs a *downdating* step, the exclusion of an existing data point from the data set. Combining these two subalgorithms results in an algorithm more than capable of tracking the dominant eigenspace of a normalized kernel matrix, requiring only $O(nm^2)$ numerical operations and $O(nm)$ memory space.

Acknowledgments

Work supported in part by projects CoE EF/05/006 Optimization in Engineering (OPTEC) and OT/03/30 of the Research Council of the Katholieke Universiteit Leuven, and the Belgian Program on Interuniversity Poles of Attraction, initiated by the Belgian Federal Science Policy Office. The scientific responsibility is assumed by its authors.

References

1. C. Blake and C. Merz, UCI repository of machine learning databases. http://www.ics.uci.edu/mlearn/MLRepository.html (1998).
2. G. Gins, I. Y. Smets and J. F. Van Impe, Efficient tracking of the dominant eigenspace of a normalized kernel matrix. *Neural Computation (accepted for publication)*, (2007).
3. L. Hoegaerts, L. De Lathauwer, J. Suykens and J. Vandewalle, Efficiently undating and tracking the dominant kernel principal components. *Neural Networks*, **20**(2), 220–229 (2007).
4. K. Kim, M. Franz and B. Schölkopf, Kernel Hebbian algorithm for iterative kernel principal component analysis. *Max-Planck-Institut für biologische Kybernetik*, **103** (2003).

5. A. Ng, M. Jordan and Y. Weiss, On spectral clustering: Analysis and an algorithm. *Advances in Neural Information Processing Systems*, **14** (2002).
6. R. Rosipal and M. Girolami, An expectation-maximization approach to nonlinear component analysis. *Neural Computation*, **13**, 505–510 (2001).
7. B. Schölkopf and A. Smola, *Learning with Kernels*. MIT Press, Cambridge (2002).
8. B. Schölkopf, A. Smola and K. Müller, Nonlinear component analysis as a kernel eigenvalue problem. *Neural Computation*, **10**, 1299–1319 (1998).
9. J. Suykens, T. Van Gestel, J. De Brabanter, B. De Moor and J. Vandewalle. *Least Squares Support Vector Machines*. World Scientific Publishing Company, Singapore (2002).
10. Y. Weiss, Segmentation using eigenvectors: A unifying view. *Proceedings IEEE International Conference on Computer Vision*, **9**, 975–982 (1999).

Appendix

Overview of the tracking algorithm

Given (i) D_n, the divisive normalization matrix of K_n, being a kernel matrix associated with the data points $\mathbf{x}_k, \ldots, \mathbf{x}_{k+n-1}$ and (ii) U_{nm} and Σ_n, the m leading eigenvectors and corresponding eigenvalues of the normalized kernel matrix $L_n = D_n^{-1/2} K_n D_n^{-1/2}$ of K_n, **calculate** (i) D_n', the divisive normalization matrix of K_n', being a kernel matrix associated with the data points $\mathbf{x}_{k+1}, \ldots, \mathbf{x}_{k+n}$ and (ii) U_{nm}' and Σ_n', the m leading eigenvectors and corresponding eigenvalues of the normalized kernel matrix $L_n' = D_n'^{-1/2} K_n' D_n'^{-1/2}$ of K_n' **by**

- **updating:**

(a) $\quad D_{n+1} \mathbf{1}_{n+1} = \begin{bmatrix} D_n \mathbf{1}_n + \mathbf{a}_u \\ \mathbf{a}_u^T \mathbf{1}_n + b_u \end{bmatrix}$

(b) $\quad U_0 = \begin{bmatrix} U_{nm} \\ \mathbf{0}_m^T \end{bmatrix}$

(c) $\quad D_u = \begin{bmatrix} \dfrac{1}{2} & 0 \\ 0 & -\dfrac{1}{2} \end{bmatrix}$

(d) $\quad A^* = \begin{bmatrix} D_n^{-1/2} \mathbf{a}_u & D_n^{-1/2} \mathbf{a}_u \\ \dfrac{b_u}{2} + 1 & \dfrac{b_u}{2} - 1 \end{bmatrix}$

(e) $Q_A R_A \overset{QR}{\longleftarrow} (I_{n+1} - U_0 U_0^T) A^*$

(f) $Q_u = [U_0 \; Q_A]$

(g) $R_u = \begin{bmatrix} I_m & \sqrt{\dfrac{n+1}{n}} \, U_0^T A^* \\ O_m^T & \sqrt{\dfrac{n+1}{n}} \, R_A \end{bmatrix}$

(h) $\Sigma_u = \dfrac{n}{n+1} \, R_u \begin{bmatrix} \Sigma_n & O_n \\ O_n^T & D_u \end{bmatrix} R_u^T$

- **downdating:**

  (a) $D_n' \mathbf{1}_n = \begin{bmatrix} \mathbf{0}_n & I_n \end{bmatrix} D_{n+1} \begin{bmatrix} \mathbf{0}_n^T \\ I_n \end{bmatrix} \mathbf{1}_n - \mathbf{a}_d$

  (b) $\begin{bmatrix} \mathbf{u}^T \\ U_{nm}'' \end{bmatrix} \leftarrow Q_u$

  (c) $M = \begin{bmatrix} \dfrac{\bar{\mathbf{u}}}{\sqrt{1 - \|\mathbf{u}\|^2}} & \bar{\mathbf{u}}_\perp \end{bmatrix}$

  (d) $M_{\text{inv}} = \begin{bmatrix} \bar{\mathbf{u}}^T \sqrt{1 - \|\mathbf{u}\|^2} \\ \bar{\mathbf{u}}_\perp^T \end{bmatrix}$

  (e) $Q_d = U_{nm}'' M$

  (f) $\Sigma_d = \frac{n+1}{n} \, M_{\text{inv}} \Sigma_u M_{\text{inv}}^T$

- **performing an SVD and a rotation:**

  (a) $\Sigma_n' \longleftarrow U_\Sigma \Sigma_n' U_\Sigma^T \overset{SVD,\ m\text{-rank}}{\longleftarrow} \Sigma_d$

  (b) $U_{nm}' = Q_d U_\Sigma$

Topological Relations on Fuzzy Regions — An Extended Application of Intersection Matrices

Jörg Verstraete*, Axel Hallez, Guy De Tré and Tom Matthé

Database, Document and Content Management, TELIN
Ghent University, Sint Pietersnieuwstraat 41
9000 GENT, Belgium
*Jorg.Verstraete@telin.ugent.be

Abstract

In traditional geographic databases and geographic information systems, a variety of different models to represent information is used. In geoscience however, many data is inherently vague or prone to uncertainty (i.e. due to limited measurements), yet the current models don't take this into account. In the chapter we examine the topological relations on a conceptual level for use with fuzzy regions, as developed before. The relations at hand stem from the nine-intersection model and are presented within the same framework as the fuzzy bitmap and fuzzy tin models for fuzzy regions.

1. Introduction

In geographic information systems, two major models are used: Field based models and entity based models.[10,11] Field based models are used to represent data spread over a wide region, for instance soil composition, altitudes, and population densities. The data structures used are commonly bitmaps and triangulated irregular networks. Entity based models are used to model objects, for instance a house, a street or a forest. The data structures used here commonly are basic geometric objects: i.e. points, lines and polygons. None of the currently used models take uncertainty or imprecision into account, despite the fact that many data are inherently uncertain or impre-cise.[9] Models that incorporate the uncertainty or imprecision have been presented in, Refs. 7 and 12.

2. Regions with Undetermined Boundaries

2.1. *Related work*

In literature, two models for regions with undetermined bound-aries have been considered. Cohn and Gotts presented the *egg-yolk* model;[2,6] Clementini considered regions with broad boundaries.[1]

The two approaches are similar in that a region A with unde-termined boundaries is defined using two crisp boundaries: an inner boundary, and an outer boundary. In the egg-yolk model, these are referred to respectively as the *yolk* and the *egg* (Fig. 1(a)); in the algebric model by Clementini, the inner region is called the interior ($A°$), the broad boundary is ΔA (Fig. 1(b)), and the exterior is A^-.

2.2. *Fuzzy regions*

2.2.1. *Fuzzy set theory*

Fuzzy regions will be defined using fuzzy set theory for the model-ing of vague and uncertain information. In fuzzy sets, each element of a domain is assigned a membership grade in the range $[0, 1]$; this grade can have different interpretations:[3] *veristic* (in which case it expresses a degree of belonging to the set, an example is the pred-icate "young"), *possibilistic* (in which case they express to which extent the element is a possible value, an example is a fuzzy age of "approximately 25") or as *degrees of truth*. A common example is the extension of the real axis, in which case possibilistic interpreted

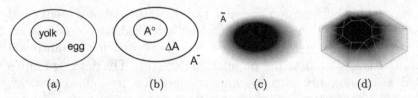

Fig. 1. Graphical representation of the egg-yolk model (a), the broad boundary model (b) and the fuzzy region model (c). A practical fuzzy region model is shown in (d).

fuzzy sets are considered to be fuzzy numbers.[8] A fuzzy region is defined similarly.

2.2.2. *Definition of a fuzzy region*

In our approaches[12] the modeling of a fuzzy region is done by defining a fuzzy set over a set of *locations*. The membership grade assigned to each location indicates the extent to which this location belongs to the fuzzy region (the fuzzy set is interpreted veristic: All points belong to the region, but some to a greater extent than others).

$$\tilde{A} = \{(p, \mu_{\tilde{A}}(p)\}, \tag{1}$$

where

$$\mu_{\tilde{A}} : U \rightarrow [0, 1]$$
$$p \mapsto \mu_{\tilde{A}}(p).$$

Here, U is the universe of all locations; the membership grade $\mu_{\tilde{A}}(p)$ expresses the extent to which p belongs to the region.

An illustration of a fuzzy region $\tilde{A}$ can be seen on Fig. 1(c); the shade of gray is related to the membership grade: A membership grade 1 is indicated by black, 0 by white, and shades in between indicate values in between: The higher the grade, the darker the color.

This approach differs from the approaches mentioned in Sec. 2.1 in that it provides additional information regarding the broad boundary. The previous models only differentiate between points belonging completely to the region (inside the inner boundary), points definitely not belonging to the region (outside the outer boundary) and points that belong to the boundary of the region. The boundary of fuzzy regions in our model is not part of the definition, but can be derived from membership grades of the elements of the fuzzy region. In this chapter, the topological aspects of such fuzzy regions are considered.

2.2.3. *Practical feasibility of fuzzy regions*

As there are an infinite number of locations in a region, practical models are required to make fuzzy regions computationally feasible in implementations for real applications. For this purpose we presented two such models: In Ref. 12 a field-based bitmap structure is adapted to model the membership grades over the region; in Ref. 12 a field-based triangulated irregular network structure is adapted for this purpose (an example is shown in Fig. 1(d)). The former approach is conceptually simple and easy to reason with (due to the fact that it is discrete), whereas the latter yields a better model at the cost of a hugely increased complexity (as this is a continuous model). For both approaches, a number of operators has been developed: Intersection, union, minimum bounding rectangle, *alpha*-cut, distance measures, surface area, etc. The results presented in this paper are the first step towards adding topological relations in the practical models.

3. Topological Relations

3.1. *Nine-intersection model (crisp)*

Topological relations — simply put — refer to the relative positions of regions. The definitions of the various intersection cases for two regions are based on three concepts; for a region A these are: the interior of the region (A°), the exterior of the region (A^-) and the boundary of the region (∂A). For intersections between two regions, and considering these three concepts, there are *nine* possible combinations; the nine-intersection matrix groups them as follows:[1]

$$\begin{pmatrix} A^\circ \cap B^\circ & A^\circ \cap \partial B & A^\circ \cap B^- \\ \partial A \cap B^\circ & \partial A \cap \partial B & \partial A \cap B^- \\ A^- \cap B^\circ & A^- \cap \partial B & A^- \cap B^- \end{pmatrix}. \tag{2}$$

By assigning each matrix element 0 if the intersection is empty, and 1 if the intersection is not empty, $2^9 = 512$ relations can be deduced. For crisp regions in a two-dimensional space R^2, only eight such intersection matrices are possible. These yield to eight possible relations:[1] Disjoint, contains, inside, equal, meet, covers, coverdBy and overlap (Fig. 2).

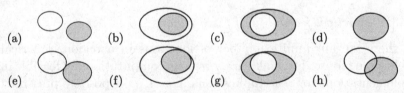

Fig. 2. Topological relations for crisp regions: (a) disjoint, (b) contains, (c) inside, (d) equal, (e) meet, (f) covers, (g) coverdBy and (h) overlap.

3.2. *Intersection model for regions with undetermined boudaries*

The intersection of regions with undetermined boundaries has been considered by Cohn and Gotts in Refs. 2 and 6 for the egg-yolk model, and by Clementini in[1] for an algebraic model for spatial objects with undetermined boundaries.

To determine topological relations, both authors started from the nine-intersection matrix as shown in Eq. (2), but due to a slight difference in definitions, Cohn and Gotts have 46 cases for intersection, whereas Clementini has 44 cases. The intersection matrix is obtained similarly to the matrix in Eq. (2), the only difference is that concepts interior, exterior and boundary are defined differently (ΔA is the adopted notation for the boundary of A).

In these approaches however, the models for the regions provided no additional information regarding points in the boundaries. As a result, no distinction is made for the regions in Figs. 3(a) and 3(b). Intuitively, one might consider point closer to the inner boundary to belong more to the region, in which case Fig. 3(b) would be less *meet* than Fig. 3(a) and more *overlap*. The fuzzy region as defined above allows to model the degree of *belonging to* the region. Consequently, it can hold additional information concerning the boundary; it is therefore to be expected that the intersection cases reflect this additional information.

3.3. *Fuzzy region intersection model*

To define topological relations for fuzzy regions, using the fuzzy region model that provides membership grades for all the points, a different approach is considered. The nine-intersection model is extended as in the above methods. However, in our approach, instead of considering a crisp intersection, the interior, exterior and boundary are considered as fuzzy regions as well, and a fuzzy intersection

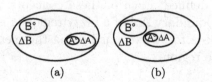

(a)   (b)

Fig. 3. Two topologies for regions with broad boundaries that yield the same intersection matrix.

is applied to obtain the different elements of the nine-intersection matrix. Appropriate concepts for interior, exterior and boundary are defined sing the membership grades as present in the fuzzy regions; an extension of the intersection has already been developed for fuzzy regions.[12] This will yield a nine-intersection matrix, but with elements in the range $[0, 1]$ instead of just mere boolean values (0 and 1).

As was already the case for the intersection models of both Clementini and Cohn and Gotts, the various relations between regions with undetermined boundaries are not named (touches, meets, ...); Clementini did however name classes of results. Interestingly, the topological relations for regions with undetermined boundaries in these models are still reflected in our model as special cases (when only values in $\{0, 0.5, 1\}$ are used).

To define the fuzzy region topology, the concept of the α-cut of fuzzy regions is often used. The α-cut stems from fuzzy set theory;[8] the *weak α-cut* of a fuzzy set A returns the elements with a membership grade greater than or equal to a given threshold α:

$$A_\alpha = \{(x, 1)|\mu_A(x) \geq \alpha, \forall x\}. \tag{3}$$

As fuzzy regions are fuzzy sets over a two dimensional domain, the same definition applies. For further definitions and usages of the α-cut for fuzzy regions, we refer to. Ref. 12. Also used in the explanation is the *core* of a fuzzy set. The core is defined as the α cut for $\alpha = 1$:

$$core(A) = A_{\alpha_1} = \{(x, 1)|\mu_A(x) \geq 1, \forall x\}. \tag{4}$$

4. Defining the Fuzzy Region Topology

4.1. *Defining the extended concepts*

In order to extend the nine-intersection model for fuzzy regions, appropriate concepts for boundary, interior and exterior of a fuzzy region need to be defined. Each of these concepts will yield a new fuzzy region. The boundary $\Delta \tilde{A}$ of a fuzzy region $\tilde{A}$ is not part of the definition, so it needs to be extracted using the membership grades of the points in the region.

$$\Delta \tilde{A} = \bigcup_{\alpha \in]0,1]} \{(p, 2(0.5 - |0.5 - \alpha|))|p \in \partial A_\alpha\}. \tag{5}$$

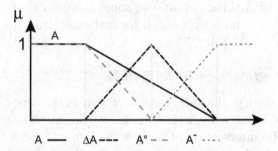

Fig. 4. Representation of the membership functions for the extended topological concepts of fuzzy regions.

Basically, points with a membership grade $\mu_{\tilde{A}}(p) = 0.5$ are assigned the value 1 as membership grade in the boundary. The more $\mu_{\tilde{A}}(p)$ differs from 0.5, the lower the membership grade is; eventually equalling 0 when $\mu_{\tilde{A}}(p) = 1$ and when $\mu_{\tilde{A}}(p) = 0$. This is illustrated on Fig. 4. It shows the membership functions for the fuzzy region $\tilde{A}$, the boundary of the region $\Delta\tilde{A}$, and also for the interior $(\tilde{A}^{\circ})$ and exterior $(\tilde{A}^{-})$.

From this boundary definition, both extended concepts of interior and exterior can be derived similarly; both concepts also yield fuzzy regions. The interior and exterior are not defined as an extension of a crisp interior using Zadeh's extension principle,[5] but are defined using the membership grades of the points. The interior $\tilde{A}^{\circ}$ (respectively exterior $\tilde{A}^{-}$) is a fuzzy region, containing only those points that have a membership grade strictly greater (respectively strictly less) than 0.5 in the original region $\tilde{A}$. In either case the membership grades are rescaled so that the result has membership grades in the range $[0,1]$, see Fig. 4.

Interior

$$\tilde{A}^{\circ} = \{(p, \mu_{\tilde{A}^{\circ}}(p)\}$$

where

$$\mu_{\tilde{A}^{\circ}} : U \to [0,1]$$

$$p \mapsto \begin{cases} 0 & \text{if } \mu_{\tilde{A}}(p) \le 0.5 \\ 1 - \mu_{\Delta\tilde{A}}(p) \\ & \text{elsewhere} \end{cases}$$

Exterior

$$\tilde{A}^{-} = \{(p, \mu_{\tilde{A}^{-}(p)}(p)\}$$

where

$$\mu_{\tilde{A}^{-}} : U \to [0,1]$$

$$p \mapsto \begin{cases} 0 & \text{if } \mu_{\tilde{A}}(p) \ge 0.5 \\ 1 - \mu_{\Delta\tilde{A}}(p) \\ & \text{elsewehere} \end{cases}$$

Note that with these definitions, some relations that are valid in the crisp case, are no longer valid, for instance: Traditionally, $A° = A \backslash \partial A$, but $\tilde{A}° \neq \tilde{A} \backslash \Delta \tilde{A}$.

4.1.1. *Intersection-operator for regions*

In fuzzy set theory, the intersection of two fuzzy sets $\tilde{C}$ and $\tilde{D}$ is performed by using a t-norm. Commonly the minimum is used as the t-norm, the intersection of fuzzy sets $\tilde{C}$ and $\tilde{D}$ using t-norm min is a new fuzzy region $\tilde{C} \tilde{\cap} \tilde{D}$, with its membership function defined as:

$$\mu_{\tilde{C} \tilde{\cap} \tilde{D}} : U \rightarrow [0, 1]$$
$$x \mapsto \min((\mu_{\tilde{C}}(x), \mu_{\tilde{D}}(x))).$$

4.2.   *Nine-intersection model for fuzzy regions*

In the crisp nine-intersection model, the matrix elements are considered to be 0 if the intersection is empty, and 1 if it is not. In our approach, the matrix elements are deduced from each intersection: Each matrix element is the value of the highest membership grade occurring in the intersection. For this, the height of a fuzzy set[4,] is used:

$$height(X) = \sup_{p}(\mu_X(p)). \tag{6}$$

Using the definitions for the topological concepts of fuzzy regions, the nine-intersection matrix can be considered as:

$$\begin{pmatrix} h(\tilde{A}° \tilde{\cap} \tilde{B}°) & h(\tilde{A}° \tilde{\cap} \Delta \tilde{B}) & h(\tilde{A}° \tilde{\cap} \tilde{B}^-) \\ h(\Delta \tilde{A} \tilde{\cap} \tilde{B}°) & h(\Delta \tilde{A} \tilde{\cap} \Delta \tilde{B}) & h(\Delta \tilde{A} \tilde{\cap} \tilde{B}^-) \\ h(\tilde{A}^- \tilde{\cap} \tilde{B}°) & h(\tilde{A}^- \tilde{\cap} \Delta \tilde{B}) & h(\tilde{A}^- \tilde{\cap} \tilde{B}^-) \end{pmatrix}, \tag{7}$$

where $h(X)$ is a shorthand notation for the *height(X)* of a fuzzy set X.

4.3.   *Interpretation*

4.3.1.   *Crisp regions*

By means of comparison, consider two crisp regions A and B. If they are disjoint (Fig. 2(a)), the intersection matrix is in given in Fig. 5(a); if they meet (Fig. 2(e)), the intersection matrix is given in Fig. 5(b);

$$
\begin{pmatrix} 0\ 0\ 1 \\ 0\ 0\ 1 \\ 1\ 1\ 1 \end{pmatrix}
\quad
\begin{pmatrix} 0\ \ 0\ \ 1 \\ 0\ \ 1\ \ 1 \\ 1\ \ 1\ \ 1 \end{pmatrix}
\quad
\begin{pmatrix} 1\ \ 1\ \ 1 \\ 1\ \ 1\ \ 1 \\ 1\ \ 1\ \ 1 \end{pmatrix}
$$
$$
\text{(a)} \qquad\qquad \text{(b)} \qquad\qquad \text{(c)}
$$

Fig. 5. Intersection matrices for some crisp cases.

finally, if they overlap (Fig. 2(h)), the intersection matrix is given in Fig. 5(b).

4.3.2. *Fuzzy regions*

Consider the fuzzy regions $\tilde{A}$ and $\tilde{B}$. The nine-intersection matrix (as defined in (7)) for the case when they are disjoint, matches the crisp intersection matrix for crisp regions (see Fig. 5(a)):

$$
\begin{pmatrix} 0\ \ 0\ \ 1 \\ 0\ \ 0\ \ 1 \\ 1\ \ 1\ \ 1 \end{pmatrix}
$$

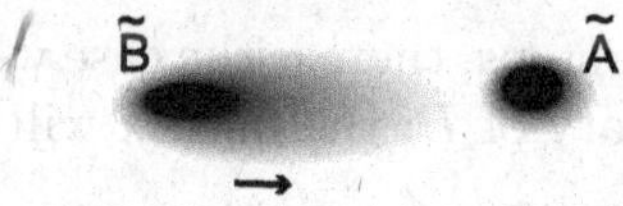

Next, consider the region $\tilde{B}$ to move closer to $\tilde{A}$. First, only the boundaries will start to overlap: $\Delta\tilde{B}$ intersects with $\Delta\tilde{A}$ but not with $\tilde{A}^{\circ}$; nor does $\Delta\tilde{A}$ intersects with $\tilde{B}^{\circ}$. On the nine-intersection matrix, this yields no change in the elements that deal with the interiors. The exteriors were already overlapping, and nothing changes here either. Consequently, the only matrix element that will change is the middle element: $height(\Delta\tilde{A}\tilde{\cap}\Delta\tilde{B})$. It will indicate a value $x > 0$ and increase the more $\Delta\tilde{B}$ will intersect with $\Delta\tilde{A}$

$$
\begin{pmatrix} 0\ \ 0\ \ 1 \\ 0\ \ a\ \ 1 \\ 1\ \ 1\ \ 1 \end{pmatrix}
$$

Here, $a \neq 0$, as equality would imply the boundaries to be disjoint. Note how this matrix does resembles the nine-intersection matrix representation for *meets*.

As $\tilde{B}$ moves closer to $\tilde{A}$, $\Delta\tilde{B}$ will start to intersect $\tilde{A}^{\circ}$. Note that $\tilde{B}$ still does not contain points with $\mu_{\tilde{A}}(p) = 1$, but points p for which $\mu_{\tilde{A}}(p) > 0.5$ are part of the interior. The region $\tilde{B}$ contains some of these points; causing $\sup_p(\mu_{\tilde{A}^\circ \tilde{\cap} \Delta \tilde{B}}(p(x,y)))$ to change to a value $b > 0$.

$$\begin{pmatrix} 0 & a & 1 \\ 0 & b & 1 \\ 1 & 1 & 1 \end{pmatrix}$$

Again, there are some constraints:

- $a \in]0,1]$: as the interior of A, $\tilde{A}^\circ$ overlaps with the boundary $\Delta \tilde{B}$; $a = 1$ if the $\tilde{A}^\circ$ overlaps sufficiently with $\Delta \tilde{B}$: This is when the core of $\tilde{A}^\circ$ overlaps with the core of $\Delta \tilde{B}$.
- $b \in]0,1]$: the boundaries $\Delta \tilde{A}$ and $\Delta \tilde{B}$ overlap, so $a > 0$; $b = 1$ if the core of $\Delta \tilde{A}$ intersects with the core of $\Delta \tilde{B}$.

Skipping some steps, there is the case where region $\tilde{A}$ is completely inside the boundary of $\tilde{B}$; the matrix will look like this:

$$\begin{pmatrix} a & b & c \\ d & e & f \\ g & h & i \end{pmatrix}$$

Where the following constraints hold:

- $a \in [0,1[$: the interiors cannot overlap with a degree 1; $a = 0$ if $\tilde{A}^\circ$ is far enough from $\tilde{B}^\circ$ (i.e. if it is in the portion where $\mu_{\tilde{B}} < 0.5$)
- $b \in]0,1]$: $\tilde{A}^\circ$ is inside $\Delta \tilde{B}$ ($b \neq 0$); $b = 1$ if both cores overlap
- $c \in [0,1[$: $\tilde{A}^\circ$ is inside $\Delta \tilde{B}$. $c = 0$ if they overlap with their cores
- $d \in [0,1[$: $\Delta \tilde{A}$ can either not overlap with $\tilde{B}^\circ$ ($d = 0$ if $\Delta \tilde{A}$ is there where $\mu_{\tilde{B}} < 0.5$), or can overlap stronger the closer $\Delta \tilde{A}$ gets to $\tilde{B}^\circ$
- $e \in]0,1]$: $\Delta \tilde{A}$ overlaps with $\Delta \tilde{B}$
- $f \in [0,1[$: $\Delta \tilde{A}$ cannot overlap completely with $\tilde{B}^-$
- $g = 1$: $\tilde{A}^-$ overlaps to the maximum extent with $\tilde{B}^\circ$
- $h = 1$: $\tilde{A}^-$ overlaps to the maximum extent with $\Delta \tilde{B}$
- $i = 1$: $\tilde{A}^-$ overlaps to the maximum extent with $\tilde{B}^-$

Notice how the matrix in this example reverts to the similar case in Ref. 1 (shown in Fig. 3) if the extreme values (i.e. 1 where the matrix element is in $]0, 1]$ and 0 where it is in $[0, 1[$) are considered.

For other topological situations, similar conclusions can be drawn. In total, 46 intersection cases can be considered, each imposing limitations on the different matrix elements. For the elements a_1, a_2, b, c_1 and c_2, the possible limitations are: Equal to 0, in $]0, 1]$ and in $]0, 1[$. For the elements d, e_1, e_2 the possible limitations are equal to 0, in $]0, 1[$ and equal to 1.

4.3.3. *Example*

Contrary to the traditional intersection matrices, both for crisp regions as for broad boundaries, the interpretation of the fuzzy intersection matrices differ. A consequence of the fact that the regions are truly fuzzy, is that the different cases are no longer mutually exclusive. This is best illustrated by means of an example; two given regions could for instance yield the following intersection matrix:

$$\begin{pmatrix} d & c_1 & e_1 \\ c_2 & b & a_1 \\ e_2 & a_2 & 1 \end{pmatrix} = \begin{pmatrix} 0.6 & 0.7 & 0.4 \\ 0.4 & 0.6 & 0.3 \\ 1 & 0.6 & 1 \end{pmatrix}. \tag{8}$$

Taken into account the values at hand, and the limitations imposed by the different cases, this particular matrix is similar to the cases:

$$\{4, 5, 10, 11\}. \tag{9}$$

It is possible to further distinguish between the cases that occur, using the values that occur in the intersection matrix. The rule we use is that values smaller than 0.5 belong more to ranges of the form $[0, 1[$ than to the range $]0, 1]$; whereas values greater than 0.5 have the opposite property (this is an intuitive rule). To work with this, match values are assigned for every matrix element x that distinguishes two groups and for every case i that is in either of the two groups.

Definition 1 (Match value m_x^i for a case i and a matrix element x).

$$m_x^i = \begin{cases} x & \text{if } x < 0.5 \text{ and range of case } i =]0, 1] \\ 1 - x & \text{if } x < 0.5 \text{ and range of case } i = [0, 1[\\ x & \text{if } x \geq 0.5 \text{ and range of case } i =]0, 1] \\ 1 - x & \text{if } x \geq 0.5 \text{ and range of case } i = [0, 1[\end{cases}. \tag{10}$$

The differences between the cases 4, 5, 10 and 11 are in the values of $a_1 = 0.3$, $c_1 = 0.7$ and $c_2 = 0.4$; for a_1 these are:

$$a_1 = 0.3 \text{ cases } 4,10: \quad 0 < a_1 \leq 1 \Rightarrow m_{a_1}^4 = m_{a_1}^{10} = 0.3$$
$$\text{cases } 5,11: \quad 0 \leq a_1 < 1 \Rightarrow m_{a_1}^5 = m_{a_1}^{11} = 0.7 \tag{11}$$

This indicates that cases 5 and 11 are a better match for the example than cases 4 and 10. For the values c_1 and c_2, the match values are :

$$c_1 = 0.7 \text{ case } 5: \qquad 0 \leq c_1 < 1 \Rightarrow m_{c_1}^5 = 0.3$$
$$\text{cases } 4,10,11: \quad 0 < c_1 \leq 1 \Rightarrow m_{c_1}^4 = m_{c_1}^{10} = m_{c_1}^{11} = 0.7$$
$$c_2 = 0.4 \text{ cases } 4,5: \qquad 0 \leq c_2 < 1 \Rightarrow m_{c_2}^4 = m_{c_2}^5 = 0.6$$
$$\text{cases } 10,11: \quad 0 < c_2 \leq 1 \Rightarrow m_{c_2}^{10} = m_{c_2}^{11} = 0.4 \tag{12}$$

According to the match values for c_1, cases 4,10,11 are a better match than case 5; whereas the match values for c_2 leads us to conclude that cases 4 and 5 are a better match than cases 10 and 11. Aggregating the match values using the minimum yields:

$$\text{case 4: } \min\{m_{a_1}^4, m_{c_1}^4, m_{c_2}^4\} = \min\{0.3, 0.7, 0.6\} = 0.3,$$
$$\text{case 5: } \min\{m_{a_1}^5, m_{c_1}^5, m_{c_2}^5\} = \min\{0.7, 0.3, 0.6\} = 0.3,$$
$$\text{case 10: } \min\{m_{a_1}^{10}, m_{c_1}^{10}, m_{c_2}^{10}\} = \min\{0.3, 0.7, 0.4\} = 0.3,$$
$$\text{case 11: } \min\{m_{a_1}^{11}, m_{c_1}^{11}, m_{c_2}^{11}\} = \min\{0.7, 0.7, 0.4\} = 0.4.$$

As the aggregated match value is the highest for case 11, the topology for the example is closer to this case, than to any of the other three cases. However, the differences between the different averages are very small, so the regions in the example still resemble the other three cases quite closely.

5.   Conclusion

In this paper, we presented a fuzzy topology model, which is an extension of the crisp nine-intersection model, and extends the intersection model as defined for objects with both boundaries[1] and the egg-yolk model.[2,6] The model reverts to these if only membership grades in $\{0, 0.5, 1\}$ are used, and back to the crisp model if only membership grades in $\{0, 1\}$ are used. The presented concept of fuzzy regions has already been applied in two practical models: A bitmap based model and a TIN based model,[12] for which operations have been defined. The fuzzy topology concept as presented, will make it possible to consider topological relationships between such fuzzy regions, and will be applied in both of these models.

References

1. E. Clementini and P. Di Felice, An algebraic model for spatial objects with undetermined boundaries. *GISDATA Specialist Meeting — revised version* (1994).
2. A. G. Cohn and N. M. Gotts, Spatial regions with undetermined boundaries. *Proc. of the 2nd ACM Workshop on Advances in GIS*, pp. 52–59 (1994).
3. D. Dubois and H. Prade, The three semantics of fuzzy sets. *Fuzzy Sets and Systems*, **90**, 141–150 (1999).
4. D. Dubois and H. Prade, *Fundamentals of Fuzzy Sets*. Kluwer Academic Publishers (2000).
5. D. Dubois and H. Prade, Possibility theory, probability theory and multiple-valued logics: A clarification. *Annals of Mathematics and Artificial Intelligence*, **32**, 35–66 (2001).
6. N. M. Gotts and A. G. Cohn, A mereological approach to representing spatial vagueness. *Working Papers, 9th Int. Workshop on Qualitative Reasoning*, pp. 246–255 (1995).
7. A. Hallez, J. Verstraete, G. De Tré and R. De Caluwe, Contourline based modeling of vague regions. *Proc. of 9th IPMU*. Annecy, France (2002).
8. G. J. Klir and B. Yuan, *Fuzzy Sets and Fuzzy Logic: Theory and Applications*, New Jersey, Prentice Hall (1995).
9. A. Morris, Why spatial databases need fuzziness. *Proceedings of Nafips*, pp. 2446–2451 (2001).
10. P. Rigaux, M. Scholl and A. Voisard, Spatial databases with applications to GIS. Morgan Kaufman Publishers (2002).
11. S. Shekhar, S. Chawla, *Spatial Databases: A Tour*. Pearson Education Inc. (2003).
12. J. Verstraete, G. De Tré, R. De Caluwe and A. Hallez, Field based methods for the modeling of fuzzy spatial data. *Fuzzy Modeling with Spatial Information for Geographic Problems*. F. Petry, V. Robinson and M. Cobb (eds.), Springer-Verlag, pp. 41–69 (2005).

Quantifier Elimination Versus Generalized Interval Evaluation — A Comparison on a Specific Class of Quantified Constraints

Carlos Grandón[*] and Alexandre Goldsztejn[†]

[*] COPRIN projet at INRIA Sophia-Antipolis, France
Carlos.Grandon@sophia.inria.fr[‡]
[†] University of Nice Sophia-Antipolis, France
Alexandre@Goldsztejn.com

Abstract

This paper presents and compares two methods for checking if a box is included inside the solution set of an equality/inequality constraint with existential quantification of its parameters. We focus on distance constraints, where each existentially quantified parameter has only one occurrence, because of their usefulness and their simplicity.

The first method relies on a specific quantifier elimination based on geometric considerations whereas the second method relies on computations with generalized intervals (intervals whose bounds are not constrained to be ordered). We show that on two-dimensional problems, both methods yield equivalent results. However, when dealing with higher dimensions, generalized intervals are more efficient.

1. Introduction

The interval theory[1,2] was born in the 1960s aiming rigorous computations with uncertain quantities. Interval constraint propagation[3,4] is a widely used technique that allows one to reduce the domains

---

[‡]This work was partially supported by CONICYT, Chile.

of variables involved in a numerical constraint without losing any solution. When this technique is coupled with a bisection algorithm, an accurate reliable outer approximation of the solution set of a numerical Constraint Satisfaction Problem (CSP) can be achieved.[5] However, when the solution set has a non-null (hyper)volume, such a branch and prune algorithm will bisect again and again the boxes included inside the solution set, leading to inefficient computations. This situation can be strongly improved using a test for detecting inner boxes so that boxes which are proved to lie inside the solution set will not be bisected any more. Furthermore, in addition to the speedup of computations, such inner boxes often have interesting interpretations.

There are different situations where the solution set of a CSP has a non-null volume, e.g. inequality constraints[6] or constraints with existentially quantified parameters like $(\exists a \in \mathbf{a}) \, c(a, x)$ where $\mathbf{a}$ is an interval.[7] In this paper, we focus on quantified distance constraints where the variables are the coordinates of a point $x \in \mathbb{R}^n$. The existentially quantified parameters are the coordinates of another point $a \in \mathbb{R}^n$ and the distance $r \in \mathbb{R}$ between them. Then, the distance constraint fixes the distance between a and x to be equal to r. The approximation of such constraints can be useful in many contexts, e.g. GPS localization or parallel robots modeling.[8,9]

We propose and compare two different methods for checking if a box is included inside the solution set of a distance equation with existentially quantified parameters. On one hand, the quantified distance constraint is changed to an equivalent nonquantified disjunction/conjunction of constraints which can be checked using interval arithmetic. On the other hand, the Kaucher arithmetic of generalized intervals,[10,11] which is the basis for a new formulation[12] of the modal intervals theory,[7,13] allows one to verify the inclusion through a generalized interval evaluation of the constraint. These two tests for inner boxes are implemented in a branch and prune algorithm and experiments have been carried out on academic examples.

Notations Following[14] intervals are denoted by boldface letters. Let $\mathcal{E} = \{e_1, \ldots, e_n\}$ be an ordered set of indices, the vector $(\mathbf{x}_{e_1}, \ldots, \mathbf{x}_{e_n})$ is denoted by $\mathbf{x}_{\mathcal{E}}$, so that $(\mathbf{x}_1, \ldots, \mathbf{x}_n)$ is denoted by $\mathbf{x}_{[1,\ldots,n]}$. If no confusion is possible, the usual notation $\mathbf{x}$ will be used in place of $\mathbf{x}_{[1,\ldots,n]}$.

2.   Problem Statement

The Euclidean distance between two points $a, x \in \mathbb{R}^n$ is defined by

$$f(a, x) = \sqrt{\sum_{k \in [1, \ldots, n]} (x_k - a_k)^2}. \tag{1}$$

Given two n-dimensional boxes **x**, **a** and an interval **r**, we are interested in the following quantified distance constraint

$$(\exists a \in \mathbf{a})\, (\exists r \in \mathbf{r})\, (f(a, x) = r), \tag{2}$$

which is denoted by $c_{\mathbf{a},\mathbf{r}}(x)$. The set of $x \in \mathbb{R}^n$ which satisfies (2) is denoted by $\rho_{\mathbf{a},\mathbf{r}}$. It is shown in diagrams (a) and (b) of Fig. 1. This paper aims to provide some sufficient conditions for the inclusion $\mathbf{x} \subseteq \rho_{\mathbf{a},\mathbf{r}}$.

It can be noted that a sufficient condition designed for one quantified distance constraint can also be used for a conjunction of quantified distance constraints $\bigwedge_{k \in [1,\ldots,m]} c_{\mathbf{a}^{(k)},\mathbf{r}^{(k)}}(x)$, where $\mathbf{a}^{(1)}, \ldots, \mathbf{a}^{(m)}$ are some n-dimensional boxes and $\mathbf{r}^{(1)}, \ldots, \mathbf{r}^{(m)}$ some intervals. Indeed, if existentially quantified parameters are not shared between different constraints, we have the following implication:

$$\bigwedge_{k \in [1,\ldots,m]} \mathbf{x} \subseteq \rho_{\mathbf{a}^{(k)},\mathbf{r}^{(k)}} \implies \mathbf{x} \subseteq \bigcap_{k \in [1,\ldots,m]} \rho_{\mathbf{a}^{(k)},\mathbf{r}^{(k)}}. \tag{3}$$

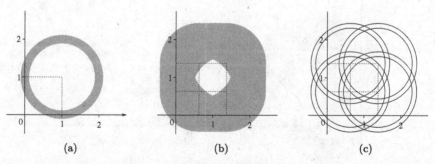

    (a)   (b)   (c)

Fig. 1. Quantified distance constraints. (a) Exact center $\mathbf{a} = (1, 1)$, and interval radius $\mathbf{r} = [0.9, 1.1]$. (b) All parameters have interval values $\mathbf{a} = ([0.8, 1.2], [0.8, 1.2])$ and $\mathbf{r} = [0.9, 1.1]$ (with a less intuitive graph). (c) The eight characteristic circles of (b).

3. A Specific Quantifier Elimination

The quantifier elimination (QE) consists in transforming a quantified constraint into an equivalent nonquantified constraint. A general QE algorithm for polynomial constraints is available.[15] However, its high complexity restricts its application to small problems. In the particular case of distance constraints, the implementation of QE proposed in Mathematica5.1 succeeds only in the one-dimensional case. For higher dimensions, the calculus could not be ended before memory overflow on a Pentium IV 2 Ghz with 512 Mb of memory. In this section, we present a specific QE for the distance constraint $c_{\mathbf{a},\mathbf{r}}(x)$. The presentation is done in the two-dimensional case. The three-dimensional case can be treated in the same way.[16,17] However, higher dimensions are still out of the scope of the proposed specific QE, because of its complexity.

The typical graph of the constraint $c_{\mathbf{a},\mathbf{r}}(x)$ is shown in Fig. 1(b), while its eight characteristic circles are presented in Fig. 1(c). These circles are obtained using the bounds of the intervals $\mathbf{a}$ and $\mathbf{r}$. The specific QE proposed in this section reconstructs the graph of Fig. 1(b) using the information available on Fig. 1(c), i.e. using only the bounds of the involved intervals.

3.1. *Decomposition of the quantified distance constraint*

The specific QE proposed here relies on the decomposition of $c_{\mathbf{a},\mathbf{r}}(x)$ into two auxiliary constraints with convex graph. The graphs of these two auxiliary constraints are illustrated on Fig. 2.

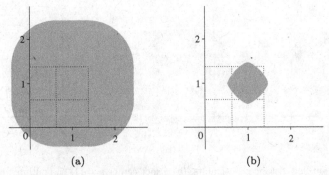

Fig. 2. Graphs of the two auxiliary constraints used in the reconstruction of $c_{\mathbf{a},\mathbf{r}}(x)$. (a) The constraint $c'_{\mathbf{a},\mathbf{r}}(x)$. (b) The constraint $c''_{\mathbf{a},\mathbf{r}}(x)$.

Notice that the boundary of Fig. 2(b) is not included in the graph of $c''_{\mathbf{a},\mathbf{r}}(x)$ so that we clearly have

$$c_{\mathbf{a},\mathbf{r}}(x) \iff c'_{\mathbf{a},\mathbf{r}}(x) \wedge \neg c''_{\mathbf{a},\mathbf{r}}(x). \tag{4}$$

(see Ref. 16 for a proof in the general case taking into account some nontypical situations). We now characterize these two auxiliary constraints using the bounds of the involved intervals.

3.1.1. *The constraint* $c'_{\mathbf{a},\mathbf{r}}(x)$

The graph of the constraint $c'_{\mathbf{a},\mathbf{r}}(x)$ is built using the four exterior circles of Fig. 2(a) and two boxes. Indeed, $c'_{\mathbf{a},\mathbf{r}}(x)$ is equivalent to the disjunction of the following six constraints:

1. $f(\underline{\mathbf{a}}_1, \underline{\mathbf{a}}_2, x) \le \overline{\mathbf{r}}$
2. $f(\overline{\mathbf{a}}_1, \underline{\mathbf{a}}_2, x) \le \overline{\mathbf{r}}$
3. $f(\underline{\mathbf{a}}_1, \overline{\mathbf{a}}_2, x) \le \overline{\mathbf{r}}$
4. $f(\overline{\mathbf{a}}_1, \overline{\mathbf{a}}_2, x) \le \overline{\mathbf{r}}$
5. $x \in ([\underline{\mathbf{a}}_1 - \overline{\mathbf{r}}, \overline{\mathbf{a}}_1 + \overline{\mathbf{r}}], \mathbf{a}_2)$
6. $x \in (\mathbf{a}_1, [\underline{\mathbf{a}}_2 - \overline{\mathbf{r}}, \overline{\mathbf{a}}_2 + \overline{\mathbf{r}}])$

This reconstruction of $c'_{\mathbf{a},\mathbf{r}}(x)$ is illustrated by Fig. 3. The first four constraints represent four disks. The graph of their disjunction is close to the graph of $c'_{\mathbf{a},\mathbf{r}}(x)$ but some gaps are present. The last two constraints fill the remaining gaps thanks to the two boxes presented in Fig. 3(b).

3.1.2. *The constraint* $c''_{\mathbf{a},\mathbf{r}}(x)$

The graph of the constraint $c''_{\mathbf{a},\mathbf{r}}(x)$ is easily obtained by intersecting four open disks corresponding to the interior circles of Fig. 1(c).

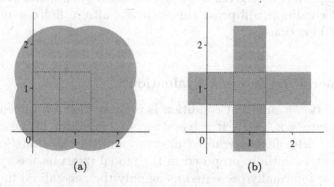

(a) (b)

Fig. 3.   Reconstruction of the constraint $c'_{\mathbf{a},\mathbf{r}}(x)$. (a) Four disks. (b) Two boxes.

The constraint $c''_{\mathbf{a},\mathbf{r}}(x)$ is equivalent to the conjunction of four constraints:

$$7.\ f(\underline{\mathbf{a}}_1, \underline{\mathbf{a}}_2, x) < \underline{\mathbf{r}} \quad 8.\ f(\underline{\mathbf{a}}_1, \overline{\mathbf{a}}_2, x) < \underline{\mathbf{r}}$$
$$9.\ f(\overline{\mathbf{a}}_1, \underline{\mathbf{a}}_2, x) < \underline{\mathbf{r}} \quad 10.\ f(\overline{\mathbf{a}}_1, \overline{\mathbf{a}}_2, x) < \underline{\mathbf{r}}$$

Thus, $\neg c''_{\mathbf{a},\mathbf{r}}(x)$ is built as the disjunction of four (nonstrict) inequalities.

3.2. *Interval arithmetic*

Now, we use classic interval arithmetic to evaluate the previously constructed expression for all x in a given box $\mathbf{x}$, in the following way:

- For constraints 5 and 6 (Sec. 3.1.1), we have $\mathbf{x} \subseteq \tilde{\mathbf{a}} \Rightarrow (\forall x \in \mathbf{x})(x \in \tilde{\mathbf{a}})$, where $\tilde{\mathbf{a}}$ is one of the two intervals involved in the constraints.
- For the other constraints, the natural extension of f is used (the real operations are replaced by their interval counterparts in the expression of f). We have $f(\tilde{a}, \mathbf{x}) \circ \tilde{r} \Rightarrow (\forall x \in \mathbf{x})(f(\tilde{a}, x) \circ \tilde{r})$ where $\circ \in \{\leq, \geq\}$ and $\tilde{a}_1 \in \{\underline{\mathbf{a}}_1, \overline{\mathbf{a}}_1\}$, $\tilde{a}_2 \in \{\underline{\mathbf{a}}_2, \overline{\mathbf{a}}_2\}$, and $\tilde{r} \in \{\underline{r}, \overline{r}\}$ are some bounds of the original intervals.

We now have a sufficient condition for $\mathbf{x} \subseteq \rho_{\mathbf{a},\mathbf{r}}$. But this is not a necessary one: a box can satisfy $\mathbf{x} \subseteq \rho_{\mathbf{a},\mathbf{r}}$ while it does not satisfy any of the six constraints presented in Sec. 3.1.1. Such a box would intersect several graphs but would be included in none of them (this flaw will be called the *decomposition flaw* from now on). However, it can be proved that given a box satisfying $\mathbf{x} \subseteq \rho_{\mathbf{a},\mathbf{r}}$, the proposed sufficient condition will prove this inclusion after a finite number of midpoint bisections.

4. Generalized Interval Evaluation

In this section a sufficient condition is proposed for a n-dimensional box $\mathbf{x}$ to satisfy $\mathbf{x} \subseteq \rho_{\mathbf{a},\mathbf{r}}$. It is based on one evaluation of the expression of $f(x, a)$ using generalized intervals and their arithmetic. This technique was initially proposed in the modal intervals theory[7,12,13] and is now informally presented using only the generalized intervals arithmetics.

4.1. Generalized intervals and quantifiers

The intervals usually considered in the interval theory are closed, bounded and nonempty. These intervals are uniquely defined by two real numbers, called their bounds. The lower bound of an interval is of course lower or equal than its upper bound. Generalized intervals are defined relaxing the constraint that bounds have to be ordered increasingly, e.g. $[-1, 1]$ is a proper interval and $[1, -1]$ is an improper interval. So, related to a set of reals $\{x \in \mathbb{R} \mid u \le x \le v\}$, where $u, v \in \mathbb{R}$, one can consider two generalized intervals $[u, v]$ and $[v, u]$. It will be convenient to use the operations $\mathtt{dual}\,[u, v] = [v, u]$ and $\mathtt{pro}\,[u, v] = [\min\{u, v\}, \max\{u, v\}]$ (called proper projection) to change the proper/improper quality of a generalized interval keeping unchanged the underlying set of reals.

The set of generalized intervals is denoted by $\mathbb{KR}$, the set of proper intervals by $\mathbb{IR}$ and the set of improper intervals by $\overline{\mathbb{IR}}$. An inclusion is defined for generalized intervals by $\mathbf{x} \subseteq \mathbf{y} \iff (\underline{\mathbf{y}} \le \underline{\mathbf{x}}) \wedge (\overline{\mathbf{x}} \le \overline{\mathbf{y}})$, e.g. $[-1, 1] \subseteq [-1.1, 1.1]$ (the inclusion corresponds to the inclusion between the underlying sets of reals), $[1.1, -1.1] \subseteq [1, -1]$ (the inclusion between the underlying sets of reals is reversed) and $[2, 0.9] \subseteq [-1, 1]$ (the underlying sets of reals have at least one common point).

Let us now consider a continuous function $g : \mathbb{R}^n \to \mathbb{R}$, a generalized interval vector $\mathbf{x} \in \mathbb{KR}^n$ and a generalized interval $\mathbf{z} \in \mathbb{KR}$. We now define the $(g, \mathbf{x})$-interpretability of $\mathbf{z}$ as following: first, if $\mathbf{x}_1, \ldots, \mathbf{x}_n$, and $\mathbf{z}$ are proper then by definition $\mathbf{z}$ is $(g, \mathbf{x})$-interpretable if and only if

$$(\forall x \in \mathbf{x})\,(\exists z \in \mathbf{z})\,(g(x) = z). \tag{5}$$

Therefore, when all involved intervals are proper, we obtain the interpretation of the classical interval theory. Second, if an improper interval is involved in place of a proper one, the related quantifier is changed in the quantified proposition to be satisfied, keeping the universal quantifiers in front of the quantified proposition. Also, when an improper interval is associated to a variable, the domain of this variable is the proper projection of the former. For example, if $\mathbf{x}_1, \mathbf{z} \in \mathbb{IR}$ (proper) and $\mathbf{x}_2 \in \overline{\mathbb{IR}}$ (improper) then by definition $\mathbf{z}$ is $(g, \mathbf{x})$-interpretable if and only if

$$(\forall x_1 \in \mathbf{x}_1)\,(\exists z \in \mathbf{z})\,(\exists x_2 \in \mathtt{pro}\,\mathbf{x}_2)\,(g(x) = z). \tag{6}$$

On the other hand, if $\mathbf{x}_1 \in \mathbb{IR}$ and $\mathbf{x}_2, \mathbf{z} \in \overline{\mathbb{IR}}$ then by definition $\mathbf{z}$ is $(g, \mathbf{x})$-interpretable if and only if

$$(\forall x_1 \in \mathbf{x}_1)\,(\forall z \in \mathbf{pro\ z})\,(\exists x_2 \in \mathbf{pro\ x}_2)\,(g(x) = z). \tag{7}$$

Thanks to the definition of $(g, \mathbf{x})$-interpretable intervals, we are able to handle quantified propositions by only performing computations on generalized intervals. This will lead to efficient computations.[12]

The next step is to construct such $(g, \mathbf{x})$-interpretable intervals. This construction follows the construction of classical interval extensions: first the construction is done for simple functions (Sec. 4.2). This leads to some formal expressions of interpretable intervals in the cases of simple elementary functions like $+, -, \times, \div, x^2, \ldots$ As in the context classical interval analysis, these expressions form a generalized interval arithmetic (that is proved to coincide with the Kaucher arithmetic). Then this generalized interval arithmetic is used to perform some generalized interval evaluation of the function (Sec. 4.3). Although it is not true in general, this evaluation is proved to compute interpretable generalized intervals when the expression used for the interval evaluation contains only one occurrence of each variable (other techniques has been proposed[12] for the treatment of expressions that contain multiple occurrences of variables). Therefore this generalized interval evaluation can be used for distance equations.

4.2. *The Kaucher arithmetic*

The Kaucher arithmetic[10] extends the classical interval arithmetic to generalized intervals. The Kaucher addition and subtraction have the same expressions than their classical counterparts, i.e. $\mathbf{x} + \mathbf{y} = [\underline{x}+\underline{y}, \overline{x}+\overline{y}]$ and $\mathbf{x}-\mathbf{y} = [\underline{x}-\overline{y}, \overline{x}-\underline{y}]$. The expressions of the Kaucher multiplication and division are a little more complicated and can be found in many references [10,11] Although it was not introduced with this goal, the Kaucher operation $\mathbf{x} \circ \mathbf{y}$, where $\circ \in \{+, -, \times, /\}$, is proved[12,13] to compute a $(\circ, \mathbf{x}, \mathbf{y})$-interpretable generalized intervals. For example, $[1, 2] + [10, 4] = [11, 6]$ is interpreted by

$$(\forall x \in [1, 2])\,(\forall z \in [6, 11])\,(\exists y \in [4, 10])\,(x + y = z), \tag{8}$$

and $[1, 2] \times [10, 4] = [10, 8]$ is interpreted by

$$(\forall x \in [1, 2])\,(\forall z \in [8, 10])\,(\exists y \in [4, 10])\,(x \times y = z). \tag{9}$$

Also, univariate functions $f(x)$ like x^2 or $\sqrt{x}$ are extended to generalized intervals in the following way: the interval $f(\mathbf{x})$ satisfies **pro** $f(\mathbf{x}) = \mathbf{range}(f, \mathbf{pro} \, \mathbf{x})$ and has the same proper/improper quality than $\mathbf{x}$, e.g. $[2, 3]^2 = [4, 9]$ is interpreted by $(\forall x \in [2, 3]) \, (\exists z \in [4, 9]) \, (x^2 = z)$ and $[3, 2]^2 = [9, 4]$ is interpreted by $(\forall z \in [4, 9]) \, (\exists x \in [2, 3]) \, (x^2 = z)$.

Now, as we can compute interpretable intervals for elementary functions, we are in position to provide interpretable intervals for more realistic functions compounded of elementary functions.

4.3. *Generalized evaluation of an expression*

Let us illustrate on an example the generalized interval evaluation of an expression. Consider the function $g(x, a, u) = (x - a)^2 + u$ and the generalized intervals $\mathbf{a} = [4, 2]$, $\mathbf{x} = [0, 1]$ and $\mathbf{u} = [2, 3]$. The interval $\mathbf{z}$ is obtained by evaluating the expression of g (the intervals $\mathbf{t}$ and $\mathbf{s}$ are intermediate intervals): $\mathbf{t} = \mathbf{x} - \mathbf{a} = [-2, -3]$, $\mathbf{s} = \mathbf{t}^2 = [9, 4]$ and $\mathbf{z} = \mathbf{s} + \mathbf{u} = [11, 7]$. These computations are interpreted by the following quantified propositions: $\mathbf{t} = \mathbf{x} - \mathbf{a} = [-2, -3]$ is interpreted by

$$(\forall x \in \mathbf{x}) \, (\forall t \in \mathbf{pro} \, \mathbf{t}) \, (\exists a \in \mathbf{pro} \, \mathbf{a}) \, (x - a = t). \qquad (10)$$

Also $\mathbf{s} = \mathbf{t}^2 = [9, 4]$ is interpreted by

$$(\forall s \in \mathbf{pro} \, \mathbf{s}) \, (\exists t \in \mathbf{pro} \, \mathbf{t}) \, (t^2 = s). \qquad (11)$$

Finally $\mathbf{z} = \mathbf{s} + \mathbf{u} = [11, 7]$ is interpreted by

$$(\forall u \in \mathbf{u}) \, (\forall z \in \mathbf{pro} \, \mathbf{z}) \, (\exists s \in \mathbf{pro} \, \mathbf{s}) \, (s + u = z). \qquad (12)$$

It is easy to see that the quantified propositions (10) and (11) imply the following one:

$$(\forall x \in \mathbf{x}) \, (\forall s \in \mathbf{pro} \, \mathbf{s}) \, (\exists a \in \mathbf{pro} \, \mathbf{a}) \, ((x - a)^2 = s). \qquad (13)$$

In the same way, the quantified propositions (12) and (13) imply the following one:

$$(\forall x \in \mathbf{x}) \, (\forall u \in \mathbf{u}) \, (\forall z \in \mathbf{pro} \, \mathbf{z}) \, (\exists a \in \mathbf{pro} \, \mathbf{a}) \, (g(x, a, u) = z) \qquad (14)$$

Therefore, the interval $\mathbf{z}$ is $(g, \mathbf{x}, \mathbf{a}, \mathbf{u})$-interpretable. The presented argumentation is easily generalized to any expression containing only one occurrence of each variable and any generalized interval arguments, and therefore to quantified distance constraints of arbitrary dimension. As a consequence, the generalized interval evaluation $f(\text{dual } \mathbf{a}, \mathbf{x})$ yields a $(f, \text{dual } \mathbf{a}, \mathbf{x})$-interpretable interval. Furthermore, thanks to the properties of the generalized intervals inclusion,[12] if $\mathbf{r}$ satisfies $f(\text{dual } \mathbf{a}, \mathbf{x}) \subseteq \mathbf{r}$ then $\mathbf{r}$ is also $(f, \text{dual } \mathbf{a}, \mathbf{x})$-interpretable, that is

$$(\forall x \in \mathbf{x})\ (\exists a \in \mathbf{a})\ (\exists r \in \mathbf{r})\ (f(a, x) = r) \tag{15}$$

is true. Finally, the inclusion $\sqrt{(\mathbf{x}_1 - \text{dual } \mathbf{a}_1)^2 + \cdots + (\mathbf{x}_n - \text{dual } \mathbf{a}_n)^2}$ $\subseteq \mathbf{r}$ is a sufficient condition for $\mathbf{x} \subseteq \rho_{\mathbf{a},\mathbf{r}}$. This condition is not necessary in general, e.g. $\mathbf{a} = ([-2, 2], [-2, 2])$ and $\mathbf{r} = [1, 1]$ so that $\mathbf{x} = ([-2, 2], [-2, 2])$ is an inner box which does not satisfy the above inclusion (in this case, the specific QE presented in Sec. 3 succeeds in proving the inclusion). However, it can be proved that the sufficient condition based on generalized interval evaluation is furthermore necessary provided that $\text{mid}(\mathbf{a}_i) \notin \mathbf{x}_i$ $(\forall i = 1, \ldots, n)$. It is likely to be satisfied for inner boxes $\mathbf{x}$ in some realistic situations.

5. Comparison of the Two Methods

Some academic examples were selected in order to compare both approaches for checking inner boxes in a CSP involving quantified distance constraints. The first and second problems are in a two-dimensional space, while the third problem is in a three-dimensional space. Problem $\mathbf{P_1}$ is composed of a single constraint $c_{\mathbf{a},\mathbf{r}}(x)$, while $\mathbf{P_2}$ and $\mathbf{P_3}$ are composed of three constraints $c_{\mathbf{a}^{(1)},\mathbf{r}^{(1)}}(x)$, $c_{\mathbf{a}^{(2)},\mathbf{r}^{(2)}}(x)$, and $c_{\mathbf{a}^{(3)},\mathbf{r}^{(3)}}(x)$. All problems have uncertainties. Table 1 shows the description of each one.

A branch and prune algorithm combining 2B-consistency and bisection techniques was used for solving each problem. The inner box checking was applied each time the consistency algorithm failed in reducing the space.

Table 2 shows the computational results[a] of the experiments, using the specific quantifier elimination (SQE) and the generalized interval evaluation (GIE). Column *Boxes* shows the total number of boxes found, while *Inner* shows the number of inner boxes. The

---

[a] Obtained on a Pentium IV 2GHz with 256Mb of RAM and 1,5Gb of swap memory, running IcosAlias v0.2b (http://ralyx.inria.fr/2004/Raweb/coprin/uid24.html).

Table 1.   Description of some academic examples.

Prob.	Variable domains	Parameters domains
P_1	$\mathbf{x} = ([-100, 100], [-100, 100])$	$\mathbf{a} = ([-0.5, 0.5], [-0.5, 1.3])$
		$\mathbf{r} = [1.3, 1.6]$
P_2	$\mathbf{x} = ([-100, 100], [-100, 100])$	$\mathbf{a}^{(1)} = (0, 0)$
		$\mathbf{r}^{(1)} = [2, 2.25]$
		$\mathbf{a}^{(2)} = ([3, 3.5], 0)$
		$\mathbf{r}^{(2)} = [2.95, 3.05]$
		$\mathbf{a}^{(3)} = ([-2.5, -2.25], 2)$
		$\mathbf{r}^{(3)} = [3.25, 3.5]$
P_3	$\mathbf{x} = ([0, 100], [-100, 100], [0, 100])$	$\mathbf{a}^{(1)} = ([-0.1, 0.1], [-0.1, 0.1], [-0.1, 0.1])$
		$\mathbf{r}^{(1)} = [4, 5]$
		$\mathbf{a}^{(2)} = ([4.9, 5.1], [-0.1, 0.1], [-0.1, 0.1])$
		$\mathbf{r}^{(2)} = [3, 4]$
		$\mathbf{a}^{(3)} = ([1.8, 2.2], [3.95, 4.05], [0.8, 1.2])$
		$\mathbf{r}^{(3)} = [4, 5]$

Table 2.   Some computational results.

Prob.	Strategy	Boxes[a]	Inner	Volume	Inner Volume	Time(s)
P_1	No Test	$> 10^7$	—	—	—	—
P_1	SQE	64877	33225	18.50312	18.49187	4.63
P_1	GIE	64877	33225	18.50312	18.49187	4.08
P_2	No Test	451655	—	0.21236	—	36,08
P_2	SQE	5481	2550	0.21236	0.21103	0.53
P_2	GIE	5481	2550	0.21236	0.21103	0.43
P_3	No Test	7717507	—	2.83133	—	803.63
P_3	SQE	503059	137900	2.83133	2.72203	87.49
P_3	GIE	501795	137799	2.83133	2.72254	58.38

[a]Precision $\epsilon = 10^{-3}$ (for 2D problems) and $\epsilon = 10^{-2}$ (for the 3D problem).

columns *Volume* and *Inner Volume* show the sum of the volume of the boxes. Some experiments have been conducted without using any inner box checking, but P_1 led to swap memory overflow (1.5 Go) before reaching the expected precision.

First of all, it is clear that the use of inner tests drastically reduces the computation times in all situations. On Problems P_1 and P_2 (Figs. 4(a) and 4(b)), the two methods for inner box checking are optimal and compute exactly the same approximations: on one hand, the bisection is performed in such a way that the *decomposition*

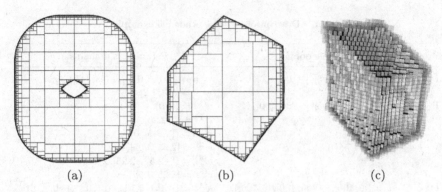

(a)   (b)   (c)

Fig. 4.   Graphical representation of the solutions of the problems.

flaw (Sec. 3.2) of the SQE is not met. On the other hand, we have $\mathbf{x} \cap \mathbf{a} = \emptyset$ for all inner boxes, so that the GIE is optimal. The running time using the GIE is always slightly lower than using the SQE because the former computes only one evaluation of the constraint. On Problem $\mathbf{P_3}$ (Fig. 4(c)), the two tests compute different approximations: the total volumes are equal with both methods but the inner volume provided by the GIE is greater, with a lower number of inner boxes. While the GIE is still optimal (because $\mathbf{x} \cap \mathbf{a} = \emptyset$), the *decomposition flaw* is now met (in 3D the decomposition of the SQE is more complicated so the *decomposition flaw* is more likely to be met). As a consequence, the speedup of GIE is more sensitive on this example.

6.   Conclusion

Equality constraints with existentially quantified parameters generally have a non-null volume solution set. Therefore, any bisection algorithm dedicated to the approximation of their solution set should incorporate a test for checking inner boxes, unless it will spend most of the time bisecting again and again boxes included inside the solution set. Focusing on the simple but useful example of quantified distance constraints, we proposed two tests: on one hand, thanks to geometric considerations, the quantified distance constraint has been changed to a nonquantified constraint. On the other hand, we presented with a new point of view a test which was initially proposed by the modal intervals theory.

Some experiments have been conducted on academic examples of conjunctions of quantified distance constraints. Although both methods are very different, they yield very similar results about both computation times and description of the solution set (with a slight advantage for the test based on generalized intervals). Moreover, the test based on generalized intervals presents two advantages: first, it is much simpler to implement. Second, it can be easily extended to a quantified distance constraint in an arbitrary dimensional space, where the proposed specific quantifier elimination fails. Our current work[17] combines both approaches in a optimal inner test.

References

1. R. Moore, *Interval Analysis*. Prentice-Hall (1966).
2. B. Hayes, A lucid interval. *American Scientist*, **91**(6), 484–488 (2003).
3. F. Benhamou and W. Older, Applying interval arithmetic to real, integer and Boolean constraints. *Journal of Logic Programming*, **32**(1), 1–24 (1997).
4. H. Collavizza, F. Delobel and M. Rueher, Comparing partial consistencies. *Reliable Computing*, **1**, 1–16 (1999).
5. L. Jaulin, M. Kieffer, O. Didrit and E. Walter, *Applied Interval Analysis with Examples in Parameter and State Estimation, Robust Control and Robotics*. Springer-Verlag (2001).
6. L. Krippahl and P. Barahona, Applying constraint programming to protein structure determination. *Proc. CP'99*, Vol. 1713. *Lecture Notes in Computer Science*, pp. 289–302 (1999).
7. P. Herrero, M. Sainz, J. Vehí and L. Jaulin, Quantified set inversion with applications to control. *IEEE International Symposium on Computer Aided Control Systems Design* (2004).
8. M. Silaghi, D. Sam-Haroud and B. Faltings, Search techniques for nonlinear constraint satisfaction problems with inequalities. Vol. 2056. *Lecture Notes in Computer Science*, pp. 183–193 (2001).
9. J.-P. Merlet, *Parallel Robots*. Kluwer, Dordrecht (2000).
10. E. Kaucher, *Uber Metrische und Algebraische Eigenschaften Einiger Beim Numerischen Rechnen Auftretender Raume*. PhD thesis, Karlsruhe (1973).
11. S. Shary, A new technique in systems analysis under interval uncertainty and ambiguity. *Reliable Computing*, **8**(5), 321–418 (2002).
12. A. Goldsztejn, *Définition et Applications des Extensions des Fonctions Réelles aux Intervalles Généralisés*. PhD thesis. Université de Nice-Sophia Antipolis (2005).
13. SIGLA/X, Modal intervals (basic tutorial). *Applications of Interval Analysis to Systems and Control (Proceedings of MISC'99)*, pp. 157–227 (1999).
14. R. Kearfott, Standardized notation in interval analysis (2002).
15. J. Davenport and J. Heintz, Real quantifier elimination is doubly exponential. *J. Symb. Comput.*, **5**, 29–35 (1988).

16. C. Grandon and B. Neveu, A specific quantifier elimination for inner box test
    in distance constraints with uncertainties. *Research Report 5883, INRIA*, url
    http://www.inria.fr/rrrt/rr-5883.html (2006).
17. C. Grandón, *Résolution de systèmes d'équations de distance avec incertitudes
    (in English)*. PhD thesis. Université de Nice-Sophia Antipolis (2007).